Dante's Education

Latin Schoolbooks and Vernacular Poetics

FILIPPO GIANFERRARI

OXFORD
UNIVERSITY PRESS

Great Clarendon Street, Oxford, OX2 6DP,
United Kingdom

Oxford University Press is a department of the University of Oxford.
It furthers the University's objective of excellence in research, scholarship,
and education by publishing worldwide. Oxford is a registered trade mark of
Oxford University Press in the UK and in certain other countries

© Filippo Gianferrari 2024

The moral rights of the author have been asserted

All rights reserved. No part of this publication may be reproduced, stored in
a retrieval system, or transmitted, in any form or by any means, without the
prior permission in writing of Oxford University Press, or as expressly permitted
by law, by licence or under terms agreed with the appropriate reprographics
rights organization. Enquiries concerning reproduction outside the scope of the
above should be sent to the Rights Department, Oxford University Press, at the
address above

You must not circulate this work in any other form
and you must impose this same condition on any acquirer

Published in the United States of America by Oxford University Press
198 Madison Avenue, New York, NY 10016, United States of America

British Library Cataloguing in Publication Data

Data available

Library of Congress Control Number: 2023951624

ISBN 9780198881766

DOI: 10.1093/oso/9780198881766.001.0001

Printed and bound by
CPI Group (UK) Ltd, Croydon, CR0 4YY

Links to third party websites are provided by Oxford in good faith and
for information only. Oxford disclaims any responsibility for the materials
contained in any third party website referenced in this work.

OXFORD STUDIES IN MEDIEVAL
LITERATURE AND CULTURE

General Editors
Ardis Butterfield, Yale University, Bruce Holsinger, University of Virginia,
and Shazia Jagot, University of York

The monograph series *Oxford Studies in Medieval Literature and Culture* showcases
the plurilingual and multicultural quality of medieval literature and actively seeks to
promote research that not only focuses on the array of subjects medievalists now
pursue—in literature, theology, and philosophy, in social, political, jurisprudential,
and intellectual history, the history of art, and the history of science—but also that
combines these subjects productively. It offers innovative studies on topics that may
include, but are not limited to, manuscript and book history; languages and
literatures of the global Middle Ages; race and the post-colonial; the digital
humanities, media and performance; music; medicine; the history of affect and the
emotions; the literature and practices of devotion; the theory and history of gender
and sexuality, ecocriticism and the environment; theories of aesthetics; medievalism.

Per Elisabetta
(e per Pietro, Giulia, Bernardo, Carlo, Andrew, e Francesco)

XIII (Dedications)
[...] I know
you are reading this poem through your failing sight, the thick
lens enlarging these letters beyond all meaning yet you read on
because even the alphabet is precious.
I know you are reading this poem as you pace beside the stove
warming milk, a crying child on your shoulder, a book in your hand
because life is short and you too are thirsty.
—Adrienne Rich, from the last section of the title poem in
An Atlas of the Difficult World

Contents

List of Illustrations	vi
Acknowledgments	vii
Abbreviations and Note on Translations	ix
Prologue: The Politics of Learning	2
1. An Introduction to Literacy and Education in Dante's Florence	18
2. Learning to Praise: The *Vita nova* as a Vernacular Reader	52
3. (Un)like Aesop: Defining the *Commedia*'s Generic Monstrosity	97
4. *Pugna pro patria*: Freeing Cato from His *Distichs*	132
5. A Lesson in Cross-Cultural Pastoral: The *Ecloga Theoduli* in *Purgatorio*	167
6. Re-Dressing Achilles, Resisting Proserpina, Surpassing Virgil: The End of the Purgatorial Curriculum	208
7. "Be Silent, Ovid" (You, Too, Statius and Claudian): Underground Voices in the Prologue to *Paradiso*	248
Epilogue: "The School That You Have Followed"	276
Bibliography	287
Index	315

List of Illustrations

Figure P.1. Ambrogio Lorenzetti, *Allegory of the Good and Bad Government: The Good City*, detail of a classroom scene, Siena, Palazzo Pubblico, Sala dei Nove   1

Figure P.2. Ambrogio Lorenzetti, *Allegory of the Good and Bad Government: The Good City*, Siena, Palazzo Pubblico, Sala dei Nove   17

Figure 1.1. Oxford, Bodleian Library, Can. Class. Lat. 72, fol. 92r   39

Figure 1.2. Florence, Biblioteca Nazionale Centrale, Magliabechi VII.931, fols. 8v–9r   40

Figure 2.1. Florence, Biblioteca Medicea Laurenziana, Plut. 33.32, fol.1   67

Figure 2.2. Florence, Archivio di Stato di Firenze, Carte Strozziane IIIa ser., 72, fol. 1r   68

Figure 2.3. Detail of Figure 2.2   72

Figure 3.1. Florence, Biblioteca Nazionale Centrale, Magliabechi VII.931, fol. 6r   105

Figure 4.1. Rome, Biblioteca Vallicelliana, F.1, fol. 28r   140

Figure 4.2. Detail of Figure 4.1   141

Figure 4.3. Rome, Biblioteca Vallicelliana, F.1, fol. 30r   143

Figure 5.1. Oxford, Bodleian, Add. A. 171, fol. 31r   173

Figure 5.2. Detail of Figure 5.1   173

Figure 6.1. Florence, Biblioteca Medicea Laurenziana, Plut. 24 sin. 12, fol. 49r   216

Figure 6.2. Florence, Biblioteca Medicea Laurenziana, Plut. 24 sin. 12, fol. 70r   220

Acknowledgments

There are very many people that I need to thank for their personal and academic help over the years. Even though these brief acknowledgments cannot encompass all of you by name, my heartfelt gratitude goes to all of you.

First and foremost, thanks are due to Zyg Barański for his unwavering mentorship and caring friendship over the years. Without his scholarship and patient advice, this book could not have come to fruition. Thank you for your generosity, patience, and for being more than a mentor. I am equally indebted to Simone Marchesi for his meticulous scrutiny of various manuscript drafts and his generous sharing of insightful ideas. His friendship and mentorship are invaluable. I am grateful to the following friends and colleagues for their comments, criticism, help, and guidance while the manuscript was completed and then revised: John Ahern, Albert Ascoli, Elisa Brilli, Christopher Cannon, Alison Cornish, Lorenzo Dell'Oso, Grace Delmolino, Enrico Faini, Camilo Gomez-Rivas, Stephen Harris, Justin Haynes, Tristan Kay, Catherine Keen, Sean Keilen, Sharon Kinoshita, Elena Lombardi, Arielle Saiber, and Justin Steinberg. The dedicated editorial team and anonymous readers at Oxford University Press also significantly contributed to improving this book. Cathy Cambron has also offered extensive copywriting advice on different versions of this manuscript. For all remaining errors, I am solely responsible.

I wish to express my gratitude also to Martin Bloomer, Ted Cachey, Ambrogio Camozzi Pistoja, Paul Gehl, David Gura, Michele Mulchahey, Hildegund Müller, Gabriella Pomaro, Daniel Sheerin, and Heather Webb for their encouragement and suggestions at the time of this book's first inception as part of my dissertation. Special thanks extend to the many friends and mentors who accompanied and advised me during my Ph.D. candidacy at the University of Notre Dame, my studies at the University of Bologna, and as an exchange student at the University of Cambridge. I hold in memory with gratitude the teachers and friends who guided me in my scholarly pursuits and are no longer with us: Andrea Battistini, Adam Foley, Robert Hollander, Emilio Pasquini, and Andrew Tallon.

To all my colleagues, past and present, at Vassar College, Smith College, and especially at the University of California, Santa Cruz, I offer my thanks for their scholarly and moral assistance over the past seven years. The support from the Department of Literature and the Humanities division at UCSC has been invaluable during challenging years marked by COVID, wildfires, strikes, and difficult housing conditions. My colleagues and the staff in the department have all been

viii ACKNOWLEDGMENTS

especially welcoming and supportive, taking much valuable time to help me operate in a new academic environment and secure financial support for this project. I am also grateful to the graduate students with whom I have had the privilege to work. They brilliantly assisted me in my teaching duties and enriched me during our many dialogues.

The research discussed in this book and its writing have been made possible through the generosity of the American Council of Learned Societies, the UCSC Academic Senate and EVC Fellows Program, The Humanities Institute, the Hellman Fellows Program, and The University of California Humanities Research Institute. The personell of the Archivio di Stato di Firenze, the Biblioteca Medicea Laurenziana, the Bodleian Library, and the Biblioteca Vallicelliana have also assisted me at the time when I was researching this book and when I was assembling its final manuscript.

In conclusion, I want to extend my special thanks to those who made it possible for me to write this book. To my parents, Paolo and Michela, who always believed in me and through their hard work and personal support provided opportunities they never had. To my brothers, Gianluca and Mattia, who have always been there for me even when I was nowhere to be found. Finally, I dedicate this book to my wife and best friend, Elisabetta, for all the personal and professional sacrifices she made to enable my career and this project; and to our children, who gave me the motivation to finish this book, and whose infectious joy and liveliness inspire me. Thank you for being you and a reason for everything.

Earlier versions of some materials incorporated into Chapter 4 have appeared in *Dante Studies* 135 (2017): 1–30; in *Dante e la cultura fiorentina: Bono Giamboni, Brunetto Latini e la formazione intellettuale dei laici*, ed. Zygmunt G. Barański, Theodore J. Cachey, and Luca Lombardo (Rome: Salerno, 2019), 173–91; and in *"Nostra maggior musa": I maestri della letteratura classica nella Commedia di Dante*, ed. John Butcher (Città di Castello: Edizioni Nuova Prhomos, 2021), 217–33.

Abbreviations and Note on Translations

The following abbreviations, editions, and translations are used throughout the book.

Inf.	*Inferno*
Purg.	*Purgatorio*
Par.	*Paradiso*
Conv.	*Convivio*
Vn.	*Vita nova*
Egl.	Dante Alighieri, *Egloghe*
Ecl. Theod.	Johann E. Osternacher, *Theoduli eclogam recensuit et prolegomenis instruxit* (Urfahr-Lenz: Ripariae prope Lentiam, 1902) *The Eclogue of Theodulus: A Translation*, trans. by George Rigg (Toronto: Centre for Medieval Studies, University of Toronto, 2005). Accessed https://www.medieval.utoronto.ca/research/online-resources/eclogue-theodulus-translation
ED	*Enciclopedia Dantesca.* 1970. Rome: Enciclopedia Treccani. Accessed at http://www.treccani.it/enciclopedia/catone-l-uticense_(Enciclopedia-Dantesca)/
MLN	Modern Language Notes

Dante Alighieri's works and their English translations have been cited according to the following editions, accessed at https://dante.princeton.edu/:

Commedia

La Commedia secondo l'antica vulgata, ed. Giorgio Petrocchi, 4 vols (Milan: Mondadori, 1966–67)
    Robert Hollander and Jean Hollander, trans., *Dante: Inferno* (New York: Doubleday/Anchor, 2000); *Purgatorio* (New York: Doubleday/Anchor, 2003); *Paradiso* (New York: Doubleday/Anchor, 2007)

Convivio

Convivio, ed. Franca Brambilla Ageno, 3 vols (Florence: Le Lettere, 1995)
    Richard H. Lansing, trans., *Dante's "Il Convivio"* (New York: Garland, 1990)

De Vulgari Eloquentia

De vulgari eloquentia, ed. Pio Rajna (Florence: Società Dantesca Italiana, 1960)
    Steven Botterill, trans., *Dante: De vulgari Eloquentia* (Cambridge: Cambridge University Press, 1996)

Egloghe

Egloghe, ed. Ermenegildo Pistelli (Florence: Società Dantesca Italiana, 1960)
   Ph. Wicksteed and E.G. Gardner, trans., *Dante: Eclogues* in *The Latin Works of Dante Alighieri* (London: Dent, 1904)

Epistule

Epistole, ed. Ermenegildo Pistelli (Florence: Società Dantesca Italiana, 1960)
   Paget Toynbee, trans., *Dante: Epistles* in *The Letters of Dante* (Oxford: Clarendon, 1920)

Monarchia

Monarchia, ed. Pier Giorgio Ricci (Florence: Società Dantesca Italiana, 1965)
Prue Shaw, trans., *Dante: Monarchia* (Cambridge: Cambridge University Press, 1995)

Questio de aqua et terra

Questio de aqua et terra, ed. Ermenegildo Pistelli (Florence: Società Dantesca Italiana, 1960)
   Ph. Wicksteed, trans., *Dante: Questio de aqua et terra* in *The Latin Works of Dante Alighieri* (London: Dent, 1904)

Vita nova

Vita nuova, ed. Michele Barbi (Florence: Società Dantesca Italiana, 1960)
   Translations of the *Vita nova* are from Dante Alighieri, *Vita nova*, trans. Andrew Frisardi (Evanston, IL: Northwestern University Press, 2012), unless otherwise noted. Accessed at https://digitaldante.columbia.edu/text/library/la-vita-nuova-frisardi/.

The following commentaries on the *Commedia* have been cited according to the *Dartmouth Dante Project*, https://dante.dartmouth.edu/:

   Pietro Alighieri (1) (1340–42)
   Pietro Alighieri (2) (1344–55 [1])
   Pietro Alighieri (3) (1359–64)
   Anonimo Fiorentino (1400[?])
   Benvenuto da Imola (1375–80)
   Giovanni Boccaccio (1373–75)
   Umberto Bosco e Giovanni Reggio (1979)
   Tommaso Casini and S. A. Barbi (1921)
   Lodovico Castelvetro (1570)
   Anna Maria Chiavacci Leonardi (1991–97)
   Francesco da Buti (1385–95)

Bernardino Daniello (1547–68)
Cristoforo Landino (1481)
L'Ottimo Commento (1333)
Nicola Fosca (2003–2015)
Robert Hollander (2000–2007)
Giovanni Andrea Scartazzini (1872–82 [2nd ed. 1900])
Francesco Torraca (1905)

All classical Latin texts and their translations, unless stated otherwise, are cited according to the editions available on the Perseus Digital Library. Accessed at https://www.perseus.tufts.edu/hopper/.

Editions and translations for the Latin school texts are provided in the footnotes and *Bibliography*.

The Latin Bible and its English translation are quoted from Douay-Rheims Catholic Bible. Accessed at http://www.drbo.org/.

Figure P.1 Ambrogio Lorenzetti, *Allegory of the Good and Bad Government: The Good City*, detail of a classroom scene, Siena, Palazzo Pubblico, Sala dei Nove.
Source: Heritage Image Partnership Ltd./Alamy Stock Photo.

Prologue

The Politics of Learning

That he may not be deceived by ambiguous signs
we shall offer some instruction.

(St. Augustine, *On Christian Doctrine*)

Squeezed in between two *botteghe* (workshops), near the center of the lively marketplace scene that animates Ambrogio Lorenzetti's fresco of "The Good City," appears a small classroom. In it a familiar scene of learning unfolds: a teacher is lecturing a tightly packed classroom. His tall figure towers over the room from the height of an imposing wooden chair, while a large lectern separates him from the rest of the small enclosure. The instructor's berth takes up half of the room, giving a measure of his authority. By contrast, the small bodies of the students are fused together into shapeless spots of red and blue robes, punctuated only by rows of upturned heads. They all appear intent on the teacher's words. Unencumbered by the books that lie open on the desks in front of them, their eyes are magnetized by the taller figure, while their necks are uncomfortably stretched upward. The symbolism of the scene is interrupted only by the realistic posture of a student in the foreground. He too has his eyes fixed on the master but is propping up his chin with the right hand—a small support for the unnatural effort of learning. Is he pondering a question or daydreaming?

This fragment of ordinary school life tends to "disappear" in the massive, and massively detailed, urban space created by the artist. The significance of this detail is easily lost on the observer and is generally concealed by the deceptively simple label "lecturer" that is offered in art book captions. Compared with the wealth of scholarship and interpretation that has probed the meaning of Lorenzetti's complex allegory, the attention devoted to the little classroom and its role in the larger symbolism of the fresco is minimal. Yet, when closely considered, the small classroom cannot fail to strike modern observers for the apparent oddity of its surroundings: a busy street full of people carrying foods or driving livestock; a shoemaker's workshop; a tavern full of patrons; a hosier busy with his products; and high, above the city's skyline, builders at work on what promises to be a monumental tower (Figure P.2). Although precarious, the naturalism of this large scene of city life invites viewers to appreciate both the centrality granted to schooling in

Dante's Education. Filippo Gianferrari, Oxford University Press. © Filippo Gianferrari (2024).
DOI: 10.1093/oso/9780198881766.003.0001

the business center and its obvious blending in with other commercial activities.[1] This captivating detail of urban life sums up the historical phenomenon whose cultural implications I set out to explore in this book. But before we can get to the heart of this story, we shall first zoom out of Lorenzetti's classroom and consider its larger iconographic and historical context.

In 1338, after being commissioned by Siena's democratic government to paint frescoes on the walls of the *Sala de' Nove*, in the *Palazzo Pubblico*, Ambrogio Lorenzetti put his signature on one of the Middle Ages' most memorable pieces of civic art—a detailed allegory of the key political doctrine behind the city's shared governance. Lorenzetti's legacy is a visual distillation of the common good that the *comune* swore to promote and protect—justice, freedom, and prosperity for "all."[2] As the good of the polity took priority over individual interests, so the democratic government of "the Nine" represented the antidote to the tyranny of one.

Justice is the key virtue that sets Lorenzetti's political allegories in contrast, creating the two antagonistic landscapes depicted in the large cycle. In the allegory of Good Government, Justice is embodied by a female figure: she is crowned and sitting on a throne, her eyes lifted to gaze up at the personification of Wisdom hovering over her in midair. In her hand, Justice holds the scale that administers fitting retribution to both the good and the bad. Conversely, in the allegory of Bad Government, she is chained and vilified; the plates of her scale lie broken at her sides. Next to each allegory, a massive representation of the city and its countryside shows the effects of each government: where the Common Good and Justice rule, a city flourishes, harmony and industriousness unite all its citizens, and the surrounding countryside is safe and productive; where Tyranny has the upper hand and Justice is shamed, a desolate city lies in ruins, while dissension and strife are the only currency its citizens exchange.

A most intriguing facet of Lorenzetti's extensive pictorial cycle is its subtle combination of realism and allegory. The civic allegories attest to the profound impact that the rediscovery of Aristotle's *Politics* had on the political thought

---

[1] The naturalism of Lorenzetti's representation has been recently reassessed and its many debts to medieval visual iconography effectively retraced. For a helpful reconstruction of the tradition Lorenzetti was working with in creating his school scene, see Robert Gibbs, "Images of Higher Education in Fourteenth-century Bologna," in "*Medieval Architecture and Its Intellectual Context*," ed. Eric Fernie and Paul Crossley (London: Hambledon Press, 1990), 269–81.

[2] It would be deceiving to think of late medieval Italian communes as democracies in modern terms. "The Nine" who met in the room that bears their name were "a coordinating committee and executive board for a large council of three hundred members and three smaller commissions of tax officials, merchants, and knights. Together these councils embodied the sovereign authority of the republic." Randolph Starn, *Ambrogio Lorenzetti: The Palazzo Pubblico, Siena* (New York: George Braziller, 1994), 15. It remains true, however, that in fourteenth-century Italian city-states "anyone ranging from simple artisans to international merchant-bankers could now participate in local politics, which had previously been entirely dominated by the *milites*, the citizen-knights." Enrico Faini, "Before the 'Primo Popolo': Politics and the Popular Movement at San Gimignano in the First Half of the Thirteenth Century," in *Disciplined Dissent in Western Europe*, ed. Fabrizio Titone (Turnhout: Brepols, 2022), 49–74, at 49.

4   DANTE'S EDUCATION

of fourteenth-century Italian city-states.[3] Lorenzetti, however, does not merely restage a traditional opposition of two abstract allegories, Justice versus Tyranny. In his depiction, Siena becomes the Good Government that prospers in the face of all tyrannies. Albeit inspired by traditional iconography, Lorenzetti's glittering vision of the good city center—its manicured architecture and its marketplace bustling with life—is modeled on the real fourteenth-century Siena. Commercial activities are reproduced in detail and occupy a large part of the scene. The realism of this depiction is interrupted only by a group of people dancing and singing in the street.[4] The frescoes deliver a clear political message in their portrayal of the effects of Good Government, celebrating the leadership of "the Nine" who met in the *Sala* and deliberated on the administration of the city.

The schoolroom scene reflects the importance that the civic administration assigned to the Sienese university (the *studium*) for the city's economic flourishing. In the year the frescoes were signed, 1338, Siena opened its doors to a great exodus of students from Bologna and was seeking to be officially recognized as the home of a *studium generale*.[5] The iconography evidences the commodification of instruction that, beginning in the thirteenth century, had propelled the growth of secular schools in the urban centers of northern Italy. Education, in other words, had become an asset that could be sold, and teaching was a remunerative profession that laypeople could pursue. In Lorenzetti's civic allegory, schooling emerges as one of the essential services that a fair and efficient communal administration was expected to provide. Education was perceived as integral to the collective pursuit of the common good—simultaneously depending on and contributing to it.

Lorenzetti was not alone in seeing education as a key engine in the life of fourteenth-century Italian city-states. According to Giovanni Villani's *Nuova Cronica*, in the same year Lorenzetti signed his frescoes, Florence boasted an impressive network of urban schools and high levels of lay literacy:

> Trovamo ch'e' fanciulli e fanciulle che stavano a leggere del continuo, da otto in dieci mila. I garzoni che stavano ad apprendere l'abbaco e algorismo in sei scuole, da mille in milledugento. E questi che stavano ad aprendere gramatica e loica in quattro grandi scuole, da cinquecentocinquanta in seicento.

[3] On the influence of Aristotle's *Politics* on Lorenzetti's fresco see Nicolai Rubinstein, "Political Ideals in Sienese Art: The Frescoes by Ambrogio Lorenzetti and Taddeo di Bartolo in the Palazzo Pubblico," *Journal of the Warburg and Courtauld Institute* 21 (1958): 179–207. Lately, however, the influence of Cicero and Brunetto Latini on Lorenzetti have also been convincingly argued. For an innovative reading of the frescoes sparked by these findings, see C. Jean Campbell, *The Commonwealth of Nature: Art and Poetic Community in the Age of Dante* (University Park: Pennsylvania State University Press, 2008).

[4] As Starn (*Ambrogio Lorenzetti*, 72) notes, "in the *real town* dancing in the street was forbidden by law."

[5] Siena would not be recognized as a *studium generale* until 1357. See Hastings Rashdall, "The University of Europe in the Middle Ages," rev. and ed. F. M. Powicke and A. B. Emden, vol. 2 (Oxford: Oxford University Press, 1969), 31–35.

(We find that the boys and girls who were learning to read numbered from 8,000 to 10,000. The boys who were learning the abacus and algorism in six schools, from 1,000 to 1,200. And those who were learning grammar and logic in four higher schools from 550 to 600.)[6]

Historians have long warned against taking these figures as reliable evidence of schooling in Florence in 1338. Paul Gehl rightly points out that Villani's claim is part of a section of his *Cronica* that celebrates the city's prosperity and progress.[7] The chronicler's propagandistic aim, however, is notable on its own terms. While Villani claims that the advancement of schooling in Florence was remarkable for the time, he also links it to the city's power and economic success. Notwithstanding the questionable accuracy of his account, Villani confirms that the key role of education for both individual and collective advancements had become a social construct in fourteenth-century Italy.[8]

A Poet Learns to Read

Dante's Education: Latin Schoolbooks and Vernacular Poetics postulates that the new attention to and financial investment in education in medieval Italian communes were key to the rise of vernacular literacy and the growth of the lay public that Dante targeted in his oeuvre. While this historical development should in no way be compared to our modern national school systems and curricula, the proliferation of urban schools in thirteenth- and fourteenth-century Florence is a documented reality. "System," in other words, may be an anachronistic term, but, for all the variety of strains and conditions that marked it, schooling in late medieval Italy offers some invariants that make it a coherent object of study.[9]

One of these invariants is the selection of Latin texts used in the teaching of language, which this book explores in relation to Dante Alighieri and his contemporary public. The realization that the body of texts read in medieval schools north of the Alps was so narrow as to constitute a standardized textbook, or "reader," has made it possible to note that vernacular poets often referenced school texts in their works. In his book *From Literacy to Literature: England 1300–1400*, Christopher Cannon argues that there is a "remarkably straight line" that links the schoolbooks

---

[6] Giovanni Villani, *Nuova Cronica* 12.94, ed. Giuseppe Porta, vol. 3 (Parma: U. Guanda, 1990–91), 198.

[7] Paul Gehl, *A Moral Art: Grammar, Society, and Culture in Trecento Florence* (Ithaca, NY: Cornell University Press, 1993), 21–26.

[8] There is a general consensus on this point. More recently, see William R. Day Jr., "Economy," in *Dante in Context*, ed. Zygmunt G. Barański and Lino Pertile (Cambridge: Cambridge University Press, 2015), 30–45.

[9] In a recent study, Sarah Lynch reached the same conclusion about the city of Lyon during the fourteenth and the fifteenth centuries. See Lynch, *Elementary and Grammar Education in Late Medieval France* (Amsterdam: Amsterdam University Press, 2017).

6   DANTE'S EDUCATION

that survive from fourteenth-century England to the most original techniques displayed by Ricardian poets.[10] The opening question of this study is whether a similar conclusion can be drawn in the case of Dante.

Since the beginning of the twenty-first century, important work on Dante has attempted to reconstruct the poet's intellectual formation. Little evidence, however, survives about his life and education. As a result, scholars have often approached this conundrum by focusing on the book collections, educational institutions, and cultural milieus to which the poet might have had access. These studies tend to explain Dante's major intellectual achievements as being informed by the different cultural environments in which he lived during his exile.[11] Although contextualizing the cultural influences that shaped Dante's formation is of paramount importance for understanding the poet's oeuvre and its contributions to the development of the vernacular, it is equally necessary to establish how and to what extent he may have had access to sources and places of learning. Since it is at present difficult to assess what the poet might have learned in different places at different times during his exile, late thirteenth-century Florence—where Dante lived from 1265 to 1302—offers a reliable point of departure for reconstructing his intellectual formation.[12] Even studying the educational context of Dante's earliest schooling, however, is not devoid of major challenges, as little information survives on Florentine cultural institutions that predate the fourteenth century. Dante, moreover, was neither a *clericus* nor a *magister*—he was a *laicus*, and our knowledge of the ways in which the laity was educated in the late Middle Ages is limited.[13] In recent years, several attempts have been made to study the cultural context of Dante's Florence. Studies, however, have often focused on his alleged "higher" education—that is, the poet's relations with contemporary universities, as well as religious *studia* and their libraries.[14] Even when discussing the poet's ideas

[10] Christopher Cannon, "From Literacy to Literature: Elementary Learning and the Middle English Poet," *PMLA* 129, no. 3 (2014): 349–64, at 350; and Cannon, *From Literacy to Literature: England 1300–1400* (Oxford: Oxford University Press, 2016), 15.

[11] Representative of this critical trend are, for instance, Enrico Fenzi, introduction to his edition of *De vulgari eloquentia*, vol. 3 of Dante Alighieri, *Opere*, ed. Enrico Malato (Rome: Salerno, 2012), xix–lxii; and Mirko Tavoni, introduction to his edition of *De vulgari eloquentia*, vol. 1 of Dante Alighieri, *Opere*, ed. Marco Santagata (Milan: Mondadori, 2011), 1067–123.

[12] As already pointed out by Zygmunt G. Barański, "Studying the Spaces of Dante's Intellectual Formation: Some Problems of Definition," in *"I luoghi nostri": Dante's Natural and Cultural Spaces*, ed. Zygmunt Barański, Andreas Kablitz, and Ülar Ploom (Tallinn: Tallinn University Press, 2015), 257–88.

[13] On this defining feature of Dante's intellectual formation and activity, see Ruedi Imbach's seminal work, *Dante, la philosophie et les laics* (Fribourg: Éditions Universitaires, Paris: Éditions du Cerf; 1996). See also Zygmunt G. Barański, "Dante commentatore e commentato: Riflessioni sullo studio dell'*iter* ideologico di Dante," in *Lettere Classensi* 23 (Ravenna: Longo, 1994), 135–58; and Robert Black, "Education," in *Dante in Context*, 260–76.

[14] The project *Dante and Late Medieval Florence: Theology in Poetry, Practice and Society*, a collaboration between the Universities of Leeds and Warwick, deserves mention. See also Claire E. Honess and Matthew Treherne, *Reviewing Dante's Theology* (Berlin: Peter Lang, 2013). Among the most recent studies on the Florentine cultural milieu, here I should mention Zygmunt G. Barański, Theodore J. Cachey, and Luca Lombardo, eds., *Reconsidering Dante and Brunetto Latini (and Bono Giamboni)*

PROLOGUE 7

concerning grammar and language, scholars have almost invariably investigated Dante's philosophy of language, with particular emphasis on the poet's indebtedness or resistance to theories by speculative grammarians. Basic questions about how and where the poet acquired literacy and grammar, in contrast, have rarely been asked.[15] Yet, while we cannot establish whether the poet received any kind of higher education, we do know that he was taught how to read and write in Latin.

We cannot assume the existence of a unified curriculum of readings adopted by the grammar teachers of late medieval Florence. Evidence, however, points to a corpus of short Latin poems that were consistently used for education or recommended for beginners and intermediate readers, as well as to less elementary texts that were simply more widely consumed at that time than they are now. The "minor" Latin poems, which were used for language instruction, were considered educational readings, propaedeutic to the study of the major Roman poets. Some of these "school texts" were among the most widely disseminated books of the Middle Ages, and they undoubtedly influenced intellectuals all over Europe. Furthermore, the practice of memorization during the first years of language training was so extensive that literate people, like Dante, retained a powerful memory of their school readings throughout their life.[16] This literary corpus, therefore, furnished a growing number of moderately educated readers with a shared "cultural literacy."

The term "cultural literacy" applies to contemporary Western societies and identifies the stock of background information that enables individuals in each society to communicate effectively through reading, writing, and speaking. Critics of this notion have contended that educational models based on the pursuit of

(Rome: Salerno, 2019); Johannes Bartuschat, Elisa Brilli, and Delphine Carron (eds.), *The Dominicans and the Making of Florence (13th–14th Centuries)* (Florence: Firenze University Press, 2020); Lorenzo Dell'Oso, "Problemi di metodo intorno alla formazione intellettuale di Dante: i cataloghi librari, le tracce testuali, il *Trattatello* di Boccaccio," *Le Tre Corone* 4 (2016): 1–32; Silvia Diacciati and Enrico Faini, "Ricerche sulla formazione dei laici a Firenze nel tardo duecento," *Archivio storico italiano* 652, no. 2 (2017): 205–37; Luca Lombardo, *Boezio in Dante: La* Consolatio Philosophiae *nello scrittoio del poeta* (Venice: Edizioni Ca' Foscari, 2013), esp. 13–79; Paola Nasti, "Storia materiale di un classico dantesco: la *Consolatio Philosophiae* fra XII e XIV secolo, tradizione manoscritta e rielaborazioni esegetiche," *Dante Studies* 134 (2016): 142–68; Anna Pegoretti, "Filosofanti," *Le Tre Corone* 2 (2015): 11–70; and Sylvain Piron, "Le poète et le théologien: une rencontre dans le *Studium* de Santa Croce," *Picenum Seraphicum* 19 (2000): 87–134, now in *Ut philosophia poesis: Questions philosophiques dans l'écriture de Dante, Pétrarque, Bocacce*, ed. Fosca Mariani-Zini and Joël Biard (Paris: Vrin, 2008), 73–112.

[15] For an overview of critical discussions of Dante and language, see Irène Rosier-Catach, Anne Grondeux, and Ruedi Imbach, ed. and trans., *De l'éloquence en vulgaire* (Paris: Fayard, 2011), 9–64.

[16] The character of Beatrice distills the methodological assumption behind this pedagogical practice in *Paradiso* 5.41–42, when she reminds the protagonist that learning is not possible without memorization: "non fa scienza, / sanza lo ritenere, aver inteso." Through repetition and the use of wax tablets, literacy education required an intense use of psychomotor memory that can hardly be compared to the learning of any modern language. See Cannon, "From Literacy to Literature: Elementary Learning and the Middle English Poet," 361; Mary J. Carruthers, *The Book of Memory: A Study of Memory in Medieval Culture* (Cambridge: Cambridge University Press, 1990), esp. xiii–xiv; and Ivan Illich, *In the Vineyard of the Text: A Commentary to Hugh's Didascalicon* (Chicago: University of Chicago Press, 1993), 70.

8 DANTE'S EDUCATION

cultural literacy generate a "rigid, tradition-based book list" that is "too elitist, too exclusionary."[17] Such a description, however, aptly represents Latin education in the Middle Ages, when the teaching of literacy hinged on the study of a tradition-based book list and contributed to defining social elites. Learning to read and write provided the basics of language and ethics, a rudimentary introduction to literature, and some notions of biblical and classical antiquities. School texts and their exegesis at the hands of medieval teachers constituted the repositories of the cultural literacy shared by most literate individuals in Latin Christendom.[18] Little, however, has been done to explore this situation in relation to Dante's literary culture, often leaving unquestioned the poet's self-representation as an exceptional reader of classical literature with few or no ties to contemporary literary sensibilities.[19] For a nuanced appreciation of Dante's actual debts to and departures from contemporary Latin education, we need to set his writings next to medieval school texts. What did the poet learn during his initiation to Latin literacy? What lifelong influence did school readings have on his cultural and moral formation?[20]

To begin answering these questions, in this book I focus primarily on Dante's reworking of medieval school texts in the *Vita nova* and in the *Commedia*. For my analysis, I have selected eight minor Latin poems that were popular school readings and whose presence in late medieval Florence is attested in surviving manuscripts: Henry of Settimello's *Elegia*, Prosper of Aquitaine's *Liber epigrammatum*, the *Disticha Catonis*, fables from the *Aesopus latinus* (also known as "elegiac *Romulus*"), the *Ecloga Theoduli*, Statius' *Achilleid*, and Claudian's *De raptu*

---

[17] Erik D. Hirsch Jr., "'Cultural Literacy' Doesn't Mean 'Core Curriculum,'" *English Journal* 74.6 (October 1985): 47–49, esp. 47. See also Hirsch, "Cultural Literacy," *American Scholar* 52, no. 2 (Spring 1983): 159–69; and Hirsch, *Cultural Literacy: What Every American Needs to Know* (Boston: Houghton Mifflin, 1987). For a criticism of this idea, see Audrey T. Edwards, "Cultural Literacy: What Are Our Goals?," *English Journal* 73, no. 4 (April 1984): 71–72.

[18] On the selection of texts in the medieval curriculum, see Marcus Boas, "De Librorum Catonianorum historia atque compositione," *Mnemosyne*, n.s., 42 (1914): 17–46; Tony Hunt, *Teaching and Learning Latin in Thirteenth-Century England: Texts*, vol. 1 (Rochester, NY: Boydell & Brewer, 1991); and, more recently, Cannon, *Literacy to Literature: England 1300–1400*. For a critique of Boas's proposal, see Rino Avesani, "Il primo ritmo per la morte del grammatico Ambrogio e il cosiddetto 'Liber Catonianus,'" *Studi Medievali* 6 (1965): 455–88.

[19] Edward Moore, *Studies in Dante. First Series: Scripture and Classical Authors in Dante* (New York: Greenwood Press, 1968) was influential in setting this trend, which is still dominant, as exemplified, for instance, by Winthrop Wetherbee, *The Ancient Flame: Dante and the Poets* (Notre Dame, IN: University of Notre Dame Press, 2008). A significantly new attention to the importance of reconsidering the label "classics" in Dante from the point of view of his contemporary culture is exemplified by Zygmunt G. Barański, "The Classics," in *The Oxford Handbook of Dante*, ed. Manuele Gragnolati, Elena Lombardi, and Francesca Southerden (Oxford: Oxford University Press, 2021), 111–26; and Simone Marchesi, "Classical Culture," in *The Cambridge Companion to Dante's Commedia*, ed. Zygmunt G. Barański and Simon Gilson (Cambridge: Cambridge University Press, 2019), 127–39.

[20] For the importance of studying Dante's intellectual formation contextually, see Bruno Nardi, *Sigieri di Brabante nella "Divina Commedia" e le fonti della filosofia di Dante* (Spianate, Pescia: Presso l'autore, 1912), 69. As Cannon observes, "the history of the schoolroom has, in fact, often been most relevant to literary history when it has been a chapter in the history of the book." Cannon, "From Literacy to Literature: Elementary Learning and the Middle English Poet," 352.

Proserpinae.[21] These are all poetic works that were preferred by medieval pedagogues on account of their moralizing content, as well as their brevity, metrical form, and the diverse array of literary genres they showcased. These poems may well have been the first poetic compositions that Dante learned by heart and that introduced him to Latin literature. At its most basic level, therefore, the present study offers the first systematic account of Dante's interaction with medieval school texts. At another level, the book shows that medieval education exerted a seminal influence on Dante's poetics throughout his career, and particularly on his attempts to develop a teaching program tailored to the need of lay readers. By concentrating on the *Vita nova* and the *Commedia*, the book shows that Dante's project of educating the reader became enmeshed in his poetics. *Dante's Education*, in other words, encompasses both the education the poet received and the one he wished to impart to his readers.

Dante's pedagogical tendencies are undeniable and color his whole literary production.[22] When the poet composed the *Commedia*, vernacular poetry could count on an expanding readership but not yet on an established book market. Few vernacular poets could have imagined a reader—or a group of readers—willing to copy a whole collection of poems by a single author.[23] Professional writing was spreading, but it still came at considerable cost and required uncommon skills. Not surprisingly, then, texts were mostly addressed either to individual readers or to specific "textual communities," as in the case of vernacular epistles and poems.[24] Although a marketable audience for vernacular poetry did exist, the full potential of that market was yet to be pursued by the young book "industry" and, arguably, by vernacular readers as well. Throughout his oeuvre, however, Dante imagines his reader as someone sitting at a desk and "reading" his works, a detail that is already revealing in the context of late medieval Italy, where most people "listened to" vernacular texts. A legitimate question is how Dante hoped to engage with the vernacular readers he had identified as his primary audience. In most cases, they lacked the cultural and critical sophistication that comes from extensive reading

---

[21] On popular school texts in medieval Italy, see Avesani, "Primo ritmo"; Robert Black, *Humanism and Education in Medieval and Renaissance Italy: Tradition and Innovation in Latin Schools from the Twelfth to the Fifteenth Century* (Cambridge: Cambridge University Press, 2001); and Gehl, *Moral Art*.

[22] For a recent discussion of Dante's pedagogical attitude and aims, see Ruedi Imbach, "Dante come allievo e maestro," in *"Minima medievalia": saggi di filosofia medievale* (Rome: Aracne, 2019), 197–217. According to Imbach, Dante's pedagogy was informed by Aquinas's idea—expressed in q. 11, a. 1 of *Questiones disputatae de veritate*—that a teacher can only help a student learn insofar as the former can inspire the latter to use reason to know something.

[23] Guittone d'Arezzo and Monte Andrea are the first who seem to have conceived anthologies of their own poems in the Italian vernacular milieu. See Olivia Holmes, *Assembling the Lyric Self: Authorship from Troubadour Song to Italian Poetry Book* (Minneapolis, MN: University of Minnesota Press, 2000), chap. 1.

[24] For the notion of "textual community" in the context of eleventh- and twelfth-century France, see Brian Stock, *The Implications of Literacy: Written Language and Models of Interpretation in the Eleventh and Twelfth Centuries* (Princeton, NJ: Princeton University Press, 1983). Paul Gehl (*Moral Art*, 4) specifically refers to grammar education in late-medieval Italy as the "ethical preparation of the student to enter a textual community."

10   DANTE'S EDUCATION

practice.[25] To address this gap, the poet instructs and to some extent constructs his readers. While implementing a new textual object, therefore, Dante needed also to train readers—and potential copyists—who could appreciate the literary sophistication of his vernacular works and find further instruction in them. As I discuss in what follows, Dante approached this humble but also strategic and self-serving task by relying on, and sometimes reacting to, what was then the only other available model of reading instruction: Latin.

Elementary education in Dante's day was education in Latin literacy. Its aim was not only to teach Latin but also to provide a pathway to literacy in the vernacular. The lay readers targeted by Dante's vernacular texts had received the same elementary language instruction, based on a handful of Latin religious, grammatical, and literary texts. Even those who had advanced to the study of Latin grammar had studied and memorized a selection of minor Latin poems. Since the teaching of literature coincided with that of grammar and rhetoric, for many of these readers—including those who eventually pursued a university degree, such as lawyers, judges, notaries, and doctors—the minor Latin texts represented their only formal literary training. Paradoxically, therefore, the introduction to literacy and grammar provided them with the bulk of their literary culture.[26] *These* texts, rather than the *auctores maiores*, gave most lay readers access to classical culture. As this book argues, Dante could rely on this shared literary culture to introduce some of his most original innovations. On the one hand, the poet depended on an audience that had been educated through Latin school texts; on the other hand, his intention was to provide a comparable option for learning in the vernacular. Dante aimed his program of instruction specifically at those who wished to educate themselves but could not read Latin or who did have some Latin proficiency but did not have the leisure and intellectual means that would allow them to pursue further learning. Latin was still a necessary means for recovering the riches of antiquity and for communicating with readers from other countries, but alternative forms of instruction in the vernacular were in high demand.

There is a further and, in my view, essential aspect of Dante's stance toward Latin education, namely that he too was a layperson and an outsider with respect to institutions of higher education. From this position, he was able to reflect on the limits and shortcomings of contemporary educational trends but also to turn this criticism to his own advantage. I emphasize this point as it explains the somewhat polemical nature of Dante's vernacular model of instruction. His educational

---

[25] Not to mention the linguistic barriers that affected non-Tuscan readers of the *Commedia* in Dante's Italy. On this see the recent essay by Alessandro Carlucci, "Who Could Understand the *Commedia*? Multilingualism, Comprehension and Oral Communication in Medieval Italy," in *Dante beyond Borders*, ed. Nick Havely, Jonathan Katz, and Richard Cooper (Oxford: Legenda, 2021), 132–44.

[26] Quintilian in his *Institutio Oratoria* explains that grammar comprises the science of speaking correctly and the detailed exposition of the poets: "recte loquendi scientiam et poetarum enarrationem" (1.4.2 but see also 2.1.4). For a general discussion on the subject, see Ernst Robert Curtius, *European Literature and the Latin Middle Ages* (London: Routledge & K. Paul, 1953), 51–52.

PROLOGUE   11

enterprise, moreover, was part of a broader lay vernacular movement that characterized late medieval Italy, and Tuscany in particular. This movement included figures such as Brunetto Latini and Francesco da Barberino—both active in Florence during Dante's time there—and resulted in the large number of vernacular translations that were produced during the fourteenth century.[27] From a historical perspective, therefore, the poet's pedagogical aim was not unique. This shared commitment informed what I would like to term his poetics of vernacular learning.

Qualifying Dante as a "teacher" may appear to diminish his self-fashioned image as an inspired prophet and exceptional poet that over the centuries has become established among readers. Unquestionably, the explicit and unifying aim of the *Commedia* is the spiritual and moral education of the reader.[28] The author's deep concern with the political and spiritual struggles of his time is evident throughout the poem and has been acknowledged by medieval and modern readers alike. Less obvious for a modern reader is the fact that Dante's spiritual and moral reformism hinged on the reading of literary texts and entailed a literary education of his contemporary audience. Yet poetry had a key role in medieval learning. Not only were pupils introduced to literacy through the act of memorizing minor Latin poems, but, as medieval treatises on education reveal, this corpus of readings also served as the first step of an intellectual, moral, and spiritual ascent that begins with the study of grammar. A well-known example is provided by the short introductions to authors and texts found in several medieval manuscripts. These *accessus ad auctores* often identify the objective of poetic fiction with the ethical instruction of the reader. In his *Dialogus super auctores*, Conrad of Hirsau (*ca.* 1130) explains that liberal studies were so named because they led to spiritual liberation: "*in libertate vocati sumus*: studiis liberalibus regi nostro serviamus" ('We have been called forth to receive freedom' [Gal. 5: 13]. Let us then serve our king by pursuing liberal studies.).[29] Similarly, in his allegorical association of the heavens with the sciences, in the second book of the *Convivio* (13–14.19), Dante envisions an epistemological pathway that begins with the study of grammar and the other seven liberal

---

[27] Notably, Florence was the first city in Europe to translate into the vernacular its entire body of laws in 1356. For the importance of vernacular translations in fourteenth-century Florence and Italy, see Alison Cornish, *Vernacular Translation in Dante's Italy: Illiterate Literature* (Cambridge: Cambridge University Press, 2010).

[28] As stated in the *Epistula* to the lord of Verona, Can Grande de la Scala, which is generally attributed to Dante, "finis totius et partis est removere viventes in hac vita de statu miserie et perducere ad statum felicitatis" (*Ep.* 13.39).

[29] R. B. C. Huygens, ed., *Accessus ad auctores, Bernard d'Utrecht, Conrad d'Hirsau: Dialogus super auctores; Édition critique* (Leiden: Brill, 1970), 122, § 1581–82. Transl. is from Alistair J. Minnis, A. B. Scott, and David Wallace, eds., *Medieval Literary Theory and Criticism, c. 1100–c. 1375: The Commentary-Tradition* (New York: Clarendon Press, 1988), 64. Conrad's view was shared by many in the Middle Ages, such as Adelard of Bath. See *Des Adelard von Bath Traktat "De eodem et diverso,"* ed. Hans Willner, vol. 4 (Münster: Aschendorff, 1903), 16. For a general discussion of the medieval conceptions of liberal arts, see Jerome Taylor's introduction to his translation of *The Didascalicon of Hugh of Saint Victor: A Medieval Guide to the Arts* (New York: Columbia University Press, 1968), 3–42, esp. 17–19.

12   DANTE'S EDUCATION

arts, continues with that of physics and metaphysics, and culminates with the contemplation of the "divine science." Instead Brunetto Latini emphasizes the moral implications of literary studies from a secular perspective in his *Rettorica*, where he states that the study of poetry ("i detti de' poeti") instructs people on "how to act well" ("insegnamento e via di ben far").[30] Thus, as it clearly appears, "medieval reading was above all an ethical activity."[31]

In the history of the West, literacy has always meant more than just the perpetuation of an alphabet. Over the past century, several studies have claimed that the introduction of writing brought about transformations in mental and social structures, and the alphabet has been defined as a "technology" that "has shaped Western reality in a most profound way." Literacy has often been seen as an essential prerequisite for the democratization of citizenship and the secularization of learning.[32] But this view has increasingly been called into question—particularly the alleged link between literacy and economic prosperity.[33] Instead literacy has been shown to be a major instrument for underwriting cultural and social hegemonies. In medieval Europe, as Martin Irvine points out, grammar provided "the discursive rules and interpretative strategies that constructed certain texts as repositories of authority and value," while contributing to the identity formation and social empowerment of an elite of *litterati*. Revisiting Pierre Bourdieu, Katharine Breen argues that medieval grammar education was geared to the formation of a moral *habitus*: "the student does not merely learn rules, but he is himself regulated, made regular, by the language he studies and the discipline of the classroom in which he studies it." Walter Ong identified Renaissance Latin instruction with a "puberty rite" that male pupils underwent as part of their initiation into a social and cultural elite of the literate, while Gary P. Cestaro has shown

[30] Brunetto Latini, *La Rettorica*, ed. and trans. Stefania D'Agata D'Ottavi (Kalamazoo, MI: Western Michigan University, 2016), 17.21, p. 47. The Italian text is quoted from *La Rettorica di Brunetto Latini*, ed. Francesco Maggini (Florence: Galletti e Cocci, 1915), 35.

[31] John Dagenais, *The Ethics of Reading in Manuscript Culture: Glossing the Libro de Buen Amor* (Princeton, NJ: Princeton University Press, 1994), 17.

[32] Illich, *Vineyard of the Text*, 93.

[33] In his influential work *Orality and Literacy: The Technologizing of the Word* (New York: Methuen, 1982), Walter Ong claimed that "the Greek alphabet was democratizing" (91). In his seminal works, Jack Goody has offered a view of the effect of literacy on society, culture, and economics that has—perhaps inexactly—been labeled as deterministic. See Goody, *Literacy in Traditional Societies* (Cambridge: Cambridge University Press, 1968), and Goody, *The Power of the Written Tradition* (Washington, DC: Smithsonian Institution Press, 2000). Harvey J. Graff's work, instead, has targeted the "literacy myth" and highlighted the hegemonic and oppressive legacies of literacy in the West. See Graff, *The Legacies of Literacy: Continuities and Contradictions in Western Culture and Society* (Bloomington: Indiana University Press, 1987). More recently, Martin Devecka has proposed that an essential key to the debate about the role of literacy in antiquity is a consideration of the literacy rates in the ancient world. See Devecka, "Literacy," in *The Oxford Handbook of the Literatures of the Roman Empire*, ed. Daniel L. Selden and Phiroze Vasunia (Oxford: Oxford University Press, 2015), https://doi.org/10.1093/oxfordhb/9780199699445.013.40 accessed February 2024.

PROLOGUE   13

how this gendered conception of grammatical instruction, as both nurturing and disciplinary, informed Dante's oeuvre.[34]

Book-based Latin instruction also helped consolidate cultural identity and cohesion among different regional elites across Western Europe. This process was bolstered by the wide diffusion of Renaissance grammar schools. Their curricula and success depended on the ideological presupposition that fluency in Latin and Greek was essential for the acquisition of all knowledge.[35] Even today, literacy meshes with wider processes of social and cultural transformation, contributing to social segregation and equipping the members of any society with notions and values endorsed by different "cultures of teaching."[36] Dante's engagement with his time's "legacies of literacy" is integral to his work as both an innovator and a reformer.[37] As I maintain in this book, by revisiting Latin school texts in his vernacular works, Dante revised popular conceptions of poetry, its significance for nurturing ethical communities, and the role of classical antiquity in Christian culture.

The minor Latin school poems, in particular, should be scrutinized with great care in relation to Dante's original stance toward the ancient poetic tradition. Since Latin school texts were also taught to introduce pupils to the study of classical antiquity, these readings offered mediated access to the classics—just as medieval glosses and commentaries did.[38] Robert Black is alone in addressing the study of

---

[34] In order of mention: Martin Irvine, *The Making of Textual Culture: "Grammatica" and Literary Theory, 350–1100* (Cambridge: Cambridge University Press, 1994), 2; Katharine Breen, *Imagining an English Reading Public, 1150–1400* (Cambridge: Cambridge University Press, 2010), 2; Walter J. Ong, "Latin Language Study as a Renaissance Puberty Rite," *Studies in Philology* 56, no. 2 (1959): 103–24, reprinted in Ong, *Rhetoric, Romance, and Technology* (Ithaca, NY: Cornell University Press, 1971), 113–41; and Gary P. Cestaro, *Dante and the Grammar of the Nursing Body* (Notre Dame, IN: University of Notre Dame Press, 2003).

[35] On the ideological legacy of the Renaissance grammar school, see Anthony Grafton and Lisa Jardine, *From Humanism to the Humanities: Education and the Liberal Arts in Fifteenth and Sixteenth-Century Europe* (London: Duckworth, 1986); and Don Paul Abbot, "Rhetoric and Writing in Renaissance Europe and England," in *A Short History of Writing Instruction: From Ancient Greece to Contemporary America*, ed. James J. Murphy (New York: Routledge, 2012), 95–120. With a focus on modern and contemporary education in England and the United States, John Guillory has discussed the school's historical function of distributing, or regulating, access to the forms of cultural capital, which served the consolidation of class division. From this perspective, "literary works must be seen rather as the vector of ideological notions which do not inhere in the works themselves but in the context of their institutional presentation, or more simply, in the way in which they are taught." Guillory, *Cultural Capital: The Problem of Literary Canon Formation* (Chicago: University of Chicago Press, 1993), ix.

[36] Rebecca W. Bushnell, *A Culture of Teaching: Early Modern Humanism in Theory and Practice* (Ithaca, NY: Cornell University Press, 1996).

[37] Graff, *Legacies of Literacy*.

[38] On the importance of studying medieval commentaries and *accessus*, the reference work remains A. J. Minnis and A. B. Scott, eds., *Medieval Literary Theory and Criticism c. 1100–c. 1375: The Commentary Tradition* (Oxford and New York: Clarendon Press, Oxford University Press, 1988). See also R. Hanna et al., "Latin Commentary Tradition and Vernacular Literature," in *The Middle Ages*, vol. 2 of *The Cambridge History of Literary Criticism*, ed. A. J. Minnis and I. Johnson (Cambridge: Cambridge University Press, 2005), 361–421. Regarding their importance for the study of Dante's classicism, see Violetta de Angelis, "'. . . e l'ultimo Lucano,'" in *Dante e la "bella scola" della poesia: Autorità e sfida*

14   DANTE'S EDUCATION

Dante's classical culture from the perspective of his Latin education in Florence.[39] My methodology and conclusions, however, differ greatly from Black's. Although recent paleographical studies of medieval schoolbooks are essential to reconstruct trends and transformations in the educational canon, their approach does not necessarily meet the need for a comprehensive understanding of school texts as literary artifacts, thereby downplaying their influence on medieval literary theory. For this reason, in *Dante's Education*, I regard medieval Latin school texts primarily as a literary corpus. I consider their medieval reception, which can be inferred from commentaries, interlinear glosses, and other manuscript evidence, such as textual layout and other marginalia. My analysis reveals a largely unexplored history. The minor Latin authors deployed in medieval education should not be seen—as historians have often done—as an alternative to the major Latin authors, whose study was eventually reestablished by Renaissance humanist education.[40] Rather, as *Dante's Education* argues, since the minor Latin poems imitate and emulate the major classical poets to a large degree, Dante's reception of these school texts represented a form of classical humanism engaged with the absorption of ancient pagan lore into a new Christian and vernacular poetics. A third goal of the present book, therefore, is to lay the groundwork for interpreting school texts' position with respect to the major classical tradition—the ways in which they mediated classical reception during the Middle Ages and particularly their influence on Dante's classicism.

Consequently, *Dante's Education* delves into larger questions concerning the practices and aims of late medieval education. These questions need to be posed with a critical eye toward the generally accepted but nevertheless anachronistic dichotomy between minor and major Latin authors. Although such a distinction is drawn in medieval reading lists, it was not meant to rank the poetic quality of these works, but rather to mark a progression within a coherent and unified process of intellectual ascent toward knowledge and wisdom.[41] Studying the *auctores minores* was meant to prepare students to read the *maiores*.

After reasserting the thesis of the "decline" of classical culture in thirteenth-century Italy, Black claims that "an extraordinary figure such as Dante may have revealed considerable knowledge of the classics, but it cannot be assumed that this was based on a grounding at school."[42] I contend that there are significant elements of continuity between the classical reception offered by medieval school

---

poetica, ed. Amilcare Iannucci (Ravenna: Longo, 1993), 95–149. Zygmunt G. Barański ("The Classics") has recently reasserted the relevance of Dante's mediated access to the classics and pointed to the importance of school texts.

[39] Black, "Education," 260–76.

[40] The same conceptual opposition between the study of minor and major Latin authors is substantially reasserted by two essential studies on the curriculum of language instruction in medieval Florence, Gehl's *Moral Art* and Black's *Humanism*.

[41] See, for instance, Conrad of Hirsau, *Dialogus*.

[42] Black, *Humanism*, 197.

texts and some of the conceptual and technical solutions employed by the poet in his *Vita nova* and *Commedia*. Thus, it is my hope to contextualize Dante's poetic and intellectual contributions in relation to broad educational movements that shaped vernacular culture.

Dante's Poetics of Vernacular Learning

The book's argument unfolds as follows:

- Chapter 1, "An Introduction to Literacy and Education in Dante's Florence," surveys the extant evidence regarding literacy and grammar instruction in thirteenth-century Florence and Dante's earliest education. The chapter demonstrates the key importance of studying minor Latin school texts in reconstructing the culture of literacy shared by the poet and his contemporaries.
- Chapter 2, "Learning to Praise: The *Vita nova* as a Vernacular Reader," argues that Dante conceived his first experimental work, the *Vita nova*, as a "vernacular reader" for the rising Florentine lay readership. To engineer this groundbreaking literary artifact, the poet drew on the sources of his own education: the Latin readers that were parsed and memorized in thirteenth- and fourteenth-century Florentine schools. In particular, the *Vita nova* closely reworks two school texts found in these anthologies, Henry of Settimello's *Elegia* and Prosper of Aquitaine's *Liber epigrammatum*. Dante's first significant literary achievement, therefore, was already informed by a pervasive didacticism.
- Chapter 3, "(Un)like Aesop: Defining the *Commedia*'s Generic Monstrosity," traces Dante's creative reworking of school texts, as this evolved from the *Vita nova* to the *Commedia*. A close assessment of the reception of Aesopic fables in medieval education reveals the theoretical significance of Dante's reference to Aesop at *Inferno* 23.4. Glosses, commentaries, and encyclopedic texts show that medieval literary theory considered this genre of fables as paradigmatic of moralizing fiction. The presence of Aesop's name in *Inferno*, I argue, plays a pivotal role in Dante's discourse about the uniqueness of the *Commedia* vis-à-vis traditional definitions of "fable" and "comedy."
- Chapter 4, "*Pugna pro patria*: Freeing Cato from his *Distichs*," reinterprets the presence of the pagan suicide Cato in Dante's Christian Purgatory from the perspective of the *Disticha Catonis*'s popularity in medieval education. This collection of moralizing aphorisms spuriously attributed to Cato was one of the most popular school texts of medieval Europe. The *Disticha Catonis* were often quoted in contemporary political discussions about a citizen's

16   DANTE'S EDUCATION

duty to die for the homeland. The chapter shows how the political reception of this school text influenced Dante's representation of Cato in the *Commedia*.

After mastering the *Disticha Catonis*, medieval pupils often parsed and memorized another minor Latin poem, the *Ecloga Theoduli*. As Chapter 5, "A Lesson in Cross-Cultural Pastoral: The *Ecloga Theoduli* in *Purgatorio*," argues, Dante mirrored this selection of readings by modeling some of *Purgatorio*'s central cantos (9–12, 28) on the *Ecloga*. My analysis shows that the *Ecloga* supplied a fitting precedent and model for Dante's distinctive habit of placing episodes from Scripture side by side with ancient pagan myths, and for his representation of a river as the ultimate boundary that Virgil is not allowed to cross. The chapter goes on to argue that first in *Paradiso* 19 and then in his last work, the second *Egloga* to Giovanni del Virgilio, Dante obliquely criticizes the *Ecloga Theoduli*'s condemnation of ancient poetic wisdom.

Chapter 6, "Re-Dressing Achilles, Resisting Proserpina, Surpassing Virgil: The End of the Purgatorial Curriculum," confirms the key role of school texts in Dante's *Purgatorio* by examining possible allusions to Statius' *Achilleid* and Claudian's *De raptu Proserpinae* in cantos 9, 21–22, and 28 of the second canticle. The chapter shows how references to the two poems mark the protagonist's rite of passage to moral maturity and fulfill metapoetic functions by informing the poet's emulative engagement with the genre of the Latin epic and his original harmonization of epic and elegy.

Chapter 7, "'Be Silent, Ovid!' (You, Too, Statius and Claudian): Underground Voices in the Prologue to *Paradiso*," highlights the extensive intertextual allusions to both the *Achilleid* and the *De raptu Proserpinae* in the first two cantos of *Paradiso*. While rewriting Ovid in the opening of the *Commedia*'s last *cantica*, Dante also engages with the models of Ovidian emulation established by Statius and Claudian. Dante's intertextual dialogue creates a poetic genealogy that begins with Ovid, outdoes the epic poems endorsed by contemporary teachers, and culminates in the *Commedia*. *Paradiso* thus emerges as an alternative to these didactic models and the new standard for vernacular epic poetry.

The book's Epilogue, "The School that You Have Followed," closes on Dante's intertextual criticism of Henry of Settimello's *Elegia* in the crucial scene of his reunion with Beatrice at the top of Mount Purgatory. Here, Dante presents his own poetics of vernacular learning as a corrective to the instruction offered by established venues of higher education.

This prospectus of chapters omits a focused discussion of the *Convivio*, which readers might have expected from this book. The *Convivio* is only marginally discussed in the following pages because *Dante's Education* is *not* about Dante's philosophy of education. That topic requires an entirely different approach and belongs in a companion work to the present volume. That study (which I hope, in time, to add to this one) will investigate Dante's pedagogical thought in relation to established medieval traditions and contemporary vernacular discussions on what, to whom, how, and why a lay person should write to educate others. While operating within the confines of an illiterate society, Dante conceived of reading and learning as a key and accessible means for realizing humanity's natural and supernatural destiny. Albeit visionary in many ways, his intuition grew out of fertile soil. The historical and cultural reality that nurtured this idea remains mostly a mystery to us.

Figure P.2 Ambrogio Lorenzetti, *Allegory of the Good and Bad Government: The Good City*, Siena, Palazzo Pubblico, Sala dei Nove.

Source: Heritage Image Partnership Ltd./Alamy Stock Photo.

1

An Introduction to Literacy and Education in Dante's Florence

Questo sarà quello pane orzato del quale si satolleranno migliaia, e a me ne soverchieranno le sporte piene. Questo sarà luce nuova, sole nuovo, lo quale surgerà là dove l'usato tramonterà, e darà lume a coloro che sono in tenebre ed in oscuritade, per lo usato sole che a loro non luce.

(Convivio 1.13.12)

(This commentary shall be that bread made with barley by which thousands shall be satiated, and my baskets shall be full to overflowing with it. This shall be a new light, a new sun which shall rise where the old sun shall set and which shall give light to those who lie in shadows and in darkness because the old sun no longer sheds its light upon them.)

With this compelling imagery, the first chapter of Dante's unfinished *Convivio* (1304–08) captures the perceived novelty of writing a commentary in the vernacular in Italy at the turn of the fourteenth century. Like bread made with barley, the prose of the *Convivio* will be poor and less refined than the Latin texts from which it is compiled, yet nutritious and accessible for a larger audience made of literate laypeople.[1] Like a new sun, the vernacular will soon shed new light where Latin once illuminated the path of learning.[2] This biblical language conveys some

[1] The image of the *pane orzato* is rich in symbolic meanings ensuing from a significant tradition in both Roman and Christian texts. Among these instances, I single out Seneca's use of the same in one of his moral epistles, where it represents a type of knowledge that is unrefined, but nonetheless nutritious for Roman philosophers (*Ad Lucilium* 2.18.10). For a recent discussion of this image's complex meaning in Dante's *Convivio*, see Ambrogio Camozzi Pistoja, "Testo come eucarestia: linguaggio parabolico nel *Convivio* di Dante," *Studi danteschi* 84 (2019): 57–99, esp. 73.

[2] Whether Dante identifies the sun with the Convivio or the vernacular has been the object of some debate. The two, however, can hardly be separated, as Dante's audience of nonspecialists requires both a new language and a new organization of the knowledge made available by the Convivio. There is little doubt, moreover, as to the symbolic correlative of the setting sun that no longer sheds light on the path. This sun is the established language of learning, Latin. For a discussion of this extensive biblical metaphor, see Gianfranco Fioravanti's comm. ad loc., Convivio 1.13.12, in Dante Alighieri, *Convivio—Monarchia—Epistole—Egloge*, ed. Gianfranco Fioravanti et al., vol. 2 of Opere, ed. Marco Santagata (Milan: Mondadori, 2014), 186–87. Karla Mallette points out that "neither Dante nor Petrarch could

Dante's Education. Filippo Gianferrari, Oxford University Press. © Filippo Gianferrari (2024).
DOI: 10.1093/oso/9780198881766.003.0002

of Dante's excitement about the momentous transformation taking place as he was writing: a vernacular readership of laypeople, both men and women, was coming into existence as a social reality. Suggesting that this burgeoning audience represented the future of literature and culture, the author compares Latin to the setting sun—its light doomed to disappear. History, as we know, confirmed Dante's prophecy only centuries after his death. At that time, his claim challenged the historical foundations of Western education. Rather than depending on a gift of prophecy, Dante's defiance of the established hierarchy of learning relied on a practical consideration. Had he written the *Convivio* in Latin,

> Lo latino non l'averebbe esposte se non a' litterati, ché li altri non l'averebbero intese. Onde, con ciò sia cosa che molti più siano quelli che desiderano intendere quelle non litterati che litterati, séguitasi che non averebbe pieno lo suo comandamento come 'l volgare, [che] dalli litterati e non litterati è inteso.
>
> (*Convivio* 1.7.12)

> (Latin would not have explained them [the philosophical *canzoni* that are the object of Dante's commentary] except to the learned, for no one else would have understood it. Therefore, since among those who desire to understand them the unlearned are far more numerous than the learned, it follows that Latin would not have fulfilled their command as well as the vernacular, which is understood by the learned and the unlearned alike.)

Dante was a keen witness of the gradual advent of a lay literate community—if not yet a society—where for centuries culture had been, and still was, primarily oral.[3] From the late tenth century until the mid- to later thirteenth century, literacy grew, and its distribution shifted. More people, among both the clergy and the laity, acquired some level of literacy, while the number of lay schools came to surpass the number of ecclesiastical ones.[4] With the expansion and consolidation of the university movement during the twelfth and the thirteenth centuries, reading and

---

have known that Latinity's moment in the sun had passed." Yet here Dante seems to have a glimpse of what was bound to come, as Latin had long ceased to be a living language. See Mallette, *Lives of the Great Languages: Arabic and Latin in the Medieval Mediterranean* (Chicago: University of Chicago Press, 2021), 69.

[3] To be more precise, as Franz Bäuml notes, while "the majority of the population of Europe between the fourth and the fifteenth centuries was, in some sense, illiterate . . . medieval civilization was a literate civilization; the knowledge indispensable to the functioning of medieval society was transmitted in writing: the Bible and its exegesis, statutory laws, and documents of all kinds. The need for writing that served a wide variety of purposes is evident in the development of the *ars dictaminis*." Bäuml, "Varieties and Consequences of Medieval Literacy and Illiteracy," *Speculum* 55, no. 2 (1980): 237–65, at 237.

[4] Harvey J. Graff, *The Legacies of Literacy: Continuities and Contradictions in Western Culture and Society* (Bloomington: Indiana University Press, 1987), chaps. 2–3 and 4. See also Erich Auerbach, "The Western Public and Its Language," in *Literary Language and Its Public in Late Latin Antiquity and in the Middle Ages*, trans. Ralph Manheim (New York: Pantheon, 1965), 237–338, esp. 292.

20   DANTE'S EDUCATION

writing became essential means for gaining access to university training, and the number of readers and writers of technical literature increased.[5] Thus, literacy had become instrumental for the pursuit of some lucrative careers.[6] As Harvey J. Graff notes, the key to the "Italian development" in the history of literacy in the West was precisely "the early emergence of *professional* laymen: teachers, lawyers, notaries, and physicians, whose business in life made it necessary for them to be educated, especially in Latin."[7]

On the one hand, Dante openly reproves the new class of literate people who pursued an education for utilitarian reasons: "E a vituperio di loro dico che non si deono chiamare litterati, però che non acquistano la lettera per lo suo uso, ma in quanto per quella guadagnano denari o dignitate" (To their shame I say that they should not be called learned, because they do not acquire learning for its own use but only insofar as through it they may gain money or honor) (*Convivio* 1.9.3). Lawyers, physicians, and clerics are deemed undeserving of the bread of knowledge bestowed by his *Convivio* (1.9.2–3, 11, and 3.11.10). On the other hand, Dante is aware that such professional lay readers represent a new audience worth cultivating.[8] In addition to this university-trained *litterati*, the poet gestured to readers from the lay nobility and the upper classes, most of whom had little proficiency in Latin (*non litterati*). Their literacy, however, was far more advanced in

[5] About the expansion of the university movement, see Helene Wieruszowski, *The Medieval University. Masters, Students, and Learning* (Princeton, NJ: Van Nostrand, 1966), chap. 7. This development was reflected in the production of more legible manuscripts, equipped with paratextual tools to ease their consultation. See Malcolm B. Parkes, "The Influence of the Concepts of *Ordinatio* and *Compilatio* on the Development of the Book," in *Medieval Learning and Literature: Essays Presented to R. W. Hunt*, ed. J. J. G. Alexander and M. T. Gibson (Oxford: Oxford University Press, 1975), 115–41, and also Richard H. Rouse and Mary A. Rouse, "*Statim invenire*: Schools, Preachers, and New Attitudes to the Page," in *Renaissance and Renewal in the Twelfth Century*, ed. R. L. Benson and G. Constable (Cambridge, MA: Harvard University Press, 1982), 201–25, republished in Mary A. Rouse and Richard H. Rouse, *Authentic Witnesses: Approaches to Medieval Texts and Manuscripts* (Notre Dame, IN: University of Notre Dame Press, 1991), 191–255.

[6] As Graff (*Legacies of Literacy*, 54) points out, "in some small ways, literacy began to be associated with limited opportunities for social mobility and changes in position. It became more useful for more persons, although in an absolute sense few required it for their livelihoods and welfare."

[7] Graff, *Legacies of Literacy*, 57.

[8] Recent studies on the intended readers of the *Convivio* and Dante's attitude toward them have shown the tension between the outspoken condemnation and exclusion of those with professional and secular learning and the author's actual intention to lure them into his program of spiritual renewal. See, for instance, Ambrogio Camozzi Pistoja, "Testo come eucarestia. Linguaggio parabolico nel Convivio di Dante," *Studi danteschi* 84 (2019): 57–99, and Enrica Zanin, "'Miseri, 'mpediti, affamati': Dante's Implied Reader in the *Convivio*," in *Dante's* Convivio, *or How to Restart a Career in Exile*, ed. Franziska Meier (Oxford: Peter Lang, 2018), 207–21. It is also essential to consider that despite Dante's protestations in *Convivio*, the members of his intellectual circle in Ravenna, during the last year of his life, belonged precisely to these professional categories. They had university-level education and were endowed with advanced literacy in the vernacular; they viewed Dante as an authority from whom they wished to learn. Important work has been done in recent years to reconstruct Dante's intellectual circles and milieus in Ravenna. For a good summary of the findings, see Marco Petoletti, *Dante e la sua eredità a Ravenna nel Trecento* (Ravenna: Longo, 2015). See also Alessandro Barbero, *Dante* (Bari: Laterza, 2020), 259–62.

the vernacular, and their desire for knowledge was hindered by domestic and civic responsibilities (*Convivio* 1.1.4 and 1.11.6).

As Erich Auerbach highlights, Dante "molded, as potential readers of his poem, a community which was scarcely in existence at the time when he wrote and which was gradually built up by his poem and by the poets who came after him."[9] On the other hand, Auerbach maintaines, Dante was able to write "a sublime poetry on a level with the great models of antiquity" *because* he could rely on an established vernacular literary language and "a public capable of understanding such poetry."[10] While the historical emergence of a lay readership is indeed at the heart of Dante's popularizing project in the vernacular—as it had already been for Brunetto Latini and Bono Giamboni—Dante makes it clear that many among this lay public could hardly have possessed the literary skills and breadth of classical culture implied by both the *Convivio* and the *Commedia*. The actual ability of Dante's most cherished readers to appreciate his groundbreaking cultural project and poetics, therefore, would have been considerably more limited than Auerbach assumed. If Latin was still the language of learning—the "old sun"—how were the lay, vernacular readers (*non litterati*) supposed to grasp Dante's remarkable philosophical and literary innovations? One of the solutions often proposed is to see Dante as someone belonging to the small elite of those with university-level training and targeting an audience that shared his same advanced education. Paradoxically, therefore, while the poet stressed the wide reach of his cultural project, in practice his works perpetuated an established social and intellectual hierarchy of readers. Such a conclusion would contradict the intentions Dante states at the opening of his *Convivio*. Had he conceived either the *Convivio* or the *Commedia* primarily for a public of university-trained *litterati*, he would have betrayed the very culture of vernacular learning he was striving to establish: the new light and new sun—an ideal, it should be noted, that the poet advocated until the end of his life.[11]

As this chapter shows, the root of this apparent conundrum lies in our limited ability to reconstruct the cultural literacy shared by Dante's lay readers. This vernacular audience and the educational landscape in which the poet operated were more nuanced and fluid than is often assumed. Furthermore, to meet the professional and intellectual needs of a growing literate society, schooling was also undergoing a significant process of transformation at that time. Instruction in the vernacular—particularly in the *abbaco* schools—was slowly emerging, but the backbone of education was still in Latin. To extend the metaphor Dante uses in the *Convivio*, lay culture was illuminated by two suns: it was suffused with the dawning light of vernacular literacy, while at the same time still pervaded by the twilight of Latin, the primary language of instruction.

[9] Auerbach, "The Western Public and Its Language," in *Literary Language*, 312.
[10] Auerbach, "Camilla, or the Rebirth of the Sublime," in *Literary Language*, 182–233, 232.
[11] As exemplified, for instance, by one of Dante's latest works, the bucolic exchange with Giovanni del Virgilio. A brief discussion of this exchange is provided in Chapter 5.

22   DANTE'S EDUCATION

Despite Dante's claim, Latin was in fact gaining new strength in some elite milieus, as in the proto-humanist Paduan circles, and was soon to have a powerful comeback.[12] The Florentine milieu in which the poet was first educated, however, featured a developed network of independent schools where language instruction, albeit still centered on a handful of minor Latin texts, was increasingly oriented toward preparing pupils for professional careers for which vernacular literacy sufficed. Reconstructing these different educational trends, as well as the types of literacy that defined the poet's contemporary audience, is pivotal to appreciating the shared literary culture on which Dante could rely to build a pedagogical program in the vernacular suitable for the laity.

The Growth of Lay Education

Literacy was relatively widespread in Italian communes on the cusp of the fourteenth century.[13] Increasingly complex bureaucratic systems required civic administrations to keep large volumes of documentation constantly updated, while the development of microcredit mechanisms intensified the need for written records in business transactions.[14] Scores of notaries, clerks, and officials had become indispensable. In the context of the civic struggles that opposed the old aristocracy to the thriving popular front—the *popolo*—and reshaped the political order of late medieval Italian cities, literacy also constituted a means for improving social mobility, as well as political stability and cohesion.[15] "New" families with

---

[12] On this point, see Ronald G. Witt, *"In the Footsteps of the Ancients": The Origins of Humanism from Lovato to Bruni* (Leiden: Brill, 2000).

[13] Graff, *Legacies of Literacy*, chap. 4.

[14] On the socioeconomic and cultural implications of literacy in the late Middle Ages, see, for example, John Ahern, "The New Life of the Book: Oral and Written Communication in the Age of Dante" (Ph.D. diss., Indiana University, 1976), 117; Auerbach, "The Western Public and Its Language," 293–96; Franz Bäuml, "Varieties and Consequences," esp. 256; Graff, *Legacies of Literacy*, chaps. 2–4; J. K. Hyde, "Some Uses of Literacy in Venice and Florence in the Thirteenth and Fourteenth Century," *Transactions of the Royal Historical Society* 29 (1979): 109–28, esp. 112–35; Lauro Martines, *Power and Imagination: City-States in Renaissance Italy* (Baltimore, MD: Johns Hopkins University Press, 1988), 81; John M. Najemy, *A History of Florence, 1200–1575* (Malden, MA: Blackwell, 2006), 45; and Armando Petrucci, *Readers and Writers in Medieval Italy: Studies in the History of Writing* (New Haven, CT: Yale University Press, 1995), esp. 132–41.

[15] The *popolo* was a pressure group that protected the interests of the commoners—wealthy merchants and businessmen—against the nobility. According to Antonio Lanci's entry, "Popolo," in the *ED*, Dante also uses the term according to its sociopolitical meaning in *Paradiso* 16.131. Two influential studies on the Italian *popolo* are John Koening, *Il "popolo" dell'Italia del nord nel XIII secolo* (Bologna: il Mulino, 1986), and Gaetano Salvemini, *Magnati e popolani in Firenze dal 1280 al 1295*, ed. Ernesto Sestan (Turin: Einaudi, 1960 [1899]). For a more recent discussion of the *popolo* in the political landscape of Dante's Italy, see Edward Coleman, "Cities and Communes," in *Italy in the Central Middle Ages*, ed. David Abulafia (Oxford: Oxford University Press, 2004), 27–57; William Caferro, "Empire, Italy, and Florence," in *Dante in Context*, ed. Zygmunt G. Barański and Lino Pertile (Cambridge: Cambridge University Press, 2015), 9–29, esp. 22; and Jean-Claude Maire Vigueur, *Cavalieri e cittadini. Guerre, conflitti e società nell'Italia comunale* (Bologna: il Mulino, 2004).

acquired wealth wished for their children to attend school. Women, too, especially those of high social status, gained relatively more access to education, either within their families, studying with independent teachers, or in religious orders.[16] To accommodate the broader social demand for literacy instruction, schooling and the production of books became increasingly urban and lay activities. The renewed attention given to the development of education as a perceived engine for the economic and political growth of cities is evidenced by the fact that some Italian communes offered and organized free instruction.[17]

As merchants, notaries, bankers, and preachers came to occupy key social and political roles in the corporate world of the Italian communes, the rich bilingual activity of these professionals created, in Bernhard Bischoff's words, "plurilingual regions" and "linguistic borders" that were natural homes to interpreters and translators. Merchants were vernacular writers, as they wrote letters and kept records for both professional and personal reasons; preachers developed forms of vernacular oratory; and notaries wrote documents both in Latin and the vernacular. The revitalized notarial class became chiefly responsible for producing and disseminating new vernacular texts. Vernacular poetry began to expand from the margins of public, professional writings—on which it was copied.[18] The cultural activity of these literate professionals is also documented by the production of *volgarizzamenti*—vernacular translations, or rather compendia with commentaries, of Latin and other foreign texts—which began toward the end of the thirteenth century and grew steadily throughout the fourteenth. The burgeoning number of *volgarizzamenti* met an increasing demand for written products in the vernacular to support independent learning.[19]

---

[16] Paul F. Grendler, *Schooling in Renaissance Italy: Literacy and Learning, 1300–1600* (Baltimore: Johns Hopkins University Press, 1989), 87–108. It seems that in some cases even the children of poor families received some degree of elementary education (102–03).

[17] Paolo Rosso, *La scuola nel Medioevo: Secoli VI–XV* (Rome: Carocci, 2018), 163.

[18] Bernard Bischoff, "The Study of Foreign Languages in the Middle Ages," *Speculum* 36 (1961): 209–24, at 210–11. On the growth of professional literacy and lay intelligentsia, see also Paul F. Gehl, "Preachers, Teachers, Translators: The Social Meaning of Language Study in Trecento Tuscany," *Viator* 25 (1994): 289–324; Najemy, *History*, 46–48; H. Wayne Storey, *Transcription and Visual Poetics in the Early Italian Lyric* (New York: Garland, 1993), 5–69; and Mirko Tavoni, "Linguistic Italy," in *Dante in Context*, 249–59. Before the twelfth century, vernacular texts were traditionally confined to occasional means of circulation—such as the margins and the "guard" pages of books and registers, or flyleaves—that rarely reached beyond restricted professional or cultural circles. Oral forms of declamations and songs remained the principal vehicles for broader circulation. See Petrucci, *Readers and Writers*, 177; Cesare Segre, "Oralità e scrittura nell'epica medioevale," in *Oralità: Cultura, letteratura, discorso: Atti del Convegno Internazionale (Urbino 21–25 luglio 1980)*, ed. Bruno Gentili and Giuseppe Paioni (Rome: Edizioni dell'Ateneo, 1985), 19–35.

[19] In the vast literature about the *volgarizzamenti* in Italy, see Sara Bischetti et al., eds., *Toscana bilingue: Storia sociale della traduzione medievale* (Berlin: De Gruyter, 2021); Alison Cornish, *Vernacular Translation in Dante's Italy: Illiterate Literature* (Cambridge: Cambridge University Press, 2010); Giuseppe De Luca, *Scrittori di religione del Trecento: Volgarizzamenti* (Turin: Einaudi, 1977); Gianfranco Folena, *Volgarizzare e tradurre* (Turin: Einaudi, 1991); Cesare Segre, *Volgarizzamenti del Due e Trecento* (Turin: UTET, 1963); and Segre, "I Volgarizzamenti del Due e Trecento," in *Lingua, stile e società: Studi sulla storia della prosa italiana* (Milan: Feltrinelli, 1976 [1963]), 49–78. The database

24 DANTE'S EDUCATION

The vernacular audience of these works was socially diversified and occupied several intermediate levels between complete illiteracy and advanced literacy. Readers in the Middle Ages could be categorized according to which type of literacy they possessed: "professional" literacy, shared by scholars and men of letters; "recreational" literacy, typical of cultivated but nonprofessional readers, often from aristocratic families and living in courts; and finally "pragmatic" literacy, practiced by those who read and wrote habitually in the exercise of recording transactions as part of their businesses.[20] Those who could read the vernacular but not Latin were labeled as *illitterati*, or *ydioti*, and were usually laypeople. Instead the term "laici" was used to designate people without substantial university-level training, as opposed to the *clerici* (clergy) and *litterati*, who had been educated in conventual schools and universities and were proficient in both the vernacular and Latin.[21] The category of those whose literacy and culture was halfway between Latin and the vernacular, the so-called *modice litterati*, was expanding in the social milieus of thirteenth-century northern Italian cities. On occasion, these people pursued careers as public functionaries. This audience of intermediate *litterati* fed into the genre of didactic and popularizing literature in the vernacular, which was written by authors with more advanced Latin literacy and culture and, sometimes, university training.[22] A key engine of the vernacular movement, therefore, was the cultural activity of the laity.[23]

Tuscan cities featured particularly high literacy rates among the laity. The density of practical writing and *volgarizzamenti* produced in Florence alone during the thirteenth and fourteenth centuries stands out.[24] A small "society of letters" appears to have been active in the city since approximately the 1260s and, by the

DiVo offers an up-to-date collection of the most ancient Italian *volgarizzamenti*. See http://divoweb. ovi.cnr.it/(S(qeoclx45nlczrr55qshbu42c))/CatForm01.aspx, accessed March 2023.

[20] Malcolm B. Parkes, "The Literacy of the Laity," in *Scribes, Scripts and Readers: Studies in the Communication, Presentation and Dissemination of Medieval Texts* (London: Hambledon Press, 1991), 275–97. On the wide variety of literacy among medieval Italian readers and scribes, see Storey, *Transcription*, 8–9.

[21] Ruedi Imbach has defined *laicus* as follows: "illiterate 'lay' people are all men and women who were not regularly enrolled in university courses in the Faculty of Arts or Theology." Imbach, *Dante, la philosophie et les laics* (Paris-Fribourg: Cerf-Éditions Universitaires, 1996), here quoted from *Dante, la filosofia e i laici*, ed. and trans. Pasquale Porro (Genova: Marietti, 2001), 131–66. See also Ruedi Imbach and Catherine König-Pralong, *La sfida laica: Per una nuova storia della filosofia medievale* (Rome: Carocci, 2016), 23–36.

[22] On the *modice litterati*, see Enrico Artifoni, "Ancora sulla *parva letteratura* tra latino e volgari," in *Toscana bilingue*, 107–24.

[23] An exception should be noted. The popularizing religious movements and orders, such as the Franciscans and the Dominicans, were also promoting the diffusion of religious texts and sermons in the vernacular. See De Luca, *Scrittori di religione*.

[24] Rosso, *La scuola*, 163. Notable, for instance, is the case of secondhand dealers who operated in considerable numbers in thirteenth-century Florence and had enough literacy in the vernacular to keep detailed shop registers. See Gianfranco Cherubini, "Un rigattiere fiorentino del Duecento," in *Studi in onore di Arnaldo d'Addario*, ed. Luigi Borgia et al. (Lecce: Conte Editore, 1995), 761–72. Based on his study of artisan life and culture in thirteenth-century Florence, Cherubini claims that "non diversamente da altri artigiani o commercianti della sua città, il rigattiere aveva dunque avuto familiarità con la penna e con la lettura" (765).

end of the 1300s, a number of citizens averaging about 50 percent of the total population shared some levels of literacy.[25] According to Giovanni Villani's account of education in Florence in 1338–39—quoted in the *Prologue*—elementary schools were attended by 8,000–10,000 children, while six schools of *abbaco* enrolled between 10,000 and 12,000 students, and four schools of grammar and logic enrolled around 600 pupils. Considering that the city's population averaged about 120,000 people before the Black Death, with a birth rate of 6,000 children every year, Villani's figures appear remarkably high for the time. Hence, scholars have long doubted their accuracy. Paul Grendler calculates that these numbers would correspond to approximately 67 to 83 percent of Florentine boys, a rather astronomical figure. Robert Black points out that Villani's numbers anticipate by nearly a century the figures disclosed by the Florentine *Catasto* of 1427, according to which approximately 69.3 percent of male city residents were apparently able to write.[26] An indisputable fact about advanced literacy in the city is that 932 notaries were enrolled in the notarial guild in 1338 (Villani sets the number of notaries and lawyers at 700), and about 1,100 were active in Florence between 1250 and 1325.[27]

Because of its size and expanding economy, Florence had a relatively high degree of social mobility, and literacy came to be perceived as significant in the pursuit of individuals' and families' ambitions.[28] The *popolo* gained control over the city's government from 1250 to 1260 and established power firmly after 1282. After the reforms passed in 1282, being officially enrolled in one of the major guilds (*arti*) allowed for participation in the city council—the *consiglio del popolo*—which was the first step of a political career. Although not among the requirements for accessing the *arti*, literacy was nonetheless instrumental to several of the

---

[25] Witt, "*In the Footsteps*," 177. See also Najemy, *History*, 45–46; Rosso, *La scuola*, 163; and Tavoni, "Linguistic Italy," 254.

[26] Giovanni Villani, *Nuova Cronica* 12.94, ed. Giuseppe Porta, vol. 3 (Parma: U. Guanda, 1990–91), 198; Grendler, *Schooling*, 71–73. Grendler's percentile is calculated on a population of 120,000, pre-Black Death, as estimated by David Herlihy and Christiane Klapisch-Zuber in *Les Toscans et leurs familles: Une étude du catasto florentin de 1427* (Paris: Fondation Nationale des Sciences Politiques, 1978), 176. Villani numbers 90,000 "mouths" in the city, but this figure conflicts with the one he provides for the number of baptisms. Grendler also notes that Villani likely inflated the enrollments of both *abbaco* and grammar schools, as Florence would have needed a disproportionate number of teachers to instruct a similar number of students. For different interpretations of these figures, see Robert Black, *Education and Society in Florentine Tuscany* (Leiden-Boston: Brill, 2007), 1, and Paul Gehl, *A Moral Art: Grammar, Society, and Culture in Trecento Florence* (Ithaca, NY: Cornell University Press, 1993), 21–26.

[27] Irene Ceccherini and Teresa De Robertis, "*Scriptoria* e cancelleria nella Firenze del XIV secolo," in *Scriptorium: Wesen, Funktion, Eigenheiten*, ed. Andreas Nievergelt et al. (Munich: Bayerische Akademie der Wissenschaften, 2015), 141–65, at 142. See also Irene Ceccherini, "Le scritture dei notai e dei mercanti a Firenze tra Duecento e Trecento: Unità, varietà, stile," *Medioevo e Rinascimento* 24 (2010): 29–68, esp. 31–32, and Franek Sznura, "Per la storia del notariato fiorentino: i più antichi elenchi superstiti dei giudici e dei notai fiorentini (anni 1291 e 1338)," in *Tra libri e carte: Studi in onore di Luciana Mosiici*, ed. Teresa De Robertis and Giancarlo Savino (Florence, Franco Cesari Editore, 1998), 437–515.

[28] See Robert Davidsohn, *Storia di Firenze*, vol. 4 t. 3 (Florence: Sansoni, 1973), 211, and Witt, "*In the Footsteps*," 174.

26   DANTE'S EDUCATION

professions that belonged to the major guilds.[29] The wealthy commercial families, instead, sought to advance their heirs' education not only through functional and practical training, but also by enriching their linguistic and literary culture, as a means to assimilate to the urban nobility. In time, this "politics" of education engendered a highly literate class of merchants and entrepreneurs that was responsible for an outpouring of practical and personal writings, particularly in Florence.[30]

Generally, however, merchants, bankers, and artisanal entrepreneurs with large-scale businesses could afford only what was essential for the education of their future apprentices. Most pupils acquired their literacy by memorizing Latin prayers, learned the rudiments of commercial record-keeping, and read pious books in the vernacular.[31] During this elementary stage of education, they learned "the technical skills of literacy without necessarily focusing on the practice of literacy," as Sarah Lynch notes.[32] Once they had mastered such elementary proficiency, they either set out to be apprentices in the *bottega* (workshop), learning from artisans and other professionals, or went on to the *abbaco* schools to study commercial mathematics. Rarely did these pupils study Latin grammar. Advanced proficiency in Latin was a skill essential only for churchmen and a very few lay professionals— notaries, physicians, and judges—but it no longer constituted the only useful type of literacy for the pursuit of a remunerative career.[33] Villani well encapsulates this state of affairs in marking a clear separation between the teaching of literacy ("stavano a leggere del continuo"), which was accessible to a large number of pupils (8,000–10,000), and the more advanced teaching of grammar, pursued instead only by a minority of students (500–600).

Villani's account, moreover, reveals that a developed network of schools supported the expansion of literacy in Florence. Schooling in Italian cities grew

---

[29] In addition, some of the *arti*, like those of the *medici* and *speziali*, could have opened their doors to professional literates on occasion. See Raffaele Ciasca, *L'arte dei Medici e Speziali nella storia e nel commercio fiorentino dal Secolo XII al XV* (Florence: Olschki, 1927).

[30] Graff, *Legacies of Literacy*, 56. Exemplary of the later development of this politics of education is the case of a 1461 document from Venice in which a rich merchant of drapery wishes his adoptive son to have the practical education of a draper, in the *bottega*, while also being educated in reading, writing, and music. See Franco Franceschi, ". . . E seremo tutti ricchi": Lavoro, mobilità sociale e conflitti nelle città dell'Italia medievale (Pisa: Pacini, 2012), 83. Franceschi (". . . E seremo tutti ricchi," 70) also points to the evidence that among the literate artisans the compilation and use of manuals known as "manuali di preparazione e consultazione" seems to have been a common practice. Antonio Montefusco and Sara Bischetti ("Prime osservazioni su *Ars dictaminis*, cultura volgare e distribuzione sociale dei saperi nella toscana medievale," *Carte romanze* 6, no. 1 [2018]: 163–240) maintain that merchants and bankers, especially from Florence, are often the ones pushing for writing documents in the vernacular, thus pointing to the role played by this productive class in the expansion of the vernacular.

[31] Gehl, *Moral Art*, 35–36.

[32] Sarah Lynch, *Elementary and Grammar Education in Late Medieval France* (Amsterdam: Amsterdam University Press, 2017), 111.

[33] Giovanni Villani (*Nuova Cronica* 12.94) indicates that those who went on studying logic and Latin in Florence did so to pursue careers in law, medicine, or the church. Interestingly, these three categories of professionals are precisely the ones attacked by Dante in *Convivio* 3.11.10 for their merely utilitarian pursuit of knowledge.

considerably during the thirteenth century and reached new levels of organization during the fourteenth. Three types of educational providers operated in Italian cities: communal schools, run by teachers who were appointed and paid by the civic government, or a university if one was in place; independent schools created by freelance masters, who taught either in their homes or in rented premises and were paid by parents; and ecclesiastical schools, sponsored either by the bishop or by religious orders in monasteries. Ecclesiastical schools, which had traditionally been the primary providers of education, sharply declined in number—only a few of them appear to have survived in Italy after 1300. Instead, lay, urban schools multiplied and gradually replaced the ecclesiastical schools.[34]

When faced with the growing and diversified demand for instruction in technical subjects, such as calculus, arithmetic, navigation, law, and measurements, church schools proved especially obsolete. A number of specialized schools run by local professionals opened to fulfill different educational needs: elementary schools taught reading and writing, grammar schools taught Latin at a more advanced level, and abacus schools prepared clerks and other employees who operated in large-scale trades and banking. Notaries and merchants founded their own schools, contributing to the formation of curricula of studies in the vernacular for advanced and technical instruction.

Some communes eventually imposed a public monopoly on instruction, whereas others favored an open and competitive market. Still others left the initiative entirely to private teachers and families, who negotiated terms and conditions among themselves.[35] Small towns and villages tended to follow the first model, whereas large cities leaned toward the other two. Professional corporations and lay confraternities became chiefly preoccupied with education. While confraternities prioritized the instruction of poor and abandoned children, corporation schools were set up to train future merchants and notaries. Where a university was in place, moreover, courses of notarial writing were taught as adjunct studies in the faculty of arts.[36]

Pre-university teaching became a profession that could be learned through apprenticeship and was mostly regulated by private contracts. Independent elementary teachers, known as *doctores puerorum*, formed a professional class organized in corporations. These teachers were mostly, although not exclusively, male and often from the notarial class. They taught the alphabet, elementary reading,

---

[34] On the importance of cathedral and bishopric schools in Carolingian Italy and their decline in the time of the free communes, see Grendler, *Schooling*, 9, and Giuseppe Manacorda, *Il Medioevo*, vols. 1–2 of *Storia della scuola in Italia* (Sandron: Milan, 1914), esp. vol. 1, chaps. 2 and 4.

[35] Grendler (*Schooling*, 11) maintains that "civil governments and parents created the schools of Renaissance Italy." See also Robert Black, *Humanism and Education in Medieval and Renaissance Italy: Tradition and Innovation in Latin Schools from the Twelfth to the Fifteenth Century* (Cambridge: Cambridge University Press, 2001), 34–35; Carla Frova, *Istruzione e educazione nel Medioevo* (Turin: Loescher, 1974), 100–05; and Najemy, *History*, 46.

[36] Rosso, *La scuola*, 70–72.

28   DANTE'S EDUCATION

and a rudimentary introduction to Latin grammar.[37] Teachers of commercial mathematics, *maestri d'abbaco*, were also very active in cities at this time. Independent teachers often moved around seeking employment from different communal administrations, thereby creating a sort of educational network throughout the urban centers of northern Italy.[38] Women also engaged in the business of elementary instruction, as shown by extant contracts.[39] As Black notes, "the horizons of elementary teachers hardly extended further than the most rudimentary knowledge of Latin; the culture of abacus masters was firmly rooted in the vernacular, which was the language of their textbooks and teaching; Latin was the province of the grammar masters whose interests and preparation were limited to Latin language, literature, and basic philology."[40] Although Latin texts continued to provide the bulk of elementary education, vernacular literacy and education gradually infiltrated teaching practices and eventually became an alternative to Latin instruction.[41]

The concomitant rise of mendicant and lay *studia* also contributed to the growth of schooling in the Italian communes. Establishing *studia* in large urban centers was paramount to the mendicants' project of theological renewal and lay evangelization at the beginning of the thirteenth century. Conventual schools provided instruction in grammar, logic, and theology and were often equipped with *scriptoria* and libraries. The *studium artium*, where grammar was taught, was sometimes located outside the convent and open to all children.[42] External schools became a common feature of Dominican education in Italy. Although the friars ran their schools and appointed grammar teachers, they often relied on financial support from local governments or wealthy patrons. The extent of laypeople's access to grammar instruction in conventual schools remains unclear. It is nonetheless evident that a mutual exchange of teachers, students, and books regularly took place between mendicant schools and their surrounding cities.[43]

---

[37] Some teachers privately tutored the children of noble and wealthy citizens and could live with the family in their home—as, for instance, in the case of Giovanni Velluti's son at the end of the fourteenth century. See Santorre Debenedetti, "Sui più antichi 'doctores puerorum' a Firenze," *Studi Medievali* 2 (1907): 327–51, 345n1.

[38] Bonvesin da la Riva, a friar and grammar teacher, reported that in mid-thirteenth-century Milan there were more than seventy elementary teachers engaged in teaching literacy and eight local teachers (*magistri*)—plus some other foreigners—who taught grammar. A similar educational and professional landscape characterized other large Italian cities, such as Venice and Florence. Quoted in Rosso, *La scuola*, 162.

[39] Rosso, *La scuola*, 164.

[40] Black, *Humanism*, 30.

[41] Robert Black, "Teaching Techniques: The Evidence of Manuscript Schoolbooks Produced in Tuscany," in *The Classics in the Medieval and Renaissance Classroom*, ed. Junita Feros Ruys, John O. Ward, and Melanie Heyworth (Turnhout, Belgium: Brepols, 2013), 245–63, at 263.

[42] Dominican sources distinguish between *noviti*, students who entered the grammar school with the intention of eventually joining the convent, and *pueri*, who enrolled in the school only for the purpose of learning grammar. See M. Michèle Mulchahey, *"First the Bow Is Bent in Study": Dominican Education before 1350* (Toronto: Pontifical Institute of Mediaeval Studies, 1998), 86.

[43] As a result of the lack of teachers among the clergy in the late fourteenth century, monasteries and convents began to hire lay teachers, who came to live and teach grammar in the convent.

The rise of universities, with their growing monopoly on higher and professional education, also helped strengthen and transform pre-university instruction. In cities where a lay *studium* was in place, grammar teachers were often on the university's payroll, and the organization of schools and their curricula increasingly fell under academic control. As a result, primary grammar instruction became more compartmentalized. The role of grammar teachers was limited to introducing students to literacy and the basics of Latin grammar in preparation for university-level training.[44]

In thirteenth-century Florence, instead, schooling developed spontaneously in response to the growing and widespread demand for professional literacy. Unlike other towns in Tuscany, the Florentine commune made no centralized attempt to run public schools and did not have elementary grammar masters on the city payroll—not even during the following century. Education in the city was a private and secular business. Several *doctores puerorum* appear to have been active from the last quarter of the thirteenth century, and they operated independently, stipulating private contracts with their students' families.[45] By 1316, *doctores puerorum*, instructors of *abbaco*, and grammar teachers organized themselves into a minor guild. The teaching of the *abbaci* in Florence was especially developed. Teachers of *abbaco* ran their schools in the *botteghe*, where they gave pupils some limited instruction in the vernacular, practical numeracy for accounting, and different modes of letter writing.[46] From Villani's account mentioned earlier, we can surmise

---

See Black, *Humanism*, 173–243. For discussions about lay participation in education in conventual schools, see Zygmunt Barański, "Studying the Spaces of Dante's Intellectual Formation: Some Problems of Definition," in *"I luoghi nostri": Dante's Natural and Cultural Spaces*, ed. Zygmunt Barański, Andreas Kablitz, and Ülar Ploom (Tallinn: Tallinn University Press, 2015), 257–88, esp. 263; Charles T. Davis, "Scuola," in the *ED*, and "Education in Dante's Florence," *Speculum* 40 (1965): 415–35, reprinted in *Dante's Italy and Other Essays* (Philadelphia: University of Pennsylvania Press, 1984), 137–65; Anna Pegoretti, "Filosofanti," *Le tre corone* 2 (2015): 11–70; Johannes Bartuschat, Elisa Brilli, and Delphine Carron, eds., *The Dominicans and the Making of Florence (13th–14th Centuries)* (Florence: Firenze University Press, 2020); Sylvain Piron, "Le poète et le théologien: une rencontre dans le *Studium* de Santa Croce," *Picenum Seraphicum* 19 (2000): 87–134, now in *Ut philosophia poesis: Questions philosophiques dans l'écriture de Dante, Pétrarque, Bocacce*, ed. Fosca Mariani-Zini and Joël Biard (Paris: Vrin, 2008), 73–112; and Rosso, *La scuola*, 174.

[44] Robert Black and Gabriella Pomaro, *La consolazione della filosofia nel Medioevo e nel Rinascimento italiano: libri di scuola e glosse nei manoscritti fiorentini* (Florence: SISMEL Edizioni del Galluzzo, 2000), esp. 24–25. Among northern Italian cities, Bologna had the largest number of elementary and secondary schools administered by the university (Grendler, *Schooling*, 26).

[45] On lay teachers and schools in Florence, see Robert Black, "Education," in *Dante in Context*, 260–76, esp. 260–61; Davidsohn, *Storia*, vol. 7, 315–16; Davis, "Scuola"; Debenedetti, "Sui più antichi"; Enrico Fiumi, "Economia e vita privata dei fiorentini nelle rilevazioni statistiche di Giovanni Villani," *Archivio Storico Italiano* 111 (1953): 239–41; Frova, *Istruzione*, 105; Gino Masi, ed., *Formularium Florentinum Artis Notariae (1200–1242)* (Milan: Vita e Pensiero, 1943); Giuseppe Papaleoni, "Maestri di grammatica toscani dei secoli XIII e XIV," *Archivio Storico Italiano* 14 (1894): 149–52; Najemy, *History*, 53–54; and Helene Wieruszowski, "*Ars Dictaminis* in the Time of Dante," in *Medievalia et Humanistica* 1 (1943): 95–108.

[46] The most ancient extant record of a Florentine *abbachista* is a 1313 contract, but the activity of *abbaco* schools in the city certainly predated this document. See Davis, "Scuola," and Debenedetti, "Sui più antichi," 345. Florence's *abbaco* teaching was so developed that, in the mid-fourteenth century, the city was providing *abbachisti* also to Venice, Verona, and Lucca (Black, *Humanism*, 153). For more

30   DANTE'S EDUCATION

that, in Florence, reading and *abbaco* were taught in different schools. This separation was not common to other Italian cities. Venetian boys, for instance, would study for several years in schools that combined education in vernacular reading and writing, Latin grammar, *abbaco*, and commercial bookkeeping. Instead, Florentine pupils between the ages of eleven and fifteen took a two-year course focused on the *abbaco*.[47] This peculiar emphasis on *abbaco* instruction points to the professional aims that informed the organization of schooling in the city and pushed Latin education to the margins.

Tellingly, advanced grammatical instruction in the city appears to have been rather underdeveloped during the thirteenth century, even in comparison to smaller Tuscan centers.[48] During the first half of that century, grammatical and rhetorical training for the laity was mostly limited to elementary literacy, while grammar was often taught as part of notarial instruction.[49] Florence's offerings in the field of higher education were also surprisingly modest when compared with what was available in nearby Tuscan cities such as Pistoia, Arezzo, and Siena. Florence lacked a university until relatively late—1321—but had three major religious *studia*, a cathedral school of canon law, and possibly one notarial school in operation during the thirteenth century.[50] When, however, one considers that by the

---

details on the *abbaco* schools in Italy and their curricula, see Alfredo Stussi, ed., *Zibaldone da Canal* (Venice: Fonti per la Storia di Venezia, 1967), and Warren Van Egmond, *Practical Mathematics in the Italian Renaissance: A Catalog of Italian Abbacus Manuscripts and Printed Books to 1600* (Florence: Istituto e museo di storia della scienza, 1980). As Franco Franceschi points out, education in the Florentine *botteghe* was one aspect of the important role these commercial realities played in the socialization of both children and adults. See Franceschi, *Oltre il "Tumulto": I lavoratori fiorentini dell'Arte della lana fra Tre e Quattrocento* (Florence: Olschki, 1993).

[47] From Boccaccio's case, it is known that after completing the *abbaco* school, pupils continued to be educated in the practice of *marcatura* (merchant work). During this phase, the apprentice merchant was taught the measurements used in different markets inside and outside of Italy and on the *portolani* (the maps of seacoasts and commercial routes). See Gehl, *Moral Art*, 21, and Grendler, *Schooling*, 77.

[48] Davis, "Scuola."

[49] Before Brunetto Latini's time, Florence's capitular school seems also to have offered grammatical instruction. For a recent reassessment of this educational offer, see Enrico Faini, "Prima di Brunetto: Sulla formazione intellettuale dei laici a Firenze ai primi del Duecento," *Reti Medievali* 18, no. 1 (2017): 189–218.

[50] The Franciscan convent of Santa Croce was a *studium generale* with the same degree of importance as the one in Bologna, albeit inferior to those in Paris, Oxford, and Cambridge. The convent was furnished with a good collection of theological books, and between 1287 and 1289 hosted influential theologians such as Pietro di Giovanni Olivi and Umbertino da Casale. The convent also provided a venue where up-to-date philosophical, scientific, and even medical theories circulated. For a reconsideration of the study of natural philosophy and medical theories among the Florentine laity before and during Dante's time, see Silvia Diacciati and Enrico Faini, "Ricerche sulla formazione dei laici a Firenze nel tardo duecento," *Archivio storico italiano* 652, no. 2 (2017): 205–37, esp. 220–37. Santa Maria Novella was also home to an expanding library and was better known for the teaching of one of St. Thomas Aquinas's students, Remigio de' Girolami, who taught there in 1274–76, 1297–98, and then again more sporadically until his death in 1319/20. It seems also likely that Ptolemy of Lucca wrote his continuation of Aquinas's *De regime principum* when residing at Santa Maria Novella. Little to nothing is known about the Augustinian *studium* of Santo Spirito or that of the Serviti of SS. Annunziata. On Santa Maria Novella, see Bartuschat, Brilli, and Carron, *The Dominicans*; Davis, "Education"; Mulchahey, *"First the Bow"*; M. Michèle Mulchahey, "Education in Dante's Florence Revisited: Remigio de' Girolami and the Schools of Santa Maria Novella," in *Medieval Education*, ed. Ronald

LITERACY AND EDUCATION IN DANTE'S FLORENCE   31

second half of that century, Florence was already one of the largest and most powerful cities in Europe, the delay in the development of grammar schools and lay institutions for higher education is striking.[51] Florence's professionally oriented educational milieu, together with the city's fast-expanding vernacular culture and its network of independent lay schools, also informed instructional practices and the selection of school readings.

School Texts in Dante's Florence

Vulgarem locutionem appellamus eam qua infantes adsuefiunt ab assistentibus cum primitus distinguere voces incipiunt; vel, quod brevius dici potest, vulgarem locutionem asserimus quam sine omni regola nutricem imitantes accipimus. [3] Est et inde alia locutio secondaria nobis, quam Romani gramaticam vocaverunt. Hanc quidem secundariam Greci habent et alii, sed non omnes. Ad habitum vero huius pauci perveniunt, quia non nisi per spatium temporis et studii assiduitatem regulamur et doctrinamur in illa.

(De vulgari eloquentia 1.1.2–3)

(I call "vernacular language" that which infants acquire from those around them when they first begin to distinguish sounds; or, to put it more succinctly, I declare that vernacular language is that which we learn without any formal instruction [literally: without rules], by imitating our nurses. (3) There also exists another kind of language, at one remove from us, which the Romans called *gramatica* [grammar]. The Greeks and some—but not all—other peoples also have this secondary kind of language. Few, however, achieve complete fluency in it,

---

B. Begley and Joseph W. Koterski (New York: Fordham University Press, 2005), 143–81; Gabriella Pomaro, "Censimento dei manoscritti della biblioteca di S. Maria Novella. Parte I: Origini e Trecento," in *Memorie domenicane* NS 11 (1980): 325–470. Relevant works on Santa Croce are Charles T. Davis, "The Early Collection of Books of S. Croce in Florence," *Proceedings of the American Philosophical Society* 107 (1963): 399–414; Davis, "The Florentine 'studia' and Dante's 'Library,'" in *The Divine Comedy and the Encyclopedia of Arts and Sciences*, ed. Giuseppe Di Scipio and Aldo Scaglione (Amsterdam-Philadelphia: Benjamins, 1988), 339–66; Giuseppina Brunetti and Sonia Gentili, "Una biblioteca nella Firenze di Dante: i manoscritti di S. Croce," in *Testimoni del vero: Su alcuni libri in biblioteche d'autore*, ed. Emilio Russo (Rome, Bulzoni, 2000), 21–55; Piron, "Le poète et le théologien"; Sonia Gentili and Sylvain Piron, "La bibliothèque de Santa Croce," in *Frontières des savoirs en Italie à l'époque des premières universités (XIII–XV siècles)*, ed. Joël Chandelier and Aurélien Robert (Rome: École française de Rome, 2015), 481–507; Anna Pegoretti, "'Nelle scuole delli religiosi': Materiali per Santa Croce nell'età di Dante," *L'Alighieri* 50 (2017): 5–55; and Pegoretti, "Filosofanti."

[51] See William R. Day Jr., "Economy," in *Dante in Context*, 30–45. On the peculiar situation of higher education in Dante's Florence, see also Faini, "Prima di Brunetto," 192, and Giorgio Inglese, *Vita di Dante: una biografia possibile* (Rome: Carocci, 2015), 56.

32 DANTE'S EDUCATION

since knowledge of its rules and theory can only be developed through dedication to a lengthy course of study.)

Dante's definition of Latin as an immutable *grammatica* in the *De vulgari eloquentia* reflects the organization of language instruction in the schools of thirteenth-century Florence, and Italy more broadly, where the only grammar to be taught was Latin. This excerpt also confirms the general state of schooling in the city delineated in the previous section: a large majority of readers acquired some literacy only in their natural language, and a minority—*pauci*—learned Latin as a secondary language. This advanced training, the poet implies, required a substantial investment of time and material resources, which only a minority of pupils could afford. Dante, however, does not describe how pupils acquired their basic literacy, useful also for writing in the vernacular, or what the study of grammar entailed: How did the two programs of instruction differ? Where did they overlap? On the one hand, acquiring vernacular literacy still implied some study of Latin texts, and similar teaching techniques were used throughout all stages of instruction. On the other hand, the rise of a widespread demand for vocationalist literacy and the advancement of the vernacular affected the traditional teaching of Latin.

During the Middle Ages, the teaching of language was carried out through a lengthy process of "immersion" in a foreign language.[52] The whole course of study comprised three stages: the first one focused on the study of phonetics; the second dealt with Latin morphology; and the third one tackled Latin syntax and composition. At all stages, pupils learned by sounding out, reading, parsing, and memorizing Latin texts and grammars. Language instruction, therefore, coincided with "the passing on of a textual heritage to serve as the basis of verbal communication and creativity," to quote Marjorie Curry Woods's felicitous phrase.[53] The selection of literary texts singled out as appropriate for instruction appears to have been remarkably consistent throughout Western Europe and England between the ninth and twelfth centuries: short texts for beginners, usually metrical (for example, the *Disticha Catonis*); literary riddles (such as St. Boniface's *Aenigmata*); Boethius' *Consolatio Philosophiae*; the principal hexametric and epic poems (usually Virgil and Statius); and the satires by Juvenal and Persius. The Christian Latin biblical epics by Juvencus and Sedulius are often presented as the culmination of this itinerary of formative readings. After the twelfth century, other ancient texts, especially Ovid, were added to this reading list, as interest in the biblical epics dwindled.[54]

---

[52] Black, *Humanism*, 173, and Suzanne Reynolds, "*Medieval Reading: Grammar, Rhetoric and the Classical Text*" (Cambridge: Cambridge University Press, 1996), esp. part I.

[53] Marjorie Curry Woods, "The Teaching of Writing in Medieval Europe," in *A Short History of Writing Instruction: From Ancient Greece to Contemporary America*, ed. James J. Murphy, 3rd ed. (New York: Routledge, 2012), 93.

[54] Martin Irvine and David Thomson, "*Grammatica* and Literary Criticism," in *The Cambridge History of Literary Criticism*, ed. A. Minnis and I. Johnson (Cambridge: Cambridge University Press,

LITERACY AND EDUCATION IN DANTE'S FLORENCE   33

Marcus Boas has observed that several manuscripts produced in northern Europe between the ninth and the thirteenth centuries feature the progressive formation of a school anthology, which he named *Liber Catonianus*.[55] In the ninth century, this Latin primer comprised only the *Disticha Catonis* and *Avianus*, but by degrees other works were added: the *Ilias Latina*, the *Ecloga Theoduli*, Maximianus' *Elegiae*, and finally Statius' *Achilleid*, along with Claudian's *De raptu Proserpinae*. These miscellaneous collections were identified as *Libri de moribus* or *Libri ethicorum* at various times, pointing to the overlap of language and moral education. The actual reality and diffusion of such a standardized curriculum, however, has been repeatedly questioned by scholars over the past century. Rino Avesani, for instance, has argued that the selection of readings was considerably more flexible than the one featured in the *Liber-Catonianus* type of anthologies. Avesani has also pointed out that medieval reading lists do not identify certain texts as "scholastic" but distinguish between major and minor Latin *auctores*.[56]

Medieval pedagogues singled out some authors as "minor" on account of their function as propaedeutic to the reading of the more advanced *auctores maiores*.[57] The eleventh-century *Ars lectoria* by Aimeric the grammarian, for instance, lists the *Disticha Catonis*, the *Ilias Latina*, Maximian, Avianus, and Aesop as the first texts that pupils should read at the beginning of their education. The same program is also found in the twelfth-century *Accessus ad auctores*, as well as in the nearly contemporary *Dialogus super auctores* by Conrad of Hirsau. At the beginning of the thirteenth century, in a sermon "ad scholares," Jacques de Vitry recommends Cato, Theodulus, Avianus, "et alii"; and Eberhard the German's *Laborintus* features a comparable program of study. Hugh of Trimberg's late thirteenth-century *Registrum multorum auctorum* lists Cato, Aesop, Avianus, Maximian, *Pamphilus*, *Ovidius puellarum*, and *Geta* as the first eight titles of his curriculum; it also includes the *Ecloga Theoduli* under the category of *poetae Christiani* and mentions Claudian's *De raptu* with Statius' *Achilleid* among

---

2005), 13–41, esp. 37–39. See also Tony Hunt, *Teaching and Learning Latin in Thirteenth-Century England: Texts*, vol. 1 (Rochester, NY: Boydell & Brewer, 1991), 60–65; and Silvia Rizzo, *Ricerche sul latino umanistico*, vol. 1 (Rome: Edizioni di storia e letteratura, 2002), 127. On the selection of texts that were more popular in the schools of Europe during the early Middle Ages, see Birger Munk Olsen, *I classici nel canone scolastico altomedievale* (Spoleto: Centro Italiano di Studi sull'Alto Medioevo, 1991).

[55] Marcus Boas, "De Librorum Catonianorum historia atque compositione," *Mnemosyne*, n.s., 42 (1914): 17–46.

[56] Rino Avesani, "Il primo ritmo per la morte del grammatico Ambrogio e il cosiddetto 'Liber Catonianus,'" *Studi Medievali* 6 (1965): 455–88.

[57] As we learn from Conrad of Hirsau's *Dialogus super auctores*—an imaginary dialogue between a teacher and his zealous student about the correct approach to the reading of the Latin authors—"the failure in studying the most unimportant authors is unpardonable, even though the student may be well-versed in the major ones, and whatever knowledge was gained from a study of the major authors would be rendered obscure by neglect of the minor ones." Quoted in Alistair J. Minnis, A. B. Scott, and David Wallace, eds., *Medieval Literary Theory and Criticism, c. 1100–c. 1375: The Commentary-Tradition* (New York: Clarendon Press, 1988), 41.

34 DANTE'S EDUCATION

the *poetae Romani* suitable for more advanced instruction.[58] Eva M. Sanford's extensive manuscript survey confirms that many of the works recommended by medieval pedagogues for elementary and intermediate instruction were in fact present in school anthologies copied and used in different parts of Europe. Sanford, however, points out that the texts consistently found in these manuscripts did not crystallize into a curriculum, such as the one identified by Boas as the *Liber Catonianus*.[59] Rather, as Jill Mann eloquently states, the *Liber* represents "a theme on which endless variations are played."[60] It seems reasonable, therefore, to assume that although no standard reading curriculum existed, certain works were consistently chosen as textbooks.

Language education in the urban schools of late medieval Italy was still organized around the study of Latin texts. Two different visions of education, however, informed alternative programs for grammatical instruction: one, linked to ecclesiastical institutions, continued to follow the traditional syllabus centered on the study of the ancient classical authors; the other, informed by the rise of professional and academic education, promoted the study of thirteenth-century manuals—as, for instance, Alexander of Villedieu's *Doctrinale* and Geoffrey of Visnauf's *Poetria Nova*—in lieu of the Roman classics.[61] Students often read these handbooks to learn formal letter writing and only after reading their way through the *auctores minores*. Since the new administrative, notarial, legal, and academic professions required advanced secondary training—as in the *artes dictaminis* and *notaria*, for instance—most pupils began their formal instruction at the age of seven and left school between the ages of twelve and fifteen to begin their professional apprenticeship. Quick progress at the elementary stages of education

---

[58] In order of mention: Harry F. Reijnders, "Americus, *Ars Lectoria*," *Vivarium* 9 (1971): 119–37; *Vivarium* 10 (1972): 41–101, 124–76; R. B. C. Huygens, ed., *Accessus ad auctores, Bernard d'Utrecht, Conrad d'Hirsau: Dialogus super auctores; Édition critique* (Leiden: Brill, 1970); Jacques de Vitry, *Sermones vulgares* 16, in *Analecta novissima*, ed. J. B. Pitra, vol. 2 (Paris, 1885–88), 365–72, at 366; for the *Laborintus*, see Edmond Faral, *Les arts póetiques du XIIe et du XIIIe siècle: Recherches et documents sur la technique littéraire du moyen âge* (Paris: Champion, 1924), 358–61, lines 602–21; and *Das "Registrum multorum auctorum" des Hugo von Trimberg: Untersuchungen und Kommentierte Textausgabe*, ed. Karl Langosh (Berlin: Ebering, 1942). For a similar curriculum, see also Louis J. Paetow, ed. and trans., *The Battle of the Seven Arts* (Berkeley: University of California Press, 1914), esp. 56.

[59] Eva M. Sanford, "The Use of Classical Latin Authors in the *Libri Manuales*," *Transactions and Proceedings of the American Philological Association* 55 (1924): 190–248.

[60] Jill Mann, "'He Knew Nat Catoun': Medieval School-Texts and Middle English Literature," in *The Text in the Community: Essays on Medieval Works, Manuscripts, Authors, and Readers*, ed. Jill Mann and Maura Nolan (Notre Dame, IN: University of Notre Dame Press, 2006), 41–74, at 48. On the flexibility of the curriculum, see also Elisabeth Pellegrin, "Les *Remedia Amoris* d'Ovide texte scholaire médiévale," *Bibliothèque de l'École des Chartres* 115 (1957): 172–79; Irvine and Thomson, "*Grammatica*," 37–41; and Lynch, *Education in Late Medieval France*, 116.

[61] During the twelfth century, new grammars, glossaries, and dictionaries were written, such as the above-mentioned *Doctrinale*, the *Papias* or *Elementarium doctrinae rudimentum*, Hugutio of Pisa's *Derivationes* or *Magnae Derivationes*, Éverard de Bethune's *Graecismus*, and Giovanni Balbi's *Catholicon*. About their use in grammatical instruction, see Black, *Humanism*, 69, and Grendler, *Schooling*, 111–17.

and in grammar instruction became paramount. The traditional method of time-consuming immersion in the Roman authors was thus no longer suitable for the pursuit of these lay careers. For the same reason, curricula of readings for grammatical education centered around the Roman classics were not the most popular in thirteenth-century Italian schools. Tradition kept certain texts in the classroom, but their selection became significantly narrower.[62]

The grammar course was "open-ended": the curriculum of readings and its extension depended on teachers' preferences, individual students' ability, and parents' wishes.[63] There clearly was a progression from the *auctores minores* to the *maiores*, but the order in which these texts were read is not otherwise evident. Minor and major authors were not usually collected together in anthologies, suggesting that these texts may have been used at different stages of instruction. A few minor Latin texts remained the most popular choice among schoolteachers, whereas a minimal teaching of the Roman *auctores maiores* might have occurred at the higher levels of education. Little evidence of this "academic" use of the major *auctores* survives, however—even for cities such as Arezzo, Bologna, and Padua, where the organization of grammar schools fell under university control. Even the curricula of Italian universities did not normally feature courses on the *auctores* until the fifteenth century.[64]

Education in Florence during the thirteenth century best exemplifies these pedagogical trends, as teachers had to adapt to the growing need for vocationalist literacy and grammatical education for university-level professional training and practical use. As noted earlier, reading instruction in Florence was the undisputed territory of the *doctores puerorum* and independent grammar teachers. The absence of a university allowed them greater autonomy in designing their own programs—often to accommodate the desires of parents who paid tuition and

[62] For different hypotheses about the reading curricula of late medieval Italy and the conflict between rhetorical training and the study of the ancient classics, see Black, "Education," 265; Black, *Humanism*; Black and Pomaro, *La consolazione della filosofia*; Eugenio Garin, *L'Educazione in Europa, 1400-1600* (Bari: Laterza, 1957); Anthony Grafton and Lisa Jardine, *From Humanism to the Humanities: Education and the Liberal Arts in Fifteenth- and Sixteenth-Century Europe* (London: Duckworth, 1986), esp. the introduction; Grendler, *Schooling*, 111, 168; Paul Oskar Kristeller, *Renaissance Thought: The Classic, Scholastic, and Humanistic Strains* (New York: Harper, 1961), 7; Louis John Paetow, *The Arts Course at Medieval Universities with Special Reference to Grammar and Rhetoric* (Urbana-Champaign: University of Illinois Library, 1910); Helene Wieruszowski, "Rhetoric and the Classics in Italian Education of the Thirteenth Century," *Studia Gratiana* 2 (1967): 169–208; Ronald G. Witt, *The Two Latin Cultures and the Foundation of Renaissance Humanism in Medieval Italy* (Cambridge: Cambridge University Press, 2012). On the study of the *Poetria nova* in Italian grammar schools, see Robert Black, "Between Grammar and Rhetoric: *Poetria nova* and Its Educational Context in Medieval and Renaissance Italy," in *La poetria del medioevo latino*, ed. Gian Carlo Alessio and Domenico Losappio (Venice: Ca' Foscari, 2018), 45–68.

[63] Gehl, *Moral Art*, 52.

[64] Black, *Humanism*, 202. According to Witt, *"In the Footsteps,"* 195–97, there was little teaching of the classics at the grammar school level in central and northern Italy before the end of the fourteenth century. Gehl (*Moral Art*) argues that education in Florence remained centered on the same few *auctores minores* throughout the trecento. Black (*Humanism*) instead contends that the *maiores* gradually had a comeback during this century, after a sharp decline in the previous one.

36 DANTE'S EDUCATION

were eager for their children to complete their instruction as quickly as possible. Children would begin school around the age of seven. First, they memorized the alphabet on a piece of paper (*carta*) pinned on a wooden board (*tabula*) and sometimes featuring the sign of the cross (*croce*).[65] Pupils then progressed to sounding and spelling out letters and syllables by reading some Latin primers, often including the psalms or a selection of them, usually the penitential ones.[66] After that, students read Donatus' *Ars minor*—a late fourth-century grammar—or its abbreviated version, known as *Ianua*.[67] Pupils at this stage were not considered to be studying Latin—they were called *non latinantes*—because they seem to have simply sounded out the Donatus (*a suono*) to study phonetics rather than to read and understand it.[68] The earliest surviving reference to this elementary stage of the curriculum in Florence is found in a document from 1304, in which the female teacher D(omina) Clementia, *doctrix puerorum*, commits to teach Andrea, brother of Lippo di Casino, to read the "Psalterium" and the "Donatus."[69] On completing this first stage, students would have been able to read the vernacular and to possess the necessary foundations for the actual study of Latin.[70] Writing was often learned after this first stage, sometimes together with the *abbaco*.[71] The focus on learning how to read as quickly as possible made elementary instruction useful in and of itself to a large variety of individuals belonging to different social classes, who pursued this training to achieve practical, and sometimes even advanced, literacy in the vernacular.[72]

---

[65] Florentines insisted on their children learning to read as early as possible. Occasionally, mothers instructed children in the alphabet at home. Black, *Education and Society*, 121–22, and Debenedetti, "Sui più antichi," 342. A classic study about reading instruction in the Middle Ages is Danièle Alexandre-Bidon, "La lettre volée: Apprendre à lire à l'enfant au Moyen Age," *Annales. Histoire, Sciences Sociales* 4 (1989): 953–92.

[66] According to Black, "in Tuscany it seems that prayers and devotional texts had definitely replaced psalms in the *salterio*" (*Humanism*, 38). Black also maintains that the Psalter had, by the thirteenth century, become synonymous with the ABC, and "psalteratus" identified a literate person (37). On the Latin primer, see also Frova, *Istruzione*, 83; Nicholas Orme, *Medieval Children* (New Haven, CT: Yale University Press, 2001), 88–90; and Reynolds, *Medieval Reading*, 8–11.

[67] Black, "Education," 262. It has long been recognized that in Italy the *Ars minor* was substituted by a manual spuriously attributed to Donatus, which Remigio Sabbadini named *Ianua* after the first line of its verse prologue: "*Ianua sum rudibus*." See Remigio Sabbadini, *La scuola e gli studi di Guarino Guarini Veronese (con 44 documenti)* (Catania: Galati, 1896), 35, 42–44. See also Black, *Humanism*, 45; Gehl, *Moral Art*, 30, 82–106; Grendler, *Schooling*, 174–82; Rizzo, *Ricerche*, vol. 1, 127.

[68] This phonetic reading was also known as reading "a veduta," "testualiter," or "cum textu." Black, "Teaching Techniques," 246; Gehl, *Moral Art*, 20; Witt, *"In the Footsteps,"* 194. With regard to education in northern Italy, Frova maintains that "per un anno gli alunni si esercitano a leggere e ripetere ad alta voce prima di praticare la scrittura e memorizzano brani in Latino prima di comprenderlo appieno" (*Istruzione*, 102).

[69] Debenedetti, "Sui più antichi," 123; Black and Pomaro, *La consolazione della filosofia*, 4.

[70] Najemy, *History*, 45–46.

[71] Children learned to trace letters, but professional writing for documentary and book production was a manual skill that required specialized training, often at the university level. On this see István Hajnal, *L'enseignement de l'écriture aux universités médiévales* (Budapest: Maison d'édition de l'Académie des Sciences de Hongrie, 1959), esp. chaps. 3–5.

[72] Lynch, *Education in Late Medieval France*, 128.

The defining moment in the education of every Florentine pupil came after reading the Donatus for the first time, which marked the end of elementary instruction. At this point, students either continued with the study of grammar or did not.[73] The second stage of the language curriculum focused on Latin morphology and started from rereading the Donatus. Students parsed and memorized it, this time reading it for comprehension—*per lo senno*. Only at this stage were pupils said to be reading and studying Latin (*latinantes*).[74] After reading the Donatus for the second time, they were introduced to short Latin texts, selected from the *auctores minores*. The third and final stage of the language curriculum focused on Latin syntax and composition. Priscian's *Institutiones Grammaticae* had provided the theoretical basis for this study in antiquity but proved unsuitable for medieval pupils who studied Latin as a second language. Grammar handbooks—such as Hilderic of Montecassino's *Adbreviatio artis grammaticae*—were composed to replace the *Institutiones*. Theoretical study of Latin syntax should have been complemented by reading of the *auctores maiores* and should have overlapped with the teaching of literature. There was, however, a considerable difference, relatively to both time and competence, between reading the Donatus *per lo senno* and reading the *auctores*. Whereas three grammar schools offered this type of advanced Latin instruction in Villani's fourteenth-century Florence, no surviving evidence indicates where laypeople could have accessed such education in the city during the previous century. As Dante claims in the *De vulgari eloquentia*, moreover, only a minority of students went on to study grammar.[75]

When compared with grammar education in other thirteenth-century cities, such as Arezzo and Siena, in the schools of Florence study of the classics seems to have been particularly poor. Paul Gehl argues that a school curriculum explicitly designed for instructing lay pupils gradually consolidated during the years between 1260–70 and 1390, a period marked by two influential teaching personalities, Brunetto Latini and Francesco da Barberino. Surveying several manuscripts of schoolbooks, Gehl found that a number of pocket-sized, inexpensive books produced in Tuscany between the late thirteenth century and the second half of the fourteenth century share a similar material format and selection of *auctores minores*. The evidence that such books were available in significant numbers,

---

[73] In some cases, boys went to grammar school after some training in the *abbaco*. See Gehl, *Moral Art*, 83.

[74] "Senno" may mean either "meaning," "intellect," or "mind." Scholars have generally taken "senno" to mean "meaning" in this context, thereby interpreting the second reading of Donato as the one in which students would have read the text for understanding rather than sounding it out. Black ("Teaching Techniques," 246) is alone in arguing that "senno" here means that at this second stage the Donatus was memorized.

[75] For Hilderic's *Adbreviatio*, see Anselmo Lentini, *Ilderico e la sua "Ars grammatica"* (Montecassino: In coenobio Casinensi, 1975). About grammar school in late medieval Florence, see Black, *Humanism*, 66; see also Gehl, *Moral Art*, 30, 67. For some hypotheses about advanced grammatical teaching offered to the laity by the capitular school in the thirteenth century, see Faini, "Prima di Brunetto." On the techniques used for teaching syntax, see Black, "Teaching Techniques," 260.

38   DANTE'S EDUCATION

presumably through stationers, shows that they were produced to meet growing market demand. Readers' interest in these booklets was driven by their use in education, which had likely been consolidating for several years.[76] It is significant that only the *auctores minores* and a few medieval grammar texts appear in these little school anthologies. The major Latin poets seem not to have been copied in this format.[77] Even Statius' *Achilleid* and Claudian's *De raptu Proserpinae*, staples of education for centuries, do not appear in this type of school manuscript before the fourteenth century.[78] Bestsellers, according to Gehl, were Cato, Prosper, and Prudentius' *Dittochaeon*. In addition to these titles, Black points also to the popularity of Aesopic fables (either from *Avianus* or the *Aesopus latinus*) and Henry of Settimello's *Elegia*.[79]

The apparent absence of epic Latin poems represents a significant difference even when compared to anthologies of the *Liber-Catonianus* type from northern Europe, in which Claudian and Statius are often found. Paul Clogan has observed that the texts in these school anthologies sampled different literary genres: the *Disticha Catonis* represented wisdom literature, Theodulus the Latin eclogue, Aesop the fable, Maximian the elegy, and Claudian and Statius offered an introduction to epic poetry.[80] Hence, the Florentine schoolbooks seem to have been designed for students who were not expected to progress to the study of advanced Latin poetry. They were presented instead with relatively simpler Latin metrical texts with which to improve their linguistic proficiency and learn essential ethical principles, as well as key biblical, mythological, and literary notions. The distinctive glossing featured in these manuscripts reinforces this impression. In contrast to the *Liber-Catonianus* type of manuscripts produced in northern Europe during the thirteenth century (Figure 1.1), which sometimes present extensive apparatuses

[76] Paul Gehl, "Latin Readers in Fourteenth-Century Florence," *Scrittura e civiltà* 13 (1989): 387–440; Gehl, *Moral Art*; Black, "Teaching Techniques," 250–51.

[77] Gehl, "Latin Readers," 401.

[78] Black, *Humanism*, 191; Gehl, "Latin Readers," 387–440; and Gehl, *Moral Art*, 54. However, we find some examples of "anthologies" containing more advanced texts, like Boethius or Virgil, which may have been used at lower levels of education (Gehl, *Moral Art*, 58). I shall return to the question of the presence of Statius and Claudian in Florentine grammar schools in Chapter 6. Black (*Humanism*, 199) also found evidence that Maximian, the *Ilias Latina*, Pamphilus, the Physiologus, and the pseudo-Boethian's *De disciplina scholarium* were also read, though they were probably less popular.

[79] Not surprisingly, the most copious glossing, particularly in the vernacular, is found in manuscripts of the *auctores minores*. Black, *Humanism*, 224. A similar curriculum of texts appears to have been popular in northern Italy during the later Middle Ages, as several other documents show. Around 1304, a Piedemontese master was required to "legere auctores vel Donatum, Catonem, Summam (perhaps Pietro Isollela's *Regulae*), Prosperum, Yssopum, Boetium." At the same time, the Florentine Domina Clementia (whose case I have mentioned above) was teaching a similar selection of readings. In Volterra, the grammar teacher was asked to teach the usual authors and to end with Boethius. In Chioggia, in 1386, the selection of Latin readings to be taught was once again "esopum, prosperum, ovidium Heroidum, et boetium." The *Statuti* of the comune of Bra required teachers to read Donatus, Cato, Prosper, Aesop, Boethius, and the *Dottrinale*. All these documents are cited and discussed in Frova, *Istruzione*, 114–15.

[80] Paul M. Clogan, "Literary Genres in a Medieval Textbook," *Medievalia et Humanistica* 11 (1982): 199–209.

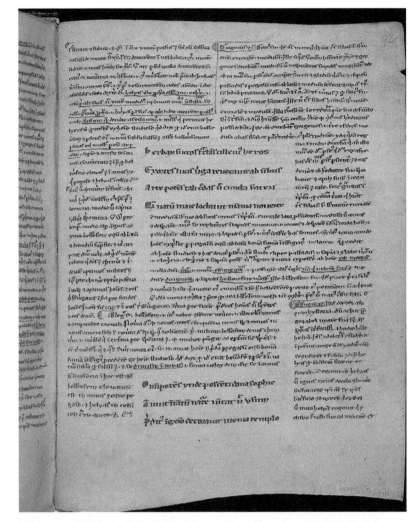

Figure 1.1 MS Oxford, Bodleian Library, Can. Class. Lat. 72, fol. 92r. *Ecloga Theoduli* 197–204, with commentary.

Source: Courtesy of the Bodleian Library, Oxford.

of marginal glosses and commentaries, manuscripts of late medieval schoolbooks in Florentine libraries display limited, mostly interlinear glossing that features only grammatical and lexicographical explanations; no moral or allegorical reading is offered in the margins of the texts.[81] Glosses provide synonyms for difficult

---

[81] A possible reason for this difference may also be in the different ownership of these textbooks. The ones in Florence were more likely student copies, whereas the few examples from northern Europe that I was able to study were more expensive copies, perhaps owned by teachers, with a commentary laid out for use during lectures. But the large number of what were likely student copies in Florence is

40 DANTE'S EDUCATION

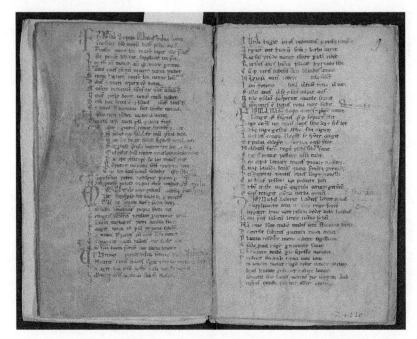

Figure 1.2 Florence, Biblioteca Nazionale Centrale, Magliabechi VII.931, fols. 8v–9r. Two folia featuring fables from the *Aesopus Latinus* (or *elegiac Romulus*) with light interlinear and marginal glosses by different hands.

Source: Courtesy of the Italian Ministry of Culture/Biblioteca Nazionale Centrale, Florence. Reproduction or duplication by any means is strictly prohibited.

words and brief mythological, geographical, or historical explanations intended to provide students with useful context (Figure 1.2). Numbers often appear over the words to help students rearrange the sentences in a more intelligible order. For Black, such peculiar glossing shows that teachers resorted to Latin texts primarily to explain grammar to their pupils and had little or no interest in the actual content of the texts. Black terms this educational approach "the triumph of philology." His view, however, is not shared by Gehl, who argues instead that grammar remained primarily a "moral art."[82] Although such a controversial point can hardly be assessed based on paratextual evidence alone, manuscripts of schoolbooks from fourteenth-century Florence do show that traditional practices of language education and school readings underwent significant transformations during Dante's generation. Florence's expanding literacy and schooling seem to have coincided with a narrowing of the curriculum. During the thirteenth century and part of the

significant in itself, as discussed in this and the following chapter. For a detailed analysis of the peculiar features of manuscripts of schoolbooks from late medieval Florence, see Black, *Humanism*, 27.

[82] Black has made this argument in several of his works. See, for instance, Black, *Humanism*, esp. 26 and chap. 5. For Gehl's thesis, see his *Moral Art*.

LITERACY AND EDUCATION IN DANTE'S FLORENCE   41

fourteenth, language instruction in the city seems to have revolved mostly around
the reading of a handful of Latin minor authors.[83]

What Dante Learned in School

In thirteenth- and fourteenth-century Florence, children were expected to follow in the social and professional footsteps of their fathers—families, in other
words, decided the type of training that their heirs received.[84] To reconstruct
Dante's earliest education, therefore, we should begin by reassessing his family's
wealth, business, and social status.[85] Received wisdom has traditionally assumed
the relative well-being of the Alighieris and Dante's means to access wealthy circles, where he came into contact with advanced cultural trends.[86] Recent studies,
however, have begun questioning this supposition.

Dante's grandfather, Bellincione, was exiled twice, a fact that suggests his lack of
powerful connections. Bellincione did not live the life of a wealthy patrician, either,
but practiced commerce and moneylending for a living. His son and Dante's father,
Alighiero, continued in this line of business, while also getting revenues from the
family's activities as landowners in the countryside.[87] Extant documents show that
the Alighieris invested in Prato and Montemurlo (not far from Florence) around

[83] This fact was also registered by contemporary witnesses. See, for instance, Boccaccio's letter to
Jacopo Pizzinga, from 1371, and a section from Giovanni Dominici's *Regola del governo di cura famil-
iare*, from around 1400 to 1405. Both will be discussed in detail in the next two chapters. See Giovanni
Boccaccio, *Epistole e lettere*, ed. Ginetta Auzzas, in *Tutte le opere*, ed. Vittore Branca, vol. 5.1 (Milan:
Mondadori, 1992), 664–68; and Giovanni Dominici, *Regola del governo di cura familiare*, ed. Donato
Salvi (Florence: A. Garinei, 1860), 134. Petrarch's *Seniles* 16.1 also reports a similar school curriculum.
[84] Boccaccio's commercial education and professional training well exemplifies this reality. For
another, later, example, of how this trend applied to most late-medieval Italian cities see Paul F.
Grendler, "What Piero Learned in School: Fifteenth-Century Vernacular Education," in *Studies in the
History of Art*, vol. 48 (Washington, DC: National Gallery of Art, 1995), 160–74, esp. 165.
[85] The exponential proliferation of new biographies of Dante over the past decade—often featuring contrasting suppositions about the poet's life and education—have only confirmed how little we
really know and can reconstruct of the poet's life. This contradiction is only set in starker relief by the
evidence that no discoveries of new documentary evidence parallel this outpour of bibliographical narratives. Innovative reconsiderations of well-known documents have constituted the only advancement
in this area. Exemplary of this latter trend is Paola Allegretti, "Dante Alighieri nell'Archivio Apostolico
Vaticano: un documento del 1320," *Dante Studies* 139 (2021): 1–23. Instead, new documentary evidence has been unearthed relative to the notaries who were associated with the poet during his time in
Ravenna. See Gabriella Albanese and Paolo Pontari, "Il cenacolo ravennate di Dante e le *Egloghe*: Fiduccio de' Milotti, Dino Perini, Guido Vacchetta, Pietro Giardini, Menghino Mezzani," *Studi danteschi* 82
(2017): 311–427. My intention in this section is to survey some of the material and biographical evidence concerning the context of Dante's earliest schooling and summarize some of the ways that this
evidence has been interpreted by scholars. In the second part, I offer my own readings of some of the
evidence that can be surmised from the poet's oeuvre.
[86] Illustrative of this trend is Giorgio Petrocchi, *Vita di Dante* (Bari: Laterza, 1983), 14. This thesis is repeated and discussed quite convincingly also in Guido Pampaloni, "Gli Alighieri, Dante e il
buon tempo antico (Il canto XVI dell'*Inferno*)," in *Esegesi e filologia*, vol. 2 of *Studi in onore di Arnaldo
d'Addario*, ed. Luigi Borgia et al. (Lecce: Conte Editore, 1995), 437–48.
[87] See Barbero, *Dante*, 31–45; Elisa Brilli and Giuliano Milani, *Dante: Les vies nouvelles* (Paris:
Fayard, 2021), 18–25, 36–45; and John Took, *Dante* (Princeton, NJ: 2020, Princeton University Press),
27–71, esp. 30–31.

42   DANTE'S EDUCATION

the middle of the thirteenth century, increasing their patrimony by charging high interest rates and foreclosing on insolvent clients.[88] Looking at the documentary evidence of the debts contracted by the Alighieri toward the end of the century, however, some historians have argued that the family could have been in social and economic decline during Dante's childhood.[89] With a history of allegiance to noble Florentine families, moreover, the Alighieris were at risk of being marginalized during the political turmoil that brought the *popolo* to power in 1250.[90]

Alessandro Barbero has countered this narrative of decline and argued that both Bellincione and Alighiero were rather successful in growing the family's wealth and in pursuing advantageous matrimonial politics. Dante and his brother would have been the first in the family to live off the revenues coming from the family's estates in the countryside. Thus, Dante would have striven to assimilate to Florence's old aristocracy by promoting the antiquity of the Alighieris' name and embracing the ideals of the urban knighthood with which the patriciate identified.[91]

For reconstructing Dante's earliest schooling in Florence, however, it is essential to appreciate that, whether on a financially sound footing or not, the Alighieris needed to be always active, both economically and politically, to increase and maintain the family's status within Florence's fluid political landscape. Their business history and precarious social standing, in between the city's new and old wealth, certainly played into the family's decisions concerning Dante's education. Furthermore, Alighiero's premature death—probably around 1277—meant that all financial and political responsibilities had to be transferred to his children rather early on.[92] The need to maintain social relevance and powerful political connections would explain why, at the age of twelve, Dante was already either legally married or engaged to Gemma Donati.[93] Alighiero's death, moreover, could have put pressure on the poet to end his formal schooling after only five years.

Before his exile in 1302, Dante's adult life in Florence was also a rather active one. By the time he wrote the *Vita nova*—during the first years of the 1290s—he

---

[88] Day, "Economy," 44.

[89] As argued by Silvia Diacciati, "Dante: relazioni sociali e vita pubblica," *Reti Medievali* 15 (2014): 243–70, particularly 246–49, and, in the same issue, by Franek Sznura, "I debiti di Dante nel loro contesto documentario," 303–21. Diacciati's thesis has been recently opposed by Barbero (*Dante*, 299, esp. n15).

[90] Enrico Faini, "Ruolo sociale e memoria degli Alighieri prima di Dante," *Reti Medievali* 15 (2014): 203–42, at 236.

[91] See Barbero, *Dante*, 31–45, and Brilli and Milani, *Dante*, esp. 21–25 and 42–45.

[92] On the date of Alighiero's death, see Inglese, *Vita*, 29. Records of the estate he left to his sons raise some questions about whether its revenues would have sufficed for the family's long-term economic well-being. Nicola Zingarelli thought they would. See Zingarelli, *La Vita, i tempi e le opera di Dante*, vol. 1 (Milan: Vallardi, 1948), 84. But he likely relies on Leonardo Bruni as an indirect witness. See Leonardo Bruni, "Della vita studi e costumi di Dante," in *Le vite di Dante*, ed. Giuseppe Lando Passerini (Florence: Sansoni, 1917), 10.

[93] Marco Santagata, *Dante: Il romanzo della sua vita* (Milan: Mondadori, 2021), 41–43; Davidsohn, *Storia*, vol. 4 t. 3, 367; and Renato Piattoli, "Donati, Gemma," in the *ED* all maintain the traditional view that at this date Dante and Gemma were legally only engaged. Recently Isabella Chabot, "Il Matrimonio di Dante," *Reti Medievali* 15 (2014): 271–302, esp. 280–300, has argued that the document binding the two actually constituted a legal marriage.

was a young man already pressed by several practical concerns and engaged in Florence's civic life. He was busy stipulating loans, either to make up for financial losses or to acquire liquidity. He also embarked on a civic and political career, which had begun with his participation in the military campaigns of Campaldino and Caprona, in 1289, and culminated with several offices in the government of the city.[94] Between 1295 and 1301, he worked as an ambassador and as a member of the *consiglio dei cento*, and eventually was elected to the highest public rank of *priore*.[95] As Dante makes clear in *Convivio* 1.1, like most laypeople at the time, he too did not enjoy the carefree conditions necessary for a life of study.

The only extant material evidence relating, although indirectly, to the poet's earliest education comes from a 1277 notarial document concerning the Alighieri family. In this document, a *doctor puerorum* named Romanus appears as a witness for the Alighieris. This evidence situates Romanus as a member of the family's entourage. Since he exercised his trade in the parish of Saint Martin—the same part of the city where the Alighieris lived—Romanus would have been a likely candidate to be Dante's teacher.[96] Under his direction, or that of any other *doctor puerorum*, the poet would have acquired literacy and the basics for the study of Latin up to the reading of Donatus.

Other evidence about Dante's earliest schooling can be surmised from the poet's oeuvre. Both in the *Convivio* and in the *De vulgari eloquentia*, Dante maintains that the vernacular first introduced him to the "path of knowledge," which in turn gave him access to Latin and, thus, to all forms of learning:

Questo mio volgare fu introduttore di me nella via di scienza, che è ultima perfezione [nostra], in quanto con esso io entrai nello latino e con esso mi fu mostrato: lo quale latino poi mi fu via a più inanzi andare.

(Convivio 1.13.5)

(This vernacular of mine was what led me into the path of knowledge, which is our ultimate perfection, since through it I entered upon Latin and with it Latin was shown to me, which then became my path to further progress.)[97]

---

[94] Notarial documents from 1297 record him and his half-brother, Francesco, as borrowers involved in the repayment of loans. For discussions of this evidence see Day, "Economy," 43; Sznura, "I debiti"; Santagata, *Romanzo*, 102–04; and Took, *Dante*, 47. Contrary to a widely shared view that these loans point to the Alighieris' financial struggles, Barbero (*Dante*, 165) argues that their purpose was to acquire liquidity for reinvestment, as the two brothers must have had enough wealth, probably in estate patrimony, to guarantee repayment of the loans.

[95] Inglese, *Vita*, 16.

[96] Like the majority of middle-class Florentine pupils, Dante probably studied with the local independent teacher. It seems that very few Florentines taught or had their children taught privately (Gehl, *Moral Art*, 230). Scholars have reacted differently to the hypothesis that Romanus was Dante's teacher. In favor of this conclusion is Pierre Antonetti, *La vita quotidiana a Firenze ai tempi di Dante* (Milan: Rizzoli, 1983), 252, and Zingarelli, *Dante*, vol. 1, 93. Less supportive are Siro A. Chimenz, *Dante* (Milan: Marzorati, 1955), 6; Robert Davidsohn, vol. 4 t. 3, 229; and Santagata, *Romanzo*, 27.

[97] I have slightly modified Richard H. Lansing's translation to give a closer rendition of the original.

44 DANTE'S EDUCATION

... vulgarem locutionem asserimus quam sine omni regola nutricem imitantes accipimus.

(*De vulgari eloquentia* 1.1.2)

(I declare that vernacular language is that which we learn without any formal instruction, by imitating our nurses.)

These two statements can be interpreted in any of three ways, or some combination of these: Dante may be suggesting (1) that the first language he heard and spoke was the vernacular; (2) that he was first taught to read in the vernacular; (3) that he was taught Latin by means of the vernacular. I am inclined to interpret Dante's words here as a generic reference to the first language he ever learned as a child by natural transmission and without any study. We cannot exclude the possibility, however, that he may also be indicating the use of the vernacular for Latin instruction. Black argues that the earliest stages of literacy instruction proceeded through the student's complete immersion in Latin, whereas the vernacular was employed in the more advanced teaching of grammar. More vernacular glosses are found in the manuscripts of school texts used for the advanced stages of grammatical instruction in fourteenth-century Florence.[98] If this was the case, then in these excerpts Dante may be referring to the key role the vernacular played in his study of Latin grammar.

Further indication that Dante was formally schooled in Latin grammar is found in the excerpt from the *De vulgari eloquentia* quoted at the beginning of the previous section: "Ad habitum vero huius pauci perveniunt, quia non nisi per spatium temporis et studii assiduitatem regulamur et doctrinamur in illa" (Few, however, achieve complete fluency in it [Latin grammar], since knowledge of its rules and theory can only be developed [literally: we learn its rules and become erudite in it] through dedication to a lengthy course of study) (*De vulgari eloquentia* 1.1.2–3). This passage presents a telling shift in the grammatical subjects of the verbs: from the third-person plural, with which Dante indicates the few who achieve a full command of Latin grammar ("pauci ... perveniunt"), to the first-person plural he deploys to describe the process by which "we," including himself, "regulamur

---

[98] Whether the vernacular was used for the elementary study of Latin in the classroom is not clear. For an overview of the available evidence, see Davidsohn, *Storia*, vol. 4 t. 3, 211; Gehl, *Moral Art*, 79 and 235; and Grendler, *Schooling*, 176. For Black's thesis mentioned earlier, see *Humanism*, 41, and Black, "The Vernacular and the Teaching of Latin in Thirteenth and Fourteenth-Century Italy," *Studi Medievali* 3 (1996): 703–51. Some historians argued that the vernacular might have been used to teach basic literacy, see Gehl, *Moral Art*, 20, and Ronald Witt, "What Did Giovannino Read and Write? Literacy in Early Renaissance Florence," *I Tatti Studies in the Italian Renaissance* 6 (1995): 83–114. Gehl's argument (*Moral Art*, 36) that the existence of manuscripts containing penitential psalms in the Tuscan vernacular would be a sign of their possible use in the teaching of elementary reading seems less persuasive when confronted with the continuous use of Latin texts like the *Donatus* for grammatical instruction. To suppose that students might have read vernacular texts in preparation for reading the *Donatus* seems rather unlikely. It is possible, however, that pupils who did not plan to attend a grammar course exercised their literacy skills on these vernacular psalms.

et doctrinamur" in the study of Latin. This shift reflects the poet's self-inclusion among those fortunate few who pursued such an uncommon training.[99] Black also notes that the sample sentence "Petrus amat multum dominam Bertam," cited in *De vulgari eloquentia* 2.6.4, could be a remnant of the poet's school lessons, as the same names are used in several samples in Pietro da Isolella da Cremona's *Summa*, a popular grammatical text at the time.[100] That Dante had received formal training in Latin grammar, therefore, is claimed by the poet himself and further proved by his literary production. The extent of his formal schooling, however, remains to be assessed.

Relevant clues can be discerned in a seemingly autobiographical section of *Convivio* 2.12. During a time of crisis following Beatrice's death, in 1290, Dante looked for consolation in the reading of two Latin works, namely Boethius' *Consolatio Philosophiae* and Cicero's *De Amicitia*. Dante not only found consolation in them but also discovered philosophy and resolved to study it further by attending the disputations in Florence's conventual schools:

E però, principiando ancora da capo, dico che, come per me fu perduto lo primo diletto della mia anima, dello quale fatta è menzione di sopra, io rimasi di tanta tristizia punto, che conforto non mi valeva alcuno. (2) Tuttavia, dopo alquanto tempo, la mia mente, che si argomentava di sanare, provide, poi che né 'l mio né l'altrui consolare valea, ritornare al modo che alcuno sconsolato avea tenuto a consolarsi; e misimi a leggere quello non conosciuto da molti libro di Boezio, nel quale, cattivo e discacciato, consolato s'avea. (3) E udendo ancora che Tulio scritto avea un altro libro, nel quale, trattando dell'Amistade, avea toccate parole della consolazione di Lelio, uomo eccellentissimo, nella morte di Scipione amico suo, misimi a leggere quello. (4) E avegna che duro mi fosse nella prima entrare nella loro sentenza, finalmente v'entrai tanto entro, *quanto l'arte di gramatica ch'io avea e un poco di mio ingegno* potea fare; per lo quale ingegno molte cose, quasi come sognando, già vedea, sì come nella Vita Nova si può vedere. (5) E sì come essere suole che l'uomo va cercando argento e fuori della 'ntenzione truova oro, lo quale occulta cagione presenta; non forse sanza divino imperio, io, che cercava di consolar me, trovai non solamente alle mie lagrime rimedio, ma vocabuli d'autori e di scienze e di libri: li quali considerando, giudicava bene che la filosofia, che era donna di questi autori, di queste scienze e di questi libri, fosse somma cosa . . . (7) E da questo imaginar cominciai ad andare là dov'ella si dimostrava veracemente, cioè nelle scuole delli religiosi e alle disputazioni delli filosofanti; sì che in picciolo tempo, forse di trenta mesi, cominciai tanto a sentire della sua dolcezza, che lo suo amore cacciava e distruggeva ogni altro pensiero.

(emphasis added)

---

[99] In support of this reading, it should be noted that Dante uses "we" for "I" also in the very first sentence of the *De vulgari*: "Cum neminem ante nos" (1.1.1).

[100] Black, "Education," 267–68.

46   DANTE'S EDUCATION

(Therefore, beginning again from the beginning, I say that when I lost the first delight of my soul, of which mention is made above, I was pierced by such sorrow that no comfort availed me. (2) Nevertheless after some time my mind, which was endeavoring to heal itself, resolved (since neither my own consolation nor that of others availed) to resort to a method that a certain disconsolate individual had adopted to console himself; and I began to read that book of Boethius, not known to many, in which, while a prisoner and an exile, he had found consolation. (3) And hearing further that Tully had written another book in which, while discussing Friendship, he had addressed words of consolation to Laelius, a man of the highest merit, upon the death of his friend Scipio, I set about reading it. (4) Although it was difficult for me at first to penetrate their meaning, I finally penetrated it as deeply *as my command of Latin and the small measure of my intellect* enabled me to do, by which intellect I had perceived many things before, as in a dream, as may be seen in the New Life. (5) And just as it often happens that a man goes looking for silver and apart from his intention finds gold, which some hidden cause presents, perhaps not without divine ordinance, so I who sought to console myself found not only a remedy for my tears but also the words of authors, sciences, and books. Pondering these, I quickly determined that Philosophy, who was the lady of these authors, sciences, and books, was a great thing. (7) I began to go where she was truly revealed, namely to the schools of the religious orders and to the disputations held by the philosophers, so that in a short period of time, perhaps some thirty months, I began to feel her sweetness so much that the love of her dispelled and destroyed every other thought.)

The author reveals his initial struggle in penetrating the meaning of these ancient texts. He also suggests that the cause of such distress was a lack of prior preparation, for which he compensated by relying on his own "ingegno" and his knowledge of Latin. Since Boethius' *Consolatio* was a popular reading in Florence's schools, the implied evidence that Dante had not read it before the age of twenty-five has suggested to some the patchy grammatical training the poet had received. For Black, for instance, the poet's admission of his lack of confidence in reading Boethius and Cicero's Latin (*Convivio* 2.12), his apparent ignorance of the *Ilias Latina* (*Convivio* 1.7.15), and the rather elementary sample sentences he deploys in *De vulgari eloquentia* 2.6.4 would all be signs of Dante's "imperfect Latin education."[101]

Different interpretations of *Convivio* 2.12 are also possible, however. The events narrated here, for instance, may be modeled on *Confessiones* 3.4.7, in which St. Augustine admits that he discovered philosophy after reading Cicero's *Hortensius*.[102] Dante's story may also reflect his critical stance vis-à-vis Florence's Scholastic milieu, as suggested by his claim that only few knew Boethius' *Consolatio*.[103]

---

[101] In support of this thesis, see Black, "Education," 267–68.
[102] As Black, too, admits ("Education," 267).
[103] See Barański, "Studying the Spaces," 269–72.

LITERACY AND EDUCATION IN DANTE'S FLORENCE   47

Since copies of the text were not lacking in the city, where the work was read and commented on, Dante's real aim here may be to fashion himself as someone exceptionally learned and ingenious, who could appreciate the meaning of texts that other untrained laymen would not have been able to navigate. The poet's account of his struggle to penetrate these works, therefore, could also be contrived.[104]

Although this passage has traditionally been interpreted as the poet's admission of his poor mastery of Latin, I would contend that Dante's claim is really the opposite: he is emphasizing the fact that his advanced Latin proficiency, "l'arte di gramatica ch'io avea," together with his own exceptional "ingegno" were key to this first, self-led approach to the study of philosophy. If genuine, Dante's acknowledgment that he had not read Boethius before the age of twenty-five may lend some key insights into the extent of his schooling in Latin grammar. Contemporary outlines of school readings suggest that, probably on account of its prosimetric form, Boethius' *Consolatio* was often read at a transitional stage of grammar education, between the study of the *auctores minores* and that of the *maiores*.[105] Dante's words, therefore, may indicate that he received formal training in Latin grammar but stopped before reading Boethius and the *auctores maiores*. It is also possible that having already read Boethius as part of his grammatical training, Dante was able to appreciate the work's philosophical meaning only after reading it a second time, at a more mature age, while focusing on its contents rather than parsing it out to learn Latin grammar. A literal reading of the poet's claim, however, supports the former interpretation.

The *Vita nova* provides evidence of Dante's distinctive confidence in his own means as a Latinist. In chapter 16 (25 in Michele Barbi's chapter division), he displays an awareness of the major Roman poets (Virgil, Lucan, Horace, and Ovid), while claiming that such literary sophistication was wanting among contemporary vernacular poets. Many of them, he argues, deployed rhetorical devices without an accurate understanding of their tradition or usage. Even supposing this to be an exaggeration, the poet certainly projects confidence in his own intellectual means and classical learning. Dante also reminds his readers of a Latin epistle he allegedly wrote on the occasion of Beatrice's death and sent to either the princes of the world

---

[104] Recent support for this interpretation has been lent by Paola Nasti, "'Vocabuli d'autori e di scienze e di libri' (*Conv.* II xii 5): percorsi sapienzali di Dante," in *La Bibbia di Dante: Esperienza mistica, profezia e teologia biblica in Dante*, ed. Giuseppe Ledda (Ravenna: Centro Dantesco dei Frati Minori Conventuali, 2011), 121–78, esp. 142. See also Luca Lombardo, "Dante, Boezio e la 'bella menzogna,'" in *L'allegoria: Teorie e forme tra medioevo e modernità*, ed. Fulvio Ferrari (Trento: Dipartimento di Studi Letterari, Linguistici e Filologici, 2010), 31–55, and Lombardo, "'Quasi come sognando': Dante e la presunta rarità del 'libro di Boezio' (*Convivio*, ii. xii, 2–7)," in *Mediaeval Sophia* 12 (2012): 141–52. About Boethius' popularity in Florence, see Brunetti and Gentili, "Una biblioteca," 176, and Paola Nasti, "Storia materiale di un classico dantesco: la *Consolatio Philosophiae* fra XII e XIV secolo: Tradizione manoscritta e rielaborazioni esegetiche," *Dante Studies* 134 (2016): 142–68.

[105] Silvia Albesano, *Consolatio Philosophiae volgare* (Heidelberg: Universitätsverlag Winter, 2006), 37–38; Black and Pomaro, *La consolazione della filosofia*, 4; and Black, "Education," 267. See also Fioravanti, comm. *Convivio* 2.12.2.

48 DANTE'S EDUCATION

or the city's most powerful and influential men (*Vita nova* 19.8 [30.1]).[106] During the first years of his exile, moreover, Dante acts as an official letter writer for the exiled White party, proving himself a competent *dictator*. His advanced skills in the field of diplomatic writing were likely instrumental in gaining him the material support and protection needed to survive many years in exile.[107] The Florentine Giovanni Villani, who wrote his *Cronica* before 1348 and was about thirteen years younger than Dante, praised the poet's Latin epistles and attested that their quality was noticed by contemporary men of letters: "furono molto commendate da' savi intenditori" (they were much praised among wise connoisseurs).[108] Dante's activity as *dictator* and deployment of the rhetorical *cursus* in his letters may indicate that, after a basic training in Latin grammar, the poet was instructed in the *ars dictaminis*, perhaps in view of further professional education in the notarial art.[109] In Florence and Italy, as observed earlier, such training was often carried out through the study of ad hoc manuals rather than by immersion in the major *auctores*. As one of such manuals, by Pietro da Isolella, shows, moreover, grammatical training already ended with an introduction to rhetoric and letter writing.[110] Hence, whether Dante read the major Roman poets that he quotes in the *Vita nova* as part of his formal schooling in Latin, rather than independently as a young adult, is questionable. Considering what I have been delineating so far, the latter seems the more plausible option.

Relying on the tenuous evidence of *Inferno* 15.82–85, where the protagonist recalls Brunetto Latini's education, some scholars have postulated that under Latini's mentorship Dante learned the *dictamen* and read a selection of the major Roman *auctores*.[111] Even if this advanced rhetorical training actually took place, however, we have no concrete details about its length and curriculum. Brunetto was certainly more invested in the study of some Latin *auctores* than most notaries

---

[106] The historical reality of this claim cannot be ascertained. It is worth considering, however, that Florentine readers of the *libello*, such as Cavalcanti, easily could have denied the claim if false.

[107] For an excellent recent reconsideration of Dante's diplomatic profession in exile, see Enrico Faini, "Dante *sapiens Tusciae*," in *Round Table, the International Dante Congress, Alma Dante 2021*, trans. Anna C. Foster, accessed January 2023, https://www.academia.edu/95721422/Dante_sapiens_Tuscie_english_version_?email_work_card=title.

[108] Villani, *Nuova Cronica*, 10.131, 118.

[109] Montefusco and Bischetti ("Prime osservazioni," 193–94) maintain that Dante's knowledge and use of the classical dictamen is "extremely precise." Dante's command of Latin and the norms of rhetorical composition is further shown in his *Monarchia* and the political epistles written in support of Emperor Henry VII. Moreover, these writings show the poet's familiarity with documents produced in the chancelleries of the imperial court, prompting scholars, particularly in recent years, to suppose his employment in that professional context while the imperial court was in Pisa in 1312. See Giuseppe Indizio, "Un episodio della vita di Dante: l'incontro con Francesco Petrarca," *Italianistica* 16, no. 3 (2012): 71–80. For an exhaustive study of Dante's letters, see Antonio Montefusco and Giuliano Milani ed., *Le lettere di Dante: Ambienti culturali, contesti storici e circolazione dei saperi* (Berlin: De Gruyter, 2020).

[110] Black, "Between Grammar and Rhetoric," 59–62.

[111] Recently on this thesis see Jelena Todorović, *Dante and the Dynamics of Textual Exchange* (New York: Fordham, 2016), chap. 2.

active in the city at the time. Yet, as Ronald Witt observes, even if Dante did in fact study with Brunetto, the latter's classical culture seems to have been somewhat limted. Particularly regarding the major Roman poets, aside from Ovid, Brunetto's knowledge does not appear nearly as extensive and direct as Dante's.[112]

The possibly limited financial and political support afforded by Dante's family, and the practical concerns he had to face rather early on, also cast some doubt on the traditional assumption that he studied in Bologna sometime between 1280 and 1286. The realization that he probably lacked the financial and educational prerequisites that granted access to higher education only set in starker relief the total absence of any documentary proof of his participation in the life of the Bolognese *studium*.[113]

In light of the clues examined so far, some provisional conclusions about the poet's earliest schooling may be drawn. Dante claimed to possess a mastery of Latin grammar that he considered, and proved to be, uncommon among vernacular laymen and intellectuals. His Latin training likely included the reading of some *auctores minores*, as suggested by references to Aesop (*Convivio* 30.4 and *Inferno* 23.4, discussed in Chapter 3) and to Priscian and Donatus (*Inferno* 15.109 and *Paradiso* 12.137–38, respectively). If he studied these texts while in school, however, he seems to have stopped short of tackling intermediate texts, such as Boethius, and thus, arguably, also the *auctores maiores*. The hypothesis that he continued his education with the study of the *ars dictaminis* in some notarial school, or simply at the end of his grammatical studies, would explain such a truncated reading curriculum. Given the Alighieris' social and financial situation, it would have been reasonable for them to invest in the poet's professional training, with an eye toward a remunerative career that also gave access to politically relevant milieus.[114] Although Dante never pursued the notarial career, his advanced Latin formation eventually allowed him to pursue the study of philosophy and a self-guided reading

---

[112] Witt, "*In the Footsteps*," 214–16.

[113] Evidence of Dante's links to Bologna is the so-called *sonetto della Garisenda*, copied by the notary Enrichetto delle Querce in 1287. His relationships with Brunetto and Guido Cavalcanti, moreover, might have given him access, either direct or indirect, to the Bolognese milieu, as they both had economical and intellectual ties with the city. Dante's journey to Bologna could have been related to his family's business in the city. In a document from October 7, 1270, we find a name that closely echoes Alighiero's listed among the Florentine moneylenders who made loans to the Bolognese commune. See Giovanni Livi, *Cultori di Dante in Bologna nei secoli XII e XIV* (Rome: Nuova Antologia, 1906), 119, and Inglese, *Vita*, 38. This document, however, has not been included in the recent edition of the *Codice Diplomatico Dantesco*. The speculation about Dante's studying in Bologna dates to the fourteenth century, when it was first asserted by Giovanni Villani and Giovanni Boccaccio. Among recent supporters of this thesis, see Luciano Gargan, *Dante, la sua biblioteca e lo studio di Bologna* (Rome: Editrice Antenore, 2014), and Pasquale Porro, "Dante e la tradizione filosofica," in *Dante*, ed. Roberto Rea and Justin Steinberg (Rome: Carocci, 2020), 307–27, esp. 309. Giovanni Livi's extensive research in the Bolognese archives, however, turned up no mention of Dante's name. Barański, "Studying the Spaces," 265–66, has cast further doubt on the likelihood of the poet's education at the *studium*.

[114] This thesis has also been suggested by Brilli and Milani in *Dante*, 45–48.

50 DANTE'S EDUCATION

of the *auctores maiores*.[115] This reconstruction of Dante's earliest Latin instruction, moreover, dovetails with the thesis put forward by some scholars that the poet deepened his classical learning only *after* his exile.[116]

Throughout all his works, Dante often claims to have been largely self-taught, as already noted with regard to *Convivio* 2.12.2. At the beginning of the *Convivio*, he presents himself as a layman whose intellectual formation did not benefit from attending the official venues of contemporary Scholastic culture (*Convivio* 1.10). He also repeatedly attacks the excesses and utilitarian aims of contemporary university learning, presenting himself as an outsider in the world of the high Latinate culture (*Convivio* 1.9.3). Even at the height of his career, while writing a Latin treatise titled *Questio de aqua et terra*, Dante describes himself as an amateur philosopher, "inter vere philosophantes minimus" (1.1), a nonspecialist, a layperson rather than a cleric, who nonetheless wishes to take part in contemporary philosophical debates. The poet's self-representation as a marginal intellectual in the Scholastic milieu of the time supports the impression, drawn from both material and textual evidence, that his formal schooling was not extensive and did not involve the study of a large variety of texts. He instead seems to have shared the same formal education as many moderately educated lay readers of his time, who were directed by their families toward professional training. The minor Latin texts he read as part of his language instruction, therefore, played a seminal role in his intellectual and literary development.

The presence—or the apparent absence—of these school texts in the poet's works should be sifted with a critical eye to Dante's own self-fashioning as a lay intellectual coming from the margins of the official academic culture. Dante is mostly silent about the *auctores* who were considered *minores*. This reticence, I argue, is intentional and serves his continual effort to connect to the major Latin tradition. Dante's critique of contemporary vernacular poets for their general ignorance of the classics (*Vita nova* 16 [25]) and Boethius' *Consolatio* (*Convivio* 12.2)

---

[115] Dante could also have relied on these skills to gain access to the guild of the *speziali*. Davidsohn observes, in his *Storia*, that knowledge of Latin was not a requirement to join the *speziali*, but it would have been highly desirable (vol. 4.3, 211). For discussion of Dante's possible links to the *speziali*, see Michele Barbi, "Dante e l'Arte dei medici e speziali," in *Problemi di critica dantesca; Seconda serie* (Florence: Sansoni, 1975), 379–84, who argued that Dante enrolled in the *arte* because of his interest in philosophy; and, more recently, Marco Santagata, "Dante e gli speziali," in *Dante und die bildenden Künste: Dialoge—Spiegelungen—Transformationen*, ed. Maria Antonietta Terzoli and Sebastian Schütze (Berlin: De Gruyter, 2016), 13–22, who instead maintained that Dante's relationship with *speziali* and painters would explain his enrollment. Diacciati (*Formazione dei laici*, 235) sides with Barbi, while Inglese (*Vita di Dante*, 15) explains that Dante could have enrolled as "medico" because medicine and philosophy were considered to be one discipline.

[116] One of the first to argue this thesis was Ulrich Leo, "The Unfinished *Convivio* and Dante's Rereading of the Aeneid," *Mediaeval Studies* 13 (1951): 41–46, which demonstrates Dante's deeper knowledge of Virgil's *Aeneid* in *Convivio* 4. Paul Renucci, *Dante disciple et juge du monde gréco-latin* (Paris: Les Belles Lettres, 1954), 61–66, esp. 70, argues that Dante first became acquainted with the classics in Bologna during the early years of his exile, between 1304 and 1306. The same thesis has also been advanced by Davis, "Scuola"; Gianfranco Fioravanti, "Introduzione," in *Convivio*, 8–19; and Mirko Tavoni, *Qualche idea su Dante* (Bologna: il Mulino, 2015), 25–50, 96–103.

shows his critical view of contemporary education, which had sidelined the study of the classics for a more pragmatic approach to language instruction. His general disregard for the minor Latin texts from the medieval school curricula, therefore, should also be interpreted in light of his challenge to established hierarchies and institutions of learning. For instance, it would have been simply impossible for the poet to be unaware of the existence of the *Ilias Latina*, as some scholars have concluded on the basis of *Convivio* 1.7.15, where Dante states that Homer had never been translated into Latin. Most late medieval lists of educational readings mention the *Ilias* among their recommended texts. The large number of its medieval manuscripts, most of which were *libri manuales* created for educational purposes, shows that this text enjoyed considerable popularity from the ninth century on.[117] Some evidence of its use in Florentine schools during the twelfth and the thirteenth centuries also survives.[118] Rather than ignorance of the existence of the *Ilias*, Dante's assertion reflects his nuanced understanding of this work.[119] The *Ilias* is indeed not a translation of Homer's *Iliad*, but rather an epitome, an "imitation," as a medieval *accessus* suggested. Medieval readers did not see the *Ilias* as an exercise in *translatio* but rather in *imitatio* by "a certain" Latin Homer: "Homerus quidam latinus."[120] Furthermore, as I have argued elsewhere, echoes of this school text may surface in the prologue to *Purgatorio* (*Ilias Latina*, 1063–65; *Purgatorio* 1.1–9).[121] Dante's silence about the *Ilias* may also reflect an opinion he expresses only a few chapters earlier, in *Convivio* 1.1.7, where he argues that poetry cannot be translated without destroying its poetic attributes. As Dante's complex relationship with the *Ilias* shows, his allusions to and silences about medieval school texts should be considered in light of his intellectual and artistic agenda.

A comprehensive assessment of the poet's debts and reactions to his earliest Latin education should look not only for Dante's direct references to or quotations from medieval school readings, but also for covert allusions to and echoes of these readings in the poet's oeuvre. The next chapters carry out this intertextual analysis of both the *Vita nova* and the *Commedia* and show Dante's creative critical engagement with popular school texts.

---

[117] Marco Scaffai, *Baebii Italici Ilias Latina*, ed. and trans. Marco Scaffai (Bologna: Pàtron, 1982), 29–36.

[118] The manuscript Florence, Biblioteca Riccardiana, 1221.2, for instance, dates from the first half of the thirteenth century and contains the text of the *Ilias* with simple interlinear vernacular glosses, as well as other annotations, all made by "an unformed hand" probably belonging to a pupil. Black, *Humanism*, 199. See also Marco Scaffai and Paolo Serra Zanetti, "Tradizione manoscritta dell'Ilias latina," in *In uerbis uerum amare: Miscellanea dell'Istituto di filologia latina e medioevale dell'Università di Bologna* (Florence: La Nuova Italia, 1980), 205–77.

[119] For the opposite thesis, see Guido Martellotti, "Omero," in the *ED*.

[120] Huygens, *Accessus*, 25–26. I thank Hildegund Müller for pointing me to this conclusive evidence.

[121] See my brief note on the subject, "Did Dante Know the *Ilias latina*? Textual Echoes in the Prologue to the *Purgatorio*," in *Dante Notes* (2017), https://dantesociety.org/node/120.

2

Learning to Praise

The *Vita nova* as a Vernacular Reader

To know a work of art or a genre well, it is of little use to take heed of the audience, of the respondent. One does not merely go wrong when relating a work of art to a specific public or to the representative of such a public; the very notion of an "ideal" receiver vitiates any theory of art. . . . For no poem is intended for its reader, no painting for its viewer, no symphony for its listener.

(Walter Benjamin, *The Task of the Translator*, 1923)

Sometime between 1290 and 1296, while still living in Florence, young Dante gathered together a selection of his poems and framed them with narrative and explanatory prose. Some of these *rime* (individual poems) had been independently circulating for several years but were now given a second life in this prosimetric *libello*, or "booklet," as the author dubs the *Vita nova* in its opening paragraph.[1] Using an evocative metaphor, Dante maintains to have compiled this small volume from the larger book of his memory, copying only a selection of the most important paragraphs listed under the rubric *Incipit Vita nova*:

In quella parte del libro de la mia memoria dinanzi a la quale poco si potrebbe leggere, si trova una rubrica la quale dice: *Incipit vita nova*. Sotto la quale rubrica io trovo scritte le parole le quali è mio intendimento d'assemplare in questo libello; e se non tutte, almeno la loro sentenzia.

(*Vita nova*, 1.1)

---

[1] The dating of the *Vita nova* revolves around two spans of years: 1292–95 and 1293–96. The later dating has most recently been supported by Stefano Carrai, in "Puntualizzazioni sulla datazione della 'Vita nova,'" *L'Alighieri* 52 (2018): 109–15. For a recent introduction to the *Vita nova* and the history of its composition, see Donato Pirovano, "Vita nuova," in *Dante*, ed. Roberto Rea and Justin Steinberg (Rome: Carocci, 2020), 37–54. For the text of the *Vita nova*, I quote Michele Barbi's edition but follow Guglielmo Gorni's chapter divisions and title (Barbi's divisions are also provided in square brackets). See Dante Alighieri, *Vita nova*, vol. 1 of *Le Opere di Dante*, ed. Michele Barbi (Florence: Società Dantesca Italiana, 1960), https://www.danteonline.it/index.html, and Alighieri, *Vita nova*, ed. Guglielmo Gorni, in *Opere; Rime; Vita nova; De vulgari eloquentia*, ed. Claudio Giunta, Guglielmo Gorni, and Mirko Tavoni, vol. 1 (Milan: Mondadori, 2011), 747–1063.

Dante's Education. Filippo Gianferrari, Oxford University Press. © Filippo Gianferrari (2024).
DOI: 10.1093/oso/9780198881766.003.0003

(In the book of my memory—the part of it before which not much is legible—
there is the heading *Incipit vita nova*. Under this heading I find the words which
I intend to copy down in this little book; if not all of them, at least their essential
meaning.)

As the title suggests, young Dante envisioned the *Vita nova* as something utterly
new in both content and form. The relatively young Italian vernacular had not yet
seen the like of the work's prosimetric form and sophisticated authorial stance. Not
only was Dante's *libello* the first single-author book in the Italian vernacular to be
entirely designed by its author, but it was also the first that instructed readers on
how to interpret, copy, and assemble the book itself.

In a move that may appear counterintuitive to our modern understanding of
"novelty," the poet drew generously from preexisting textual models, both in Latin
and the vernacular: Provençal *vidas* and *razos*, the Bible, Scholastic commentaries,
and classical and medieval elegiac poetry, to mention only a few. He also har-
monized different cultures that were normally considered to be in opposition,
such as the vernacular and the Latin, the lay and the academic, the secular and
the theological. Since Dante's purpose was to transcend and harmonize these different traditions, the *Vita nova*'s groundbreaking experimentalism neither can nor
should be reduced to any one of its models. Most original to the *libello* is the prose's
assimilation of paratextual elements—such as *commentum, accessus ad auctores*,
and *divisio textus*—that were forms of academic and Scholastic exposition. In the
extended book metaphor that opens the work, moreover, the author reveals that
the *Vita nova* is but a compendium of his book of memory, and although he will
not copy all the words in the original, he will write their essential meaning: "non
tutte, almeno la loro sentenzia" (if not all of them, at least their essential meaning).
Thus, Dante presents himself as both a "compiler" and a "commentator." The *Vita
nova*'s most innovative contribution to the history of Western literature lies in its
double nature as self-made anthology and self-commentary.[2]

---

[2] On the importance and novelty of the *Vita nova* as self-commentary, see Albert Ascoli, *Dante
and the Making of a Modern Author* (Cambridge: Cambridge University Press, 2008), 185; Zygmunt
Barański, "'Lascio cotale trattato ad altro chiosatore': Form, Literature, and Exegesis in Dante's *Vita
nova*," in *Dantean Dialogues: Engaging with the Legacy of Amilcare Iannucci*, ed. Maggie Kilgour and
Elena Lombardi (Toronto: University of Toronto Press, 2013), 1–40; Steven Botterill, "'. . . però che
la divisione non si fa se non per aprire la sentenzia de la cosa divisa' (*V.N.* XIV, 13): The *Vita nuova*
as Commentary," in *"La gloriosa donna de la mente": A Commentary on the "Vita Nuova"*, ed. Vincent Moleta (Florence: Olschki, 1994), 61–76; and Robert Hollander, *Dante: A Life in Works* (New
Haven, CT: Yale University Press, 2001), 14. In regard to the *Vita nova*'s relationship to the earlier
Provençal and vernacular tradition, see Guglielmo Gorni, "Una *Vita nova* per Cavalcanti, da Beatrice alla Donna Gentile," in *Guido Cavalcanti: Dante e il suo "primo amico"* (Rome: Aracne, 2009),
11–29, esp. 24–26; Olivia Holmes, *Assembling the Lyric Self: Authorship from Troubadour Song to
Italian Poetry Book* (Minneapolis: University of Minnesota Press, 2000), particularly chaps. 1 and
6; Tristan Kay, *Dante's Lyric Redemption: Eros, Salvation, Vernacular Tradition* (Oxford: Oxford
University Press, 2016), 93–154, esp. 98; Caterina Menichetti, "Le citazioni liriche nelle biografie
provenzali (per un'analisi stilistico-letteraria di vidas e razos)," *Medioevo Romanzo* 36, no. 1 (2012):

54   DANTE'S EDUCATION

In the literary and cultural tradition that proceeded Dante's *libello*, adding prose to poetry amounted to an act of explanation and instruction. Brunetto Latini makes this fact plain at the beginning of his *Tesoretto*, written between 1271 and 1272:

> E perció che 'l me' dire
> io lo voglio ischiarire
> sí ch'io non dica motto
> che tu non sappie 'n tutto
> la verace ragione
> e la condïzione,
> farò mio detto piano
> che pur un solo grano
> non sia che tu non sacci;
> ma vo' che tanto facci
> che lo mio dire *aprendi*,
> sí che tutto lo 'ntendi;
> E s'io parlassi iscuro
> di dicerlo in aperto,
> sí che ne sie ben certo.
> Ma perciò che la rima
> si stringe a una lima

128–60, esp. 156–60; Michelangelo Picone, "La *Vita Nuova* fra autobiografia e tipologia," in *Dante e le forme dell'allegoresi*, ed. Michelangelo Picone (Ravenna: Longo, 1987), 59–69; Picone, "*Vita Nuova*" *e tradizione romanza* (Padua: Liviana, 1979); Donato Pirovano, "Nota introduttiva," in *Vita Nuova: Rime*, ed. Donato Pirovano, poems ed. Marco Grimaldi (Rome: Salerno, 2015), 30–31; and Jelena Todorović, *Dante and the Dynamics of Textual Exchange: Authorship, Manuscript Culture, and the Making of the "Vita Nova"* (New York: Fordham University Press, 2016), 102–34. Boethius' *Consolatio* has also traditionally been seen as a central inspiration to Dante's project. The specific quality of this model's influence, however, has increasingly come under scrutiny. For a discussion of Boethius in the *Vita nova*, see Luca Lombardo, *Boezio in Dante: la "Consolatio philosophiae" nello scrittoio del poeta* (Venice: Edizioni Ca' Foscari, 2013); Lombardo, "'Alcibiades quedam meretrix': Dante lettore di Boezio e i commenti alla *Consolatio philosophiae*," *L'Alighieri* 52 (2018): 5–36; Pirovano ("Nota introduttiva," 29), who also points to the relevance of Martianus Capella's *De nuptiis Mercurii et Philologiae*; and Todorović, *Dante*, 18–101. Picone suggests that some manuscripts of Ovid's *Remedia amoris* surrounded by commentaries could have informed the genesis of the *libello*. See Picone, "La *Vita nova* come prosimetro," in *Percorsi della lirica duecentesca* (Fiesole: Cadmo, 2003), 238–41. Finally, on the *Vita nova* and the biblical and liturgical traditions, see, among others, Barański, "'Lascio cotale trattato'"; Vittore Branca, "Poetica del rinnovamento e tradizione agiografica nella *Vita nuova*," in *Studi in onore di Italo Siciliano* (Florence: Olschki, 1966), 1:123–48; Sergio Cristaldi, *La "Vita nuova" e la restituzione del narrare* (Soveria Mannelli: Rubbettino, 1994), chap. 4; Ronald L. Martinez, "Mourning Beatrice: The Rhetoric of Threnody in the *Vita nuova*," *MLN* 113 (1998): 1–29; Martinez, "The Poetics of Advent Liturgies: *Vita Nuova* and *Purgatorio*," in *Le culture di Dante: Studi in onore di Robert Hollander*, ed. Michelangelo Picone, Theodore J. Cachey, and Margherita Mesirca (Florence: Cesati, 2004), 271–304; Paola Nasti, *Favole d'amore e "saver profondo": La tradizione salomonica in Dante* (Ravenna: Longo, 2007), 43–85; Charles S. Singleton, *An Essay on the "Vita nuova"* (Cambridge, MA: Harvard University Press, 1949; repr. Baltimore: Johns Hopkins University Press, 1977); and Thomas C. Stillinger, *The Song of Troilus: Lyric Authority in the Medieval Book* (Philadelphia: University of Pennsylvania Press, 1992), chaps. 2–3.

THE *VITA NOVA* AS A VERNACULAR READER   55

di concordar parole
come la rima vuole,
sí che molte fïate
le parole rimate
ascondon la *sentenza*
e mutan la 'ntendenza,
quando vorrò trattare
di cose che rimare
tenesse oscuritate,
con bella brevetate
ti parlerò per prosa
e disporrò la cosa
parlando in volgare,
che tu intende ed apare.

(395–426; emphasis added)

(And because it is my speech, / I wish to clarify it / So that I will not say a word / By which you will not entirely know / The true reasoning / And the condition; / I will make my speaking plain, / So that not even a single grain / May exist without your knowing: / But I want you to do this much, / That you will learn from my speech / So that you will *understand* everything; / And if I were to speak obscurely, / I will make you sure / By telling it openly, / So that it may be truly right. / But since rhyme / Is polished by a file / For making words agree / As the rhyme wills, / So that many times / The rhymed words / Conceal their *meaning* / And alter the intent, / When I would treat / Of things that rhyming / Would make obscure, / With beautiful brevity / I will explain the matter to you, / *And I will speak in prose, / Speaking in the vernacular, / So that you may understand and learn.*)[3]

As Brunetto explains, poetry requires unpacking, especially when written to fulfill an educational purpose. Prose, instead, is by nature explanatory and can uncover the poem's *sententia*. The *Tesoretto*'s relevance and possible influence on the first inception of the *Vita nova*'s project is apparent. It has even been suggested that Dante conceived the *Vita nova* as the prose commentary that Brunetto never accomplished. Given the historical circumstances surrounding the birth of the *libello*, such a move would have appeared especially timely. After Brunetto's death, in 1294, Dante gradually moved to occupy the intellectual and civic void that the

---

[3] Brunetto Latini, "Tesoretto," in *Poesie*, ed. Stefano Carrai (Turin: Einaudi, 2016), 26–27. The translation is from Brunetto Latini, *Il Tesoretto (The Little Treasure)*, ed. and trans. Julia Bolton Holloway (New York: Garland, 1981), 23–25.

56   DANTE'S EDUCATION

older master's demise left in Florence's public scene. With the *Vita nova*, therefore, Dante could have attempted to endorse the role of "maestro" of the Florentines, which had hitherto belonged to Brunetto.[4] Whether in the wake of Brunetto's death or autonomously, there can be little doubt that at the heart of Dante's decision to write this self-commentary lies an urge to instruct readers on how to handle his poems. No attempt, however, has been made to interpret Dante's educational stance in the context of elementary language instruction in late thirteenth-century Florence. When we look at the sources, aims, and implications of the *Vita nova*'s didacticism, however, the importance of Florence's educational context becomes apparent.

Dante's appropriation of Scholastic forms of commentary has often been interpreted as the poet's innovative expedient to address previous receptions and misreadings of his poems, as well as to subsume traditional authority in the paradigm of his new vernacular authorship.[5] Pointing to the *divisio textus* featured by the prose, and to the classical *auctoritates* Dante quotes in chapter 16 [25], scholars have generally assumed that the educational models imitated by the poet coincided with the academic brand of textual criticism informed by Scholastic philosophy and the study of classical *auctores*.[6] This conclusion, however, should be questioned in light of the cultural milieu in which and for which Dante wrote the *Vita nova*. As discussed in Chapter 1, such an advanced classical and philosophical learning would have been unusual for a layperson whose education had taken place entirely within the confines of thirteenth-century Florence. By Dante's own admission in *Convivio* 2.12.2, we know that he made up for his own lack of classical and philosophical training only as an adult, of his own accord, and by attending places of learning that were generally outside the reach of the laity. It is also unclear to what extent Dante's own philosophic training in Florence's religious schools informed the project of the *Vita nova*.[7] To some who have considered Dante's

---

[4] Giovanni Villani's description of Brunetto as "cominciatore e maestro in digrossare i Fiorentini" (*Nuova Cronica* 8.10) is well known. On the *Tesoretto*'s influence on the *Vita nova*, see Gorni, "Introduzione," in Alighieri, *Vita nova*, 773. Domenico De Robertis noted an echo of Brunetto's *Rettorica* in *Vita nova* 1.24. See De Robertis, *Il libro della Vita nuova* (Florence: Sansoni, 1970 [1961]), 211–12. On Dante's attempts to inherit Brunetto's public and civic role among the Florentine intelligentsia, see Enrico Fenzi, "*Sollazzo* e *leggiadria*: Un'interpretazione della canzone dantesca *Poscia ch'amor*," *Studi danteschi* 63 (1991): 191–280, and, more recently, Silvia Diacciati, "Dante: Relazioni sociali e vita pubblica," *Reti medievali rivista* 15, no. 2 (2014): 243–70.

[5] Ascoli, *Dante*, 3–64, 175–226; Kay, *Dante's Lyric Redemption*, 13–59; Justin Steinberg, *Accounting for Dante: Urban Readers and Writers in Late Medieval Italy* (Notre Dame, IN: University of Notre Dame Press, 2007); and Steinberg, "Dante's First Dream between Reception and Allegory: The Response to Dante Da Maiano in the 'Vita Nova,'" in *Dante the Lyric and Ethical Poet. Dante Poeta Lirico e Etico*, ed. Zygmunt G. Barański and Martin McLaughlin (London: Legenda, 2010), 92–118.

[6] Gorni, "Introduzione"; Todorović, *Dante*, 67–101. Paolo Cherchi has recently written against this well-established idea. See Cherchi, "The *divisioni* in Dante's *Vita nuova*," *Le tre corone* 5 (2018): 73–88.

[7] A crucial discrepancy, for instance, appears in Dante's interpretation of the "donna gentile" episode in the *Convivio*, which seems to contradict his own reading of the same event in the *Vita nova*. On the influence of this philosophical training on the *Vita nova*, see Peter Dronke, *Verse with Prose: From Petronius to Dante* (Cambridge, MA: Harvard University Press, 1994), 107–11; Robert M. Durling

THE *VITA NOVA* AS A VERNACULAR READER   57

contemporary culture of literacy, his *libello* appears as an innovative attempt to reach out to a growing but still marginal lay readership. Hence, the *Vita nova*'s imitation of Scholastic techniques of textual exposition should also have fulfilled the purpose of instructing moderately educated lay readers.[8] In designing the instructional program of the *Vita nova*, therefore, Dante would have also considered the models provided by his own education, as they defined the horizon of expectation for his intended audience.

The linguistic and literary training Dante had received as part of his earliest education provided a convenient resource for designing the instructional components of the *libello* in ways intelligible to his Florentine audience. In particular, the small Latin readers that were parsed and memorized in the urban schools at that time offered suitable models for such purpose. Two especially popular school texts, Henry of Settimello's *Elegia* and Prosper of Aquitaine's *Liber epigrammatum*, display significant, and largely unexplored, similarities with the *Vita nova*. Before we focus our attention on these parallels, however, we need to define the *Vita nova*'s educational aims in light of its implied audience.

The Implied Readers of the *Vita nova* (and Their Implied Education)

A long-standing critical view defines the *Vita nova* "as a treatise by a poet, written for poets, on the art of poetry."[9] Dante's claim that he wrote the *Vita nova* to clarify the "subtle" meanings—*sententia* (19.7; 22.2; 30.9 [30.4; 33.2; 39.6; 41.9])—and to remove "alcuna dubitazione" (some doubts) (26.4 [37.4]) surrounding his poems seems to address a concern expressed only a few years earlier by an older poet, Bonagiunta da Lucca, with regard to the impenetrability of Guido Guinizzelli's and his followers' new doctrinal poems:

---

and Ronald L. Martinez, *Time and the Crystal: Studies in Dante's* Rime petrose (Berkeley: University of California Press, 1990), 53–71. Most recently, Lorenzo Dell'Oso has uncovered important evidence of the *Vita nova*'s possible dialogue with some of the theological disputations that were being debated in Santa Croce at the time. See Lorenzo Dell'Oso, "How Dante Became Dante: His Intellectual Formation between 'Clerici' and 'Laici' (1294–1296)" (Ph.D. diss., University of Notre Dame, 2020).

[8] John Ahern, "The New Life of the Book: The Implied Reader of the 'Vita Nuova,'" *Dante Studies* 110 (1992): 1–16; but see also his "The New Life of the Book: Oral and Written Communication in the Age of Dante" (Ph.D. diss., University of Indiana, 1976). Holmes (*Assembling the Lyric Self*, 123) endorses Ahern's thesis; and see, recently, Elena Lombardi, *Imagining the Woman Reader in the Age of Dante* (Oxford: Oxford University Press, 2018), esp. 60–77.

[9] Dante Alighieri, *La "Vita nuova,"* trans. Barbara Reynolds (Harmondsworth, Middlesex: Penguin, 1969), 11. Also of this persuasion are Botterill, "'Però che'"; H. Wayne Storey, "Di libello in libro: Problemi materiali nella poetica di Monte Andrea e Dante," in *Da Guido Guinizzelli a Dante: Nuove prospettive sulla lirica del Duecento: atti del convegno di studi, Padova-Monselice, 10–12 maggio 2002*, ed. Furio Brugnolo and Gianfelice Peron (Padua: Il poligrafo, 2004), 271–90; Storey, "Following Instructions: Remaking Dante's *Vita Nova* in the Fourteenth Century," in *Medieval Constructions in Gender and Identity: Essays in Honor of Joan M. Ferrante*, ed. Teodolinda Barolini (Tempe, AZ: MRTS, 2005), 117–32; and Todorović, *Dante*, 101.

58   DANTE'S EDUCATION

> Così passate voi di sottigliansa,
> e non si può trovar chi ben ispogna,
> cotant'è iscura vostra parlatura.
>   Ed è tenuta gran dissimigliansa,
> ancor che'l senno venga da Bologna,
> traier canson per forsa di scrittura.
>
> > (*Voi ch'avete mutata la mainera* [You, who have
> > modified the style], 9–14)

> (Your subtleties are so pronounced / that none can make out what
> you mean, / because your speech is so obscure. / And it is thought
> quite fanciful, / despite Bologna's learnedness, / to quote theology
> in verse.)[10]

Bonagiunta reproaches Guinizzelli for his densely conceptual poetry, which required a level of erudition uncommon for most vernacular readers and could use the support of glosses. Even a vernacular poet such as Bonagiunta felt left outside of Guinizzelli's audience, which should have more appropriately included people with university training, as implied by the mention of Bologna.

The first act of poetic writing recounted in the *Vita nova* may also appear to confirm the impression that Dante targeted only a select coterie of vernacular poets.[11] He explains that he first wrote the sonnet "A ciascun alma presa e gentil core" (To all besotted souls, my counterparts) for the "molti li quali erano famosi trovatori in quello tempo" (several of the well-known poets of that time) (1.20 [3.9]) and that a good number of poets replied. The most notable among them was Guido Cavalcanti, who eventually became, in Dante's words, his "first" friend: "primo de li miei amici" (somebody whom I consider my best friend) (2.1 [3.14]). The poet alludes to Cavalcanti on a few other occasions throughout the *Vita nova* (15.3; 16.26 [24.3; 25.10]), singling him out among the readers of the *libello*. The adjective "molti," however, suggests that Dante had already aimed his sonnet to a larger audience of poets. More notably, he claims that his initial readers turned out to be ill-suited to understanding the poem's actual meaning, whereas, by the time of its second edition in the *Vita nova*, the poem's message had become clear to everyone, even to the least trained among the readers: "Lo verace giudicio del detto sogno non fue veduto allora per alcuno, ma ora è manifestissimo a li più semplici" (The correct interpretation of my dream was not understood by anyone at first, but now it is clear to even the most simpleminded) (2.2 [3.15]). By the time he wrote the *Vita nova*, therefore, "A ciascun alma" had already reached far beyond the audience of

---

[10] Donato Pirovano, *Poeti del Dolce stil novo* (Rome: Salerno, 2012), 54–56. The translation is by Richard Lansing, "Purgatorio 24," *Digital Dante*, accessed March 11, 2021, https://digitaldante. columbia.edu/dante/divine-comedy/purgatorio/purgatorio-24/.

[11] As argued by Storey, "Di libello in libro," 271–90.

THE *VITA NOVA* AS A VERNACULAR READER   59

poets that the sonnet had originally targeted. The history of its failed reception suggests that Dante conceived the *Vita nova* for a broader readership than the initial one to whom he addressed the sonnet "A ciascun alma."[12]

John Ahern argues that, by depicting a series of different fictional readers in the *Vita nova*, Dante meant to reach out to an increasingly broad and popular audience for the *libello*. Ahern also suggests that by addressing the *canzone* "Donne ch'avete intelletto d'amore" (Women who understand the truth of love) (10.15 [19.4]) to the social category of ladies—rather than to one individual lady, as was customary— Dante targeted a whole spectrum of different readers, including the less trained ones: the *idiotae*—both men and women—who could read vernacular but had little or no understanding of Latin, and who were traditionally associated with women. Other *laici* with intermediate or advanced Latin literacy and learning but no academic training would also have fit into this category. The rapprochement of the female addressees with the philosophical term "intellectus," however, would have elicited the interest of readers belonging to different and traditionally divided milieus—from the humblest, ladylike lay reader to the *litterati*, who included cler- ics and lay people with advanced Latin literacy and university-level training.[13] Confirming that he foresaw a broad readership for his *libello*, whose reception was bound to escape his control, Dante writes of his concern about having com- municated the meaning of this *canzone* far and wide: "ché certo io temo d'avere a troppi comunicato lo suo intendimento pur per queste divisioni che fatte sono, s'elli avvenisse che molti le potessero audire" (I fear I have already communicated its meaning to too many people simply by analyzing it as I have—assuming, that is, that it should ever have a large audience) (10.33 [19.22]). After this central episode, however, the *Vita nova* keeps reaching out to an increasingly broad and diversified readership: more women, individual friends of the poet's, illustrious—and likely powerful—citizens of Florence, and finally pilgrims who are crossing Florence on their way to Rome. The identification of the last-named fictional readers as pil- grims also suggests that the *Vita nova* was aimed at an increasingly nondescript audience.[14]

---

[12] See Steinberg, *Accounting*, chaps. 1–2.

[13] Ahern, "The New Life of the Book," particularly 199 and 208; Ahern, "The Reader on the Piazza: Verbal Duels in Dante's *Vita Nuova*," *Texas Studies in Literature and Language* 35 (1990): 18–39; and Ahern, "Singing the Book: Orality in the Reception of Dante's *Comedy*," in *Dante: Contemporary Perspectives*, ed. Amilcare Iannucci (Toronto: Toronto Press, 1997), 214–39.

[14] Elena Lombardi has recently discussed the cultural implications of Dante's address to the ladies in the context of female readership in medieval Europe. See Lombardi, *Imagining*, 60–77, and Lombardi, "L'invenzione' del lettore in Dante," in *C'è un lettore in questo testo? Rappresentazione della lettura nella letteratura italiana*, ed. Giovanna Rizzarelli and Cristina Savettieri (Bologna: il Mulino, 2016), 23–41. Lombardi, too, supports the thesis that at different stages of the *Vita nova* Dante imagines different readers (27). Martinez ("Mourning Beatrice," 3–5) provides a different interpretation of the pilgrims in light of *Lamentations*. It should also be noted that, about ten years later, Dante's own perception of the *Vita nova*'s fortunes confirms that the *libello*'s readership outgrew professional, gender, and civic boundaries. In his *Convivio*, Dante assumes the reader's knowledge of the *Vita nova*, and he frames

60 DANTE'S EDUCATION

The only restriction the *libello* applies to its implied audience is the ability to read.[15] For the first time in any of his works, here Dante addresses specifically those who can read: "ricordisi *chi ci legge* che di sopra è scritto" (I ask my *readers* to recall what I explained earlier) (10.31 [19.20]; emphasis added). After Beatrice's death, moreover, Dante envisions his *libello* as circulating in written form among readers who may wish to add glosses or commentaries on it, "e però lascio cotale trattato ad altro chiosatore" (I leave this subject [literally: this tract] to another commentator) (10.2 [28.2]). In a culture in which listening was considered a form of reading, the specific notion of readers who could leaf through a copy of the book and go back to reread something was a prescriptive indication of the kind of reception that the poet envisioned for his work.[16] To address those who could read was no small restriction for the time. In the particular milieu of Florence at the end of the thirteenth century, Dante's move would have appeared both timely and ambitious.

As outlined in Chapter 1, the city of Florence displayed growing literacy among the laity and featured highly developed educational offerings. Unlike other large cities in northern Italy, however, Florence still lacked a university and featured instead some of the most advanced *abbaco* instruction in Europe. This state of things suggests that a large number of literate people received only limited language instruction, mostly for vocational reasons. These vocational readers populated the intermediate space between the two extremes of the literacy spectrum—non-Latinized and advanced Latinized readers. They could, in some cases, reach advanced reading proficiency in the vernacular but had little understanding of Latin or experience with literary criticism. Besides dealing with professional writings, however, these lay literates were interested in reading for pleasure and self-instruction.[17]

---

the former as a sort of sequel to the latter (1.4.13). Some exchanges between contemporary vernacular poets also show knowledge of the *Vita nova*—for instance, Cino da Pistoia's sonnet to Onesto da Bologna, "Bernardo, quell gentil che porta l'arco." Recent archival discoveries also point to a broader dissemination of the booklet at an earlier stage than hitherto supposed. See Luca Azzetta, "'Fece molte canzoni per lo suo amore et come pare a uno suo librecto cui ei pose nome la Vita Nova'; Note sui primi lettori della 'Vita nova,'" *Studi Romanzi* 14 (2018): 57–91.

[15] I follow Ahern's "The Implied Reader" in my use of the term "implied reader" in this chapter. An illustrative definition is also provided by Wolfgang Iser, *The Act of Reading: A Theory of Aesthetic Response* (Baltimore: Johns Hopkins University Press, 1978), 34: "The concept of the implied reader is therefore a textual structure anticipating the presence of a recipient without necessarily defining him."

[16] On the different types of reading in the Middle Ages and the different social functions, circumstances, and milieus that these types of reading served, see Armando Petrucci, *Readers and Writers in Medieval Italy: Studies in the History of Writing* (New Haven, CT: Yale University Press, 1995), 133. Dante uses terms such as "dire" and "scrivere" as basically interchangeable and does the same with "udire" and "leggere." See, for instance, *Vita nova* 10.33 [19.22].

[17] As witnessed by the burgeoning number of vernacular translations of ancient and foreign texts produced in Tuscany at the end of the thirteenth century and during the fourteenth. On this, see Alison Cornish, *Vernacular Translation in Dante's Italy: Illiterate Literature* (Cambridge: Cambridge University Press, 2010), and Giuseppe De Luca, *Scrittori di religione del Trecento: Volgarizzamenti* (Turin: Einaudi, 1977).

The overwhelmingly female audience Dante addresses and fictionalizes in the *Vita nova* fittingly embodies this expanding and self-teaching lay public. In chapter 16 [25], for instance, Dante states that the first author who wrote in the vernacular did so to be understood by a lady: "E lo primo che cominciò a dire sì come poeta volgare, si mosse però che volle fare intendere le sue parole a donna, a la quale era malagevole d'intendere li versi latini" (And the first one who started to write poetry in the vernacular started to do so because he wanted to make his words comprehensible to women, who found it difficult to follow Latin verses) (16.6 [25.6]). Women were not expected to read Latin, and since this was the language of learning in the Middle Ages, they were essentially cut off from any form of advanced or academic education. As Elena Lombardi points out, however, Dante here suggests not that women could not read Latin, but that they could do so only with much difficulty. Although evidence of female literacy in Dante's Florence remains scant, several sources indicate that it was not unusual for women to possess either basic or advanced reading skills and, in some cases, even to have had some degree of Latin instruction.[18] Girls were admitted to reading instruction, and mothers were often the first to introduce children to the alphabet. Some women, especially among the urban patrician families, also received instruction in grammar.[19] One should not, therefore, overlook the historical implications of Dante's decision to fictionalize female readers among his primary interlocutors and partners in launching the *Vita nova*'s new groundbreaking poetics (10.4–33 [18.1–19.22]). By extension, through these poetics, the author identifies as his intended audience insightful readers, both men and women, with no advanced Latin or academic training. Thus, in the *Vita nova* Dante initiated the educational program he overtly endorsed in his *Convivio*, in which he maintains that he is writing for the instruction of "not only men but women, of whom there are many in this language who know only the vernacular and are not learned" (non solamente maschi ma femmine, che sono molti e molte in questa lingua, volgari, e non litterati) (1.9.5). Moreover, the evidence that in the *Convivio* Dante assumes his readers' familiarity with the *Vita nova* further supports the hypothesis that in both works he envisioned a public with similar cultural and social characteristics.

The limited reading proficiency and literary education shared by many of such readers, however, posed no small challenge to Dante's project. In the *Vita nova*, he claims that the very "subtlety" that characterizes his poetics invites sharp readers. Ahern observes that the *libello* repeatedly calls for readers to reach a perception of Beatrice's divine nature, and of her current status within the order of eternity, "as

---

[18] For an assessment of female literacy and the different contexts, instances, and forms of women reading in the Middle Ages, see Lombardi, *Imagining*, chap. 1. On the education of women in late medieval and Renaissance Italy, see Paul F. Grendler, *Schooling in Renaissance Italy: Literacy and Learning, 1300–1600* (Baltimore: Johns Hopkins University Press, 1989), 87–108.

[19] Chapter 1 mentions the interesting case of the Florentine Domina Clementia, *doctrix puerum*. Clementia, however, may represent an exceptional case.

62 DANTE'S EDUCATION

the result of a minute examination of the text."[20] Dante, however, had to negotiate with the reality that the very task of navigating a complex literary text—let alone appreciating its subtle philosophical and theological meanings—already presented some challenges to his lay vernacular readers. Such a realization lies behind the poet's steady and at times pedantic efforts to instruct readers on how to handle not only the poems but the whole of the *Vita nova.*

The *divisiones*, for instance—a feature so innovative as to prove especially puzzling for both medieval and modern readers of the *Vita nova*—are obvious pedagogical tools, as they guide readers through the basic, literal interpretation of the poem.[21] That one of the very few poems to be equipped with both divisions and subdivisions is addressed to "Women who understand the truth of love" is, in my view, revealing of the intended aim of this paratextual tool. The "exclusive" readership of this *canzone*, made up primarily of women, is a nonspecialist one. The "emphasis on the female audience," as Justin Steinberg observes, "testifies to the expanded readership afforded by composing in the vernacular . . . the *donne* may stand for the new vernacular audience." The divisions of "Donne ch'avete," therefore, would reflect a "spirit of cultural democratization" that informs Dante's renewed poetics and, perhaps, the project of the *Vita nova.*[22] A key aim of the divisions is didactic rather than prescriptive: they are meant to assist inexpert readers.[23]

The *Vita nova* also features several instances of prose sections in which the author prompts his reader to go back and reread a given passage or to wait for a forthcoming explanation.[24] Dante also marks digressions from the proposed subject matter and gives concise treatments of theoretical questions—as in chapter 16 [25], where he justifies his use of the prosopopoeia of Love in the *Vita nova.*[25] In this central chapter—according to Guglielmo Gorni's divisions—Dante defines and legitimizes the work tools of the "poete volgare" (vernacular poets) and furnishes vernacular readers with the crucial means to exercise literary criticism. In addition, he gives them a succinct overview of the history of contemporary poetry

[20] Ahern, "The New Life of the Book," 211.

[21] For an excellent history of the *divisio textus* in the Middle Ages, see Stillinger, *The Song of Troilus*, chap. 3.

[22] Steinberg, *Accounting*, 62.

[23] For a more detailed discussion of the division and subdivisions of "Donne ch'avete intelletto d'amore" and the didactic aim of the *divisioni*, see Filippo Gianferrari, "*Donne e divisioni*: The Instructional Aim of the *Vita nova*," in *Dante's "Vita nova": A Collaborative Reading*, ed. Zygmunt G. Barański and Heather Webb (Notre Dame, IN: University of Notre Dame Press, 2023), 170–77. Paolo Cherchi has argued that the *divisioni* are not "explanations" but rather "a necessary step" of the reading process to grasp the meaning of the text. See Cherchi, "The *divisioni*."

[24] See, for instance, "And so I say that I still intend to resolve and clarify this ambiguity in an even obscurer section of this little book" (5.24 [12.17]); "it is not part of the present topic, if we look back at the proem that precedes this little book" (19.2 [28.2]).

[25] For an example of marked digressions, see "Changing the subject a little, I now want to explain the miraculous effect that her salutation had on me" (5.3 [10.3]).

and its ties with the canon of ancient literature. The *Vita nova*, moreover, collected for its readers an impressive "compendium of vernacular written forms," as Zygmunt Barański fittingly puts it, in both prose and verse.[26] Finally, Dante's practice of indicating the poems' different metrical forms would have also appeared highly instructive. Not only did this provide guidelines to the scribes, as Wayne Storey argues, but it also allowed readers to learn the different metrical forms that were characteristic of vernacular poetry.[27]

Among the several, intertwining discourses and aims that mark Dante's complex experiment in the *libello*, and have been teased out by readers over the centuries, the *Vita nova* could also be seen to operate as a "vernacular reader"—a book "containing extracts of a particular author's work or passages of text designed to give learners of a language practice in reading."[28] While explaining the poems, the prose of the *Vita nova* also educates readers "in the proper way of reading," as Ahern suggests, and offers a vernacular tutorial on how to navigate any complex literary text.[29] The very term that Dante uses to define the *Vita nova* in his opening paragraph, "libello," also implies the work's overall instructional aims.

The *libello* and the *opuscula*

Dante's introduction of the *Vita nova* based on its material form as a "libello" served not merely a poetic function but also a practical one, allowing him to

---

[26] Zygmunt Barański, "Vita nova," in *Dante's "Other Works": Assessments and Interpretations*, ed.Zygmunt G. Barański and Theodore J. Cachey Jr. (Notre Dame, IN: University of Notre Dame Press, 2022), 71–124, at 71.

[27] Readers and scribes of vernacular texts virtually coincided at that time, and directions on how to copy the *Vita nova* were, first and foremost, guidelines for how to read it. Dante himself provides the model of his ideal reader when, in the opening paragraph, he envisions himself reading *and* copying from his own book of memory. His self-representation encapsulates a major feature of reading at the time: "People read *to* write: this is the sense of the *compilatio*," as Armando Petrucci has it (*Readers*, 279). It appears that the copying of vernacular works was a more or less occasional event, left to the will of readers—addressees, dedicatees, patrons—the correspondents, in other words, of poetic exchanges, who copied and anthologized vernacular texts for personal consumption and informal distribution (Ahern, "The New Life of the Book," 12). As is well known, Italian poems were likely never sung, and they were modeled on the epistolary forms—as is obvious, for instance, with the *tenzoni*. See, among others, Ahern, *Reader on the Piazza*, 23; Holmes, *Assembling the Lyric Self*, 12; and Storey, "Di libello in libro," 279. The importance of epistolary exchanges in Florence is evidenced by Brunetto's *Rettorica*, 76.14 (Brunetto Latini, *La rettorica*, ed. Francesco Maggini [Florence: Galletti e Cocci, 1915]). Some scholars, however, have also talked of "officina scrittoria" (writing workshop) to describe the phenomenon of different vernacular manuscripts copied by the same hand. See Sandro Bertelli, "Nota sul canzoniere provenzale P e sul Martelli 12," *Medioevo e Rinascimento, Annuario del Dipartimento di Studi sul Medioevo e Rinascimento dell'Università di Firenze* 18 (2004): 369–75. On the first copiers of Dante's works, see Giovanna Frosini's recent reassessment in "Il volgare di Dante," in *Dante*, ed. Roberto Rea and Justin Steinberg (Rome: Carocci, 2020), 245–65, esp. 256.

[28] See the entry the entry "Reader" in *Oxford Learner's Dictionaries*, accessed March 2023, https://www.oxfordlearnersdictionaries.com/definition/english/reader?q=reader.

[29] Ahern, "The New Life of the Book," 199.

64   DANTE'S EDUCATION

introduce the work in a way familiar to his readers without, however, placing it in any traditional literary genre. The mixed form of the prosimetrum prevented the *Vita nova* from being identified with any specific metric or stylistic genres—in contrast to the poems contained in this work, the metrical forms of which are always indicated by the author. The *Vita nova*'s multifaceted appearance—as poetic anthology, *compilatio*, commentary, and chronicle—also precludes a clear-cut generic definition based on the work's content. Instead of juggling several generic descriptors—as in the *Commedia*, in which he deploys terms such as "canzone," "comedìa," and "poema sacro" (song, comedy, sacred poem)—the author consistently refers to the *Vita nova* as a *libello*. The term itself is far from prescriptive and leaves readers with very little indication of the particular nature of the text. The Latin word and its vernacular equivalent generically meant any piece of writing, from a legal petition or accusation to a message, to a short treatise or commentary.

Dante's contemporary readers, however, would have pictured the *libello* as a precise material object. Storey argues that the poet envisioned the *Vita nova* as a small gathering of manuscript folia (two or three *quaderni*)—presumably the format in which anthologies of vernacular poems circulated among restricted groups of readers. No extant copy of such a genre of *libello* survives to support Storey's thesis, however. It is also revealing, I believe, that when describing his *Tesoretto* as a similarly small gathering of leaves, Brunetto Latini calls it a *quaderno* rather than a *libello* (*Tesoretto*, 109–12). Storey's contribution nevertheless highlights the fact that the term *libello*, although its exact meaning is elusive, is nonetheless descriptive.

In the eyes of Dante and his readers, the material appearance of a text was closely bound to its genre, audience, and intended aims.[30] Dante's uses of the same term throughout his oeuvre are illuminating. In the *Vita nova*, the poet refers to the work as a *libello* (5.24; 16.9; 19.2 [12.7; 25.9; 29.2]) to point the reader to different sections of the text that shed light on a given issue. The *libello* thus appears as a book that can be either read according to its narrative progression or consulted like a coherent tract, following different topical inquiries.[31] In *Convivio* (2.2.2), moreover, Dante again refers to the *Vita nova* as a *libello*, but he also uses the term to designate his own *De vulgari eloquentia* (1.5.10), as well as Cicero's *De senectute* (2.8.9). Finally, in *Paradiso* 12.135, the poet deploys the term to define Petrus Hispanus's *Summulae logicales*. Dante therefore quite consistently uses the term "libello" to mean short treatise or handbook, rather than an anthology of poems.

---

[30] Storey, "Di libello in libro," 271–81. In his poem "Infra gli altri difetti del libello," Cino uses the term "libello," it seems, to identify Dante's *Commedia*.

[31] The multiformity of the *Vita nova* has been generally identified with the options of reading it either as narrative prose interpolated with poems or, vice versa, as poems framed by a prose commentary (see, for instance, Stillinger's discussion of these two options in *Song of Troilus*, 44–73). Rarely, however, have critics acknowledged that the *libello* also offers the option of reading it as a sort of reference book.

THE *VITA NOVA* AS A VERNACULAR READER 65

One may then reasonably ask what the handbook of the *Vita nova* was supposed to teach. As already noted, scholars have often proposed viewing the work as a handbook of poetic composition. With the exception of chapter 16 [25], however, the *libello* offers little or no technical instruction on how to write poetry. This hypothesis appears even less persuasive when one considers the *Vita nova* vis-à-vis the *De vulgari eloquentia*. The latter contains more relevant and practical information about poetic composition in the vernacular and was written in Latin, thus targeting readers with advanced grammar learning and a keener interest in issues of language, rhetoric, and poetics.[32]

Dante's interpolation of critical apparatuses typical of medieval Latin textuality in the prose of the *Vita nova* provides another important indication of its intended fruition. For Ahern, Dante's references to rubrics and larger paragraphs reveal the sophisticated world of medieval universities as a key model of Dante's project. This hypothesis, however, needs to be scrutinized in relation to the material indication provided by the author through the term "libello." Academic books—that is, books used for advanced, university-level study—were generally large, heavy, hard to handle, and difficult to transport; they also required solid and fixed support in order to be consulted. Obviously, therefore, they did not resemble anything like a small *libello*. Ahern does point out that Dante would rather have envisioned a small gathering of folia, the *quaderno*, that constituted the unit handed out for copying in the *pecia* system. Albeit more suitable material equivalents of the *libello* than a whole academic book would be, these small gatherings were subunits of a larger volume, often containing different texts, rather than independent and self-contained booklets.[33] Most important, however, only very few Florentine readers had some experience with this type of textuality and its critical paratexts, more common, for instance, in Bologna's university milieu. In Florence, these academic books typically belonged in the conventual libraries. Academic books would have been excessively costly, difficult to understand, and largely irrelevant for the type of lay readers for whom Dante seems to tailor the instructional sections of the *Vita nova*.[34] These readers tended either to possess no books or to own small books

---

[32] Storey, "Di libello in libro," and Todorović, *Dante*, have recently reiterated the hypothesis that Dante envisioned the *Vita nova* as a handbook of poetic composition.

[33] Ahern, "The New Life of the Book," 11. On the *pecia* system, see Peter Beal, "pecia system," in *A Dictionary of English Manuscript Terminology 1450–2000* (Oxford: Oxford University Press, 2008), https://www-oxfordreference-com.oca.ucsc.edu/view/10.1093/acref/9780199576128.001.0001/acref-9780199576128-e-0746, and Graham Pollard, *The Pecia System in the Medieval Universities* (London: Scolar Press, 1978).

[34] It is not obvious, moreover, what kind of access a layperson like Dante would have had to religious libraries. For Guglielmo Gorni, the *divisiones* are a by-product of the poet's earlier Scholastic formation, ("Introduzione," *Vita nova*, 747–82). On the poet's possible access to *quodlibetal* disputations in one of the conventual schools of Florence, see Dell'Oso, *How Dante Became Dante*. We cannot, however, assume that he also had access to conventual libraries. In her recent study "'Nelle scuole delli religiosi': Materiali per Santa Croce nell'età di Dante," *L'Alighieri* 50 (2017): 5–55, Anna Pegoretti argues that outsiders were not generally allowed to consult these books, and external lending seems to have been granted only in exceptional cases. On the cultural exchanges between the laity and the convents, see

66 DANTE'S EDUCATION

containing, together or independently, the hours, the small *psalterium*—which served also for teaching the alphabet in the earliest stages of a child's education—and other devotional texts. Lay readers also owned quivers of parchment folia, which sometimes were sewn together, containing vernacular texts. Other books that lay people knew well, and came increasingly to own copies of, were their little schoolbooks, which were poorly bound together and often made from recycled parchment or paper. These pamphlets featured small anthologies of minor Latin poems with some rudimentary glosses. These instructional booklets, I contend, represented a more suitable material analogue of the *Vita nova* handbook than academic books.[35]

A significant number of pocket-sized, inexpensive books produced in thirteenth- and fourteenth-century Florence share a similar format and selection of minor *auctores* (see Figures 2.1 and 2.2).[36] Several of these elementary school texts appear today in one, two, or three fascicles containing single texts. Some also survive in fragments, suggesting that they were often used without a binding. Ownership marks are often found in them, testifying to an increase in the laity's private ownership of these booklets, a meaningful transformation when one considers that only few households possessed any books at all.[37] Bestsellers among school texts, often found in this particular format, were Cato, Prosper's *Liber epigrammatum*, and Prudentius' *Dittochaeon*. A few similar booklets featuring Aesop and Henry of Settimello are also found.[38] In his commentary on Dante's *Commedia*, written at the end of the fourteenth century, Francesco da Buti—who had been educated in Pisa, not far from Florence—refers to Aesop precisely as "uno *libello* che si legge a' fanciulli che imparano grammatica" (a *booklet* usually read to children who are studying grammar) (emphasis added).[39] In similar fashion, in his late fourteenth-century *Liber de civitatis Florentiae et eiusdem*

Sonia Gentili, "Poesia e filosofia a Firenze tra Santa Croce e Santa Maria Novella," in *The Dominicans and the Making of Florence (13th–14th Centuries)*, ed. Johannes Bartuschat, Elisa Brilli, and Delphine Carron (Florence: Firenze University Press, 2020), 225–41, esp. 225–26. On the conventual libraries of Dante's Florence, see also Charles T. Davis, "The Early Collection of Books of S. Croce in Florence," *Proceedings of the American Philosophical Society* 107 (1963): 399–414, and Davis, "The Florentine 'studia' and Dante's 'Library,'" in *The Divine Comedy and the Encyclopedia of Arts and Sciences*, ed. Giuseppe Di Scipio and Aldo Scaglione (Amsterdam: Benjamins, 1988), 339–66.

[35] For an extended discussion of the different codicological features of books in late medieval Italy, see Petrucci, *Readers*, esp. 137, 179–81, and 224.

[36] See Chapter 1.

[37] Harvey J. Graff, *The Legacies of Literacy: Continuities and Contradictions in Western Culture and Society* (Bloomington: Indiana University Press, 1987), 88. Particularly instructive is the example of a thirteenth-century secondhand dealer with a decent-size business, whose *libro di bottega* (shop register) shows that although he possessed written proficiency in the vernacular, as witnessed by his extensive record-keeping activity, he did not seem to own any books either in the shop or at home. See Gianfranco Cherubini, "Un rigattiere fiorentino del Duecento," in *Studi in onore di Arnaldo d'Addario*, ed. Luigi Borgia et al. (Lecce: Conte Editore, 1995).

[38] Paul Gehl, "Latin Readers in Fourteenth-Century Florence," *Scrittura e civiltà* 13 (1989): 387–440, and Gehl, *A Moral Art: Grammar, Society, and Culture in Trecento Florence* (Ithaca, NY: Cornell University Press, 1993), 397–401.

[39] Francesco Da Buti, comm. *Inferno* 23.4.

THE *VITA NOVA* AS A VERNACULAR READER 67

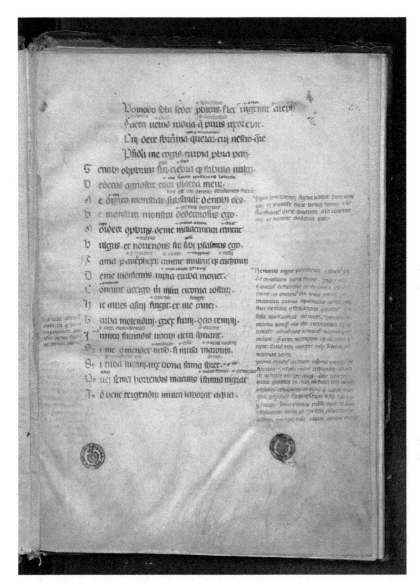

Figure 2.1 Florence, Biblioteca Medicea Laurenziana, Plut. 33.32 (XIII–XIV century, Italy), fol. 1, incipit of Henry of Settimello, *Elegia*.

Source: Courtesy of the Italian Ministry of Culture/Biblioteca Medicea Laurenziana, Florence. Reproduction or duplication by any means is strictly prohibited.

famosis civibus, Filippo Villani—a Florentine born and bred—refers to Henry of Settimello's *Elegia*: "Hic *libellus*, cui titulus 'Henriguethus' est, primam discentibus artem aptissimus per scholas Ytaliae continuo frequentatur" (This booklet, titled "Little Henry," is perfect for those who are learning the first art and is consistently

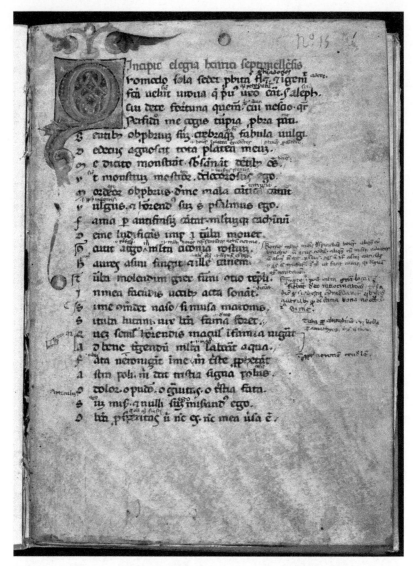

Figure 2.2 Florence, Archivio di Stato di Firenze, Carte Strozziane IIIa ser., 72 (XIV century, Italy), fol. 1r. Incipit of Henry of Settimello, *Elegia*.

Source: Courtesy of the Archivio di Stato, Florence.

read in schools all over Italy).[40] The term *libellus* is also used to define Statius' *Achilleid* in a medieval *accessus* preserved in the manuscript Florence, Biblioteca Medicea Laurenziana, Pluteo 24 Sin. 12, fol. 49r (figure 6.2) that presents the poem as written for educational goals.[41]

---

[40] Philippi Villani, *Liber de origine civitatis Florentiae et eiusdem famosis civibus*, ed. Giuliano Tanturli (Padua: Antenore, 1997), 142.
[41] For a transcription and brief discussion of the *accessus* to the *Achilleid*, see Chapter 6.

THE *VITA NOVA* AS A VERNACULAR READER   69

Individual ownership of these school folders among the laity was perhaps not yet as common during the years of Dante's schooling—in the 1270s—as it would become during the following century. The booklets survive in more exiguous numbers from the thirteenth century—unsurprisingly, as they were usually made of cheap materials and intensely used by several generations of pupils. As Gehl notes, however, the considerable number of extant copies from the fourteenth century shows that these pamphlets were produced to meet an increased market demand, which reflected educational practices that had already been in place since at least the second half of the previous century. No evidence, moreover, indicates a dramatic shift in the presence of these *auctores minores* in schools between the thirteenth century and the fourteenth.[42] It is probable, therefore, that by the time Dante wrote his *Vita nova*, these little schoolbooks were already becoming popular objects in Florentine society and culture. Florentine readers of the *Vita nova* would have associated the term "libello" with the genre of the Latin school reader. Even moderately educated laypeople, therefore, would have felt invited to approach a small booklet, like the *Vita nova*, which resembled one of their elementary readers.

Corroboration for this thesis comes from the words of Giovanni Boccaccio, who had been educated between Certaldo and Florence during the first half of the fourteenth century. Born forty-eight years after Dante, and the most influential among the first copiers of the *Vita nova*, Boccaccio witnesses a perceived bond between the minor Latin authors who were popular in contemporary education and Dante's classicizing poetics. In his epistle to the fellow poet Jacopo Pizzinga, Boccaccio constructs a succinct canon of Italian poetry from Homer and Virgil to Dante and Petrarch:

> Fuit enim illi continue spiritus aliqualis, tremulus tamen et semivivus potius quam virtute aliqua validus, ut in Catone, Prospero, Pamphilo et Arrighetto florentino presbitero, terminus quorum sunt *opuscula* parva nec ullam antiquitatis dulcedinem sapientia. Verum evo nostro ampliores a celo venere viri, si satis adverto, quibus cum sint ingentes animi, totis viribus pressam relevare, et ab exilio in pristinas revocare sedes mens est: nec frustra. Videmus autem, nec te legisse pigebit, ante alios nota dignos, seu vidisse potuimus, celebrem virum, et in phylosophie laribus versatum Dantem Allegherii nostrum.
>
> (Giovanni Boccaccio, *Letter to Iacopo Pizzinga*, 1371; emphasis added)[43]

---

[42] Paul Gehl, in *A Moral Art*, maintains that there was a substantial continuity in the school texts used in the years between Brunetto Latini and Filippo da Barberino. Even Robert Black, who instead notes a return of the *auctores maiores* in Florentine manuscripts from the fourteenth century, does not see any decline in the study of the *minores*. See Black, *Humanism and Education in Medieval and Renaissance Italy: Tradition and Innovation in Latin Schools from the Twelfth to the Fifteenth Century* (Cambridge: Cambridge University Press, 2001). The number of manuscripts containing the *auctores maiores* from the fourteenth century is also higher, which if anything shows that more school manuscripts survive from this century than from the previous one.

[43] In Giovanni Boccaccio, *Epistole e lettere*, ed. Ginetta Auzzas, vol. 5 of *Tutte le opere*, ed. Vittore Branca (Milan: Mondadori, 1992), 664–68.

70   DANTE'S EDUCATION

(In Italy there was always a spirit, though tremulous and but partly alive, rather than strong and vigorous, as in Cato, Prosper, Pamphilo, and Henry the Florentine priest; all they accomplished are *petty volumes* with little or none of the sweetness of the ancient wisdom. Truly, in our own time more illustrious men came from heaven—if I am not mistaken—who, as people of magnanimous spirit, aim to lift the oppressed [Italy] and lead her back from exile and to her ancient seat, and not in vain. Furthermore, we consider, before anyone who deserves note, if we can see—and you would not be unhappy to read this—a famous man, well versed also in philosophy, our Dante Alighieri.)

In Boccaccio's history of poetry, Dante represents the first step in the return of Italy's poetry to its ancient splendor. His advent marks the end of a line of minor Latin poets—all school texts—whose works are defined as *opuscula* (petty volumes). It is suggestive that these school readings are so described, in a way that encapsulates both their quality and their extent; pettiness was commonly associated with this genre of educational texts, as attested also by Buti's and Villani's already-mentioned use of the term "libello." More significant, however, is that a proto-humanist such as Boccaccio should acknowledge the crucial role played by these minor school texts in keeping alive the half-dead poetic fire. This fact testifies to the role played by school readings in nourishing a shared literary culture across the politically fragmented and culturally diversified Italian peninsula during the Middle Ages. Dante and his readers, including Boccaccio, would have all been introduced to literature and practiced literary criticism through the study of these *opuscula*, or *libelli*. For centuries, moreover, the Latin *auctores minores* mediated access to the major Latin tradition, on which Dante draws in his *Vita nova*—particularly in chapter 16 [25]—in order to establish the authority of vernacular poetry. Since Dante wished to elevate vernacular poetry to the status of literature—as, for instance, in *Vita nova* 16.7 [25.7], where he defines the "dicitori in rima" (writers of vernacular rhymes) as "poete volgari" (vernacular poets)—he was bound to engage with the canon of educational readings and their place in his readers' culture. Whereas Boccaccio does so by dismissing them in his own account of the reawakening of classical poetics in fourteenth-century Italy, Dante reworks them into his own vernacular reader.

In these school pamphlets, Dante and his readers found examples of the kind of critical apparatuses that he integrates into the prose of the *Vita nova*. Several of their manuscripts present rudimentary glosses, such as the *accessus ad auctorem*, interlinear translations of words, as well as short paraphrases, *divisiones textus*, and concise historical background information in the margins (see Figures 2.1, 2.2, and especially 2.3). The *ragioni* and *divisioni* in the *Vita nova*'s prose often provide the same information: narrative and contextual background to the poems,

THE *VITA NOVA* AS A VERNACULAR READER   71

as well as succinct paraphrases and summaries.[44] It is often assumed that Dante looked at Scholastic commentaries as the primary models for his *divisioni* in the *Vita nova*—"like a Dominican in Santa Maria Novella," as Peter Dronke has it.[45] It is essential to appreciate, however, that although these forms of Scholastic textuality were not the most widely available and familiar to lay Florentine readers, academic and Scholastic techniques of textual exposition had infiltrated the earliest stage of education through the teaching of grammar.[46] An eloquent example of the use of this type of textual analysis at a more elementary level is found in the glosses added to the margins of Henry of Settimello's *Elegia* in the fourteenth-century manuscript Florence, Archivio di Stato di Firenze, Carte Strozziane IIIa ser., 72, fol. 1r (Figure 2.3): "*In parte prima ponit* multa generalia loca . . . . et in *secunda dicit* quod si ab istis commendaretur" (*In the first part he lays out* many general arguments. . . . and *in the second he says* that if he were to be commended by these) (emphasis added). The resonance of this type of logical division in Dante's prose is evident: "ne la prima dico e soppongo" (in the first part I say and lay out) (*Vita nova* 6.10 [13.10]). Dante, therefore, might have looked closely at the specific brand of literary criticism contained in contemporary school booklets as the one most familiar to educated Florentine readers.

In light of this observation, it appears rather fitting that one of the *Vita nova*'s most influential models should be Boethius' *Consolatio Philosophiae*.[47] Robert Black and Gabriella Pomaro's study of Florentine manuscripts of the *Consolatio* has argued that Boethius was primarily used as a school text, with a focus on language rather than philosophical content.[48] The *Consolatio*, moreover, appears to

---

[44] See Gehl, *Moral Art*, 138; Robert Black, "Teaching Techniques: The Evidence of Manuscript Schoolbooks Produced in Tuscany," in *The Classics in the Medieval and Renaissance Classroom*, ed. Junita Feros Ruys, John O. Ward, and Melanie Heyworth (Turnhout, Belgium: Brepols, 2013), 245–63, esp. 247; and Black, *Humanism*, 298–99. About the *divisiones* in the *Vita nova*, see Botterill, ". . . però che la divisione."

[45] Dronke, *Verse with Prose*, 95–97. See also Pio Rajna, "Per le 'divisioni' della Vita Nuova," in Giuseppe Passerini and Orazio Bacci ed., *Strenna Dantesca*, vol. 1 (Florence, Ariani, 1902), 111–14.

[46] Even the glossed Psalter, which Thomas Stillinger (*Song of Troilus*) argues informed Dante's *divisioni*, was not a book readily available to laypeople, who often possessed either partial collections of psalms or Psalters with no glosses.

[47] Among the most recent studies of the *Vita nova*'s debts to the *Consolatio*, see Stefano Carrai, *Dante elegiaco: Una chiave di lettura per la "Vita nova"* (Florence: Olschki, 2006); Luca Lombardo, *Boezio in Dante: La "Consolatio philosophiae" nello scrittoio del poeta* (Venice: Edizioni Ca' Foscari, 2013); and Todorović, *Dante*, chap. 1.

[48] See Robert Black and Gabriella Pomaro, *La consolazione della filosofia nel Medioevo e nel Rinascimento italiano: Libri di scuola e glosse nei manoscritti fiorentini* (Florence: SISMEL Edizioni del Galluzzo, 2000), 24–25. About the the textual dissemination and exegesis of Boethius' *Consolatio* in Florence and Tuscany, see Paola Nasti, "Storia materiale di un classico dantesco: la *Consolatio Philosophiae* fra XII e XIV secolo: Tradizione manoscritta e rielaborazioni esegetiche," *Dante Studies* 134 (2016): 142–68; Luca Lombardo, "'Alcibiades quedam meretrix': Dante lettore di Boezio e i commenti alla *Consolatio philosophiae*," *L'Alighieri* 52 (2018): 5–36; Lombardo, "'Talento m'è preso di ricontare l'insegnamento dei phylosophi': Osservazioni sulla prosa dottrinale a Firenze nell'età di Dante," in *Dante e la cultura fiorentina*, ed. Zygmunt G. Barański, Theodore J. Cachey Jr., and Luca Lombardo (Rome: Salerno, 2019), 33–58; and Lombardo, "Primi appunti sulla *Vita nova* nel contesto della prosa del Duecento," *L'Alighieri* 60 (2019): 21–41.

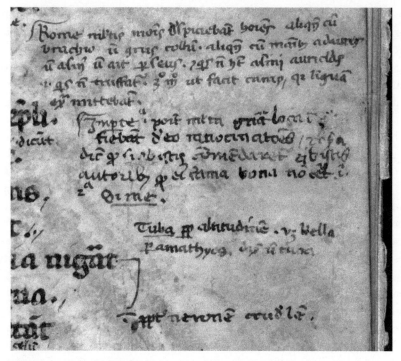

Figure 2.3 Detail of Florence, Archivio di Stato di Firenze, Carte Strozziane IIIa ser., 72 (XIV century, Italy), fol. 1r. Detail of marginal glosses, second from the top: "In parte prima ponit multa generalia loca ... et (in) secunda dicit quod si ab istis commendaretur ...

Source: Courtesy of the Archivio di Stato, Florence.

have been read in between a first stage of elementary Latin readings and a second one in which more advanced classical texts were tackled, a transition that often coincided with the progression from the Latin *auctores minores* to the *maiores*.[49] Reading Boethius, pupils were expected to refine both their grammatical and rhetorical skills. The *Consolatio*, therefore, functioned as a "bridge" text between elementary and more advanced Latin readings, as well as between the minor and the major *auctores*. Black and Pomaro show that at this intermediate stage of Latin instruction, glosses on school manuscripts begin to introduce complex rhetorical figures, such as prosopopoeia, and that *sententiae* from *auctoritates*, such as Virgil, Ovid, Horace, and Lucan, were also collected in the glossing of the *auctores minores*.[50] Remarkably, in *Vita nova* 16 [25], Dante defines precisely the meaning

---

[49] See Chapter 1.
[50] See Black and Pomaro, *La consolazione della filosofia*, 286–322. Naming these four *auctores maiores* is a feature shared by several elementary school texts, such as the *Disticha Catonis* and Henry of Settimello's *Elegia*, but the insertion of actual quotations from their writings as examples of figures

THE *VITA NOVA* AS A VERNACULAR READER   73

of prosopopoeia and its use by ancient poets, which he documents with examples from those same four Latin *auctores maiores*. The *libello*, in other words, featured critical notions that Florentine pupils would have met while reading Boethius' prosimetrum or similarly intermediate texts. It seems reasonable, therefore, to posit that Dante envisioned the *Vita nova* as a bridge text, like Boethius, designed to help lay readers enhance their reading skills in preparation for tackling more difficult vernacular texts, such as the one Dante promises to write at the end of the *libello*.[51]

This hypothesis appears less surprising when one considers that a few years later, in *Convivio* 1.2.17, Dante offered to train readers to interpret difficult allegorical texts, not only the ones he penned but those by other authors as well: "sottile ammaestramento e a così parlare e a così intendere *l'altrui scritture*" (useful instruction concerning both this mode of speaking and this mode of understanding *the writings of others*) (emphasis added). We can once again appreciate that a shared educational purpose unites the *Vita nova* and the *Convivio* into a reading curriculum, which Dante designed in order to introduce lay readers to increasingly complex poetical texts, by means of commentaries that advance their training and empower them as readers and critics of texts by other authors as well.

What the *Vita nova* owed to Dante's education can be further gauged through the *libello*'s significant parallels with some of the texts that were read in Italian schools, and particularly in Florence, at the end of the thirteenth century. Two of the *opuscula* mentioned by Boccaccio represented influential models for the *Vita nova*: Henry of Settimello's *Elegia* and Prosper of Aquitaine's *Liber epigrammatum*.

Henry of Settimello's *Elegia*

Traditionally known as the *Elegia de diversitate fortunae et philosophiae consolatione*, Henry of Settimello's poem was popular in Florentine education from the thirteenth to the fifteenth century. The *Elegia* is divided into four short books of elegiac distich lines. The first book features an extended *planctus* (plaint) for the poet's current misery, thus imitating the opening of Boethius' *Consolatio*. As the title, *Elegia*, makes plain, Henry draws on Ovid's *Tristia* and *Ex Ponto*, but other models also intrude, creating satirical and comic interludes.[52] Book 2 begins

---

of speech or rhetorical devices was a feature of more advanced stages of learning, as it is found in the glosses on the *auctores* and in didactic texts like Matthew of Vendome's *Ars versificatoria*. When defining the *schemata* (3.3), for instance, Matthew cites examples from Virgil, Horace, and Ovid.

[51] This would also dovetail with Dante's apparent downplay of the *Vita nova*'s relevance in both the *Convivio* and the *Commedia* (*Purgatorio* 30.115).

[52] As for Henry's incorporation of Ovidian elements in the *Elegia*, see Robert Black, "Ovid in Medieval Italy," in *Ovid in the Middle Ages*, ed. James G. Clark and Frank T. Coulson (Cambridge: Cambridge University Press, 2011), 123–42, and Gehl, *Moral Art*, 181–85.

74   DANTE'S EDUCATION

with the poet's violent invective against the goddess Fortune, followed by viru-
lent and offensive exchanges between the two. Only at the beginning of Book
3 does the personification of Wisdom finally make her appearance, offering the
Boethian moment of instruction and consolation. The last book features a collection of ethical teachings in elegiac couplets—strongly reminiscent of the *Disticha
Catonis*—which Wisdom imparts to the protagonist. The book turns the theological and philosophical message of the *Consolatio* into a prescriptive handbook of
the good Christian citizen.[53]

Henry's *Elegia* is a learned and classicizing exercise but also a poetic and
rhetorical experiment, which mixes together classical and late antique sources
with the biblical lamentation—chiefly drawn from the books of Job and
Lamentations—and the practical wisdom of school texts such as the *Disticha
Catonis* and *Aesop*. Henry also takes freely and abundantly from medieval texts,
especially Alan of Lille's *De planctu Naturae* and *Anticlaudianus*. Like Alan, moreover, Henry proves his poetic and rhetorical ability by spanning a wide variety of
genres and rhetorical forms, with the principal ones being elegy, invective, and
eulogy. The insertion of an episode from the genre of the Latin comedy in the first
book (195–208) represents the best evidence of the author's display of technical
virtuosity. As it clearly appears, the *Elegia* features the kind of experimentalism
and "plurilingualism" that has been rightly seen as a key feature of Dante's *Vita
nova*.[54]

Most relevant for the *Vita nova*, however, is the *Elegia*'s peculiar specimen of
poetic autobiography. What is known about Henry of Settimello is indeed derived
from the text of the *Elegia* itself, and internal references to historical events allow us
to date the work between 1191 and 1193. The wealth of autobiographical and historical references punctuating Henry's *Elegia* sets a valuable precedent for Dante's
Vita nova, which presented an innovative blending of autobiography and fiction in
the context of thirteenth-century vernacular literature. Models for such a project
of vernacular autobiography, as is well known, were not very many at the time,
with Boethius and Augustine being the usual suspects in the Latin tradition, and
the troubadours' *vidas* providing but a pale precedent in the Provençal vernacular.
Henry's *Elegia*, instead, represented a well-known example of a Boethian remake

---

[53] About Henry's rewriting Boethius' *Consolatio*, see Lombardo, *Boezio in Dante*, 103, 108. For a discussion of Boethius' influence on Henry's last two books, see Rocco Murari, *Dante e Boezio: Contributo
allo studio delle fonti dantesche* (Bologna: Zanichelli, 1905), 190. About the stronger presence of elegiac
elements in Henry's work in comparison with that of Boethius, see Lombardo, *Boezio in Dante*, 106.

[54] On Henry's remarkable literary experimentalism, see Giuseppe Chiecchi, *La parola del dolore:
Primi studi sulla letteratura consolatoria tra Medioevo e Umanesimo* (Rome: Antenore, 2005), 75–87.
On the *Vita nova*'s plurilingualism, see Zygmunt G.Barański, "The Roots of Dante's Plurilingual-
ism: 'Hybridity' and Language in the *Vita nova*," in *Dante's Plurilingualism: Authority, Knowledge,
Subjectivity*, ed. Sara Fortuna, Manuele Gragnolati, and Jürgen Trabant (Oxford: Legenda, 2010),
98–121.

THE *VITA NOVA* AS A VERNACULAR READER   75

that expands precisely on the autobiographical potential of the *Consolatio* (especially Books 1 and 2) and brings the author's life to the forefront.[55] Like the *Vita nova*, moreover, the *Elegia* was penned by a Florentine author for a Florentine audience.[56] Hence, in many ways the *Elegia* was an experiment comparable to the one attempted a century later by young Dante in the *Vita nova*.[57]

The function of Henry's *Elegia* in the grammar schools of late medieval Florence is especially significant for gauging its influence on Dante's *libello*.[58] According to Gehl, most manuscripts of the *Elegia* currently preserved in Florentine libraries transmit the text alone, rather than anthologized with other *auctores minores*; this is also the case with most manuscripts of this work outside of Florence. Black and Pomaro, however, unveiled a rather different situation, in which six out of nine manuscripts of the *Elegia* present Henry anthologized with other school texts. They nonetheless all agree that Henry was likely read at an intermediate or advanced stage of grammatical education and that the work's educational use and reception were closely bound to that of Boethius' *Consolatio*. As it appears, the *Elegia* also provided a valuable alternative to the reading of the *Consolatio*.[59] I have already suggested that Dante might have envisioned his *Vita nova* as an intermediate, vernacular text alternative to the *Consolatio* in the instruction of lay readers. If so, then Henry's *Elegia* represented an important precedent that offered a similar alternative in the milieu of Florence's grammar schools.

Stefano Carrai points out that during the Middle Ages, Boethius' *Consolatio* was considered a canonical example of elegiac poetry. It is from this perspective, he

---

[55] As Holmes (*Assembling the Lyric Self*, 6) rightly points out, autobiography as a vernacular genre was scant and very much *in fieri* before the thirteenth century. Autobiographical allusions are also present, albeit in very limited proportions, in the Boethian archetype. They do not amount, however, to a narrative account of the author's disgrace. See, for instance, *Consolatio* 1.4, 43–46. About the relevance of Henry's autobiographical take on the elegiac genre, see Salvatore Battaglia, "Introduzione," in *Il Boezio e l'Arrighetto* (Turin: UTET, 1929), vii–xxxv, and Chiecchi, *La parola del dolore*, 53–54.

[56] The work is addressed to the bishop of Florence, who is aptly named "Florentinus" in the envoy that closes the poem. Clara Fossati, "Introduzione," in Arrigo da Settimello, *Elegia*, ed. and trans. Clara Fossati (Florence: SISMEL, 2011), xi–lxii.

[57] About Henry's possible influence on Dante, see Enzo Bonaventura, *Arrigo da Settimello e l'*Elegia de diversitate fortunae et philosophiae consolatione, *Studi medievali* 4 (1912–13): 110–92, esp. 166; G. Toja, "Noterelle dantesche," *Studi danteschi* 42 (1965): 248–55; Chiecchi, *La parola del dolore*, 103–05; Lombardo, *Boezio in Dante*, 109; Pier Vincenzo Mengaldo, "L'elegia 'umile' (*De vulgari eloquentia*, II, iv)," *Giornale storico della letteratura italiana* 118 (1966): 177–98; and Enrico Malato, "Dante," in *Storia della letteratura italiana*, vol. 1, *Dalle origini a Dante*, ed. Enrico Malato (Rome: Salerno, 1995), 773–1052, at 871. As Chiecchi notes (103), signs of the influence of Henry's *Epistle* can be found in all three major authors of the Italian Trecento: Dante, Petrarch, and Boccaccio. Other important evidence of the work's popularity in Florence at Dante's time and during the following two centuries is the large number of vernacular translations—several of which were produced in Florence between the fourteenth and the fifteenth centuries. See Cremaschi's edition and also Silvia Albesano, *"Consolatio philosophiae" volgare: Volgarizzamenti e traduzioni discorsive del Trecento italiano* (Heidelberg: Winter, 2006), 36.

[58] On the use of Henry's *Elegia* for education in Florence and northern Italy, see Gehl, *Moral Art*, 53, 181–85; Black and Pomaro, *La consolazione della filosofia*, 4; and Black, *Humanism*, 224.

[59] Gehl, *Moral Art*, 185, and Black and Pomaro, *La consolazione della filosofia*, 4–8.

76   DANTE'S EDUCATION

argues, that we should reconsider the nature of Boethius' influence on the *Vita nova*.[60] In line with other studies of Boethius' presence in the *libello*, however, Carrai downplays the role of Henry's intermediation in the poet's reception of the *Consolatio*. Yet, as noted by Pier Vincenzo Mengaldo, Henry's *Elegia* constituted an accessible and influential source for Dante's definition of the elegiac genre.[61] Henry's work might, for instance, have informed Dante's definition of elegy as "stilum . . . miserorum" (the style of the unhappy) in the *De vulgari eloquentia* (2.4.5–6). In contrast to his treatment of other poetic genres, Dante defined elegy in terms of subject matter rather than style. This choice, however, would have appeared rather conventional to medieval readers, especially those trained on Henry's *Elegia sive de miseria* (*Elegy or On Misery*), as the work is titled in several manuscripts. The bond between the genre and its subject matter is further established in *Elegia* 1.43, where Henry plays paronomastically with the Latin word "miser," providing both a clear genre indicator and a handy grammatical exercise for studying the declension of a first-class adjective: "Sum miser et miseri nullus miserans miseretur" (I am miserable and nobody, though merciful, feels mercy for miserable me).[62] As Mengaldo shows, the identification of elegy as the song of misery was unique neither to Dante nor to Henry. Other medieval texts—for instance, John of Garland's *Poetria*—also helped establish this content-based definition of elegy.[63] Henry's unique place in Florentine schooling, however, made the *Elegia* particularly accessible to Dante and his readers. A close comparative reading of this school poem and the *Vita nova* further reveals Henry's influence on Dante's reworking of the elegiac genre.

Dante's choice to announce Beatrice's death abruptly by truncating the *canzone* "Sì lungiamente m'à tenuto Amore" (So long a time has Love kept me a slave) and inserting the line from Lamentations 1.1, "Quomodo sedet sola civitas plena populo! Facta est quasi vidua domina gentium" (How doth the city sit solitary that was full of people! How is she become a widow, she that was great among the nations!) (19 [28.1]), closely recalls the opening line of Henry's *Elegia*, where an adaptation of the same biblical subtext is also found: "Quomodo sola sedet probitas! Flet et ingemit, aleph! Facta velud vidua que prius uxor erat" (How doth honesty sit solitary! She cries and laments, alas! How is she become a widow, she that was married) (1.1–2). Henry's *Elegia* featured a well-known—and for many readers the only—precedent for the *Vita nova*'s combination of the biblical subtext of Jeremiah's Lamentations with the genre of classical elegy. Thus, Dante's choice to begin the *Vita nova*'s most defining elegiac moment, the mourning for Beatrice's death, by mimicking Henry's reuse of Jeremiah as the incipit of his *Elegia* is

---

[60] Carrai, *Dante elegiaco*.

[61] Mengaldo, "L'elegia 'umile,'" 178.

[62] The Latin text is quoted from Fossati's critical edition, *Elegia*. The translation is mine.

[63] Mengaldo, "L'elegia 'umile,'" 190. William of Conches also identifies elegy with misery in his commentary on Boethius. See Lombardo, *Boezio in Dante*, 434.

THE *VITA NOVA* AS A VERNACULAR READER   77

revealing.[64] Through this intertextual echo, Dante marks a crucial turning point of the *Vita nova*, where the *libello* more decisively resembles a *planctus*. Henry's *exordium* would have offered a recognizable placeholder for the genre. In order to appreciate the importance of this rhetorical strategy, however, it is essential to appreciate the place that elegy occupies in the structure of the *Vita nova*.

Two recognizably elegiac moments punctuate the narrative and thematic unfolding of the *libello*. The first one follows Dante's second encounter with Beatrice (*Vita nova* 1.3–9.11 [2.1–16.11]) and features the traditional *topoi* of love sickness, which find their primary sources in Ovid and had well-known epigones among Provençal, old French, and Italian poets. Other elegiac models also intrude at this stage—for instance, the biblical Lamentations in the sonnet "O voi che per la via d'Amore passate" (2.14–17 [7.3–6]). Since love in this section emerges primarily as a destructive force, scholars have seen here Dante's close engagement with the legacy of Cavalcanti's poetics and philosophy of love.[65] The *canzone* "Donne ch'avete intelletto d'amore" (Women who understand the truth of love) marks the end of this first phase of the *libello* and has long been read next to Guido's poem "Donna me prega," either as its inspiration or as a fitting reply to it.[66] "Donne ch'avete" opens a series of poems in praise of Beatrice, which is interrupted only by a brief elegiac interlude on the topic of death (*Vita nova* 13–14 [22–23])—a foreboding of the lady's own death. Beatrice's demise begins the second elegiac section of the *libello*, which develops through the protagonist's meeting with the "donna gentile," his two divinely inspired visions of Beatrice, and ends with the sonnet "Oltre la spera" (Beyond the sphere) with which the poet wishes to write something new—"una cosa nuova"—for two noble ladies (30 [41]). Whereas the first elegiac section centers around the subject of the pain and misery caused by love sickness and points to its Ovidian source, the second one focuses on the themes of death and consolation—as revealed by the protagonist's meeting with the "donna gentile"—that instead had their primary model in Boethius' *Consolatio*.[67] Dante's

---

[64] See Chiecchi, *La parola*, 77–78.

[65] The so-called Cavalcantian section of the *libello* has been identified with chapters 3–17 (according to Barbi's divisions). See Hollander, *Life in Works*, 31.

[66] On Dante's ideological opposition to Cavalcanti in the *Vita nova*, see, for example, Robert Pogue Harrison, *The Body of Beatrice* (Baltimore: Johns Hopkins University Press, 1988), 69–90; Robert Durling, "Guido Cavalcanti in the *Vita nova*," in *Guido Cavalcanti tra i suoi lettori*, ed. Maria Luisa Ardizzone (Florence: Cadmo, 2003), 176–86; Gorni, "Una Vita nova"; and Manuele Gragnolati, "'Rime trasformate e rime assenti': La *performance* della *Vita nova* e le figure di Dante e Cavalcanti," in *Dante the Lyric and Ethical Poet. Dante Poeta Lirico e Etico*, ed. Zygmunt G. Barański and Martin McLaughlin (London: Legenda, 2010), 74–91. Whether Guido's *canzone* "Donna me prega" predates or postdates the *Vita nova* is a matter of debate. For two opposing views, see Enrico Malato, *Dante and Guido Cavalcanti: il dissidio per la Vita Nuova e il "Disdegno" di Guido* (Rome: Salerno, 1997), and Mario Marti, "Da 'Donna me prega' a 'Donne ch'avete': non viceversa," in *Da Dante a Croce: proposte, consensi e dissensi* (Galatina: Congedo, 2005), 7–15.

[67] Scholars have advanced different views on the "sections" of the *Vita nova*—most famously, Singleton has proposed a reading that hinges on Barbi's chapters (*Essay*). The different chapter division proposed by Gorni, however, has significantly undermined the numerological significance of Singleton's thesis. For an alternative proposal on how to divide the *Vita nova* into two different parts, which

78 DANTE'S EDUCATION

mimicry of Henry's use of Lamentations, therefore, announces a pivotal switch between two different types of elegiac laments. The same shift from Ovidian to Boethian elegy, it should be noted, had its most popular precedent precisely in Henry's *Elegia* (particularly in Books 1 and 3).[68]

A more obvious, and unnoted, parallel between the *Vita nova* and the *Elegia* confirms Dante's striking retention of this school model as a generic signpost in the *libello*. After recounting his second meeting with Beatrice, Dante gives voice to his own three biological spirits. All three of them react differently to this sudden vision: the vital spirit (heart) trembles, the animal spirit (brain) wonders, and the natural one (stomach) weeps. All speak Latin, each one in a different register and style, in accordance with the canonical *tria genera dicendi* (three types of speeech)—high, middle, low—into which poetry was generally categorized.[69] The vital spirit follows the tragic style, which Dante molds on biblical and philosophical subtexts, and exclaims: "'Ecce Deus fortior me, qui veniens dominabitur michi'" ('Here is a god stronger than I, who comes to rule me'); the animal spirit announces: "'Apparuit iam beatitudo vestra'" ('Your beatitude [or bliss] has now appeared'); whereas, in elegiac style, the natural spirit laments: "'Heu miser, quia frequenter impeditus ero deinceps'" ('What misery, since from now on I will often be blocked [in my digestion]!') (*Vita nova* 1.5–7 [2.4–6]).[70] Leo Spitzer notes that an indication of the lower, elegiac register characterizing the natural spirit's utterance is to be found not only in the reference to misery but also in its awkward phrasing. Spitzer points out that a more elegant and classicizing formulation would have been "Heu me miserum."[71] He argues that Dante here means to signal a descent into the elegiac genre. If this is the case, then we should appreciate that to achieve this effect Dante quotes the same "awkward" wording of another important passage from Henry's *Elegia*. In *Elegia* 1.77–80, Henry cries out in anguish:

> Heu miser, heu demens, heu cecus! Semina mundi
> iratos animos in mea fata trahunt:
> est michi terra nocens, ignis gravis, unda nociva;
> aer tristitia perfidiore nocet.

---

the poet would have completed at two different times, see Gorni, "Una *Vita nova*." Without entering this critical discussion, I would only note that the three *canzoni* fittingly divide the *libello* into three parts. The first and the last sections, moreover, are undoubtedly elegiac in tone.

[68] For the Ovidian influences on the first part of the *Vita nova*, see Picone, "*Vita nova* come prosimetro." For the Boethian ones, see Lombardo, *Boezio in Dante*, and Todorović, *Dante*.

[69] Gorni, comm. ad loc.; Barański, "Roots."

[70] On the biblical sources of the "Ecce deus fortior," see Branca, "Poetica del rinnovamento e tradizione agiografica"; De Robertis, *Il libro*, 17; Ronald Martinez, "Poetics of Advent," 281–82; Michelangelo Picone, "Rito e 'narratio' nella 'Vita nuova,'" in *Miscellanea di studi in onore di Vittore Branca*, vol. 1 (Florence: Olschki, 1983), 154–57; and Leo Spitzer, "Osservazioni sulla *Vita Nuova* di Dante," in *Studi italiani* (Milan: Vita e Pensiero, 1976), 95–146, esp. 108–09. An innovative reconsideration of the possible theological implications of these words has been recently proposed by Lorenzo Dell'Oso, "Tra Bibbia e 'letteratura di costumanza': un'ipotesi su 'Ecce Deus fortior me' (*Vita nova*, II 4)," in *Dante e la cultura fiorentina*, 221–40.

[71] Spitzer, "Osservazioni," 108–09.

(Oh unhappy, oh foolish, oh blind! The elements of the world / unleash wrathful feelings against me: / the earth only harms me, fire is a burden, water is noxious, / the air injures me with more treacherous gloom.)

Right after this interjection, Henry claims that all the natural elements are harmful to him, not unlike the concern expressed by Dante's natural spirit that he will be frequently impeded in his natural functions. Furthermore, Henry's cry concludes a list of physiological symptoms that reveals his deeply disturbed inner state:

> Est cibus anxietas, lacrime sunt pocula, pena
>   panis, vina dolor, est mihi vita mori.
> Quod patior, pallor loquitur maciesque figurat;
>   indicat exsanguis turpiter alba cutis;
> nam facies habitum mentis studiumque fatetur,
>   mensque quod intus agit nuntiat illa foris;
> internique status liber est et pagina vultus;
>   exterior macies intus amara legit.
>
> (*Elegia* 1.69–76)

(Anguish is my food, tears are my drink, suffering / is bread, pain wine, life is death to me. / Pallor gives away my sufferance and emaciation gives form to it; / my livid and bloodless skin shamefully reveals it; / for the face mirrors the soul and its activities, / and what the mind elaborates within the face shows on the outside; / our internal state is a book and the face is the page; / the external thinness reads the interior torments.)

The complaint against the torturous natural elements and the list of Henry's bodily dysfunctions have their source in the Ovidian symptomatology of love (*Metamorphoses* 2.775), which finds significant echo also in the first elegiac section of the *Vita nova*—for instance, in the sonnet "Ciò che mi 'ncontra ne la mente more" (Whatever might restrain me when I feel drawn to see you, my heart's bliss, dies from my mind), in which the poet writes: "Lo viso mostra lo color del core, / che tramortendo ovunque pò s'appoia; / e per l'ebrïetà del gran tremore / le pietre par che gridin: Moia, moia!" (My blanching face reveals my fainting heart / which weakly seeks support from where it may, / and as I tremble in this drunken state the stones / in the wall I lean on shout back: "Die!") (*Vita nova* 8.5.5–8 [15.4.5–8]). Dante's and Henry's similar imitation of Ovid is even more relevant as this does not feature as prominently in Boethius' *Consolatio*. By redeploying Henry's interjection "Heu miser," therefore, Dante draws on a known formula to reveal the specific brand of elegy that informs the *Vita nova*'s first section. As it clearly appears, twice Dante returns to the subtext of Henry's *Elegia* to mark the beginnings of both

80   DANTE'S EDUCATION

elegiac sections of the *libello*: the first section, which opens with the interjection "Heu miser" and is modeled on Ovid's psychopathology of love, and the second, which is marked instead by the echo of Jeremiah's Lamentations and is informed by Boethius' *Consolatio*.

One more telling parallel with Henry's *Elegia* documents the school-text influence on the *Vita nova*. As Carrai notes, Dante's enigmatic exchange with the God of Love, after the loss of Beatrice's greeting, echoes, yet again, Henry's *Elegia*. Dante has a vision of Love dressed in a white garment and sitting at the foot of his bed—a scene closely recalling Boethius' first encounter with Lady Philosophy in the *Consolatio*. A remarkable exchange ensues between the two—while Love addresses the poet in Latin, Dante answers in the vernacular. This bilingual dialogue continues until the former recites the enigmatic line: "'Ego tanquam centrum circuli, cui simili modo se habent circumferentie partes; tu autem non sic'" ('I am like the center of a circle, to which the parts of the circumference stand in equal relation; but you are not so'). To which the puzzled protagonist replies: "'Che è ciò, signore, che mi parli con tanta oscuritade?'" ('Why, lord, do you speak to me in such an obscure way?'). Prompted by the poet's question, Love switches to the vernacular: "'Non dimandare più che utile ti sia'" ('Do not ask me more than might be useful to you') (*Vita nova* 5.11–12 [12.4–5]). In a moment loaded with metaliterary and metalinguistic implications, we find that the protagonist's words and rhetorical construction are nearly identical to Henry's own rewriting of the Boethian dialogue with Wisdom: "'Quid et hoc est, vera sophya, / quod dicis? Nimis est hic mihi sermo gravis'" ('What is this, oh true Wisdom, that you are speaking? These words are too difficult to me') (3.101–2). The wisdom Henry cannot fathom here is the Christian acceptance of his own unjust suffering at the hands of others. From a literary perspective, we could also say that Henry is unable to move past his own elegiac lament. Some scholars suggest that, in *Vita nova* 5[12], Love tries to show Dante that he has not yet learned to love selflessly, thus inviting him to move beyond the dissimulations typical of courtly love poetry: "'Fili mi, tempus est ut pretermictantur simulacra nostra'" ('My son, it is time for our false images [or simulations] to be put aside') (5.10 [12.4]). Once more, Henry's *Elegia* surfaces at a turning point in the narrative and generic development of the story. In both the *Elegia* and the *Vita nova*, the protagonist's inability to understand the teaching of the prosopopoeia of Wisdom and Love, respectively, derives from the unexpected injection of Christian ideas into the elegiac–courtly love genre.[72] Dante, therefore, returns to Henry's text in order to signpost three consecutive thematic stages that were already featured in the school text: the love elegy, the Christianization of the elegiac lament, and finally Boethius' *planctus* and consolation.

[72] Carrai, *Dante elegiaco*, 18, and Lombardo, *Boezio in Dante*, 433.

THE *VITA NOVA* AS A VERNACULAR READER   81

Henry's intermediary model also compensates for another important feature of the *Vita nova* that the Boethian text lacks: namely, a narrative plot.[73] Whereas the latter centers almost entirely around the exchange between Boethius and Philosophy, the *Vita nova* tells the story of the events that brought the protagonist to his spiritual maturity. In Henry's *Elegia*, only Book 3 features a dialogue fashioned after the one that Boethius has with Lady Philosophy, whereas Books 1 and 2 provide a skeletal plot. The first book is particularly relevant for the *Vita nova*. Here Henry sketches an urban landscape, in which the protagonist experiences public humiliation at the hands of his fellow citizens. As Henry escapes from the "facundis vocibus" (from loquacious voices) (1.16), constantly gossiping about his disgrace, so does Dante when blaming the "soverchievole voce" (the excessive gossip) (5.2 [10.2]) of those envious people who have caused him to lose Beatrice's greeting. As Henry becomes the *fabula vulgi*, so does Dante, in the episode of the "gabbo" (mockery) (7 [15]). As Henry runs away from the public space to a solitary corner, "qui gente vacaret" (deserted) (1.119)—a typical elegiac motif—Dante too, after falling into disgrace with Beatrice, goes to a solitary place to weep: "partito me dalle genti, in solinga parte andai a bagnare la terra d'amarissime lagrime" (withdrawing from people, I went to a solitary place to soak the ground with the bitterest of tears) (5.8 [12.1], and then again at 7.9 [14.9]). Furthermore, Henry's suggestion at the end of the poem that the public space where the disgrace he narrates took place may indeed be Florence (*Elegia* 4.241–54), and the defamatory voices those of its citizens, creates a meaningful contrast with Dante's decision entirely to omit the name of the "cittade" (city) from the *Vita nova*, while alluding to Florence all along.

Dante's and Henry's shared investment in narrative, as well as their integration of comic episodes into a general elegiac context, do not find correspondence in the Boethian archetype.[74] Hence, the role of this intertext in the *Vita nova* cannot be correctly assessed without considering Henry's intermediation. Dante's recurring references to Henry's *Elegia* at key moments of the *Vita nova* are not merely coincidental; they are instrumental to the poet's reworking of the elegiac genre. These interpolations suggest the influence of this school text on the poet's literary formation and on his metaliterary reflection at the time of the *Vita nova*. Given the popularity of Henry's poem in Florentine education, Dante could draw on this subtext to guide even his moderately educated readers through the stylistic and generic shifts he experimented with in the *libello*, thus helping them appreciate its creative reworking of traditional literary genres, styles, and tropes. It also provided a valid vernacular alternative to the two popular elegiac school texts, Boethius's and Henry's.

---

[73] De Robertis (*Il libro della Vita nuova*, 68) remarks that the actual narrative or literal parallels between the *Vita nova* and the *Consolatio* are in fact not abundant.

[74] On some key differences between Henry's *Elegia* and Boethius' *Consolatio*, see Lombardo, *Boezio in Dante*, 105–08.

82   DANTE'S EDUCATION

Prosper of Aquitaine's *Liber epigrammatum*

In the words of the most recent editor of Prosper's *Liber epigrammatum* (also known as *Epigrammata ex sententiis S. Augustini*), "Prosper exercised the greatest influence on Medieval society by becoming a standard part of the school curriculum.... Like the Distichs of Cato, Aesop's fables, and the poems of Juvencus and Sedulius, the epigrams had an extraordinary influence, because they were the first books a student would ever read."[75] Written during the final years of Prosper's life, around 455 AD, the *Liber* became a fundamental school text in the early Carolingian period, proving especially suitable to the needs of monastic education. This work remained a popular choice also for the instruction of the laity during the late Middle Ages. Extant manuscript evidence shows that the *Liber* was a bestseller among Florentine masters during the thirteenth and fourteenth centuries. Its use for education, next to moralizing poems such as Cato and Aesop, is also supported by surviving evidence. Prosper's *Liber* presents foundations of Christian faith and morality drawn from Saint Augustine's works in a rather simplified and memorable form, suitable for beginners. While teaching the rudiments of Latin grammar, therefore, teachers could also drill into pupils an essential catechism based on Prosper's succinct definitions of Christian tenets.[76] Prosper became part of Florentine popular culture to such an extent that beautiful and expensive copies of the *Liber* were presented as wedding gifts during the fourteenth century. This catechism represented an essential, edifying text to be passed on from one generation to the other, for the preservation of Christian morality and beliefs.[77]

The *Liber* has also been described "as a testament to Late Antiquity's decadent predilection for strange new literary forms."[78] It is divided into more than one hundred poetic units, each consisting of a short prose passage discussing one moral or theological topic, a *sententia*, followed by a poem in elegiac couplets that elaborates on the same *sententia*. Prosper had previously written a *Liber sententiarum* compiled from Augustine's oeuvre. Eventually he composed short poems based on a selection of these *sententiae*, and finally added a brief prose paraphrase

---

[75] Albertus G. A. Horsting, "Introduction," in *Prosper Aquitanus: Liber epigrammatum*, ed. Albertus G. A. Horsting, Corpus Scriptorum Ecclesiasticorum Latinorum, 100 (Berlin: De Gruyter, 2016), 26.

[76] Gehl, *Moral Art*, 31, 141.

[77] Paul Gehl, "An Augustinian Catechism in Fourteenth-Century Tuscany," *Augustinian Studies* 19 (1988): 93–110. Prosper's popularity in Florentine education is confirmed by Boccaccio's aforementioned *Letter to Jacopo Pizzinga*, as well as by a later witness, the fifteenth-century Dominican friar Giovanni Dominici, from Florence. See Giovanni Dominici, *Regola del governo di cura familiare*, ed. D. Salvi (Florence: A. Garinei, 1860), 134. For a later example of the popularity of Prosper's *sententiae* in Florentine culture, see Cristoforo Landino's comm. ad loc., *Par.* 20.77–78, where he quotes a famous saying generally believed to be by St. Augustine, "onde Agostino: tales amat nos Deus, quales facti sumus dono eius, et non quales sumus nostro merito," which was in fact from Prosper's *Sententiae* 46.

[78] Horsting, "Introduction," 1.

THE *VITA NOVA* AS A VERNACULAR READER   83

to accompany each of them.[79] Like the *Vita nova*, therefore, Prosper's *Liber* is a prosimetrum in which prose had been added to explain the meaning (*sententiae*) of previously composed poems. Prosper, moreover, is a compiler of the sayings of Saint Augustine, as the title *Epigrammata ex sententiis S. Augustini* indicates and a medieval *accessus* made plain: "factus Augustini discipulus hoc opus composuit ex diversis sententiis illius" (A disciple of Augustine, he compiled this work from several of his sayings).[80] But Prosper is also the author and commentator of the poems. Given the popularity of this work among Florentine readers, the relevance of its uncommon format and authorial stance for Dante's *Vita nova* is apparent.[81] Not only did the *Liber* constitute a well-known precedent of didactic prosimetrum, with a similar hierarchy between prose and poetry, but it also foreran the *Vita nova* in the threefold role of its author (compiler, author, commentator) and self-commentary. Prosper explains his complex authorial stance in the work's preface:

Praefatio

Dum sacris mentem placet exercere loquelis,
    coelestique animum pascere pane iuvat.
Quosdam, ceu prato, libuit decerpere flores,
    distinctisque ipsos texere versiculis,
ut proprias canerent epigrammata singula causas,
    et pars quaeque suo congrueret titulo.
Nec nostrae hoc opis est, sed ab illo sumitur hic ros,
    qui siccam rupem fundere iussit aquas,
ut quod in affectum cordis, pietate magistra,
    venerit, hoc promat carmine laeta fides.[82]

(While it is good to exercise the intellect in sacred discourse, and it profits the soul to feed on celestial bread. / It pleased me to collect certain flowers, as from a meadow, / and then arrange them in well-ordained little lines, / so that each epigram may sing its own theme / and each part may comply with its title. / This is not of our own doing, but this dew is drawn from Him / who ordered

---

[79] Gehl, *Moral Art*, 138.

[80] R. B. C. Huygens, ed., *Accessus ad auctores, Bernard d'Utrecht, Conrad d'Hirsau: Dialogus super auctores; Édition critique* (Leiden: Brill, 1970), 28.

[81] This feature is especially relevant when compared with other possible models of Dante's *Vita nova*—most notably, the Provençal *razos* and *vidas*, which, although crucial precedents, were not written by the authors of the poems. On this topic, see Maria Luisa Meneghetti, *Il pubblico dei trovatori: Ricezione e riuso dei testi lirici cortesi fino al XIV secolo* (Modena: Mucchi, 1984).

[82] The Latin text is quoted from the edition edite by Stefania Santelia, in Prospero d'Aquitania, *Ad coniugem suam. In appendice: Liber epigrammatum* (Naples: Loffredo, 2009), 106–193. The translation is mine.

84   DANTE'S EDUCATION

> that water should spring from dry rock, / so that whatever feeling
> is in the heart, with piety for guide, / faith may joyfully express in
> verses.)

Prosper envisions himself as a compiler, who has collected some "flowers" from a meadow and some "dew" from the abundant water that gushes forth from God's providence.[83] As has already been seen, Dante too pictures himself in the act of compiling a small volume in which he will copy only some parts from the larger repository of his memory. He does not clarify whether the author of the archetype is God or himself. Through the use of the possessive "my," Dante may imply that he is also the author of the original book of memory. But it could just as well be argued that whereas Dante's mind wrote the book of memory, God is really the author of the events recorded in it.[84] As Dante claims agency in assembling the *libello*, so does Prosper with his poems—after "collecting some flowers from a field," he arranges them into metrical lines, "distinctisque ipsos texere versiculis."

The popularizing aim of Prosper's *compilatio* is also relevant in relation to the *Vita nova*. Prosper presents poetry as a tool with which to exercise one's mind while learning "sacred sayings." These didactic aims shape his work's prosimetric form and make the nourishing "celestial bread" available to the readers. Use of this particular image to represent the work of compiling and digesting wisdom for readers is closely recalled in another, later prosimetrum by Dante, in which he aims to make philosophical learning more accessible to his lay readers. The *Convivio* begins with the image of the author collecting crumbs from the table where the "bread of the angels" is being consumed:

> Oh beati quelli pochi che seggiono a quella mensa dove lo pane delli angeli si manuca! e miseri quelli che colle pecore hanno comune cibo! . . . E io adunque, che non seggio alla beata mensa, ma, fuggito della pastura del vulgo, a' piedi di coloro che seggiono ricolgo di quello che da loro cade. (1.1.7–10)[85]

---

[83] It is interesting to note that in *Par.* 24.7–9, Dante has Beatrice use the same metaphor of the "dew" drawn from the "gushing spring" of God's grace and wisdom to represent the access to the divine vision that, through the saints' mediation, she invokes for the pilgrim: "ponete mente a l'affezione immensa / e *roratelo* alquanto: voi bevete / sempre del *fonte* onde viene quel ch'ei pensa" (emphasis added).

[84] For a discussion of both interpretations, see Enrico Fenzi, "Il libro della memoria," in *Dante in lettura*, ed. Giuseppe De Matteis (Ravenna: Longo, 2005), 15–38.

[85] Dante's opening metaphor of the celestial banquet, the crumbs of which feed people to different degrees—or not at all—and particularly the image of the "bread of the angels" elude specific interpretation but have clear eucharistic nuances. The purpose of my reference here is only to note the suggestive parallel use of this image by both Prosper and Dante to symbolize their project of popular instruction. To this end, it is also noteworthy that in *Epigrammata* 8, Prosper uses the same image of the banquet to discuss the *De doctrina apostolica*. For a close and extensive analysis of the governing metaphor of Dante's *Convivio*, most instructive is Ambrogio Camozzi Pistoja, "Testo come eucarestia. Linguaggio parabolico nel *Convivio* di Dante," *Studi danteschi* 84 (2019): 57–99.

(Blessed are the few who sit at the table where the bread of the angels is eaten, and most unfortunate those who share the food of sheep! . . . Therefore I, who do not sit at the blessed table, but, having fled the pasture of the common herd, gather up a part of what falls to the feet of those who do sit there.)

Neither of these parallel features is probative of Prosper's influence on the *Vita nova*, but they confirm Dante's assimilation of the prosimetric textual complex as essentially instructional in nature.

The relevance of the *Liber epigrammatum* as a potential model for the *Vita nova*'s overall design is not limited to its peculiar format and Prosper's authorial stance. Some of its contents overlap in meaningful ways with those of Dante's *libello*. Prosper gives lessons on a fairly simple catechism that covers a broad range of Christian doctrines in basic and practical terms. Some discourses, however, are more insistently carried out over multiple epigrams. Two are especially relevant to the *Vita nova*: the authentic praise of God, "De vera dei laudatione" (6, 73), and the supreme good a Christian can never be deprived of (14, 20, 24, 60, 63, 81, 87, 94). One of the most crucial episodes of the *Vita nova* is predicated precisely on these two topics. I am referring to the protagonist's dialogue with the ladies, during which Dante breaks away from the core aim of courtly love poetry—the satisfaction of the poet's erotic desire—and introduces his new poetics centered on the gratuitous praise of the lady: the so-called poetics *della loda*, which is inaugurated by the *canzone* "Donne ch'avete intelletto d'amore." As already discussed in the previous section, this event also marks a movement away from the elegiac theme, to which the author returns after Beatrice's death. The theoretical and poetic reflection underpinning this episode remains central to the whole of Dante's oeuvre.[86] It may be surprising, therefore, to see the possible debt this reflection owes to such a basic school text as Prosper. Yet, when one closely observes Dante's exchange with the ladies, resemblances with some of the *Epigrammata*'s core teachings become apparent.

In *Vita nova* 5.2 [10.2], Dante is denied Beatrice's greeting, which was the source of the poet's bliss ("nello quale stava tutta la mia beatitudine"). Right after that, the protagonist is dealt another unexpected blow in the already-mentioned episode of the "gabbo" (mockery) (7 [15]). At this point, while wandering alone and in anguish, the poet meets a group of ladies who question him on a crucial issue of both poetics and ethics. In what Ahern has fittingly termed a "tenzone" (a poetic dispute), one of the ladies asks the poet about the aim of his love for Beatrice. She argues that if the poet could find satisfaction in loving without being loved back— and while being mocked—the end of his love must be truly new: "novissimo." Challenged by the lady's question, Dante unexpectedly answers:

---

[86] Dante insistently reframes this *canzone* throughout his oeuvre (*Vita nova* 19; *De vulgari eloquentia* 2.8.8, and 2.12.3; and *Purgatorio* 24.50), pointing to its crucial role in shaping his innovative poetics.

86 DANTE'S EDUCATION

Madonne, lo fine del mio amore fue già lo saluto di questa donna, forse di cui voi intendete, e in quello dimorava la beatitudine, ché era fine di tutti li miei desiderii. Ma poi che le piacque di negarlo a me, lo mio segnore Amore, la sua merzede, ha posto tutta la mia beatitudine in quello che non mi puote venire meno.

(Vita nova 10.6 [18.4])

(Ladies, the goal of my love once consisted in receiving the greeting of this lady to whom you are, perhaps, referring, and in this greeting rested the bliss which was the goal of all my desires. But since it pleased her to deny it to me, my lord, Love, through his grace, has placed all my bliss in something that cannot fail me.)

In reply, the ladies demand to know what the source of such an unshakable bliss would be. Hoping to impress them, Dante claims that his satisfaction lies entirely in the words that praise Beatrice: "In quelle parole che lodano la donna mia" (In words that praise my lady) (*Vita nova* 10.8 [18.6]). At this point, the ladies reveal themselves to be both close readers and sharp logicians, posing a question that will grant them victory in the *tenzone* with the poet: "Se tu ne dicessi vero, quelle parole che tu n'hai dette in notificando la tua condizione, avrestù operate con altro intendimento" ("If you are telling us the truth, then those words you addressed to her describing your condition must have been written with some other intention") (10.9 [18.7]).[87] The poet leaves the debate without further reply, dumbstruck by the realization of the utter discrepancy between his moral principles and his poetic and personal behavior. He is, however, determined to make amends and become the poet he claims to be: "Poi che è tanta beatitudine in quelle parole che lodano la mia donna, perché altro parlare è stato lo mio? E però propuosi di prendere per matera de lo mio parlare sempre mai quello che fosse loda di questa gentilissima" (Since there is so much bliss in words that praise my lady, why have I ever written in any other way? Therefore, I resolved that from then on I would always choose as the theme of my poetry whatever would be in praise of this most gracious one.) (10.10–11 [18.9]). The first outcome of this new poetic resolution is the ground-breaking *canzone* "Donne ch'avete intelletto d'amore," which the poet addresses to all ladies who understand love.

One of the first epigrams of Prosper's *Liber* (6) is devoted precisely to the topic of the *De vera Dei laudatione* (The true praise of God). In the prose paragraph introducing this *sententia*, Prosper states, "Vera est confessio benedicentis, cum idem sonus est et oris et cordis. *Bene autem loqui, et male vivere, nihil est aliud quam sua se voce damnare*" (Authentic is the confession of he who praises the Lord, when heart and mouth speak as one. *But to speak well and live badly is nothing else than condemning oneself with one's own voice*) (emphasis added). In the related elegiac poem, he further explains:

---

[87] On the historical and cultural significance of Dante's representation of the women as close critical readers of Dante's poems, see Lombardi, *Imagining*, 60–77.

Laus vera in Dominum depromitur ore precantis,
　si quae voce fluunt, intima cordis habent.
Non prodest cuiquam solis bona dicere verbis,
　ni pia mens habeat, quod bene lingua sonat.
Nam fari recte, miserum est, et vivere prave.

(The true laud of God is drawn from the mouth of he who prays /
if the words that flow from the voice inhabit the heart's innermost
part. / There is no gain in saying good things only in words, /
unless the pious mind has in itself what the tongue sounds well. /
For it is miserable to speak well and live badly.)

One can almost hear the ladies' reproach to Dante. Even taking into consideration that Prosper here is concerned with the true praise of God, whereas Dante's
ladies are interested in the true praise of Beatrice, it is undeniable that the two
moral arguments substantially coincide: "There is no gain in saying good things
only with words / unless the pious mind has in itself what the tongue sounds well.
/ For it is miserable to speak well and live badly." The simplicity of the epigram's
message resonates with the directness of the ladies' critique of Dante, which is
based on the same moral truism, evident even to the simplest reader: when one
truly praises, whether God or Beatrice, words and actions are consistent. Blessedness originates from this unity—a pious mind, Prosper explains, is one who lives
"quod bene lingua sonat"—whereas misery comes from the separation of words
and actions: "Nam fari recte, miserum est, et vivere prave." One reasonable objection to the apparent parallelism linking the two texts could be that Dante did
not even praise Beatrice with his words, as he himself admits. If, however, one
closely considers the specific terms of the lady's criticism, the parallel appears more
clearly: "Se tu ne dicessi vero, quelle parole che tu n'hai dette in notificando la tua
condizione, avrestù *operate* con altro intendimento" (If what you're saying is true,
those poems that you wrote about your condition must have been *written* with
some other aim in mind) (emphasis added). The lady is denouncing the inconsistency between the poet's claim, "dicessi," and his poetic actions, "operare" (to
operate/act). Dante seems precisely to address this lack of consistency in the following *canzone*. In "Donne ch'avete," he assures his audience that when he speaks
about Beatrice, Love possesses him to such a degree that, if it were not for his own
weakness, he could make people love by means of his words alone: "Io dico che
pensando il suo valore, / amor sì dolce mi fa sentire, / che s'io allora non perdessi
ardire, / farei parlando innamorar la gente" (Her worth is so above / the rest, I feel
such lightness in my heart, / that if speech didn't stammer I'd impart / new love to
those who are not lovers yet) (*Vita nova* 10.16. 5–8 [19.5.5–8]). Now Dante's poetic
"operations" are consistent with his mind.

It is also noteworthy that, in Prosper's words, the consequence of Dante's moral
fallacy is that one "miserum est" (is unhappy). One could say, therefore, that a

88   DANTE'S EDUCATION

poet who praises only with his words becomes the subject and author of elegiac poetry, since, as we have seen, Dante defines elegy as the "stilum . . . miserorum." It is not a coincidence that the *canzone* "Donne ch'avete intelletto d'amore" concludes the first elegiac section of the *Vita nova* and begins one in praise of Beatrice.

The most relevant overlapping between this central episode of the *Vita nova* and Prosper's *Liber epigrammatum*, however, is in their identical definition of the ultimate and undeniable good for a Christian. When the ladies ask Dante what is the "fine . . . novissimo" (the unprecedented . . . end) of his love for Beatrice, the protagonist replies that Love "ha posto tutta la mia beatitudine in quello che non mi puote venire meno" (has transferred my bliss to that which cannot fail me). The question that most frequently returns in Prosper's *Liber epigrammatum* is precisely what constitutes the "verum bonum" of the Christian life (14, 20, 24, 60, 63, 81, 87, 94). In the epigram 87, "De diligendo Deum" (The Love of God), Prosper defines humanity's ultimate good with a formulation close to Dante's own: "Non poterit hominis labor finiri, *nisi hoc diligat quod ei non possit auferri*" (Humanity's labor will never end, *if humans do not love what cannot be taken away from them*) (emphasis added). People's lives are always fraught with anxieties unless they recognize the true good that cannot be taken away from them. Prosper later returns to the same issue in the epigram 94, "De bonis quae nemo amittit invitus" (The Goods that Nobody Loses Unwillingly), in which he explains that "potest homo invitus amittere temporalia bona; numquam vero, nisi, volens, perdit aeterna" (humans can against their will lose temporal goods; but never, unless they want to, can they lose the eternal ones). Of one piece with this advice, in epigram 20, "De praemio Christianae religionis" (The Prize of the Christian Faith), Prosper maintains that the true prize of one's faith in God is faith itself, not some other thing one may wish to gain from believing in God. Before Dante turned his interest to the solace that comes from venerating Beatrice per se, the purpose of his love had been to receive her greeting. In light of Prosper, we can appreciate that Dante's ulterior motive falsified his veneration for Beatrice:

> Hoc affectu et hoc desiderio colendus est Deus: ut sui cultus ipse sit merces. Nam qui Deum ideo colit, ut aliud magis quam ipsum promereatur, non Deum colit, sed id quod assequi concupiscit.

> (God must be worshipped with this single affection and desire: so that to venerate Him may in itself be the recompense. For one who worships God to gain something other than God himself do not venerate God, but that which one desires.)

Prosper's advice, therefore, fittingly encapsulates the moral and poetic renewal pursued by Dante after losing Beatrice's greeting.

THE *VITA NOVA* AS A VERNACULAR READER   89

The discussion of humanity's ultimate good is common to a large array of biblical and classical texts.[88] Yet, Prosper's source is remarkable in two ways: first, its treatment of the true good belongs to a theoretical discussion of both true praise and true love, as in the *Vita nova*; second, since, as I argue, the ladies represent the educated lay audience with no advanced Latin and university-level training, Dante's decision to have them echo a schoolbook might have produced a peculiar effect on his Florentine audience. When read next to Prosper, the whole episode of Dante's exchange with the group of ladies in the *Vita nova* appears in a rather comic light. Not only is Dante's renewed poetic proposition de facto undermined by the ladies' critique, but their criticism hinges on a moral platitude that any pupil in Florentine grammar schools would have known and that had likely infiltrated popular culture in the form of proverbial wisdom. Remarkably, Dante explains that he decided to narrate the episode of his meeting with the ladies because it is "delightful to hear": "E però che la cagione de la nuova materia è dilettevole a udire, la dicerò, quanto potrò più brevemente" (And since the occasion for the new subject matter is delightful to hear, I will write it down, as briefly as I know how) (*Vita nova* 10.2 [17.2]). In this light, Dante's *tenzone* with the ladies appears as a fitting culmination of the *gabbo* episode that precedes it—a comic interlude, therefore, between the first elegiac section of the *libello* and the second part, which is centered instead on the praise of Beatrice.

Prosper's *Liber epigrammatum* also sheds meaningful light on the practical, ethical implications of Dante's response to the ladies, "Donne ch'avete intelletto d'amore." As we learn from the introductory prose, this *canzone* aims to correct the fault of the poet's moral and poetic inconsistency. As a result, Dante does not address the poem to any particular lady, but to all ladies who understand love and have spiritual nobility—"che sono gentili" (*Vita nova* 10.12 [19.1]). Such ladies, as the beginning of the *canzone* reveals, are those gifted with an "intellect of love":

> Donne ch'avete intelletto d'amore,
> i' vo' con voi de la mia donna dire,
> non perch'io creda sua laude finire,
> ma ragionar per isfogar la mente.
> Io dico che pensando il suo valore,
> Amor sì dolce mi si fa sentire,
> che s'io allora non perdessi ardire,

---

[88] It is, for instance, Philosophy's central teaching to Boethius in the *Consolatio* ("quod nequeat *auferri*", 2.4) (emphasis added), as Todorović has recently pointed out (*Dante*, chap. 1). In a sense, the same belief undergirds also Bonaventure's *Itinerarium mentis in Deum*, which Singleton (*Essay*) has famously linked to the three stages of Dante's spiritual progress in the *Vita nova*. Two biblical precedents deserve special mentioning here: Luke 10:42 and Isaiah 55:13. In the passage from Luke, Jesus praises Mary's contemplative attitude as opposed to her sister Martha's active life: "optimam partem elegit, quae non auferetur ab ea." Isaiah, instead, speaks of a "signum aeternum quod non auferetur."

90   DANTE'S EDUCATION

> farei parlando innamorar la gente.
> E io non vo' parlar sì altamente,
> ch'io divenisse per temenza vile;
> ma tratterò del suo stato gentile
> a respetto di lei leggeramente,
> donne e donzelle amorose, con vui,
> ché non è cosa da parlarne altrui.
>
> (Vita nova 10.15–17 [19.4–6], lines 1–14)

> (Women who understand the truth of love, / I want to talk with
> you a while about / my lady—not because I could run out / of
> words and ways to praise her, but to set / my mind at ease. Her
> worth is so above/the rest, I feel such lightness in my heart, / that
> if speech didn't stammer I'd impart / new love to those who are
> not lovers yet. / And I won't speak so far above my head/that I go
> giddy and get lost in haze: / instead I'll talk about her gracious
> ways— / nimbly, approaching her with lightest tread— / to you,
> the amorous and wise of us, / since no one else can grasp what we
> discuss.)

The poet insists that his audience be made of readers who understand love not only
in theory, but also in practice—that is, those who are in love, "donne e donzelle
amorose." In the closing lines of the *canzone*, he also broadens his audience to
include courteous men as well, as he explains that he wishes to talk about Beatrice
only with people who are endowed with courtesy:

> E se non vuoli andar sì come vana,
> non restare ove sia gente villana:
> ingegnati, se puoi, d'esser palese
> solo con donne o con omo cortese,
> che ti merranno là per via tostana.
>
> (Vita nova 10.25 [19.14], lines 64–68)

> (And to avoid a waste of time don't go / where everyone you meet
> is coarse and dumb; / try, if you're able, only being seen / by men
> and women versed in what you mean, / whose guidance will be
> swift, not burdensome.)

As this *canzone* argues, love ennobles and infuses with virtues those who love Beatrice.[89] The poet, therefore, chooses his interlocutors based on their commitment

---

[89] This idea had already been expressed by Guido Guinizzelli, particularly in the *canzone* "Al cor
gentil rempaira sempre amore." In the *sonetto* "Amore e 'l cor gentil sono una cosa," Dante further
articulates Guinizzelli's theory of love.

to love and courtesy. Dante wishes to speak to those who not only understand but also pursue love. The definition of this ethical and gnoseological bond as "intelletto d'amore" could mirror a specific theological concept. This fact can be most easily discerned if we consider Prosper's epigram 13, in which the author discusses the topic of the "De bono intellectu" and explains that the only "good" intellect is one that informs actions:

> Bonum intellectum habet qui quod faciendum recte intelligit facit: alioquin talis est sine opere intelligentia, qualis est sine timore sapientia; cum sit scriptum, "Initium sapientiae timor Domini."

> Scriptorum Domini plene videt omne profundum,
>   implet qui factis cognita verba piis.
> Nam nimis a sensu doctrinae devius errat,
>   si quae curavit scire, fugit facere.

> (One who acts upon his right understanding of what must be done possesses good intellect: otherwise, intelligence without works is like wisdom without fear; since it is written, "The fear of God is the beginning of Wisdom." Fully understands all the depth of God's writings, / he who fulfills in pious actions the words learned. / For one who does not act upon the things he has cared to learn / wanders far from the meaning of doctrine.)

Wisdom is good not in and of itself, but only when it is humble—that is, when it is acted on. Once again, Prosper's practical definition of what constitutes "good intellect" aptly describes the spiritual, moral, and poetic progress undergone by Dante after losing Beatrice's greeting and being reproached by the ladies. Thus, Dante's choice to address the ladies as those who have an "intellect of love" acknowledges their superior understanding of love, in contrast to his own vitiated one. The *canzone* "Donne ch'avete" encapsulates the poet's transformation from a condition of ethical inconsistency to one of perfect consistency between knowledge of the good and poetic action. As Prosper's epigram 24 on "De scientia boni" (On Knowing What Is Good) clarifies, such coherence is necessary for Dante to find blessedness in the praising of Beatrice. Prosper explains that those who know the supreme good, and act accordingly, can indeed love their own actions: "qui quod novit agens, diligit id quod agit" (the one who knows what he is doing, loves what he is doing).

The *canzone* "Donne ch'avete intelletto d'amore" is unquestionably a complex and revolutionary experiment, in which the poet articulates an autonomous poetics from the influence of older vernacular poets such as Guittone d'Arezzo, Guido Guinizzelli, and Guido Cavalcanti. Our perception of the *canzone*'s importance,

92   DANTE'S EDUCATION

however, is also influenced by Dante's own estimation of the poem's unparalleled relevance for the development of his career and, more broadly, of the poetics of the "dolce stil novo" (the sweet new style) (*Purgatorio* 24.57). Hence, we should not fail to appreciate the practical and moral teaching that this poem imparted on contemporary readers of the *Vita nova*. By reframing "Donne ch'avete intelletto d'amore" in the particular narrative context of the *Vita nova*, Dante foregrounded the poem's ethical message about the unity of poetry and love in a way that resembled some of the moral tenets of his readers' and his own education. When justifying his decision not to provide all subdivisions of "Donne ch'avete intelletto d'amore," so as to open the *canzone*'s full meaning only to some among his readers, Dante seems to imply that the *Vita nova* is a work meant to communicate differently to different readers.[90] Reading it through the filter of Prosper's *Liber epigrammatum* helps unveiling what would have been a popular reception of this central episode of the *libello*.

Notwithstanding the importance of the *canzone* "Donne ch'avete intelletto d'amore," the birth of the poetics of praise represents neither the culminating nor the resolutive event of the *Vita nova*. After Beatrice's death, the poet falls into a second moment of crisis, which results in another elegiac section of the book. This crisis eventually leads him almost to betray the memory of Beatrice as a result of the new, surging love that the poet feels for the "donna gentile." At this point, a "powerful vision" brings him back to Beatrice, and then another, divinely inspired vision of the lady in the glory of Heaven persuades him to cease writing about her until he has the means to do so more adequately. The *libello* concludes with an open ending that foreshadows another, more important and more sophisticated work that Dante is yet to compose:

> Appresso questo sonetto apparve a me una mirabile visione, ne la quale io vidi cose che mi fecero proporre di non dire più di questa benedetta infino a tanto che io potesse più degnamente trattare di lei. E di venire a ciò io studio quanto posso, sì com'ella sae veracemente. Sì che, se piacere sarà di colui a cui tutte le cose vivono, che la mia vita duri per alquanti anni, io spero di dicer di lei quello che mai non fue detto d'alcuna.
>
> (*Vita nova* 31.1–2 [42.1–3])
>
> (After writing this sonnet a marvelous vision appeared to me, in which I saw things that made me decide not to say anything more about this blessed lady until I was capable of writing about her more worthily. To achieve this I am doing all that I can, as surely she knows. So that, if it be pleasing to Him who is that for

---

[90] "Dico bene che, a più aprire lo intendimento di questa canzone, si converrebbe usare di più minute divisioni; ma tuttavia chi non è di tanto ingegno che per queste che sono fatte la possa intendere, a me non dispiace se la mi lascia stare, ché certo io temo d'avere a troppi comunicato lo suo intendimento pur per queste divisioni che fatte sono, s'elli avvenisse che molti le potessero audire" (10, 33 [19, 22]).

THE *VITA NOVA* AS A VERNACULAR READER   93

which all things live, and if my life is long enough, I hope to say things about her that have never been said about any woman.)

The events ensuing from Beatrice's death prove that further steps are necessary for the poet to keep up with the marvelous story of which God is the author. Dante's final words reveal his newfound awareness that true poetic novelty is yet to come, and that God alone can grant it.

Remarkably, the end of the *Vita nova* fittingly follows Prosper's exhortation at the end of the *Liber epigrammatum*. The final epigram in the collection, "De quaerendo perseveranter Deo" (On Searching for God with Perseverance) (106), conveys the same sense of openness and need for a continuous progress that also characterizes the end of the *Vita nova*. Prosper exhorts his readers to persevere in the search for God, because no one can presume to have reached full knowledge of Him, even after making great progress:

> Nemo fidelium, quamvis multum profecerit, dicat Sufficit mihi. Qui enim dixerit, remansit et haesit in via ante finem, qui non perseverabit usque in finem.

> Cum pia mens *in laude Dei* superata laboras,
> gaude, quod tantum te bene vincit opus.
> *Teque aliquid superi cognosce hauisse vigoris,*
> *si tibi non satis est, quod cupis atque sapis.*
> Quaere bonum sine fine bonum, et persiste reperto:
> quaerere non habeant talia vota modum.
> Nam qui se nullo iam munere credit egere,
> crescere non cupiens, perdit adepta tepens.
>
> > (emphasis added)

> (None of the faithful, no matter how considerably they have pro-gressed, should say "This is enough for me." For whoever did say so has remained stuck on the way before the end and will not perse-vere until the end. Rejoice when your pious mind is overwhelmed by the labor *of praising God,* / because only this effort rightfully tires you up. / *Be aware that you have obtained some strength from above* / *if you are not satisfied with the things that you know and desire.* / Search for the unending good, and, having found it, per-sist: / may such vows be sought that are boundless. / For one who believes he no longer needs any gift, / not desiring to improve and growing cold, loses what he has gaines.)

The mind—or soul—of those who strive to praise God, Prosper explains, should gladly keep endeavoring to find suitable ways to praise God, as this is the mind's

94   DANTE'S EDUCATION

highest purpose. A mind that perceives that its desire and knowledge are inherently wanting has received a divine illumination. Dante ends his *Vita nova* precisely by claiming to have received a divine vision and stating that his poetry is still unable to say what this new experience means. The poet, moreover, gladly welcomes such an illumination and the lifelong endeavor that the proper praise of Beatrice requires. The *Vita nova*'s surprising ending, therefore, may meet a spiritual requirement for anyone who sincerely wishes to praise God. Dante's conclusion indeed seems to honor Prosper's spiritual imperative.

Prosper's influence on Dante's *Vita nova* should not surprise. The *Liber*'s popularity in Florence's cultural milieu and education, and the relative simplicity of its theological teachings, made it a relevant model for the educational goals that Dante wished to pursue with his *libello*. The peculiar format of Prosper's prosimetric compilation possibly left a durable impression on the poet. Albeit Dante did not need to learn from Prosper what a prosimetrum looks like, he must nonetheless have been keenly aware of the *Vita nova*'s resemblance to the *Liber epigrammatum*. Furthermore, Prosper's original authorial stance represents an exceptional precedent for Dante's multifaceted authorship and self-exegesis in the *libello*. The moral and theological parallels between the two texts also deserve consideration. They by no means prove that Dante needed to rely on Prosper for treating such core tenets of the Christian faith as those implied by key passages of the *Vita nova*. Yet their analogies with Prosper's epigrams shows that the theological and moral principles on which they hinged were not too distant from the moral and doctrinal ABCs that pupils learned in Florentine grammar schools. The resemblance, moreover, of Dante's discussion of what constituted the true praise of Beatrice with Prosper's teachings about the true praise of God might have appeared striking and unorthodox to contemporary readers. Finally, I suggest that as Prosper's *Liber* was parsed and memorized to advance students' reading skills in Latin, while also teaching them a basic Augustinian catechism, so the *Vita nova* offered Florentine lay readers both an intermediate vernacular reader and an essential catechism. Its doctrine concerning Christian love and Boethian consolation directly opposed secular views on the destructive power of eros and love advanced by other vernacular poets and chiefly by the *libello*'s first intended reader, Guido Cavalcanti.

Conclusion

Ahern maintains that "Dante ... provides the readers of the *Vita nova* with a new role: he thinks of them as people who regularly read material written out of motives that are not strictly utilitarian, and who will in succeeding years await another book of his on the same topic .... Dante was the first to see that such a public

THE *VITA NOVA* AS A VERNACULAR READER   95

existed potentially, and by being the first to engage it, he created it."[91] Although studies have shown that a vernacular readership was already in place by the time the poet began the *Vita nova*, we should not underestimate the challenges entailed by Dante's project: not only had most lay readers virtually never seen the like of the *Vita nova*'s textual and editorial product in the vernacular, but they had limited experience with any kind of literary text.[92] The several parallels that I have been drawing between the *libello* and medieval schoolbooks show that Dante envisioned the *Vita nova* as a sort of vernacular reader, the equivalent of texts such as Henry, Prosper, and Boethius—a bridge text, in other words, between elementary and more advanced vernacular readings. Those who had received at least intermediate Latin training could have recognized in the *Vita nova* some elements akin to their school texts. To the less educated, instead, the *libello* provided a vernacular substitute for these propaedeutic texts. Dante's evangelical claim that the meaning of his poems, such as "A ciascun alma e gentil core," could now be grasped by the simplest readers also points to some practical implications: the *libello* was designed to help its readers progress beyond their reading and interpretative skills. I would contend, therefore, that if Dante did not "create" a readership for the *libello*, he certainly wished to train one. Hence, we can see in the project of the *Vita nova* the seeds of that didactic responsibility that the poet endorsed only a few years later in the *Convivio*. While advancing the literary culture and reading skills of its lay audience, the *Vita nova* aimed to direct them in the path of spiritual salvation.

Ambrogio Camozzi Pistoja has recently argued that Dante conceived the *Convivio* primarily as an instrument for the spiritual edification of its readers and that the text selects its intended readers based on their moral inclinations rather than intellectual abilities. As Enrica Zanin notes, moreover, "the process of reading" becomes "a central issue in the *Convivio*," and the work "does not only supply knowledge, but it invites the reader to convert to it." The *Vita nova*, I maintain, marks the poet's first reckoning with the historical reality that cultivating advanced reading skills in the vernacular had become a means for the moral and spiritual formation of the laity. In the *Vita nova*, therefore, Dante laid the foundations of his educational project, by preparing his lay audience to take on more complex readings. The popularizing project at the heart of both the *Vita nova* and *Convivio* reflected a wider intellectual movement that interested the milieu in which Dante was formed. Here, as Anna Pegoretti points out, "the growing interest for the *Consolation of Philosophy* could react with the technical language of Scholasticism and

---

[91] Ahern, "The New Life of the Book," 240. This conclusion has recently been echoed by Elena Lombardi, *L'invenzione del lettore in Dante*. See also Erich Auerbach, "The Western Public and Its Language," in *Literary Language and Its Public in Late Latin Antiquity and in the Middle Ages*, trans. Ralph Manheim (New York: Pantheon, 1965), 237–338, esp. 312.

[92] On the *Vita nova*'s textual novelty see, among others, H. Wayne Storey, *Transcription and Visual Poetics in the Early Italian Lyric* (New York: Garland, 1993), 11–17.

96   DANTE'S EDUCATION

nourish the debate on the universality of knowledge."[93] In the *Commedia*, Dante took this project even further, integrating the didactic function of the prose into a coherent poetic whole, also suitable for oral and collective forms of "reading," thus reaching a more universal audience.[94] As we turn to the *Commedia*, we can appreciate the evolutions of Dante's intertextual dialogue with medieval school texts and his shifting attitude toward his own education.

[93] In order of mention, Camozzi Pistoja, "Testo come eucarestia"; Enrica Zanin, "'Miseri, 'mpediti, affamati': Dante's Implied Reader in the *Convivio*," in *Dante's* Convivio: *or How to Restart a Career in Exile*, ed. Franziska Meier (Oxford: Peter Lang, 2018), 207–21, at 207, 212; Anna Pegoretti, "'Da questa nobilissima perfezione molti sono privati': Impediments to Knowledge and the Tradition of Commentaries on Boethius's Consolatio Philosophiae," in *Dante's* Convivio: *Or How to Restart a Career in Exile*, 77–97.

[94] On the *Commedia's* ability to "explain itself" without the aid of the author's commentary, see Ascoli, *Dante*, 218–26. On the different forms of "reading" in the Middle Ages, see Lombardi, *Imagining the Woman Reader*, chap. 1. As for the first oral diffusion of the *Commedia*, see Ahern, "Singing the Book."

3

(Un)like Aesop

Defining the *Commedia*'s Generic Monstrosity

An obvious point of departure for my analysis of Dante's engagement with Latin school texts in the *Commedia* is *Inferno* 23.4–6, where the protagonist has a sudden recollection of Aesop's fable "The Frog and the Mouse":

> Vòlt'era in su la favola d'Isopo
> lo mio pensier per la presente rissa,
> dov'el parlò de la rana e del topo.

> (The brawl played out before our eyes / put me in mind of Aesop's fable / in which he told the tale of frog and mouse.)

Dante had already drawn on the Aesopic corpus in *Convivio* 4.30.4, where he cited the fable "The Cock and the Pearl" to reassert the biblical warning against casting pearls before swine (Matthew 7:6): "e come dice Esopo poeta nella prima Favola, più è prode al gallo uno grano che una margarita, e però quella lascia e quello coglie" (and as the poet Aesop says in his first fable, a grain is worth more than a pearl to a cock, and he therefore leaves the one and takes the other).[1] Whereas this allusion fits the context of *Convivio* 4.30.4, lending proverbial support to Dante's argument, the suitability and purpose of recalling Aesop's frog and mouse in the context of the fifth *bolgia* (pit), at *Inferno* 23, have long perplexed readers of the poem. In this chapter, I read this direct encroachment on the territory of fable as a key moment in Dante's definition of the *Commedia*'s unconventional stance toward literary genres and realism.[2] To appreciate this fact, however, we need to locate the mention of Aesop in *Inferno* 23 within the larger metapoetic discourse that Dante begins to articulate at *Inferno* 16, when facing the unbelievable monster Geryon.

---

[1] I follow Jill Mann in applying the term "Aesopic" to the "classic fables belonging to the genre as it is established by the historical tradition." Jill Mann, *From Aesop to Reynard: Beast Literature in Medieval Britain* (Oxford: Oxford University Press, 2009), 4.

[2] For lack of a better term, and for clarity's sake, throughout this book I use the term "genre" and other related expressions, such as "generic," even though medieval views on literary *genus* and *stilus* little resembled our modern use of these terms. For a comprehensive and insightful discussion of "genre" in medieval literature and Dante, see Zygmunt Barański, "'Tres sunt enim manerie dicendi . . .': Some Observations on Medieval Literature, Genre, and Dante," in Barański, *Dante, Petrarch, Boccaccio: Literature, Doctrine, Reality* (Oxford: Legenda, 2020), 209–56.

Dante's Education. Filippo Gianferrari, Oxford University Press. © Filippo Gianferrari (2024).
DOI: 10.1093/oso/9780198881766.003.0004

98   DANTE'S EDUCATION

Geryon, Aesop, and "comedìa"

When the protagonist is about to descend into the lower part of Hell, where fraud is punished according to its many forms, he meets the astonishing monster Geryon. Beholding this most amazing of beasts—a mix of different human and animal forms, with its skin covered in intricate and colorful patterns, resembling Turkish drapes—Dante feels compelled to address his readers and swear on the authority of his own poem that his encounter with Geryon really took place. While facing this momentous challenge to his own credibility as a witness, the author discloses a surprising detail about the poem's genre and perhaps its title:

> Sempre a quel ver c'ha faccia di menzogna
> de' l'uom chiuder le labra fin ch'el puote
> però che sanza colpa fa vergogna;
>   ma qui tacer nol posso; e per le note
> di questa comedìa, lettor, ti giuro,
> s'elle non sien di lunga grazia vote,
>   ch'i' vidi per quell'aere grosso e scuro
> venir notando una figura in suso,
> maravigliosa ad ogne cor sicuro.
>
> (Inferno 16.124–32)[3]

(Faced with that truth which seems a lie, a man / should always close his lips as long as he can— / to tell it shames him, even though he's blameless; / but here I can't be still; and by the lines / of this my Comedy, reader, I swear— / and may my verse find favor for long years— / that through the dense and darkened air I saw / a figure swimming, rising up, enough / to bring amazement to the firmest heart, / like one returning from the waves where he /

---

[3] Whether Dante intends to swear on the authority of his poem or by offering its success to God is a point of contention. For a recent reassessment of this critical debate in support of the latter interpretation, see Pietro Cagni, "Osservazioni su un giuramento dantesco (*Inferno* XVI, 124–36)," *L'Alighieri* 55 (2020): 5–22. Teodolinda Barolini instead has famously proposed a metapoetic interpretation of the whole episode. See Barolini, *The Undivine Comedy: Detheologizing Dante* (Princeton, NJ: Princeton University Press, 1992), 48–73. Justin Steinberg has sought to move beyond this duality by arguing that the success of Dante's poem "does not depend on a transcendent divine judge but is instead contingent on the same readers to whom he is swearing." Steinberg, *Dante and the Limits of the Law* (Chicago: Chicago University Press, 2013), 158. See also Luca Fiorentini, "Il Silenzio di Gerione (*Inferno* XVI-XVII)," *Rivista di Storia e Letteratura Religiosa* 2 (2016): 213–40. Scholars have occasionally questioned whether at *Inferno* 16.127 Dante wished to indicate the title or simply the genre of the poem, and whether the title "comedìa" should refer to the whole work or just the first cantica. The history of the poem's reception supports the traditional title. This tradition, however, documents the "vulgate" reception of the poem rather than Dante's actual intention, as pointed out by Alberto Casadei, "Il titolo della *Commedia* e l'Epistola a Cangrande," in *Dante oltre la* Commedia (Bologna: il Mulino, 2013), 15–44. Hence, Casadei argues, "comedìa" should not be assumed as the poem's title. The same thesis is further developed by Mirko Tavoni, "Perché il poema di Dante è una *Commedia*?," in *Qualche idea su Dante* (Bologna: il Mulino, 2015), 335–69.

DEFINING THE *COMMEDIA*'S GENERIC MONSTROSITY 99

> went down to loose an anchor snagged upon / a reef or something
> else hid in the sea, / who stretches upward and draws in his feet.)

The author introduces this solemn oath by rehearsing a classical rhetorical topos—
and proverbial wisdom—warning speakers and writers against reporting incredi-
ble events that are likely to prompt disbelief in listeners or readers.[4] In describing
Geryon, moreover, Dante disobeys the opening prescription of the *Ars poetica*,
where Horace discourages poets from creating unbelievable monsters that blend
together different natures; besides showing a lack of taste, Horace explains, such
a mix prompts disbelief in the reader.[5] In the *Commedia*, however, the monster
Geryon displays beastly features that are reminiscent of Horace's examples and
has the marks of artistic creation "painted" over its very skin:[6]

> La faccia sua era faccia d'uom giusto,
> tanto benigna avea di fuor la pelle,
> e d'un serpente tutto l'altro fusto;
>   due branche avea pilose insin l'ascelle;
> lo dosso e 'l petto e ambedue le coste
> dipinti avea di nodi e di rotelle.
>   Con più color, sommesse e sovraposte
> non fer mai drappi Tartari né Turchi,
> né fuor tai tele per Aragne imposte.
>
> (Inferno 17.10–18)

> (The face he wore was that of a just man, / so gracious was his fea-
> tures' outer semblance; / and all his trunk, the body of a serpent; /
> he had two paws, with hair up to the armpits; / his back and chest
> as well as both his flanks / had been adorned with twining knots
> and circlets. / No Turks or Tartars ever fashioned fabrics / more
> colorful in background and relief, / nor had Arachne ever loomed
> such webs.)

By rejecting Horace's norms and creating a beast that looks like a piece of art, Dante
asserts the novel and hybrid nature of his own *Commedia* vis-à-vis traditional

---

[4] For a discussion of this rhetorical trope and its use in Dante's predecessors, see Andrea Battistini,
"Il 'ver c'ha faccia di menzogna': lettura di 'Inferno' XVII," *L'Alighieri*, n.s., 40 (2012): 67–87, esp. 69–71,
and Cagni, "Osservazioni."

[5] Horace begins his *Ars* with the following warning: "Humano capiti ceruicem pictor equinam /
iungere si uelit et uarias inducere plumas / undique collatis membris, ut turpiter atrum / desinat in
piscem mulier formosa superne, / spectatum admissi, risum teneatis, amici? ... Pictoribus atque poetis /
quidlibet audendi semper fuit aequa potestas. Scimus, et hanc ueniam petimusque damusque uicissim,
/ sed non ut placidis coeant immitia, non ut / serpentes auibus geminentur, tigribus agni" (Horace, *Ars
poetica* 1–13).

[6] On the metapoetic significance of Geryon's skin and of its reference to the myth of Arachne, see
Barolini, *The Undivine Comedy*, 48–77, 122–42.

100 DANTE'S EDUCATION

literary genres and transgresses the established boundaries between realism and fiction.[7] Theodore Cachey argues that Geryon belongs to Dante's reuse of the "liminal genre of travel . . . for travel had long served as a context for the exploration and exploitation of the ever-negotiable frontier between truth and fiction." While acknowledging that his encounter with Geryon may damage his credibility as a reliable witness and a poet, Dante nonetheless asks readers to believe him. As Andrea Battistini notes, moreover, the whole of canto 16 is devised to persuade the reader of the poet's multiple claims concerning the nature and truthfulness of the *Commedia*: both Geryon and the poem may appear to be "maraviglie" (wonders) even to those with a steadfast heart.[8] By identifying his poem as a "comedìa" in connection with Geryon, therefore, Dante binds together the definition of the poem's genre and an appeal for the reader's trust.

The same bond between comedy and realism is reestablished at *Inferno* 21.2, at the outset of a triptych of cantos that narrates the pilgrim's transition through the fifth, and central, *bolgia* of the barrators (grafters) into that of the hypocrites. Here, the author refers in passing to a conversation he had with Virgil but does not wish to report:

> Così di ponte in ponte, altro parlando
> che la mia comedìa cantar non cura,
> venimmo; e tenavamo 'l colmo, quando
>   restammo per veder l'altra fessura
> di Malebolge e li altri pianti vani;
> e vidila mirabilmente oscura.

> *(Inferno* 21.1–6)

> (Thus from one bridge to the next we came / until we reached its highest point, speaking / of things my Comedy does not care to

[7] For the reading of Geryon as an image of Dante's literary "monster" with its generic and stylistic hybridity, and in opposition to Horace's norms, see Zygmunt Barański, "The 'Marvelous' and the 'Comic': Toward a Reading of *Inferno* XVI," *Lectura Dantis* 7 (1990): 72–95; Barański, "*Sole nuovo, luce nuova*": *Saggi sul rinnovamento culturale in Dante* (Turin: Scriptorium, 1996), 157–65; and Claudia Villa, "Per una tipologia del commento mediolatino: L'*Ars poetica* di Orazio," in *Il commento ai testi: Atti del seminario di Asona 2–9 ottobre 1989*, ed. Ottavio Besomi and Carlo Caruso (Basel: Birkhäuser, 1992), 19–42, esp. 39. Emilio Pasquini instead argues that Dante devises Geryon's episode as a way to represent the comic genre. See Pasquini, "Il canto di Gerione," *Atti e Memorie dell'Arcadia* 4 (1967): 346–68, esp. 348.

[8] Theodore J. Cachey Jr., "Dante's Journey between Fiction and Truth: Geryon Revisited," in *Dante, da Firenze all'aldilà: Atti del Terzo Seminario Dantesco Internazionale, Firenze 9–11 giugno 2000*, ed. Michelangelo Picone (Florence: Franco Cesati Editore, 2001), 75–92, at 90. Battistini, "Il 'ver c'ha faccia di menzogna.'" Robert Hollander also argues that the Geryon episode is intended to support Dante's claim to truth at the heart of the poem's fiction. See Hollander, "Dante Theologus-poeta," in *Dante Studies* 94 (1976): 91–136, esp. 112. On this particular issue, see also Barański, "*Sole nuovo*," 177. In Franco Ferrucci's view, Dante's claim in fact means the opposite. See Ferrucci, *Il poema del desiderio: Poetica e passione in Dante* (Milan: Leonardo, 1990), 91–124, esp. 99, originally published as "Comedìa," *Yearbook of Italian Studies* 1 (1971): 29–52. For Teodolinda Barolini (*The Undivine Comedy*, 59), the meeting with Geryon represents Dante's reflection on the "inauthenticity inherent in all narrative."

DEFINING THE *COMMEDIA*'S GENERIC MONSTROSITY   101

sing. / We stopped to look into the next crevasse / of Malebolge and heard more useless weeping.)

While at *Inferno* 17 Dante names his *comedìa* in connection with an appeal for readers' trust in the face of Geryon, here he implies the historical reality of the journey beyond what he chose to report in the poem. After opening with another passing remark on the *Commedia*'s realism, however, the triptych of the barrators closes with the author's note on the parallelism between the episode he just narrated and one of Aesop's fables—"la favola d'Isopo" (*Inferno* 23.4). This Aesopic reference sparked a large critical debate over the centuries. The discussion, however, has tended to explain away rather than explore the poet's counterintuitive move, thus obscuring its theoretical implications. A look at the specific episode and its glosses helps appreciate this fact.

Naming Aesop in *Inferno*

In *Inferno* 21, at the outset of Dante's adventures in the *bolgia* of the grafters, a group of frightful-looking devils, the Malebranche (Evil Claws), offer to "escort" Dante and Virgil to a standing pathway over the next infernal pit. A decidedly naive Virgil proves incapable of reading the devils' true intentions and, against Dante's counsel, accepts their offer. Two cantos later, after the Malebranche devils begin scuffling among themselves, Dante and Virgil, silently and unnoticed, part with their dangerous company. The brutal rage of their escort, however, does not seem to have affected Virgil's naive confidence. As they hurry on their way to the next pit, Dante is once more the first to sense the imminent peril. Inspired by a recollection perhaps dating back to his school days, the pilgrim has a sudden realization:

> Taciti, soli, sanza compagnia
> n'andavam l'un dinanzi e l'altro dopo,
> come frati minor vanno per via.
>   Vòlt'era in su la favola d'Isopo
> lo mio pensier per la presente rissa,
> dov'el parlò de la rana e del topo;
>   ché più non si pareggia "mo" e "issa"
> che l'un con l'altro fa, se ben s'accoppia
> principio e fine con la mente fissa.
>   E come l'un pensier de l'altro scoppia,
> così nacque di quello un altro poi,
> che la prima paura mi fé doppia.
>   Io pensava così: "Questi per noi
> sono scherniti con danno e con beffa

102   DANTE'S EDUCATION

> sì fatta, ch'assai credo che lor nòi.
>   Se l'ira sovra 'l mal voler s'aggueffa,
> ei ne verranno dietro più crudeli
> che 'l cane a quella lievre ch'elli acceffa."
>
> (Inferno 23.1–18)

(Silent, alone, and unescorted / we went on, one in front, the other following, / as Friars Minor walk along the roads. / The present fracas made me think of Aesop— / that fable where he tells about the mouse / and frog; for "near" and "nigh" are not more close / than are that fable and this incident, / if you compare attentively the end / of one with the beginning of the second. / And even as one thought springs from another, / so out of that was still another born, / which made the fear I felt before redouble. / I thought: "Because of us, they have been mocked, / and this inflicted so much hurt and scorn / that I am sure they feel deep indignation. / If anger's to be added to their malice, / they'll hunt us down with more ferocity / than any hound whose teeth have trapped a hare.")

At this point, a strikingly comic episode unfolds: the most sacred and revered of all Roman poets, Virgil, finally understands his protégé's sense of foreboding and, offering his own body as a sled, grabs Dante and slides down a slope![9]

Dante's reference to Aesop's tale of "the mouse / and frog" presupposed this fable's popularity among contemporary readers, who were expected to recall the ill-fated journey of the mouse and frog and to guess the cause of the protagonist's anxiety. Which versions of this tale Dante read remains difficult to assess, however, as evidence does not allow us to single out one tradition in the vast Aesopic corpus. During the Middle Ages, Aesop's name identified the beast fable genre rather than a specific author or text. None of the fable collections circulating during this period was in fact Aesop's.[10] Instead, his authority labeled a vast and heterogeneous corpus of texts that had penetrated the medieval literary canon through

---

[9] Many scholars have followed Robert Hollander's view that Virgil's humiliation at the hands of the Malebranche represents the inadequacy of his high, tragic poetry to deal with the reality of lower Hell (see Hollander's commentary on *Inferno* 21). It is debatable, however, whether Dante condemns Virgil for his overconfidence, thus undermining his epic poetry, or instead depicts him as a tragic hero at odds with the comic world of Malebolge (the latter view, for instance, is proposed by Steinberg, *Dante and the Limits of the Law*, 164). I find that both readings are equally convincing, as the suspension of the narrator's point of view on this matter is deliberate. Unlike Steinberg, I believe that Virgil's failure should be interpreted in light of the overarching comic quality of these cantos.

[10] McKenzie ("Dante's References to Aesop," *Annual Report of the Dante Society* (1898): 1–14, at 2) maintains that "to the mediaeval mind as to the ancient mind, all fables were Aesop's fables." As it will become apparent in the next section, however, this generalization is too sweeping. See also Mann, *From Aesop to Reynard*, 2–3. Aesop's original fables (sixth century BC) are lost. Modern critics even doubt that Aesop actually existed and suspect that he may have been no more than a legendary figure. In what follows, I present only a brief summary of the complex history of Aesop's reception in Western

DEFINING THE *COMMEDIA*'S GENERIC MONSTROSITY   103

two distinct traditions: one deriving from Phaedrus' fable collection, composed in Latin iambic senarii during the first century AD, and the other from Avianus' fables (fourth to fifth century AD), which followed instead a subsidiary tradition originating with the Greek writer Babrius (second century AD?).[11] Phaedrus' fables were recast into two prose collections during the Carolingian period. The most popular of these prose versions was the so-called *Romulus vulgaris*, which became a key source for later fable collections.[12] Sometime between the twelfth and thirteenth centuries, the *Romulus vulgaris* was converted back into poetry, this time in the elegiac meter.[13] The author of the so-called elegiac *Romulus* is unknown but has been traditionally, albeit erroneously, identified as Walter of England, bishop of Sicily.[14] Because of its suitability for teaching verse and morality, on account of its polished style and relative brevity, the elegiac *Romulus* acquired such an overwhelming popularity that in the late Middle Ages it eclipsed almost all other fable

literary history. For a more comprehensive account of this history, see Niklas Holzberg, *The Ancient Fable: An Introduction* (Bloomington: Indiana University Press, 2002).

[11] Although in the opening lines of his collection Phaedrus defines the matter of his work as "Aesopic," his actual source remains unknown (Mann, *From Aesop to Reynard*, 7). Avianus also acknowledges Aesop as the father of the genre but names Phaedrus and Babrius as his primary sources, albeit the former remains only a nominal source. In 1217, Alexander Neckam reworked six of Avianus' fables in a small collection known as *Novus Avianus*, which was clearly meant for teaching. See Jill Mann, "La favolistica latina," in *Aspetti della letteratura latina nel secolo XIII (Atti del primo Convegno Internazionale di studi dell'Associazione per il Medioevo e l'Umanesimo, Perugia 3–5 ottobre 1983)*, ed. Claudio Leonardi and Giovanni Orlandi (Florence: La Nuova Italia, 1986), 193–219, esp. 194. See also Léopold Hervieux, *Les fabulistes latins, depuis le siècle d'Auguste jusqu'à la fin du Moyen Âge* (New York: Burt Franklin, 1965).

[12] Three versions of the *Romulus vulgaris* are known: the *Wissemburgensis*, the *Gallicana*, and the *Vetus*. All three have been edited by Georg Thiele in his *Der lateinische Äsop des Romulus und die Prosa-Fassungen des Phädrus. Kritischer Text mit Kommentar und einleitenden Untersuchungen* (Hildesheim: Georg Olms, 1985). A prose version that had a considerable influence on the later beast fable tradition is the so-called *Romulus Nilantii*. Even though the date of its composition is uncertain, the *Nilantii* appears to have been written no later than the eleventh century. From the *Nilantii*, Marie de France derived the first forty fables of her collection, and Alexander Neckam reworked thirty-seven fables of his *Novus Aesopus*. Ademar of Chabannes (988–1034), a monk of Saint Cybard in Angoulême, copied a collection of sixty-seven fables into a composite manuscript that includes works on grammar and other educational texts. Ademar's wording reveals contacts with both Phaedrus and the *Romulus vulgaris*. See Ferruccio Bertini, *Il monaco Ademaro e la sua raccolta di favole fedriane* (Genoa: Tilgher, 1975), 58, and *Ademaro di Chabannes, Favole*, ed. Ferruccio Bertini (Genoa: Università degli Studi, Facoltà di Lettere, Dipartimento di Archeologia, filologia classica e loro tradizioni, 1988), 31.

[13] The date of the elegiac *Romulus* is uncertain, but Jill Mann (*From Aesop to Reynard*, 11n55, 102n19) notes that it was quoted in Nigel of Longchamp's *Speculum stultorum*. This fact would indicate that it was composed sometime before 1190. It is also worth noting that the elegiac *Romulus* features elements derived from Ademar of Chabannes's collection. See Sandro Boldrini, "L'Aesopus' di Gualtiero Anglico," in *La favolistica latina in distici elegiaci Atti del Convegno Internazionale, Assisi, 26–28 ottobre 1990*, ed. Giuseppe Catanzaro and Francesco Santucci (Assisi: Accademia Properziana del Subasio, 1991), 79–106.

[14] The author of this collection was long known as the Anonimus Neveleti, from one of its early editors, Nicholas Nevelet, until Léopold Hervieux claimed to have identified the author as "Walter the Englishman" (*Les fabulistes latins*, I², 475–95). The evidence in support of this identification has been generally called into doubt; see Klaus Grubmüller, *Meister Esopus: Untersuchungen zu Geschichte und Funktion der Fabel im Mittelalter* (Munich: Artemis, 1977), 78, and Paola Busdraghi, *L'Esopus attribuito a Gualtiero Anglico* (Genoa: Pubblicazioni del Dipartimento di Archeologia, Filologia classica e loro Tradizioni, 2005), 11–15. The elegiac *Romulus* was edited by Hervieux (*Les fabulistes latins*, II², 316–51). The most recent critical edition is by Paola Busdraghi.

104   DANTE'S EDUCATION

collections and came to be known as the *Aesopus latinus*. Before the elegiac *Romulus* gained this prominence, however, Avianus' poetic fables had been the most popular "Aesop" in medieval grammar schools.[15] The success of the elegiac *Romulus* never entirely eclipsed Avianus, which continued to appear in fourteenth- and fifteenth-century school anthologies.[16]

As shown by extant manuscripts, these two poetic collections represented Aesop in the classrooms of late medieval Florence. Worth mentioning here is a thirteenth-century manuscript, Florence, Biblioteca Nazionale Centrale, Magliabechiano VII.931 (Figure 3.1; also Figure 1.3), that transmits fables from the elegiac *Romulus*, glossed in the school manner by two principal hands writing at about the same time as the copyist. The interlinear glosses consist of simple Latin paraphrases, word-order marks, and vernacular equivalents; the marginalia feature grammatical explanations, and there is also a short conventional *accessus* to Aesop.

---

[15] From the seventh to the tenth century, Avianus' fables were used in schools almost everywhere in Europe, as is apparent from the large number of surviving manuscripts and from the fables' presence alongside the *Disticha Catonis* in the *Liber Catonianus*-type of anthologies from the ninth century on. See Marcus Boas, "De Librorum Catonianorum historia atque compositione," *Mnemosyne*, n.s., 42 (1914): 17–46; Edith C. Jones, "Avianus in the Middle Ages: Manuscripts and Other Evidence of Nachleben" (Ph.D. diss., University of Illinois, 1944); and Eva M. Sanford, "The Use of Classical Latin Authors in the *Libri Manuales*," *Transactions and Proceedings of the American Philological Association* 55 (1924): 190–248. Instead, manuscripts of Aesop—that is, of the *Romulus*, in its different versions and rewritings—are rare before the tenth century. Thereafter, references to Aesop in lists of school texts, as well as Aesop's presence in school miscellanies, become increasingly frequent. See Armando Bisanti, "La tradizione favolistica mediolatina nella letteratura italiana dei secoli XIV e XV," *Schede Medievali* 24–25 (1993): 34–51, esp. 35. In her edition, Busdraghi lists 190 manuscripts of the elegiac *Romulus* that date between the thirteenth and the fifteenth centuries and are preserved in libraries across Europe (*L'Esopus*, 203–24). Some manuscripts feature the text of the elegiac *Romulus* alone, but several others transmit it together with other school texts such as the *Disticha Catonis*, the *Ecloga Theoduli*, and the *Facetus*. In his *Laborintus* (609–10), Heberard the German quotes the prologue of the elegiac *Romulus* to identify Aesop among other school texts. See Edmond Faral, *Les arts póetiques du XIIe et du XIIIe siècle: Recherches et documents sur la technique littéraire du moyen âge* (Paris: Champion, 1924), 358. The first lines from this prologue are also quoted by Hugh of Trimberg in his *Registrum multorum auctorum*: *Das "Registrum multorum auctorum" des Hugo von Trimberg; Untersuchungen und Kommentierte Textausgabe*, ed. Karl Langosh (Berlin: Ebering, 1942), 5. The work's popularity lasted into the age of print, as it was included in the school anthology known as "Auctores octo," first published at Lyon in 1488 and reprinted in as many as fifty editions by 1544. See Rino Avesani, *Quattro miscellanee medioevali e umanistiche* (Rome: Edizioni di Storia e Letteratura, 1967), 21, and Aaron E. Wright, *The Fables of "Walter of England"* (Toronto: Pontifical Institute of Mediaeval Studies, 1997), 1–5.

[16] In his *Dialogus super auctores* (*ca.* 1130), Conrad of Hirsau prescribes both *Aesopus* and Avianus for instructing beginners in Latin. Conrad also explains that students should read Aesop first, and only thereafter should they move on to Avianus (R. B. C. Huygens, ed., *Accessus ad auctores, Bernard d'Utrecht, Conrad d'Hirsau: Dialogus super auctores; Édition critique* [Leiden: Brill, 1970], 455). School anthologies often featured both Aesop and Avianus rather than Aesop alone. See Bonnie Fisher, "A History of the Use of Aesop's Fables as a School Text from the Classical Era through the Nineteenth-Century" (Ph.D. diss., University of Indiana, 1987), 103–24. On the coexistence of the two collections in the classrooms of medieval Italy, see Paul Gehl, *A Moral Art: Grammar, Society, and Culture in Trecento Florence* (Ithaca, NY: Cornell University Press, 1993), 241–79.

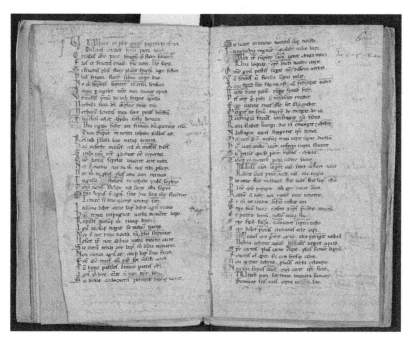

Figure 3.1 Florence, Biblioteca Nazionale Centrale, Magliabechi VII.931 fol. 6r. Detail of the fable "De mure et rana" from the elegiac *Romulus*: "Muris iter rumpente lacu, venit obvia muri…" (right folio, third line from the top).

Source: Courtesy of the Italian Ministry of Culture/Biblioteca Nazionale Centrale, Florence. Reproduction or duplication by any means is strictly prohibited.

Scholars have increasingly pointed to the relevance of the elegiac *Romulus* for Dante's knowledge of Aesop's "The Frog and the Mouse."[17] This collection, however, had many medieval imitators, commentators, and vernacular translators

---

[17] Worth noting among Dante's medieval commentators is the author of *Commento d'Anonimo Fiorentino*, who defines the *Isopetto* as a collection of "fioretti come piacque allo scrittore," echoing the first line from the elegiac *Romulus*. Kenneth McKenzie argues that the elegiac *Romulus* "is undoubtedly the *parvus libellus* mentioned by Benvenuto, and probably also the Isopo di Buti." McKenzie, "Dante's References," 8. More recently, Armando Bisanti ("Tradizione," 39) returned to support Da Buti's and Benvenuto's view insisting on the overwhelming popularity of Aesop's *De iuvene et Thaide* as a source for Dante's representation of Thais (*Inferno* 18.127–35). Critics, however, have increasingly doubted the validity of Bisanti's proposal, either reasserting the relevance of Terence's *Eunuchus* as the model of Dante's Thais or pointing to other, more suitable medieval sources, such as John of Salisbury's *Policraticus*. See Zygmunt G. Barański, "'Primo tra cotanto senno': Dante and the Latin Comic Tradition," *Italian Studies* 46, no. 1 (1991): 1–36, and Ezio Raimondi, "Notarella dantesca (a proposito di Taide)," in *Lettere Italiane* 17 (1965): 443–46, reprinted as "La Bibbia e Taide" in Raimondi, *Metafora e storia: studi su Dante e Petrarca* (Turin: Einaudi, 1970), 199–207. Guglielmo Barucci has recently argued for the importance of the *Romulus vulgaris* as source for Dante's reference to Aesop. See Barucci, "Dante e la favolistica esopica: Mondo classico e tradizione medioevale," in *"Nostra maggior musa": I maestri della letteratura classica nella Commedia di Dante*, ed. John Butcher (Città di Castello: Edizioni Nuova Prhomos, 2021), 21–36. Lately, it has been suggested that Dante read some versions of both the *Romulus vulgaris* and the elegiac *Romulus* at different times during his intellectual formation—the former probably while in school and the latter later in life. See Barucci, "Dante e la favolistica esopica," esp. 29,

106 DANTE'S EDUCATION

whose works might have mediated his knowledge of it.[18] Furthermore, Aesopic morals were part of Florence's popular culture and independently circulated, both orally and in various genres of texts.[19]

It is precisely on account of the popularity of "The Frog and the Mouse" among Dante's contemporary readers that his reference to this fable at *Inferno* 23 appears somewhat puzzling. The fable's different versions all share the same basic plot: an evil frog takes a mouse across a pond with the treacherous intention of drowning it; a bird of prey (a kite in most versions) spots the two animals struggling in the water and snatches both in its claws.[20] Despite the poet's insistence, this fable does not afford an entirely suitable parallel with the events narrated in this canto, and medieval commentators have struggled to explain Dante's emphasis on the close parallelism that would unite the two stories—"più non si pareggia 'mo' e 'issa'" (for "near" and "nigh" are not more close).[21] Even Benvenuto da Imola, who endeavors to justify Dante's claim, cannot avoid stumbling on some evident incongruities between the two stories.[22] Most commentators bypass the issue by interpreting this reference as a moralizing conclusion to the episode narrated in the preceding canto, which ended in the brawl ("rissa") between the Malebranche. There is some disagreement, however, over whether the character of the sinner Ciampolo would represent the mouse or the frog, or whether the devils Calcabrina and Alichino fighting in the pitch should be associated with the frog and the mouse while either

and Luca Marcozzi, "Dante ed Esopo," in *Dante e il mondo animale*, ed. Giuseppe Crimi and Marcozzi (Rome: Carocci, 2013), 131–49. This, however, remains on the level of speculation.

[18] This large corpus includes Marie de France's Old French Ysopet and about twenty vernacular translations in Provençal, French, Veneto, and Tuscan. See Bisanti, "Tradizione," 36–40; Sandro Boldrini, "Introduzione," in Gualtiero Anglico, *Uomini e bestie, le favole dell'Aesopus latinus* (Lecce: Argo, 1994), 8; Vittore Branca, "Introduzione," in *Esopo toscano dei frati e dei mercanti trecenteschi* (Venice: Marsilio, 1989), 9–62; and Carlo Filosa, *La favola e la letteratura esopiana in Italia: Dal medio evo ai nostri giorni* (Milan: Vallardi, 1952), 6. McKenzie ("Dante's References," 10n5) argues that in *Convivio* 4.30 Dante may be quoting an Italian version of the *Romulus*. Recently, Mariangela Semola pointed to Dante's possible knowledge of a fable by Odo of Cheriton. See Semola, "Dante e l'exemplum animale: Il caso dell'aquila," *L'Alighieri* 31 (2008): 149–59.

[19] For a brief overview of some significant examples of Aesopic quotations in medieval texts from Tuscany, see Barucci, "Dante e la favolistica esopica."

[20] The fable of the mouse and the frog is number 382 in Ben E. Perry, ed., *Aesopica* (Urbana: University of Illinois Press, 1952), and number 244 in Émile Chambry, ed., *Aesopi fabulae* (Paris: Les Belles Lettres, 1925–26). The original plot was already in Phaedrus and can be found in the several rewritings of the *Romulus*, such as those by Alexander Neckam and Odo of Cheriton. The versions of the fable differ regarding elements such as whether the mouse is alive or already dead at the moment the kite grabs the two. All versions present a similar moral, which focuses on the theme of fraud and deception. Alexander Neckam, for instance, concludes: "Quisquis credentem sibi prodit, proditur; ille, / sicut rana suo iure perit laqueo." See Alexander Neckam, *Novus Aesopus*, ed. Giovanni Garbugino (Genoa: Dipartimento di Archeologia, Filologia classica e loro Tradizioni, 1987), 65, lines 11–12.

[21] For a discussion of the differences between the two texts, see Enzo Mandruzzato, "L'apologo 'della rana e del topo' e Dante," *Studi Danteschi* 33 (1955): 147–65.

[22] Benvenuto, comm. *Inferno* 23.7–9. In the same gloss, Benvenuto adds that he does not see the similarity between the beginning and end of the two stories: "Sed dices forsan, lector: nescio per me videre quomodo istae duae fictions habeant inter se tantam convenientiam circa principium et finem Aesopi."

DEFINING THE *COMMEDIA*'S GENERIC MONSTROSITY   107

Barbariccia or the hot pitch would play the role of the kite. Both ancient and modern commentators have often endorsed some version of the latter interpretation.[23] More recently, instead, some scholars have pointed to similarities between Dante and the mouse, on the one hand, and Virgil and the frog, on the other.[24] But even this reading is not entirely persuasive and leaves substantially unchallenged Ludovico Castelvetro's criticism that Dante simply did not draw a suitable parallel here.[25]

In Sam Guyler's view, the elegiac *Romulus*'s version of this fable holds the key to deciphering the author's insistence on the close resemblance between his adventure with the Malebranche and Aesop's "The Frog and the Mouse." Dante's son, Pietro Alighieri, quotes several lines from this version in his commentary ad locum, thus supporting the hypothesis that this was the fable more familiar to his father. A look at the elegiac version of "The Frog and the Mouse," I believe, helps assess the soundness of Guyler's argument:[26]

> De mure et rana
>
> Muris iter rumpente lacu venit obvia muri
> > rana loquax et opem pacta nocere cupit.
> Omne genus pestis superat mens dissona verbis,
> > cum sentes animi florida lingua polit.
> Rana sibi murem filo confederat; audet
> > nectere fune pedem, rumpere fraude fidem.
> Pes coit ergo pedi, sed mens a mente recedit.
> > Ecce natant. Trahitur ille, sed illa trahit.
> Mergitur ut secum murem demergat: amico

---

[23] Benvenuto is the first to draw parallels between the characters in the two stories (Calcabrina with the frog, Alichino with the mouse, and Barbariccia with the kite). They, however, appear weak, especially the parallel of Barbariccia with the kite. Among modern critics who support this or similar views, see McKenzie, "Dante's References to Aesop," and Marcozzi, "Dante ed Esopo," 131–49, esp. 143. Among modern readers, Mandruzzato ("Apologo," 158–60) objects to the mainstream interpretation endorsed by McKenzie. For yet another parallel reading, see Neil M. Larkin, "Another Look at Dante's Frog and Mouse," in *Modern Language Notes* 77, no. 1 (1962), 94–99. For an exhaustive summary of different glosses on Dante's reference to Aesop, see Robert Hollander (who lists eleven of them), "Virgil and Dante as Mind-Readers (Inferno XXI and XXIII)," *Medioevo Romanzo* 9 (1984): 85–100, esp. 92–93n15.

[24] Slightly different versions of this thesis have been proposed by Sam Guyler, "Virgil the Hypocrite—Almost: A Re-Interpretation of *Inferno* XXIII," *Dante Studies* 90 (1972): 25–42; Hollander, "Virgil and Dante"; and Juan Varela-Portas de Orduña, "Función y rendimiento de la fábula de Esopo en la 'Divina Commedia' ('Inf.' XXIII 1–9)," *Medioevo y Literatura* 4 (1995): 439–51.

[25] Castelvetro, comm. *Inferno* 23.4–6.

[26] Sam Guyler, "Virgil the Hypocrite." For the relevant passages in Pietro Alighieri's commentaries, see Pietro Alighieri (2) (1344–55[?]), *Inferno* 23.4–6, and (3) (1359–64), *Inferno* 23.4–9. In her critical edition, Paola Busdraghi titles the fable "De mure et rana" in observance of the larger number of manuscripts carrying this title. Some manuscripts, however, transmit the alternative title "De rana et mure," which more closely recalls Dante's formulation: "de la rana e del topo" (*Inferno* 23.4). See Busdraghi, L'Esopus, 50.

108   DANTE'S EDUCATION

naufragium faciens naufragat ipsa fides.
Rana studet mergi, sed mus emergit et obstat
naufragio: vires suggerit ipse timor.
Milvus adest miserumque truci rapit ungue duellum:
hic iacet, ambo iacent, viscera trita fluunt.

Sic pereant qui se prodesse fatentur et obsunt.
Discat in auctorem pena redire suum.[27]

(A mouse finds his way blocked by a pond. / A croaking frog, while offering him help, secretly wishes to harm. / A mind that is not in harmony with words is the worst plague, / when embellished language polishes a soul filled with thorns. / The frog binds the mouse to itself by means of a string; it dares / to tie a foot with a rope and break faith with fraud. / Their feet are together like one, but one mind withdraws from the other. / They swim now: one is pulled, while the other pulls. / The frog plunges to submerge the mouse: by drowning the friend, trust itself drowns. / The frog tries to dive in, but the mouse resurfaces and fights against being drowned: / fear heightens its strength. / A kite flying by snatches the two miserable fighters with its deadly talons: / one dies, both die, their entrails flowing away. / Thus may perish those who offer to help and instead harm, / thus may sorrow return to its maker.)

The narrative setting and key ingredients of this story provide the first significant parallel with Dante's adventure: the fable begins with a mouse whose journey is hindered by an insurmountable obstacle, a frog who promises to help but has a treacherous mind, and the mouse's naive faith in the frog. The same situation leads to the unbecoming alliance between Virgil and the Malebranche. Both stories, moreover, end with a fight, "rissa," between two characters in a liquid: Aesop's mouse and frog struggle in the water, while Dante's devils fight in the pitch. The narrative parallel between the two stories is also key to their rapprochement in the protagonist's mind, as it is the event of the "rissa" that prompts Dante's memory of the fable. Whereas this narrative setting and development are not exclusively found in the elegiac version of "The Frog and the Mouse," its twofold moral— featured both at the beginning, the *promythium* (A mind that is not in harmony with words is the worst plague, / when embellished language polishes a soul filled with thorns), and at the end, the *epimythium* (Thus perish those who offer to help

---

[27] Busdraghi, *L'Esopus*, 50. The translation is mine. Busdraghi does not include the following four-line epimythium in her edition of Aesop's fables: "Incidit in foveam quam fecerit insidiator; / in laqueum fraudator cadit ipse suum. / In proiectorem proiectus dat lapis ictum, / quando venenosa prosilit ille manu." This ending can be found instead in Julia Bastin's edition *Recueil Général des Isopets*, vol. 2 (Paris: H. Champion, 1930), 9–10.

DEFINING THE *COMMEDIA*'S GENERIC MONSTROSITY   109

and instead harm, / thus may sorrow return to its maker)—is specific to this version and fits Dante's insistence on the relevance of the story's "beginning and end"
(*Inferno* 23.10).[28] When set next to each other, promythium and epimythium show
that not only are Dante's and Aesop's narratives similar, but so are also their moral
lessons. At the end of *Inferno* 23, the Malebranche episode concludes with the
revelation—made by the hypocrite friars in the following *bolgia*—that no standing bridge connects the pit of the grafters with that of the hypocrites. Like Aesop's
frog, therefore, the Malebranche devils had been meaning to deceive Virgil and
Dante all along. In both stories, moreover, the fraudulent guides fall victim to his
own deceptions.

If Dante's devils act like Aesop's frog and kite, then Dante and Virgil would play
the mouse's part. Yes and no. The narrative situation of their arrival to the fifth *bolgia*, and Virgil's mouselike naivete in dealing with the Malebranche, set them up
to become the victims of a straightforward remake of Aesop's "The Frog and the
Mouse." With Ciampolo's intervention, however, the story takes a different spin,
leaving the Aesopic moral premise partially unfulfilled—Dante and Virgil escape
the trap unhurt. The spectacle of the devils' fighting in the pitch and lifted up in
midair reminds Dante of the fable's end, thus causing a second thought to spring
from this first one ("And even as one thought springs from another, / so out of
that was still another born"): like the innocent mouse of the fable, who shares
the evil frog's fate, Dante and Virgil too had been in danger of becoming victims
of the devils. They made a narrow escape, however, and now have an opportunity to rewright the end of the story. The pilgrim is able to avert the tragic end of
the fable *because* he has read Aesop and learned the fable's lesson—unlike Virgil,
apparently.[29] One of the defining characteristics of Aesop's fables is the "belated
quality" of their morals: usually characters cannot learn from the disasters that
befall them.[30] While Virgil, with his caricatural naivete, perfectly embodies the
Aesopic type, Dante instead is able to break free from the fable's narrative and
moral determinism.

Commentators on the *Commedia* have often attempted to reconcile the apparent inconsistencies of Dante's Aesopic parallel from a narrative, a moral, or an
allegorical perspective. I argue instead that such incongruities point to Dante's

---

[28] Tellingly, these are precisely the excerpts of the elegiac fable quoted by Pietro Alighieri in the
third version of his commentary ad locum (Pietro Alighieri [3] [1359–64], *Inferno* 23.4–9). The first
distich is also quoted, though slightly modified, in the famous *Compendium moralium notabilium* by
the Paduan Geremia da Montagnone (1250–1321). Quoted in Barucci, "Dante e la favolistica esopica,"
34.

[29] With regard to Virgil's evident lack of preparation in facing the ethical situation mirrored by
Aesop's "The Frog and the Mouse," Steinberg rightly points out that "confronted with the true nature
of evil, higher learning and reason prove less effective than proverbial truths" (*Dante and the Limits of
the Law*, 162).

[30] Mann, *From Aesop to Reynard*, 38.

110   DANTE'S EDUCATION

creative appropriation of the fable genre.[31] Dante calls on readers to pay attention to his close reinterpretation of Aesop's plot, which, like "mo" and "issa," is both similar to and crucially different from the original. This emulative exercise evokes a popular practice in medieval Latin instruction. Composition was the crowning activity in the study of Aesop's fables: after analyzing and summarizing a given tale, pupils would proceed to rewrite it, while retaining the story's general moral. Interpretation, in other words, led to reinterpretation. If, however, "the fable-moral is closely tied to the fable-fiction," as Jill Mann has it, and "each fiction yields its own specific conclusion," by changing the end of "The Frog and the Mouse" Dante altered one of the genre's most defining traits and a well-established educational practice. The theoretical implications of such a creative appropriation become more apparent when considered from the perspective of Aesop's reception in medieval education.

"Finzioni d'Esopo": Fable and Fiction in Medieval Education

Two principal channels of instruction contributed to the popularity of Aesop's fables in medieval and Renaissance Italy: preaching and grammar. According to Aristotle's *Rhetoric*, fables are a type of oratorical example; together with parables, fables rely on made-up events as a persuasive mode of discourse, a type of proof common to all branches of rhetoric (1393b). Vernacular homiletics continued to draw on the power of Aesop's fables to engage and persuade. The use of fables in sermons increased steadily during the thirteenth century and was consolidated by the concurrent diffusion of exemplary literature.[32] As a result, the morals of the stories often underwent considerable changes, and new, detailed interpretations were provided by medieval preachers and writers. Dante shows great distress at the widespread misuse of fables among contemporary preachers. In *Paradiso* 29, the poet uses the term "favola" to condemn the practice of making up stories to include in sermons: "quante sì fatte favole per anno / in pergamo si gridan quinci

---

[31] For a narrative interpretation, see Giorgio Padoan, "Il 'Liber Esopi' e due episodi dell'"Inferno,'" in *Il Pio Enea, l'empio Ulisse* (Ravenna: Longo, 1977), 151–69. Lucia Battaglia Ricci has recently re-endorsed Padoan's thesis; see Battaglia Ricci, "Canto XXIII: 'Imagini di fuor / imagini d'entro'; Nel mondo della menzogna," in *Lectura Dantis romana: Cento canti per cento anni; Inferno; 2; Canti XVIII–XXXIV*, ed. Enrico Malato and Andrea Mazzucchi (Rome: Salerno, 2013), 740–69. For a different narrative reading, see Hollander, "Virgil and Dante," 95. Juan Varela-Portas de Orduña instead argues that an allegorical interpretation is the key to solving this conundrum. See Varela-Portas de Orduña, "Función y rendimiento."

[32] Filosa, *La favola*, 6, 35–36. Vincent of Beauvais's *Speculum historiale* and his *Speculum doctrinale* are often quoted as evidence of the increased use of Aesopic fables in thirteenth-century homiletic and exemplary literature. In both works, the author incorporates twenty-nine fables from the *Romulus vulgaris*. See Mann, *From Aesop to Reynard*, 14–16.

DEFINING THE *COMMEDIA*'S GENERIC MONSTROSITY   111

e quindi" (as it has tales like these that are proclaimed / from the pulpit, here and there, throughout the year) (104–05).[33]

While preachers were drawn to fables because of their simplicity, their persuasive force, and the vivid impression they made on listeners, teachers were interested in the fables' suitability for exercising elementary Latin composition and versification. Parsing and paraphrasing fables had been a common educational practice since antiquity. Both Quintilian and Priscian, for instance, recommended that young pupils' first assignment should include fables.[34] From Isidore to Alcuin, the fable was granted a definitive place in elementary education, which became the primary context of its medieval reception. Alexander Neckam's *Novus Aesopus* helps illustrate this point, as it features a clearly didactical format; it provides different versions of each fable, suggesting that, to practice composition and versification, pupils were expected to paraphrase, summarize, or expand on narratives while retaining the original moral. Thus, Aesop became a staple of the *Liber Catonianus*-type anthology and a favorite of teachers in late medieval Europe. Several outlines for programs of study from the eleventh to the thirteenth century recommended that Aesopic fables, together with the *Disticha Catonis*, should be among the first texts that pupils read after mastering the *Donatus*.[35] This pedagogical practice was also popular in the schools of Dante's Florence, as can be surmised from the fourteenth-century commentary on the *Commedia* by Francesco da Buti, already quoted in Chapter 2: "Isopo è uno libello che si legge a' fanciulli che imparano Grammatica, ove sono certe favole moralizzate per arrecarli a buoni costumi" (Aesop is a booklet that is read to children when they are learning grammar and that contains some moralized fables that teach them how to live a decent life).[36]

Francesco da Buti's remark shows that, while suitable for teaching grammar, fables were also ideal for moral instruction. Their notable status in medieval education depended also on their reputation for inspiring probity, a virtue that was traditionally linked to Aesop's name.[37] Aesop was chiefly seen as the teacher of a

---

[33] Another relevant passage from *Paradiso* is "Per apparer ciascun s'ingegna e face / sue invenzioni; e quelle son trascorse / da' predicanti" (Each strives to gain attention by inventing new ideas, / expounded by the preachers at some length) (94–95).

[34] Quintilian, *Institutio Oratoria* 1.9.2 and 5.2.19, and Priscian, *Praexercitamina* 551–60, "De fabula."

[35] See Chapter 1.

[36] Francesco da Buti, comm. *Inferno* 23.1–18. The translation is mine. Boccaccio also confirms Aesop's popularity in his letter to Jacopo Pizzinga, also quoted in Chapter 2. In support of the thesis that Dante read Aesop while in school are Marcozzi, "Dante ed Esopo," 136, and Padoan, "Il 'Liber Esopi,'" 157–60, esp. 160. On the steady presence of the *Aesopus latinus* in late medieval Florentine schools, see Robert Black, *Education and Society in Florentine Tuscany* (Leiden: Brill, 2007), 144, and Gehl, *Moral Art*, 135–58.

[37] Ironically, the opposite is true for Aesop's traditional portraits in the ancient *Vitae*, where the character of Aesop is represented as a Frigian slave, famous for his trickery and indecency. Tradition also claims that Aesop's ingenuity gained him a monument. See Edward Wheatley, *Mastering Aesop: Medieval Education, Chaucer, and His Followers* (Gainesville: University Press of Florida, 2000), 18–31, esp. 21.

112 DANTE'S EDUCATION

practical and earthly form of wisdom, as asserted by Conrad of Hirsau: "Hesopus iste claruit in Frigia, *seculari admodum* peritus scientia" (This Aesop flourished in Phrygia, a man who had a considerable grasp of *secular learning*).[38] Mann points out that fables' practical wisdom and ingenuity were "invoked in order to recommend or warn against some course of action in a specific historical situation."[39] Thus, the genre was seen as a vehicle for spreading traditional wisdom.[40] On account of their easy memorability and proverbial flavor, fables appealed to a broad audience. Aesop's morals also had independent lives and circulated as proverbs, which are often found quoted in vernacular texts from medieval Italy.[41]

Besides perpetuating established wisdom, fables had a major educational advantage: reading them entertained students. In Cicero's *De Inventione*, the fable is presented as a type of narrative that, albeit recited or written for amusement, also provides valuable training.[42] The dedicatory epistle that opens the *Romulus* also singles out this key feature of fable narrative: "Id ego Romulus transtuli de graeco (sermone) in latinum. Si autem legeris, Tiberine fili, et pleno animo advertas, invenies apposite ioca, que tibi *multiplicent risum* et *acuant satis ingenium*" (I, Romulus, have translated this from Greek to Latin. If you read it, Tiberinus, my son, and give it your undivided attention, you will find well-devised entertainments, *which will make you laugh and will sharpen your intellect*).[43] Amusement coupled with instruction sets the fable apart from other narrative genres, as further clarified by the verse prologue to Walter's *Liber Aesopi*: "Ut iuvet et prosit pagina presens: / dulcius arrident seria picta iocis" (May this page give profit and assistance; / sweeter are serious teachings when embellished with jokes).[44]

What makes fables amusing and particularly appealing to children is their fiction. Children, Quintilian explains, do not yet object to the rading of fiction (*Institutio Oratoria* 5.11.19). The very term *fabula* was used in medieval Latin to signify "narrative," "fiction," "myth," and "fable." It also became the standard

---

[38] Huygens, *Accessus*, 383 (emphasis added). Translation in Alistair J. Minnis, A. B. Scott, and David Wallace, eds., *Medieval Literary Theory and Criticism, c. 1100–c. 1375: The Commentary-Tradition* (New York: Clarendon Press, 1988), 47.

[39] Mann, *From Aesop to Reynard*, 5. See also Wheatley, *Mastering Aesop*, 12.

[40] Georg Thiele has well encapsulated this idea in the term "kulturhistorischen Fablen." See Thiele, *Der lateinische Äsop*, 78.

[41] In *Tresor* 2.64.3, for instance, Brunetto quotes one of Aesop's apologues within a list of authoritative texts, including Seneca and Salomon, to support the practical advice that one should never be eloquent around one's enemies. Dante too, as already mentioned, reports the epimythium from Aesop's "The Cock and the Pearl" as a proverb in *Convivio* 4.30.4. Other similar examples of Aesopic proverbs that might have been known to Dante are in Henry of Settimello's *Elegia* (1.251, 2.225, 2.238, 4.94, and 4.139). For other contemporary examples, see Barucci, *Dante e la favolistica esopica*, 21–24.

[42] Cicero, *De Inventione*, 1.19.27.

[43] Quoted and translated in Wheatley, *Mastering Aesop*, 64; emphasis added. For textual variants of the *Romulus*'s epistle, see Thiele, *Der lateinische Äsop*, 2–4. The same purpose is offered also in the dedicatory epistle introducing Avianus. See Avianus, "Fabulae," in *Minor Latin Poets*, ed. J. Wight Duff and Arnold M. Duff (Cambridge, MA: Harvard University Press, 1968), 669–749, esp. 680–82.

[44] Busdraghi, *L'Esopus*, 8n7.

DEFINING THE *COMMEDIA*'S GENERIC MONSTROSITY   113

translation of the Greek "μῦθος" (mûthos). Dante too sometimes uses the vernacular term *favola* with the same meaning of mythological fable. In *Convivio* 2.4.5, "la favola di Fetonte" (Phaeton's fable) identifies ancient myth with allegorical meanings. In *Convivio* 2.1.3, instead, Dante deploys the term more broadly to identify poetic fictions with allegorical meaning: "L'altro si chiama allegorico, e questo è quello che] si nasconde sotto 'l manto di queste favole, veritate ascosa sotto bella menzogna" (The next is called the allegorical, and this is the one that is hidden beneath the cloak of these fables, and is a truth hidden beneath a beautiful fiction). This definition relies on the theory of *integumentum*, or *cortex* (wrapping or shell) that was developed in twelfth-century Platonic allegorical commentaries of classical texts produced in the milieu of Chartres.[45] Hence, *fabula* identified both specific genres of fictional narratives, such as Aesop's or mythological fables, and also the fiction common to poetry and literature in general. Conrad of Hirsau provides an eloquent example of the universal adaptability of the term to any fictional narrative: "fabula enim ficta res est, non facta, unde a fando nomen accepit" (for fable is fiction, not fact, hence it gets its name from *fando* [speaking]).[46] *Fabula*, therefore, encapsulated the medieval understanding of poetry and of literature more broadly, as fiction whose purpose "ethice subponitur" (pertains to ethics).[47]

In his *Etymologiae*, Isidore of Seville points out that fables are fictitious because they break the laws of nature: "fabulae vero sunt quae nec factae sunt nec fieri possunt, quia *contra naturam sunt*" (fables are things that have not happened and cannot happen, because they are *contrary to nature*).[48] Within the realm of "unnatural" fiction, the Aesopic fable is consistently defined by late antique and medieval writers on account of three features: the presence of speaking beasts

---

[45] For the influence of the twelfth-century concept of *integumentum* on the *Convivio*, see Gianfranco Fioravanti, comm. ad loc., in Dante Alighieri, *Convivio; Monarchia; Epistole; Egloge*, ed. Gianfranco Fioravanti et al., vol. 2 of *Opere*, ed. Marco Santagata (Milan: Mondadori, 2014), 215. For recent studies on Dante's peculiar use of allegory and the language of *integumentum*, see Veronica Albi, *Sotto il manto delle favole: la ricezione di Fulgenzio nelle opere di Dante e negli antichi commenti alla Commedia*, (Ravenna: Longo editore, 2021); Francesco Zambon, "Allegoria e linguaggio dell'ineffabilità nell'autoesegesi dantesca dell' 'Epistola a Cangrande,'" in *L'autocommento*, ed. G. Peron (Padua: Esdra, 1994), 21–30; and Zambon, *Allegoria: una breve storia dall'antichità a Dante* (Rome: Caocci, 2021), esp. 149–63. For an "applied" study of the allegorical interpretation that developed in the milieu of Chartres see Justin Haynes's recent study *The Medieval Classic: Twelfth-Century Latin Epic and the Virgilian Commentary Tradition* (Oxford: Oxford University Press, 2021).

[46] Huygens, *Accessus*, 390. Translation from Minnis, Scott, and Wallace, *Medieval Literary Theory*, 47. Macrobius, in his *Commentarii in Somnium Scipionis*, had already explained that "fabulae, quarum nomen indicat falsi professionem." Ambrosius Aurelius Theodosius Macrobius, *Commentarii in Somnium Scipionis*, ed. J. Willis (Leipzig: Teubner, 1963), 1.2, 7–9.

[47] The *Accessus Aviani* openly states this moral aim: "Materia eius [of the fables] sunt ipsae fabulae et commune proficuum allegoriae, intentio eius est *delectare* nos in fabulis et prodesse in correctione morum. . . . *Ethicae subponitur*, quia tractat de corretione morum." Huygens, *Accessus*, 22–25; emphasis added.

[48] Isidore, *Etymologiae*, 1.44.5. The Latin text is quoted from the online edition in *The Latin Library*, accessed February 2022, https://www.thelatinlibrary.com/. Translation is from Stephen A. Barney, J. A. Beach, and Oliver Berghof, eds., *The Etymologies of Isidore of Seville* (Cambridge: Cambridge University Press, 2006). Emphasis added.

114   DANTE'S EDUCATION

(*fabula Aesopica*) or speaking beasts and men (*fabula libica*), moral instruction coupled with playful entertainment, and the fable's status as a merely fictitious narrative.[49] Conrad of Hirsau defines the Aesopic fable's specific type of fiction in terms that help readers set it apart from other literary genres:

> Differunt autem Hesopi fabulae ad morum finem relatae et delectandi gratia confictae a commentis mendacibus Terentii, Plauti et aliorum similium poetarum, quia, etsi aliquo modo veritati compendebat quod isti de negotiis humanarum rerum vel personarum confixerunt, quod Hesopus confinxit nec fuit umquam nec fieri potuit.[50]

> (However, Aesop's fables, related for the purpose of moral instruction, differ from the deceptive inventions created for the sake of entertainment by Terence, Plautus, and other similar poets, because, although in some way Aesop condensed truth regarding the affairs of human things or characters that those poets invented, what Aesop fabricated never was nor could ever be.)

Especially notable is Conrad's distinction between fable and the genre of the ancient Latin comedy, "commentis mendacibus Terentii, Plauti." As Conrad explains, fable and comedy present different degrees of fiction: although both genres feature fictitious narratives, fables tell stories that never happened and are utterly impossible, while comedies' fictitious stories are verisimilar. Cicero points out that *fabula* differs from the other two types of narrative, *historia* and *argumentum*, in that it recounts neither true nor verisimilar facts.[51] Cicero's distinction is echoed in the *volgarizzamento* of Brunetto Latini's *Tresor*, where "fabula" is said to recount "cose che non sono vere, né a vero somigliano" (things that are neither true nor verisimilar) (8.38).[52] On the same presupposition, in the *Vita nova* Dante steers clear from including details that might come across as "parlare fabuloso" (fable-like language) (2.10) and taint the realism of his autobiographical narrative. The same distinction remained in use in late medieval exegesis, as shown by a fourteenth-century commentary on Avianus that is contained in the manuscript Erfurt, Amplon. Q. 21: "fabula est sermo fictus qui nec est verus nec verisimilis" (the fable is a made-up discourse that is neither true nor verisimilar).[53]

The same conception of fable as synonymous with sheer fiction is echoed in Giovanni Dominici's *Regola del governo di cura familiare*, written in Florence

---

[49] Jan Ziolkowski, "The Form and Spirit of Beast Fables," *Bestia: Yearbook of the Beast Fable Society* 2 (1990): 4–18, esp. 7.

[50] Huygens, *Accessus*, 398–404. The translation is mine.

[51] Cicero, *De Inventione* 1.19.27.

[52] *Il Tesoro di Brunetto Latini volgarizzato da Bono Giamboni* (Venice: Co' tipi del Gondoliere: 1839), 304.

[53] Robert Gregory Risse, "An Edition of the Commentary of the Fables of Avianus in Erfurt MS., Amplon Q.21: The Text and its Place in Medieval Literary Culture" (Ph.D. diss., Washington University, 1964), 101–02.

DEFINING THE *COMMEDIA'S* GENERIC MONSTROSITY   115

between 1400 and 1405. Complaining about contemporary humanist education and expressing nostalgia for the books that children used to read in school in the good old days of Florence, Dominici lists a traditional curriculum of readings. Among the canonical school texts, Aesop is featured with the eloquent label "finzioni d'Esopo" (Aesop's fictions):

> La prima cosa che insegnavano era il salterio e la dottrina sacra; e se gli mandavano più oltre, avevano moralità di Catone, *finzioni d'Esopo*, dottrina di Boezio, buona scienza di Prospero tratta di santo Agostino, e filosofia d'Eva columba, o Tres leo naturas, con un poco di poetizzata scrittura santa nello Aethiopum terras; con simili libri, de' quali nullo insegnava il mal fare.[54]

> (The first thing they were taught was the Psalter and the sacred doctrine. Then, if they went on with their education, they would read: Cato's morality [i.e., the Distichs of Cato]; *Aesop's fictions*; Prosper's Epigrammata, drawn from Saint Augustine; philosophy from Prudentius' Dittochaeon; the Phisiologus; a little poetic Scripture from the Eclogue of Theodulus; with such books, in other words, that taught nothing wrong.)

Readers who had been trained on Aesop's "finzioni," and who knew the essential difference between fables and comedies, might have found puzzling Dante's reference to the fable "The Frog and the Mouse" at the end of his adventure with the Malebranche. After he had sworn in front of Geryon that his "comedy" recounts unbelievable but nonetheless true events, and after he confirmed the poem's genre at the outset of the grafters' three cantos ("la mia comedìa," *Inferno* 21.2), his ending the same episode by pointing out the close similarity between his and Aesop's narratives represented a theoretical contradiction. Dante, I argue, referenced the father of the fable at *Inferno* 23 to signal his deliberate blowing up of the traditional boundaries imposed on literary genres by medieval education and exegesis: his *comedìa* is not a fable, yet it amuses and instructs readers with an impossible narrative, like one of Aesop's fables. Medieval treatises, such as Isidore's *Etymologiae*, taught that fable breaks natural rules, as it is *contra naturam*, whereas comedy preserves a status of verisimilitude. Clearly, by recounting a miraculous journey to the otherworld, Dante's *Commedia* was an exception to this rule from the outset.[55] Dante's engagement with the Aesopic *fabula* extends far beyond his reference

---

[54] Giovanni Dominici, *Regola del governo di cura familiare*, ed. D. Salvi (Florence: A. Garinei, 1860), 134; emphasis added. The translation is mine.

[55] Early commentators clearly perceived this apparent contradiction in Dante's mixing of literary genres with different degrees of verisimilitude and tried to explain it. Boccaccio (*Inferno*, "Introductory Note"), for instance, maintains: "Sono ancora le cose che nelle comedìe si racontano cose che per avventura mai non furono, quantunque non sieno sì strane da' costumi degli uomini che essere state non possano: la sustanziale istoria del presente libro, dell'essere dannati i peccatori, che ne' loro peccati

116   DANTE'S EDUCATION

to "The Frog and the Mouse" in *Inferno* 23, creating a large intertextual network underlying his representation of lower Hell.

The Frog, the Mouse, and Dis

Aesop's name resounds in Malebolge at a key narrative transition in the pilgrim's descent through lower Hell, as Dante's enterprise is threatened by the devils' insubordination. Let us briefly consider the major narrative elements that make up the three cantos of the grafters:

1. Dante's journey is threatened by the devils.
2. Dante and Virgil disagree on how to deal with their present circumstances (*Inferno* 21, 127–35).
3. Virgil is incapable of bringing about a resolution to their impasse, thereby jeopardizing Dante's trust in his guide's authority.
4. The sinners are compared to frogs in a pond: "E come a l'orlo de l'acqua d'un fosso / stanno i ranocchi pur col muso fuori" (And just as in a ditch at water's edge / frogs squat with but their snouts in sight) (*Inferno* 22.25–26); "ch'una rana rimane e l'altra spiccia" (that one frog stays while yet another plunges) (33).
5. The events narrated take three *canti* to unfold, thereby creating a sort of "structural enjambment."[56]
6. In the preceding canto—before the unfolding of the quarrel that prompts the poet's recollection of Aesop's fable "de la rana e del topo"—Dante addresses the reader with an invitation to prepare for a new "ludo": "O tu che leggi, udirai nuovo ludo" (Now, reader, you shall hear strange sport) (*Inferno* 22.118). The term "ludo" introduces the events that follow as a form of "play." I shall return to this obscure address later.
7. In the following canto, *Inferno* 23.9, the author provides an important hermeneutic key for interpreting the events that are unfolding in light of Aesop's intertextual parallel. Dante warns that these events should be interpreted "con la mente fissa" (with circumspection) to appreciate their parallels with Aesop's fable "The Frog and the Mouse."

Dante's ordeal with the Malebranche, however, is not the first time that the devils threaten his journey. Already at *Inferno* 8–9, when the protagonist is about to pass through the city of Dis and descend from upper to lower Hell, a new kind of devil shows up and refuses to grant him passage. Here again, Virgil appears clueless and

---

muoiono, a perpetua pena, e quegli, che nella grazia di Dio trapassano, essere allevati alla eterna gloria, è, secondo la catolica fede, vera e stata sempre."

[56] Battistini, "Il 'ver c'ha faccia di menzogna,'" 68.

DEFINING THE *COMMEDIA'S* GENERIC MONSTROSITY   117

unable to overcome the unexpected obstacle, and Dante's mission is on the verge of being jeopardized, until a powerful messenger from God arrives to free the way for the pilgrim. The parallel between the two impasses narrated at *Inferno* 8–9 and 21–23 has long been noted—not so, however, the evidence that the two sets of cantos feature identical narratives and similar extradiegetic elements:

1. Dante's journey is threatened by the devils almost to the point of being compromised at the gates of Dis.
2. Dante and Virgil do not agree on how to overcome this perilous impasse (*Inferno* 8.97–108).
3. Virgil's authority is undermined by the devils when they shut him out of Dis (*Inferno* 8.112–17). Although trusting in God's certain aid, Virgil is puzzled and disquieted by the devils' resistance and his own powerlessness (8.118–20). As a result, for the first time since the beginning of their journey, Dante doubts Virgil's ability to guide him through the underworld (*Inferno* 9.1–3).
4. Here, too, the sinners are compared to frogs (*Inferno* 9.76).
5. The events around the city of Dis take up three *canti*.
6. Finally, the poet introduces the arrival of the celestial "messo" (messenger) with an address to the reader, this time with an invitation to look for the truth hidden under the "velame de li versi strani" (veil of these strange verses) (*Inferno* 9.61–63).

The mirroring quality of *Inferno* 8–10 and 21–23 sheds a light on the correlation between the poet's addresses to the reader in these two sets of cantos and their entanglements with the genre of Aesop's fable. At *Inferno* 9, Dante apparently invites readers to interpret his poem as an allegory, discarding the literal surface of the story in favor of its moral meaning: "O voi ch'avete li 'ntelletti sani, / mirate la dottrina che s'asconde / sotto 'l velame de li versi strani" (O you who have sound intellects, / consider the teaching that is hidden / behind the veil of these strange verses) (*Inferno* 9.61–63). Giorgio Padoan notes the similarity between the poet's summoning of those with "sound intellects" here and his subsequent admonition, at *Inferno* 23, to observe with "mente fissa" (circumspection) the analogy between Aesop's fable "The Frog and the Mouse" and the "rissa" (brawl) of the devils. Padoan, moreover, explains that "Dante here [*Inferno* 23] refers to the allegorical and moral meaning rather than to the literal sense of this episode" and observes that "Aesop too . . . is a book filled with teachings in which the events narrated are not as relevant as the morality they teach."[57] I take Padoan's suggestion even further and argue that, by means of a subtle intertextual reference, Dante already confronts the genre of Aesop's moralized fictions at *Inferno* 9.

[57] Padoan, "Il 'Liber Esopi,'" 98–99.

118   DANTE'S EDUCATION

The poet's invitation to the reader to look "behind the veil of these strange verses," in *Inferno* 9.61–63, is followed by the arrival of the "messo celeste" (messenger from Heaven), which terrorizes the wrathful—who are submerged in the bog of the Styx, outside of Dis—and causes them to leap out of the marsh. Dante compares them to frogs fleeing a water snake:

> Come le rane innanzi a la nimica
> biscia per l'acqua si dileguan tutte,
> fin ch'a la terra ciascun s'abbica,
> vid'io più di mille anime distrutte
> fuggir così dinanzi ad un ch'al passo
> passava Stige con le piante asciutte.
>
> (*Inferno* 9.77–81)

> (As frogs, before the snake, / all scatter through the water / til each sits huddled on the bank, / I saw more than a thousand lost souls flee / before one who so lightly passed across the Styx / he did not touch the water with his feet.)

Most medieval commentators explain the simile of wrathful-frogs and *messo*-snake with a moral interpretation drawn from either the medieval *Physiologus* or another moralized bestiary. The *Ottimo commento*, for instance, claims that the snake is a fitting comparison for the celestial messenger, as in Scripture the snake often represents wisdom and intelligence: "per la quale proprietate della sapienza ch'elli ebbe, sono molto saputi li serpenti" (this is on account of the messenger's wisdom, as snakes are full of wisdom). In contrast, as Benvenuto argues, frogs always represent impurity and evil: "ranae sunt nigrae, turpes, infectae . . . rana est animal foedum" (frogs are black, dirty, and deformed . . . the frog is a filthy animal).[58] Modern commentators instead point to the classical origin of Dante's simile and suggest that its source may be a passage from Ovid's version of the story of Latona and the rustics who are turned into frogs (*Metamorphoses* 6.370–81). Whereas Ovid's frogs provide a suitable source for Dante's representation of the wrathful quarreling under the bog (especially *Metamorphoses* 6.374–76), one conspicuous absence undermines the relevance of this source for the simile of the frogs chased by the snake: no mention of a snake is made in Ovid's story.[59]

---

[58] Ottimo, comm. *Inferno* 9.76; Benvenuto, comm. *Inferno* 9.76. The translation is mine. For an exhaustive discussion of the sources that informed with moral significance Dante's reference to the frogs in *Inferno*, see Giuseppe Ledda, *Il bestiario dell'aldilà* (Ravenna: Longo, 2019), 138–49.

[59] Reference to this source can often be found among modern commentators, as in Charles S. Singleton, for instance (comm. *Inferno* 9.76–78). Ledda (*Il bestiario dell'aldilà*, 144–49) rereads Ovid's precedent as relevant for understanding the metapoetic significance of Dante's reference to the frogs here.

DEFINING THE *COMMEDIA*'S GENERIC MONSTROSITY   119

I believe that Dante's simile of the frogs and the snake may instead constitute a precise reference to Aesop's fable "De ranis et ydro" ("The Frogs and the Snake"), as suggested by the title's close resemblance to the poet's simile. A look at the elegiac *Romulus*'s version of this story further substantiates this impression:

De ranis et ydro

Cum nichil auderet ludentes ledere ranas,
    supplicuere Iovi ne sine rege forent.
Iupiter huic voto risum dedit. Ausa secundas
    rana preces subitum sensit in amne sonum.
Nam Iove dante trabem, trabis ictu flumine moto
    demersit subitus guttura rauca timor.
Placato rediere metu, videre tigillum,
    stando procul regem pertimuere suum.
Ut novere trabem per se non posse moveri,
    pro duce fecerunt tertia vota Iovi.
Ira Iovem movit, regem dedit, intulit ydrum.
    Ydrus hiante gula cepit obire lacum.
Clamitat ecce lacus: "Morimur, pie Iupiter, audi
    Iupiter, exaudi Iupiter, affer opem!
Nos sepelit venter, nostri sumus esca tyranni,
    aufer cedis opus, redde quietis opes."
Ille refert: "Emptum longa prece ferte magistrum,
    vindicet eternus otia spreta metus."

Omne boni pretium nimio vilescit in usu,
    fitque mali gustu dulcius omne bonum.
Si quis habet quod habere decet, sit letus habendo.
    Alterius non sit, qui suus esse potest.

(When nothing dared bother the playing frogs, / they implored Zeus lest they should remain without a king. / Zeus laughed at their prayer. / A frog, encouraged, dared repeat these prayers and heard a sudden noise in the river. / Since Zeus had given them a log for a king, the water, hit, was set in motion. / Immediately fear submerged the croaking throats. / When their terror ceased, they came back; they saw the little log. / From a distance, they had feared their king. / Once, however, they understood that the log couldn't move on its own, / for the third time they begged Zeus for a king. / Outraged, Zeus gave them a king: he sent the snake. / The snake began to swim around the lake with its mouth open. / And

120 DANTE'S EDUCATION

from the lake rose a loud cry: "We die, o good Zeus, hear us, Zeus, grant us, oh Zeus, give help! / His belly is our grave, we are food for the tyrant, take away the author of the massacre, / give us our peace back." / The god replies: "Bear the master you begged for so long, / may eternal fear vindicate the peace you have despised." / The value of every good decreases with continuous enjoyment / and every good becomes sweeter when evil is tasted. / If someone has what is decent, may he be satisfied. / May he belong to no one, he who is the master of himself.)

On closer examination, "The Frogs and the Snake" presents remarkable narrative and moral parallels with *Inferno* 8 and 9. Blind and irrational, the frogs beg Zeus for a king, when they could instead enjoy freedom and independence. Warned a first time by Zeus' mocking message—the log falling from heaven—the frogs keep on begging for a king. They finally succeed in rousing Zeus' fury, and the god sends them the deadliest messenger of his rage, the snake. As soon as the snake reaches the pond and starts swimming in it with its mouth open, terror overcomes the frogs as they cry out to Zeus, this time asking him to free them from their new tyrant. But the request comes too late.

When one substitutes Dante's devils for Aesop's frogs, the two stories overlap in interesting ways: like the frogs of the fable, the devils try to oppose God's will by blocking the pilgrim's way; they also ignore God's first warning in Virgil's attempt to parley with them (*Inferno* 8.86–93, 112–20); finally, their insistence causes God to send a powerful messanger. Like the snake of the story, the celestial *messo* approaches the water of the Styx; like Aesop's frogs, sinners and devils flee in terror. Although the devils never ask for God's intervention, and do not wish to be ruled by a divinely appointed sovereign, their relative independence, too, is disrupted as a result of their pointless stubbornness.[60] Thus, by comparing the souls of the wrathful to the frogs being chased by the snake (*Inferno* 9.77), Dante points readers' attention to the evident parallel with Aesop's fable.

Dante's allusion to Aesop's fable "The Frogs and the Snake" should also inflect our understanding of the poet's address to the reader only a few lines before, when he invites them to consider "la dottrina che s'asconde / sotto 'l velame de li versi strani" (the teaching that is hidden / behind the veil of these strange verses) (*Inferno* 9.62–63). This enigmatic authorial intervention is among the most obscure and glossed passages of the whole poem and has often been at the center

---

[60] Moreover, both Dante's and Aesop's stories can be suitably interpreted as political allegories of the independent cities that proudly oppose a superior, transregional power, such as the emperor, and in so doing lose their privileges and freedom. The moral theme of Walter's fable and its variants was sometimes read in explicitly political and historical terms. The commentary on Walter of England's fables transmitted in the MS Wolfenbüttel, Herzog August Bibliothek, Codex Guelferbytanus 185 Helmstadiensis, interprets a version of this fable, titled *De ranis regem petentibus*, as the historical allegory of Athens. See Wright, *Fables*, 70.

of the critical debate about Dante's stance regarding medieval allegory and its role in the poem. Most medieval commentators take Dante's address as an invitation to read allegorically the events of the "siege" of Dis—particularly the advent of Medusa and the other furies—the literal and narrative meaning of which should be discarded merely as *ficta res* (fiction) devised for the moral instruction of the reader. As Veronica Albi notes, Dante's address draws on the allegorical lexicon developed by Bernardus Silvester and William of Conches for mythographic exegesis, which similarly informs the passage from *Convivio* that I have mentioned above (2.1.3). Some of these earliest commentators draw on Fulgentius and interpret Medusa as an allegory of terror, while others follow the Vatican mythographers and see her as embodying *oblivium* (forgetfulness). Both interpretations, therefore, present Medusa as the allegory of a major obstacle in Dante's journey of spiritual knowledge.[61] Applying a similar hermeneutic key, while also drawing on the Pauline opposition of literal and spiritual understandings of the Bible, John Freccero has seen Dante's address to the reader as an invitation to move beyond a faithless, literalist reading of the text to embrace instead the journey of conversion traced by the pilgrim.[62]

Other modern critics have argued that the whole episode of the divine messenger of *Inferno* 9 would reenact, both typologically and liturgically, Christ's descent into Hell—*descensio Christi ad inferos*. This biblical precedent provides a fitting model for the advent of the divine *messo*, at the end of the canto.[63] This typology also allows the recovery of the literal meaning of Dante's "siege" of Dis as historically true, in the fashion of biblical allegory. Dante, therefore, would claim that the divine envoy did in fact come down from Heaven to free the way for the pilgrims. The mysterious events typologically and liturgically reenact Jesus's storming of Hell.

I would like to contribute to the rich and ongoing scholarly conversation on these cantos by observing that Dante's allusion to Aesop's fable "The Frogs and the Snake" complicates his address to the reader, only a few lines earlier, by bringing yet another type of fictional narrative into the spectrum of hermeneutic possibilities thematized by this canto. As already noted, the address features terminology proper to medieval allegorical exegesis. A similar process of interpretation is also proposed by the prologue of the elegiac *Romulus*: "Verborum levitas morum fert / pondus honestum, et nucleum / celat arida testa bonum" (the lightness of the words bears / the honest weight of morals, / and the arid head covers a good kernel) (*Aesopus*, 1.11–12). Unlike Dante's verses, which are "strange" and heavy

---

[61] Albi, *Sotto il manto*, 176–78.

[62] John Freccero, "Medusa: The Letter and the Spirit," in *Dante: The Poetics of Conversion*, ed. Rachel Jacoff (Cambridge, MA: Harvard University Press, 1986), 119–35, at 135.

[63] This thesis has been recently reassessed by Pietro Cagni, "Il messo celeste e la liturgia alle porte di Dite (*Inferno* IX)," *Le Forme e la storia* 9, no. 2 (2016) [*Lecturae Dantis: Dante oggi e letture dell'*Inferno]: 229–50.

122   DANTE'S EDUCATION

with doctrine, however, Aesop's fiction is "light." Such lightness seems out of place within the allegorical weight of this canto.

It is also necessary to note that Aesop's brand of moralized stories is technically not allegorical. As Mann convincingly argued, Aesop's type of *fabula* is "fundamentally and avowedly a fiction," and would be misleading to classify it as allegory. In beast fables, Mann continues, "there is no sense of penetrating to an 'underlying reality.'" As described in the previous section, unlike mythological and biblical allegories, Aesop's fables cannot be explained historically, nor can they be viewed as exemplifying universal truths. Their fiction is outspoken, irreversible, and the very heart of their mode of discourse.[64] Mann's distinction of a specific brand of Aesopic *alieniloquium* foregrounds its relevance in Dante's narrative thematization of the difficulties and perils entailed by hermeneutics in *Inferno* 9. Here, not only does the poet engage with biblical and mythological allegories, as readers have often pointed out about his address to the readers, but he also gestures toward Aesop's type of unnatural fiction. Dante's dangerous meddling with this type of fiction may cause the poem to stall, as symbolized by Medusa's advent. It also foreruns Geryon's appearance and the poet's acknowledgment of the poem's genre and complicated relationship with truth. Aesop's veiled presence in *Inferno* 9, therefore, belongs to the overarching discourse the poet articulates across the two clusters of cantos of Dis (*Inferno* 8–10) and the grafters (21–23). Both contain Aesopic references and have Geryon at their center. Dante's close dialogue with the genre of the Aesopic fable in these cantos may hold the key to unlocking this theoretical complex.

"Mia comedìa," "nuovo ludo," and "favola d'Isopo"

After addressing readers at *Inferno* 9 and 16, Dante turns to them again at *Inferno* 22, when the culminating act of his adventure with the Malebranche devils is about to unfold. In anticipation of their "rissa" (brawl), which prompts the pilgrim's memory of Aesop's fable "The Frog and the Mouse," Dante warns readers to prepare for the ludicrous spectacle of Ciampolo's race against the devils, when the former tricks the latter into setting him free: "O tu che leggi: udirai nuovo ludo"

---

[64] Mann, *From Aesop to Reynard*, 33. Mann's clarification is helpful for our purposes but should not be generalized, as the term "allegoria" is used by both ancient and medieval writers to refer to Aesop's fables. At least in theory, fable's chief trope was considered allegory, in the sense of Isidore of Seville's standard definition of *allegoria* as *alieniloquium*—a speech that says one thing to mean something different (*Etymologiae* 1.1.37.22). Quintilian, for instance, maintains that Aesopian apologues that are used like proverbs should be understood allegorically (*Institutio Oratoria* 5.11.21). Also, medieval *accessus* and glosses on Aesop's fables deploy this terminology, as exemplified by the *accessus* to Avianus quoted earlier. Pietro Alighieri explains that Dante's reference to Aesop's "The Frog and the Mouse" is supposed to recall the allegorical meaning of the fable and illustrate the sin of barratry: "qui [the grafters] pleni sunt omnibus fallaciis et deceptionibus, de quibus allegorice sensit Ysopus in illa sua fabula *De Mure et Rana* quam tangit hic auctor."

(Now, reader, you shall hear strange sport) (*Inferno* 22.118). In classical Latin, "ludus" means "game" or "drama," and in medieval sources the same word denotes either "sport" and "competition" or "sacred drama."[65] Scholars have suggested that Dante's use of the term "ludo"—hapax legomenon in *Inferno*—is possibly a specific indication of literary genre. More recently, Mira Mocan has linked the word to the ancient French genre of the *jeu*, a theatrical form that was both comic and moralizing, while Lino Pertile has described the three cantos of the grafters as Dante's experiment with the genre *eroicomico* (comic epic). For Leo Spitzer, the "ludo" instead introduces a farcical "interlude" in Dante's otherwise serious comedy. The poet's reference to Aesop in the following canto would also belong to this momentary generic "descent" of the poem into the realm of farce. Spitzer argues that Dante perceives a "kinship between farce and fable," an argument certainly in tune with the "lightness" traditionally attributed to Aesop's narratives.[66] Yet some medieval sources describe farce and fable as akin only to a certain extent but different on a crucial point: while a defining feature of the genre, the "ludic" component of fables fulfilled a primarily educational objective. The elegiac *Romulus* encapsulates this intrinsically twofold nature of fable in the already-quoted introductory poem of the collection (*Aesopus* 1.1–6). Here fables are defined as "seria picta *iocis*" (serious things embellished with *jokes*), confirming that the fable's jokes and entertainment served moral and didactic purposes.[67]

The fact that Dante deploys the generically charged term "ludo" precisely one canto after referring to his poem as a "comedìa" (*Inferno* 21.2), and one canto before comparing it to Aesop's fable (*Inferno* 23.4), may provide further clues to the term's theoretical meaning. One more look at Isidore of Seville's *Etymologiae* further highlights the significance of Dante's sequential use of these three technical terms:

Fabulas poetae quasdam delectandi causa finxerunt, quasdam ad naturam rerum, nonnullas ad mores hominum interpretati sunt. Delectandi causa fictas, ut eas,

---

[65] For examples of this use in medieval texts, see the entries "jocum" and "jocari" in Du Cange et al., *Glossarium mediae et infimae latinitatis* (Niort: Le Favre, 1883–87), consulted online at http://ducange.enc.sorbonne.fr/. The same conceptual overlapping is also detectable in Dante's use of the terms "gioco" and "ludo." For the different meanings of this term, see Antonio Lanci's entry "ludo" in the *ED*.

[66] In order of mention, see Mira Mocan, "Il 'nuovo ludo' dei diavoli e dei dannati: Lettura di *Inferno XXII*," *Dante Studies* 138 (2020): 152–75; Lino Pertile, "Canti XXI–XXII–XXIII: Un esperimento eroicomico," in *Esperimenti Danteschi: Inferno 2008*, ed. Simone Invernizzi (Genoa: Marietti, 2009), 157–72; Lino Pertile, *Dante popolare* (Ravenna: Longo, 2021), 165–82; and Leo Spitzer, "The Farcical Elements in Inferno, Cantos XXI–XXIII," *Modern Language Notes* 59, no. 2 (1944): 83–88, at 85.

[67] For classical uses of the word "jocus," see the entry in Charlton T. Lewis and Charles Short's *A Latin Dictionary* (Oxford: Clarendon Press, 1879), Perseus Digital Library, Tufts University, http://www.perseus.tufts.edu/.

124   DANTE'S EDUCATION

quas vulgo dicunt, vel quales Plautus et Terentius conposuerunt. . . . Unde et
Aesopi talessunt fabulae ad morum finem relatae.

(*Etymologiae* 1.40.3)

(Poets have made up some fables for the sake of entertainment, and expounded
others as having to do with the nature of things, and still others as about human
morals. Those made up for the sake of entertainment are such as are commonly
told, or that kind that Plautus and Terence composed. . . . Whence Aesop's fables
are the kind told for the purpose of a moral.)

The distinction Isidore proposed between two different types of *fabula* centers
on one crucial opposition: whereas the Latin comedians invented fictional (but
verisimilar) stories solely to entertain their readers, Aesop did so for moral instruction.[68] While the ludic element represents a key means for the fable's educational
aims, amusement is thought to be comedy's main goal. As fiction represents the
source of such entertainment, its meaning and function also differ between the two
genres. Comedy represents the lowest type of narrative because its use of fiction
has no ethical justification.

From this perspective, Dante's exhortation to enjoy the forthcoming "ludo" in
conjunction with his definition of the poem as a comedy would seem to abide
by the traditional assumption that with comedy comes amusement simply for
the sake of entertainment. Hence, the whole Malebranche episode appears to
be devised only to entertain his readers, as Spitzer argues. This interpretation, I
believe, is complicated only one canto later, when Dante claims that the devils'
ludic commotion ("rissa" [brawl]) has a parallel in Aesop's fable "The Frog and
the Mouse." The author, as already discussed, points readers' attention to the textual loci where the moral of a fable is usually explained—the beginning and the
end—as the places where the parallels between the two stories are more apparent.
Thus, while preparing his readers for a new *ludo*, at *Inferno* 22, Dante also marks
his peculiar conflation of *comedìa* and *favola*: his story amuses like a comedy but
instructs like a fable. Furthermore, in a realistic twist, he distances his comedy from
traditional fables by dramatizing the protagonist's ability to learn from Aesop's
wisdom and escape the trap set up for him by the Malebranche devils. Dante's
emphasis on the newness and strangeness of this play—"*nuovo* ludo"—may point
precisely to such an innovative reworking of the fable genre.[69]

---

[68] Macrobius makes the same distinction in his *Commentarii in Somnium Scipionis*, 1.2, 7–9.

[69] I, therefore, disagree with Giuseppe Mazzotta's argument that the "nuovo ludo" would refer to the
devil's "comedy," which enacts the "dangerousness of aesthetics" entailed by Dante's comic enterprise.
For Mazzotta, in these cantos Dante would reject "the profanities" of the comic style as interpreted by
the medieval comic traditions of the *carmina Burana* and the comic and parodic genres, typical of the
vernacular poetry of court jesters. See Mazzotta, *Dante's Vision and the Circle of Knowledge* (Princeton,
NJ: Princeton University Press, 1993), 235–37. The same interpretation had already been proposed by

DEFINING THE *COMMEDIA*'S GENERIC MONSTROSITY   125

At the outset of the three cantos of the grafters, Dante claims that there are some incidents that his comedy does not care to report ("comedìa cantar non cura") (*Inferno* 21.2). In Spitzer's view, this statement implies that the forthcoming farce of the Malebranche is a "whimsical inclusion . . . a 'stuffing'" of Dante's comedy.[70] The opposite, however, seems to be true: the poet's disclosure that he omitted other unimportant facts reinforces the perceived relevance of the following ludic interlude. Dante, I argue, has chosen to include it for the purpose of defining the exceptional nature of his "comedìa," as revealed by the succession of generic markers—*comedìa*, *ludo*, *favola*. Further proof of the metapoetic discourse undergirding the three cantos of the grafters comes from the last lines of the preceding canto, where the character Virgil refers to the *Aeneid* as a tragedy (*tragedìa*) and maintains that Dante knows it well: ". . . così 'l canta / l'alta mia tragedìa in alcun loco: / ben lo sai tu che la sai tutta quanta" (. . . and thus he is sung / in certain verses of my lofty tragedy, / as you know very well, who know it well) (*Inferno* 20.112–14). The adjective "lofty" leaves little doubt as to the theoretical opposition that readers are meant to draw between Virgil's high tragedy and Dante's low "comedìa," named at the opening of the following canto.

Dante had already discussed this generic opposition years before, in his *De vulgari eloquentia*, where he argued that the tragic style is the most suitable for treating lofty subject matters, as opposed to the humble language and subject matter that are characteristic of the comedy: "per tragediam superiorem stilum inducimus; per comediam inferiorem" (*De vulgari eloquentia* 2.4). In *Malebolge*, however, Dante shows no intention of operating according to these strict classifications. At the opening of the same canto, *Inferno* 20, for the first time since the beginning of the poem Dante provides some indications of the *Commedia*'s structure. The technical language adopted by the author, however, associates his poem with the lofty genre of the epic—or tragic—song: "Di nova pena mi conven far versi / e dar matera al ventesimo *canto* / de la prima *canzon* ch'è d'i sommersi" (Of strange new pain I now must make my verse, / giving matter to the canto numbered twenty / of this *canzone*, which tells of those submerged) (*Inferno* 20.1–3; emphasis added). Following this solemn opening is another address to the reader, which suggests that the *Commedia*'s subject matter is indeed a tragic one and should provoke tears in readers, but for the purpose of instruction rather than entertainment: "Se Dio ti lasci, lettor, prender frutto / di tua lezione, or pensa per te stesso / com'io potea tener lo viso asciutto" (Reader, so may God let you gather fruit / from reading this, imagine, if you can, / how I could have kept from weeping) (*Inferno* 20.19–21). In *De vulgari eloquentia*, Dante defines the "cantio" precisely as "tragica coniugatio" ("the *canzone* . . . is a connected series of equal stanzas in the tragic style"), whereas

---

Nino Borsellino, "Un nuovo ludo," in *La tradizione del comico: Letteratura e teatro da Dante a Belli* (Milan: Garzanti, 1989), 25–31.

[70] Spitzer, "Farcical Elements," 86.

126   DANTE'S EDUCATION

the *canzone* in the comic style should be called "cantilena" (2.8.8).[71] One cannot help but sense in Virgil's praise of Dante's deep knowledge of the *Aeneid* an invitation for the reader to look back at the opening of the same canto and realize that the author of the *Commedia* has mastered the tragic style and incorporated it in his own poem. Yet, the tragic register that opens *Inferno* 20 clashes with the very different subject matter of the following three cantos of the grafters, where the poet discloses the ludic side of his morally edifying *comedìa*. This generic shift is anticipated in Dante's invitation to "gather fruit" (*Inferno* 20.19) from the horrible vision of the soothsayers, which closely recalls Aesop's exhortation to "carpe fructum" from his amusing fables.

If, for a moment, we zoom out of the *bolgia* of the grafters to consider all the generic markers that Dante disseminates in the cantos hitherto discussed, the outcome is a series of striking theoretical contradictions. At *Inferno* 9, outside the gates of Dis, the author invites readers to interpret the events narrated through a seemingly allegorical process (the teaching "hidden / behind the veil of these strange verses"); this exhortation is followed, only a few lines later, by an allusion to Aesop's fable "The Frogs and the Snake." At *Inferno* 16, before the wonderful monster Geryon appears, the poet creates a technical oxymoron by swearing on his comedy—a genre traditionally defined by verisimilitude—that he truly saw that wonderful monster. At the outset of *Inferno* 20, the author describes the *Commedia* as an epic poem; while beholding the tragic deformity of the soothsayers, moreover, the reader is invited to sympathize with the protagonist's feelings and to draw instruction from the poem; the canto ends with a reference to Virgil's *Aeneid* as *the* tragic (epic) poem. At the beginning of the following canto, *Inferno* 21, Dante calls his poem a comedy once more. *Inferno* 22 contains a third address to the readers to enjoy the forthcoming *ludo*. Finally, at *Inferno* 23, Aesop's fable— fiction that should be read for moral instruction—becomes the reference model for interpreting the violent quarrel that breaks out between the Malebranche devils and endangers Dante's journey. In light of this brief overview, one may conclude that in defining the genre of his poem throughout *Malebolge*, Dante has created a theoretical monster as marvelous and unorthodox as Geryon.

Dante places his meeting with Geryon and titling of the *Commedia* at *Inferno* 16, exactly seven cantos after and seven before two allusions to Aesop's fables—the first at *Inferno* 9 and the other at *Inferno* 23. This evidence suggests that Aesop's fables provide an essential model (and antimodel) in Dante's definition of his

---

[71] Zygmunt G. Barański also notes the generic significance of the technical language Dante deploys at the opening of this canto. See Barański, "The Poetics of Meter: *Terza Rima*, 'Canto,' 'Canzon,' 'Cantica,'" in *Dante Now: Current Trends in Dante Studies*, ed. Theodore J. Cachey Jr. (Notre Dame, IN: University of Notre Dame Press, 1995), 3–41. Other studies have also highlighted the significance of the canto of the soothsayers as a discussion of correct and incorrect ways of reading, particularly with regard to classical texts. See, for instance, Teodolinda Barolini, "True and False See-ers in *Inferno* XX," *Lectura Dantis* 4 (1989): 42–54, and Alison Cornish, *Reading Dante's Stars* (New Haven, CT: Yale University Press, 2000), 43–53.

poem's peculiar genre. The extraordinary instances of beasts that speak, act, and go through all sorts of "risse," as if they were human, were the principal source of diversion (*ludus*) in Aesop's fables. In the *canti* of the grafters, Dante engages with just such subject matter and expects his readers to be amused and amazed. In preparation for his reference to Aesop's fable "The Frog and the Mouse," at *Inferno* 23, Dante fills the preceding canto with a notable concentration of beast similes. Here, sinners and devils are compared to "dalfini," "ranocchi," "lontra," "porco," "gatte," "sorco," "uccello," "anitra," "falcon," "sparvier" (dolphins, frogs, otters, pig, cats, mouse, bird, duck, falcon, sparrow hawk). Together with the two references to Aesop, these may serve as placeholders for the genre of the ancient fable.[72] By introducing in his *Inferno* beast-like demons that speak, fight, and trick one another just as Aesop's beasts do, Dante is aware of violating the generic boundaries between comedy and fable. The evidence that Aesopic echoes begin at the gates of Dis, on the threshold of lower Hell, and concentrate in *Malebolge*, the part of Hell where fraud is punished, provides further proof of the metapoetic significance of this intertextual dialogue.[73] The poet's purpose and invitation to the reader is to move beyond the "ludo" (sport) and observe with "mente fissa" (with circumspection) the miraculous nature of the author's all-encompassing *Commedia*, which entertains and instructs its readers, like a conventional comedy or a fable, and yet surpasses all canonical norms in matters of genre and style.

But Aesop's memories also belong to the daring literary experimentalism that distinguishes these cantos. I concur with Pertile that the cantos of the grafters contain the seeds of a very different poem than the *Commedia* turned out to be. Similarly, Dante's meddling with different degrees of fiction and allegory between *Inferno* 9 and 23 provides a window onto his work in progress, when he was still grappling with different literary genres and contradictory degrees of fiction in the attempt to negotiate a form for the *Commedia*'s marvelous realism.[74]

Three more facts strike me about the Aesopic moments of *Inferno*. First, both times that Aesop surfaces through the text, Dante's journey is on the verge of failing. Perhaps the danger that threatens the protagonist symbolizes the one run by the poem itself when it pushes the boundaries between literary genres. As we learn from the protagonist in front of Geryon, Dante's comedy would indeed fail should the readers interpret it as a fable—that is, as mere fiction. Second, just as in each

---

[72] A different reading is offered by Simone Marchesi, who instead points out that all this animal imagery would reflect the author's close engagement with Ovid, the poet of exile, in coincidence with the sin of which Dante had been accused and for which he was consequently exiled. See Marchesi, "Distilling Ovid: Dante's Exile and Some Metamorphic Nomenclature in Hell," in *Writers Reading Writers: Intertextual Studies in Medieval and Early Modern Literature in Honor of Robert Hollander*, ed. Janet Smarr (Newark, NJ: University of Delaware Press, 2007), 21–39, at 34. For a parodic interpretation of Dante's reference to animals in these cantos, see Ledda, *Il bestiario dell'aldilà*, 129–37.

[73] Besides the two cases that I have just discussed (*Inferno* 9 and 23), critics have noted other covert allusions to Aesop in *Inferno* 18.127–35 and 22.58.

[74] See Pertile, *Dante popolare*, 182.

128 DANTE'S EDUCATION

one of Aesop's fables the author addresses the readers directly either at the fable's beginning or at its end to explain the moral of the story, so also does Dante in the Aesopic cantos of his *Inferno*. The narrator's interventions in these *canti* imitate those of the author in Aesop's fables: namely, they provide a key to interpreting the meaning of the narrative, usually a moral reading, either at the beginning of the fable, through the *promythium*, or at its end, through the *epimythium*. The practice of authorial intervention is a fundamental characteristic of the genre. Finally, it does not seem a coincidence that the three *canti* in which Dante evokes Aesop, meets Geryon, and points to the fluid relationship between literary fiction and truth in *Inferno* should all feature references to frogs and other amphibious beasts. The souls punished in the Styx, outside of Dis, and the barrators are both compared to frogs living across two elements:

> Come le rane innanzi a la nimica
> biscia ...

(Inferno 9.77–78)

(As frogs confronted by their enemy, / the snake ...)

> E come a l'orlo de l'acqua d'un fosso
> Stanno i ranocchi pur col muso fuori,
> sì che celano i piedi e l'altro grosso,
>   sì stava d'ogne parte i peccatori;
> ma come s'appressava Barbariccia,
> così si ritraén sotto i bollori.

(Inferno 22.25–30)

(And just as in a ditch at water's edge / frogs squat with but their snouts in sight / their bodies and their legs all hidden, / So here on every side these sinners crouched; / but faster than a flash, when Barbariccia / drew near, they plunged beneath the boiling pitch.)

Geryon, too, is compared to a beaver as, with his body half on the rim and half floating over the abyss, he waits for the protagonist:[75]

> E quella sozza imagine di froda
> sen venne, e arrivò la testa e 'l busto,
> ma 'n su la riva non trasse la coda.
>   ...
> Come talvolta stanno a riva i burchi,

---

[75] For the moral symbolism implied by Geryon's association with the beaver in relation to medieval sources, see Ledda, *Il bestiario dell'aldilà*, 108–12.

che parte sono in acqua e parte in terra,
e come là tra li Tedeschi lurchi
  lo bivero s'assetta a far sua guerra,
così la fiera pessima si stava
su l'orlo ch'è di pietra e 'l sabbion serra.
  Nel vano tutta sua coda guizzava,
torcendo in sù la venenosa forca
ch'a guisa di scorpion la punta armava.

(Inferno 17.7–27)

(And he came on, that filthy effigy / of fraud, and landed with his head and torso / but did not draw his tail onto the bank. . . . As boats will sometimes lie along the shore, / with part of them on land and part in water, / and just as there, among the guzzling Germans, / the beaver sets himself when he means war, / so did that squalid beast lie on the margin / of stone that serves as border for the sand. / And all his tail was quivering in the void / while twisting upward its envenomed fork, / which had a tip just like a scorpion's.)

That beasts in medieval texts also had metapoetic significance is not news and this fact certainly holds true for the *Commedia*, as Giuseppe Ledda has shown.[76] It seems reasonable, therefore, to suppose that through these references to amphibious animals, Dante may wish symbolically to hint at the amphibious nature of his poem, which crosses over traditionally imposed boundaries among literary genres and specifically between comedy and fable.[77]

Dante's repeated mention of frogs in connection with his forays into the realm of the Aesopic fable could have been polemically addressed against a tradition that originated with early Christian biblical exegesis. Origen of Alexandria, for instance, interprets the frogs that God sent to plague the Egyptians in the book of Exodus as an allegory of the pagan poets, who wrote beautiful but deceiving fables: "Per secundam uero plagam, in qua ranae producuntur, indicari figuraliter arbitror carmina poëtarum qui, inani quadam et inflata modulatione velut ranarum sonis et cantibus, mundo huic deceptionis fabulas intulerunt" (I deem the second plague, when the frogs are sent, to be an allegory of the songs of poets who,

---

[76] See Giuseppe Ledda, "Per un bestiario di Malebolge," in *Dante e il mondo animale*, 92–113; Ledda, "Un bestiario metaletterario nell'Inferno dantesco," *Studi Danteschi* 78 (2013): 119–53, and Ledda, *Il bestiario dell'aldilà*, chap. 4.

[77] Mira Mocan provides a fitting moral explanation to the obsessive presence of frogs and other amphibious animals in the cantos of the barrators. See Mocan, "Il 'nuovo ludo.'" It should also be noted that Dante repeatedly compares Geryon's tail to that of a scorpion (*Inferno* 16.1, 27), and Virgil sits between Dante and the tail in order to shield his disciple from it (*Inferno* 16.83–84). Given Geryon's central place in this network of Aesopic references, one cannot help connecting this particular to the famous Persian fable—not Aesop's this time—of the turtle and the scorpion.

130 DANTE'S EDUCATION

with a certain empty and inflated melody, akin to the noise and songs of frogs, introduced stories of deception). Origen's allegorical interpretation is echoed by medieval exegetes. Caesarius of Arles adds that poets are like frogs in that they make reprobate and inconvenient shouts, and Rupert of Deutz compares croaking frogs to the histrionic performances of poets in theaters.[78] Against the grain of this apologetic tradition, Dante is unafraid of associating himself with the ancient croaking poets and concocting similarly entertaining and fictional stories within the monstrous belly of his own comedy.

Epimythium

Dante's tendency to mix different literary genres and degrees of fiction did not escape the attention of some of his contemporary readers and critics, such as the vernacular poet known as Cecco d'Ascoli.[79] Francesco Stabili was Cecco's real name, and he was a professor of astrology in Bologna. In 1327, only six years after Dante's death, Cecco was burned at the stake in Florence, condemned by the Inquisition as a relapsed heretic. Before his execution, he had been working on a vernacular poem, the *Acerba*, which features a wide range of cosmological, natural, ethical, and theological topics. The project remained unfinished but appears to be conceived as a polemic against the *Commedia*. The *Acerba* targets Dante's use of poetic fiction with particular vehemence and aims to replace it with a new kind of poetry, which popularizes accurate scientific and theological notions. The essence of Cecco's poetics is expounded at the end of Book 4, where the author launches a direct attack against Dante's *Commedia*:

> Qui non se *canta al modo de le rane*,
> qui non se canta al modo del poeta,
> chi finge, imaginando, cose vane:
> ma qui resplende e luce onne natura
> che a chi intende fa la mente lieta;
>
> ...
>
> qui non se sogna per la selva obscura.

---

[78] For the three passages mentioned, see, in order, Origenes, *Homiliae in Exodum (latine Rufino interprete)*, 4.6, in *Sources Chrétiennes* 321, ed. Maurcel Borret (Paris: Éditions du Cerf, 1985), 134, 143–46; Caesarius Arelatensis, *Sermones Caesarii uel ex aliis fontibus hausti*, 99.2, ed. G. Morin, Corpus Christianorum, Series Latina, 103 (Turnhout, Belgium: Brepols, 1953), 404–09; Rupertus Tuitiensis, *Liber Exodus*, (1.32). In *Commentariorum de operibus S. Trinitatis libri XLII*, in *Patrologia Latina*, vol. 167 (Paris: 1854), 565–742. The translations are mine. Manfred Bambeck quotes these and other sources in his study on the apologetic theme of the croaking poets. See Bambeck, "Zur Polemik des Cecco d'Ascoli gegen Dante oder von der Allgengenwart der Allegorese," *Romanistiches Jahrbuch* 31 (1980): 73–77.

[79] I thank Simone Marchesi for graciously pointing me to this conclusive piece of evidence.

DEFINING THE *COMMEDIA*'S GENERIC MONSTROSITY   131

Lasso le çançe e torno un el vero:
la *fabulle* me fon sempre inimiche.
(*Acerba* 4.13.1–18 [4669–86]; emphasis added)[80]

(Here, we don't *sing like frogs*, here we don't sing like the poet,
who invents and imagine vain things. But here all nature shines
and glows, delighting the mind of those who understand. Here we
don't dream in the dark wood. . . . I leave nonsense behind and
return to truth. *Fables* were always my enemies.)

Cecco, a keen reader and critic of the *Commedia*, frowned on Dante's unconventional meddling with the genre of the ancient fable. Cecco points precisely
to Dante's reference to Aesop's "The Frog and the Mouse," at *Inferno* 21, and
denounces him as one of the croaking pagan poets who had been cast out by
Christian exegetes.[81]

As implied by the constant presence of frogs and other amphibious creatures,
such as Geryon, Dante's references to Aesop's frogs in *Inferno* carry greater significance than mere narrative or moral analogies. Aesopic references serve instead as
generic placeholders for the fable. By drawing on this well-known school text, the
poet made plain the groundbreaking nature of his all-encompassing *Commedia*,
which amuses and instructs, like a fable, and breaks all canonical rules in matters
of genre and style, as it claims to be not just a verisimilar comedy but a true one.
The *Commedia*, in other words, is both like and unlike Aesop.

---

[80] Text quoted from Cecchus Asculanus, *Acerba* [*Acerba etas*], ed. Marco Albertazzi (Trento: La
Finestra, 2002). The translation is mine.

[81] Seth Fabian also links Cecco's particular wording to Aesop's mention in *Inferno* 21. See Fabian,
"Cecco vs. Dante: Correcting the Comedy with Applied Astrology" (Ph.D. diss., Columbia University,
2014). Following Bambeck ("Zur Polemik"), Ercole Erculei argues that Cecco was pointing to the larger
apologetic theme of the "croaking poets." See Erculei, "Frogs' Fairy Tales and Dante's Errors: Cecco
d'Ascoli on the Florentine Poet and the Issue of the Relationship between Poetry and Truth," in *Miscellanea Mediaevalia* 40: *Irrtum—Error—Erreur*, ed. Andreas Speer and Maxime Mauriège (Berlin:
De Gruyter, 2018), 669–80. A brief mention of Cecco's possible reference to Dante's frogs and their
metapoetic significance is also in Ledda, *Il bestiario dell'aldilà*, 152–54. Our readings of Dante's frogs
and Cecco's attack, however, differ greatly.

4

Pugna pro patria

Freeing Cato from His *Distichs*

> If you're talking about evil thoughts, give them the Gospel: *De corde exeunt cogitations malae*, "Evil thoughts spring forth from the heart." If your subject is the fickleness of friends, well, you've got Cato . . .
>
> (Cervantes, *Don Quixote*)

Purgatorio—the *Commedia*'s second canticle—describes Dante's journey through the realm of purgation, the only transitory realm of the three that constitute his afterlife. Unlike Hell and Paradise, Purgatory will cease to be in operation after Judgment Day. The way that souls experience the purgatorial space is also in transition: only there are they supposed to move from one place to another, like pilgrims. The sole purpose of this journey is to purge their vices while winding their way up Mount Purgatory. At its summit, they will enter the Earthly Paradise, which provides the gateway to Heaven. That Purgatory should be transitory in nature was not Dante's invention. Some biblical sources hint at the possibility of expiating one's sins after death and the efficacy of praying for the dead, while accounts of medieval visions of the afterlife, as well as theological writings, reiterate the necessarily provisional nature of this redemptive place.[1] The emergence of the doctrine of Purgatory in the thirteenth century extended the possibility of transformation or development to the afterlife, which, according to Caroline Walker Bynum, had traditionally been seen as "the realm of stasis."[2] The idea, however, that Purgatory should coincide with a process of learning and moral edification, in the course of which souls are forced to study an entire curriculum of exemplary stories from the Bible, ancient history and literature, and mythology, is one of Dante's most innovative contributions to the development of this relatively new doctrine—the Catholic Church defined it for the first time in 1274, at the Second Council of

---

[1] Purgatory is not mentioned in the scriptures. Three biblical passages, however, have been foundational for the development of this Catholic doctrine: 2 Maccabees, Matthew 5.25–6 and 12.31–2, and 1 Corinthians 3.10–17. On the development of the concept of Purgatory in medieval visions, see Alison Morgan, *Dante and the Medieval Other World* (Cambridge: Cambridge University Press, 1990), chap. 5.

[2] Caroline Walker Bynum, *The Resurrection of the Body in Western Christianity, 200–1336* (New York: Columbia University Press, 1995), 14.

Dante's Education. Filippo Gianferrari, Oxford University Press. © Filippo Gianferrari (2024).
DOI: 10.1093/oso/9780198881766.003.0005

Lyon. Dante, in other words, succeeded in turning a place of pain, a temporary hell, into a place of education and edification.

At the end of his purgatorial ascent, Dante-the-pilgrim learns from Beatrice how dangerously effective bad "schools" can be in leading one to damnation (*Purgatorio* 33.85). Thus, in representing Purgatory, the poet counters the moral corrosiveness of his contemporary education to offer a reformed and reformative program of instruction. George Corbett proposes to read Dante's *Purgatorio* as a text that educates readers on Christian ethics.[3] In particular, Corbett draws important parallels with medieval oral preaching practice, a key means for vernacular instruction in Dante's time.[4] To complement this view, the next chapters argue that allusions to medieval school texts also mark several pivotal moments throughout *Purgatorio*'s narrative development. In presenting a new moral and spiritual education, "in pro del mondo che mal vive" (to serve the world that live so ill) (*Purgatorio* 32.103), Dante engages in a dialogue with the foundational texts of his own linguistic and literary formation to represent his *Purgatorio* as a Christian school that offers an education for achieving salvation and an alternative to the worldly "scuola" (school) that almost damned him (*Purgatorio* 33.85).

A Christian Cato

When Dante and Virgil emerge from the infernal pit to approach the feet of the Purgatorial Mountain, they are confronted with the figure of an unnamed old man whose mere appearance inspires respect and deference. As the reader learns from Virgil's words, the usher for this antechamber of Purgatory is none other than Cato Uticensis, who committed suicide in Utica in 46 BC, while campaigning against Julius Caesar in defense of the Roman republic. Several features of Dante's representation of Cato have puzzled readers throughout the centuries. His appearance as an old man, to begin with, is rather ill-suited to someone known to have died at a young age.[5] This discrepancy has prompted scholars to wonder whether Dante might have, either willingly or not, confused Cato Uticensis with his great-grandfather, Cato the Censor, a senator of the Roman republic renowned for his moral strictness and conservativism.[6] The most striking peculiarity of the purgatorial Cato, however, is his very place among the saved souls in the Christian afterlife.

---

[3] George Corbett, *Dante's Christian Ethics: Purgatory and Its Moral Contexts* (Cambridge: Cambridge University Press, 2020).

[4] See esp. chap. 5.

[5] The iconography of the bearded Cato had important precedents, such as Lucan's *Pharsalia* 2.374–75, and Cato's fierce appearance was meant to symbolize his moral rigidity. But the fact that Dante presents him as an old man—"veglio" (*Purgatorio* 1.31)—constituted an interesting choice.

[6] The argument about Dante's confusion of the different Catos is an old and rather superseded one. For a more recent revival of this thesis, see Betsy Bowden, "Dante's Cato and the *Disticha Catonis*," *Deutsches Dante-Jahrbuch* 75, no. 1 (2000): 125–30.

134   DANTE'S EDUCATION

Erich Auerbach famously explained the Cato paradox as *figura* of the providential redemption of the pagans. Giuseppe Mazzotta took Auerbach's—as well as Charles Singleton's—biblical hermeneutic further and interpreted Cato's suicide as a "secular reenactment of the Exodus." While these readings have heightened our perception of Dante's renewed understanding of Roman history through the lenses of biblical typology and providential history, they have tended to distract us from the role played by contemporary education and local political discourse in shaping Dante's meditation on Cato's self-sacrifice.[7]

Robert Hollander argued that Dante's Christianization of Cato was unprecedented and that "whatever rationale we may find for his salvation by Dante, we must remember that the poet expected us to be amazed."[8] Dante's transformation of the pagan suicide into a type of Christian martyr did elicit some disquiet among the ancient commentators on the *Commedia*, sometimes stirring up critical reactions.[9] The poem itself contributes to the suspense surrounding the afterlife destiny of Cato Uticensis. In *Inferno* 14, Dante leaves the wood of the suicides and squanderers to enter the fiery desert where violence is punished. The author compares the new landscape to the Libyan desert crossed by Cato when trying to join forces with the Numidian king against Julius Caesar, as recounted by Lucan in the ninth book of his *Pharsalia*:

> Lo spazzo era una rena arida e spessa,
> non d'altra foggia fatta che colei
> che fu da' piè di Caton già soppressa.
>
> (*Inferno* 14.13–15)

> (At an expanse of deep and arid sand, / much like the sand pressed long ago / beneath the feet of Cato.)

Cato's name here calls attention to his conspicuous absence in the place where medieval readers would have expected to find him, among the suicides.

---

[7] Erich Auerbach, "Figura," in *Scenes from the Drama of European Literature: Six Essays*, trans. Ralph Manheim (New York: Meridian Books, 1959), 11–76; Giuseppe Mazzotta, *Dante, Poet of the Desert: History and Allegory in the Divine Comedy* (Princeton, NJ: Princeton University Press, 1979), chap. 1, esp. 58–65; and Charles S. Singleton, "In Exitu Israel de Aegypto," *78th Annual Report of the Dante Society of America* (1960): 1–24.

[8] Robert Hollander, *Allegory in Dante's Commedia* (Princeton, NJ: Princeton University Press, 1969), 124–26. More recently, Hollander argued again that "it is so vital to understand that no one other than Dante was of the opinion that Cato's virtues were specifically Christian, much less that he was destined for salvation." See Robert Hollander, "Dante's Cato Again," in *Dantean Dialogues: Engaging with the Legacy of Amilcare Iannucci*, ed. Maggie Kilgour and Elena Lombardi (Toronto: University of Toronto Press, 2013), 66–124, at 66.

[9] Examples of this tendency are Anonimo Fiorentino, comm. *Purgatorio* 1.31–6, and Cristoforo Landino, comm. 1.31–3. See also Francesco da Buti's allegorical justification, comm. *Purgatorio* 1.40–48. For a brief discussion of Cato in the ancient commentaries, see Hollander, "Dante's Cato Again," 69.

FREEING CATO FROM HIS *DISTICHS*   135

The hypothesis that Dante's Christianization of Cato would have surprised medieval readers still finds support in current critical literature.[10] As I would like to show, however, such a cultural appropriation was unprecedented only with regard to the poet's ancient and late antique sources. Contrary to received wisdom, Christianizing Cato was a well-rehearsed practice in medieval education.[11] In his commentary on the *Disticha Catonis* (*Distichs of Cato*), for instance, the ninth-century monk and *magister* Remigius of Auxerre reports that some of his sources shared the assumption that in ancient Rome there was a certain Cato—the author of the *Disticha*—who was a Christian: "quidam eum Christianum esse profitentur."[12] Since the *Disticha Catonis*'s fortunes in medieval education paved the way for Cato's Christian afterlife, we need to reflect on Dante's engagement with this tradition. Even a protohumanist such as Benvenuto da Imola, who criticizes Dante's very great mistake in saving Cato—"error satis enormis"—points out that the Purgatorial Cato—that is, Cato Uticensis—should not be confused with the author of the *Disticha Catonis*, as some, such as Vincent of Beauvais, had done.[13] As Benvenuto's clarification reveals, late medieval culture was divided between two traditional views of Cato: a learned and classicizing one that acknowledged the historical significance of Cato Uticensis' life, and a rather popular tradition that loosely associated the name "Cato" with the ethical universe taught by the *Disticha Catonis*. As we will see, even intellectuals from Dante's Florence, such as Brunetto Latini and Remigio De' Girolami, were not immune from the influence of the *Disticha Catonis*.

Thanks to its popularity among grammar teachers, the *Disticha Catonis* became one of the most quoted texts in medieval Europe, thereby intensifying the confusion surrounding the identity of the different Catos from antiquity.[14] For many in

[10] See, for instance, Justin Steinberg, *Dante and the Limits of the Law* (Chicago: University of Chicago Press, 2013), 112–13. But some scholars have also pointed to the several ambiguities surrounding Dante's representation of Cato. See, for instance, Angelo Mangini, "Quel che Catone non sa: Per una nuova lettura di *Purgatorio* I e II," *Studi e problemi di critica testuale* 89 (2014): 111–49.

[11] On the Christianization of the *Disticha Catonis* and its author in medieval education, see Richard Hazelton, "The Christianization of 'Cato': The *Disticha Catonis* in the Light of Late Mediaeval Commentaries," *Mediaeval Studies* 19 (1957): 157–73.

[12] This excerpt is transmitted in the eleventh-century manuscript Lucca, Biblioteca Statale, MS 1433, fol. 85r. It is also trasncribed in Augusto Mancini, "Un commento ignoto di Remy d'Auxerre ai Disticha Catonis," *L'Accademia* 11 (1902): 175–98, at 179.

[13] Benvenuto da Imola, comm. *Purgatorio* 1.28–33. He vehemently accuses Vincent of Beauvais in the following terms, "Nota etiam quod Vicentius Beluacensis in suo speculo historiali, quod fuit opus vere gallicum, scribit, quod hic Cato Uticensis fecit libellum quo pueri scholastici utuntur; quod non solum est falsum sed impossibile, quia in illo libello fit mentio de Lucano, qui fuit tempore Neronis" (Benvenuto, comm. *Purg.* 1.73–75).

[14] The fundamental manuscript studies on the *Disticha*'s diffusion and use in medieval schools are those by Marcus Boas, "De librorum catonianorum historia atque compositione," *Mnemosyne*, n.s., 42 (1914): 17–46, and Boas, "Cato und die Grabschrift der Allia Potestas," *Rheinisches Museum für Philologie* 81 (1932): 178–86. Among the more recent contributions on the subject of the *Disticha* in medieval and Renaissance education, see Rino Avesani, "Il primo ritmo per la morte del grammatico Ambrogio e il cosiddetto 'Liber Catonianus,'" *Studi Medievali* 6 (1965): 455–88; Michael Baldzuhn, *Schulbücher im Trivium des Mittelalters und der Frühen Neuzeit: Die Verschriftlichung von Unterricht*

136   DANTE'S EDUCATION

Dante's time, especially lay readers without extensive training in classical literature, Cato's name identified the moralizing voice that had instructed them through the homonymous distichs. Surprisingly, however, scholars who have grappled with Dante's enigmatic representation of Cato in *Purgatorio* 1 and 2 have seldom noted this fact.[15] Those who did take stock of this cultural construct, moreover, did not consider the nuanced and often contradictory receptions of this school text in late medieval Italy. John Scott, for instance, argued that "the author of the *Commedia* was convinced—primarily through his reading of the *Pharsalia* and the *Disticha Catonis* . . . that Cato had been granted the grace of implicit faith."[16] Scott, however, does not evaluate the actual extent and quality of the *Disticha*'s influence on Dante. His passing note also lacks any appreciation of the controversial reuses of this source in medieval political discourses. At a time when anti-elite and popular movements, particularly in Florence, promoted political ideas of common good and justice modeled on the ancient Roman republic, quoting the *Disticha Catonis* was neither culturally nor politically neutral. If Dante hoped to surprise his readers

---

in der Text- und Überlieferungsgeschichte der "Fabulae" Avians und der deutschen "Disticha Catonis" (Berlin: De Gruyter, 2007); Robert Black, *Humanism and Education in Medieval and Renaissance Italy: Tradition and Innovation in Latin Schools from the Twelfth to the Fifteenth Century* (Cambridge: Cambridge University Press, 2001), 40–63; Black, "The School Miscellany in Medieval and Renaissance Italy," *Segno e Testo* 2 (2004): 213–44; Black, "The Vernacular and the Teaching of Latin in Thirteenth and Fourteenth-Century Italy," *Studi Medievali* 3 (1996): 703–51; Paul Gehl, *A Moral Art: Grammar, Society, and Culture in Trecento Florence* (Ithaca, NY: Cornell University Press, 1993); Gehl, "Humanism for Sale: Making and Marketing Schoolbooks in Italy, 1450–1650" (2008), accessed February 2022, http://www.humanismforsale.org/text/; Gehl, "Latin Reader in Fourteenth-Century Florence," *Scrittura e civiltà* 13 (1989): 387–440.

[15] Significant exceptions to this trend are Zygmunt G. Barański, "Purgatorio 1," in *Lectura Dantis Bononiensis*, vol. 5, *Inferno XXIX–Purgatorio I–II*, ed. Emilio Pasquini and Carlo Galli (Bologna: Bologna University Press, 2015), 105–33, esp. 21–27; Betsy Bowden, "Dante's Cato and the *Disticha Catonis*"; Charles Grandgent, "Cato and Elijah: A Study in Dante," *PMLA* 17 (1902): 71–90, esp. 84; Mazzotta, *Dante, Poet of the Desert*, 58; Nicola Scarano, *Saggi danteschi* (Livorno: Giusti, 1905), 134; John A. Scott, *Dante's Political Purgatory* (Philadelphia: University of Pennsylvania Press, 1996), 69–84, esp. 76–78; Gustav Wolff, "Cato der Jüngere bei Dante," *Jahrbuch der Deutschen Dante-Gesellschaft* 2 (1869): 227–29. For a concise yet pointed survey of their different arguments, see Hollander, "Dante's Cato Again," esp. 97n10. In addition to the studies just mentioned, other influential contributions to the interpretation of Dante's Cato that informed my reading are Auerbach, "Figura"; Delphine Carron, "Le héros de la liberté: Les aventures philosophiques de Caton au Moyen Âge latin, de Paul Diacre à Dante" (Ph.D. diss., Université Paris IV et Neuchâtel, 2010), 709–921, https://doc.rero.ch/record/21170/files/00002181.pdf; Carron, "Une vie de philosophe philosophique? Le *Comentum super Dantis Aldigherii Comoediam* de Benvenuto da Imola et l'élaboration de la figure du *Catone Dantesco* au XIVᵉ siècle italien," in *Vie philosophique et vies de philosophes*, ed. Bruno Clément (Paris: Sens & Tonka, 2010), 177–94; Violetta de Angelis, ". . . E L'ultimo Lucano," in *Dante e la "bella scola" della poesia: Autorità e sfida poetica*, ed. Amilcare Iannucci (Ravenna: Longo, 1993), 145–202; Mario Fubini, "Catone l'Uticense," in the *ED*; Robert Hollander, "Ancora sul Catone Dantesco," *Studi Danteschi* 75 (2010): 187–204; Hollander, "Cato's Rebuke and Dante's Scoglio," *Italica* 52 (1975): 348–63; Antonio Martina, "Catone il Vecchio," in the *ED*; Enrico Proto, "Nuove ricerche sul Catone dantesco," *Giornale storico della letteratura italiana* 59 (1912): 193–248; Ezio Raimondi, "Il Canto I del *Purgatorio*," in *Lectura Dantis Scaligera* (Florence: Le Monnier, 1963); Raimondi, "Rito e storia nel I canto del *Purgatorio*," in *Metafora e storia: Studi su Dante e Petrarca* (Turin: Aragno, 2008), 98–132; Nunzio Vaccaluzzo, "Fonti del Catone dantesco," *Giornale storico della letteratura italiana* 40 (1902): 140–50.

[16] Scott, *Dante's Political Purgatory*, 78.

FREEING CATO FROM HIS *DISTICHS*   137

by redeeming Cato Uticensis in *Purgatorio*, he had to engage with contemporary receptions of this didactic text.

"Cato Says . . .": Which Cato? The *Disticha Catonis* in Medieval Education

Cato's name was exceedingly popular in medieval culture, where it epitomized wisdom and rigid moral virtue. The roots of this idealization were ancient. Plutarch's biography of Cato the Elder explains that "his third name was not Cato at first, but Priscus. Afterwards he got the surname of Cato for his great abilities. The Romans call a man who is wise and prudent, catus" (*Marcus Catus* 1.2).[17] Late republican and imperial Roman writers contributed to saturating Cato's name with a specific moral, civic, and political complex of virtues. In his *De finibus bonorum et malorum* (4.44), Cicero presents Cato Uticensis as "omnium virtutum auctor[e]" (father of all virtues), while in the *De officiis* (1.31.112), Cato presents superhuman qualities—"incredibilem gravitatem" (austerity beyond belief) and "perpetua constantia" (unswerving consistency)—which compelled him to commit suicide rather than capitulating to Caesar. In the third book of his *De finibus*, moreover, Cicero identifies Roman Stoicism with Cato's rigid ethics and unshaken resolution. His unequaled virtues were glorified by Virgil in the *Aeneid*, where Cato features as the ruler of the blessed souls in the Elysian fields: "dantem iura Catonem" (Cato, giving judgments and decrees) (*Aeneid* 8.670).[18] In Seneca's view, instead, Cato embodies supreme wisdom: he is a model set by the gods for mankind (*De constantia sapientis* 2.2.1). More important, however, Seneca celebrates Cato as the ultimate hero of freedom who fought against the demise of the Roman republic— "neque enim Cato post libertam vixit nec libertas post Cato" (neither Cato lived after freedom nor did freedom live after Cato) (2.2.2)—a definition that likely played an important role in Dante's representation of Cato Uticensis in *Purgatorio* 1 and *Monarchia* 2.[19] Among Roman authors, therefore, Cato increasingly emerges as the last protector of republican freedom, the *defensor patriae* who sacrificed his own life to the cause of the Roman people, as he is celebrated in Lucan's *Pharsalia* (2.306–13) and Sallust's *Bellum Catilinae*. The latter's popularity in medieval education, moreover, helped spread this political view.

---

[17] Bernadotte Perrin, trans., *Plutarch's Lives*, vol. 2 (Cambridge, MA: Harvard University Press, 1914).

[18] Which of the two Catos Virgil had in mind here is a matter of some contention. Whereas ancient exegetes, and most importantly Servius, identified him as the Censor, modern commentators point out that the reference to Catilina in the line before Cato makes his appearance (*Aeneid* 8.868) would reveal him to be Cato Uticensis. Dante also appears to follow the latter reading. See, for instance, Ettore Paratore's comm. ad locum, Virgilio, *Eneide*, trans. Luca Canali and commentary by Ettore Paratore (Milan: Mondadori, 1985), 677.

[19] For Seneca's influence on Dante's representation of Cato, see Proto, "Nuove ricerche."

138   DANTE'S EDUCATION

Cato's medieval afterlife was equally informed by a progressive abstraction and idealization. His name became a synonym for rigid morality—as encapsulated by Boethius' epigraphic reference to the "rigidus Cato" in the *Consolatio Philosophiae* (1.M7)—and for perfect wisdom and virtue—as in Benvenuto da Imola's gloss, drawn on Valerius Maximus, also a popular school text: "Valerius vero dicit quod qui unum bonum ac sapientem nominare voluerit sub Catonis nomine diffiniat" (But truly Valerius says that whoever wishes to name one good and wise person should use Cato's name).[20]

Education was chiefly responsible for advancing an idealized and dehistoricized image of Cato in late antiquity and the Middle Ages. Already in the schools of ancient Rome, "Cato" had been turned into a favorite subject of model sentences for linguistic drills and rhetorical exercises. In the mind of medieval schoolboys, however, the contours of Cato's image largely overlapped with those of the author of the *Disticha Catonis*, which they had to read, parse, and memorize. The *Disticha*, or *Dicta Catonis*, feature four books of distich hexameters containing moralizing *sententiae* addressed by an unnamed father to his son. The *Disticha* became a "bestseller" of the genre of wisdom literature and was one of the most popular school readings in medieval Western Europe. Its hexameters provided an elementary text with which pupils could exercise their proficiency in Latin grammar while acquiring rudiments of morality. In the schools of northern Italy, as in the rest of Europe, Cato belonged to the first stages of language studies and was read either together or immediately after the *Donato*.[21] Seven vernacular translations (*volgarizzamenti*) of Cato's distichs that were produced in Tuscany between the twelfth and fifteenth centuries witness the popularity of this work in the milieu where Dante received his first education.[22] The work left "an indelible imprint on the minds of the young," as shown by hundreds of quotations from the *Disticha* in

---

[20] Benvenuto da Imola, comm. *Purgatorio* 1.34–36. The translation is mine. In the *Anticlaudianus*, Alan of Lille names Cato as the chief example of both insistence and intransigence (2.355 and 6.230). Evidence of this moralistic tradition of Cato in medieval culture is everywhere. To mention only two examples, which might have been notorious at Dante's time, I cite Henry of Settimello's *Elegy* 3.85–86 ("Tu nimium tuus es, nimis et tibi credis, inepte, / et solus credis *providus esse Cato*"; emphasis added); and the anonymous twelfth-century Italian *Cantilena giullaresca* ("Salva lo vescovo senato, / lo mellior c'umque sia nato," / che da l'ora fue sagrato / tutt'allumma 'l chericato. / Né Fisolaco né *Cato* / non fue sì *ringratïato*," 1–6; emphasis added). Quoted in Alfredo Giuliani, *Antologia della poesia italiana. Dalle origini al Trecento* (Milan: Feltrinelli, 1975), 11.

[21] See Black, *Humanism*, 40–63; Paul F. Grendler, *Schooling in Renaissance Italy Literacy and Learning, 1300–1600* (Baltimore: Johns Hopkins University Press, 1991), 174–82, and Silvia Rizzo, *Ricerche sul latino umanistico*, vol. 1 (Rome: Edizioni di storia e letteratura, 2002), 127.

[22] Laura Fontana, "Un inedito volgarizzamento toscano dei *Disticha Catonis*," in *In ricordo di Cesare Angelini; Studi di letteratura e filologia* (Milan: Il Saggiatore, 1979), 46–64; Cesare Segre and Mario Marti, *Prosa del Duecento* (Milan: Ricciardi, 1959), 187–94. Worth mentioning here is also Bonvesin da la Riva's thirteenth-century vernacular commentary *Expositiones Catonis*. As Bonvesin taught grammar in Milan and wrote primarily moral and didactic works in both vernacular and Latin, the choice to comment in the vernacular on the *Disticha* confirms the work's popularity as a didactic text in late medieval Italy. See Bonvesin da la Riva, "Expositiones Catonis," in *Le opera volgari di Bonvesin da la Riva*, ed. Gianfranco Contini (Rome: Società filologica romana, 1941), 323–60.

medieval texts.[23] It would not be an overstatement to say that, from the ninth to the sixteenth century, most European schoolboys read, parsed, and memorized the *Disticha Catonis*.[24]

Although some of the *Disticha's* basic material may be as early as the second century, scholars tend to date the work to the third century AD.[25] The identity of the author also remains unknown. As the introduction to the second book refers to Lucan's *Pharsalia*, however, it seems obvious that neither Cato the Censor nor Cato Uticensis lived long enough to write the eponymous distichs. Yet the name "Cato" was added to the title as early as the ninth century.[26] As evidenced by a large variety of sources, the two famous Catos from antiquity were consistently associated with it.

The distinction between the identities of the different Catos began to blur already in the first century. Glosses on the *Disticha*, moreover, together with the practice of quoting its *sententiae* in medieval texts, promoted the substantial assimilation of the ancient Catos.[27] Lacking precise historical information, medieval *accessus* to the *Disticha Catonis* identify as many as twelve different Catos, six of whom are indicated as the possible authors of the work.[28] These *accessus* usually

---

[23] Hazelton, "Christianization," 159. Max Manitius listed several hundred references to the *Disticha Catonis* from medieval philosophical works, sermons, religious and secular poetry, chronicles, encyclopedias, and commentaries. See Manitius, "Beiträge zur Geschichte Römischer Dichter in Mittelalter," *Philologus* 51 (1892): 166–71.

[24] On the importance of the *Disticha* in the genre of medieval wisdom literature see David Wells, "Fatherly Advice: The Precepts of 'Gregorius,' Marke, and Gurnemanz and the School Tradition of the 'Disticha Catonis'; with a Note on Grimmelshausen's 'Simplicissimus,'" *Frühmittelalterliche Studien* 28 (1994): 296–332. Several medieval outlines of educational programs—quoted in Chapter 1—confirm that this work played an essential role in medieval education. On the history of the *Disticha's* influence on medieval culture, see Robert Bolgar, *The Classical Heritage and its Beneficiaries* (Cambridge: Cambridge University Press, 1954), 197; Paul Clogan, "Literary Genres in a Medieval Textbook," *Medievalia et Humanistica* 11 (1982): 199–209; J. Wight Duff and Arnold Duff, "Introduction to Dicta Catonis," in *Minor Latin Poets*, ed. J. Wight Duff and Arnold Duff (Cambridge, MA: Harvard University Press, 1968), 586; Hazelton, "Christianization"; Giuseppe Manacorda, *Storia della scuola in Italia: Il Medioevo* (Milan: R. Sandron, 1914), vol. 2, 281–82; Henri-Irénée Marrou, *Histoire de l'éducation dans l'antiquité* (Paris: Le Seuil, 1948), 69–73; Paolo Roos, *Sentenza e proverbio nell'antichità e i "Distici di Catone": Il testo latino e i volgarizzamenti italiani* (Brescia: Morcelliana, 1984), 198–204; Eva Matthews Sanford, "The Use of Classical Latin Authors in the *Libri Manuales*," *Transactions and Proceedings of the American Philological Association* 55 (1924): 190–248; Elisabeth Schulze-Busacker, "Des *Disticha Catonis* dans l'Occident au Moyen Âge," *Actes de langue francaise et de linguistique* 2 (1989): 155–66.

[25] On the dating of the *Disticha Catonis*, see Richard Hazelton, "Two Texts of the Disticha Catonis and Its Commentary, with Special Reference to Chaucer, Langland and Gower" (Ph.D. diss., Rutgers University, 1956), vii–viii, and Franz Skutsch, *Dicta Catonis*, in *Realencyclopädie*, ed. August Pauly and Georg Wissowa (Stuttgart: Metzler, 1905), col. 358.

[26] Hazelton, "Two Texts," vi.

[27] See Serena Connolly, "Disticha Catonis Uticensis," *Classical Philology*, 107 (2012), 119–30. Marcia Colish gives the example of Tertullian's *Apologeticum* 39.12–13, in which Tertullian clearly confuses Cato Uticensis with his ancestor Cato the Elder. See Colish, *The Stoic Tradition from Antiquity to the Early Middle Ages* (New York: Brill, 1985), vol. 1, 16. Comprehensive studies on the reception and tradition of Cato from antiquity are Robert J. Goar, *The Legend of Cato Uticenis from the First Century B.C. to the Fifth Century A.D. with an Appendix on Dante and Cato* (Brussels: Latomus, 1987); Piero Pecchiura, *La figura di Catone Uticense nella letteratura latina* (Turin: Giappichelli, 1965). More recently, see the monumental study by Carron, *Le héros*.

[28] On the different attributions of the *Disticha Catonis* attempted by medieval commentaries, see Delphine Carron, "À la recherche de Caton: Essais médiévaux de reconstruction de biographies

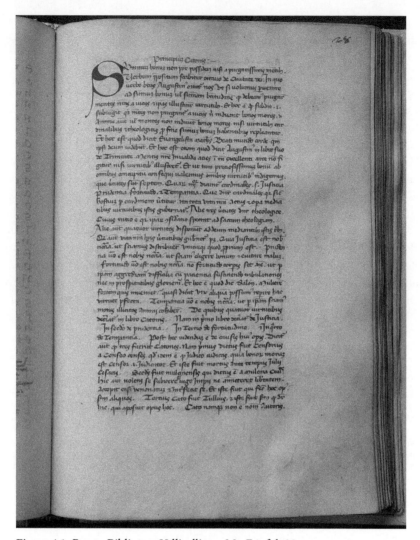

Figure 4.1 Rome, Biblioteca Vallicelliana, Ms. F.1, fol. 28r.

Source: Courtesy of the Italian Ministry of Culture/Biblioteca Vallicelliana, Rome. Reproduction or duplication by any means is strictly prohibited.

single out at least Cato the Elder, also known as the Censor, and Cato Uticensis: "Duo Catones erant Romae, Censorius Cato et Uticensis Cato" (There were two Catos at Rome, Cato the Censor and Cato of Utica). These *accessus* also succinctly

antiques," in *Actualiser le passé: Figures antiques du Moyen Âge à la Renaissance*, ed. Jean-Claude Mühlethaler and Delphine Burghgraeve (Lausanne: Centre d'Études Médiévales et Post-Médiévales de l'Université de Lausanne, 2012), 47–62, https://serval.unil.ch/resource/serval:BIB_34DBDAE31C15. P001/REF, and Paola Navone, "Catones Perplurimi," *Sandalion: Quaderni di cultura classica, cristiana e medievale* 5 (1982): 311–27.

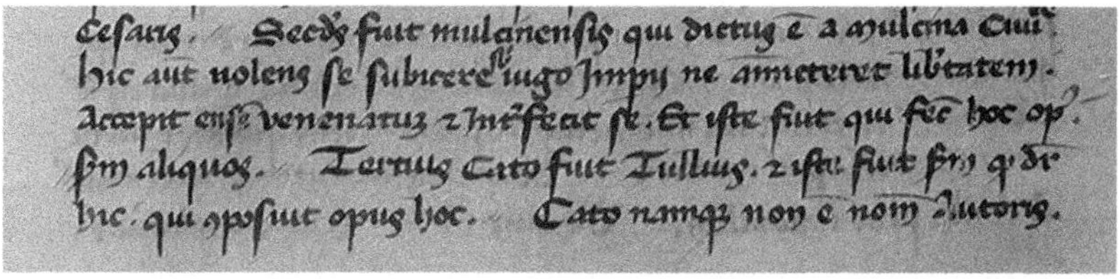

Figure 4.2 Rome, Biblioteca Vallicelliana, Ms. F.1, fol. 28r. Detail of the last five lines, "Secundus fuit mulcinensis . . ."

Source: Courtesy of the Italian Ministry of Culture/Biblioteca Vallicelliana, Rome. Reproduction or duplication by any means is strictly prohibited.

distinguish the deeds of the two Catos: "Ideo Censorius dicitur Cato, quia bonus iudex erat et bene et iuste de omnibus iudicabat; ideo autem Uticensis Cato dicitur, quia devicit Uticam" (Cato the Censor is so called because he was a good judge and decided well on all matters; Cato of Utica is so called because he conquered Utica).[29] As for the *Disticha*, these *accessus* attribute its authorship either to the Censor ("Sed Censorius Cato cum videret iuvenes et puellas in magno errore versari, scripsit hunc libellum ad filium suum" [But when Cato the censor saw that the young men and girls were living very wicked lives, he wrote this book to his son]) or to a third "Cato" known only for his distichs ("neuter illorum fuit iste Cato" [neither of them was this Cato]), or else simply admit uncertainty on this matter ("vel Cato vel alius—nam auctor incertus est" [either one Cato or the other—for the author is unknown]).[30] Vincent of Beauvais instead identified the author of the booklet with Cato Uticensis. As already noted, such an association appalled early humanists.[31] It was, however, a widespread notion that was hard to eradicate, as witnessed not only by the above-mentioned Benvenuto da Imola but also by the *accessus* transmitted in the fourteenth-century manuscript, F.1 of the Biblioteca Vallicelliana of Rome: "Secundus fuit mulcinensis [*sic*] qui dictus est a mulcina [*sic*] ciuitate. hic autem nolens se subicere sub iugo imperii ne amicteret libertatem accepit ense venenatum et interfecit se. Et iste fuit qui fecit hoc opus secundum aliquos" (The second one was Cato "Mulcinensis" [*sic*] who

---

[29] See R. B. C. Huygens, ed., *Accessus ad auctores, Bernard d'Utrecht, Conrad d'Hirsau: Dialogus super auctores; Édition critique* (Leiden: Brill, 1970), 21. All translations from the medieval *Accessus* to Cato are from A. J. Minnis, A. B. Scott, and David Wallace, eds., *Medieval Literary Theory and Criticism, c. 1100–c. 1375: The Commentary-Tradition* (New York: Clarendon Press, Oxford University Press, 1988), 15.

[30] Huygens, *Accessus ad auctores*, 21. The second quotation is from Remigius of Auxerre's commentary on the *Disticha* (Mancini, *Un commento*, 179). The last quotation is from John of Salisbury's *Policraticus* 7.9, ed. Clement C. J. Webb, *Ioannis Saresberiensis episcopi Carnotensis Policratici sive De nvgis cvrialivm et vestigiis philosophorvm libri VIII*, vol. 2 (Oxford: Clarendon Press, 1909), 125. All translations are mine. On the identity of the *Disticha*'s author, see also Conrad of Hirsau, *Dialogus*, 328–50, in Huygens, *Accessus ad auctores*, and Hazelton, *Christianization*, 164n35.

[31] Vincent de Beauvais, *Speculum historiale* VI [v], 107: De Catone stoyco et dictis eius, accessed August 2023, http://atilf.atilf.fr/bichard/.

142   DANTE'S EDUCATION

is so named from the city of "Mulcina" [*sic*]. Since he did not want to be subjugated by the empire and did not renounce his freedom, poisoned, he killed himself with a sword. According to some, he was the one who wrote this work) (fol. 28r; see Figures 4.1 and 4.2). Other commentators instead suggested that some other famous Roman author, such as Cicero, was responsible for writing the distichs: "solet dici quod Tullius hoc opus composuit, et nomine persona Catonis hoc opus intitulavit" (it is often said that Tully wrote this work, and titled it under Cato's name).[32] The work nonetheless became inseparably linked to Cato's name more on account of its content than on the basis of his supposed authorship: "alii dicunt quod huic libello nomen non ab auctore, sed a materia sit inditum: '*catus* enim sapiens est'" (others say that this book got its name, not from its author, but from the subject matter: "for *catus* means 'wise'").[33]

Despite the efforts of the commentary tradition to pin down the identity of its author, most medieval writers cite the *Disticha* simply as "Cato dicit." Furthermore, many quotations attributed to "Cato" in thirteenth-century texts are in fact drawn from the *Disticha*.[34] This loose citation practice contributed to the confusion surrounding the identity of the Cato who penned the *Disticha* and the two famous Catos from antiquity. As Delphine Carron states, "These three Catos were easily confused or assimilated during the Middle Ages, sharing their Roman origins and love for moral integrity."[35] Depending on the different context in which the distichs were quoted, therefore, they were attributed to one or the other Cato.

The *Disticha Catonis* did not merely help dehistoricize Cato in medieval culture, turning him into the embodiment of honesty, prudence, and human wisdom; it also fostered his Christianization.[36] Although the morality distilled by the *Disticha* is worldly and has no significant religious dimension, medieval commentaries assimilated it to the Christian worldview. They draw parallels between Cato and biblical characters, including Christ. Solomon's *Proverbs* are often found quoted in the margins of manuscripts of the *Disticha* or in tandem with Cato's distichs in medieval texts, thus equating their authority and wisdom.[37] A good example of this syncretistic reception can again be found in the glosses on the *Disticha* transmitted by the manuscript F.1 of the Biblioteca Vallicelliana in Rome. The introduction to the work, "principium Catonis" (fol. 28r), opens with a quotation drawn from *De*

---

[32] Bodleian Library, Can. Bibl. Lat. MS 72, fol. 60r (XIII c.), quoted in Hazelton, "Two Texts," vi, and then again in Hazelton, "Christianization," 163n27. The translation is mine. Commentators also attributed the *Disticha* to Seneca and John Chrysostom, as in Città del Vaticano, Biblioteca Apostolica Vaticana, Vat. Lat. MS. 1663, fol. 6v.

[33] Huygens, *Accessus ad auctores*, 21. The translation is mine. Hazelton ("Christianization," 164n34) remarks that "most of the commentaries contain the 'etymology': 'Cato enim grece, ingeniosus vel sapiens dicitur latine.'"

[34] See Carron, *Le héros*, 356.

[35] Carron, "À la recherche de Caton," 49. The translation is mine.

[36] See Hazelton, "Christianization."

[37] Hazelton, "Two Texts," xx.

civitate Dei, notwithstanding Augustine's famous condemnation of Cato Uticensis in the same work. The text of the distichs is also interpolated with *sententiae* drawn from the biblical book of Proverbs, Augustine, Gregory the Great, Seneca, and Cicero (see Figure 4.3).

Through a combination of militant readings of the *Disticha Catonis* and Sallust's *Bellum Catilinae*, medieval education also infused Cato's virtues with political consequence. Sallust was, together with Cicero, a key model for teaching

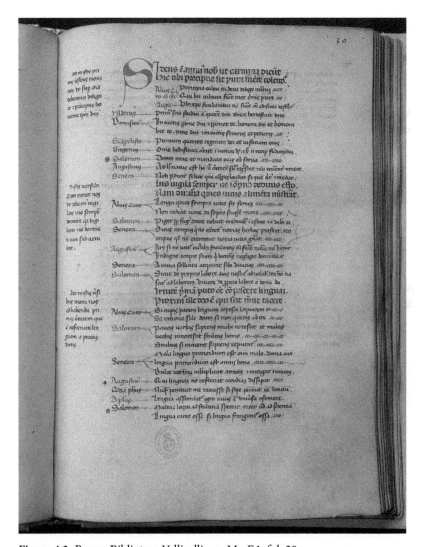

Figure 4.3 Rome, Biblioteca Vallicelliana, Ms. F.1, fol. 30r.

Source: Courtesy of the Italian Ministry of Culture/Biblioteca Vallicelliana, Rome. Reproduction or duplication by any means is strictly prohibited.

144   DANTE'S EDUCATION

Latin prose in medieval Italian schools, where it maintained steady popularity throughout the thirteenth century.[38] Sallust's *Bellum Catilinae* provided an account of Cato's crucial role in breaking down Catiline's conspiracy (42–41 BC). In particular, the *Bellum* featured Cato's speech in favor of executing Catiline and his followers for the protection of the Roman republic and the commonweal. This section of the *Bellum*, which is titled *Oratio Catonis* in some manuscript rubrics, was a staple text for the study of grammar and rhetoric.[39] Sallust's account of Cato's speech was translated and further popularized by the anonymous author of the thirteenth-century French compilation known as *Les Fais des Rommains*.[40] Through the study of the *Disticha* and Sallust's *Oratio Catonis*, the late medieval grammar curriculum linked Cato to pro-republican ideals and particularly to the much-debated theological and political doctrine of the common good. Dante's contemporary culture was pervaded by this political reception of Cato. To draw on the authority of the *Disticha Catonis*, therefore, was in no way ideologically neutral. Different sources gave access to slightly different Catos, which were then adapted to opposite and conflicting cultural and political agendas.[41] To appreciate this fact, we should turn to Brunetto Latini's representation of Cato. Brunetto was a champion of republican ideals and a public figure that helped reshape the political and cultural life of Dante's Florence. In *Inferno* 15, Dante acknowledges the important influence played by Latini's magisterial authority and describes him as a father and a teacher. But this representation also implied Dante's criticism of the master's secular worldview and conception of civic rhetoric.[42] Brunetto's appropriation of the *Disticha Catonis* and Sallust sheds light on the reception of Cato in the cultural milieu in which Dante was educated.

---

[38] Robert Black, "Classical Antiquity," in *Dante in Context*, ed. Zygmunt G. Barański and Lino Pertile (Cambridge: Cambridge University Press, 2015), 277–96, esp. 313, and Black, "Education," in *Dante in Context*, 260–76, esp. 267–70. See also Beryl Smalley, "Sallust in the Middle Ages," in *Classical Influences on European Culture A.D. 500–1500: Proceedings of an International Conference Held at King's College, Cambridge, April 1969*, ed. R. R. Bolgar (Cambridge: Cambridge University Press, 1971), 165–75, and Leighton D. Reynolds and N. G. Wilson, *Texts and Transmission: A Survey of the Latin Classics* (Oxford: Clarendon Press, 1983), 341–47.

[39] Quotations from the *Oratio* can also be found in the *Florilegium Gallicum*. See Rosemary Burton, *Classical Poets in the "Florilegium Gallicum"* (Frankfurt am Main: Lang, 1983), 188–99. Sallust, as Smalley notes, was commonly classified as *ars grammatica*. Medieval teachers and glossators were particularly keen also on extracting proverbial wisdom from Sallust, as noted by Smalley, "Sallust in the Middle Ages," at 168–170.

[40] Thomas J. McCormick, ed., *A Partial Edition of "Les Fais des Rommains" with a Study of its Style and Syntax* (Lewiston, NY: Mellen Press, 1995).

[41] As Charles Davis maintains, "an encyclopedist . . . is not expected to be original: it is his choice of subjects and authorities that is significant." Charles T. Davis, "Brunetto Latini and Dante," in *Dante's Italy, and Other Essays* (Philadelphia: University of Pennsylvania Press, 1984), 166–97, at 169.

[42] Although much has been written on Dante's complex relationship with Brunetto and inclusion of the latter in the *Commedia*, for a recent, comprehensive, and nuanced overview of this topic, see Catherine Keen, "'Parlando vommi / con ser Brunetto' (*Inf.* XV 100–101): Dante in dialogo con Brunetto Latini," *Studi danteschi* 83 (2018): 73–94.

Brunetto's Cato Says: Fight for the Fatherland

Cato's example and authority play an important role in Brunetto's magnum opus, the *Tresor*. Brunetto's aim was to offer an innovative educational program in the vernacular for the urban ruling elites. As revealed by the epithet "maestro," with which he identifies himself throughout the whole work, Brunetto aspired to be the teacher of a rising urban class made up of lay professionals employed in public administration, particularly those appointed to the office of *podestà* in the northern Italian communes.[43] In Brunetto's educational program, Cato constitutes one of the most quoted authorities and recurrent examples of civic virtues.

Throughout the *Tresor*, Brunetto uses Cato's name without distinction to identify both Cato Uticensis and the moral *auctoritas* of the *Disticha*, which is simply reported as "Cato dicit." Cato Uticensis surfaces briefly in the first book of the *Tresor* and features prominently in the third one, where he emerges as one of the principal defenders of the Roman republic against Catiline and his fellow conspirators. In Book 1, the episode of the conspiracy emerges as the watershed event in the history of Rome: Catiline nearly succeeded in overturning a republic that had lasted for 465 years. Brunetto keeps on returning to these events with telling insistence, as, in his account, they are at the origin of Florence's founding and the city's natural proclivity for war and conflict, which led to the author's exile (*Tresor* 1.37.2–3).[44] The hero of this story, for Brunetto, is Cicero, who was consul at the time and succeeded in defeating Catiline. Cato draws his relevance in this historic drama chiefly from his association with Cicero, whose authority in Brunetto's view is second only to Aristotle's. In Book 3, Brunetto reports Cato's speech against Catiline—drawing it almost entirely from *Les Fais de Rommains*—and analyzes it as a perfect example of the civic rhetoric featured in that book.[45] In his oration, Cato rebukes his fellow senators for the greed that blinded them to the imminent danger threatening the freedom of the republic and condemns the corruption of both public and individual morality. Rome's mighty army, he maintains, did not lead the city to its current power and wealth; its citizens' moral integrity and love for justice did (*Tresor* 3.37.8). That virtuous life, however, has long been forsaken

---

[43] Pietro G. Beltrami, "Introduzione," in Brunetto Latini, *Tresor*, ed. Pietro G. Beltrami (Turin: Einaudi, 2007), vii–xxvi.

[44] The thirteenth-century *Chronica de origine civitatis Florentiae* also draws on Sallust's *Bellum Catilinae* to trace the historical origin of the opposition between Florence and Fiesole. See Riccardo Chellini, ed., *Chronica de origine civitatis Florentiae* (Rome: Istituto Storico Italiano per il Medioevo, 2009), 64–67. But this is not the only source to propose such a connection. For a critical survey of Catiline's key role in medieval accounts of Florence's origins, see Delphine Carron, "La figure de Catilina et l'histoire de Florence dans les chroniques (début XIIIᵉ–milieu du XIVᵉ siècle)," *Rassegna Europea di Letteratura Italiana* 51–52 (2018): 11–60.

[45] Brunetto also quotes Cato's reference to Torquatus (*Bellum Catilinae* 52.30), who condemned his son to death in retaliation for his disobedience, as an example of digression (3.13.9), an effective prologue (29.7), and persuasive confutation (61.17). Other fragments from Cato's speech against Catiline make cursory appearances as examples of speech division (3.48.2), confutation through comparable proofs (65.2), and arguments that inspire piety in the listener (69.17).

146   DANTE'S EDUCATION

by nearly everybody (*Tresor* 3.37.3), and Cato alone seems to have remained faithful to it.[46] Thus, civic and religious piety gradually emerges as the conspirators' real target and the victim that Cato, as the guardian of civic morality, intends to rescue (*Tresor* 3.37.12). In Sallust's peculiar account of political and moral crises, as Beryl Smalley notes, "Cato appeals not for himself, but as a relic of ancient virtue and as a foil to his contemporaries"; in a time of moral lassitude, he is the last defender of traditional Roman values, on which depended the freedom of the republic.[47]

This portrait of Cato Uticensis, which Brunetto derives from Sallust—via *Les Fais de Rommains*—overlaps in meaningful ways with that of the author of the *Disticha Catonis*. In the introductory epistle to his son, the father who allegedly penned Cato's distichs presents himself precisely as someone striving against the moral degradation of his time, "cum animadverterem quam plurimos graviter in via morum errare" (as I noticed the very great number of those who go seriously astray in the path of conduct) (*Epistula Catonis*).[48] Thus, Catiline and his followers, who in Cato's words appear as a youthful generation who no longer honor God and family and show no mercy to others, resemble the imagined audience of young people that the author of the *Disticha* sets out to reform. Not surprisingly, therefore, the same cardinal values defended by Sallust's Cato are also prescribed at the opening of the *Disticha*: "Deo supplica / Parentes ama / Cognatos cole . . . Maledicus ne esto" (Pray to God / Love your parents / Respect your kindred . . . Do not be abusive) (*Disticha Catonis, Breves sententiae*).

Brunetto's reworking of *Disticha* 1.30 in three different passages of the *Tresor* furthers the substantial overlapping between Cato Uticensis and the author of the *Disticha* (*Tresor* 2.62.4, 2.69.3, 3.98.1). The original distich warns against moral inconsistency and explains that it is especially reproachable to accuse another of one's own vices: "Que culpare soles ea tu ne faceris ipse: / turpe est doctori, cum culpa redarguat ipse" (Do not yourself what you are wont to blame: / when sin convicts the preacher's self, 'tis shame). The warning featured in the second line of the distich is echoed by Sallust's Cato, in a passage (*Tresor* 52.8) that Brunetto quotes once again through the intermediation of *Les Fais* (1454–56, p. 70): "carje ne pardone pas volentiers a autrui le meffait dontje ne sentoie nulle teche en moi" (I do not willingly forgive in others the crimes of which I am completely innocent) (*Tresor*, 3.37.3).[49] It is on account of his own moral perfection that Cato is allowed

---

[46] Sallust's Caesar, for instance, had proclaimed his disbelief in any form of afterlife retribution to argue against executing Catiline and his allies.

[47] Smalley, "Sallust in the Middle Ages," 165, 166. On Sallust's moralizing reading of Rome's decline, see Donald C. Earl, *The Political Thought of Sallust* (Cambridge: Cambridge University Press, 1961), 44.

[48] The text and translation of the *Disticha Catonis* are from J. Wight Duff and Arnold Duff, eds., "Dicta Catonis," in *Minor Latin Poets*, 585–639.

[49] The translation is from Brunetto Latini, *The Book of the Treasure (Li Livres dou Tresor)*, trans. Paul Barrette and Spurgeon Baldwin (New York: Garland, 1993).

FREEING CATO FROM HIS *DISTICHS*   147

to rebuke the lassitude of his fellow senators. Brunetto's selective use of Sallust's *Bellum* and the *Disticha Catonis*, therefore, invites readers to identify Cato Uticensis, who features prominently in Books 1 and 3, with the *auctoritas* of the *Disticha*.[50]

The majority of Brunetto's quotations from the *Disticha Catonis* are concentrated in Book 2, which instructs readers in moral philosophy—vices and virtues (2.1)—and reports wise *sententiae* to educate them about the four "active" virtues, as Brunetto defines prudence, temperance, fortitude, and justice (*Tresor* 2.1.2-3).[51] The medieval reception of the *Disticha Catonis* presented this work precisely as a handbook on the four cardinal virtues: "materia Catonis in hoc opere sunt quatuor virtutes principales, scilicet iusticia, prudencia, fortitudo, temperancia" (Cato's subject matter in this book is the four cardinal virtues, i.e., justice, prudence, fortitude, and temperance).[52] Copyists began to divide the *Disticha* into four books, one for each virtue: "Nam in primo libro determinatur de Iustitia. In secondo de prudentia. In tertio de fortitudine. Et in quarto de temperantia" (For in the first book justice is discussed. In the second book prudence. In the third one fortitude. And in the fourth one temperance) (Rome, Biblioteca Vallicelliana, ms. F1, 28r; see Figure 4.1). Among the many quotations from the *Disticha* that punctuate *Tresor* 2, one is especially worth considering in order to appreciate the particular image of Cato that Brunetto wishes to convey. In *Tresor* 2.99.1, in the context of a discussion about the virtue of piety, Brunetto writes:

> pitié est une vertu qui nos fait aimer et servir diligenment nos parans et nostre païs. Et ce nos vient par nature, car nos naisons premierement a Dieu, et puis a nos parans et a nostre pais. *Caton dit: Filz, combate toi por ton païs.* L'en doit faire tot son povoir por le comun profit de son païs et de sa ville.
>
> (emphasis added)

> Pity is a virtue which makes us love and serve diligently our relatives and our country, and this comes to us through nature, for first of all we are born for God and then for our parents and our country. *Cato says: fight for your country;* one must do everything in one's power for the common profit of one's country and city.

---

[50] Carron (*Le héros*, 683) notes that Brunetto's reference to Cato in the opening of the *Tesoretto* (55–62) also substantiates the identification of Cato with the author of the *Disticha*. Carron correctly notes that Brunetto never clearly distinguishes between the two.

[51] Four of the distichs quoted in *Tresor* 2.62–64 are in fact drawn from Albertano da Brescia's *Liber de doctrina dicendi et tacendi*, a popular handbook on disciplining the tongue that Brunetto translates almost in full to discuss the virtue of "garde." *Tresor* 2.62.2, 3, 4, and 64.4 translate, respectively, Albertano's *Doctrina* 1.10, 23, 27, and 3.18. See Albertano da Brescia, *Liber de doctrina dicendi et tacendi: la parola del cittadino nell'Italia del Duecento*, ed. Paola Navone (Florence: SISMEL, 1998). Brunetto, however, also borrows from the *Disticha* independently and according to his own ideological agenda. In *Tresor* 2.60.5, for instance, he quotes *Disticha Catonis*, 114, which is not in Albertano's text. Furthermore, at *Tresor* 2.60.5, Brunetto clearly echoes—consciously or not—*Disticha* 125.

[52] Quoted in Hazelton, "Two Texts," 19n89.

148   DANTE'S EDUCATION

Drawing on this exhortation from the *Disticha*, Brunetto showcases Cato Uticensis primarily as a patriotic icon and republican hero.

Sallust's *Oratio Catonis*, on which Brunetto dwells at length in Book 3, reinforces the depiction of Cato as a patriot, whose love for his city is rooted in the doctrine of the common good. In his speech, Cato argues for the absolute superiority of the commonweal, which supersedes in value all personal interests. All citizens must protect their commune in order to defend their own private interests, for "se vos ces choses que vos tant amez volez garder et retenir, et vos volez mantenir vos delis par ordre et par repos, esveilliez vos ci, et pensez dou comun guarantor" (if you wish to keep and retain those things which you care for so much, and if you wish to preserve what gives you pleasure in an orderly and peaceful fashion, wake up here and now, and think of how to preserve the common good [literally, the commune]) (*Tresor* 3.37.2).[53] Tellingly, Brunetto already placed the same emphasis on Cato's patriotism in an earlier handbook on civic rhetoric, the *Rettorica*. Here, through the words of the *Sponitore*—that is, Brunetto himself, commenting on Cicero's *De inventione*—the author explains that "come disse Cato parlando della congiurazione di Catellina: 'Congiurato ànno i nobilissimi cittadini incendere e distruggere la *patria nostra*'" (as Cato said, talking about Catilina's conspiracy: "Our most noble citizens have conspired to burn and destroy *our fatherland*") (102.1; emphasis added).[54] Charles Davis observes that through his emphasis on Catiline's conspiracy, Brunetto was likely the initiator of the Florentine cult of Cicero the patriot.[55] I would argue, however, that Brunetto also encouraged the Florentine reception of Cato Uticensis as a patriotic icon. The authority of the *Disticha* proved especially instrumental to this end, as it put the exhortation to fight for the fatherland in Cato's mouth: "Cato dicit: pugna pro patria."

This distich was frequently quoted in contemporary debates about the commonweal, leading to the recurrent exploitation of Cato's name and example in pro-republican Florentine discourses.[56] A case in point is Remigio de' Girolami's *De bono comuni*—a work the Dominican friar addressed to the people of Florence immediately after the political turmoil that led to Dante's exile. The central thesis of this work is the superiority of the common good over the private one. To

---

[53] Carron shows how Brunetto adds small nuances to Cato's speech to transform him into the ideal civic orator and defender of the commonweal. See Delphine Carron, "Le metamorfosi di un cittadino eccezionale: Immagini verbali nel Medioevo del Catone dell'affaire' Catilina," *Storia del pensiero politico* 2 (2013): 425–44, at 436–44.

[54] Brunetto Latini, *La Rettorica italiana di Brunetto Latini*, ed. Francesco Maggini (Florence: Galletti e Cocci, 1915). The translation is mine.

[55] Davis, "Brunetto Latini and Dante," 177.

[56] This *sententia Catonis* was widely popular and frequently quoted in contemporary texts, particularly in legal glosses and in political treatises defining the commonweal and individuals' duties toward the fatherland. See Ernst H. Kantorowicz, "'Pro patria mori' in Medieval Political Thought," *American Historical Review* 56 (1951): 472–92, revised and expanded in Kantorowicz, *The King's Two Bodies: A Study in Medieval Political Theology* (Princeton, NJ: Princeton University Press, 1957), 232–72; and Gaines Post, "Two Notes on Nationalism in the Middle Ages," *Traditio* 9 (1953): 281–320.

support this argument, Remigio mentions Cato's example twice. In chapter 2, in the context of a florilegium of classical quotations, Remigio attributes the famous *sententia* from the *Disticha* to "Cato": "Et Cato dicit: 'pugna pro patria.'"[57] In chapter 5, the author includes the example of Cato Uticensis' suicide as part of a list of illustrious men who sacrificed themselves for the common good.[58] Like Brunetto in the *Tresor*, Remigio deems it unnecessary to identify the two Catos as separate individuals. In fact, it could be argued that the quotation from the *Disticha* reinforces Remigio's presentation of Cato Uticensis' suicide as a patriotic action for the well-being of the Roman republic—a powerful example of the self-sacrifice that is required of any citizen wishing to contribute to the common good.[59] By quoting Cato's exhortation "pugna pro patria" in the context of his *Tresor*, therefore, Brunetto set an important precedent for using the example of Cato in discourses, such as Remigio's, that encouraged the identification of Florence with the fatherland.[60]

The use of Cato as a patriotic icon suited Brunetto's political reinterpretation of Roman history. Catherine Keen observes that "Brunetto, like other Guelf ideologues, responded strongly to [Florence's] foundation story's alternative potential emphasis on Roman republicanism, as incarnated by Cicero and Cato, as part of the city's special legacy."[61] The representation of a patriotic Cato, therefore, would have been consistent with Brunetto's project of identifying Florence with Rome and himself with Cicero and Cato. Like them, Brunetto served the commonweal with his rhetorical skills and was eventually cast out of his country. Like Cicero, however, Brunetto eventually returned and adapted to the changed political landscape. Dante's personal and political story, instead, resembled Cato's rather than Cicero's—as Dante died outside of his *patria*, unable to come to terms with his political opponents. Not surprisingly, the complex evolution of this ancient

---

[57] Remigio de' Girolami, *De bono comuni II*, in Emilio Panella, *Dal bene comune al bene del comune: I trattati politici di Remigio dei Girolami († 1319); Nella Firenze dei Bianchi-Neri* (Florence: Nerbini, 2014), 152. On Remigio's political ideas, see Delphine Carron, "Remigio de' Girolami dans la Florence de Dante (1293–1302)," *Retie Medievali* 18, no. 1 (2017): 443–71, and Charles T. Davis, "An Early Florentine Political Theorist: Fra Remigio de' Girolami," in *Dante's Italy and Other Essays*, 198–223.

[58] A list that resembles Dante's in *Convivio* 4.5 and *Monarchia* 2.5 has an important model in Augustine's *De civitate Dei* 5.18.

[59] Remigio de' Girolami, *De bono comuni*, 18.11.

[60] Through his representation of Cato, Brunetto had already argued that for the sake of the common good virtually anything can be justified. For instance, in *Tresor* 3.38.1–2, where he begins his rhetorical analysis of Cato's speech against Catiline, Brunetto claims that to achieve an honest end—namely, rescuing the Roman republic—Cato pursued what may appear as a dishonest argument. In Brunetto's reading, therefore, Cato becomes a skillful orator who might even twist the truth for the good of the fatherland.

[61] Catherine Keen, "Vernacular Eloquence and Roman Rhetoric between Brunetto and Dante," in *Dante e la cultura Fiorentina*, ed. Zygmunt G. Barański, Theodore J. Cachey Jr., and Luca Lombardo (Rome: Salerno, 2019), 151–72, at 155. Keen also argues that in his translations of Cicero's orations *Pro Ligario, Pro Marcello*, and *Pro rege Deiotaro*, Brunetto displays a keen interest in Cicero's capacity to return to work in post-republican Rome, submitting to the practical necessity of collaborating with his former opponents (161–67).

150   DANTE'S EDUCATION

figure throughout Dante's oeuvre leads to a very different representation of Cato than Brunetto's.

The *Patria* and the World: Cato in *Convivio* 4

In the fourth book of the *Convivio*, Dante insistently returns to the ancient exemplary figure of Cato. Compared with the limited references to Cato in both the *Commedia* (three) and the *Monarchia* (two), the eight occurrences in *Convivio* 4 alone deserve notice. Cato's relevance is one of several significant parallels uniting *Convivio* 4 and the second book of the *Tresor*.[62] As both works deal with the ethical principles that define a virtuous life and argue for the relationship between virtue and true nobility, both authors insistently return to Cato as the quintessential example of the perfectly virtuous man.[63] Yet, their representations of this ancient figure differ in important respects.

Convivio 4, as Dante states, fulfills a practical, educational purpose: "propuosi di gridare alla gente che per mal cammino andavano acciò che per diritto calle si drizzasse[ro]" (I resolved that I would cry out to those who were walking along this evil path so that they might place themselves back on the right way) (4.1.9).[64] With the booming voice of a prophet, the author sets out to correct some mistaken and ingrained assumptions about human nobility: "Oh come è grande la mia impresa in questa canzone, a volere omai così trifoglioso campo sarchiare, come quello della comune sentenza, sì lungamente da questa cultura abandonato!" (O how great an enterprise have I undertaken in this canzone by desiring now to weed an overgrown field like that of common opinion, so long deprived of cultivation) (4.7.4). Later, in chapter 24, Dante clarifies that among the designated readers of *Convivio* 4 are young men who would not be able to keep on the right path without

---

[62] Davis ("Brunetto Latini and Dante," 180–88) points out that in *Tresor* 2.114, Brunetto Latini deals with the theory of nobility and seems to have closely influenced *Convivio* 4.23. To the parallel highlighted by Davis, Claudio Giunta also adds the relevant loci of *Tresor* 2.54.7 and 3.75.3. See Giunta's commentary on *Le dolci rime d'amor ch'i' solia*, in Dante Alighieri, *Opere*, ed. Marco Santagata (Milan: Mondadori, 2011), 1, 522. See also Keen, "Vernacular Eloquence," 168–69.

[63] Both *Convivio* 4 and *Tresor* 2 present the highest concentrations of references to Cato in the two authors' respective oeuvres. Among recent interpretations of the sources and aims of *Convivio* 4, see Albert R. Ascoli, *Dante and the Making of a Modern Author* (Cambridge: Cambridge University Press, 2008), esp. chaps. 2–3, and Ambrogio Camozzi Pistoja, "Il quarto trattato del *Convivio*: O della satira," *Le tre corone* 1 (2014): 27–53; see also Paolo Falzone, *Desiderio della scienza e desiderio di Dio nel "Convivio"* (Bologna: il Mulino, 2010); Gianfranco Fioravanti, "La nobiltà spiegata ai nobili: una nuova funzione della filosofia," in *Il Convivio di Dante*, ed. Johannes Bartuschat and Andrea Aldo Robiglio (Ravenna: Longo, 2015), 157–63; Sonia Gentili, *L'uomo aristotelico alle origini della letteratura italiana* (Rome: Carocci, 2005), 127–49; Laurence E. Hooper, "Dante's *Convivio*, Book 1: Metaphor, Exile, *Epoche*," Supplement, *MLN* 127 (2012), 86–104; and Andrea Mazzucchi, "Per una nuova edizione commentata del *Convivio*," in *Leggere Dante oggi*, ed. Enrico Malato and Andrea Mazzucchi (Rome: Salerno, 2012), 81–107, esp. 100–05.

[64] Franziska Meier argues that Dante wrote the *Convivio* for young adults who were nonspecialized and outside the university environment but who wished nonetheless to receive an education. See Meier, "Educating the Reader: Dante's *Convivio*," *L'Alighieri* 45 (2015): 21–34.

the example offered by older and wiser people: "così l'adolescente che entra nella selva erronea di questa vita, non saprebbe tenere lo buono cammino, se dalli suoi maggiori non li fosse mostrato" (so an adolescent who enters into the meandering forest of this life would not know how to keep the right path unless it were shown to him by his elders) (4.24.12). Dante sets out to deal with what was considered "oppinione del vulgo" (opinion ... so ingrained in the common people) (4.7.2) to clear away incorrect assumptions and to point his readers to the right authorities and examples. The way Dante formulates his main purpose in the *Convivio* echoes the alleged author of the *Disticha Catonis* in his dedicatory epistle:

"Cum animadverterem quam plurimos graviter *in via morum errare, succur-rendum opinioni* eorum et consulendum famae existimavi, maxime ut *gloriose* viverent et honorem contingerent".

(*Epistula Catonis*; emphasis added)

(As I noticed the very great number of those who *go seriously astray in the path of conduct,* I decided that I should come to the aid of their belief and take thought for their reputation, so that they might live with the utmost glory and attain honor.)

Like Dante in *Convivio* 4, "Cato" wishes to help those who are being sidetracked *in via morum* and take them back to the right path. The two texts also define their aims using identical terms, albeit according to different meanings: as Dante aims to reform the "*opinione* del volgo," so Cato writes his distichs in order to rescue "*opinioni* eorum."[65] In addition, the last chapters of *Convivio* recommend several of the moral values also taught by the *Disticha Catonis*, including the need to discipline the tongue (*Disticha Catonis* 1.3: *Convivio* 4.2.8); the scorn of wealth and avarice (*Disticha Catonis* 2.19: *Convivio* 4.13.6–17); the mandate of piety, which requires one to show deference to fathers, older people, and teachers (*Brevis sententia, Disticha Catonis* 4.6: *Convivio* 24.18); old men's obligation to serve as positive examples to young people (*Disticha Catonis* 1.16: *Convivio* 4.24.12); and, finally, the importance of obedience and modesty—*verecundia* (*Brevis sententia*: *Convivio* 4.25.10, 4.26.2). Some of these prescriptions are, of course, common features of the genre of gnomic and didactic literature, but the number of moral values endorsed by both *Convivio* and the *Disticha* is at least worth noting.[66]

In his treatment of nobility, Dante increasingly refers to *auctoritates* from the genre of wisdom literature, as, for instance, the biblical books of Proverbs and

---

[65] The term "opinioni" in the *Epistula Catonis* may also be interpreted as "reputations" rather than "opinions."

[66] As demonstrated by Simone Marchesi, Cicero's *De officiis* represents another crucial source for Dante's treatment of some of the ethical matters discussed in *Convivio* 4. See Marchesi, "La rilettura del 'De officiis' e i due tempi della composizione del 'Convivio,'" *Giornale storico della letteratura italiana* 177 (2001): 84–107.

152   DANTE'S EDUCATION

Ecclesiastes, the Gospels, Cicero and Seneca, and finally Aesop.[67] Among these authorities, Solomon and his Proverbs feature prominently. Starting in chapter 16, Dante increasingly refers to the biblical king as the third major authority of *Convivio* 4—the other two being Aristotle and the Emperor Frederick II. Dante even identifies with Solomon: "E però io nel cominciamento di questo capitolo posso parlare con la bocca di Salomone" (I am therefore at the beginning of this chapter able to speak with Solomon's voice) (4.5.2).[68] As mentioned earlier, medieval glosses quoted *sententiae* from the Proverbs and Ecclesiastes next to the distichs and deemed the author of the school booklet "the wisest of men since Solomon, old Cato."[69] Brunetto followed this practice in *Tresor* 2, where he regularly places the *Disticha* next to Solomon's sayings, as well as those of other authors of wisdom literature. Furthermore, in *Convivio* 4.24.16, Dante remarks that Solomon's purpose in the Proverbs is to correct the moral conduct of the young in order to make them "glorious": "E però scrive Salomone nelli Proverbii che quelli che umilemente e obedientemente sostiene [d]al correttore le sue corrett[iv]e riprensioni, 'sarà *glorioso*'; e dice 'sarà,' a dare a intendere che elli parla allo adolescente, che non puote essere nella presente etade" (therefore Solomon writes in Proverbs that he who humbly and obediently endures his chastener and his just reproofs "shall be glorified," and he says "shall be," to indicate that he is speaking to an adolescent, one who in the present age of life cannot be glorified). The author of the *Disticha Catonis* embraces the same purpose in his introductory *Epistula*, where he maintains that his moral reform will help young people "ut *gloriose* viverent" (so that they might live with the utmost glory and attain honor). The parallel is worth noting even though Dante invests the term "glory" with radically different meanings from those implied in the *Disticha*. A semantic rewriting of the *Disticha*'s educational aims and moral teachings might have been precisely the poet's purpose.

The extraordinary number of references to Cato that pepper *Convivio* 4 reproposes medieval education's celebrated pair, Solomon and Cato. While the subject

---

[67] Jill Mann defines "wisdom literature" as "a term denoting works that impart moral instruction by means of proverbs or exemplary anecdotes." Jill Mann, "'He Knew Nat Catoun': Medieval School-Texts and Middle English Literature," in *The Text in the Community: Essays on Medieval Works, Manuscripts, Authors, and Readers*, ed. Jill Mann and Maura Nolan (Notre Dame, IN: University of Notre Dame Press, 2006), 41–74, at 41. Barry Taylor provides the following "working definition" of the proverb collection: "a text which gives advice on conduct, expressed in brief sentences paratactically arranged." See Taylor, "Medieval Proverb Collections: The West European Tradition," *Journal of the Warburg and Courtauld Institutes* 55 (1992): 19–35, esp. 19.

[68] The translation is mine. For the influence of Solomon's authority and the medieval exegesis of the Song of Songs on *Convivio* 4, see Peter Dronke, *Dante's Second Love: The Originality and the Contexts of the "Convivio"* (Leeds: Maney, 1997); Paola Nasti, *Favole d'amore e "saver profondo": La tradizione salomonica in Dante* (Ravenna: Longo, 2007), 93–130; and Nasti, "'Vocabuli d'autori e di scienze e di libri' (*Convivio* II xii 5): Percorsi sapienzali di Dante," in *La Bibbia di Dante: Esperienza mistica, profezia e teologia biblica in Dante*, ed. Giuseppe Ledda (Ravenna: Centro Dantesco dei Frati Minori Conventuali, 2011), 121–78.

[69] Walter Map, *De nugis Curialium*, ed. Frederick Tupper and Marbury B. Ogle (London: Chatto & Windus, 1924), 287, quoted in Hazelton, "Two Texts," xx.

FREEING CATO FROM HIS *DISTICHS*   153

matter of the fourth book compels Dante to appropriate *the* medieval *auctoritas* in matters of wisdom, Solomon, it also impels him to draw on *the* medieval *exemplum* of wisdom and moral righteousness, Cato. Hence, Cato's massive presence in *Convivio* 4 reflects a conventional practice of medieval gnomic literature. After all, Dante is trying to expound on the moral ABCs that his readers should have already acquired while learning to read and write.[70] Tellingly, after celebrating Cato's name (4.28.19), the fourth book of the *Convivio* closes on a reference to "Esopo poeta" (the poet Aesop), who is presented as the ultimate *auctoritas* against those who refuse to learn: "più è prode al gallo uno grano che una margarita, e però questa lascia e quello coglie" (a grain is worth more than a pearl to a cock, and he therefore leaves the one and takes the other) (*Convivio* 4.30.4). As the first texts assigned to medieval pupils, Cato and Aesop represented the ABCs and repositories of practical wisdom for any medieval reader.

Despite Dante's rather conventional use of Cato's example and the possible echoes of the *Disticha Catonis* in *Convivio* 4, the author never directly quotes the famous school text. This fact seems particularly striking in comparison with Brunetto's *Tresor* 2, where "Cato" coincides with the authoritative voice of the *Disticha*. Dante was likely aware that the *Disticha Catonis* is a spurious work, having little to do with the two famous Catos from antiquity, but so also was Brunetto, arguably. The reason for Dante's apparent disregard for the *Disticha* may lie in his original approach to the classics and the history of Rome. In *Convivio* 4, for the first time, he shows a deeper knowledge of Virgil's *Aeneid* and, more broadly, of the classical authors. For the first time, moreover, Dante articulates his belief that Rome did not achieve universal *imperium* with violence but received it from God to fulfill his providential design.[71] The *Disticha Catonis* would have appeared unfitting to Dante's renewed classicism. First, Dante's reading in the Latin *auctores* made him aware of the key role of Cato Uticensis' life and suicide in terms of the history of the salvation of mankind.[72] Whereas the *Disticha* features Cato as *auctoritas*—a Christian moralist, in fact—the Latin poets presented him instead as a

---

[70] As Dante argues, misunderstandings of the nature and source of nobility come from flawed premises, which a reeducation of the reader should attempt to correct, as "molti idioti che non saprebbero l'a.b.c. e vorrebbero disputare in geometria, in astrologia e in fisica" (*Convivio* 4.15.16).

[71] On Dante's greater knowledge of Virgil's *Aeneid* in *Convivio* 4, see Ulrich Leo, "The Unfinished *Convivio* and Dante's Rereading of the Aeneid," *Mediaeval Studies* 13 (1951): 41–64. Marchesi ("La rilettura del 'De officiis,'" 84–87) convincingly argues that Dante's renewed knowledge of classical authors in *Convivio* 4 is also demonstrated by a deeper knowledge of Cicero's *De officiis*. See also Marchesi, "Distilling Ovid: Dante's Exile and Some Metamorphic Nomenclature in Hell," in *Writers Reading Writers: Intertextual Studies in Medieval and Early Modern Literature in Honor of Robert Hollander*, ed. Janet Smarr (Newark, NJ: University of Delaware Press, 2007), 21–39, at 35. About the poet's new awareness of the providential role of the Roman empire, see, for instance, *Convivio* 4.6.13, where he states that "per due apertissime ragioni vedere si può, le quali mostrano quella civitade imperatrice, e da Dio avere speziale nascimento, e da Dio avere speziale processo."

[72] On Dante's interpretation of the providential meaning of Rome's *imperium* and its radical difference from Augustine's view in *De civitate Dei*, see Mazzotta, *Dante, Poet of the Desert*, esp. chap. 4, and Simone Marchesi, *Dante and Augustine: Linguistics, Poetics, Hermeneutics* (Toronto: Toronto University Press, 2011), 157.

154   DANTE'S EDUCATION

historical character and example. The poet, therefore, elects Solomon as the *auctoritas* of this book and retains Cato primarily as an example of perfect morality and nobility and as a key player in the providential history of Rome.

Second, contemporary receptions of the *Disticha Catonis* made it an especially problematic source for interpreting Cato Uticensis' suicide as a step in the providential realization of Rome's universal empire. Certainly, Dante was aware of the exploitation of the *Disticha* in contemporary republican propaganda, particularly in debates on the civic and theological definition of the common good, which we already noted with regard to Brunetto's *Tresor* and Remigio's *De bono comuni*. To support his new providential view of the empire, Dante relies instead on portraits of Cato provided by Cicero, Seneca, and especially Lucan. Lucan's *Pharsalia* lends Dante crucial aid for deconstructing the patriotic Cato encapsulated in the distich "pugna pro patria." To shatter the patriotic limits imposed by the *Disticha* on Cato's suicide and to give a universal horizon to his sacrifice, Dante translates almost to the letter Lucan's *Pharsalia* 2.380–83 and writes "onde si legge di Catone che non a sé, ma *alla patria e a tutto 'l mondo* nato esser credea" (hence we read of Cato that he thought of himself as born not for himself, but *for his country and for the whole world*) (4.27.3; emphasis added).[73] Perhaps these lines from Lucan's *Pharsalia*—as well as Dante's own experience as an exile—helped the poet reach a new awareness of the historical and providential significance of Cato's suicide: Cato, Dante seems to argue, lived not just for his fatherland but for all humanity. This interpretation is underpinned by the evidence that in his nearly contemporary treatise on vernacular eloquence, Dante had claimed, as a rebuke of his own exile, that "nos autem, cui *mundus est patria*" (to me, however, *the whole world is a homeland* (*De vulgari eloquentia* 1.6.3; emphasis added). The author, therefore, had already showed a keen interest in promoting a cosmopolitan concept of homeland that crosses over urban and regional boundaries and coincides with the sense of belonging to the human community at large. The model of this humanistic counter-patriotism is the exiled poet Ovid, in *Fasti* 1.493: "Omne solum forti patria est, ut piscibus aequor" (to the brave every land is their country, as the sea to fish). Simone Marchesi argues that Dante's close rewriting of Ovid in the *De vulgari eloquentia* 1.6.3 would be directed precisely at Brunetto's rather hypocritical reuse of the same sentence in *Tresor* 2.84.11.[74]

Another important piece of evidence reveals Dante's efforts to redirect Cato's reception away from the heavily politicized trajectories drawn by Brunetto. Whereas Cato Uticensis appears as the hero of the war against Catiline in both Brunetto's *Rettorica* and his *Tresor*, Dante's Cato is never linked to those events. The poet's only reference to Catiline's conspiracy is at *Convivio* 4.5.19, but, notably,

---

[73] The excerpt from Lucan's text echoed in Dante's words is the following: "Hi mores, haec duri inmota Catonis / secta fuit, seruare modum finemque tenere / naturamque sequi *patriaeque* inpendere uitam / nec sibi sed *toti* genitum se credere *mundo*" (*Phars.* 2.380–83; emphasis added).

[74] Marchesi, "Distilling Ovid," 25.

FREEING CATO FROM HIS *DISTICHS*   155

it features Cicero as the main protagonist of that story, not Cato: "E non puose Iddio le mani quando uno nuovo cittadino di picciola condizione, Tulio, contra tanto Cittadino quanto era Catellina la romana libertate difese? Certo sí" (Was the hand of God not evident when a new citizen of small means, namely Tully, defended the liberty of Rome against so great a citizen as Catiline? Most certainly). In direct opposition to Brunetto's *Tresor*, Dante disregards the two major sources of Cato endorsed by medieval education, Sallust and the *Disticha Catonis*. Hence, Dante's renewed understanding of the legacy of Cato's sacrifice coincides with an increasing rejection of his celebration as a patriotic icon. On the one hand, Dante endorses the abstract idealization of Cato's name disseminated by the *Disticha*. The poet, for instance, elects Cato the Elder as the example of perfect disposition for receiving the divine gift of true nobility (*Convivio* 4.21.9) and claims that Cato Uticensis bears the name: "di cui è bello terminare ciò che de li segni de la nobiltade ragionare si convenia" (It is good to bring to a close what I have had to say about the signs of nobility) (4.28.19). On the other hand, throughout *Convivio* 4, Dante celebrates the example of Cato Uticensis' life and death in its full historical, allegorical, and providential significance. To glorify Cato, moreover, the author corrects the *Disticha*'s patriotic exhortation that was attributed to Cato and harnessed by contemporary republican discourse. Dante's effort to free Cato from the patriotic use of his distichs is apparent and culminates in the *Monarchia* and the *Commedia*.

Dante's Cato Says: Fight for Freedom (*Purgatorio* 1–2 and *Monarchia* 2)

In the minds of medieval readers, some of the elements that introduce Cato's character in *Purgatorio* would have conjured up the author of the *Disticha Catonis*. The four brilliant stars that shine on Cato's face and symbolize his full possession of the four cardinal virtues are strongly reminiscent of the *Disticha*, as medieval copyists arbitrarily divided the distichs into four books and identified each book with one of the four cardinal virtues.[75] Furthermore, Dante likens his Cato to a venerable father who inspires reverence from his son: "che più non dee a padre alcun figliuolo" (that no son owes his father more) (1.33). As I have already mentioned, in his introductory epistle the author of the *Disticha* also qualifies himself as a father writing to his son: "Nunc te, fili carissime, docebo" (now I will teach you, dearest son) (*Epistula Catonis*).[76] Fittingly, the character Virgil immediately instructs Dante to show reverence to Cato: "e con parole e con mani e con cenni / reverenti

---

[75] Already noted by Scott, *Dante's Political Purgatory*, 78.
[76] Throughout the *Commedia*, Dante uses the appellative "padre" to address both his teachers, Virgilio (e.g. *Inferno* 8.110) and Brunetto Latini (*Inferno* 15.31); they, in turn, call Dante "figliuol mio" (*Inferno* 3.121).

156   DANTE'S EDUCATION

mi fé le gambe e'l ciglio" (and by his words and signs and with his hands / made me show reverence with knee and brow) (1.50–51). One of the most important precepts of the *Disticha* was the unconditional submission that sons, students, and the young in general owe to fathers, teachers, and older people: "Maiori concede / Magistratum metue" (Yield to your senior; honor a magistrate) (*Breves sententiae*). The third symbolic element in Dante's representation of Cato—the old man's "oneste piume" (venerable locks) (1.42)—also reflects one of the *Disticha Catonis's* most cherished tenets. Already in *Convivio* 4.6.9–10, Dante explains that for the ancient Stoic philosophers the purpose of human life was the "rigida *onestade*. . . . E diffiniro così questo onesto: 'quello che sanza utilitade e sanza frutto, per sé di ragione è da laudare.' E costoro e la loro setta chiamati furono Stoici, e fu di loro quello glorioso Catone di cui non fui di sopra oso di parlare" (strict *integrity*. . . . And they defined this integrity as "that which apart from utility or profit is for its own sake praiseworthy according to reason." They and their sect were called Stoics, and to them belonged that glorious Cato of whom I did not dare to speak above) (emphasis added). This *onestade* seems to be the primary and most distinctive virtue of the purgatorial Cato, as confirmed by the epithet "onesto" with which this character is identified in the following canto (*Purgatorio* 2.119). The Stoic *honestas* is unmistakably the core of the *Disticha's* educational agenda, as this represents the foundational virtue that binds any individual to moral and civil laws: "Quod iustum est petito vel quod videatur *honestum* / nam stultum est petere, quod possit iure negare" (Ask what is right or fair to human eye: / for it is foolish to ask what may rightly be denied) (1.31; emphasis added); "patere legem quam ipse tuleris" (accept the law which you yourself made); "illiud adgredere quod iustum est" (undertake what is fair) (*Breves sententiae*); "Dat legem natura tibi, non accipit ipsa" (Nature gives you a law, it does not receive it from you) (1.31a).[77]

More similarities between the first two *canti* of Dante's *Purgatorio* and the *Disticha* can be observed. Cato's harsh reply, "non c'è mestier *lusinghe*" (there is no need of *flattery*) (*Purgatorio* 1.92–93; emphasis added), to Virgil's *captatio benevolentiae* also recalls one of Cato's central teachings in the *Disticha*, where he repeatedly criticizes sycophants and warns that one must be one's own severest judge: "Virtutem primam esse puta compescere linguam; / Proximus ille deo est, qui scit ratione tacere" (To rule the tongue I reckon virtue's height: / he's nearest God who can be dumb aright) (*Disticha Catonis* 1.3); "Cum te aliquis laudat, iudex tuus esse memento; / Plus aliis de te quam tu tibi credere noli" (When someone praises you, be judge alone: / trust not men's judgment of you, but your own)

---

[77] See also, for instance, the *brevis sententia* "mundus esto" often translated in the *volgarizzamenti* as "sia onesto." But see also the distichs: "Si famam servare cupis, dum vivis, honestam / fac fugias animo, quae sunt mala gaudia vitae" (4.17). Virgil's character also shares Cato's rigid *honestas*. The former's embarrassment at the beginning of *Purgatorio* 3 reveals an unspoken ethical system that unites the two characters and is signaled by the word "onestade" (3.11).

(*Disticha Catonis* 1.14); "Noli homines blando nimium sermone probare: / fistula dulce canit, volucrem dum decipit auceps" (Approve not men who wheedling nothings say: / fowlers pipe sweetly to delude their prey) (*Disticha Catonis* 1.27).[78] Since Virgil is a pagan, and Christian salvation is not granted to him in the poem, distich 1.3 fittingly describes what his character fails to grasp in front of Cato: "to rule the tongue" when one reckons with "virtue's height: he's nearest God who can be dumb aright."

The first cantos of Dante's *Purgatorio* and the *Disticha Catonis* also share a similar vision of corporal punishment and pain as means for self-purification and edification. In several places, the *Disticha* teaches the need to endure patiently the productive pain that comes from fitting punishment: "Quod merito pateris, patienter ferre memento / cumque reus tibi sis, ipsum te iudice damna" (What you deserve to bear, with patience bear: / and, when you're judge of self, you must not spare) (*Disticha Catonis* 3.17); "Cum quid peccaris, castiga te ipse subinde; / vulnera dum sanas, dolor est medicina doloris" (For faults committed, oft yourself arraign: in treating wounds, the cure of pain is pain) (*Disticha Catonis* 4.40). The opening of Dante's *Purgatorio* is informed by this same vision of corporal punishment as a source of therapeutic pain: souls are invited to endure it patiently, as evoked by the symbolic "giunco schietto" (a straight reed) that, "umile" (humble) and without "fronda" (leaf), can welcome the blows it receives (in order of mention, 1.95, 135, 103). The *Disticha Catonis* envisions its ideal pupil as having these same characteristics: "infantem nudum cum te natura creavit, / paupertatis onus patienter ferre memento" (A naked babe since nature fashioned thee, / with patience bear the load of poverty) (*Disticha Catonis* 1.21); "Verbera cum tuleris discens aliquando magistri, / fer patris imperium, cum verbis exit in iram" (At school you sometimes bear the teacher's cane: / so 'gainst a father's angry words don't strain) (*Disticha Catonis* 4.6).[79]

Finally, but most important, Cato's role at the threshold of the purgatorial world would have summoned memories of the *Disticha Catonis* in medieval readers. In *Purgatorio* 1, Cato "ushers" Dante and Virgil into the new world by introducing them to the preparatory rituals of purification.[80] Cato then reappears in *Purgatorio* 2 and urges the souls to head back to the right path. Cato's double task—first to

---

[78] Evidence of the popularity of *Disticha* 1.14 and 1.27 in the Florentine milieu at Dante's time can be found in Brunetto's *Tresor* 2.60.5, where the author echoes both.

[79] It should be noted that whereas the *Disticha*'s conception of corporal punishment fits the one provided in the Ante-*Purgatorio*, it does not fully relate to the rest of *Purgatorio*. Throughout the second canticle, pain is increasingly envisioned as an experience that should not only be endured but also joyfully embraced. A telling example is found in the *cornice* of gluttony, where Forese corrects his own definition of punishment: "io dico pena, e dovria dir sollazzo" (*Purgatorio* 23.72). For a comprehensive study on the symbolism and significance of Dante's reflection on the purpose of pain in Purgatory, see Manuele Gragnolati, *Experiencing the Afterlife: Soul and Body in Dante and the Medieval Afterlife* (Notre Dame, IN: Notre Dame University Press, 2005), chap. 3.

[80] See Raimondi's interpretation of Cato's double duty as examiner and instructor ("Il Canto I del *Purgatorio*," 29).

158   DANTE'S EDUCATION

indicate the path and then to exhort souls to tread it—recalls the commitment the *Disticha*'s author takes in the introductory *Epistle* quoted earlier. In one of the most popular medieval *accessus* to the *Disticha Catonis*, Cato is presented as someone who shows the way *ad veram salutem*:

> Materia eius sunt precepta bene et caste vivendi. Intentio eius est representare nobis qua via tendamus ad veram salutem et ut diligenter eam appetamus et omni studio inquiramus, non ad tempus, sed perseveranter, utilitas est hunc librum legentibus ut vitam suam sapienter instituere agnoscant.[81]

> (Precepts for living a good and moral life form the subject matter of this book. Its intention is to show us by what way we may reach true salvation, encouraging us to earnestly seek after it and zealously search for it, not just for a time but with perseverance. The usefulness of this book is that those who read it should learn to order their lives wisely.)

As explained by yet another medieval *principium Catonis*, the way to the final blessedness requires the purging of vices and the acquisition of virtues:

> Summum bonum non potest possideri nisi a purgatissimis mentibus. . . . In quo uerbo beatus Augustinus hortatus est nos ut si uolumus peruenire ad summum bonum uel summam beatitudinem quod debeamus purgare mentes nostras a uicijs et ipsas illustare uirtutibus. . . . De quibus quatuor uirtutibus determinantur in libro Catonis.
>
> (Rome, Biblioteca Vallicelliana, F.1, fol. 28r, Figure 4.1)

> (The supreme good cannot be possessed but by the most purged minds [souls]. . . . With these words Saint Augustine exhorts us so that, if we wish to reach the supreme good—or supreme blessedness—we should purge our minds [souls] from vices and enlighten them with virtues. These four virtues are treated in Cato's book.)

Hence, to find that the solicitous doorkeeper of the realm of purgation should be the authoritative, fatherlike Cato, whose face is drenched in the lights of the four cardinal virtues, may not have appeared all that surprising to medieval readers steeped in the *Disticha*'s teachings.

More surprising, however, would have been the absence of the sacred name "Cato" in *Purgatorio*. In an unexpected twist, Dante never names Purgatory's doorkeeper and instead celebrates his suicide, which unmistakably qualifies him as the historical Cato Uticensis. Given the ethical significance of the *nomen Catonis* in

---

[81] Huygens, *Accessus ad auctores*, 21. The translation is mine.

the cultural milieu of late medieval Italy, and the confusion between the different Catos discussed earlier, Dante's choice never to name this character "Cato" seems rather deliberate. This conspicuous absence makes plain that the Purgatorial Cato is *not* the crypto-Christian moralist and author of the distichs but precisely the historical Cato who committed suicide in Utica. However, as already mentioned, Dante does not refrain from naming Cato in *Inferno* 14. I will return to this important difference in due course.

The *Disticha Catonis* and its medieval exposition help shed a light on another meaningful feature of Virgil's initial exchange with Cato:

> "Or ti piaccia gradir la sua venuta:
> libertà va cercando, ch'è sì cara,
> come sa chi per lei vita rifiuta.
>   Tu 'l sai, ché non ti fu per lei amara
> in Utica la morte, ove lasciasti
> la vesta ch'al gran dì sarà sì chiara."
>
> (*Purgatorio* 1.70–75)

> ("May it please you to welcome his arrival, / since he's in search of liberty, which is so dear, / as he well knows who gives his life for it. / You know this well, since death in Utica / did not seem bitter, there where you left / the garment that will shine on that great day.")

On the one hand, Virgil praises the stoic *virtus* that compelled Cato to give up his life in the name of freedom: "come sa chi per lei vita *rifiuta*" (*Purgatorio* 1.72; emphasis added).[82] All four books of the *Disticha* forcefully condemn living a life without virtue and urge readers not to fear death, since, far from being an evil in itself, death brings an end to evil and suffering: "Fac tibi proponas mortem non esse timendam / quae bona si non est, finis tamen illa malorum est" (Be this thy motto—Do not dread death: / death, if no boon, our troubles finisheth) (*Disticha Catonis* 3.22); "non metuit mortem, qui scit contemnere vitam" (he fears no death who knows how life to spurn) (*Disticha Catonis* 4.22).[83] These moral principles suit Virgil's justification of Cato's suicide as an act of renouncing a life that could no longer be virtuous without freedom. On the other hand, when stating the reason behind Cato's suicide, Virgil sharply departs from the *auctoritas* of the *Disticha*; according to Virgil, Cato died *pro libertate* and not *pro patria*.

---

[82] Romano Manescalchi offers a compelling interpretation of the importance of Cato's Stoic indifference to death. See Manescalchi, "Una nuova interpretazione del Catone dantesco," *Critica Letteraria* 140 (2008): 419–46; also in Manescalchi, *Studi sulla Commedia, Le tre fiere, Enea, Ciacco, Brunetto, Catone, Piccarda ed altri problemi danteschi* (Naples: Loffredo, 2011), 133–60.

[83] See also *Disticha Catonis* 1.22, 3.22, 4.22, and 37.

160   DANTE'S EDUCATION

As witnessed by Brunetto's *Tresor* 2 and Remigio de' Girolami's *De bono comuni*, the *Disticha*'s exhortation "pugna pro patria" was in some cases deployed together with Cato Uticensis' example of martyrdom for the common good. In the *Convivio*, Dante broadens this overly narrow civic interpretation of Cato's suicide by electing the more cosmopolitan *auctoritas* of Lucan's *Pharsalia* over that of the *Disticha*. In *Purgatorio* 1, Dante further distances Cato's example from any patriotic connotation derived from the *sententia* "pugna pro patria" and turns his suicide into a sacrifice motivated by love for freedom. In the context of Purgatory, this love also acquires spiritual significance, as it points to humanity's emancipation from sin through a correct use of free will and the exercise of virtues—both of which will become central to Dante's ethical discussion in both *Purgatorio* and *Monarchia*. Thus, with his example, Cato urges souls to pursue the freedom that represents the final goal of their purgatorial expiation. Yet, even here the freedom championed by Cato does not transcend history and politics. Dante provides the same rational for his suicide also in the *Monarchia*, where Cato's sacrifice is presented as "illud inenarrabile sacrifitium *severissimi libertatis tutoris* Marci Catonis" (and that sacrifice [words cannot express it] of the *most stern guardian of freedom*, Marcus Cato) (*Monarchia* 2.5.15; emphasis added). The author also explains that Cato's action was exemplary, as he sacrificed himself "ut mundo libertatis amores accenderet, quanti libertas esset ostendit dum e vita liber decedere maluit quam sine libertate manere in illa" (in order to set the world afire with love of freedom, showed the value of freedom when he preferred to die a free man rather than remain alive without freedom) (*Monarchia* 2.5.15). Significantly, Dante juxtaposes the motivation for Cato's suicide with that of the Deci's self-sacrifice for the sake of the fatherland: "quorum alteri *pro salute patrie* mortis tenebras non horruerunt" (the former *for deliverance of their fatherland* did not recoil from the shadows of death) (*Monarchia* 2.5.15; emphasis added). The *Monarchia* not only restates that the true motivation behind Cato's suicide was an unconditional love for humanity's freedom, but also qualifies Cato's example in opposition to the heroism of the Deci, whose sacrifice was out of love for the fatherland. Dante's treatment of Cato's suicide in the *Monarchia*, therefore, appears consistent with *Purgatorio* 1 and shows the poet's evolving perception of the key role played by Cato's suicide in the history of Rome's contribution to the "redemptive process" of the world's "temporal order."[84]

Dante's word choice appears even more significant when we consider it in its historical and cultural context. Several medieval legists, canonists, and theologians who wrote about politics argued that dying for the *patria* was an act of *caritas*. Dante was likely familiar with an important formulation of this theory in Tolomeo da Lucca's *De regimine principum*. In the third book, Tolomeo writes:

---

[84] Mazzotta, *Dante, Poet of the Desert*, 64.

FREEING CATO FROM HIS *DISTICHS* 161

Amor patriae in radice charitatis fundatur, quae communia propriis, non propria communibus anteponit, ut beatus Augustinus dicit exponens verbum Apostoli de charitate. Virtus autem charitatis in merito antecedit omnem virtutem, quia meritum cuiuscumque virtutis ex virtute charitatis dependet. Ergo amor patriae super caeteras virtutes gradum meretur honoris.

(De regimine principum 4.c.3)[85]

(Love for the fatherland is founded in the roots of a charity, which puts the common good before one's own, not one's own before the common good, as Saint Augustine says when commenting the Apostle's words on charity. Deservedly the virtue of charity precedes all other virtues with regard to merit, because the merit of any virtue depends upon that of charity. Therefore, the love for the fatherland deserves a rank of honor above all other virtues.)

Since *caritas* is the mother of all Christian virtues, those who die for the fatherland and fellow citizens win eternal salvation in the afterlife. As Brunetto did in *Tresor* 3, Tolomeo quotes Sallust's Cato to prove how dear the *amor patriae* was deemed among the ancient Romans: "Quantus vero fuerit amor patriae in antiquis Romanis Salustius refert in *Catilinario* ex sententia Catonis, quasdam de eis connumerando virtutes, in quibus dictus amor includitur" (Sallust reports how sincere the love of the fatherland was in the ancient Romans from Cato's words in the *Catilinario*, enumering their virtues, in which said love is included) (*De regimine principum* 4.c.3). In the *De bono comuni*, Remigio takes Tolomeo's argument even further and maintains that the personally guiltless citizen, if he could prevent his country from being punished, should readily accept his own damnation (even to Hell), rather than being saved at the expense of his commune:

Et dicendum quod pena in damnato presupponit culpam in eo etiam simul cum pena remanentem; et ideo est ibi offensa Dei, quem tenemur preamare toti mundo, et propter amorem ipsius gaudere de pena inflicta etiam infernali quantocumque comuni a Deo propter offensam ipsius Dei, iuxta illud *Ps.* [57.11] "Letabitur iustus cum viderit vindictam." Si autem quantacumque pena posset esse sine culpa, ex virtute amoris ordinati homo deberet potius ipsam velle pati cum immunitate comunis quam quod comune suum ipsam incurreret cum immunitate sui, in quantum est pars comunis."

(Remigio de' Girolami, *De bono comuni* 18.11)

(And it must be said that in the man who is damned the punishment presupposes a fault, even simultaneously with the remaining punishment. Thus, there is there an offense against God Himself, Whom we must love above all, and for the love of

---

[85] Joseph Mathis, ed., *Divi Thomae Aquinatis De Regimine Principum* (Turin: Marietti, 1971), 41. The translation is mine.

162   DANTE'S EDUCATION

Him we are required to love the inflicted punishment, even the infernal one, as a common one from God the offense against God; *Ps.* 57.11, "The just shall rejoice when he shall see the revenge." However, let us suppose that a punishment is given without sin. On account of ordinate love, a man should be willing to suffer the punishment and spare his commune rather than let his community suffer it and he himself be spared; this because he is part of the commune.)

Other medieval sources present even more extreme elaborations of the idea that patriotic love is an act of charity, while almost invariably invoking Cato's *auctoritas* and example to support their argument. For instance, the famous jurist and professor at the University of Bologna, Accursius, quotes the distich "Cato says 'pugna pro patria'" several times in his *Glossa ordinaria* on Justinian's *Corpus juris civilis*.[86] Accursius's student and successor, Odofredus, relies on the same authority in his *Summa in usus feudorum Compluti*, and goes so far as to claim that, for the *res publica*, a thing is lawful that would otherwise be unlawful.[87] Such a line of reasoning—which had already been adopted by Brunetto and substantiated by Cato's example (*Tresor* 3.38.1–2)—would have offered Dante suitable grounds for redeeming Cato's suicide in *Purgatorio* and representing him as the virtuous citizen who sacrifices everything out of charity for the fatherland. Remarkably, however, the poet does not rely on such an argument to Christianize his Cato; in fact, Dante openly disregards it by transforming Cato's suicide from patriotic martyrdom into the self-sacrificial act of an uncompromising lover of freedom.

Scholars have discussed at length the meaning of Dante's statement that Cato died for the love of freedom, as well as the sources that might have influenced the poet.[88] To my knowledge, it has not been noted before that, by making such a claim, Dante clearly dismisses a patriotic justification endorsed by contemporary lawyers and theologians.[89] I take issue with Mazzotta's thesis that, in saving Cato, Dante endorsed existing theological and legal arguments that patriotic death was a work of *caritas*.[90] On the contrary, I argue that Dante's word choice in both *Purgatorio* and *Monarchia* is meant to counter those who claimed that *caritas* toward the *patria* was to be placed above all other Christian mandates. His objection to this argument might also have been motivated by the renewed political views he formed after the exile. In the context of the late medieval urban struggles in

---

[86] "Et iste incidit in crimen laesae maiestatis . . .; et Cato dicit, 'pugna pro patria.'" *Glos. ord.* To C. 9.43 (42), 3 par. 4. Quoted in Post, "Two Notes on Nationalism," 288.

[87] Odofredo, *Summa in usus feudorum*, is quoted in Post, "Two Notes on Nationalism," 288. Medieval historiographers, such as Henry of Ghent and Geoffrey of Mommouth, also support the interpretation of patriotic death as an act of charity. See Kantorowicz, *The King's Two Bodies*, 240–41.

[88] One of the best contributions on this subject remains Theodore Silverstein, "On the Genesis of *De Monarchia* II,5," *Speculum* 13, no. 3 (1938): 326–49.

[89] The opposite thesis has actually been suggested by many—for instance, Proto, "Nuove ricerche," 213–15, and Silverstein, "On the Genesis," esp. 346–47.

[90] Mazzotta, *Dante, Poet of the Desert*, 60–61. Gaines Post provides several examples of such a nationalistic claim in his essay "Two Notes on Nationalism."

FREEING CATO FROM HIS *DISTICHS*   163

Italy, the term "patria" was often used to refer to the city and to promote forms of civic patriotism against the universalist and conflicting claims of church and empire. By disengaging his purgatorial Cato from the ideal of the earthly *patria*, therefore, Dante contrasted the use of this ancient example for factional political discourses. The poet's antipatriotic aims stand out more clearly when we consider again *Inferno* 14, where the *nomen Catonis* is mentioned for the only time in the *Commedia*. If read next to Tolomeo da Lucca's patriotic argument, the particular wording that opens the canto and anticipates the appearance of the "sacred name" of Cato is revealing:[91]

Poi che la *carità del natio loco*
mi strinse, raunai le fronde sparte
e rende' le a colui, ch'era già fioco.
   Indi venimmo al fine ove si parte
lo secondo giron dal terzo, e dove
si vede di giustizia orribil arte.
   Lo spazzo era una rena arida e spessa,
non d'altra foggia fatta che colei
che fu da' piè di Caton già soppressa.
      (*Inferno* 14.1–15; emphasis added)

"*Amor patriae* in radice *charitatis*
fundatur"
(Tolomeo of Lucca, *De regimine principum*, III c.4; emphasis added)

(Urged by the *love I bore my place of birth*,
/ I gathered up the scattered leaves and gave them back / to him, who had by this time spent his breath. / Then we came to the boundary that divides / the second circling from the third. / And here the dreadful work of justice is revealed.

. . .

at an expanse of deep and arid sand, / much like the sand pressed long ago / beneath the feet of Cato.)

("*Love for the fatherland* is founded
in the roots of a *charity*")

The specific terminology deployed by the poet does not seem accidental. Moved by the *caritas* for his own *patria*, Dante the character consents to reassemble the torn branches that constitute the spiritual body of an unnamed Florentine suicide. With these words, the poet evokes the power of the patriotic love that should bind individuals to the other members of their civic community. As the reader learns from Virgil's reproach to Dante in *Inferno* 20, however, there should be no pity for those whom God condemns to Hell: "Qui vive la pietà quand'è ben morta; / chi

---

[91] For evidence of Tolomeo's possible influence on Dante, see Silverstein, "On the Genesis."

164   DANTE'S EDUCATION

è più scellerato che colui / che al giudicio divin passion comporta?" ("Here piety lives when pity is quite dead. / Who is more impious than one who thinks / that God shows passion in His judgment?") (*Inferno* 20.28–30).[92] Hence, the situation that the poet describes in the first lines of *Inferno* 14 uncovers the tension between devotion to the earthly fatherland and respect for God's eternal law. In such a context, the reference to Cato stresses his absence among the suicides by evoking the patriotic charity of which the Roman senator himself served as the supreme example. The poet instead seems to suggest that had Cato's suicide been merely for the sake of his earthly *patria*, his place would have been in Hell with the other suicides. Tellingly, Dante-the-pilgrim is about to meet some of the most influential public citizens from Florence's previous generation, including Brunetto, who are punished in the same subcircle of violence that opens on Cato's name and the mention of patriotic charity. These Florentine souls had laid the foundations of the political and institutional life of Dante's Florence. Judging from their dialogues with the protagonist, they still care more about the well-being of their earthly fatherland, Florence, than about God's will and their eternal damnation.[93]

In *Purgatorio* 1, therefore, Dante frees Cato's suicide from partisan propaganda and transforms him into the champion of a moral freedom that transcends geographical and political boundaries.[94] Dante's reinterpretation of Cato in the *Commedia* endorses one of two readings that medieval commentaries on the *Disticha Catonis* give to the exhortation "pugna pro patria." One is featured in Remigius d'Auxerre's commentary and offers a political and temporal reading of

---

[92] These lines present some ambiguities that have caused considerable discussion among modern commentators. First, the Italian "pietà" could mean either "pity" or "piety." Second, readers do not agree on whether Virgil's invitation to abandon "pietà" should be limited only to the *bolgia* of the diviners or applied to Hell more broadly—either in its entirety or only with regard to its lower part. There is also a philological issue that obscures the exact reading of line 30. For a summary of these problems, see Hollander's commentary ad locum. Giorgio Inglese (comm. ad loc.) notes that whereas "qui" would refer to lower Hell, line 30 refers to this particular *bolgia*. It should be noted, however, that ancient commentators do not find these lines nearly as problematic, reading them instead as a generic invitation not to pity those whom God's justice condemns. Unlike many among modern critics, moreover, early commentaries extend Virgil's invitation to the whole of Hell and its inhabitants. I opt to follow the latter as the most logical interpretation.

[93] See, for instance, Dante's dialogue with Jacopo Rusticucci, Guido Guerra, and Tegghiaio Aldobrandi in *Inferno* 16.

[94] This is not a new interpretation of Dante's Cato. Proto ("Nuove ricerche," 230) claimed that "la libertà per la quale si uccise Catone, si trasforma nella libertà morale, spirituale del cristiano." I am not persuaded, however, by the allegorical interpretation provided by Proto, as I believe that Dante's new vision of Rome's providential history informs the purgatorial Cato with a typological meaning. A typological reading of Cato's suicide would be in line with a fundamental theological distinction that Dante makes about the Roman "miracles" in *Convivio*. Justin Steinberg has noted that in *Convivio* 4, Dante lists Cato's suicide among the miracles that are "the 'strumenti' through whom we can discern the force of God's outstretched arm, 'più volte parve esse braccia di Dio essere presenti' (4.5.17)." Cato's "miracle" is presented in opposition to other Roman miracles that instead have been carried out by men with "le mani proprie." See Justin Steinberg, "Dante's Constitutional Miracles (*Monarchia* 2.4 and *Inferno* 8–9)," *Lettere Italiane* 3 (2016): 431–44, esp. 436. Such a distinction allows Dante to present Cato's suicide as a divinely inspired action, an argument that had already been made by theologians to justify a biblical suicide like Samson's. On the association of Cato and Samson, see Barański, "Purgatorio I." This complex issue, however, reaches beyond the limits of this chapter.

FREEING CATO FROM HIS *DISTICHS*   165

this exhortation: "*Pugna pro patria* id est pugnando defende patriam" (*Fight for the fatherland*, that is, defend your fatherland by fighting).[95] The other, altogether different, is provided by another anonymous commentary: "*Pugna pro patria*, id est celesti, quia ista patria terrena non est habitatio nostra, quia aliena et advena est habitatio terrena. Nichil enim decentius est hominibus quam pro patria pugnare" (*Fight for your homeland*, that is, the heavenly one, because this earthly homeland is not our dwelling, because the earthly dwelling is foreign and alien to us. Nothing is more decent for men than fighting for the homeland).[96] Immediately on entering Purgatory, therefore, souls find in Cato a living invitation to embrace the process of purification—"Correte al monte a spogliarvi lo scoglio" (Hurry to the mountain and there shed the slough) (2.122)—that leads to ultimate freedom from sin and to the virtuous life needed to access the heavenly fatherland. As I have shown, however, if the purgatorial Cato simply embodied the moral and spiritual attitude required of the souls in Purgatory to reach the ultimate freedom, Dante did not need to identify the character precisely as Cato Uticensis. The mere name "Cato" would have sufficed to evoke the moral universe endorsed by the *Disticha Catonis*—its promotion of the virtuous life and scorn of vice as the path that leads to God. Dante, instead, avoids mentioning this name altogether here.

On the one hand, by celebrating Cato's suicide in the context of *Purgatorio*, Dante certainly infuses the former's love for political freedom with moral significance. On the other hand, Cato Uticensis' uncompromising love for freedom points to the political and historical grounds on which free will might also be exercised in the present life. Through Cato's example, Dante also directs readers to Rome's providential history and its role in allowing for the political order that is required for both the social and individual pursuits of virtue. To make this point, however, he has to address the traditional image of the patriotic Cato, promoted by propagandistic exploitations of the *sententia* "pugna pro patria," and to emancipate the historical Cato Uticensis from contemporary civic discourses. In the *Monarchia*, Dante opposes even more openly his vision of the providential meaning of Cato's suicide to the patriotic interpretation offered by the *Disticha*. The continuity between the political, historical value of Cato's suicide and its eschatological significance hinges on Dante's conception of the universal *monarchia* as the uncorrupted political system that protects freedom and peace and allows its citizens to exercise free will and live the life of virtue. Hence, Rome is not *any* fatherland, but *the* fatherland common to all Christians, for which any Christian should be ready to fight.

To conclude, we can agree with Hollander that the purgatorial Cato was meant to surprise contemporary readers. We should also appreciate, however, that Dante

---

[95] Lucca, Biblioteca Statale, MS 1433, fol. 85r.
[96] This gloss is transmitted in Oxford, Bodleian Library, MS. Canonicus Bibliotheca Latina 72, fol. 62v, and quoted by Hazelton, "Christianization," 166. The translation is mine.

166   DANTE'S EDUCATION

reached this effect in a close dialogue with the *Disticha Catonis* and the reception of Cato fostered by contemporary education. The poet had no need of special instruction by the *Disticha* in granting Cato "the grace of implicit faith," as Scott maintains, but was nonetheless aware of the close relationship that, in the imagination of contemporary readers, tied the name "Cato" to the teachings of this popular school text.[97] As this chapter has shown, even though Dante does not reject the ideal vision of the perfectly virtuous Cato widely disseminated by the *Disticha*, the poet fundamentally diverges from this tradition in his presentation of Cato's suicide: first, by historicizing the purgatorial Cato as the Uticensis and, second, by providing a justification for his suicide that is not strictly patriotic and better fits the providential theory of Rome's universal empire. As the next two chapters discuss, the *Disticha Catonis* is by no means the only school text that occupies a relevant place in Dante's representation of Purgatory: the poet's engagement with contemporary education in this *cantica* is extensive and in dialogue with several other medieval school texts.

---

[97] Scott, *Dante's Political Purgatory*, 78. As many excellent studies have already argued, Dante's understanding of Cato's example and its historical significance, beginning with *Convivio* 4, appears to be increasingly shaped by Virgil, Lucan, Seneca, Sallust, and their medieval glosses. Delphine Carron has recently provided a comprehensive account of the importance of Lucan's reception for the medieval interpretation of Cato's virtues. See Delphine Carron, "Réinterprétations médiévales de Lucain (XIe–XIVe s.), à propos de la vertu catonienne," in *Des nains ou des géants? Emprunter et créer au Moyen Âge*, ed. Claude Andrault-Schmitt, Edina Bozoky, and Stephen Morrison (Turnhout, Belgium: Brepols, 2015), 65–90. Elisa Brilli recently argued that Sallust's theory about Rome's decadence influenced Dante's explanation of the causes behind the decadence of Florence in Cacciaguida's *canti*. See Elisa Brilli, *Firenze e il profeta: Dante fra teologia e politica* (Rome: Carocci, 2012), 205–07, and Brilli, "Memorie degli antenati e invenzioni dei posteri: Cacciaguida tra Dante e Firenze," *Letture Classensi* 14 (2015): 67–84, esp. 78. On the importance of Sallust's representation of Cato in civic discussions between Brunetto and Dante, see also Silvia Diacciati and Enrico Farini, "Ricerche sulla formazione dei laici a Firenze nel tardo Duecento," *Archivio storico italiano* 651, no. 2 (2017): 205–38, esp. 209.

5

A Lesson in Cross-Cultural Pastoral

The *Ecloga Theoduli* in *Purgatorio*

> The end then of learning is to repair the ruins of our parents by regaining to know God aright.
>
> (John Milton, *Of Education*)

In the opening remarks of his short treatise *Of Education*, John Milton highlights a foundational point of Christian pedagogy: the ideal—and thus ultimately unachievable—end of learning is the restoration of humanity to its prelapsarian state of moral perfection. Dante's journey through *Purgatorio* leads precisely back to the lost Garden of Eden. To regain their place in the Earthly Paradise, penitent souls must shed their fallen habits and learn to live according to their true moral nature. To this end, each of the Purgatorial terraces where penitents purge their past vices is built around a specific program of exemplary stories on which the souls must meditate. *Exempla* and *sententiae* represented essential teaching devices of medieval education, wherein they fulfilled three primary purposes: to teach history through the most memorable *facta* and *dicta* of the ancients; to support and demonstrate a given argument; and, finally, to exhort students with moral examples either to imitate or to reject. Popular examples were often drawn freely from both biblical and pagan traditions.[1]

After leaving Cato behind, and while contemplating *Purgatorio*'s *exempla*, medieval readers would soon have recognized echoes of another familiar school text that was also built around a formidable collection of biblical and pagan stories: the *Ecloga Theoduli*. This eclogue is a poem from the Carolingian period,

---

[1] There is an abundance of scholarly literature on this subject. Some I have quoted with regard to the *Disticha Catonis*, in Chapter 4. Due to its specific relevance for the field of Dante studies, here I should mention Carlo Delcorno, *Exemplum e letteratura: tra Medioevo e Rinascimento* (Bologna: il Mulino, 1989), particularly 195–257, and Delcorno, "Dante e il linguaggio dei predicatori," *Letture Classensi* 25 (1996): 51–74. See also Delcorno's useful bibliographic surveys, "Nuovi studi sull' 'exemplum,'" *Lettere italiane* 36, no. 1 (1984): 49–68, and "Nuovi studi sull' 'exemplum,'" *Lettere italiane* 46, no. 3 (1994): 459–97. A more recent review of critical literature on the subject is in Filippo Conte, "Studi sull'*exemplum*," *Le forme e la storia* 6, no. 1 (2013): 277–92. Classic studies on the subject include Claude Bremond, Jaques Le Goff, and Jean-Claude Schmitt, eds., *L'exemplum* (Turnhout, Belgium: Brepols, 1982); F. C. Tubach, "Exempla in the Decline," *Traditio* 18 (1962): 407–17; and Peter Von Moos, *Geschichte als Topik: Das rhetorische Exemplum von der Antike zur Neuzeit und die historiae im "Policraticus" Johannes von Salisbury* (New York: G. Olms, 1988).

Dante's Education. Filippo Gianferrari, Oxford University Press. © Filippo Gianferrari (2024).
DOI: 10.1093/oso/9780198881766.003.0006

168   DANTE'S EDUCATION

whose impact on medieval pastoral poetry cannot be overstated. It also offered a convenient survey of scriptural and ancient history that celebrated one while condemning the other. For these reasons, the *Ecloga* became a particularly popular school text in medieval Europe. A reader who had been educated on the *Ecloga Theoduli* could have noticed that a number of the mythological and biblical stories referenced in Dante's *Purgatorio* were also featured in the popular school text.[2] As scholars observed, the *Ecloga* may also inform Dante's representation of two key places and narrative situations of his *Purgatorio*: the gate of Purgatory proper (*Purgatorio* 9), and its end on the banks of the river Lethe in Eden (*Purgatorio* 28).[3] In both *canti*, Dante highlights intriguing points of contact between Christian and pagan traditions, while, at the same time, remarking the latter's tragic fate outside of eternal salvation.

Since a systematic study of the *Ecloga Theoduli*'s influence on Dante's *Purgatorio* has never been attempted, we are yet to appreciate the actual extent of the poet's engagement with this school text in the poem. As I propose in this chapter, however, the *Ecloga Theoduli* represents a pivotal model for Dante's construction of parallel biblical and pagan examples in *Purgatorio*, particularly for the examples of pride and humility in cantos 10–12. Echoes of the *Ecloga*, moreover, play a structural role throughout the whole of *Purgatorio* and shed light on the key syncretism that characterized the didactic program designed by Dante for this second otherworldly kingdom. As *Purgatorio*'s many entanglements with the *Ecloga Theoduli* reveal, Dante confronted the authority of this popular schoolbook to negotiate his own vision of the place of pagan wisdom in Christian education. To appreciate this fact, however, some familiarity with the *Ecloga*'s structure, its contents and essential message, as well as with the history of its fortunes as a school text in medieval Europe, is in order.

---

[2] The following is a list of biblical and mythological stories that are present in both texts; the majority of these are not treated in this chapter but suggest the *Ecloga*'s possible influence on Dante's culture: *Purg.* 14.133, Cain (*Ecl. Theod.* 57–60); *Purg.* 17.19–21, Tereus and Procne (*Ecl. Theod.* 271–72), 25–27, Haman (*Ecl. Theod.* 281–84); *Purg.* 18.133–35, Israelites in the wilderness (*Ecl. Theod.* 137–140; 145–48); *Purg.* 20.109–11, Joshua (*Ecl. Theod.* 169–72); *Purg.* 22.146–47, Daniel (*Ecl. Theod.* 257–60), 148–50, Golden Age (*Ecl. Theod.* 45–48); *Purg.* 25.130–32, Diana (*Ecl. Theod.* 261–64); *Purg.* 26.40–42, Sodom and Gomorrah (*Ecl. Theod.* 109–16); *Purg.* 27.22, Geryon (*Ecl. Theod.* 174), 76–87, pastoral scene—shepherd overseeing his flock (*Ecl. Theod.* 76–87), 93, prophetic dreams (*Ecl. Theod.* 131), 95, Venus Citharea (*Ecl. Theod.*117), 115, Edenic *pome* (*Ecl. Theod.* 51), 135, prelapsarian nature (*Ecl. Theod.* 50), 142, crowning (*Ecl. Theod.* 231); *Purg.* 28.47, pastoral scene—men and women divided by a river (*Ecl. Theod.* 15), 50, Proserpina (*Ecl. Theod.* 317), 93, Eden, and 94, after the fall (*Ecl. Theod.* 41–44), 130, Lethe (*Ecl. Theod.* 311), 140, Golden Age (*Ecl. Theod.* 38).
[3] For the first proposition, see Zygmunt G. Barański, "Reading the *Commedia*'s IXs 'Vertically': From Addresses to the Reader to the *Crucesignati* and the *Ecloga Theoduli*," *L'Alighieri* 44 (2014): 5–35, esp. 31; for the second one, see Ambrogio Camozzi Pistoja, "Il veglio di Creta alla luce di Matelda: una lettura comparativa di *Inferno* XIV e *Purgatorio* XXVIII," *Italianist* 29 (2009): 27–28.

THE *ECLOGA THEODULI* IN *PURGATORIO*   169

The *Ecloga Theoduli* in Medieval Education

The *Ecloga Theoduli* was written sometime between the second half of the ninth century and the beginning of the tenth. Its authorship continues to elude scholars, who generally consider "Theodulus" to be a fictional name. Medieval glosses on the *Ecloga* describe its author as a scholar who studied and wrote his poem in Athens before 529.[4] The poem stages a poetic contest between two shepherds, in the wake of Virgil's third *Eclogue*. The outcome, however, could not be more distant from its Virgilian model, as Theodulus turns the two contenders into the allegories of Christian Truth and Pagan Falsehood, embodied respectively by the shepherdess Alithia and the shepherd Pseustis.[5] From the outset, the *Ecloga Theoduli* displays the marks of an original reworking of the classical pastoral:

> *Æthiopum terras* iam fervida torruit æstas,
> in Cancro solis dum volvitur aureus axis,
> compuleratque suas *tiliæ* sub amœna *capellas*
> natus ab Athenis pastor cognomine Pseustis,
> pellis pantheræ corpus cui texit utrimque
> discolor et rigidas perflavit *fistula* buccas
> emittens sonitum per mille foramina vocum.
> Ad fontem iuxta pascebat *oves* Alithia,
> virgo decora nimis David de semine regis,
> cuius habens *citharam* fluvii percussit ad undam.
>
> > (*Ecloga Theoduli* 1–10; emphasis added)[6]
>
> (The summer's heat scorched the *Ethiopian land*, / The time the sun's gold orb revolves in Cancer's sign. / A shepherd born in

---

[4] Some have attributed the poem to Godescale or Gottschalk of Orbasis. On the authorship and dating of the *Ecloga Theoduli*, see R. B. C. Huygens, "Introduction," to Bernard d' Utrecht, *Commentum in Theodolum (1076–1099)*, ed. R. B. C. Huygens, 2nd ed. (Spoleto: Centro italiano di studi sull'alto Medioevo, 1977), 4–6. See also Max Manitius, *Geschichte der Lateinischen Literatur des Mittelalters*, vol. 1 (Munich: Beck, 1911), 573; Johann E. Osternacher, "Die Überlieferung der 'Ecloga Theoduli,'" *Neues Archiv* 45 (1915): 329–76, esp. 331; Betty N. Quinn, "Ps. Theodolus," in *Catalogus Translationum et Commentariorum*, ed. Paul O. Kresteller, Virginia Brown, and Ferdinand E. Cranz, vol. 2 (Washington, DC: Catholic University of America Press, 1971), 383–408; Frederic J. E. Raby, *A History of Secular Latin Poetry in the Middle Ages*, vol. 1 (Oxford: Clarendon Press, 1957), 228; Karl Strecker, "Ist Gottschalk der Dichter der 'Ecloga Theoduli,'" *Neues Archiv* 45 (1924): 18–23.

[5] R. P. H. Green claims that "no poem in the large class of Latin poems in which a pastoral framework is made the vehicle for a debate takes more care in recreating the Virgilian milieu." See R. P. H. Green, "The Genesis of a Medieval Textbook: The Models and Sources of the *Ecloga Theoduli*," *Viator* 13 (1982): 49–106, esp. 51. For a criticism of this view, see Francesco Mosetti Casaretto, "Il caso controverso dell'*Ecloga Theoduli*," *Studi Medievali* 54, no. 1 (2013): 329–64.

[6] The *Ecloga Theoduli* is quoted from Johann E. Osternacher, *Theoduli eclogam recensuit et prolegomenis instruxit* (Urfahr-Lenz: Ripariae prope Lentiam, 1902). The translation is from *The Eclogue of Theodulus: A Translation*, trans. George A. Rigg (Toronto: Centre for Medieval Studies, University of Toronto, 2005), accessed August 2023, https://www.medieval.utoronto.ca/research/online-resources/eclogue-theodulus-translation. I have modified Rigg's translation of the first line to reflect more closely the Latin original. Rigg translated it as follows: "The summer's heat, like Africa, scorched all the earth."

170   DANTE'S EDUCATION

> Athens—Falsehood was his name— / Had brought his herd of
> goats beneath the *lime tree*'s shade. / A spotted panther skin he'd
> wrapped around himself; / A *pipe* puffed out his stiffened cheeks,
> emitting sounds / Of many notes, dispelled from out a thousand
> holes. / Just by the spring the maiden Truth gave sheep their food,
> / A lovely girl, descended from King David's line / Whose *harp* she
> held and played it by the river's stream.)

The distinctive incipit "Aethiopum terras," by which the poem came to be known, already marks a sharp departure from the Virgilian archetype, as it relocates the pastoral landscape to the far and mysterious land of Ethiopia—a land described in the Bible as pagan, idolatrous, and the enemy of Israel.[7] Even though Ethiopia had become Christian long before Rome did, and the country's rich monastic tradition had made sporadic contact with the West, for medieval readers this exotic name pointed to multiple and fantastic locations at the antipodes of the world, both in the East and South.[8] Ethiopia was often associated with India and placed in the so-called torrid zone, which is described by different sources as either accessible or lying beyond humanity's reach. In classical Latin texts, the word "Aethiops" identifies "dark-complexioned races" living near Egypt and is also used as synonym of "sunburnt" or "black man." The term, however, not only has geographical, physical, and racial connotations but also was used as a plain deprecatory attribute to indicate "a coarse, dull, awkward man, a blockhead."[9] Medieval maps and other sources imagine the "torrid" regions of the world as inhabited by monstrous human races, deformed by the extreme heat or marked by unrestrained sexual habits.[10] Some medieval commentators of the *Ecloga*, such as the so-called Anonymous Teutonicus, also contributed to this bodily, spiritual, and moral disparagement of the Ethiopians:

> *Ethyopum* id est peccatorum . . . Eciam peccato res [*sic*] bene comparantur Ethyopibus, quia sicud Ethyopes sunt homines nigri et horribilem prebent videntibus aspectum, sic eciam peccatores denigrati labe peccati . . . *Ethyopum*, id est hominum nigrorum per peccatum.[11]

---

[7] See, for instance, Psalms 67.32; Isaiah 11.10, 20.3–6, 43.3, and 45.14; Jeremiah 46.8–9; Ezekiel 29.10 and 30.4.

[8] In his commentary, Bernard of Utrecht explains that there are three lands called Ethiopia: one in the East, one in the West, and one in the South. Bernard d'Utrecht, *Commentum in Theodulum*, § 1.1–3. For the long history of Ethiopian monasticism, see Gianfrancesco Lusini, "The Ancient and Medieval History of Eritrean and Ethiopian Monasticism: An Outline," in *A Companion to Medieval Ethiopia and Eritrea*, ed. Samantha Kelly (Leiden: Brill, 2020), 194–216.

[9] Charlton T. Lewis and Charles Short, "Aethiops," in *A Latin Dictionary* (Oxford: Clarendon Press, 1879), Perseus Digital Library, Tufts University, accessed February 2022, http://www.perseus.tufts. edu/hopper/text?doc=Perseus%3Atext%3A1999.04.0059%3Aentry%3DAethiops.

[10] See Adolfo Cecilia, Luigi Vanossi, and Enrico Cerulli, "Etiopia," in the *ED*.

[11] Anonimus Teutonicus, *Commentum in Theodoli Eclogam*, 1.3, in Árpád Órban, "Anonymi Teutonici Commentum in Theodoli Eclogam e Codice Utrecht, U.B. 292 editum," *Vivarium* 11, no. 1 (1973): 1–41. The translation is mine.

(*Of the Ethiopians*: namely, belonging to sinners . . . Sinners well compare to Ethiopians, because as Ethiopians are black men and appear horrible to those who see them, so too sinners, blackened by the tent of sin. . . . *Of the Ethiopians*: namely, of blackened people, through sin.)

In the Anonymous Teutonicus's reading, physical traits and racial stereotypes become a degrading mark of moral sinfulness, while allegorically they identify the sin of heresy. Paradoxically, however, medieval culture understood Ethiopia also to be a place central to salvation history. This remote and mysterious land was associated with the Queen of Sheba, loved by King Solomon and often identified as the bride of the Song of Songs; one of the Magi who first adored Jesus; and one of Queen Candace's court officials, whose conversion is narrated in Acts 8:26–40. As Suzanne Conklin Akbari maintains, from a theological perspective "Ethiopia was understood as a place of special grace and apocalyptic expectations."[12] The unconventional Ethiopian setting in which the *Ecloga Theoduli*'s poetic contest takes place, therefore, immediately unveils the poem's core theme: the clash between Christianity and paganism.

Other elements in the *Ecloga Theoduli*'s narrative exordium also forerun the poem's antagonistic message. The pagan Pseustis, originally from Athens, is shepherding his goats under a linden tree, which represents a curious variation on the canonical Virgilian beech tree (*Eclogues* 1.1). According to the Anonymous Teutonicus commentator on the *Ecloga*, the linden tree symbolizes Satan's temptations, because it puts out beautiful flowers but does not produce fruit. Pseustis in turn would represent the devil, or the false preacher, who lures others into perdition by means of beautiful lies.[13] Instead, the shepherdess Alithia, a holy virgin born from the lineage of King David, drives a flock of sheep to a spring of water. The reference to the two different flocks (*oves* and *capellas*) has classical precedents in both Virgil and Ovid.[14] In the particular context of the clash between paganism and Christianity represented in the *Ecloga*, however, the opposition of the two flocks acquires eschatological significance, as it reflects a specific biblical symbolism derived from the Gospel of Matthew.[15] In Matthew 25.31–34, Jesus explains that on Judgment Day, God will separate the saved from the damned, as a shepherd separates sheep from goats:

---

[12] Suzanne Conklin Akbari, "Where Is Medieval Ethiopia? Mapping Ethiopic Studies within Medieval Studies," in *Toward a Global Middle Ages: Encountering the World through Illuminated Manuscripts*, ed. Bryan C. Keene (Los Angeles: Getty Publications, 2019), 82–93, at 88. Eventually Ethiopia came also to be associated with the legendary Prester John, whose Christian kingdom was located somewhere in the East.

[13] "Tylia enim est arbor valde pulchra, habens multos flores et nullum fructum producens. Sic Pseustis, i. dyabolus vel falsus praedicator, falsitate disputat, que falsitas nullum fructum gerit et dulcor ymaginarius ei inesse videtur." Anonimus Teutonicus, *Commentum in Theodoli Eclogam*, 1.3.

[14] See, for instance, the Virgilian precedent of *Eclogues* 1, where Tityrus has sheep (1.8) and Meliboeus goats (1.12), and *Eclogues* 7, where Thyrsis drives sheep and Corydon goats.

[15] On Theodulus's adaptation of this key biblical subtext, see Francesco Mosetti Casaretto, "Introduzione," to Theodulus, *Ecloga: Il canto della verità e della menzogna* (Florence: SISMEL Edizioni del Galluzzo, 1997), liii–cxvii, at lix.

172 DANTE'S EDUCATION

Cum autem venerit Filius hominis in majestate sua, et omnes angeli cum eo, tunc sedebit super sedem majestatis suae: et congregabuntur ante eum omnes gentes, et separabit eos ab invicem, sicut pastor *segregat oves ab haedis*: et statuet oves quidem a dextris suis, haedos autem a sinistris. Tunc dicet rex his qui a dextris ejus erunt: Venite benedicti Patris mei, possidete paratum vobis regnum a constitutione mundi.

(emphasis added)

(And when the Son of man shall come in his majesty, and all the angels with him, then shall he sit upon the seat of his majesty. And all nations shall be gathered together before him, and he shall separate them one from another, as the shepherd *separateth the sheep from the goats*: And he shall set the sheep on his right hand, but the goats on his left. Then shall the king say to them that shall be on his right hand: Come, ye blessed of my Father, possess you the kingdom prepared for you from the foundation of the world.)

The beginning of the *Ecloga Theoduli*, therefore, anticipates the fateful separation of the two eschatological flocks, sets the apologetic theme of the whole poem, and foretells the outcome of the poetic contest: the Christian Alithia is destined to win and lead her sheep to the spring of eternal life, whereas the pagan Pseustis is condemned to lose and drive his goats under the shadow of eternal perdition. How pervasive this eschatological interpretation of the poem's opening imagery was in medieval education can be surmised by the interlinear glosses of a schoolbook that was produced in fourteenth-century Italy. Here, a medieval glossator added the interlinear gloss "Christians" over the word "sheep" and "baptism" over "spring" (Figures 5.1 and 5.2).

Pseustis, moreover, emerges from the opening scene of the poem as a remarkably composite figure. On the one hand, the shepherd from Athens embodies classical antiquity in general, and Virgil in particular, as clearly alluded to by the shepherd's pipe (*fistula*) that Pseustis plays. On the other hand, the remote Ethiopian landscape he inhabits, and the black-spotted panther skin he wears, turn Pseustis into a figure not only of the ancient, pagan poet but also of the ethnically and culturally distant "other"—the humanity living in the mysterious Orient, beyond Christendom's southern and eastern borders.[16] Pseustis' Virgilian *fistula*, moreover, is opposed to Alithia's *cithara*. The symbolic relevance of this opposition of instruments is apparent: the *cithara* famously belonged to King David, as well as to Apollo, and thus represents a sacred instrument for both traditions. The *fistula*, on the contrary, is a vapid instrument, full of air and vanity. In Greek

---

[16] Although the panther skin may also turn Pseustis into a figure of Bacchus, it should be noted that the god was traditionally represented wearing a tiger skin.

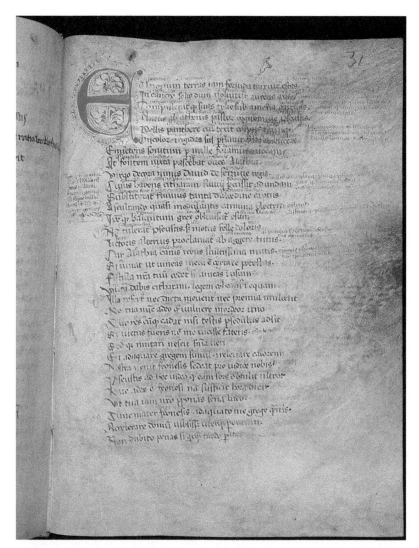

Figure 5.1 Oxford, Bodleian, Addenda Add. A. 171 (XIV century), fol. 31r. Incipit of the *Ecloga Theoduli*: "Ethiopum terras iam."
Source: Courtesy of the Bodleian Library, Oxford.

Figure 5.2 Oxford, Bodleian, Addenda Add. A. 171 (XIV century), fol. 31r. Detail of interlinear gloss: the gloss "baptismus" has been added over the word "fontem," and the abbreviated word "christianis" over the Latin "oves."
Source: Courtesy of the Bodleian Library, Oxford.

174   DANTE'S EDUCATION

mythology—but the story is also briefly referenced in Ovid's *Metamorphoses* 6 (383–400)—the faun Marsyas plays the flute, which had been created and then cast away by Athena, in a poetic contest with Apollo, who instead plays his stringed instrument, a *cithara* or a lyre. The former is judged the loser in the musical duel and is skinned alive by the latter, while his tears turn into a river. Similarly, Pseustis with his *fistula* challenges Alithia, armed with her *cithara*, to a poetic duel held in front of the allegory of Prudence, Fronesis, and is likewise doomed to fail.

Following the model of Virgil's seventh *Eclogue*, the contest between Pseustis and Alithia unfolds in a series of quatrains, whose lines, however, feature a unique variant of Leonine hexameters. Pseustis sings twenty-nine mythological stories drawn from Ovid, Virgil, Statius, and several other classical and late antique sources, and Alithia answers each one of them with a quatrain containing episodes from the Old Testament that parallel Pseustis' more or less explicitly. To Pseustis' account of the Golden Age, for instance, Alithia replies with the story of Adam and Eve in the Earthly Paradise. The result is a sequence of parallel stories across Christian and pagan traditions, until Alithia overcomes pagan lies and Pseustis loses his flute and the ability to sing, losses that betoken the end of pagan poetry and the beginning of a new Christian poetics. Finally, the time of the day when the story takes place—the duel starts at midday and ends at sunset—is rather atypical of the pastoral genre and symbolizes the twilight of pagan culture. As paganism no longer constituted a real threat when the poem was written, Theodulus's actual target was classical poetry.

The *Ecloga Theoduli* is a remarkable product of erudition and unprecedented poetic experiment that had a long-lasting influence on the medieval pastoral genre. Not only did its author draw on a variety of different sources, harmonizing them into a single, original poem, but he also readapted the topos of the pastoral contest into a medium for representing a clash between Christian and pagan cultures, in patristic-like apologetic spirit. The Christian poets Sedulius and Alcuin had already exploited the potential of the amoebean eclogue for carrying out a debate, and Theodulus further implemented this trend, while drawing on a wide range of literary genres and styles. Another close model for its format and content was offered by Prudentius' *Dittochaeon* or *Tituli Historiarum*, also a medieval school text. Like the *Ecloga Theouduli*, Prudentius' poem features a sequence of quatrains alternating stories from the Old and the New Testaments, but the pastoral setting and pagan mythology are entirely missing, as Prudentius collects only biblical stories. While Prudentius' practice of drawing parallels between the Old and the New Testaments found its roots and legitimation in Jerome's system of biblical correspondences, the *Ecloga Theoduli*'s systematic rapprochement of similar pagan and biblical stories has no precedent in Latin Christian poetry.[17] The *Ecloga*, therefore,

---

[17] The influence of Prudentius' *Dittochaeon* on the genesis of the *Ecloga* is still a matter of debate. R. P. H. Green is in favor of counting Prudentius among the models of the *Ecloga*, but he also acknowledges

THE *ECLOGA THEODULI* IN *PURGATORIO*   175

offered medieval readers a uniquely cross-cultural storehouse of ancient examples and wisdom.[18] Through the study of Prudentius' *Dittochaeon* and Theodulus, medieval educators joined the teaching of grammar with basic historical notions. While learning the most momentous events in both sacred and pagan antiquities, pupils were also introduced to a providential view of universal history as a process of fall, decline, and redemption with Christ's incarnation at its center.

The *Ecloga Theoduli*'s memorable synthesis of universal history and edifying stories contributed to its considerable success in the medieval schoolroom. Students were probably introduced to the *Ecloga Theoduli* sometime after studying the *Disticha Catonis*—at a stage, that is, when they were able to read full Latin sentences. Alexander Neckam considered the poem to be appropriate for pupils who had already digested some elementary Latin readers and were ready to move on to more advanced texts in preparation for readings of greater complexity:

> Postquam alphabetum didicerit et ceteris puerilibus rudimentis imbutus fuerit, Donatum et illud utile moralitatis compendium quod Catonis esse vulgus opinatur addiscat, et ab Ecgloga Theodoli transeat ad eglogas Bucolicorum, prelectis tamen quibusdam libellis informationi rudium necessariis.

> (After he has learnt the alphabet and been imbued with certain other boyish rudiments, let him learn Donatus and that useful moral compendium which is generally believed to be the work of Cato, and from the *Eclogues* of Theodolus let him move on to the *Bucolics* [of Virgil], having first however read some shorter works which are necessary for the instruction of the unlearned.)[19]

---

that, given their similar forms and contents, it is surprising to find that the two poems share no further commonalities. Even the biblical stories only partially overlap: a quarter of Theodulus's references coincide with those chosen by Prudentius. See Green, "Genesis," 61. Ian Thomson and Louis Perraud instead rule Prudentius out of the major sources of the *Ecloga*. See Thomson and Perraud, *Ten Latin Schooltexts of the Later Middle Ages: Translated Selections* (Lewiston, NY: Mellen Press, 1990), 111. They follow Morton Y. Jacobs's argument in "Bernard's Commentum in Theodulum, editio princeps" (Ph.D. diss., University of North Carolina at Chapel Hill, 1963). Sedulius' *Carmen Paschale* and Prudentius' *Contra Symmachum* also offered seminal models for the *Ecloga* (Green, "Genesis," 61). In addition, Harry Vredeveld has noted verbal parallels with nine Christian poems and with ten Carolingian works. See Harry Vredeveld, "Pagan and Christian Echoes in the 'Ecloga Theoduli': A Supplement," *Mittellateinisches Jahrbuch* 22 (1987): 109–13. The *Ecloga* also draws on a wide array of classical sources, among which Ovid, Virgil, Servius, Statius, and the Vatican Mythographers are the most relevant ones. Vredeveld ("Pagan and Christian Echoes") offers a list of verbal parallels between the *Ecloga* and seventeen classical poets. Instead, Huygens ("Introduction") emphasizes the relevance of the Vatican Mythographers.

[18] The uniqueness of the *Ecloga*'s experiment should be seen in light of the distaste for and general avoidance of the embarrassing parallels between biblical and mythological stories displayed by early Christian authors. Besides the system of parallel examples in Dante's *Purgatorio*, another late medieval exception worth mentioning is Baudri of Bourgueil. See Ernst Robert Curtius, *European Literature and the Latin Middle Ages* (London: Routledge & Kegan Paul, 1953), 46, 220, 362–363. Curtius also argues that the poem had been written by a schoolmaster who devised it to teach mythology while at the same time warning students against it (46).

[19] The Latin original is quoted in Charles H. Haskins, "A List of Text-Books from the Close of the Twelfth Century," *Harvard Studies in Classical Philology* 20 (1909): 75–94, at 90. The translation is by

176   DANTE'S EDUCATION

Reading the *Ecloga*, therefore, coincided with the early stages in the reading curriculum and provided a sample of the Latin bucolic genre.[20]

The *Ecloga* also purveyed a paradigm of classicizing Christian poetry that aimed to defuse the threat entailed in studying pagan poetry and mythology in the Christian classroom.[21] As a medieval *accessus* clearly states, Theodolus juxtaposes Christian and pagan beliefs to extol one and lambaste the other:

> Materia eius sunt sententiae de ecclesiasticis et paganis scriptis collatae et ipsae in eis certantes personae, intentio eius est ostendere vires veritatis et defectum falsitatis et tantum katholicam traditionem excellere ritum gentilem, quantum veritas falsitatem. Utilitas est ut cum viderimus victam succumbere falsitatem, ipsam relinquamus et lumen veritatis assequamur.[22]

> (His subject-matter is a comparison of profound sayings drawn from ecclesiastical and from pagan writings, and the characters who debate in these. His intention is to show the strength of truth and the inadequacy of falsehood, and that traditional Catholic teaching excels the pagan religion as truth excels falsehood. The usefulness is that, when we have seen falsehood vanquished, we may abandon it and follow the light of truth.)

Yet the text itself may be shown to display an ambivalent attitude toward pagan antiquity. As the narrative unfolds, the reader presides over a poetic clash between opposing traditions and poetics; the outcome of this pastoral contest is an interlocking chain of parallel stories that foregrounds both opposition and similarity between pagan and Christian traditions. As a result, the actual aim of this work (*intentio operis*) has been at the center of a heated debate among scholars. The most recent editor of the *Ecloga*, Francesco Mosetti Casaretto, has no doubt that Theodulus wishes to represent ancient mythology as demonic, prompting readers to reject it *in toto*. Others, like Peter Dronke, suggest instead that the *Ecloga* may pass a more nuanced judgment on the value and significance of pagan mythology in Christian culture.[23] The *Ecloga* does present some ambiguity on this point. Toward

---

Suzanne Reynolds in her *Medieval Reading: Grammar, Rhetoric and the Classical Text* (Cambridge: Cambridge University Press, 1996), 7.

[20] Paul M. Clogan, "Literary Genres in a Medieval Textbook," *Medievalia et Humanistica* 11 (1982): 199–209, esp. 202.

[21] Birger Munk Olsen explained the role of the *Ecloga* in medieval education as "another remedy against the Classics." Olsen, *L'atteggiamento medievale di fronte alla cultura classica* (Rome: Unione internazionale degli istituti archeologici, storia e storia dell'arte in Roma, 1994), 26–27.

[22] R. B. C. Huygens, ed., *Accessus ad auctores, Bernard d'Utrecht, Conrad d'Hirsau: Dialogus super auctores; Édition critique* (Leiden: Brill, 1970), 27. The translation is in A. J. Minnis, A. B. Scott, and David Wallce, eds., *Medieval Literary Theory and Criticism c. 1100–1375: The Commentary Tradition* (Oxford: Oxford University Press, 1991 [1988]), 18.

[23] For a good summary of the critical debate on the interpretation of the *Ecloga*, see Mosetti Casaretto, "Il caso controverso dell'*Ecloga Theoduli*." Also by Mosetti Casaretto, see "Alle origini del genere pastorale cristiano: L'*Ecloga Theoduli* e la demonizzazione del paganesimo," *Studi Medievali*

THE *ECLOGA THEODULI* IN *PURGATORIO*   177

the end of the poem, while the specter of defeat looms large for Pseustis, and he is compelled to surrender to the Christian truth, the judge of the duel, Fronesis, enigmatically appeals to Alithia for mercy, lest Pseustis be fatally wounded by despair:

FRONESIS

> Mortales cuncti quod contendunt adipisci
> nec, si perficiant, vitæ discrimina curant,
> ex insperato dominus tibi contulit ultro:
> ut cessare velis devictus supplicat hostis.
> Treicius vates commovit pectine Manes,
> te moveant lacrimæ; iam tollit cornua Phœbe;
> sol petit Oceanum frigus succedit opacum:
> desine quod restat, ne desperatio lædat.
>
> (Ecloga Theoduli 337–44)

> (What every mortal yearns to gain and doesn't care / about the risk to life, if they achieve the prize, / the Lord, unhoped, has granted you of his own will. / Your rival, conquered, begs that you should now desist. / The Thracian bard, with thumb on harp, moved shades long dead, / so now let tears move you! The moon lifts up her horns, / the sun sinks in the sea, and chilly dark comes next. / Now don't say any more, lest desperation hurt.)

Fronesis' advice insinuates a mitigating effect on the *Ecloga*'s outspoken opposition to pagan mythology: her care to ensure that Pseustis should not be cast into despair can be allegorically interpreted as a suggestion for Christian poets to draw moral profit from pagan stories and to subsume them into their poetics.[24] Thus a tension is at play in the *Ecloga* between the overt condemnation of pagan poetry and its preservation for practical purposes.

---

33 (1992): 469–536, and "Introduzione"; and "Discussione sulla lezione di Dronke," in *Ideologie e pratiche del reimpiego nell'Alto Medioevo: Atti della XLVI Settimana di Studio del Centro Italiano di Studi sull'Alto Medioevo; Spoleto, 16–21 Aprile 1998* (Spoleto: Centro di Studi sull'Alto Medioevo, 1999), 313–19. For an opposite view, see Peter Dronke, "Riuso di forme e immagini antiche nella poesia," in *Ideologie e pratiche del reimpiego*, 283–312; Michael Herren, "Reflections on the Meaning of the *Ecloga Theoduli*: Where Is the Authorial Voice?," in *Poetry and Exegesis in Premodern Latin Christianity: The Encounter between Classical and Christian Strategies of Interpretation*, ed. Willemien Otten and Karla Pollmann (Boston: Brill, 2007), 199–230; Lean Meyers, "L'Églogue de Théodule: 'Démonisation' ou 'sacralisation' de la mythologie?," in *L'allégorie de l'antiquité à la Renaissance*, ed. Brigitte Pérez-Jean and Patricia Eichel-Lojkine (Paris: Champion, 2004), 335–47; Alan Soons, "The Didactic Quality of *Theoduli Ecloga*," *Orpheus* 20 (1973): 149–61; Jean-Yves Tilliette, "Grecia Mendax," in *La Grèce antique sous le regard du Moyen Âge Occidental, Actes du 15e Colloque de la Villa Kérylos (Beaulieu-Sur-Mer, 8 et 9 Octobre 2004)*, ed. Jean Leclant and Michel Zink (Paris: Diffusion De Boccard, 2005), 11–22.

[24] Medieval discussions of mnemotechnics taught that memory was instrumental to the virtue of prudence. On the link between the art of memory and the virtue of prudence in medieval culture, see

178   DANTE'S EDUCATION

The medieval commentators of the *Ecloga* similarly display ambivalence on this point and often highlight elements of continuity between pagan and Christian traditions. For instance, Bernard of Utrecht—an obscure schoolmaster who furnished the poem with a commentary at the end of the eleventh century—argues that Alithia forgives Pseustis, in observance of Fronesis' advice, but that the author does not openly say so for reasons of prudence.[25] Instead of discarding ancient poetry entirely, commentators strive to show the wisdom conveyed by mythological stories. In their commentaries, Bernard of Utrecht, Alexander Neckam, and the Anonymous Teutonicus all propose allegorical or euhemeristic interpretations of the mythological lore related by Pseustis.[26] Bernard of Utrecht appears to be mostly concerned with providing grammatical explanations, textual expositions, and narrative summaries of the biblical episodes quoted in the *Ecloga*. He classifies the pagan stories as *fabulae* and the biblical ones as *historiae*, thereby acknowledging their different epistemological values. He interprets most of the fables etiologically, often highlighting their moral meaning, which he terms *misterium*. He also provides moral and allegorical readings for each *historia*.[27] Instead of setting pagan mythology and biblical stories in opposition, Bernard values the former tradition as a source of learning and the latter as a source of revelation. The Anonymous Teutonicus retains Bernard's main division between *fabulae* and *historiae* and explains that both can have allegorical and moral truths, albeit regularly introducing scriptural episodes in terms of "hystoria vera." Notwithstanding this classification, he often draws comparisons between pagan and Christian traditions and points to their parallel elements. The same critical attitude can be detected also in Conrad of Hirsau's brief *accessus* to Theodulus, where the commentator explains that

> intentio eius (Theoduli) est sacrae paginae veritatem commendare et fabularum commenta dissuadere, non quidem ut non legantur, sed ne lectae credantur vel in actum transferantur. . . . Proprium quidem est servo dei veritatem a falsitate descernere, ut *omnia probet, quod bonum est teneat, ab omni specie mala*

Mary Carruthers, *The Book of Memory: A Study of Memory in Medieval Culture* (Cambridge: Cambridge University Press, 2008), esp. chap. 5, and Pier Massimo Vescovo, "Ecfrasi con spettatore (Dante, 'Purgatorio' X–XVII)," *Lettere Italiane* 45 (1993): 335–60, esp. 336.

[25] "Patet ergo Alithiam Pseusti ignovisse, cum de quo cuncta pendeant iudex legatur hoc voluisse, et ex hoc Theodolum prudenter tacuisse." Bernard d'Utrecht, *Commentum in Theodolum*, §§ 1542–44.

[26] For a comprehensive overview of the medieval commentaries on the *Ecloga*, see Quinn, "Ps. Theodolus." Judging from the extant manuscripts, Bernard's commentary circulated mostly in the schools of England and northern Europe and was eventually supplanted by a commentary attributed to Alexander Neckam. Neckam's authorship, however, is recorded only in two manuscripts. This commentary enjoyed wide circulation during the late Middle Ages. See Christopher J. McDonough, "Alexander Neckam and the Commentary on the *Ecloga Theoduli*: A Question of Attribution," *Filologia Mediolatina* 15 (2008): 249–67. A later commentary by the Anonymous Teutonicus is preserved only in two manuscripts and was certainly circulating in Germany and some parts of northern Europe. Finally, Odo Picardus composed (1406–07) a gloss for the son of Charles VI as an introduction to the duties and responsibilities of the king.

[27] See Bernard d'Utrecht, *Commentum in Theodolum*, §§ 1076–99.

THE *ECLOGA THEODULI* IN *PURGATORIO*   179

abstineat. . . . Primum igitur in hoc opere a docente sensus ponendus est in litera, deinde ipsa litera per allegoriam elucidanda, inde per moralitatem vita legentis instituenda.

(emphasis added)[28]

(Theodulus's intention is to celebrate the truth of the sacred page and dissuade from the fictions of fables, not because they should not be read, but lest, once read, they be believed in and acted upon. . . . Appropriate to the servant of God is to discern the truth from the lie, *to test everything, retain what is good, and refrain from all sorts of evils.* . . . Hence, in this work, the first meaning is to be found by the teacher in the letter, then this same letter ought to be interpreted allegorically, and from it the reader should be instructed on how to live morally.)

Echoing Saint Paul's invitation to test everything and retain what is good (1 Thessalonians 5:21–23), Conrad advocates for finding moral edification and wisdom anywhere, without needing to discard non-Christian sources of learning. It would not be an overstatement, therefore, to maintain that medieval readers generally endorsed Fronesis' invitation to Alithia in the poem to spare the pagan poet and mythographer Pseustis.[29] Given the *Ecloga Theoduli*'s status as a school text, its ambivalent stance toward pagan poetry had a significant influence on medieval culture and specifically on Dante's syncretistic system of *exempla* of his *Purgatorio*.

The poem's popularity is documented by many extant manuscripts across the whole of Europe and a rich tradition of medieval and early modern commentaries.[30] A large majority of surviving manuscripts date from the

---

[28] Huygens, *Accessus*, 94–95. The translation is mine.

[29] A noticeable variation in the layouts of medieval manuscripts of the *Ecloga Theoduli* should also be mentioned here as possible evidence of the different trends in the poem's reception. Among the manuscripts of the *Ecloga Theoduli* that I have been able to survey, I have noticed that twelfth- and thirteenth-century expensive copies, mostly produced in central and northern Europe, tend to leave space among the quatrains, to be filled with glosses, and mark the initial letters of each quatrain with different colors to distinguish Pseustis from Alithia—usually one in red and the other in blue. See, for instance, Vatican City, Biblioteca Apostolica Vaticana, Vat. Lat. 1633 (XIII), fols. 7r–12v. This layout helps readers visualize the opposition between pagan and Christian traditions. Instead, later and cheaper manuscripts of schoolbooks from Italy now preserved in Tuscan libraries were generally copied without commentary. The quatrains are all laid out one after the other as one uninterrupted poem. Moreover, the initial letters are all the same color. See for instance Lucca, Biblioteca Statale, MS 1400 (XIV); Florence, Biblioteca Medicea Laurenziana, Plut. 91, sup. 4 (XIV–XV), fols. 28r–33r; Florence, Biblioteca Nazionale Centrale 1,45 (XIII–XIV); Florence, Biblioteca Riccardiana, MS 630 (XIV²), fols. 23r–28v; and Florence, Biblioteca Riccardiana, MS 725, fols. 33r–40v. This layout did not help readers visualize the poetic contest between pagan lie and Christian truth and rather presented the *Ecloga* as a single, continuous poem, thus heightening the ambiguity of its assimilation of classical antiquity.

[30] The manuscript production and diffusion of the *Ecloga* across Europe grew considerably during the later centuries of the Middle Ages: the only eighteen extant manuscripts of the *Ecloga* written between the ninth and the thirteenth centuries were followed by 150 that were produced between the thirteenth and fifteenth centuries. See Birger Munk Olsen, *I classici nel canone scolastico altomedievale* (Spoleto: Centro Italiano di Studi sull'Alto Medioevo, 1991), 119–22. For a discussion of Olsen's census, see Mosetti Casaretto, "Introduzione," xv. About the commentary tradition on the *Ecloga*, see George

180 DANTE'S EDUCATION

thirteenth through the fifteenth century. This fact suggests that, although a product of high medieval monastic culture, the *Ecloga* reached its widest circulation during the late Middle Ages.[31] As already noted in Chapter 1, Theodulus is steadily cited—often by the work's incipit—in medieval reading lists, either among the *auctores minores* or the Christian poets.[32] The poem also became a stable component in manuscripts of the *Liber Catonianus* anthology, as observed by Marcus Boas, and eventually was added to the *Auctores Octo*.[33] The popularity of the *Ecloga* remained sustained in central and northern Europe, where it was studied, printed, and translated well into early modern times. Less evident is the poem's actual circulation in late-medieval and Renaissance Italy, where it appears to have been gradually set aside by educators and readers alike. Theodulus is also missing from the list of early-printed books produced in the peninsula.[34] Extant manuscripts and other evidence suggest that Theodulus enjoyed some circulation in the Tuscan schools of Dante's time. As Paul Gehl maintains, however, it seems that "by the fourteenth century this northern European 'best seller' was merely an extra or elective text, perhaps in the process of losing what scant popularity it ever had in Italy."[35] Giovanni Dominici's *Regola del governo di cura familiare*, written in Florence in 1400–05, states that "ancient" Florentine pupils used to learn "un poco di poetizzata scrittura santa nello *Aethiopum terras*" (a little poetic Scripture from the Eclogue of Theodulus). Whereas in the humanistic milieu of Dominici's Florence pupils were no longer exposed to the *Ecloga*, and the other old and decent

L. Hamilton, "Theodulus: A Medieval Textbook," *Modern Philology* 7 (1909): 169–85; and Quinn, "Ps. Theodolus," 384. For a discussion of the *Ecloga*'s suitability for teaching, see Soons, "Didactic Quality," 150.

[31] On the monastic origin of the poem, see Green, "Genesis," 51–55. The list of books by the Benedictine Abbot of Monte Cassino, Desiderius (1058–87), mentions "Virgilium cum egloga Theodori"—another name for the *Ecloga*—next to "Donatum." See *Chronica Cassinensis* 6, cap. 63 (ed. Wattenbach, 746), quoted in Elias A. Lowe, *The Beneventan Script: A History of the South Italian Minuscule* (Oxford: Clarendon Press, 1914), 81–82. Further evidence of the *Ecloga*'s ties to monastic education is that, according to Árpád Órban, the manuscript of the Anonymous Teutonicus's commentary, Utrecht U.B. 292, belonged to a Carthusian monastery outside Utrecht. See Órban, "Anonymi Teutonici Commentum," 2.

[32] In his *Dialogus super auctores*, for instance, Conrad of Hirsau lists Theodulus among the essential readings of the school curriculum. See Huygens, *Accessus*, 93–96.

[33] Marcus Boas, "De Librorum Catonianorum historia atque compositione," *Mnemosyne*, n.s., 42 (1914): 17–46.

[34] Paul Gehl, *A Moral Art: Grammar, Society, and Culture in Trecento Florence* (Ithaca, NY: Cornell University Press, 1993), 159.

[35] Gehl, *Moral Art*, 254 (see also 261, 263). Gehl (268) also records a fourteenth-century copy of the poem in the manuscript Lucca, Biblioteca Statale, MS 1400. The manuscript was written in Italy and was used in schools. Glosses around the text are written in both Latin and the vernacular and are also from the fourteenth century. See also the manuscript Oxford, Bodleian, Add. A. 171 (XIV century), which appears to have been written in Italy and presents marks of school use. On the *Ecloga*'s fading status in late-medieval education, see also Robert Black, *Humanism and Education in Medieval and Renaissance Italy: Tradition and Innovation in Latin Schools from the Twelfth to the Fifteenth Century* (Cambridge: Cambridge University Press, 2001), 219.

THE *ECLOGA THEODULI* IN *PURGATORIO*   181

school texts "de' quali nullo insegnava il mal fare" (that taught nothing wrong), he claims that this had still been the case for previous generations of Florentines.[36]

The *Ecloga*, moreover, remained a key paradigm of Christian bucolic and the only other widely known pastoral poem besides Virgil's. Hence, its relevance for Dante's poetics cannot be overstated, especially considering that during the last year of his life the author penned two Latin eclogues as part of a poetic exchange with a professor of classics in Bologna, known as Giovanni del Virgilio. With his first eclogue, Dante set off a bucolic exchange that played a key role in resuscitating the genre and restoring it to its Virgilian archetype. Inspired by that exchange, del Virgilio would go on to address an eclogue to Albertino Mussato, a famous poet from Padua, and both Petrarch and Boccaccio wrote their own collections of eclogues. In his bucolic poem addressed to Mussato, del Virgilio identifies Dante as responsible for bringing the genre back to life after the centuries of silence following Virgil's eclogues.[37] In many ways, this was no exaggeration, as neither the ancient imitators of Virgil—Calpurnius and Nemesianus—nor his Carolingian epigones circulated in late medieval Italy before the time of Petrarch. The *Ecloga Theoduli* was the only exception to this general silence, thus providing a key precedent to Dante's experiment with the genre. Not surprisingly, an echo of the *Ecloga* has been detected in Dante's second *Egloga*, and I will return to its significance in the conclusion to this chapter.[38] A study of Dante's engagement with the *Ecloga*'s paradigm of classical pedagogy should begin with a discussion of *Purgatorio*'s program of *exempla* and bucolic representation of Eden.

A Model for the Examples of Humility and Pride
(*Purgatorio* 10–12)

The clearest and most compelling evidence of the *Ecloga Theoduli*'s influence on Dante's *Purgatorio* is a formal one: both texts feature sequences of alternating parallel mythological and biblical examples. Both, moreover, draw biblical stories from both the Old and the New Testaments, thus inserting, either directly or implicitly, classical culture into the system of biblical typology. On entering each terrace of Mount Purgatory, Dante and Virgil are presented with a series of famous stories exemplifying the virtue antithetical to the vice purged in that particular place. Symmetrically, examples of the same vice are recalled as the two leave each terrace. The medium of this edifying contemplation changes with every moral cycle. In *Purgatorio* 10, for instance, the pilgrims enter the cornice of pride and are

---

[36] Giovanni Dominici, *Regola del governo di cura familiare*, ed. Donato Salvi (Florence: A. Garinei, 1860), 134.

[37] See Marco Petoletti, "Nota introduttiva" to his edition of Dante's "Egloge/Egloghe" in Opere di Dante, ed. Marco Baglio et al., vol. 4 (Rome: Salerno, 2016), 491–504, at 496–97.

[38] Petoletti, comm. ad loc., *Egl.* 4.10.

182   DANTE'S EDUCATION

first instructed about the virtue of humility through a series of bas-reliefs carved on the side of the mountain and representing stories about Mary, King David, and the emperor Trajan. In *Purgatorio* 12, close to the terrace's exit, an extensive sculptural cycle, this time carved on the floor, exemplifies pride through the stories of Lucifer, Briareus, the Gigantomachy, the Tower of Babel, Niobe, Saul, Arachne, Rehoboam, Eriphyle, Sennacherib, Cyrus, Holofernes, and Troy. Edward Moore has famously remarked that here Dante displays the "curious habit to place side by side quotations from Scripture and so-called profane authors, balancing one against the other, as though they had something like co-ordinate authority."[39] For Carlo Delcorno, instead, Dante's use of *exempla* owes more to medieval culture than ancient and modern commentators have generally appreciated.[40] Rather than looking for the sources of individual *exempla*, Delcorno searches for medieval texts that feature similar sequences of examples.[41] He demonstrates, for instance, that William Peraldus's *De superbia* represents a suitable precedent for the sequence of biblical examples of pride in *Purgatorio* 12.[42] Peraldus's *De superbia*, however, presents one major limitation: it features only biblical *exempla* of pride. As for the classical stories that Dante alternates with the scriptural ones, Delcorno concludes that the poet was not influenced by medieval intermediaries and drew directly on Virgil, Statius, Ovid, and Orosius. Thus, Moore's argument about Dante's peculiar syncretism remains fundamentally untroubled by the evidence of the poet's reliance on medieval collections of *exempla*.

[39] Edward Moore, *Studies in Dante, First Series: Scriptures and Classical Authors in Dante* (Oxford: Oxford University Press, 1886), 26. The same idea has been reiterated in more recent time as, for instance, in Hollander's commentary. Hollander maintains that the idea of placing pagan examples next to biblical ones is an idiosyncratic feature of Dante's approach. See Hollander, comm. on *Purg.* 12.13–15.

[40] Carlo Delcorno, "Dante e Peraldo," in *Exemplum e letteratura*, 204. Carlo Delcorno showed that the increased use of *exempla* and similitudes in homiletics during the thirteenth century played an important role in Dante's use of *exempla* in *Purgatorio*. See also Carlo Delcorno, "Dante e l'exemplum' medievale," *Lettere italiane* 35 (1983): 3–28, and Delcorno, "Dante e il linguaggio." His methodological suggestions have been followed by several scholars, for instance, Lucia Battaglia Ricci, "'Come . . . le tombe terragne portan segnato': Lettura del dodicesimo canto del *Purgatorio*," in *Ecfrasi: Modelli ed esempi fra Medioevo e Rinascimento*, ed. Giovanni Venturi (Rome: Bulzoni, 2004): 33–63. On the purgatorial *exempla* more broadly, see also Claudia Crevenna, "Strategie ricorsive negli *exempla* del *Purgatorio* dantesco," *ACME: Annali della Facoltà di Lettere e Filosofia dell'Università di Milano* 57 (2004): 33–54; Nicola Longo, "L'*exemplum* fra retorica medievale e testo biblico nel *Purgatorio*," in *Memoria biblica nell'opera di Dante*, ed. Enzo Esposito et al. (Rome: Bulzoni, 1996), 57–98; Mariangela Semola, "Maria e gli altri *exempla* biblici nei canti X–XXVI del *Purgatorio* Dantesco," in *Memoria biblica e letteratura italiana*, ed. Vincenzo Placella (Naples: Istituto Universitario Orientale, 1998), 9–32; and Semola, "Dante e l'*exemplum* animale: Il caso dell'aquila," *L'Alighieri* 31 (2008): 149–59. On the relationship between the medieval theory of the *imagines agentes* and Dante's use of *ecfrasis* in *Purgatorio*, see Giovanni Venturi, "Una *lectura Dantis* e l'uso dell'ecfrasi: *Purgatorio* X," in *Ecfrasi: Modelli ed esempi fra Medioevo e Rinascimento*, 15–31, and Vescovo, "Ecfrasi con spettatore," 335–60.

[41] Delcorno, "Dante e Peraldo," 204.

[42] Delcorno, "Dante e Peraldo," 210–12. Delcorno ("Dante e il linguaggio," 61) also notes verbal echoes between the two texts, although the source for both could be in Gregory's *Moralia*. Before him the importance of Peraldus was explored by Franco Mancini, "Un'*auctoritas* di Dante," *Studi Danteschi* 14 (1968): 95–119, and Siegfried Wenzel, "Dante's Rationale for the Seven Deadly Sins, *Purg.* XVII," *Modern Languages Review* 60 (1965): 529–33.

THE *ECLOGA THEODULI* IN *PURGATORIO*   183

To date, no medieval text has been identified that features the same kind of systematic juxtaposition of parallel biblical and classical stories found in *Purgatorio* 12. As in Peraldus's case, some medieval collections of *exempla* present the same biblical stories, albeit arranged in different order and without significant verbal echoes, while a few other sources may be shown to inform Dante's retelling of individual examples, both pagan and biblical.[43] Among them, John of Salisbury's *Policraticus* is worth noting, as it presents several pagan and biblical *exempla* that appear in *Purgatorio*; they, however, are not alternated to suggest the same kind of parallelism that Dante foregrounds in his work.[44] On the contrary, the *Ecloga Theoduli* features the same continuous and systematic juxtaposition of biblical and pagan stories, thus supplying a unique precedent to Dante's peculiar use of *exempla* in *Purgatorio*. On closer inspection, the *Ecloga* and *Purgatorio* appear to be united by more than just a general resemblance. This medieval school text represents an obvious formal and structural precedent particularly for *Purgatorio* 10 and 12 and may also have inspired Dante's selection of examples in these cantos.[45]

The *Ecloga Theoduli* and Dante's *Purgatorio* share two defining characteristics that set them apart from other medieval collections of *exempla*: they are both poetic works that alternate pagan and biblical examples in an uninterrupted chain, inscribed within a narrative frame. In both poems, moreover, narrative and metrical units coincide. In the *Ecloga* each example corresponds to one quatrain, while in *Purgatorio* 12 each story covers one *terzina*.[46] Most important, however, the

---

[43] Critics have noted the relevance of texts such as Prudentius's *Dittochaeon* and *Contra Symmachum*, the *Fiore e vita de' filosofi*, John of Salisbury's *Policraticus*, John of Wales's *Communiloquium*, and also Brunetto Latini's *Tresor*. All these sources, however, have been proposed almost exclusively as models for the examples in *Purgatorio* 10, 20, and 23. Curtius (*European Literature*, 364) was perhaps the first to notice that John of Salisbury's *Policraticus* collects together the example of Trajan, the unusual story of the Jewess Mary who "bit into" her own son during Titus' siege of Jerusalem (*Purgatorio* 23.30), and the story of the prostitute Thais (*Inferno* 18.30). Uzzah is also mentioned in John's *Policraticus*, but Curtius does not note it. Umberto Bosco also highlights the similarity between Dante's representation of Hadrian IV in *Purgatorio* 19 and John's treatment of Hadrian V in *Policraticus*. See Umberto Bosco, "Adrian IV and V," in *Dante vicino* (Rome: Sciascia, 1979), 378–91. Giovanni Fallani, followed by Gianni Venturi, pointed out that in the *Fiore e vita de' filosofi* there is a version of the story of Trajan and the widow that is almost a verbatim source for Dante's *exemplum* of Trajan in *Purgatorio* 10. See Giovanni Fallani, *Il Canto X del Purgatorio* (Turin: Società Editrice Internazionale, 1964); Mario Pastore Stocchi, "Traiano," in the *ED*; and Venturi, *Una lectura*, 28. Delcorno ("Dante e Peraldo," 205–06) discusses other possible models for the examples of Trajan's and Fabricius' stories, in *Purgatorio* 12 and 20.

[44] *Policraticus* 8.20–21 features a sequence of biblical examples almost identical to that in *Purgatorio* 12. See Filippo Gianferrari, "Pride and Tyranny: An Unnoted Parallel between *Purgatorio* 12 and *Policraticus* 8.20–21," *Dante Notes* (May 2016), https://www.dantesociety.org/publicationsdantenotes/pride-and-tyranny-unnoted-parallel-between-purgatorio-12-and-policraticus.

[45] The *Ecloga Theoduli*'s possible influence on Dante's purgatorial examples has been suggested, but never investigated, by Rino Avesani, "Il primo ritmo per la morte del grammatico Ambrogio e il cosiddetto 'Liber Catonianus," *Studi Medievali* 6, no. 2 (1965): 455–88, at 458; Curtius, *European Literature*, 362–63, and Nicola Zingarelli, *La Vita, i tempi e le opera di Dante*, vol. 1 (Milan: Vallardi, 1948), 96. See also Carlo Delcorno, *Exemplum e letteratura*, 239.

[46] Delcorno, "Dante e Peraldo," 201.

184   DANTE'S EDUCATION

Ecloga features the same interlocking pattern of parallel pagan and biblical stories that also regulates Dante's sequences of examples of humility and pride. The
Ecloga opens its poetic contest with a pagan example, sung by Pseustis, followed
by a biblical one, by Alithia; pagan and biblical traditions continue to intertwine
following this order for the rest of the poem. Dante, instead, begins his series on
pride with a biblical story, Lucifer's rebellion against God, which is followed by a
pagan one, the Gigantomachy.[47] The author, however, devotes two *terzine* to the
story of the Gigantomachy—one to Briareus' defeat alone and the other to that of
all giants:

> Vedëa Brïareo fitto dal telo
> celestïal giacer, da l'altra parte,
> grave a la terra per lo mortal gelo.
>   Vedea Timbreo, vedea Pallade e Marte,
> armati ancora, intorno al padre loro,
> mirar le membra d'i Giganti sparte.
>
> *(Purgatorio* 12.28–33)

> (My eyes beheld Briarèus, on the other, / transfixed by the celestial
> bolt, / now heavy on the earth in chill of death. / My eyes beheld
> Thymbraeus, Pallas, and Mars, / still armed, together with their
> father, / astounded by the giants' scattered limbs.)

The example of the giants is then followed by that of Nimrod and Babel. Hence,
by means of the double account of the Gigantomachy, Dante reverses the order
of the examples, from biblical-pagan (Lucifer-Briareus) to pagan-biblical (Giants-
Nimrod), and then maintains that order until the end of the series on pride. He,
therefore, closely imitates the *Ecloga Theoduli*'s organization of examples. This
evidence is most notable because it occurs in the exemplary pair of the Gigantomachy and the Tower of Babel, which had already been made famous by the
Ecloga (85–92): that Dante should echo Theodulus here, when reversing the order
of the examples in *Purgatorio* 12 to reflect the order in the *Ecloga*, is revealing.[48]

---

[47] According to Giorgio Inglese in his commentary on *Purgatorio* 12, in *De civitate Dei* 11.15 Augustine maintains that Lucifer's rebellion marks the entrance of pride into history. See Dante Alighieri,
Commedia: Purgatorio, ed. Giorgio Inglese (Roma: Carocci, 2016 [2011]), 160n27.

[48] There is no agreement on whether Dante's two *terzine* on the Gigantomachy should be read as
one example or two discrete ones. Most recently, for instance, Inglese (comm. *Purgatorio* 12.32) has
argued that in the two *terzine* about the Gigantomachy, Dante rewrites Statius' *Thebaid*, which would
suggest that they should be read as two parts of one single episode. Delcorno ("Dante e Peraldo," 207)
instead argues that they constitute two distinct examples. This is also Anna Maria Chiavacci Leonardi's
reading (comm. ad loc.). This division is also supported by the recurrence of three words—*vedea, o,*
and *mostrava*—each beginning four consecutive *terzine*. The initial letters of these three words form
the acrostic "VOM" (man), which is then recreated by the three initial letters of the tercet that closes the
entire exemplary series. The discovery of the acrostic is relatively recent. See Lia Baldelli, "acrostico,"

THE *ECLOGA THEODULI* IN *PURGATORIO*   185

The precedent of the *Ecloga Theoduli* also sheds some light on the rationale behind the selection and pairing of the examples in *Purgatorio* 12. Critics have found it difficult to explain their organization, as it does not fully match any of the theological divisions available to the poet.[49] As in the *Ecloga Theoduli*, however, in *Purgatorio* 12 similar themes or narrative elements establish the correspondences between pagan and biblical episodes: Lucifer's fall recalls Briareus'; the gods are stunned in front of the fallen giants, as Nimrod is stunned in front of the fallen tower; Niobe's desperation recalls Saul's; Arachne's defeat is set next to that of Roboam; Almeon kills his mother, as Sennacherib's sons kill their father; and Cyrus is beheaded by a woman just like Holophernes. It is reasonable, therefore, to conclude that Dante is operating in accordance with the "theory of the parallelism of exemplary figures," of which the *Ecloga Theoduli* was the primary poetic example.[50]

Theodulus also represents a clear predecessor for Dante's condensed and dramatic approach to exemplary narrative. *Purgatorio* 12 offers but a memorable glimpse of each episode by staging only their most dramatic events, which are depicted either *in medias res* or at their conclusion. The *Ecloga*, too, focuses on the most memorable scenes of each story, creating particularly strong and memorable images. Both texts, therefore, feature a paratactic rather than diegetic approach to exemplary narrative. Dante and Theodulus both rely on the popularity of their examples, expecting readers to fill in each story's missing narrative.

The most notable evidence of Theodulus's influence on *Purgatorio* 12 is provided by the several mythological and biblical stories the two texts have in common. Although their order and pairing mostly differs, the fact that ten out of Dante's sixteen examples of humility and pride are also mentioned in the *Ecloga* with the same moral meaning is arresting:

Exempla	*Purgatorio* 10	*Ecloga Theoduli*
Orpheus and Eurydice	5–6	189–92
Mary and the Incarnation	40–42	330–32
David	64–66	193–96

---

in the *ED*, and Moore, *Studies in Dante*, 268. See also Chiavacci Leonardi's *Nota di approfondimento* at the end of her commentary on *Purgatorio* 12.

[49] Relying on Aquinas's *Summa Theologiae* (II ii q. 130, 131, 132), Eugenio Parodi suggests that the three groups of examples of pride follow the categories of *praesumptio, inanis gloria*, and *ambitio*. See Eugenio Parodi, "Gli esempi di superbia punita e il 'bello stile' di Dante," *Atene e Roma* 18 (1915): 97–107, reprinted in *Poesia e storia nella* Divina Commedia (Venice: 1965), 147–61. Chiavacci Leonardi ("Introduzione" to *Purgatorio* 12) instead divides the examples into the three categories of "pride against God, oneself, and others." Such a division, however, appears unprecedented in medieval culture. Lucia Battaglia Ricci ("Come le tombe," 53) shows a suggestive parallel between Dante's twelvefold division of the examples of pride and Saint Bernard of Clairveaux's *Liber de gradibus humilitatis et superbiae*. Saint Bernard distinguishes twelve degrees of pride. On this issue, see also Delcorno, "Dante e Peraldo," 208.

[50] Curtius, *European Literature*, 363.

186 DANTE'S EDUCATION

Exempla	*Purgatorio* 12	*Ecloga Theoduli*
Gigantomachy	28–33	85–88
Tower of Babel	34–36	89–92
Niobe	37–39	261–64
Saul	40–42	193–96
Eriphyle	49–51	149–52
Judith and Holofernes	58–60	274–76
Troy	61–63	319–20

As this quick comparative look reveals, one pair that is identical in both the *Ecloga* and *Purgatorio* 12 is the one linking the myth of the Gigantomachy with the episode of the Tower of Babel from Genesis:

Vedëa Brïareo fitto dal telo
celestïal giacer, da l'altra parte,
grave a la terra per lo mortal gelo.
  Vedea Timbreo, vedea Pallade e
                    Marte,
armati ancora, intorno al padre loro,
mirar le membra d'i Giganti sparte.
          (*Purgatorio* 12.28–33)

(My eyes beheld Briarèus, on the other, / transfixed by the celestial bolt, / now heavy on the earth in chill of death. / My eyes beheld Thymbraeus, Pallas, and Mars, / still armed, together with their father, / astounded by the giants' scattered limbs.)

Surrexere viri terra genitrice creati,
Pellere cælicolas fuit omnibus una
                    voluntas;
Mons cumulat montem, sed totum
                    Iuppiter hostem
Fulmine deiectum Vulcani trusit in
                    antrum.
          (*Ecloga Theoduli* 85–88)

(Men born from Mother Earth rose up; the common will / of all was to expel the heaven-dwelling gods. / They heaped the mountains up, but Jupiter cast down / the foe by bolt, and thrust them into Vulcan's cave.)

Vedea Nembròt a piè del gran
                    lavoro
quasi smarrito, e riguardar le genti
che 'n Sennaàr con lui superbi fuoro.
          (*Purgatorio* 12.34–36)

(My eyes beheld Nimrod at the base of his great work, / as though bewildered, and the people, / who in Shinar shared his pride, all looking on.)

Posteritas Adæ summa Babilonis in arce Turrim construxit, quæ cælum tangere possit. Excitat ira Deum: confusio fit labiorum, Disperguntur ibi, nomen non excidit urbi. (*Ecloga Theoduli* 89–92)

(In Babel's lofty citadel a tower was built / by Adam's race: its top, they hoped, would reach the sky. / God's wrath was roused: confusion fell upon their tongues / and they were scattered, but the city's name survives.)

The two accounts do not present significant verbal echoes, and scholars have singled out Statius and Ovid as likely sources of Dante's compressed version of the myth.[51] Since the *Ecloga*, however, constitutes the oldest and most popular medieval text to draw a parallel between the Gigantomachy and the Tower of Babel, its possible influence on Dante cannot be underestimated. I am aware of two other occurrences of this exemplary pair, in Albertino Mussato's epistle on the theological relevance of poetry and in one of Jacopo Passavanti's sermons. Jacopo's sermons were delivered several years after Dante's death, and there is no evidence that Dante ever read Mussato's epistle, which was addressed to a Venetian grammar teacher, probably after 1315.[52] It seems more reasonable, therefore, to suppose that the teaching of the *Ecloga Theoduli* had helped shape the parallelism between these two stories in medieval culture.[53]

Also worthy of attention are the four classical examples of punished pride referenced by both poems: the Gigantomachy, Niobe, Eriphyle, and Troy. No other medieval source among the ones hitherto singled out by scholars and commentators shares as many classical examples in common with *Purgatorio* 12. In addition, the two works' account of Niobe's story presents a notable commonality:

O Nïobè, con che occhi dolenti
vedea io te segnata in su la strada,
tra sette e sette tuoi figliuoli spenti!
(*Purgatorio* 21.37–39)

(Ah, Niobe, I saw you sculpted in the roadway, / your eyes welling up with grief, / amidst your dead, seven sons and seven daughters.)

Thura cremate focis, si quos servare velitis
Fetus incolumes: iubet hoc Latonia proles.
Ex humero Triviæ dependent spicula mille
Cum totidem nervis, Niobæ vindicta loquacis.
(*Ecloga Theoduli* 261–64)

(Burn incense on your hearths, if you would keep alive / your children'—so Diana bade Latona's child. / A thousand darts, a thousand strings, hung from her arm / to take revenge on Niobe for boastful words.)

---

[51] Dante seems to have closely reworked the text of Statius' *Thebaid* 2.596–600 to create his own *terzine* on Briareus and the giants and to have relied on Ovid's *Metamorphoses* 10.150–51 for Zeus' thunderbolts. Pietro Alighieri had already noted some of these classical quotations in his 1359–64 comment on *Purgatorio* 12.1–72. George Butler instead proposes a few loci from Claudian's *De raptu Proserpinae* as possible sources. See George Butler, "Claudian's *De Raptu Proserpinae* and Dante's Vanquished Giants," *Italica* 84, no. 4 (2007): 661–78. Theodulus seems instead to have mixed together different sources. See Green, "Genesis," 83.

[52] Jacopo Passavanti could have derived the association of these two stories precisely from Dante's *Purgatorio* 12. See Michèle Mulchahey, "Dominican Education and the Dominican Ministry in the Thirteenth and Fourteenth Centuries: Fra Jacopo Passavanti and the Florentine Convent of Santa Maria Novella" (Ph.D. diss., University of Toronto, 1988). Mussato's epistle *Ad Johannem professorem gramaticae* is number 6 in the new edition by Luca Lombardo; the lines in question are 49–50: "Quid movisse Iovi quondam fera bella Gigantes / astructam celo quam Babilona fuit?" See Albertino Mussato, *Epistole metriche*, ed. Luca Lombardo (Venice: Ca' Foscari, 2020), 198.

[53] This idea has already been suggested by Curtius, *European Literature*, 215.

188　DANTE'S EDUCATION

Both authors rewrite the same portion of Ovid's account of the myth in *Metamorphoses* 6.146–312, namely the aftermath of Latona's revenge, carried out by Apollo's and Diana's arrows. Moreover, the *Ecloga* condemns Niobe's "loquacitas" as a manifestation of the pride that brought her to disregard the piety due to the goddess. In Dante's *Purgatorio*, Niobe is also punished for the same sin.[54]

Both *Purgatorio* 12 and the *Ecloga Theoduli* also feature a reference to the story of Amphiaraus' betrayal by his wife, Eriphyle, and her subsequent assassination at the hands of their son. This example from the Theban epic saga is rare in medieval *summae exemplorum*.[55] A few narrative elements in Dante's account of Eriphyle's story, moreover, are also present in Theodulus's version:

Mostrava ancor lo duro pavimento
come Almeon a sua madre fé caro
parer lo sventurato addornamento.
(*Purgatorio* 12.49–51)

(Now was shown, on that hard floor, / how Alcmaeon made that necklace, ill-omened, / seem not worth the price his mother paid.)

Uxoris stimulos luis, Aimphiaræ sacerdos,
Pectore flagrantis dum splendet baca
monilis
Haurit te subitus specus ex Acheronte
profundo;
Mactat eam tenebris orbatæ dextera prolis.
(*Ecloga Theoduli* 149–52)

(Priest Amphiaraus, your wife, inflamed by greed / for gleaming necklace, made you pay for what she urged: / A cave from Acheron's great depth soon swallows you. / Your orphaned child's right hand dispatches her to Hell.)

Both poems mention the divine necklace that Eriphyle proudly desired to wear and that was the cause of her death at the hands of her son—also an element mentioned by both texts.

The example of Troy is also quoted in both texts. This fact is relevant even if the two mentions differ greatly in content and form. The *Ecloga* refers to the "secret of Troy"—possibly the Palladium—as the ultimate mystery of pagan culture, which Pseustis evokes as his final weapon against Alithia. Alithia responds by mentioning Mary and the Incarnation. In *Purgatorio* 10 and 12, Mary and Troy occupy the opposite extremes of the moral spectrum that separates humility and

---

[54] Green ("Genesis," 92) believes that Theodulus rewrote Ovid's *Metamorphoses* 6.146 here. The story of Niobe is introduced as a cautionary tale about the necessity of honoring the Penates, which reflects the function that this story also performs in *Purgatorio* 12, where it exemplifies pride. For the sources of Dante's Niobe in *Purgatorio* 12, Pietro Alighieri (comm. *Purgatorio* 12 [1359–64]) points to Ovid's *Metamorphoses* 6.169, 184–86, and 301–02. He also suggests Ovid's *De Ponto* 1.2.29–30.

[55] Among ancient texts, Statius provides an extensive account of this story in *Thebaid* 2.265–66, 294, 297–305, 4.192–213, and 7.785–88. Conversely, Ovid (*Met.* 9.406–46) succinctly reports the story, and Virgil offers only a fleeting reference to it in *Aeneid* 6.445–46.

THE *ECLOGA THEODULI* IN *PURGATORIO*   189

pride. Mary represents the supreme example of humility, which allowed for Christianity's ultimate mystery, the Incarnation, whereas Troy marks the highest point in the history of human pride. In the *Ecloga* too, Mary and Troy are presented respectively as the two focal moments of Christian and pagan history respectively.

Another notable feature of both poems is a sequence of examples of (in)famous women. In the *Ecloga*, this theme links together one of the longest sequences of *exempla*: in the two quatrains 261–68, Niobe is mentioned next to Susanna; in lines 269–76, Procne and Medea (*malae mulieres*) are paired with Judith; and finally, in lines 277–84, Scylla is coupled with Esther. Pseustis attacks the women as a retort to Alithia, who is winning the contest. The Christian shepherdess fires back by turning the theme into a celebration of famous biblical women who fulfilled God's plan and punished evil men. Dante also presents a pair of famous women from both traditions, Tamiri and Judith (lines 55–60), who carried out the assassination of tyrants. Dante's reworking of the theme, however, aligns biblical and classical traditions in a celebration of virtuous women.

The parallels linking *Purgatorio* 12 to the *Ecloga Theoduli*, therefore, are structural, formal, and thematic, and are also evinced in the selection and pairing of a significant number of examples across pagan mythology and the two Testaments. While Dante often draws directly on the classical *auctores* and the Bible, disseminating their verbal echoes in the intertextual fabric of the canto, he is also closely refashioning the *Ecloga*'s paradigm. I would suggest that the *Ecloga* provides Dante with an "intertextual script," which Umberto Eco defines as "rhetorical and narrative schemes that belong to a selected inventory" shared by readers of the same cultural background.[56]

In light of this conclusion, we should now reconsider Moore's claim that Dante displays a "curious habit of placing side by side quotations from Scripture and so-called profane authors, balancing one against the other, as though they had something like co-ordinate authority." On the one hand, as we have seen, such a practice would not have appeared at all curious to a reader familiar with the *Ecloga Theoduli*; on the other hand, Dante's comparison of pagan and biblical traditions differs from Theoudulus's on one fundamental point. Whereas, in several instances, the *Ecloga* opposes pagan and Christian stories as if they exemplified vices and virtues respectively, in *Purgatorio* Dante does not merely reproduce this cultural clash. He instead uses both traditions to exemplify either vices or virtues—as if they had "co-ordinate authority"—thereby breaking down the sharp opposition of pagan vice and Christian virtue staged in the *Ecloga*. Thus, if Dante relies on the archetype provided by the *Ecloga*, he adapts it to fit his own harmonizing view on the relationship between Christianity and paganism. He clearly denies

---

[56] In Umberto Eco's words, "sceneggiature intertestuali" are "schemi retorici e narrativi che fan parte di un corredo selezionato." Eco, *"Lector in fabula": La cooperazione interpretativa nei testi narrativi* (Milan: Bompiani, 1979), 81–84, at 84. The translation is mine.

190 DANTE'S EDUCATION

the *Ecloga*'s rejection of pagan poetry and mythology and exploits instead the syncretism and figuralism that are only implicit in the school text. But things are hardly this simple in Dante's critical engagement with Theodulus's authority. As we should see next, in correspondence with the physical and fictional boundaries of *Purgatorio* proper—in *Purgatorio* 9 and 28—Dante rearticulates the *Ecloga*'s inner tension between antagonistic and syncretistic views of universal history.

The *Ecloga Theoduli* and *Purgatorio*'s Liminalities: A Text across Cultural Borders

The topography of *Purgatorio* features three macro zones, each one fulfilling a different purpose: the ante-Purgatory, wherein souls who delayed repenting in life are compelled to wait before undertaking their penitential journey; Purgatory proper, in which souls suffer painful purgation and receive their moral reeducation; and the Garden of Eden, where the water of the river Lethe washes away the memory of past sins, while that of the Eunoè restores remembrance of good deeds. The vision and the organization of these three spaces are original to Dante and highlight the transitory and transitional nature of this otherworldly realm. The many liminalities that give life to *Purgatorio*'s stratified landscape—further bisected by the terraces shaping its moral and physical structure—amplify the moral drama of conversion and transformation that is at the heart of this world. The drama on stage, however, is also a cultural one. The history of humanity's redemption, which Christ brought about, and which is constantly renewed on the sides of the Purgatorial Mountain, casts a long shadow, whose tragic mystery comes increasingly under scrutiny in this *cantica*: the loss of pagan culture, with its wisdom and virtue. As we will see, Dante's reflection on this thorny question surfaces more powerfully in conjunction with Purgatory's liminal spaces and is accompanied by his evolving critical engagement with the *Ecloga*'s reading of universal history.

I have already discussed how the *Ecloga Theoduli* influenced the series of parallel examples of virtues and vices that unfold at the intersections of each terrace. The *Ecloga*'s relationship with *Purgatorio*'s liminalities, however, extends also to the two main borders of Purgatory proper. Memories of the *Ecloga* surface in *Purgatorio* 9, where the protagonist transitions from the ante-Purgatory into Purgatory proper. To mark this fictional locus as one of "uncertain liminality, of obstacles, and exceptional miraculous intervention," Dante intersperses the whole canto with seemingly unrelated references and allusions to both mythological and biblical stories. Several of them, as Zygmunt Barański has pointed out, are also in the *Ecloga Theoduli*.[57] Of the many classical characters alluded to in *Purgatorio* 9, only Achilles is absent from the *Ecloga*:

---

[57] Barański, "Reading," 7, 31.

THE *ECLOGA THEODULI* IN *PURGATORIO*   191

Example	Purgatorio 9	Ecloga Theoduli
Aurora and Tithonus	1–6	221–24
Tereus and Procne	13–15	271–72
Ganymede	22–24	77–80
Orpheus and Eurydice	131–32	189–92

In addition, both poems mention the following biblical stories:

Example	Purgatorio 9	Ecloga Theoduli
Adam	10	41, 50, 89
Lot's wife	131–32	115–16
Angel doorkeeper with fiery sword	76–84	51–52
Chromatic sequence recalling the fall (Gold– silver–ash)	115, 118–19	38, 47, 50

The evidence that all stories represent standard motifs in medieval literature cautions us against overstating the importance of their parallel use between the two texts. The *Ecloga's* standing in medieval education, however, makes the likeliness of its influence more plausible. Furthermore, *Purgatorio* 9 exploits a systematic comparison of mythological and biblical stories that reflects unfavorably on the pagan tradition—an approach that seemingly contradicts Dante's reverence toward classical antiquity and reflects instead the *Ecloga's* disparaging rejection of this tradition.[58]

Memories of the *Ecloga Theoduli* resurface at the opposite end of Purgatory proper, on the bank of the river Lethe in Eden. Here, the protagonist and his two guides, the Roman poets Virgil and Statius, meet a mysterious lady who is singing and picking flowers on the opposite side of the river from them. Matelda explains that the magnificent forest they have just entered is really the Garden of Eden, which had become inaccessible to humanity after the fall of Adam and Eve. Matelda introduces the new Edenic space by celebrating the syncretistic parallel between the biblical story of the fall and the myth of the Golden Age:

> Quelli ch'anticamente poetaro
> l'età dell'oro e suo stato felice
> forse in Parnaso esto loco sognaro.
> Qui fu innocente l'umana radice;
> qui primavera sempre e ogni frutto;
> nettar è questo, di che ciascun dice.
>
> (*Purgatorio* 28.139–44)

---

[58] Barański, "Reading," 7, 31. Hollander (comm. *Purgatorio* 9) also noted Dante's unusual treatment of the classics in this canto: "Rarely in the *Commedia* is the contrast between classical and Christian views ... more present than in these classicizing passages that open this canto."

192   DANTE'S EDUCATION

(Those who in ancient times called up in verse / the age of gold
and sang its happy state / dreamed on Parnassus of perhaps this
very place. / Here the root of humankind was innocent, / here it
is always spring, with every fruit in season. / This is the nectar of
which the ancients tell.)

Among the pagan poets who sang of the lost Golden Age, Virgil, with his fourth
Eclogue, stands out as the main target of Matelda's praise. The prophetic quality
of this poem is already celebrated by the character Statius in *Purgatorio* 22, whose
conversion to Christianity was sparked precisely by its reading:

> Facesti come quei che va di notte
> che porta il lume dietro e sé non giova,
> ma dopo sé fa le persone dotte,
>   quando dicesti: "Secol si rinova
> torna giustizia e primo tempo umano,
> e progenïe scende da ciel nova."
>   Per te poeta fui, per te cristiano.
>
>   (*Purgatorio* 22.67-73)

(You were as one who goes by night, carrying / the light behind
him—it is no help to him, / but instructs all those who follow—
/ when you said: "The centuries turn new again. / Justice returns
with the first age of man, / new progeny descends from Heaven."
/ Through you I was a poet, through you a Christian.)

Virgil's merits, moreover, are evoked in Dante's bucolic representation of Eden.
Like Christian writers before him, Dante borrows heavily from the depiction of
the Golden Age in Virgil's fourth *Eclogue*.[59] This precedent allowed Dante to envi-
sion the pastoral genre as a medium to reconcile pagan and biblical traditions in
a syncretistic form. Throughout the poem, he consistently draws an overarching
parallel between Virgil's "Saturna regna" (Saturn's reign) (*Eclogues* 4.8) "sotto 'l
cui rege fu già 'l mondo casto" (under its king the world was innocent), as stated
in *Inferno* 14.96, and Eden, where "è l'uom felice" (man lives in joy), as Beatrice
reminds the protagonist in *Purgatorio* 30.75. The key role of Virgil's *Eclogues* in

---

[59] Dante's celebration of Virgil in Eden culminates in *Purgatorio* 30, where references to both the
Aeneid and the *Georgics* abound. For an enlightening discussion of these intertextual tributes to Vir-
gil and their engagement with Statius' celebration of Virgil at the end of the *Thebaid*, see Ronald L.
Martinez, "Dante and the Two Canons: Statius in Virgil's Footsteps (*Purgatorio* 21–30)," *Comparative
Literature Studies* 32, no. 2 (1995): 151–75, esp. 167. On the role of the Golden Age motif in Dante's
Purgatorio, see Teodolinda Barolini, *Dante's Poets: Textuality and Truth in the Comedy* (Princeton, NJ:
Princeton University Press, 1984), 258–60; Camozzi Pistoja, "Il veglio di Creta"; and Richard Shoaf,
"'Auri sacra fames' and the Age of Gold (*Purg.* XXII, 40–41 and 148–150)," *Dante Studies* 96 (1978):
195–99, esp. 196–97.

THE *ECLOGA THEODULI* IN *PURGATORIO*   193

Dante's pastoral vision of Eden is already anticipated in *Purgatorio* 27, where the author narrates the events of the night before his entrance into Eden. The pilgrim is getting ready to sleep on the mountain slope, while the two Roman poets prepare to watch over him. The whole scene is described through a pastoral simile: Dante is like a sheep and his guardians like shepherds.[60] The presence of classical poetry in Eden, however, is also riddled with tension. In his encounter with Matelda, for instance, the protagonist recalls memories of unhappy love stories sung of by Ovid, such as between Proserpina and Pluto, Venus and Adonis, and Hero and Leander.[61] Most important, here is where Virgil's part in the history of salvation reaches its tragic end, as he is not allowed to pass the river Lethe and continue his journey to Heaven with Dante and Statius.

I argue that Dante's contrasting use of the bucolic space, first as a medium for the syncretistic recovery of ancient poetics and then for its apologetic exclusion, finds a defining model in the *Ecloga Theoduli*. The popular school text also begins by echoing Virgil's bucolic Golden Age, highlights precisely the parallelism with the biblical story of the fall, and ends with the exclusion of the pagan poet Pseustis, who, like Virgil, is left on the other side of the river that represents Christian baptism and salvation.[62] The contest between Alithia and Pseustis opens with a parallel account of the Golden Age and the fall:

Pseustis
Primus Cretæis venit Saturnus ab oris
Aurea per cunctas disponens sæcula terras;
Nullus ei genitor nec quisquam tempore maior;
Ipso gaudet avo superum generosa propago.

Alithia
Incola primus homo fuit in viridi paradiso.
Coniuge vipereum donec suadente venenum
Hausit eo cunctis miscendo pocula mortis:
Sentit adhuc proles, quod commisere parentes.

---

[60] For a comprehensive discussion of Dante's rewriting of Virgil's *Eclogues* in Eden, see Caron Ann Cioffi, "'Il cantor de' bucolici carmi': The Influence of Virgilian Pastoral on Dante's Depiction of the Earthly Paradise," in *Lectura Dantis Newberryana*, ed. Paolo Cherchi and Antonio Critodemo Mastrobuono, vol. 1 (Evanston, IL: Northwestern University Press, 1988), 93–122.

[61] Charles S. Singleton famously argued that Matelda would represent the goddess of justice, Astraea, whose return is prophesized by Virgil in *Eclogues* 4.6. See Singleton, "Virgo or Justice," in *Dante Studies: Journey to Beatrice*, vol. 2 (Cambridge, MA: Harvard University Press), 184–203. For a reading of these tragic classical subtexts, see Peter Hawkins, "Transfiguring the Text: Ovid, Scripture and the Dynamics of Allusion," *Stanford Italian Review* 5 (1985): 115–39, revised and expanded in Hawkins, "Watching Matelda," in *The Poetry of Allusion: Virgil and Ovid in Dante's Commedia*, ed. Rachel Jacoff and Jeffrey Schnapp (Stanford, CA: Stanford University Press, 1991), 181–201, and revised and reprinted in Hawkins, *Dante's Testaments: Essays in Scriptural Imagination* (Stanford, CA: Stanford University Press, 1999), 159–79.

[62] Camozzi Pistoja ("Il veglio di Creta," 26–28) also notes the *Ecloga Theoduli* as Dante's possible source here.

194   DANTE'S EDUCATION

Pseustis

Splendorem tanti non passus Iuppiter auri
Expulit illatis patrem crudeliter armis:
Decolor argento mundi successit imago
Et iam primatum dedit illi curia divum.

Alithia

Exulat eiectus de sede pia protoplastus
Ac cinis in cinerem naturæ mutat honorem.
Ne tamen æterni temeremur stipite pomi,
Flammeus ante fores vetat ensis adire volentes.

(*Ecloga Theoduli* 37–52)

(From Cretan shores came Saturn; he was first of all / and then he
spread the age of gold throughout the earth. / He had no sire: no
one preceded him in time; / the noble race of gods enjoys descent
from him. / The first man dwelt and lived in verdant paradise /
until, persuaded by his wife, the serpent's draught / he drank and
mixed the cup of death for all mankind. / We offspring feel today
what once our parents did. / Jove could not bear the brilliance of
all this gold; / he took up arms and, cruel, drove his father out. /
Then silver came and changed the colour of the world: / the court
of gods gave Jupiter the primacy. / From kindly place exiled, the
first-made was expelled / and, dust-to-dust, forsakes the honour
Nature gave. / Lest we be tempted by the age-old apple's stock, / a
flaming sword forbids all those that would approach.)

While opposing the two traditions, the *Ecloga Theoduli* foregrounds their evident
parallels. Medieval commentators were receptive to the syncretistic interpretation of the fall implied by the poem.[63] The *Ecloga* and its commentators reflect
a medieval vision of universal history that identified the myth of a remote time
of justice and bliss with the biblical Eden. Dante, too, endorses such a harmonizing view, as highlighted by Matelda's declaration quoted earlier (*Purgatorio*
28.139–44).

In their reworking of the fall–Golden Age motif, the two texts also share similar treatments of the myth of Proserpina. Dante introduces Matelda's character
by comparing her to Proserpina, when she was picking flowers on the meadows

---

[63] See, for instance, the Anonymous Teutonicus's gloss on these lines: "Nam Saturnus primus deo-
rum fuit, Adam primus hominum fuit; Saturnus expulsus de regno, Adam de paradyso. . . . Postquam
Pseustis proposuit fabulose quomodo primus homo sue legis, puta Saturnus, expulsus est a regno suo,
hic Alithia respondet Pseusti per veram Historiam, quomodo primus homo sue legis, puta Adam,
expulsus est de paradyso." Órban, "Anonymi Teutonici Commentum," 19–21.

THE *ECLOGA THEODULI* IN *PURGATORIO*   195

of Enna only instants before Ades kidnapped her: "'Tu mi fai rimembrar dove e qual era / Proserpina nel tempo che perdette / la madre lei, ed ella primavera'" ("You make me remember where and what / Proserpina was, there when her mother / lost her and she lost the spring") (*Purgatorio* 28.49–51). The reference to Proserpina as the one who "perse primavera" alludes once more to the implicit parallelism between the Christian fall and the pagan Golden Age, which the ancients conceived of as an eternal spring. There can be little doubt that the eternal "primavera" sung by the ancient poets who wrote about the Golden Age (139–44), and celebrated by Matelda a few lines later, is the same one lost by Proserpina. Curiously, Dante seems to suggest that she had some responsibility in this irreparable loss: while Ceres lost Proserpina, her daughter was the one who lost spring. Thus, she emerges as a mythological version of Eve standing in opposition to Matelda, who embodies a type of unfallen Eve. Dante, therefore, characterizes the myth of Proserpina as another version of the fall–Golden Age motif.[64] The *Ecloga Theoduli* suggests a similar reading of this myth, allotting it two quatrains. Theodulus's highly condensed summary of the story focuses on its aftermath, which provides yet another mythological account of the end of a remote age of bliss, when humanity could live off the spontaneous gifts of the earth, and the beginning of agricultural labor. In the first quatrain, Ceres donates agriculture to mankind, whereas in the second one the *Ecloga* emphasizes the moment of the story when Proserpina, like Eve, eats the forbidden fruit, an action that seals her periodic confinement in Hell: "Dic mihi: dum tristes adiit Proserpina sedes / Lege data matri, si vellet nata reverti. / Gustum perfidiæ quis primum prodidit ore?" (When Proserpine went down to gloomy hell, a law / was given Ceres for her daughter's safe return. / Now say who first, in treachery, revealed her meal?) (*Ecloga Theoduli* 317–19).[65] Theodulus also hints at the presence of a tempter-traitor, like the snake in the biblical story. The *Ecloga*, therefore, associates Proserpina with both the myth of the Golden Age and the story of the fall, thus preparing the ground for the goddess's evocation in *Purgatorio* 28.

Theodulus's influence on Dante's syncretistic account of the fall–Golden Age motif in Eden may also explain the *Ecloga*'s apparent ties with *Purgatorio* 9—the gate of Purgatory proper. Three of the four stories mentioned at the opening of this canto (Aurora and Tithonus, Thetis and Achilles, and Ganymede)—two of which are also in the *Ecloga*—exemplify humanity's fallen nature, the human aspiration to achieve eternity, and the necessity of divine intervention: the Thetis Aurora

---

[64] For a compelling discussion of the mythological-biblical parallel embodied by Dante's mention of Proserpina in *Purgatorio* 28, see Emerson Brown Jr., "Proserpina, Matelda, and the Pilgrim," *Dante Studies* 89 (1971): 33–48.

[65] In its first reference to the myth, the *Ecloga* states the following: "Gnosia cum raros quateret Dodona racemos, / Mater larga Ceres miserata fame pereuntes / Triptolemum mundo misit serpente ministro, / Qui primum terræ spem demonstravit aristæ" (*Ecl. Theod.* 205–08). Proserpine is also mentioned in a third quatrain, which is dedicated to the myth of Orpheus. Here she is presented as the infernal queen (*Ecl. Theod.* 189–92).

196   DANTE'S EDUCATION

wants to acquire eternal life for her mortal husband, Tithonus, but all she obtains for him is to age forever without dying (1–9), and the goddess Thetis attempts without success to prevent her demigod son, Achilles, from undertaking his ill-fated journey to Troy (34–39), whereas the mortal Ganymede is snatched from Mount Ida by Zeus and given immortality (19–33). In the midst of these mythological references, Dante inserts one fleeting allusion to the biblical story of the fall: "quand'io, che meco avea di quel d'Adamo / vinto dal sonno, in su l'erba inchinai" (when I, who had with me something of Adam, / lay down, overcome by sleep, there on the grass) (*Purgatorio* 9.10–11). Tellingly, after this reference, Dante meets an angel who is guarding the door of Purgatory and resembles the one set by God in front of Eden's gates after the fall. Notwithstanding Dante's open reference to Adam a few lines earlier, readers have been surprisingly averse to construing the second half of *Purgatorio* 9 as a symbolic and narrative reverse of the fall (Genesis 3.24):

> vidi una porta, e tre gradi di sotto
> per gire ad essa, di color diversi,
> e un portier ch'ancor non facea motto.
>   E come l'occhio più e più v'apersi,
> vidil seder sovra 'l grado sovrano,
> tal ne la faccia ch'io non lo soffersi;
>   e una spada nuda avea in mano,
> che reflettea i raggi sì ver' noi,
> ch'io drizzava spesso il viso in vano.

(Purgatorio 9.76–84)

> (I now saw was a gate, with three steps leading / up to it, each one of a different color. / The keeper of that gate as yet said not a word. / And, when my eyes could make him out more clearly, / I saw that he was seated above the topmost step, / his face so bright I could not bear to look. / In his hand he held a naked sword, / which so reflected his bright rays / I often had to turn my eager eyes away.)

Although critics tend to link this guardian to the mysterious angel seen by St. John in Revelation 1.16, the gatekeeper also shares some interesting similarities with the angel from Genesis: his sword resembles the "flammeus gladius" held by the guardian of Eden in Genesis 3.24; the gate itself marks the entrance to a forbidden place, like the lost garden of Eden; and finally, the reference to Adam's body a few lines earlier hints at the relationship between the gate Dante is approaching and the one through which the first parents were cast out.[66] Theodulus also refers to

---

[66] Only modern commentators have noted the intertextual relevance of the passage from Genesis, highlighting the similarity between the dazzling sword carried by the purgatorial guardian angel and

THE *ECLOGA THEODULI* IN *PURGATORIO*   197

the guardian angel from Genesis in the line "Flammeus ante fores vetat ensis adire volentes" (a flaming sword forbids all those that would approach) (*Ecloga Theoduli* 52).[67] Thus, in the second half of *Purgatorio* 9, Dante appears as a new Adam, who enters the unlocked gate and begins his path back to the lost Earthly Paradise.[68]

Dante's typological rewriting of this theme in conjunction with the two borders of Purgatory proper invites him to articulate a confrontation between pagan and biblical traditions as well as with the influential model of the *Ecloga Theoduli*. Theodulus was by no means the only medieval source that featured a syncretistic account of the fall–Golden Age motif. The Christianizing reception of Virgil's *Eclogue* 4, as already noted, provided a positive alternative. Whereas Virgil's pastoral Golden Age pervades Dante's representation of Eden, on the two banks of the river Lethe the poet clearly conjures up the narrative setting of the *Ecloga Theoduli*: a bucolic landscape and a river that separates a Christian woman (Matelda) from a pagan man (Virgil) who never gets to cross it. Mosetti Casaretto interprets the river in the *Ecloga Theoduli* as a cultural boundary and the allegorical equivalent of the unbridgeable gulf that separates Christianity from paganism. As the river signifies the purifying water of the Christian baptism, the fact that Pseustis never crosses it suggests that he never converts.[69] Mosetti Casaretto also points out that, given the role of the bucolic subtext as the key reference model of the *Ecloga*, the pagan poet left on the other side of salvation may specifically represent Virgil.

---

the *flammeum gladium*. The first to propose this parallel was Giovanni Scartazzini (1900). Scartazzini's interpretation was then followed by several other commentators. For more detailed discussions of the sacramental function of the angel in *Purgatorio* 9 and his sword, see Erminia Ardissino, *Tempo liturgico e tempo storico nella Commedia di Dante* (Vatican City: Libreria editrice vaticana, 2009), 86; Peter Armour, *The Door of Purgatory: A Study of Multiple Symbolism in Dante's Purgatorio* (New York: Clarendon Press, 1983), 39; Anna Pegoretti, "Immaginare la veste di un angelo: Il caso di *Purg.* 9, 115–116," *L'Alighieri* 27 (2006): 141–51.

[67] This line is an obvious calque of Genesis 3.24. In its intertwined accounts of the stories of the fall and the Golden Age (*Ecloga Theoduli* 37–52, quoted earlier), Theodulus also features a sequence of colors—gold, silver, dust—symbolizing the decline of both humanity and nature. The same chromatic series, although inverted, is found in the scene of *Purgatorio* 9.115–20. The angel's dress appears to Dante like "cenere, o terra" (ashes or earth) colors that allude to Genesis 3.19–20, and the two keys used by the guardian angel are gold and silver. Although they symbolize the sacerdotal power that God bestowed on St. Peter, the symbolic meaning of the keys' sequential usage—first the silver and then the gold key—is more obscure. In light of the *Ecloga Theoduli*, the chromatic sequence ash gray–silver–gold in *Purgatorio* 9 could symbolize the reversal of the fall and the return to the Golden Age–Edenic world. For the penitential symbolism implied by the angel's colors, see Ardissino, *Tempo*; Giuseppe Ledda, "Sulla soglia del *Purgatorio*: Peccato, penitenza, resurrezione; Per una 'lectura' di *Purgatorio* IX," *Lettere Italiane* 46 (2014): 3–36; Pegoretti, "Immaginare"; and Ezio Raimondi, "Analisi strutturale e semantica del canto IX del *Purgatorio*," *Studi Danteschi* 45 (1968): 121–46. For the symbolism implied by the two keys see Ardissino, *Tempo*, 84–85; Armour, *The Door*, 39; and Raimondi, *Analisi*, 141–42.

[68] In *Purgatorio*, Dante meets no other angel who performs the same duty of guardian *stricto sensu* as the one in *Purgatorio* 9; the angel who presides over the border between the first and second ledge does not carry a sword and acts in a distinctively welcoming fashion, which eventually becomes the defining feature of all the "guardian" angels present in the remaining cornices (*Purgatorio* 12.91–92). Furthermore, while this angel uses his sword to mark Dante's forehead with seven Ps, the symbols of human sin that originated with the fall, all other angels symbolically reverse the effects of the fall as they remove the marks from Dante's forehead.

[69] Mosetti Casaretto, "Introduzione," xxv.

198   DANTE'S EDUCATION

In *Purgatorio* 30, therefore, the character Virgil reenacts the tragedy of the pagan poet and shepherd who is never allowed to cross the river and access Christian salvation.

By reproposing the *Ecloga*'s narrative setting, Dante characterizes his Eden as the last liminal space shared by Christianity and paganism. Even in *Monarchia* 3.16.7, Dante defines the Earthly Paradise as the place where humanity fully achieves its earthly goal—the virtuous life—and where secular and spiritual dimensions perfectly overlap.[70] In *Purgatorio*'s version of Eden, however, the Christian and pagan worlds overlap only in their parallel accounts of a lost Golden Age. This is true also for the *Ecloga*, which, as already noted, begins with a syncretistic account of the fall–Golden Age motif and then shows the two traditions progressively diverging. In *Purgatorio* 9 and 28–31, Dante evokes the same tension between the apparent overlapping of pagan and Christian accounts of the fall and also their growing distance. His pastoral representation of Eden, therefore, not only engages with the syncretism afforded by the authority of Virgil's *Eclogue* 4, as critics have long noted, but also confronts the *Ecloga Theoduli*'s apologetic reworking of Virgil.

Dante's apparent reproduction of the *Ecloga*'s hostile exclusion of pagan poetry from salvation is puzzling at best, as it contradicts the more tolerant attitude displayed in the parallel examples of vices and virtues at the heart of *Purgatorio*'s education, as well as in Matelda's celebration of the ancient poets' visions of the Golden Age. An adequate explanation of the reasons behind Dante's abrupt turn away from pagan antiquity in Eden transcends the purpose of the present study and would require addressing two interrelated issues of notable complexity: the tragic destiny assigned to the character Virgil in the *Commedia* and the troubling question of the salvation of virtuous pagans, which returns at several intervals throughout the poem but finds its most extensive articulations in Limbo (*Inferno* 4) and the Heaven of Justice (*Paradiso* 18–20). On the other hand, an obvious, albeit partial, reason for Dante's treatment of Virgil in Eden should at least be mentioned here. Virgil's reenactment of Pseustis' exclusion from the side of salvation dramatizes the tragedy of the fall itself and the mysterious circumstances of its redemption through Christ's sacrifice. Something valuable was lost in this process: ancient wisdom and virtue. Virgil's tragedy in Eden dramatizes Dante's bereavement for this loss. Clearly, Dante does not engage in the *Ecloga*'s same critical exercise of pitting the errors of paganism against its virtues only to condemn its unredeemable limitations. He, moreover, takes Theodulus's challenge to the ecumenic reading of Virgil's *Eclogue* 4 beyond the banks of the Lethe.

---

[70] Andrea Ciotti points to the same parallel between the two texts in his entry "Paradiso Terrestre" in the *ED*.

The Ethiopian Shall Condemn Such Christians
(*Paradiso* 19.109)

Dante returns to discuss the salvation of the virtuous pagans a few years later, while writing *Paradiso*. In the Heaven of Jupiter, in canto 18, the protagonist meets the blessed souls who loved and practiced justice during their earthly lives. Together, they form the image of the Eagle of Jupiter and talk with one voice, speaking God's mind to the pilgrim. As a crucial question about justice burns in Dante's mind, the Eagle summarizes it as follows:

> "Un uom nasce a la riva
> de l'Indo, e quivi non è chi ragioni
> di Cristo né chi legga né chi scriva;
> e tutti suoi voleri e atti buoni
> sono, quanto ragione umana vede,
> sanza peccato in vita o in sermoni.
> Muore non battezzato e sanza fede:
> ov' è questa giustizia che 'l condanna?
> ov' è la colpa sua, se ei non crede?"
>
> (Paradiso 19.70–78)

("A man is born / upon the bank along the Indus, with no one there / to speak, or read, or write of Christ, / and all that he desires, everything he does, is good. / As far as human reason can discern, / he is sinless in his deeds and in his words. / He dies unbaptized, dies outside the faith. / Wherein lies the justice that condemns him? / Wherein lies his fault if he does not believe?")

Dante names India as a metaphor of the world beyond the geopolitical and cultural limits of Latin Christendom.[71] Thus, after Limbo, here he reapproaches the question of salvation from a cultural and geographical perspective. The issue of the "cultural other" is already anticipated in Limbo by the presence of the virtuous Muslims (*Inferno* 4.129 and 143–44).[72] By the same token, in the Heaven of Jupiter the matter of eternal salvation for the virtuous pagans from antiquity—and, most important, Virgil—is equally at stake.

In reply to the protagonist's question, the Eagle begins by positing the presumption of those who wish to search the mysterious depths of God's predestination.

---

[71] See Brenda Deen Schildgen, *Dante and the Orient* (Urbana: University of Illinois Press, 2002), 92–109.

[72] On this, see Teodolinda Barolini, "Dante's Limbo and the Cultural Other, Or: Injustice on the Banks of the Indus," in *Dante Worlds: Echoes, Places, Questions*, ed. Peter Carravetta (Rome: "L'Erma" di Bretschneider, 2019), 21–34.

200 DANTE'S EDUCATION

It then proceeds to restate the necessity of believing in Christ in order to achieve eternal salvation (*Paradiso* 19.103–05). At this point, however, the Eagle's lecture takes a radically different turn:

> Ma vedi: molti gridan "Cristo, Cristo!"
> che saranno in giudicio assai men *prope*
> a lui, che tal che non conosce Cristo;
>   e tai Cristian dannerà l'Etïòpe,
> quando si partiranno i due collegi,
> l'uno in etterno ricco e l'altro inòpe.
>
> (*Paradiso* 19.106–11)

> (But observe that many shout out "Christ, O Christ!" / who shall be farther off from Him, / on Judgment Day, than such as know not Christ. / The Ethiopian shall condemn such Christians / when the two assemblies go their separate ways, / the one forever rich, the other poor.)

Although faith in Christ is necessary to be saved, the Eagle warns that God's final judgment is as mysterious as his predestination: many who know and proclaim Christ's name on earth will be excluded from the Kingdom of Heaven, whereas some who come from the ends of the world and were never reached by the Gospel will be numbered among the saints. The Eagle's unsettling opening toward the possibility of eternal salvation for non-Christians rephrases several biblical subtexts and closely echoes the Gospel of Matthew.[73] However, Dante's choice to have the Ethiopian represent the humanity that will come forth from the antipodes to judge the Christian hypocrites constitutes an original reworking of his biblical source.[74]

---

[73] Matthew 7:21; 8:11–12; 12:41–42. Deen Schildgen (*Dante and the Orient*, 103) also points to the possible intertext of Paul, Romans 2:13.

[74] Since the "queen of the south" was often identified as the sovereign of Ethiopia, a reference to Matthew's subtext may be at the heart of Dante's phrasing here. It is in light of this biblical subtext that I read this passage as claiming that some Ethiopians will be saved and in the position to condemn bad Christians, rather than being themselves condemned together with bad Christians. For a discussion of these two readings, see Teodolinda Barolini, *Dante's Multitudes: History, Philosophy, Method* (Notre Dame, IN: Notre Dame University Press, 2022), 39–44. The habit of naming Ethiopia in conjunction with India, which Dante reflects in *Purgatorio* 26.21, might also have prompted him to name the Ethiopian in direct reply to the apparent condemnation of the Indian a few lines earlier (*Paradiso* 19.71). India and Ethiopia were often associated with the Far East and South, respectively, as, for instance, in the eighth-century *Mappamondo* drawn by Paolo Orosio. Yet, news that Ethiopia was in fact a Christian kingdom had come to circulate more widely in the West after the fall of Acri in 1290, and Dante's decision to single out the Ethiopian at this particular point in the poem's treatment of universal salvation appears surprising. See Cecilia, Vanossi, and Cerulli, "Etiopia," in the *ED*. This would not be the first instance of Dante's deliberate omission of well-known descriptions of Asia and the Near East to create symbolic rather than realistic geographies. See Deen Schildgen, *Dante and the Orient*, esp. 105–06; Paolo Pecoraro argues that Dante creates his own "Geografia dantesca." See Pecoraro, *Le stelle di Dante: Saggio d'interpretazione di riferimenti astronomici e cosmografici della Divina commedia* (Rome: Bulzoni, 1987). Theodore J. Cachey Jr. notes that Dante's map of the world in

When we consider that in these cantos the author is also contemplating the destiny of the virtuous pagans who lived before Christ, and thus coming to terms with the trauma of Virgil's tragedy in Eden, the fact that the popular incipit of the *Ecloga Theoduli* evoked precisely the lands of the Ethiopian—"Aethiopum terras"—requires close inspection. As already seen, the *Ecloga* popularized the view that the remote and mysterious land of Ethiopia constituted the place where the line between the saved and the damned was going to be clearly drawn. In *Paradiso* 19, Dante seems also to question Theodulus's authority when referring to the two eschatological "assemblies" in which the damned and the saved will be divided and will "go their separate ways" on the last day (*Paradiso* 19.110). Dante alludes here to the same passage from Matthew's gospel (25.31–34) that Theodulus conjures up in the opening of the *Ecloga*, when the pagan Pseustis leads a flock of goats and the Christian Alithia drives sheep instead. The passage from Matthew discusses the importance of both faith and works for individual salvation. Unlike the *Ecloga Theoduli*, which equates the division between the two flocks to the one between Christians and pagans, the Evangelist Matthew promises shocking revelations on Judgment Day: some nominally Christians will be condemned for their lack of charity, while others will be saved on account of their good work rather than their professed faith. Thus, to their mutual astonishment, the former will be marched to their eternal damnation, whereas the latter will be saved:

> Then shall the king say to them that shall be on his right hand: Come, ye blessed of my Father, possess you the kingdom prepared for you from the foundation of the world. For I was hungry, and you gave me to eat; I was thirsty, and you gave me to drink; I was a stranger, and you took me in; naked, and you covered me; sick, and you visited me; I was in prison, and you came to me. Then shall the just answer him, saying; Lord, when did we see thee hungry, and fed thee; thirsty, and gave thee drink? And when did we see thee a stranger, and took thee in? or naked, and covered thee? Or when did we see thee sick or in prison, and came to thee? And the king answering, shall say to them: Amen I say to you, as long as you did it to one of these my least brethren, you did it to me.
>
> (Matt. 34–46)

In *Paradiso* 19, therefore, Dante proves himself a more charitable reader of this scriptural passage than Theodulus, who disingenuously misinterpreted it to fit his own apologetic bill. By drawing on a more comprehensive interpretation of Matthew 25, Dante contradicts Theodulus on his own scriptural ground. Whereas the *Ecloga Theoduli* turns the torrid planes of Ethiopia into the stage where the

---

the poem is informed by "a Roman and Italocentric 'projection'" and displays the poet's "underlying cultural-political theory." See Cachey, "Cartographic Dante: A Note on Dante and the Greek Mediterranean," in *Italica* 87, no. 3 (2010): 325–54, revised and reprinted in Jan M. Ziolkowski, ed., *Dante and the Greeks* (Washington, DC: Dumbarton Oaks, 2014), 197–226.

202   DANTE'S EDUCATION

pagan Pseustis comes to be judged by the Christian Alithia, Dante calls on the Ethiopian *to be* the judge of uncharitable Christians. After leaving his own Virgil/Pseustis on the other bank of the river Lethe, in Eden, Dante brings him back with the Ethiopian for a surprise epilogue on Judgment Day, when all souls will be judged on the basis of their charitable works.[75]

Pastoral Epilogue

Dante's face-off with the *Ecloga Theoduli* in the Heaven of Justice, however, is not the final chapter of this story. Significant evidence of a continued engagement with this school text can also be seen in Dante's last poem. As noted earlier, during the final year of his life he embarked on a bucolic correspondence with Giovanni del Virgilio, effectively resuscitating a poetic genre that had been dormant since Carolingian times. Del Virgilio, a Latinist and classical enthusiast who at some point held a public teaching appointment in Bologna, had been the first one to reach out, around 1319.[76] In a Latin metrical epistle modeled on Horace's, he exhorts Dante to cease writing in the vernacular and to devote himself instead to composing a Latin epic poem about the conflict between Guelfs and Ghibellines that unfolded after the death of Henry VII. The prize that del Virgilio offered was the poetic crowning in Bologna. Dante, instead, replies with a Latin eclogue in which the poet fashions himself a new Tityrus—Virgil's bucolic disguise—and kindly declines the flattering proposal. The move follows Virgil's own refusal to write epic in *Eclogue* 6.3–5, where Apollo commands the poet-shepherd to limit himself to the humbler subject matter of pastoral poetry. By invoking the bucolic Virgil,

---

[75] Virgil is clearly evoked in these cantos by means of his proxy, the Trojan Ripheus, who, together with the emperor Trajan, is among the blessed souls in the Heaven of Jupiter and epitomizes the possibility of the gift of implicit faith, or spiritual baptism, that God could grant to the non-Christians who lived a virtuous and charitable life either before or after Christ (*Paradiso* 20.43–47, 67–72). This doctrine had already been theorized by some of the major Christian theologians, such as, to mention only a few, Augustine, Albert the Great, Thomas Aquinas, and Bonaventure. For a brief summary of this theological debate, see Chiavacci Leonardi's "Introduction" to *Paradiso* 19. For a thorough discussion of Virgil in relation to the Heaven of Justice, see Edoardo Fumagalli, *Il giusto Enea e il pio Rifeo: Pagine dantesche* (Florence: Olschki, 2012), 1–33 and 215–45. Deen Schildgen (*Dante and the Orient*, 94) offers a different reading of these cantos in light of Dante's imperial argument in the *Monarchia* and the *Commedia*.

[76] For this particular dating of del Virgilio's metrical epistle, see Marco Petoletti, "Nota introduttiva," 493. Contrary to received wisdom, Gabriella Albanese and Paolo Pontari have recently uncovered evidence that Giovanni del Virgilio was appointed as professor of poetry and versification with a public salary in Bologna *as a result of* his correspondence with Dante. See Albanese and Pontari, "Il notariato bolognese, le *Egloghe* e il Polifemo dantesco: nuove testimonianze manoscritte e una nuova lettura dell'ultima egloga," *Studi Danteschi* 81 (2016): 13–130, and Albanese and Pontari, *L'ultimo Dante e il cenacolo ravennate: Catalogo della Mostra*, Ravenna, Biblioteca Classense, September 9–October 28, 2018 (Ravenna: Longo, 2018), 48. For an excellent introduction and new reading of Dante's exchange with Giovanni del Virgilio, see David G. Lummus, "Egloghe," in *Dante's Other Works: Assessments and Interpretations*, ed. Zygmunt G. Barański and Theodore J. Cachey Jr. (Notre Dame, IN: Notre Dame University Press, 2022), 306–32.

whose mouthpiece Giovanni "del Virgilio" claimed to be, Dante refuses to conform his own poetic project to the civic epic proposed by del Virgilio. Hence the pastoral genre becomes an allegory for Dante's poetic enterprise in the vernacular. Del Virgilio welcomes the pastoral challenge and replies with an eclogue inviting Dante to leave Ravenna—where the Florentine exile had found refuge during the last years of his life—and go to Bologna. The poem ends with del Virgilio's polite threat to offer the poetic crowning to the Paduan poet Albertino Mussato instead. Dante's last reply was delivered after his death and represents a manifesto for the independence and dignity of vernacular poetry.

Readers have often pointed out that Dante's second eclogue opens with a series of distinctively non-Virgilian elements. What has mostly gone unnoted, however, is that all these eccentric elements bespeak the author's close engagement with the *Ecloga Theoduli*:

> Velleribus Colchis prepes detectus Eous
> alipedesque alii pulcrum Titana ferebant.
> Orbita, qua primum flecti de culmine cepit,
> currigerum canthum libratim quemque tenebat;
> resque refulgentes, solite superarier umbris,
> vincebant umbras et fervere rura sinebant.
> Tityrus hoc propter confugit et Alphesibeus
> ad silvam, pecudumque suique misertus uterque,
> fraxineam silvam tiliis platanisque frequentem.
> Et dum silvestri pecudes mixteque capelle
> insidunt herbe, dum naribus aera captant,
> Tityrus hic, annosus enim, defensus acerna
> fronte soporifero gravis incumbebat odori;
> nodosoque piri vulso de stirpe bacillo
> stabat subnixus, ut diceret, Alphesibeus.
>
> (Egloga 4.1–15)

(Their Colchian fleeces doffed, Eous swift and th' other / steeds the beauteous Titan bore. And momently the track / in equal poise held either chariot-bearing orb, / what point it felt the first down-swerving from the height. / Sun-smitten things, but now by self-cast shade out-lengthed, / their shadows overpassed; the fields, all unprotected, burned. / And woodward now had Tityrus and Alphesibaeus fled, / themselves compassionating and their herds seeking the copse where, / 'twixt the ash's growth, linden and plane find frequent space. / And there—the while reposing on the woodland grass, / cattle, with goats between, sniff the cool air— / Tityrus, drowsed by odours somnolent, with maple leaves, /

204   DANTE'S EDUCATION

> reclining, shields his age; and, to discourse, / Alphesibaeus stands,
> leaning upon / a gnarled pear-wood staff wrenched from its stock.)

The astronomical periphrasis is the first unconventional element in this opening scene. Commentators have generally argued that it reflects one of the hallmarks of Dante's poetry in the *Commedia*, where such astronomical references are indeed common, showing the cross-fertilization between his poetic experiments with different genres and languages.[77] The fictional hour when the meeting between the two shepherds takes place, noon, is also outside the conventions laid out by Virgil for the genre.[78] The heat of the meridian hour, moreover, causes the shepherds to find respite in a forest under the shade of a linden tree, a botanical element that is also distinctively non-Virgilian. A linden tree, however, is precisely the tree under which Pseustis pushes his flock of goats in the opening scene of the *Ecloga Theoduli*: "compuleratque suas *tiliæ* sub amœna *capellas* / natus ab Athenis pastor cognomine Pseustis" (A shepherd born in Athens—Falsehood was his name— / Had brought his herd of *goats* beneath the *linden tree*'s shade.) (3–4).[79] The subtext of the *Ecloga* also accounts for the other two non-Virgilian elements in this prologue scene: the astronomical opening, also found in Theodulus—"in Cancro solis dum volvitur aureus axis" (the time the sun's gold orb revolves in Cancer's sign) (2)—as well as the noon hour and scorching midday heat. If, as I contend, Dante here is integrating elements from the *Ecloga Theoduli* in his rewriting of Virgil, then it is all the more intriguing to find that Dante-Tityrus and his companion are leading a mixed flock of sheep and goats: "pecudes mixteque capelle."[80] An obvious model for Dante's rewriting is in Virgil's *Eclogue* 1.74: "Ite, meae, felix quondam pecus, ite, capellae" (Away, my goats! Away, once happy flock!).[81] Yet, given the author's apparent engagement with Theodulus in this scene, the image of the mixed flock carries theoretical implications that are too significant to be ignored. Dante represents himself acting exactly like the character Pseustis at the beginning of the *Ecloga Theoduli*: to find shelter from the heat, he leads his mixed flock under the shade of the linden tree.[82]

---

[77] See Gabriella Albanese, comm. ad loc. in her edition of Dante's "Egloge," in Dante Alighieri, *Opere*, ed. Marco Santagata, vol. 2 (Milan: Mondadori, 2014), 1593–783, and Petoletti, comm. ad loc., in "Egloge/Egloghe."

[78] Albanese, comm. ad *Egl.* 4.7–9.

[79] Petoletti, too, notes the important precedent of the *Ecloga Theoduli* in his commentary ad locum.

[80] I identify Tityrus with Dante, even though at the end of the poem the narrator reveals that he was not present at the events recounted in the eclogue but was filled in by another eyewitness. This confusing allegorical play is hard to interpret and might point to the poem's unedited state. For a discussion of this and other puzzling elements of this eclogue, see Lino Pertile, "Le Egloghe di Dante e l'antro di Polifemo," in *Dante the Lyric and Ethical Poet: Dante lirico e etico*, ed. Zygmunt G. Barański and Martin McLaughlin (London: Legenda, 2010), 153–67.

[81] Gabriella Albanese argues that Dante here may be echoing Ovid's *Metamorphoses* 13.927, "oves hirtaeve capellae." Albanese, comm. ad loc.

[82] Similarly, Jonathan Combs-Schilling argues that in his *Egloghe* Dante "affords Virgil an alternate ending—a second resting place—within Dante's *oeuvre*," a place beyond the *Commedia*'s theological

THE *ECLOGA THEODULI* IN *PURGATORIO*   205

One may rightfully ask why Dante should wish to break the division of Matthew's two eschatological flocks in the context of a poem that is really just an elegant refusal to move to Bologna and receive the poetic crowning. Clearly, there is more in this eclogue than meets the eye. Dante does not simply compare the political and cultural advantages of Ravenna with those of Bologna: he opposes a different vision of poetry to the one promoted by Giovanni del Virgilio. In the bucolic allegory, Ravenna is identified with the Sicilian pastures, whereas Bologna has become Mount Etna, home of the Cyclopes. Dante removes the pastoral landscape of this eclogue from both the real geography of Ravenna and the bucolic one of Virgil's Italy and Arcadia, relocating it in Theocritus' Sicily. The Sicilian muses, it should be noted, had already been invoked by Virgil in the incipit—"Sicelides musae paulo maiora canamus" (Muses of Sicily, essay we now / a somewhat loftier task!) (*Eclogue* 4.1)—of the same fourth *Eclogue* whose Christianizing reception had been opposed by the *Ecloga Theodulis*. Dante's evocation of Sicily in his second eclogue, therefore, indirectly points to the fundamental text proving the wisdom and prophetism of the ancient poets, whose perplexing place in the history of salvation is at the center of the *Commedia*'s representation of Limbo, Eden, and the Heaven of Jupiter.[83]

The character of Amphesibeus, moreover, argues against the idea of Tityrus relocating to Mount Etna because this move would be against the poet's very nature. He then provides four examples to illustrate that all things act according to their different natures:

> "Quod mentes hominum" fabatur "ad astra ferantur
> unde fuere, nove cum corpora nostra subirent,
> quod libeat niveis avibus resonare Caistrum
> temperie celi letis et valle palustri,
> quod pisces coeant pelagi pelagusque relinquant
> flumina qua primum Nerei confinia tangunt,
> Caucason Hyrcane maculent quod sanguine tigres,
> et Libies coluber quod squama verrat arenas,
> non miror, nam cuique placent conformia vite,
> Tityre, sed Mopso miror, mirantur et omnes
> pastores alii mecum Sicula arva tenentes,
> arida Ciclopum placeant quod saxa sub Ethna."
>
> (*Egloga* 4.16–27)

"exigencies." Combs-Schilling, "Tityrus in Limbo: Figures of the Author in Dante's Eclogues," *Dante Studies* 133 (2015): 1–26.

[83] And obviously in Statius's cantos in *Purgatorio* 21–22, where Statius presents Virgil's fourth eclogue as the reason of his own conversion.

206   DANTE'S EDUCATION

> ("That souls," quoth he, "of men make for the stars, / whence they were newly come when first our frames / they entered; that white swans love to make ring Cayster / with their joy in temperate heavens and in plashy vale; / that fishes of the sea gather, and quit that sea, / just where the streams first touch the realm of Nereus; / that the Caucasus is dabbed with blood Hyrcanian-tiger-spilt, / the sands of Lybia swept by serpent-scales, I not admire; / for, Tityrus, each thing delights in what / to its own life conforms; but I marvel, and marvel / all my fellow-swains holding Sicilia's pastures, that the rocks / that parch 'neath Etna's summit should delight Mopsus.")

The selection of examples is rather singular, even within Dante's oeuvre, and may carry deeper significance than generally acknowledged.[84] First, Amphesibeus quotes the Platonic doctrine of the soul's return to the star from which it originated. This choice appears especially striking because Dante had respectfully denied this belief in *Paradiso* 4. All the other examples, instead, imply animals and exotic locations: the white swans that love singing along the Cayster River in Turkey; the fish that gather around the rivers' estuaries, where the two different waters meet; the Hyrcanian tigers that dab with blood the land of Caucasus; and, finally, the snakes that slither on the sand of the Libyan desert. Albeit all classical topoi, these references also map a geographical and cultural space that lies far away from the gravitational pull of the Bolognese university. Notably, in his previous eclogue, Dante had already opposed Giovanni del Virgilio's noble pursuit of classical poetry to the legal culture that dominated the *studium* (*Egloga* 2.29–31). Thus, through the allegory of Tityrus' choice to inhabit the free Sicilian pastures, rather than moving into the Cyclops' caves, Dante claims vernacular poetry's fundamental independence: its authority lies at the peripheral and permeable boundaries of poetic culture, where Christian poetry and ancient wisdom freely mix and overlap. Unlike the Bolognese university milieu represented by del Virgilio, which in the allegory is ruled by the despotic Polyphemus, vernacular poetry emerges as a place of cultural freedom and syncretism.[85]

The intertextual echo of Theodulus that opens Dante's last *Egloga* also points readers back to *Purgatorio* 27, in which Dante the character is obliged to rest in the transitional space between Purgatory proper and Eden. As already mentioned,

[84] As Pertile ("Le *Egloghe* di Dante," 157–61) points out, several of these classical and mythological references have no precedent in Dante's oeuvre.

[85] For a different but equally compelling interpretation of Dante's resistance to the Bolognese milieu, as one dominated by incipient humanist culture see David Lummus, *The City of Poetry: Imagining the Civic Role of the Poet in Fourteenth-Century Italy* (Cambridge: Cambridge University Press, 2020), 63–111.

here the author deploys a pastoral simile to describe himself, Virgil, and Statius settling down for the night:

> ciascun di noi d'un grado fece letto;
> ché la natura del monte ci affranse
> la possa del salir più e 'l diletto.
>   Quali si stanno ruminando manse
> le capre, state rapide e proterve
> sovra le cime avante che sien pranse,
>   tacite a l'ombra, mentre che 'l sol ferve,
> guardate dal pastor, che 'n su la verga
> poggiato s'è e lor di posa serve;
>   e quale il mandrïan che fori alberga,
> lungo il peculio suo queto pernotta,
> guardando perché fiera non lo sperga;
>   tali eravamo tutti e tre allotta,
> io come capra, ed ei come pastori,
> fasciati quinci e quindi d'alta grotta.
>
> (*Purgatorio* 27.73–86)

(Each of us made, of a step, a bed, / for the nature of the mountain took from us / the power and the urge for climbing higher. / As goats that have been quick and reckless / on the heights before they grazed / now peacefully chew their cud, / silent in the shade while the sun is burning, / guarded by the shepherd, leaning on his staff, / who lets them take their rest, / and as the herdsman who lives out in the open / passes the night beside his quiet flock, / watching lest a beast should scatter them, / such were the three of us, / I like a goat and they like shepherds, / shut in on all sides by walls of rock.)

This pastoral scene is identical to the one that Dante would eventually repurpose in the *Egloga* 4. But whereas in *Purgatorio* Virgil and Statius shepherd the vernacular poet—who, it should be noted, compares himself to a goat—in his last poem Dante takes this role for himself.

6

Re-Dressing Achilles, Resisting Proserpina, Surpassing Virgil

The End of the Purgatorial Curriculum

After falling asleep in the Valley of the Princes—as the last known region in the ante-Purgatory is commonly referred to—Dante wakes up in a strange new place. While he was fast asleep, Saint Lucy took him on a miraculous flight and carefully laid him near the gate of Purgatory proper. To describe his sense of confusion at waking up in a foreign place, the author compares himself to young Achilles waking up on Scyros' shores, after his mother had carried him there from Chiron's cave:

> Non altrimenti Achille si riscosse,
> li occhi svegliati rivolgendo in giro
> e non sappiendo là dove si fosse,
>   quando la madre da Chirón a Schiro
> trafuggò lui dormendo in le sue braccia,
> là onde poi li Greci il dipartiro;
>   che mi scoss' io, sì come da la faccia
> mi fuggì "l sonno, e diventa" ismorto,
> come fa l'uom che, spaventato, agghiaccia.
>
> (*Purgatorio* 9.34–42)

> (Not otherwise Achilles started up, / moving his startled eyes in a wide circle, / not knowing where he was / that time his mother carried him, / sleeping in her arms, from Chiron to Scyros, / where later the Greeks would take him away— / than I awoke, the sleep gone from my eyes, / and then went pale, / like a man frozen in his terror.)

Dante's recollection of this famous scene from the first book of Statius' *Achilleid* (1.247–50) carries greater cultural and metaliterary significance than commentators and scholars have generally acknowledged.[1] To appreciate this fact, we need

---

[1] A notable exception is represented by Suzanne C. Hagedorn, "A Statian Model for Dante's Ulysses," *Dante Studies* 115 (1997): 19–43.

Dante's Education. Filippo Gianferrari, Oxford University Press. © Filippo Gianferrari (2024).
DOI: 10.1093/oso/9780198881766.003.0007

THE END OF THE PURGATORIAL CURRICULUM   209

to consider the poem's role and fortunes in medieval education. Statius' short epic provided a sample of the genre that was often administered to medieval pupils either in tandem with or alternatively to Claudian's *De raptu Proserpinae*. It seems rather significant, therefore, to find a dramatic evocation of Claudian's poem precisely at the opposite side of Purgatory proper, when the protagonist is about to cross the river Lethe in Eden. As discussed in the previous chapter, Dante compares Matelda, who is picking flowers and lovingly singing in the Edenic forest, to Proserpina in the meadows of Henna, only moments before she is abducted by Pluto (*Purgatorio* 28.49–51). The fact that direct references to both the *Achilleid* and the *De raptu Proserpinae* appear at the two opposite ends of Dante's purgatorial ascent invites further scrutiny.

In light of the presence of the *Disticha Catonis* and the *Ecloga Theoduli* retraced in the previous two chapters, we are now better positioned to appreciate the substantial role played by medieval school texts throughout *Purgatorio*. To some degree, their order mimics the ideal one often found in medieval reading lists: the *Disticha Catonis* at the beginning of the reading curriculum; the *Ecloga Theoduli* at a more intermediate level; and the *Achilleid* and the *De raptu Proserpinae*—or Latin epic more generally—at a more advanced stage.[2] Thus a discussion of medieval school texts constitutes one of the underlying themes of Dante's representation of Purgatory as a place of spiritual, moral, and intellectual reformation. As the next pages show, the evocations of Statius' and Claudian's unfinished epics also fulfill key symbolic and metapoetic functions: at the narrative level, these references mark the beginning and the end of the protagonist's fictional rite of passage to moral maturity; from a metapoetic perspective, they support the author's self-representation as the vernacular equivalent of the Latin epicists—embodied in *Purgatorio* by the characters of Statius and Virgil.

For the benefit of the reader, throughout this chapter and the following one, I use the label "epic" to designate the genre of the *Achilleid* and the *De raptu Proserpinae* in accordance with our modern understanding of literary genres. As Michael Barnes points out, however, epic "is an omnivorous species: it incorporates into itself the voices, tropes, and themes of other genres as it evolves (as it must) over the centuries." Hence, epic coincides with "whatever the culture in which it is embedded decides it is."[3] If the genre's boundaries are by its very definition flexible and porous, this is even more true of the genre's medieval reception. In the Middle Ages, Zygmunt Barański warns, literary genres "did not have fixed meanings

---

[2] As featured in manuscripts of the *Liber Catonianus* type, as well as by medieval lists of readings, such as Conrad of Hirsau's *Dialogus super auctores*. See R. B. C. Huygens, ed., *Accessus ad auctores, Bernard d'Utrecht, Conrad d'Hirsau: Dialogus super auctores; Édition critique* (Leiden: Brill, 1970), 119–20.

[3] Michael H. Barnes, "Claudian," in *A Companion to Ancient Epic*, ed. John Miles Foley (Malden, MA: Blackwell, 2005), 538–49, at 545.

210   DANTE'S EDUCATION

and did not consistently designate one particular kind of text."[4] Dante never uses the generic marker "epic." In the *De vulgari eloquentia* (2.4.5–6), he divides the poetic genres and styles into "tragic, comic, and elegiac," and in the *Commedia* he labels Virgil's *Aeneid* as a "tragedìa" (*Inferno* 20.113). Hence, what modern readers would call "epic" poetry, Dante would have probably termed "tragedy." He also argues that three lofty themes pertain to this style and meter: "integrity," "love," and "arms" (2.2.8). This selection of lofty subjects reflects the two branches of epic poetry that Latin poets had inherited from their Greek predecessors: Hesiod's didactic epos and Homer's heroic one.[5] No Italian vernacular poet, Dante claims, had written on the subject of war: "Arma vero nullum latium adhuc invenio poetasse" (as for arms, I find that no Italian has yet treated them in poetry) (2.2.9). This line points to the incipit of Virgil's *Aeneid* "Arma virumque cano . . ." Dante indeed derived his understanding of the ancient epic genre from the works of its major Latin representatives—Virgil's *Aeneid*, Ovid's *Metamorphoses*, Lucan's *Pharsalia*, Statius' *Thebaid*—and, as I argue in this chapter, from its representatives in the medieval school room, the *Achilleid* and the *De raptu Proserpinae*.[6] Statius' and Claudian's unfinished epics are emulative of the major Roman epicists, displaying a self-conscious mastery of the rhetorical and stylistic standards of the genre, as well as its conventional tropes and imagery. The two short poems, therefore, offered a succinct handbook of the genre—one with which Dante would

[4] Zygmunt Barański, "'Tres enim sunt manerie dicendi . . .'": Some Observations on Medieval Literature, Genre, and Dante," in Barański, *Dante, Petrarch, Boccaccio: Literature, Doctrine, Reality* (Oxford: Legenda, 2020), 209–56, at 219.

[5] On this classification, see Richard Jenkyns, "Epic and Other Genres in the Roman World," in *A Companion to Ancient Epic*, 562–73.

[6] On the reception of classical literary genres in the Middle Ages, see, among others, Ronald Martinez, "Rhetoric, Literary Theory, and Practical Criticism," in *Dante in Context*, ed. Zygmunt Barański (Cambridge: Cambridge University Press, 2015), 277–96. On Dante's understanding and division of genres, see Zygmunt G. Barański, "'Comedìa': Notes on Dante, the 'Epistle to Cangrande,' and Medieval Comedy," *Lectura Dantis* 8 (1991): 26–55, revised and expanded in Barański, "*Chiosar con altro testo*" (Florence: Cadmo, 2001), 41–76; Barański, ed., "*Libri Poetarum in Quattuor Species Dividuntur*": *Essays on Dante and "Genre*" (Reading, UK: University of Reading, 1995); Barański, "'Tres enim sunt manerie dicendi . . .'"; Ambrogio Camozzi Pistoja, "Il quarto trattato del *Convivio*: O della Satira," *Le tre corone* 1 (2014): 27–53; Camozzi Pistoja, "Profeta e satiro: A proposito di *Inferno* 19," *Dante Studies* 133 (2015): 27–45; Rossella D'Alfonso, "Fra retorica e teologia: Il sistema dei generi letterari nel basso medioevo," *Lingua e stile* 17, no. 2 (1982): 269–93; Amilcare Iannucci, *Forma ed evento nella "Divina Commedia*" (Rome: Bulzoni, 1984), 13–50; Iannucci, "Dante's Theory of Genres and the 'Divina Commedia,'" *Dante Studies* 91 (1973): 1–25; Vittorio Russo, "Strutture innovative delle opere letterarie di Dante nella prospettiva dei generi letterari," *L'Alighieri* 20, no. 2 (1979): 46–63, revised and expanded in Russo, *Il romanzo teologico* (Naples: Liguori, 2002), 31–53; Francesco Tateo, "*Il poema sacro ("Par." XXV 1–3*)," in *Versi controversi*, ed. Domenico Cofano and Sebastiano Valerio (Foggia: Edizioni del Rosone, 2008), 345–68; Claudia Villa, "Il problema dello stile umile (e il riso di Dante)," in *Dante the Lyric and Ethical Poet*, ed. Zygmunt G. Barański and Martin McLaughlin (London: Modern Humanities Research Association and Maney Publishing, 2010), 138–52, revised and expanded in Villa, *La protervia di Beatrice* (Florence: SISMEL, 2009), 215–32. Dante experiments with the martial subject matter in several passages of *Inferno*. The "siege" of Dis, narrated at *Inferno* 7–9, is an obvious example, as well as the introduction to the incomparable carnage related at *Inferno* 28. Whereas, the adventure with the Malebranche devils, in the cantos of barratry, at *Inferno* 21–22, contains clear satirical plays on the epic genre.

THE END OF THE PURGATORIAL CURRICULUM   211

have been eager to engage, especially in *Purgatorio* where he represents himself as the vernacular alternative to Virgil.

Epic ABCs

Statius' *Achilleid* and Claudian's *De raptu Proserpinae* figured prominently in late medieval education, as shown by their relatively stable presence in extant lists of school readings and in later versions of *Liber Catonianus*-type anthologies.[7] The pedagogical fortunes of the *Achilleid* reached an apogee during the twelfth and the thirteenth centuries.[8] Likewise, use of the *De raptu Proserpinae* in the schools of medieval Europe really picked up during the twelfth century and continued for at least two more centuries. The two poems fulfilled a similar function in medieval Latin instruction, as they both proved suitable readings to combine with the study of syntax at the most advanced stages of grammar learning. Together with the *Ilias Latina*, the two poems provided a fitting introduction to the study of the major Roman epics. Some of the poems' common features were especially fitting for this task: both are unfinished and thus short; they present an epic subject matter but with strong elegiac themes; and they display the self-conscious artistry of Silver Age Latin poetry, as Claudian often strives to imitate Statius (more on this shortly).[9] As a result of their stylistic similarities, combined use in the classroom,

[7] Both poems feature in reading lists from the eleventh century on. Different evidence, however, points to the *Achilleid*'s presence in medieval schools already in the tenth century. Some scant evidence of Claudian's inclusion among school readings dates back to the ninth century. See Paul M. Clogan, "Literary Genres in a Medieval Textbook," *Medievalia et Humanistica* 11 (1982): 199–209, at 204; Amy Key Clarke and Phyllis M. Giles, eds., *The Commentary of Geoffrey of Vitry on Claudian "De raptu Proserpinae"* (Leiden: Brill, 1973), 5. Conrad of Hirsau (1070–1150) and Aimeric of Auxerre (1086), however, do not mention him in their lists. On Statius' and Claudian's place in the medieval Latin curriculum and in the text of the *Liber Catonianus*-type anthologies, see Rino Avesani, "Il primo ritmo per la morte del grammatico Ambrogio e il cosiddetto 'Liber Catonianus,'" *Studi Medievali* 6 (1965): 455–88, esp. 469–88; Robert Black, *Humanism and Education in Medieval and Renaissance Italy: Tradition and Innovation in Latin Schools from the Twelfth to the Fifteenth Century* (Cambridge: Cambridge University Press, 2001), esp. 190, 218; Marcus Boas, "De Librorum Catonianorum historia atque compositione," *Mnemosyne*, n.s., 42 (1914): 17–46; Clogan, "Literary Genres," esp. 205–06; Clogan, "The Manuscripts of the *Achilleid*," *Manuscripta* 8 (1964): 175–79; Clogan, "Medieval Glossed Manuscripts of the *Achilleid*," *Manuscripta* 9 (1965): 104–09; Clogan, "Introduction," in *The Medieval Achilleid of Statius, Edited with Introduction, Variant Readings, and Glosses*, ed. Clogan (Leiden: Brill, 1968), 1–18; Violetta de Angelis, "Lo Stazio di Dante: poesia e scuola," *Schede umanistiche* 16, no. 2 (2002): 29–69; and Munk Olsen Birger, *I classici nel canone scolastico altomedievale* (Spoleto: CISAM, 1991), 69–74.

[8] See Haral Anderson, *Reception: The Vitae and Accessus*, vol. 3 of *The Manuscripts of Statius* (self-pub., 2009), 31; Boas, "De Librorum," 17. Claudian's *De raptu* seems to have become firmly established in the elementary curriculum only after the twelfth century. On Claudian's twelfth-century fortunes in medieval schools, see Marco Onorato, "Introduzione," in *Claudio Claudiano, De raptu Proserpinae*, ed. Marco Onorato (Naples: Loffredo, 2008), 75–81.

[9] Some of the characteristics common to both Statius' and Claudian's poems are excessive use of hyperbole and pathos, extensive use of figures of speech, lively descriptive narrative. Their technique often border on the mannerist and artificial, especially in Claudian's case. See Onorato, "Introduzione," 11–107, at 40–56.

212 DANTE'S EDUCATION

and physical proximity in manuscripts of school anthologies, some elements from Statius' medieval *accessus* and glosses were transferred to Claudian's, thus binding the two poems together in medieval culture.[10]

Statius' works were already much admired and studied in Roman schools during the poet's lifetime (*ca.* AD 45–*ca.* 96). Although he did not always enjoy steady popularity over the centuries, his influence on European literature can hardly be overstated. His epics were frequently copied during the Carolingian renaissance and entered school reading lists as early as the tenth century. Gerbert of Aurillac (946–1003), for instance, names Statius next to Virgil as one of the "tragic" poets in his canon of *auctores*, while Pierre Maurice (abbot of Cluny in 1122) lists Statius among the illustrious representatives of ancient philosophy and poetry.[11] During the twelfth century, his fame achieved stable prominence, and his works were studied alongside the great Roman authors.[12] In his *Dialogus super auctores* (*ca.* 1130), Conrad of Hirsau lists the *Thebaid* and the *Achilleid* among the foundational readings that any pupil should master, while a medieval *accessus* claims that Statius' popularity was second only to Virgil's in the thirteenth century.[13] The *Thebaid* and *Achilleid* circulated separately and, toward the end of the thirteenth century, the latter began to be copied alongside the *Ilias Latina*. Together, they provided a convenient introduction to the Homeric saga.[14] As a result of the poem's growing popularity in the scholastic milieu, the name "Statius" became practically synonymous with the *Achilleid*—also known as *Stacius minor*—and this association remained well into the fifteenth century.[15]

A substantial exegetical tradition developed to help readers interpret the *Achilleid*; a fifth-century commentary by Lactantius Placidus and four anonymous twelfth-century glosses survive. These glosses, which are rarely transmitted apart from the poem, provide short paraphrases, vocabulary explanations, grammatical

---

[10] A few identical glosses can be found in both poems. See, for instance, Clark and Giles, *Commentary of Geoffrey of Vitry*, 128–129n5. I will discuss some of these in due course. For a more detailed analysis of this phenomenon, see Amy Key Clarke, "Introduction," in Clarke and Giles, *Commentary of Geoffrey of Vitry*, 11.

[11] See Günter Glauche, *Schullektüre im Mittelalter* (Munich: Bei der Arbeo Gesellschaft, 1970), 62–65. On Statius' medieval popularity, see also de Angelis, "Lo Stazio," 36; Huygens, *Accessus ad auctores*, 119–20; Claudia Villa, *La "lectura Terentii,"* vol. 1, *Da Ildemaro a Francesco Petrarca* (Padua: Antenore, 1984), 121–23.

[12] William J. Dominik, "Statius," in *A Companion to Ancient Epic*, 514–27, at 525.

[13] Anderson, *Manuscripts of Statius*, vol. 3, 35. The growing interest of medieval readers in Statius' works also shines through the rich accounts of the author's life and oeuvre featured in medieval *accessus*. For a comprehensive reconstruction of the different *accessus* to Statius and their diffusion and circulation during the Middle Ages, see Anderson, introduction to vol. 2 of his *Manuscripts of Statius* (i–vii), as well as pp. 1–65 in the same volume.

[14] De Angelis, "Lo Stazio," 38; Anderson, *Manuscripts of Statius*, introduction to vol. 1, xi–xiii.

[15] De Angelis, "Lo Stazio," 34. On the medieval use and circulation of Statius' two poems, see de Angelis's paleographic analysis ("Lo Stazio," 34); and also Anderson, *Manuscripts of Statius*, introduction to vol. 1, v–xiii.

THE END OF THE PURGATORIAL CURRICULUM 213

notes, mythological and geographical information, and intertextual references.[16] A large number of *accessus* and *vitae* complete the rich exegetical tradition on Statius. On occasion, these forms of ancillary paratexts were copied independently from his two epics and collected in miscellaneous manuscripts. Prose summaries of the different parts of the *Achilleid*—known as *periochae*—were also in circulation, often without marginal or interlinear commentaries.

At least four traditions of *accessus* to the *Achilleid* attest that the work was unfinished.[17] Although Statius introduces the *Achilleid* as an epic poem on the entire life of Achilles—from his childhood in Scyros, through the Trojan War, until his death—the work remains incomplete, cut short in Book 2 by the poet's death. The only events recounted in the poem are the following: Thetis attempts to save Achilles by disguising him as a girl at the king's court in Scyros; Achilles rapes Deidamia, and she eventually yields to his request that they enter into a romantic relationship; Ulysses and Diomedes find out Achilles' hiding place and persuade him to join the military expedition against Troy; the heroes depart for Troy while, in the distance, Deidamia, joined by her sisters, laments the loss of her love. Despite its incompleteness, the poem was often presented as a finished work, divided in five books, and with a definitive ending.[18] Some other *accessus*, however, show uncertainty as to how the poem should be divided, and the state of the *Achilleid* remained a quarrel even among Italian humanists.[19]

In medieval schools, the poem was received as the story of Achilles' youth, a sort of *bildungsroman*, which offered a narrative preamble to the Trojan War—conveniently summarized by the often-accompanying *Ilias Latina*—and was meant to provide helpful instructions for the education of boys:

> Intencio Stacii in hoc libro est ergo ut describendo puericiam Achillis qualiter nutritus sit in puericia intendit nos docere puerilem erudicionem et qualiter pueri

---

[16] Anderson, *Manuscripts of Statius*, vol. 3, 1. See also Birger Munk Olsen, "La réception de la littérature classique: travaux philologiques," vol. 4, part 1, of *L'Étude des auteurs classiques latins aux XIe et XIIe siècles* (Paris: CNRS, 2009), 106. For the text of Lactantius' commentary, see *Lactantii Placidi qui dicitur commentarios in Statii Thebaida et Commentarium in Achilleida: Recensuit Ricardus Jahnke* (Leipzig: Teubner, 1898). Exemplars of the *Achilleid* copied in the *Libri Catoniani* are often surrounded by glosses that were developed for scholastic use. Some of them are ancient but independent from Lactantius' commentary (Clogan, "Literary Genres," 205).

[17] Anderson, *Manuscripts of Statius*, vol. 3, 24–25, 29, 38–41, and 61. See, for instance, the *accessus* transmitted in the manuscript Lincoln College, Oxford, Lat. 27, fol. 62r.: "Materia huius libri gesta sunt achillis. que omnia quidem statius a primeua etate usque ad eius obitum scribere proposuit. sed morte preuentus opus incepit non expleuit"—quoted in Marjorie Curry Woods, *Weeping for Dido* (Princeton, NJ: Princeton University Press, 2019), 57–58n18. See also the *accessus* quoted by Clogan in *Medieval Achilleid*, 9.

[18] For this purpose, in medieval manuscripts, the spurious line "Aura silet, puppis currens a litora venit" was often added at the end of the poem (De Angelis, "Lo Stazio," 37).

[19] Uncertainty, for instance, is expressed by the *accessus* transmitted in the manuscript London, British Library, Harley 2744, fol. 193r—quoted in Woods, *Weeping for Dido*, 58. For the humanist quarrel on how to divide the *Achilleid*, see Violetta de Angelis, "Magna questio preposita coram Dante et domino Francisco Petrarca et Virgiliano," *Studi Petrarcheschi* 1 (1984): 103–210.

214 DANTE'S EDUCATION

sunt nutriendi ut postmodum fiant virtuosi et robusti. Materia eius est thetis et achilles. Vtilitas huius libri est ut cognito qualiter achilles nutritus fuit qui postea fortissimus grecorum fuit sciamus et nos simili modo pueros nutrire et erudire.[20]

(The intention of Statius in this book is, therefore, that, in describing the boyhood of Achilles and how he was brought up during boyhood, he intends to teach us the education of boys and how boys are to be brought up so that afterwards they be made manly and strong. His subject is Thetis and Achilles. The usefulness of the book is so that, having learned how Achilles was brought up, who afterwards was the bravest of the Greeks, we know how to bring up and teach boys in a similar way.)

According to this reading, the *Achilleid* featured an epic of upbringing, with the hero going through different stages of maturation that correspond to his different adult mentors. Marjorie Curry Woods observes that "Achilles is quasi-feral with Chiron, girlish after Thetis's instructions on comportment, and more manly by the minute with Ulysses and Diomedes."[21] The *Achilleid*'s interpretation as a guide for the education of young men likely contributed to its success among medieval pedagogues. It also informed the view of Statius as *poeta doctus*—a poet teacher who offered useful advice on the upbringing of children. This notion affected the reception of the *Thebaid*. In some of the poem's *accessus*, Statius is presented as a learned poet and moral philosopher, whose works provide many lessons on a wide variety of subjects and are especially rich in moral examples to be either imitated or rejected. For instance, one of the moral subjects discussed by the *Thebaid* would be the necessity for children to avoid anger.

A medieval *accessus* to the *Achilleid*, preserved in the manuscript Plutei 24 sin. 12, fol. 49r of the Biblioteca Medicea Laurenziana in Florence (Figure 6.1), explains that Statius wrote the *Achilleid* to satisfy the emperor Domitian's request that the learned poet solve the philosophical question "utrum ea que predestinata sunt euitari" (whether the things that are predestined can be avoided), which was being debated in the imperial court. To illustrate that the question should be answered in the negative, the *accessus* continues, Statius composed a poem about Thetis's failed attempt to avert her son's fate: "qui [Statius] imperatori suisque fidelibus questionem soluere cupiens hunc libellum composuit, ostendendo qualiter Thetis fatis resistere voluit et nequivit" (wishing to solve the matter for the emperor and his faithful servants, Statius wrote this booklet, in which it is shown how Thetis wished and failed to resist fate). The bond

---

[20] Vienna, Österreichische Nationalbibliothek Cod. 3114, fol. 110r. Text and translation are quoted from Woods, *Weeping for Dido*, 62–63. On the manuscript tradition of the *Achilleid* as a complete epic about the education of Achilles, see also De Angelis, "Lo Stazio," 36–37, 50.

[21] Woods, *Weeping for Dido*, 61.

THE END OF THE PURGATORIAL CURRICULUM   215

between Statius and moral education, therefore, was profoundly felt in medieval culture.[22]

The fame of the unfinished *Achilleid*, however, did not rest on its pedagogical value alone. This "last epic poem of the classical period," as it has been defined, represents a remarkable experiment and challenge to previous poetic models.[23] Although medieval *accessus* emphasize its "grandiloquus stilus"—the lofty style typically associated with tragedy and epic—in its unfinished form, the *Achilleid* features an epic with an erotic and elegiac core. It thus mixes subjects and styles that were traditionally kept separate, at least in theory.[24] As Richard Jenkyns points out, none of the Latin epicists from the Flavian period attempted to revise the standards of the genre as these had been established by Virgil and Ovid: the only exception to this trend is Statius' *Achilleid*.[25]

In his *De raptu Proserpinae*, Claudian took Statius' experiment in the *Achilleid* even further, as he made eros and elegy the core themes of his unconventional epic.[26] The author's original intention—as suggested by the prooemium—was to tell the story of Proserpina: her abduction, her crowning as queen of the underworld, her mother Ceres' desperate search for her lost daughter, and the end of the Golden Age with the concomitant beginning of agriculture. However, the *De raptu Proserpinae*, too, was interrupted by its author's death in the middle of Book 2. For centuries before Claudian, the story of Ceres and Proserpina had enjoyed great popularity in Greek culture, when it was made the subject of a Homeric hymn to Demeter and of Orphic poems; all of which are now lost. To this myth are also devoted several episodes in Ovid's *Metamorphoses*. Yet, Claudian's version differs substantially from Ovid's and constitutes the most extensive account of the myth to have survived.[27]

Although Claudian's *De raptu Proserpinae* has traditionally been associated with the epic genre, its style and subject matter bear little resemblance to the

---

[22] The translation is mine. Dominik, "Statius," 526. Dante, too, is affected by this particular perception of Statius' poetics, as is apparent from *Convivio* 4.25, where the author draws on the first book of the *Thebaid* to provide examples of *stupore*, *pudore*, and *verecundia*. Another example is in Pietro Alighieri's commentary on *Purgatorio* 21, where Dante's son describes Statius' poems as handbooks of moral examples. See Paratore, "Stazio," in the *ED*. As Dominik notes, moreover, "Statius was also regarded in medieval *accessus* as a poeta historiographus which reflected the prevailing view of the *Thebaid* as a history with moral overtones" ("Statius," 526).

[23] The definition is used by Alessandro Barchiesi, *Speaking Volumes: Narrative and Intertext in Ovid and Other Latin Poets* (London: Duckworth, 2001), 129.

[24] De Angelis, "Lo Stazio," 53; Anderson, *Manuscripts of Statius*, vol. 3, 14–29 and 50–62.

[25] Jenkyns, "Epic and Other Genres," 571.

[26] As critics have often been willing to acknowledge, Claudian takes Statius as his primary model. See P. Papinius Statius, *Achilleid*, ed. and trans. O. A. W. Dilke (Exeter: Bristol Phoenix Press, 2005 [1954]), 19. J. B. Hall also agrees on this point and brings up the example of Claudian's Ceres, who resembles Statius' Thetis. See Hall's "Introduction," to his critical edition of Claudius Claudianus, *De Raptu Proserpinae*, ed. J. B. Hall (London: Cambridge University Press, 1969), 3–114, esp. 110.

[27] See Hall's "Introduction," 106. Hall also points out that Claudian's verbal imitations of Ovid's *Metamorphoses* do not come from Proserpina's episode (108n1).

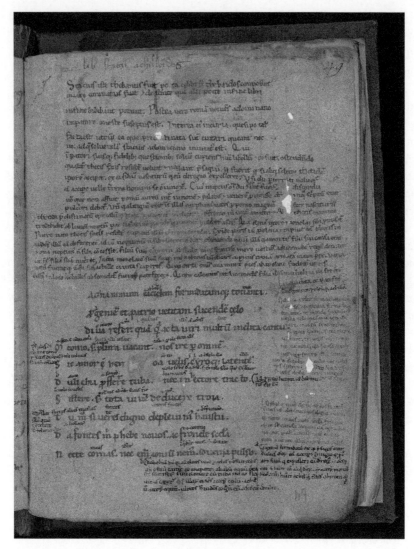

Figure 6.1 Florence, Biblioteca Medicea Laurenziana, MS Plut. 24 sin. 12, fol. 49r. Statius, *Achilleid* with *accessus* and glosses.

Source: Courtesy of the Italian Ministry of Culture/Biblioteca Medicea Laurenziana, Florence. Reproduction or duplication by any means is strictly prohibited.

grand Homeric and Virgilian tradition.[28] The poem follows instead in the tradition of post-Virgilian epics: it features a rather fragmentary and underdeveloped

---

[28] On Claudian's eccentric relation to the ancient epic genre, see Barnes, "Claudian," 538–49, esp. 543–45; Claire Gruzelier, "Introduction," in Claudian, *De Raptu Proserpinae*, ed. and trans. Claire Gruzelier (Oxford: Clarendon Press, 1993), xvii–xxxi, esp. xxvii; and Hall, "Introduction," 110.

THE END OF THE PURGATORIAL CURRICULUM   217

plot made up of loosely connected episodes and lacks the central figure of a hero. The poem is bound together by a series of main interrelated themes: the conflict between the heavens and the underworld, military imagery, which heightens the brutality of Proserpina's abduction; an atmosphere of mystery; and an underdiveloped narrative plot.[29] Claudian's poem draws its dynamic force from the author's learned and sophisticated style, which is characterized by brilliant descriptions, extended speeches, and subtle intertextuality. As the poem's style marks a decisive penetration of oratory into epic poetry, it features countless similes, metaphors, and personifications—all key elements, it should be noted, of Dante's poetry in the *Commedia* as well. On account of Claudian's rhetorical prowess and colorful style, bits and pieces of his poems also circulated independently, as models for composition or aphorisms to be quoted. He is often cited in medieval grammatical commentaries and excerpted in florilegia.[30]

Claudian's sophisticated literary culture shines through the intricate web of intertexts that the poem engages with, as does the author's ability to play with established themes and tropes. The hallmarks of his poetics are allusions and intertextuality: he borrows, quotes, and imitates language, imagery, and topoi from previous literature.[31] He articulates several stock poetic themes in dialogue with the major Roman epics, thus creating a "literary pastiche," as Claire Gruzelier terms it.[32] Virgil, Ovid, and especially Statius' *Achilleid* represent Claudian's primary models in the *De raptu Proserpinae*. He displays toward them the kind of agonistic attitude that was typical of Silver Age poetry and a mark of Statius' influence. Claudian's literary erudition and stylistic ability turned the *De raptu Proserpinae* into a "touchstone" of late antique education—a handy treasure trove of literary themes and rhetorical forms for medieval pupils to digest and assimilate.[33] Thus, the poem's wide circulation came increasingly to bear on its use for instructional purposes, particularly in the *Liber Catonianus* type of anthologies.[34]

---

[29] Gruzelier, "Introduction," xxvi–xxvii; Hall, "Introduction," 110; and Gabriella Ryser, "A Wedding in the Underworld of Claudian's *De Raptu Proserpinae*," in Ilinca Tanaseanu-Döbler et al., eds., *Reading the Way to the Netherworld: Education and the Representations of the Beyond in Later Antiquity* (Göttingen: Vandenhoeck & Ruprecht, 2017), 282–300, at 294.

[30] Tony Hunt, *Teaching and Learning Latin in Thirteenth-Century England: Texts*, vol. 1 (Woodbridge, UK: Boydell & Brewer, 1991), 69.

[31] See A. K. Clarke, "Claudian's Method of Borrowing in *De raptu Proserpinae*," *Proceedings of the Cambridge Philological Society* 1 (1952): 4–7; O. A. W. Dilke, "Patterns of Borrowing in Claudian's *De raptu Proserpinae*," *Revue belge de philologie et d'histoire* 43, no. 1 (1965): 60–61; and C. Ware, *Claudian and the Roman Epic Tradition* (Cambridge: Cambridge University Press, 2012), 171.

[32] Gruzelier, "Introduction," xxiii. On these characteristics of Claudian's style, see also Hall, "Introduction," 106–09.

[33] Ryser, "A Wedding in the Underworld," 298.

[34] Onorato, "Introduzione," 77.

218   DANTE'S EDUCATION

In the twelfth century, Geoffrey of Vitry wrote a commentary on Claudian's *De raptu Proserpinae* that was suitable for classroom use.[35] The commentary's minimal treatment of philosophical points and the absence of any critical appreciation of the poem are indications of the elementary character of its intended audience. Discussions of meter and grammar are few and sporadic. Geoffrey shows no interest in treating grammar from a logical perspective. Some of the variant readings of Claudian's text that Geoffrey offers may be simplifications designed to assist Latin beginners. Mythological allusions are fully explained, and quotations from classical authors are abundant. Little, however, has been established with regard to the circulation of Geoffrey's commentary in late medieval Europe. Thanks to its continued use in medieval education, therefore, Claudian's *De raptu Proserpinae* exerted an important influence on medieval Latin poetry and the reception of the ancient epic genre, as well as of Proserpina's myth.

In their unfinished poems, both Statius and Claudian tamper with the epic genre by blending in elegiac and erotic themes. They celebrate both the disruptive and edifying power of love, as well as its crucial role in the rite of passage from youth to maturity. They also share a tendency to model their poetics on the emulation of the major Roman *auctores*: outdoing these authorities means proving themselves worthy of being called poets. Given the influence they exerted on late medieval literary education, an assessment of Dante's reception of their epic model is essential to appreciate his particular assimilation of classical poetics into a new vernacular literature.

Doubts remain, however, as to when the *Achilleid* and the *De raptu Proserpinae* became popular readings in Florentine schools, and whether Dante's first acquaintance with them dated back to his school days. Only a handful of extant thirteenth-century manuscripts of the two poems survive in Florentine libraries today. This fact has been interpreted by some as a sign of the poems' relative neglect in Florence's schools during this century. Robert Black, for instance, found little evidence that Statius was a popular school text in the city and argues that Claudian's poem firmly established itself in the Italian classroom only during the fourteenth century.[36] Their educational use in Florence may be witnessed by at least one surviving manuscript predating the fourteenth century and bearing marks of its use in the school context. The already mentioned manuscript Florence, Biblioteca Medicea Laurenziana Plutei 24 sin. 12, formerly a volume in

---

[35] See Clogan, "Literary Genres," 205, and Clarke and Giles, *Commentary of Geoffrey of Vitry*, 5–7. Geoffrey was a master at Vitry, near Cluny, an active center of learning during the twelfth century. See Clarke and Giles, *Commentary of Geoffrey of Vitry*, 2. The entire commentary is transmitted in a thirteenth-century manuscript (Oxford, Bodl. Lat. Class. C. 12) and in abbreviated form in nine manuscripts from the twelfth to the fourteenth centuries. Four of these manuscripts are *Liber Catonianus*-type anthologies, proving that the commentary was used for teaching purposes. See Clogan, "Literary Genres," 204.

[36] Black, *Humanism*, 219–20.

THE END OF THE PURGATORIAL CURRICULUM   219

the Santa Croce library, collects together a Christian epic by Sedulius, the *Carmen Paschale*, Statius' *Achilleid* (Figure 6.1), and Claudian's *De raptu Proserpinae* (Figure 6.2). Hence, the miscellaneous anthology looks like a small handbook of epic poetry designed for Christian readers. Black, however, excludes this manuscript from his census of medieval school texts. He argues that the sections containing Statius' and Claudian's poems belong to different manuscripts, one of which was produced outside of Italy, and were bound together only later. Other scholars, however, have reached different paleographical conclusions about the history of the composition and circulation of this miscellaneous volume, locating either part of its production or at least its glossing in Italy before the fourteenth century.[37] It is also important to note that later manuscripts currently held in Florentine libraries show that the two poems were copied together in school anthologies during the first half of the fourteenth century.[38] This fact implies that both the *Achilleid* and the *De raptu Proserpinae* had already reached some limited circulation in the city over the preceding century.[39]

Dante's reception of the *Achilleid* has gained some critical attention in relation to the character Statius in *Purgatorio*. Scholars have been particularly keen on investigating the metapoetic implications of this character's function as filter and catalyst in Dante and Virgil's evolving relationship.[40] Yet the importance of the

---

[37] The manuscript Florence, Biblioteca Medicea Laurenziana Plut. 24 sin. 12 is one of the most ancient manuscripts of Claudian's *De raptu Proserpinae*. At least this section of the manuscript dates from between the eleventh and the twelfth centuries. See Hall, "Introduction," 49–64. L. D. Reynolds suggested that Claudian's poem had been transcribed by an Italian copyist. See Reynolds, *Texts and Transmission: A Survey of the Latin Classics* (Oxford: Clarendon Press, 1983), 143. Violetta de Angelis ("Lo Stazio di Dante," 40) also believed the manuscript was produced and glossed in Italy during the twelfth century. However, the three poems collected in it were originally copied independently of one another, and we do not know when they were bound together. More recently, Black argued that this might have occurred as late as the fifteenth or even the eighteenth century. Moreover, while the first two poems are written in two different Italian hands, Black argues that Claudian's poem is in a distinctively non-Italian hand and was probably written by a French scribe. According to Black, the same Italian hand glossed Sedulius and Statius, whereas the glosses on Claudian's poem would be by a different hand. See Robert Black, "The School Miscellany in Medieval and Renaissance Italy," *Segno e Testo* 2 (2004): 213–44, at 214. Black assumes that while Sedulius and Statius might have been present in Florence since the twelfth century, Claudian was not (Black, *Humanism*, 395). In a more recent study, *Manuscripts of Statius* (vol. 1, 104), Anderson argues that all three poems were written outside Italy, probably in France, in the twelfth century, but the same hand glossed both Statius and Claudian during the fourteenth century. If true, Anderson's conclusion—combined with Black's analysis of the Italian hand of the glossator—would prove that the three texts were circulating together as an anthology in Italy as early as the fourteenth century. Hall ("Introduction," 7–11) lists several other manuscripts still in Florentine libraries that were written before the fourteenth century. This fact may provide further evidence of the poem's circulation in Dante's Florence. Among these, the manuscript Florence, Biblioteca Medicea Laurenziana Plutei 33.4 dates from the thirteenth century.

[38] See Paul Gehl, "Latin Readers in Fourteenth-Century Florence," *Scrittura e civiltà* 13 (1989): 387–440.

[39] The considerable number of manuscripts of the *Achilleid* that were copied and glossed in the school manner in Italy during the late Middle Ages also points to the poem's established place in the curriculum. For some interesting examples, see Woods, *Weeping for Dido*, chap. 2.

[40] A footnote cannot do justice to the wealth of studies on both Statius in Dante and Dante's Statius. For a general introduction to this topic, see Ettore Paratore's entry "Stazio, Publio Papinio" in the *ED*, and also William Stephany's entry "Statius," in *Dante Encyclopedia*, ed. Richard Lansing (New York:

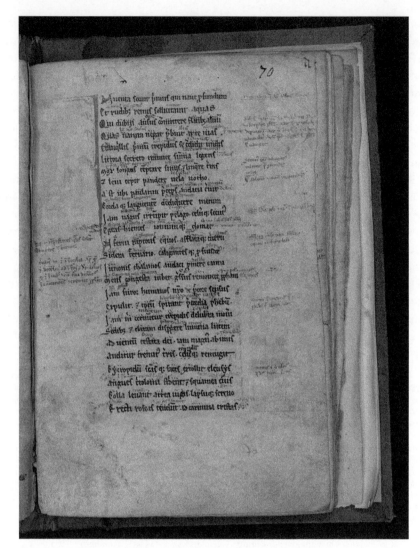

Figure 6.2 Florence, Biblioteca Medicea Laurenziana, MS Pluteo 24 sin. 12, fol. 70r. Claudian, *De raptu Proserpinae*, surrounded by interlinear and marginal glosses.

Source: Courtesy of the Italian Ministry of Culture/Biblioteca Medicea Laurenziana, Florence. Reproduction or duplication by any means is strictly prohibited.

Garland, 2000), 798–800. For brevity's sake, I will leave aside several studies that focus on Statius' presence in *Inferno*, and I will mention only some of the essays on the character Statius in *Purgatorio* that have been especially relevant in the preparation of this chapter: Teodolinda Barolini, *Dante's Poets: Textuality and Truth in the Comedy* (Princeton, NJ: Princeton University Press, 1984), 256–69; Alessandro Boccia, "Appunti sulla presenza di Stazio nella *Divina Commedia*," *Annali dell'Istituto Italiano per gli Studi Storici* 18 (2001): 29–45; Giorgio Brugnoli, "Stazio in Dante," *Cultura Neolatina* 29 (1969): 117–25; Brugnoli, "Statius Christianus," *Italianistica* 17 (1988): 9–15; de Angelis, "Magna questio";

THE END OF THE PURGATORIAL CURRICULUM   221

Achilleid in these cantos has been overshadowed by excessive scholarly focus on the *Thebaid*. Very little attention, moreover, has been devoted to the influence of Claudian's *De raptu Proserpinae* on Dante—a trend that stems from the latter's apparent disregard for the late Roman poet. Whether Dante knew Claudian's *De raptu Proserpinae* is still a matter of debate, and *Dantisti* have often assumed that he did not.[41] The poem's success in medieval education, however, raises the

de Angelis, "Lo Stazio"; Diana Glenn, "Women in Limbo: Arbitrary Listings or Textual Referents? Mapping the Connections in *Inferno* 4 and *Purgatorio* 22," *Dante Studies* 117 (1999): 85–115; Hermann Gmelin, "Dante und die römischen Dichter," in *Deutsches Dante-Jahrbuch* 31–32 (1953): 42–65; Denise Heilbronn, "The Prophetic Role of Statius in Dante's *Purgatory*," *Dante Studies* 95 (1977): 58–65; Craig Kallendorf and Hilaire Kallendorf, "'Per te poeta fui, per te cristiano' (*Purg.* 22.73): Statius as Christian, from 'Fact' to Fiction," *Deutsches Dante-Jahrbuch* 77 (2002): 61–72; C. S. Lewis, "Dante's Statius," in *Medium Aevum* 25 (1956): 133–39, now in *Studies in Medieval and Renaissance Literature*, ed. Walter Hooper (Cambridge: Cambridge University Press, 1979), 94–102; Simone Marchesi, *Dante and Augustine: Linguistics, Poetics, Hermeneutics* (Toronto: University of Toronto Press, 2011), 117–53; Ronald Martinez, "La 'sacra fame dell'oro' (*Purgatorio* 22, 41) tra Virgilio e Stazio: dal testo all'interpretazione," *Letture Classensi* 18 (1989): 177–93; Martinez, "Dante and the Two Canons: Statius in Virgil's Footsteps (*Purgatorio* 21–30)," *Comparative Literature Studies* 32 (1995): 151–75; Manlio Pastore Stocchi, "Il cristianesimo di Stazio (Purg. XXII) e un'ipotesi del Poliziano," in *Miscellanea di studi offerta a Armando Balduino*, ed. Lorenzo Renzi et al. (Padua: Seminario di Filologia Moderna dell'Università, 1962), 41–45; Luca Carlo Rossi, "Prospezioni filologiche per lo Stazio di Dante," in *Dante e la "bella scola" della poesia: Autorità e sfida poetica*, ed. Amilcare Iannucci (Ravenna: Longo, 1993), 205–24; Richard Shoaf, "'Auri sacra fames' and the Age of Gold (*Purg.* XXII, 40–41 and 148–150)," *Dante Studies* 96 (1978): 195–99; Arthur Woollgar Verrall, *Collected Literary Essays, Classical and Modern*, ed. Matthew Bayfield and James Duff (Cambridge: Cambridge University Press, 1913): 160–66; Winthrop Wetherbee, *The Ancient Flame: Dante and the Poets* (Notre Dame, IN: University of Notre Dame Press, 2008), 159–202.

[41] The number of studies on Dante and Claudian is considerably more exiguous than that of studies on Stazio. One of the earliest disputes about Dante's knowledge of Claudian revolved around a quotation from Claudian's *De bello Gildonico* that appears in the epistle to Guido da Polenta and was spuriously attributed to Dante—the *Epistola* 8 in Pietro Fraticelli's edition, *Il Convito di Dante Alighieri e le Epistole* (Florence: Barbera, 1857), 500–06. See also Julius Schück, "Dantes classische Studien und Brunetto Latini," *Neue Jahrbücher für Philologie und Paedagogik* 92 (1865): 262–63; Paget Toynbee, "Was Dante Acquainted with Claudian?," *Academy* 44 (1893): 488–89, republished in *Dante Studies and Researches* (London: Methuen, 1902), 282–83; Toynbee, "Claudianus," in *A Dictionary of Proper Names and Notable Matters in the Works of Dante* (Oxford: Clarendon Press, 1898), 165. In his entry "Claudiano" in the *ED*, Michele Coccia follows Paget Toynbee's opinion and maintains that there are no echoes of Claudian's poems in Dante's works. Some of Claudian's hemistiches, however, seem to surface in *Convivio* 1.3.5–6 and 4.1–12 (see Giovanni Busnelli, "Il Convivio di Dante e un suo nuovo commento," in *La Civiltà Cattolica* 86, no. 1 [1935]: 135–46), but Dante could have drawn them from medieval collections of *exempla* or *sententiae*. For Claudian's quotations that were most popular during the Middle Ages, see, for instance, Jean-Thiébaut Welter, *L'exemplum dans la littérature religieuse et didactique du Moyen Age* (Paris-Toulouse: Guitard, 1927), 111, 126, 369–74. Welter contradicts Michele Scherillo, who maintained that Claudian was unknown to the "centonisti." See Michele Scherillo, *Alcuni capitoli della biografia di Dante* (Turin: Loescher, 1896), 426–27. Edward Moore (*Studies in Dante: First Series. Scripture and Classical Authors in Dante* [New York: Haskell House Publishers, 1968], 240n1) argues that Dante never read Claudian's works. Curiously, however, although Dante's knowledge of Claudian has often been doubted by modern scholars, ancient and early modern commentaries on the *Commedia* have often noted the presence of possible echoes of the Roman poet in Dante's poem. For a detailed summary of Claudian's presence in the history of the *Commedia*'s exegesis, see George F. Butler, "Claudian's *De raptu Proserpinae* and Dante's Vanquished Giants," *Italica* 48, no. 4 (2007): 661–78. Several commentators have associated Claudian with Dante's *Inferno*, noting parallels between the two poets' treatment of the Furies and the Giants, and the tremendous size and utter helplessness of Pluto and Satan. The name "Efialte" in *Inferno* 31.94 has also been discussed as a possible reference to Claudian's *De bello Pollentino sive Gothico* 75. Although this intertextual link was already noted by Pietro Alighieri, Raffaello Fornaciari proposes that Claudian's *In Rufinum*

222   DANTE'S EDUCATION

question of whether he could possibly have ignored it. The intertextual evidence discussed in this chapter and the following one should help define this matter and show Dante's assimilation of Claudian's *De raptu Proserpinae*. His apparent disregard of this popular school text can be shown to be deliberate.

Re-Dressing Achilles, Resisting Proserpina: Dante's Purgatorial Rite of Passage

Purgatorio 9 represents a liminal space Dante-the-pilgrim needs to cross in order to move from the ante-Purgatory into Purgatory proper and thus begin his journey of purgation. This canto also encapsulates a crucial narrative moment of personal decision and commitment, as the protagonist is required to face the angel door-keeper and comply with his instructions. The pilgrim is also warned not to look back after crossing Purgatory's gate, lest his journey end even before it begins. Dante's path of moral and spiritual maturity, therefore, begins on this threshold, where he lives his moment of epic resolution. Similarly, the moment when Achilles wakes up in Scyros, he is confronted with his mother's injunction that he hides in women's clothes to avert his heroic destiny. His decision to follow the path traced for him by Thetis sets off a psychological chain of reactions in which he will first rape and marry Deidamia and then embrace military virtue by following Ulysses and Diomedes to Troy. It has been speculated that Statius' *bildungsroman* of Achilles provided a suitable narrative for exciting the imagination of medieval schoolboys and arousing their spirit of competition. It has also been abundantly shown, however, that medieval readers glossed and interpreted literary texts that featured obvious erotic contents in ways that often defy and puzzle modern readers' expectations.[42] I contend that Dante's identification with Achilles at *Purgatorio* 9.34–39 conjures up the social and emotional rite of passage that in medieval education coincided with the reading of the *Achilleid*.

1.123–28 influenced Dante's depiction of Ulysses, as these lines narrate Ulysses' journey to the end of the *Oceano* and his meeting with the dead. See Raffaello Fornaciari, *Studi su Dante* (Florence: Sansoni, 1901), 112. Antonino Pagliaro (*Ulisse: Ricerche semantiche sulla Commedia* [Messina-Florence: D'Anna, 1967], 406), however, brings several legitimate objections to Fornaciari's thesis; whereas Stefano Carrai (*Dante e l'antico: L'emulazione dei classici nella Commedia* [Florence: SISMEL Edizioni del Galluzzo, 2012], 32–34) has recently proposed new evidence in favor of Fornaciari's argument. Olindo Ferrari ("Il mondo degli inferi di Claudiano," *Athenaeum* 4 [1916]: 33–337) proposes that Claudian's *In Rufinum* 2.482–90 presents a form of punishment that recalls Dante's *contrapasso*. Emerson Brown ("Proserpina, Matelda, and the Pilgrim," *Dante Studies* 89 [1971]: 33–48) has argued that Claudian's *De raptu* is the source of Dante's representation of Proserpina in *Purgatorio* 28. Finally, Guglielmo Bellaira ("Un'eco Claudianea in Dante?," *L'Alighieri* 1 [1974]: 50–52) has shown convincing intertextual affinities between Dante's use of the navigation metaphor in *Paradiso* 2 and Claudian's preface to *De raptu Proserpinae* 1. I will discuss Claudian's echoes in *Paradiso* more closely in the next chapter.

[42] To mention but one illuminating study of this hermeneutic practice based on medieval manuscripts, see John Dagenais, *The Ethics of Reading in Manuscript Culture: Glossing the Libro de Buen Amor* (Princeton, NJ: Princeton University Press, 1994). The first book of Augustine's *Confession* offers an extended discussion of how ambiguous texts, such as *Aeneid* book 4, where read for the purpose of linguistic education but presented Christian pupils with moral snares.

THE END OF THE PURGATORIAL CURRICULUM   223

As Walter Ong argued, medieval and Renaissance Latin instruction represented a "puberty rite" that male pupils underwent as part of their initiation into a social and cultural elite of literates.[43] In time, with the expansion and consolidation of the vernacular, the exclusivity of this Latinized caste increased. The use of corporal punishment heightened the perception of Latin instruction as toughening one's character and moral fiber, but so also did the selection of school readings: poetry appealed to the "weak" minds of boys but was taught to get them *over* their weakness.[44] The genre of the ancient epic helped fuel the kind of competitive mentality instilled by Latin education. A short poem such as the *Achilleid*, for instance, perfectly illustrated the temptations of love and femininity—as dramatized by Achilles' cross-dressing—but exalted the hero's decision to leave his mother's tutelage, re-dress in his male clothes, abandon his newly wedded wife, and embrace the life and fate of a warrior.[45] Achilles' initial bewilderment and progressive movement away from his mother's care and into Ulysses' tutelage mirrors the psychological and social trajectory that medieval pupils were expected to follow as part of their Latin training—in contrast to the vernacular, often perceived as maternal.[46] Hence, in the eye of readers who had been educated on the *Achilleid*, Dante's self-identification with Statius' Achilles at the moment when his heroic journey is about to begin evoked precise social and cultural implications. Contemporary readers would have perceived that, at *Purgatorio* 9, the pilgrim is about to set out on a process of education and initiation into a new moral order, which is first introduced in the cantos of Eden and then represented in *Paradiso*.

Suzanne Hagedorn has already noted the importance of Dante's self-fashioning as *alter Achilles* throughout the *Commedia*, but she stops short of suggesting a particular reason for it.[47] The association is worth pondering, however, especially given that Dante locates Achilles among the lustful in Hell (*Inferno* 4.65). Rather than providing a model to follow, Achilles' upbringing shows some serious shortcomings and appears ill-suited for someone such as Dante, who is going through Purgatory in search of moral freedom, as claimed by Virgil in *Purgatorio* 1.71. Dante's self-identification with young Achilles at *Purgatorio* 9, therefore, implies a specific criticism of the type of education featured in Statius' poem. The

---

[43] Walter J. Ong, "Latin Language Study as a Renaissance Puberty Rite," *Studies in Philology* 56, no. 2 (1959): 103–24, reprinted in Ong, *Rhetoric, Romance, and Technology* (Ithaca, NY: Cornell University Press, 1971), 113–41.

[44] Ong, "Latin Language Study," 113–17.

[45] As Woods eloquently points out, Achilles' "time with his mother was a literal and figurative deviation from his manly path. At the end of the text he heads off to war with his new mentors, Ulysses and Diomedes, respectively the smartest leader and an archetypal warrior of the Greeks, who will, it is implied, turn him into a man" (*Weeping for Dido*, 85–86).

[46] As evidenced by Dante at different moments throughout his oeuvre. On this, the seminal study is Gary P. Cestaro, *Dante and the Grammar of the Nursing Body* (Notre Dame, IN: University of Notre Dame Press, 2003).

[47] Hagedorn, "A Statian Model," 36–40.

224   DANTE'S EDUCATION

poet, for instance, displays keen awareness of the unhappy fate of the heroine and victim of the *Achilleid*, Deidamia. Her name is invoked twice in the poem: first, at *Inferno* 26.62, where Virgil mentions her abandonment in the list of Ulysses' sins, and a second time by Statius, at *Purgatorio* 22.114, where she features as one of the souls in Limbo. Both mentions are notable. In the first case, Dante thinks enough of Deidamia's abandonment to make it one of the reasons for Ulysses' eternal damnation. The second instance is remarkable in two ways. First, Deidamia's presence in Limbo should probably be seen in opposition to Dido's damnation among the lustful. Statius conceived the second book of the *Achilleid* as a reworking of the fourth book of the *Aeneid*, in which Aeneas and Dido become lovers; the hero then abandons the queen of Carthage to fulfill his epic fate, and she kills herself. The relationship between Achilles and Deidamia in the *Achilleid* follows an almost identical trajectory. In the *Commedia*, however, the two couples' otherworldly destinies do not perfectly align and create instead a suggestive chiasmus: whereas Aeneas and Deidamia are in Limbo, Achilles and Dido are punished in the circle of lust.

The other interesting aspect about Statius' mention of Deidamia at *Purgatorio* 22.114 is that she is not the only female character from the *Achilleid* who enjoys a place among the virtuous pagans of Limbo. All her sisters and Achilles' mother, Thetis, are also with her: "e Teti, e con le suore sue Deïdamia" (and Thetis, and Deïdamia with her sisters).[48] Their names complete a list of unhappy heroines from antiquity now in Limbo, and their presence there can be seen as a self-tribute to the character Statius. Yet the evidence that they are all women and victims of Achilles' decision to follow his heroic call cannot be inconsequential, and it adds to Dante's self-identification with Achilles in *Purgatorio* 9. Hagedorn suggests that Dante's insistent focus on the *Achilleid*'s female victims throughout *Inferno* represents the hallmark of his "comic mode," which "implicitly questions the price of epic adventure."[49] Dante's criticism appears especially notable when compared to the *Achilleid*'s reception in medieval education. As Woods shows in her study of medieval glosses on the *Achilleid*, the poem was generally viewed as proposing a positive model of upbringing. Glosses paid little to no attention to Deidamia's sorrow at being raped and eventually abandoned by Achilles to care for their son. Dante's rereading of Achilles' *bildungsroman*, therefore, appears rather at odds with this scholastic reception.

More evidence of Dante's "comic" revision of the *Achilleid* is his implicit inversion of the poem's ending in the culminating cantos of *Purgatorio*. In Statius' poem, after luring Achilles out of his disguise and persuading him to join the Greek army

---

[48] This revelation belongs to a set of particularly puzzling lines that strike modern readers for their apparent inconsistency with *Inferno*. For a detailed discussion of the issues implied by Statius' mention of female characters from his own poem, see Mario Martelli, *Ragione e talento: Studio su Dante e Petrarca* (Cosenza, Italy: Falco Editore, 2009), 63–70.

[49] Hagedorn, "A Statian Model," 36.

THE END OF THE PURGATORIAL CURRICULUM   225

in the siege of Troy, Ulysses and Diomedes lead the young hero away from Dei-damia to the battlefield. The character Dante, on the contrary, is led by Virgil and Statius *to* Beatrice. This narrative inversion seems significant when observed from the perspective of Dante's self-identification with Achilles at *Purgatory* 9; Dante's heroic journey does not require him to abandon the woman he loves and make her a victim. Rather, the heroic path and love converge in *Purgatorio*. This fact has also important metapoetic implications that I discuss in the next section. From a narrative and symbolic perspective, however, it is essential to note that, by recast-ing himself as a new Achilles, Dante highlights the altogether different nature and purpose of his purgatorial "upbringing," which leads him to embrace an opposite type of moral and sexual maturity from the one the *Achilleid* proposed to medieval pupils. The culminating stage of this reeducation is represented by Beatrice's les-son, in Eden, on the true purpose of Dante's love for her, which, after her demise, should have directed him to God, rather than weighed him down (*Purgatorio* 30.121–44).

As part of his initiation into a new moral and emotional maturity, the pilgrim must shed the deceiving understanding of eros that through Achilles' story had been ingrained in medieval pupils as part of their education.[50] After figuratively re-dressing Achilles' clothes in *Purgatorio* 9, Dante is also called on to resist Pros-erpina. Narratives of sexual violence represented a common feature of some texts in the medieval Latin curriculum. This theme had been inherited from ancient education and was closely intertwined with the study of rhetorical forms, such as declamations.[51] A key event in the *Achilleid*'s narrative development, as already noted, is the scene of Deidamia's rape at the hands of young Achilles (1.640–45). This episode coincides with the hero's recovery of his masculinity after being forced by his mother to wear female clothes. It also marks a rite of passage and the "onset of his manhood," as Achilles then persuades Deidamia to accept their relationship, which will eventually be sanctioned by her father and turned into a legitimate union.[52] That violence was an acceptable means to obtain sexual satisfaction and, with some cunning, nuptial reparation was a message implied by several other texts adopted in medieval education—for instance, Ovid's *Ars amatoria* (1.673–78) and the medieval comedy known as *Pamphilus* (681–96). As a medieval gloss on Ovid's *Ars amatoria* explains, however, "the learned man teaches it [Ovid's *Ars*] not for use but as a warning." As noted earlier, moreover, some medieval *accessus* explained that the main lesson to be gained from Statius' poem about young Achilles is to not resist fate as Thetis instead did. The way in

---

[50] An essential study on Dante's reconciliation of sexual and theological conceptions of love is Tristan Kay, *Dante's Lyric Redemption: Eros, Salvation, Vernacular Tradition* (Oxford: Oxford University Press, 2016).

[51] On this subject, see Marjorie Curry Woods, "Rape and the Pedagogical Rhetoric of Sexual Violence," in *Criticism and Dissent in the Middle Ages*, ed. Rita Copeland (Cambridge: Cambridge University Press, 1996), 56–86.

[52] Woods, "Rape," 60.

226 DANTE'S EDUCATION

which these texts were taught and received—or the possible discrepancy between teachers' exposition and pupils' reception—remains difficult to assess.[53]

Pupils, however, did find a similar narrative of sexual violence in Claudian's account of Proserpina's abduction and forced marriage to Hades.[54] It seems significant, therefore, that at the end of his journey through Purgatory proper, and on entering Eden, Dante the character is presented with a new incarnation of Proserpina, Matelda, who clearly entices him:

> subitamente cosa che disvia
> per maraviglia tutto altro pensare,
>   una donna soletta che si gia
> e cantando e scegliendo fior da fiore
> ond' era pinta tutta la sua via.
>   "Deh, bella donna, che a' raggi d'amore
> ti scaldi, s'i' vo' credere a' sembianti
> che soglion esser testimon del core,
>   vegnati in voglia di trarreti avanti,"
> diss'io a lei, "verso questa rivera,
> tanto ch'io possa intender che tu canti.
>   Tu mi fai rimembrar dove e qual era
> Proserpina nel tempo che perdette
> la madre lei, ed ella primavera."

(Purgatorio 28.38–51)

(and there appeared to me, as suddenly appears / a thing so marvelous / it drives away all other thoughts, / a lady, who went her way alone, singing / and picking flowers from among the blossoms / that were painted all along her way. / "Pray, fair lady, warming yourself in rays of love— / if I am to believe the features / that as a rule bear witness to the heart," / I said to her, "may it please you / to come closer to this stream, / near enough that I may hear what you are singing. / You make me remember where and what / Proserpina was, there when her mother / lost her and she lost the spring.")

---

[53] For the *accessus* to the *Achilleid*, see the one in the manuscript Florence, Biblioteca Medicea Laurenziana, Pluteo 24 Sin. 12, fol. 49r, transcribed earlier. The gloss on Ovid's *Ars amatoria* is quoted in Dagenais, *The Ethics*, 84–85. An interesting example of contemporary concern with the real implications of poetic rape can be found in Guido Guinizzelli's poem "Chi vedesse a Lucia un var capuzzo." To get a sense of the reception of Ovid's *Ars amatoria* in medieval school glosses, see Ralph J. Hexter, *Ovid and Medieval Schooling: Studies in Medieval School Commentaries on Ovid's Ars Amatoria, Epistulae Ex Ponto, and Epistulae Heroidum* (Munich: Bei der Arbeo-Gesellschaft, 1986), esp. 15–82.

[54] Another famous example of the relevance of Claudian's *De raptu* in the medieval imaginary concerning the tension between lawful marriage and the pursuit of sexual pleasure is offered by Chaucer's "The Merchant's Tale."

THE END OF THE PURGATORIAL CURRICULUM   227

The attractive "features" of this beautiful lady basking all alone in the "rays of love" threaten to drive Dante astray from the vision of Eden—"disvia." The author recreates here the typical narrative situation found in the old French poems of the genre known as *reverdie* and in the Occitan *pastorella*. More precisely, the words that describe Matelda's first appearance are a direct reference to his fellow Florentine poet Guido Cavalcanti's *pastorella*, "In un boschetto trova' pasturella" (in wood-way found I once a shepherdess).[55] Cavalcanti's encounter with the attractive shepherdess in his poem ends in the consensual consummation of their carnal desire. Traditionally, however, a *pastorella* could also end in rape, and perhaps Matelda's identification with Proserpina alludes precisely to this possible resolution. Dante then goes on to compare Matelda to two Ovidian heroines: Venus in love with Adonis (64–66), as recounted in *Metamorphoses* 10; and Hero, Leander's unhappy lover in Ovid's *Heroides* (18). All three classical comparisons allude to destructive sexual desire and materialize Dante's erotic temptation in this *pastorella*-like situation. After Matelda reveals that her love is really for God and an expression of the Christian virtue of charity, however, the protagonist is immediately free from his "self-produced temptation," and the much-anticipated scene of either sexual violence or consensual consummation never unfolds. Dante subverts the expectation of the genre.[56]

Intertextual memories of both vernacular and classical texts induce the protagonist into temptation and create a precise, yet deceiving, expectation in the reader. As critics note, the negative role of both vernacular and Latin literary traditions in preparing Dante for his meeting with Matelda implies both a criticism and a correction he wishes to propose through his new theological vision of eros and love.[57] I argue that Dante's reversion of a rape scene here also engages with the narrative of sexual violence that is key to both Statius' *Achilleid* and Claudian's *De raptu Proserpinae*. By overcoming this specific pedagogical tradition, Dante symbolizes the completion of his purgatorial education. He also shows to have assimilated the moral lesson of these texts in the way that learned men were

---

[55] Scartazzini is the first commentator to call attention to Dante's rewriting of Cavalcanti's poem "In un boschetto trova' pasturella" in *Purgatorio* 28 (comm. to *Purg.* 29.1) Among other contributions that support this thesis, see Barolini, *Dante's Poets*, 148–53; Massimiliano Chiamenti, "Corollario oitanico al canto ventottesimo del *Purgatorio*," *Medioevo e rinascimento* 13 (1999): 207–20; Patrizia Grimaldi Pizzorno, "Matelda's Dance and the Smile of the Poets," *Dante Studies* 112 (1994): 115–32; Renato Poggioli, "Dante *poco tempo silvano*: Or a 'Pastoral Oasis' in the *Commedia*," *Annual Report of the Dante Society* 80 (1962), 1–20; and Charles Singleton, *Journey to Beatrice* (Cambridge, MA: Harvard University Press, 1967 [1958]), 214–16.

[56] Hollander, comm. ad *Purg.* 28.70–75. For the discussion of pleasure underlying Dante's Eden, see Giuseppe Mazzotta, *Dante's Vision and the Circle of Knowledge* (Princeton, NJ: Princeton University Press, 2014), 219–41.

[57] See, for instance, Justin Steinberg, *Accounting for Dante: Urban Readers and Writers in Late Medieval Italy* (Notre Dame, IN: University of Notre Dame Press, 2007), 171–79, and Peter Hawkins, "Transfiguring the Text: Ovid, Scripture and the Dynamics of Allusion," *Stanford Italian Review* 5 (1985): 115–39, revised and expanded in Hawkins, "Watching Matelda," in *The Poetry of Allusion: Virgil and Ovid in Dante's Commedia*, ed. Rachel Jacoff and Jeffrey Schnapp (Stanford, CA: Stanford University Press, 1991), 181–201.

228 DANTE'S EDUCATION

expected to read them. Dante, therefore, re-proposes a literary "rape situation" and "passes the test."[58]

Evidence of Dante's engagement with Claudian's text in *Purgatorio* 28 provides key support to this thesis. Critics have generally identified Ovid's *Metamorphoses* 5.385–401 as the subtext evoked by Dante's comparison of Matelda with Proserpina (*Purgatorio* 28.50). The relevance of Claudian's *De raptu Proserpinae*, instead, has mostly been doubted.[59] The latter, however, featured the most extensive account of this myth, and its popularity in medieval education makes it unlikely that Dante could altogether have ignored it.[60] Although Ovid provides a key source for Dante's representation of Eden and Matelda, the interference of Claudian's poem in this intertextual dialogue can be picked up. Dante presents Proserpina's story as another account of a lost age when the earth freely produced fruits and humans did not need to survive through agricultural labor. This mythological association, however, is not as obvious in Ovid's account of Proserpina's abduction in *Metamorphoses* 5.385–401. On the contrary, Ovid recounts that after Ceres finally realizes her daughter is missing, in a rage she commands the Sicilian earth to bear corn no longer and, more important, she destroys agricultural tools (*Metamorphoses* 5.477–80).[61] Claudian's version of the story, instead, suggests that Proserpina's kidnapping coincided with the moment when humanity left behind its dependence on spontaneous fruits and began to live on corn and other products of agriculture: "unde datae populis fruges et glande relicta / cesserit inventis Dodonia quercus aristis" (whence corn was given to man whereby he laid aside his acorn food, / and the new-found ear made useless Dodona's oaks) (*De raptu Proserpinae* 1.30–31).[62] Since Claudian defines Ceres' gift to humankind as agriculture, his poem anticipated Dante's interpretation of Proserpina's abduction as the reason behind the loss of the Golden Age.[63]

---

[58] Dagenais, *The Ethics*, 214–15.

[59] Matelda's words "qui primavera sempre" may allude to *Metamorphoses* 5.107: "vere furor sempre." This Ovidian reference is only one among several included in Dante's representation of Eden in this canto. See Mariapina Settinari, "Influssi ovidiani nella *Divina Commedia*," in *Siculorum Gymnasium* 12 (1959): 62. Enrico Proto ("Dante e i poeti latini," *Atene e Roma* 12 [1909], col. 288) also points to possible echoes from *Fasti* 4.425–30 and 437–42; Carrai (*Dante e l'antico*, 42), too, argues that in the line "ond'era pinta tutta la sua via" there is also a verbatim echo of Ovid's other account of Proserpina's story in *Fasti* 4.430: "pictaque dissimili flore nitebat humus."

[60] On the key place of Claudian's poem for the reception of this myth in the Latin West see Hall, "Introduction," 106.

[61] "Ergo illic saeva vertentia glaebas / fregit aratra manu, parilique irata colonos / ruricolasque boves leto dedit arvaque iussit / fallere depositum vitiataque semina fecit."

[62] The translation is quoted from Maurice Platanauer, ed. and trans., *Rape of Proserpine*, in *Claudian*, vol. 2 (Cambridge, MA: Harvard University Press, 1922), https://www.theoi.com/Text/ClaudianProserpine.html#1.

[63] Emerson Brown maintains that Dante's remark about Proserpina's responsibilities in the loss of eternal spring also points to Claudian's portrayal of Proserpina. See Brown, *Proserpina*, 37. In his entry "Proserpina" in the *ED*, Roberto Mercuri, too, underlines this interpretative trend. As already observed, moreover, in the context of medieval education, the particular reading of Proserpina's myth as another account of the lost Golden Age was reinforced by other school texts, such as the *Ecloga Theoduli*.

THE END OF THE PURGATORIAL CURRICULUM   229

Some specific elements in Dante's representation of Matelda and her Edenic surroundings also point to the source of Claudian's subtext. Robert Durling and Ronald Martinez, for instance, highlight the fact that, like Matelda, Claudian's Proserpina (*De raptu Proserpinae* 2.125–50) is picking flowers to weave into garlands, whereas Ovid's Proserpina puts them in a basket or lets them fall in her lap.[64]

Claudian's depiction of the meadows of Henna, moreover, features interesting similarities with Dante's description of the Edenic forest:[65]

> Forma loci superat flores: curvata tumore
> parvo planities et mollibus edita clivis
> creverat in collem. Vivo de pumice fontes
> roscida mobilibus lambebant gramina rivis
> silvaque torrentes ramorum frigore soles
> temperat et medio brumam sibi vindicat aestu:
>
> . . .
>
> Haut procul inde lacus (Pergum dixere Sicani)
> panditur et nemorum frondoso margine cinctus
> vicinis pallescit aquis: admittit in altum
> cernentes oculos et late pervius umor
> ducit inoffensos liquido sub flumine visus
> imaque perspicui prodit secreta profundi.
>
> (*De raptu Proserpinae* 2.101–17)

> (Even more lovely than the flowers in the country. The plain, with gentle swell and gradual slopes, rose into a hill; issuing from the living rock gushing streams bedewed their grassy banks. With the shade of its branches a wood tempers the sun's fierce heat and at summer's height makes for itself the cold of winter.... Not far from here lies a lake called by the Sicani Pergus, girt with a cincture of leafy woods close around its pallid waters. Deep down therein the eye of whoso would can see, and the everywhere transparent water

---

[64] See Robert M. Durling and Ronald L. Martinez, *The Divine Comedy of Dante Alighieri: Purgatorio*, vol. 2 (Oxford: Oxford University Press, 2003), comm. ad *Purg.* 28.50, 486. Durling and Martinez's note appears even more significant if one considers that Matelda's behavior is prefigured by the character Leah's in the preceding canto. In a prophetic dream, Dante sees the biblical Leah weaving garlands of flowers: "ch'i' mi son Lia, e vo movendo intorno / le belle mani a farmi una ghirlanda" (I am Leah, / and here I move about, using my fair hands / to weave myself a garland) (*Purgatorio* 27.101–02). However, it should be noted here that the prophetic quality of the dreams in *Purgatorio* has been a matter of some critical debate. See, for instance, Zygmunt G. Barański, "Dante's Three Reflective Dreams," *Quaderni d'Italianistica* 10 (1989): 213–36.

[65] As also noted by Ernst Robert Curtius, *European Literature and the Latin Middle Ages* (London: Routledge & Kegan Paul, 1953), 218.

230   DANTE'S EDUCATION

invites an untrammeled gaze into its oozy depths and betrays the uttermost secrets of its pellucid gulfs.)[66]

Both Dante and Claudian are conditioned by the literary topos of the *locus amoenus*, which was widespread in ancient literature. Michele Coccia argues that Ovid provides the model for both Dante's and Claudian's reuse of the trope of the clear water: "Invenio sine vertice aquas, sine murmure euntes, / perspicuas ad humum, per quas numerabilis alte / calculus omnis erat, quas tu vix ire putares" (I chanced upon a stream, / that flowed without a ripple or a sound / so smoothly on, I hardly thought it moved) (*Metamorphoses* 5.587–89).[67] Yet there is a detail in both Dante's and Claudian's readaptations of this trope that is missing from Ovid's. Before seeing Matelda, Dante describes the river Lethe as more transparent than any other clear water on earth: "Tutte l'acque che son di qua più monde, / parrieno avere in sé mistura alcuna / verso di quella, che nulla nasconde" (all the streams that run the purest here on earth / would seem defiled beside that stream, / which reveals all that it contains) (*Purgatorio* 28.28–30). But the forest that surrounds the river is so wonderfully thick that the water running closest to the banks appears pitch dark, thus creating a wonderful contrast: "avvegna che si muova bruna bruna / sotto l'ombra perpetüa, che mai / raggiar non lascia sole ivi né luna" (even though it flows in darkness, / dark beneath perpetual shade / that never lets the sun or moon shine through) (*Purgatorio* 28.31–33). The prodigious water of the Lethe, at once exceptionally dark, near the banks, and exceptionally transparent, near the center, resembles the water of Lake Pergus described by Claudian in the above-quoted passage, where the same contrast is produced between the clarity of the water and the darkness produced by the "cincture of leafy woods close around its pallid waters."

Finally, the role of the wind in Dante's Edenic forest recalls that of the wind Zephyrus in Claudian's Henna. In *Purgatorio* 28.106–14, Matelda explains how the wind is created in Eden and serves as a means for sowing new plants:

> in questa altezza ch'è tutta disciolta
> ne l'aere vivo, tal moto percuote,
> e fa sonar la selva perch'è folta:
> e la percossa pianta tanto puote,
> che de la sua virtute l'aura impregna
> e quella poi, girando, intorno scuote;
> e l'altra terra, secondo ch'è degna
> per sé e per suo ciel, concepe e figlia

---

[66] The English translation is by Maurice Platnauer, *Claudian*, Vol. II, Loeb Classical Library Volume 136 (Cambridge, MA: Harvard University Press, 1922), accessed March 2024, https://www.theoi.com/Text/ClaudianProserpine.html

[67] See Coccia, "Claudiano," in the *ED*.

di diverse virtù diverse legna.
(That movement strikes upon this summit, / standing free in the living air, and makes / the forest, because it is so dense, resound. / The wind-lashed plants have such fecundity / that with their power they pollinate the air, / which after, in its circling, scatters seed abroad. / Your earth below, according to its qualities / and climate, conceives and then brings forth / from various properties its various plants.)

When Proserpina is led by the nymphs to the meadows of Henna, Etna asks Zephyrus to fly and spread new plants and flowers everywhere in order to welcome the divine guests:

> "Nunc adsis faveasque, precor, nunc omnia fetu
> pubescant virgulta velis, ut fertilis Hybla
> invideat vincique suos non abnuat hortos.
> Quidquid turiferis spirat Panchaia silvis,
> quidquid odoratus longe blanditur Hydaspes,
> quidquid ab extremis ales longaevus harenis
> colligit optato repetens exordia saeclo,
> in venas disperge meas et flamine largo
> rura fove. Merear divino pollice carpi
> et nostris cupiant ornari numina sertis."
> Dixerat. Ille novo madidantes nectare pennas
> concutit et glebas fecundo rore maritat,
> quaque volat, vernus sequitur rubor; omnis in herbas
> turget húmus medioque patente convexa sereno.
>
> (*De raptu Proserpinae* 2.90–104)

("Grant that now all the trees be thick with newly-grown fruit, that fertile Hybla may be jealous and admit her paradise surpassed. All the sweet airs of Panchaea's incense-bearing woods, all the honied odours of Hydaspes' distant stream, all the spices which from the furthest fields the long-lived Phoenix gathers, seeking new birth from wished for death—spread thou all these through my veins and with generous breath refresh my country. May I be worthy to be plundered by divine fingers and goddesses seek to be decked with my garlands." So spake she, and Zephyrus shook his wings adrip with fresh nectar and drenches the ground with their life-giving dew. Wheresoe'er he flies spring's brilliance follows.)

232 DANTE'S EDUCATION

Once again, the source for both Dante and Claudian may be found in Ovid, who also represents Zephyrus caressing new flowers born without seeds during the eternal spring of the mythical Golden Age (*Metamorphoses* 1.107–08). Yet, in no way does Ovid link this description to Proserpina's story. Hence, while drawing on the Ovidian archetype in his description of Eden and Matelda, Dante also alludes to Claudian's rewriting of the same model, thus creating what has been termed an "imitative series."[68]

The vanquishing of the protagonist's lustful imagination, kindled by the memories of both vernacular and classical poems evoked by Matelda's appearance, represents a precise inversion of Claudian's narrative of rape, and thus also an implicit rebuke of the central ingredient in the *Achilleid*'s recipe for achieving heroic maturity. As John Freccero explains, in his encounter with Matelda, Dante recovers a "prelapsarian Persephone." "Whatever else she may represent," Freccero argues, "the pastoral landscape and erotic feelings of the pilgrim would indicate the recapture, or near recapture, of a pastoral (and therefore poetic) innocence, a return to Eden after a long *askesis* . . . short of Eden, there is not erotic—or poetic—innocence."[69]

Dante's education in Purgatory proper culminates with an explicit rite of passage: before entering Eden, Virgil crowns Dante and celebrates his newly reconquered moral perfection:

> Non aspettar mio dir più né mio cenno;
> libero, dritto e sano è tuo arbitrio,
> e fallo fora non fare a suo senno:
> per ch'io te sovra te corono e mitrio.
>
> (*Purgatorio* 27.139–42)

---

[68] The concept of "imitative series and clusters" has also been defined as "two-tier allusion" or "window reference." All these labels point to different instances of the same poetic process of rewriting that takes place "when author 'C' simultaneously imitates or alludes to a passage or text by author 'A' and its imitation by author 'B.'" See Colin Burrow, "Virgil, from Dante to Milton," in *The Cambridge Companion to Virgil*, ed. Charles Martindale (Cambridge: Cambridge University Press, 2000), 79–90; Burrow et al., *Imitative Series and Clusters from Classical to Early Modern Literature* (Berlin: De Gruyter, 2020); and Elisabetta Tarantino, "*Fulvae Harenae*: The Reception of an Intertextual Complex in Dante's *Inferno*," *Classical Receptions Journal* 4, no. 1 (2012): 90–126. I offer more examples of this intertextual practice in the next chapter. Scholars have also pointed to other elements in Dante's representation of the Earthly Paradise that may reveal Claudian's influence. Edoardo Coli suggests the possibility that Claudian's representation of Olympus, in *Panegyricus dictus Manlio Theodoro consuli* 206–10, may have influenced Dante's representation of Eden. See Coli, *Il Paradiso Terrestre dantesco* (Florence: Carnesecchi, 1897), 171. Peter Dronke also lists Claudian among the possible sources of Dante's Earthly Paradise. See Dronke, "*Viaggi al Paradiso terrestre*," in *Dante: Da Firenze all'aldilà: atti del terzo Seminario dantesco internazionale, Firenze, 9–11 giugno, 2000* (Florence: Cesati, 2001), 93–103. He also points to Claudian's *Epithalamium*, 60–68, as a possible precedent for Dante's "aura dolce." See Dronke, "Dante's Earthly Paradise: Towards an Interpretation of *Purgatorio* 28," in *The Medieval Poet and His World* (Rome: Edizioni di Storia e Letteratura, 1984), 387–405.

[69] John Freccero, *Dante: The Poetics of Conversion*, ed. Rachel Jacoff (Cambridge, MA: Harvard University Press, 1986), 125–26.

(No longer wait for word or sign from me. / Your will is free, upright, and sound. / Not to act as it chooses is unworthy: / over yourself I crown and miter you.)

In this graduation ceremony, the guide and magister Virgil sends off his student, who has now become a doctor. As soon as the ceremony is over, the protagonist enters Eden and is already presented with a test: he has to resist Matelda, the new Proserpina. Dante's epic upbringing in *Purgatorio*, therefore, concludes with the explicit requirement that he unpack and act upon what Statius and Claudian had taught him.

Statius' Failure and Claudian's Silence: Dante's Epic Ascent

Dante's narrative inversion of Statius' *Achilleid* and Claudian's *De raptu Proserpinae* in *Purgatorio* also has significant metapoetic implications. By fashioning himself as a novel Achilles on the path to becoming a new type of hero, Dante revisits the genre of the Latin epic, readapting it to his vernacular poem. His meddling in the generic realm of the ancient epic dovetails with the theoretical discourse articulated through Statius' appearance at *Purgatorio* 21. In Statius' cantos, the author dramatizes his own ascent to authority and presents himself as a Christian poet at the intersection of both classical and vernacular traditions.[70] Through the several fictional encounters with poets that punctuate the culminating part of his purgatorial climb, Dante quietly supersedes both his vernacular predecessors, who excelled in the humble genre of love poetry, and his Latin master, Virgil, who set the standard for the loftier epic genre. Dante achieves this double goal by raising the content and style of his own vernacular poetry to the level of the ancient epic—the "lofty tragedy," as the character Virgil defines his *Aeneid* at *Inferno* 20.113 ("alta . . . tragedìa"). The emulation of the ancients in *Purgatorio* also coincides with Dante's self-representation as the latest member of the "fair school" of the ancient poetry. This "scola" is introduced at *Inferno* 4—where it counts as members Homer, Virgil, Ovid, Lucan, and Horace—and is then completed by Statius at *Purgatorio* 21. Virgil, too, is often referred to as "maestro" throughout *Inferno*, and in *Purgatorio* he introduces himself to Statius as Dante's "scola" (school) (*Purgatorio* 21.31–33).[71] The term "scola" also evokes a pedagogical model. For Dante, to rise to the level of the ancient epicists meant to become in turn a didactic model for other vernacular poets to imitate and try to emulate, thus filling the void of vernacular epics he denounced in the *De vulgari eloquentia* (2.8).

---

[70] Albert Ascoli, *Dante and the Making of a Modern Author* (Cambridge: Cambridge University Press, 2008), 60, 315.

[71] On the parallels between *Purgatorio* 21–22 and *Inferno* 4.103–05, see Ascoli, *Dante and the Making*, 317, and Martinez, "Two Canons."

234   DANTE'S EDUCATION

It seems only reasonable that, in order to set a vernacular standard for the emulation of the ancient epic, Dante would wish to engage with the two epic poems
sanctioned by medieval education. Before tackling the major Roman epicists, such
as Virgil, Ovid, and Lucan, pupils would have "cut their teeth" on the *Achilleid*
and the *De raptu Proserpinae*. They offered exemplary models of epic emulation
based on a subtle intertextuality and the cross-fertilization of epic, erotic, and elegiac genres.[72] Their particular brand of epic must have elicited Dante's interest,
as in *Purgatorio* he attempts to reconcile the Latin and vernacular canons and
their respective subject matter. While Dante-the-pilgrim is following in Virgil's and
Statius' footsteps, he meets two of the major Italian vernacular love poets from the
previous generation, Bonagiunta da Lucca and Guido Guinizzelli. In a fictional
dialogue with Bonagiunta, Dante claims a new way of writing in relation to Love:

> E io a lui: "I' mi son un che, quando
> Amor mi spira, noto, e a quel modo
> ch'e' ditta dentro vo significando."
>   "O frate, issa vegg'io," diss'elli, "il nodo
> Che 'l Notaro e Guittone e me ritenne
> Di qua dal dolce stil novo ch'I' odo!"
>
> *(Purgatorio* 24.52–57)

> (And I to him: "I am one who, when Love / inspires me, take
> note and, as he dictates / deep within me, so I set it forth." / "O
> my brother," he said, "now I understand the knot / that kept the
> Notary, Guittone, and me / on this side of the sweet new style I
> hear.")

While Dante represents himself as the vernacular successor to the great Latin epicists, therefore, he also reasserts his fundamental authority as a love poet. This
innovative synthesis of contrasting genres, I contend, had some of its ancient
precursors in Statius' *Achilleid* and Statius' *De raptu Proserpinae*.

The two works' relevance in Dante's quest to become a poet at the intersection of
the Latin and vernacular canons becomes manifest through the character Statius
in *Purgatorio*. Most critics agree that the interactions between the characters of
Dante, Virgil, and Statius in these cantos dramatize the relationship between the
Commedia, the *Aeneid*, and the *Thebaid*. The fictional Statius, moreover, acts as
a "testimonial to" Virgil, allowing Dante to revise the *Aeneid* for Christian ends.[73]

---

[72] Clogan, "Literary Genres," 206. On the significance of Statius' and Claudian's poems as late examples of Roman epic poetry, see Dominik, "Statius," and Barnes, "Claudian," in *A Companion to Ancient
Epic*, 514–27 and 538–49.
[73] Barolini, *Dante's Poets*, 256–69. See also Martinez, "Two Canons," 151–75.

THE END OF THE PURGATORIAL CURRICULUM   235

This metapoetic reading takes the deference exhibited to the *Aeneid* by the closing lines of the *Thebaid* as the key to understanding Statius' function in Dante's own emulation of Virgil. An argument, however, should be made for the theoretical weight borne by the *Achilleid* in the cantos where Statius makes his first appearance.

References to the *Achilleid*, as already noted, fulfill key narrative and symbolic functions in *Purgatorio*. This fact is especially notable when compared to the relatively little impact that memories of this poem—as opposed to the *Thebaid*—seem to make on *Inferno* and its apparent absence from Dante's earlier works. Dante's interest in this school epic seemingly increases around his representation of Statius in *Purgatorio*.[74] The relevance of the *Achilleid* becomes apparent already in Statius' detailed autobiography:

> "Nel tempo che 'l buon Tito, con l'aiuto
> del sommo rege, vendicò le fóra
> ond'uscì 'l sangue per Giuda venduto,
>   col nome che più dura e più onora
> era io di là," rispuose quello spirto,
> "famoso assai, ma non con fede ancora.
>   Tanto fu dolce mio vocale spirto,
> che, tolosano, a sé mi trasse Roma,
> dove mertai le tempie ornar di mirto.
>   Stazio la gente ancor di là mi noma:
> cantai di Tebe, e poi del grande Achille;
> ma caddi in via con la seconda soma.
>   Al mio ardor fuor seme le faville,
> che mi scaldar, de la divina fiamma
> onde sono allumati più di mille;
> de l'Eneïda dico, la qual mamma
> fummi, e fummi nutrice, poetando:
> sanz'essa non fermai peso di dramma.
>   E per esser vivuto di là quando
> visse Virgilio, assentirei un sole
> più che non deggio al mio uscir di bando."
>
> (*Purgatorio* 21.82–102)

---

[74] Obvious references to Statius' *Achilleid* are in *Inferno* 12.71, 26.62; *Purgatorio* 9.34, 21.92, 22.109–14. Scholars have also argued that echoes of the poem can be found in *Inferno* 5.65, 12.108, 25.85–87; *Purgatorio* 32.28–30; *Paradiso* 1.52–54, 2.7–9, 2.13–15, 9.82–84, 10.61–63, 23.1–9, 28.19–21. See Paratore, "Stazio," in the *ED*. Dante never mentions the *Achilleid* in his "minor" works, where he openly refers only to the *Thebaid*. In *De vulgari eloquentia* 2.6, Dante generically names Statius among the *poeti regulates*, without mentioning any of his works. In the *Convivio* (3.8.10, 3.9.16, 4.25.6, and 4.27.21), Dante uses the *Thebaid* as a repository of moral examples.

("In the time when worthy Titus / aided by the King most high, / avenged the wounds / from which had poured the blood that Judas sold, / on earth I bore the name that most endures / and honors most," replied that spirit, / "Fame I had found, but not yet faith / So sweet was my poetic recitation that Rome / drew me from Tolouse and deemed me worthy / to have my brows adorned with myrtle. / My name is Statius. On earth men often speak it. / I sang of Thebes and then of great Achilles, / but fell along the way with the second burden. / The sparks that kindled the fire in me / came from the holy flame / from which more than a thousand have been lit— / I mean the *Aeneid*. When I wrote poetry / it was my *mamma* and my nurse. / Without it I would not have weighed a dram. To have lived on earth when Virgil lived / I would have stayed one year's sun longer / than I owed before I came forth from my exile.")

Statius presents the *Achilleid* and the *Thebaid* as equally significant poetic achievements—"cantai di Tebe, e poi del grande Achille"—thus confirming the relevance the former had for Dante. In the following line, moreover—"ma caddi in via con la seconda soma"—the unfinished epic stands out, as it comes to embody the poet's sudden death and highlights the sense of incompleteness that envelops Statius' poetic career. Hence, Dante rejects the popular interpretation of the *Achilleid* as a complete epic that was promoted in contemporary education.[75]

The fact that Dante defines the *Achilleid* as Statius' "second burden" is also significant. The expression seems to be a calque of the *Achilleid*'s exordium, where the author expresses his hope for a second poetic crowning: "da fontes mihi, Phoebe, novos ac fronde secunda" (give me, o Phoebus, new springs and a *second* laurel) (*Achilleid* 1.9; emphasis added). This line also represented Dante's only accessible source of information concerning Statius' first poetic crowning, which is mentioned in the line "dove mertai le tempie ornar di mirto" (to have my brows adorned with myrtle) (*Purgatorio* 21.75).[76] Yet Dante's decision to have the late Roman poet crowned with myrtle is puzzling; its symbolic meaning remains hard to decipher, as the *Thebaid* should have earned Statius the laurel—a more fitting

---

[75] Judging from the lack of surprise among the first commentators of the *Commedia*, one may surmise that Dante was not trying to shock his readers by making such a revelation. Dante would have likely encountered both sides of the debate, since, as Amanda Weppler argues, he drew on multiple *accessus* for his representation of Statius. See Weppler, "Dante's Stazio: Statius and the Transformations of Poetry" (Ph.D. diss., University of Notre Dame, 2016), 25. See also de Angelis, "Lo Stazio," 29–69, at 36–37.

[76] The other source of information about Statius' first poetic crowning would be the *Silvae*, which, however, was unknown at Dante's time. Weppler ("Dante's Stazio," 64–69) points to the existence of at least one other medieval text that could have informed Dante of Statius' crowning.

prize for a great epic.[77] Regardless of the way one interprets the symbolic meaning of the myrtle, it is evident that Dante wishes to present Statius as someone who had failed to win the laurel: if he had received a crown of myrtle, then the "second leafy branch" he is eager to conquer in the prologue to the *Achilleid* coincides with the laurel crown. By acknowledging that he "fell along the way with the second burden" (*Purgatorio* 21.93), therefore, Dante's Statius admits that he never achieved the laurel. This particular formulation also contains an implicit reference to Horace's *Ars poetica* (38–40), which Dante had already quoted in *De vulgari eloquentia* 2.4.4:

> Ante omnia ergo dicimus unumquenque debere materie pondus propriis humeris coequare, ne forte humerorum nimio gravata virtute, in cenum cespitare necesse sit. Hoc est quod magister noster Oratius precipit, cum in principio Poetrie *Sumite materiam dicit.*

> (First of all, I declare that anyone must adjust the weight of his material to suit his own shoulders, lest the excessive burden bearing down upon them overcome his strength and send him sprawling in the mud; and this is what our master Horace teaches at the beginning of his Ars poetica, where he says "Choose your subject.")

By drawing on Horace's warning, Dante colors Statius' words with the veiled admission of his unsuitability for the task undertaken with the *Achilleid*. On the contrary, medieval glosses do not consider the *Achilleid's* incompleteness to be a *vitium* (defect), on account of the poet's death.[78] Once again, Dante goes against the poem's traditional reception to highlight Statius' responsibility in this poetic fiasco. Yet, why Statius' failure with the *Achilleid* should be so relevant for Dante's own claim to poetic authority in *Purgatorio* is a question that remains to be fully addressed.

Scholars generally note that Statius' praise of Virgil in *Purgatorio* 21 (94–102) dramatizes the admiration for the *Aeneid* expressed by the *Thebaid*, particularly in its last lines. The canto ends on a narrative reenactment of this envoy, in which the personified *Thebaid* looks at the *Aeneid* as its ideal yet unreachable model:

> uiue, precor; nec tu diuinam Aeneida tempta,
> sed longe sequere et uestigia semper adora.

---

[77] Scholars have proposed several possible interpretations of the "myrtle." De Angelis ("Lo Stazio," 56–58), for instance, has shown that, because myrtle was the plant designated to celebrate love poets, this was the poetic genre in which the character Statius maintains he had achieved his greatest success. See also Vincenzo Tandoi, "Il ricordo di Stazio 'dolce poeta' nella *Satira* VII di Giovenale," *Maia* 21 (1969): 103–22. Another interesting discussion of this mysterious crowning has been more recently proposed by Edoardo Fumagalli, "Il lauro e il mirto," in *Il giusto Enea e il pio Rifeo: Pagine dantesche* (Florence: Leo S. Olschki, 2012), 89–108. For an exhaustive summary of interpretations see Hollander, comm. *Purgatorio* 21.90, and Fosca, comm. *Purgatorio* 21.90.

[78] As shown by de Angelis, "Lo Stazio," 36–37.

238   DANTE'S EDUCATION

> mox, tibi si quis adhuc praetendit nubila liuor,
> occidet, et meriti post me referentur honores.
>
> *(Thebaid* 12.816–19)[79]

> (Live on, I pray! Do not try to surpass the *Aeneid* divine, / but, at a distance, follow and always revere Her imprint. / Soon, if some bruised Envy still spreads clouds before you, it will / set; after I'm gone, you'll win your well-deserved honors.)

In *Purgatorio*, on discovering Virgil's identity, Dante's Statius attempts to embrace his teacher's feet—"Già s'inchinava ad abbracciar li piedi" (already he was stooping to embrace my teacher's feet) (*Purgatorio* 21.130)—only to be turned away: "frate, non far" (Brother, do not do so) (131). This scene reproduces the *Thebaid*'s pedestrian metaphor: "Do not try to surpass the *Aeneid* divine, / but, at a distance, follow and always revere Her imprint." The same trope is also repeated in Statius' description of his own conversion, in the following canto, where he claims that, though a pagan, Virgil lighted the way to the true God for those who came after him—"Facesti come quei che va di notte, / che porta il lume dietro e sé non giova / ma dopo sé fa le persone dotte" (You were as one who goes by night, carrying / the light behind him—it is no help to him / but instructs all those who follow) (22.67–69). Finally, Dante extends the metaphor from Statius to himself, by fictionalizing his own climb on Statius' and Virgil's trails: "Elli givan dinanzi, e io soletto / di retro, e ascoltava i lor sermoni / ch'a poetar mi davano intelletto" (They went along in front and I alone, / came on behind, listening to their discourse / which gave me understanding of the art of verse.) (127–29).[80] As scholars have acknowledged, Statius stands in between Virgil and Dante, according to a precise hierarchy of texts.

Dante's extended reworking of the *Thebaid*'s metaphor of tradition, however, does not flatten out the *Commedia*'s complex representation of his own and Statius' relationship with Virgil as one of inflexible subordination.[81] The hierarchy between the three poets is marred by instability. Statius' Christianity and his superior knowledge of Purgatory underscores Virgil's limitations. From his first appearance, moreover, Statius acts like a teacher, instructing Virgil and Dante on

---

[79] The translation is taken from P. Papinius Statius, *Thebaid: A Song of Thebes*, trans. Jane W. Joyce (Ithaca, NY: Cornell University Press, 2008). In addition to this passage, *Thebaid* 10.445–48 is the other instance in which Statius openly states his admiration for the *Aeneid*: "uos quoque sacrati, quamuis mea carmina surgant / inferiore lyra, memores superabitis annos. / forsitan et comites non aspernabitur umbras / Euryalus Phrygiique admittet gloria Nisi."

[80] Benvenuto da Imola reads Statius' reply to Virgil at the end of *Purgatorio* 21.133–36 as a calque of Virgil's *Aeneid*: "Or puoi la quantitate / comprender de l'amor ch'a te mi scalda / quand'io dismento nostra vanitate, / trattando l'ombre come cosa salda."

[81] Ronald Martinez rightly points out that "as it passes from Virgil to Stazio," this imagery "develops from the topic of following in the master's footsteps and adopts the iconography of inspiration by the Holy Spirit." Martinez, "Two Canons," 155.

THE END OF THE PURGATORIAL CURRICULUM 239

the nature of Purgatory. This role certainly reflects Statius' deeper understanding of the place that, according to the fiction, he had inhabited for centuries. Arguably, however, it also symbolizes the reputation of *poeta doctor* that Statius had acquired as a result of the *Achilleid*'s fortunes in medieval education. Statius' didactic authority in the *Commedia* reaches its apogee when he reinterprets Virgil's *Aeneid* 3.57 and fourth *Eclogue* in light of the Christian revelation—he emulates Virgil by giving a different meaning to the same *littera*.[82] Finally, both Statius and Dante surpass their master and leave him behind in the Earthly Paradise. They, in other words, contradict the limits imposed by Statius' pedestrian metaphor in the envoy of the *Thebaid*. I contend that Dante's extended narrative correction of this metaphor may reflect the different attitudes toward Virgil that separate the end of the *Thebaid* from the prologue of the *Achilleid*. In the latter, Statius moves from an attitude of imitation to one of emulation.[83]

In the proem of the *Achilleid*, Statius sets his work in direct continuity with Homer:

> Magnanimum Aeaciden formidatamque Tonanti
> progeniem et patrio vetitam succedere caelo,
> diva, refer. quamquam acta viri multum inclita cantu
> Maeonio (sed plura vacant), nos ire per omnem—
> sic amor est—heroa velis Scyroque latentem
> Dulichia proferre tuba nec in Hectore tracto
> sistere, sed tota iuvenem deducere Troia.
>
> (*Achilleid* 1.1–7)[84]

> (Achilles—bring back the story, Goddess, / of the formidable hero descended through Aeacus / from thundering Jupiter, but denied

[82] Martinez argues—and he is not alone—that Statius the character's "misinterpretation" of *Aeneid* 3.56–7 in *Purgatorio* 22.40–41 is actually a legitimate reinterpretation. See Martinez, "La 'sacra fame,'" 177–93. See also Marchesi, *Dante and Augustine*, 117–44.

[83] Statius' subordination and deference to Virgil is the hallmark of *Purgatorio* 21–22. Besides being an obvious reference to the end of the *Thebaid*, Statius' relationship with Virgil also dramatizes the hierarchy of texts that was observed in medieval education. In *Purgatorio* 22.94–114, while in dialogue with Statius, the character of Virgil completes the census of the ancient poets in Limbo and lists a selection of *auctores minores* that mirrors that of the *maiores* met by Dante at *Inferno* 4. See Martinez, "Two Canons," 155. It could be argued that the character Statius expands the sway of Latin literature over the *Commedia*, just as the *Achilleid* marked the end of the medieval Latinizing curriculum and ushered pupils into the universe of the major Latin literature. On Dante's division between the *auctores maiores*, at *Inferno* 4, and the *minores*, at *Purgatorio* 22, see Barański, "Tres enim sunt," 236. On Dante and the *auctores*, see also *Dante e la "bella scola" della poesia*, ed. Amilcare A. Iannucci (Ravenna: Longo, 1993); Michelangelo Picone, "Dante e il canone degli *Auctores*," *Rassegna Europea di letteratura italiana* 1 (1993), 9–26; and Claudia Villa, "Il canone poetico mediolatino (e le strutture di Dante, *Inf.* IV e *Purg.* XXII)," in *La protervia*, 17–38.

[84] The translation is quoted from P. Papinius Statius, *Achilleid*, trans. Stanley Lombardo (Indianapolis: Hackett, 2015), lines 1–10.

240 DANTE'S EDUCATION

> His heaven, / his deeds indeed famous through Homeric song, / but with much more to celebrate. May it be / your pleasure that I encompass, as is my desire, / the entire hero, trumpeting him forth / from his hiding in Scyros and not stopping / with the dragging of Hector, but going on to hymn / the great warrior through the whole tale of Troy.)

The poem aims to fill the *lacunae* in Achilles' story left by Homer—"sed plura vacant." The conspicuous absence of Virgil from this prologue should not fail to strike readers, especially when compared to the envoy of the *Thebaid*. In his commentary, Lactantius Placidus remarks that Statius' bold claim echoes Virgil's in the *Aeneid*:

> IN HECTORE TRACTO SISTERE tacere. Homerus enim usque ad mortem Hectoris descripsit Iliados et tacuit unde superius: "cantu Maeonio, sed plura vacant." Unde et Virgilius (Aen. 1.456): "uidet Iliacas ex ordine pugnas" id est: non usque ad mortem Hectoris, sed usque ad excidium Troiae pictas.[85]

> (STOPPING WITH HECTOR'S DEATH. Homer indeed narrated the *Iliad* up to Hector's death and was silent about the rest, hence above it says: "in the Homeric song, but much more is missing." For the same reason Virgil says: "he sees according to the order of the war" (*Aeneid* 1.456), which means: depictions not only up to Hector's death but to Troy's destruction.)

According to Lactantius, therefore, by providing the missing parts of Achilles' story, in the *Achilleid* Statius emulates Virgil's attempt to fulfill the Homeric saga. Statius, therefore, claims for his poem a place equal to that of the *Aeneid* in the ancient epic genealogy and presents himself as the latest heir in the Homeric lineage.[86] The continuity of this poetic tradition was further asserted by the poem's textual transmission and reception. From the thirteenth century, the *Achilleid* was often copied next to the *Ilias Latina*. An *accessus* to the *Ilias Latina*, copied in an

---

[85] Lactantius Placidus, *Commentarios in Statii*, 487.

[86] On the emulative stance toward Virgil implied by the opening lines of the *Achilleid*, see Alessandro Barchiesi, "La guerra di Troia non avrà luogo: Il proemio dell'*Achilleide* di Stazio," *Annali dell'Istituto Universitario Orientale di Napoli* 18 (1996): 45–62, at 50; Peter Heslin, *The Transvestite Achilles: Gender and Genre in Statius' Achilleid* (Cambridge: Cambridge University Press, 2005), 101; and Stephen Hinds, *Allusion and Intertext: Dynamics of Appropriation in Roman Poetry* (Cambridge: Cambridge University Press, 1998), 91–96. In his gloss on the first line of the poem, O. A. W. Dilke argues that "Magnanimum" is used by Virgil as an epithet of Aeneas in *Aeneid* 1.260. See his comm. ad loc., 79. Alessandro Barchiesi notes that the *Achilleid* is atypical in that it is highly unusual for epic proems to explicitly name their models. As he points out, Statius' direct naming of Homer as his model is more a cunning move than an acknowledgment of debt. Some passages from Book 1 may also be read as metapoetic references to "Statius's assimilation of the epic tradition." See Barchiesi, *Speaking Volumes*, 129, 186n3. For other interpretations of this opening, see François Ripoll and Jean Soubiran, eds., *Stace Achilléide* (Louvain: Peeters, 2008), 151–54, and Renée Uccellini, *L'arrivo di Achille a Sciro: Saggio di commento a Stazio. Achilleide 1, 1–396* (Pisa: Edizioni della Normale, 2012), 34–36.

THE END OF THE PURGATORIAL CURRICULUM   241

Italian manuscript from 1343, shows that Statius' *Achilleid* had indeed gained a place next to the *Aeneid* in fulfilling Homer's epic:

> Auctor huius est homerus. Materia est historia troiana, ab illo loco ubi greci exierunt ab aulide insula cum suis carinis, usque ad illum locum vbi achilles interfecit hector circum civitatem deductum. Nota quod stacius incepit istam materiam ab illo loco in quo paris rapuit helenam. Et achilles ade<m>ptus usque ad hoc quod greci fuerunt in aulide. Ubi actor iste incipit usque ad interfectionem hectoris. Vbi incipit Virgilius in secondo eneidos usque ad destructionem troje etc. Tres hystoriam troie partim tractant omnem.[87]

> (The author of this book [the *Ilias Latina*] is Homer. The subject matter is the history of Troy from where the Greeks left the island of Aulis with their ships up to the place where Achilles killed Hector led around the city. Note that Statius started the story from where Paris snatched Helen, and Achilles was taken away [by Thetis], up to the point where the Greeks were at Aulis. Here this author begins, continuing to the killing of Hector, when Virgil in Book 2 of the *Aeneid* begins, continuing to the destruction of Troy, etc. The three [authors] treat the whole story of Troy in parts.)

Together with the *Aeneid* and the *Ilias Latina*, the *Achilleid* gave primary access to the Trojan epic before the Latin West regained Homer. The appeal of the *Achilleid*'s precedent to Dante is obvious, as he, too, attempts to carve a space for his vernacular epic in the Homeric lineage. To this end, Dante feels compelled to fashion himself not only as a new Aeneas (*Inferno* 2), but also as a new Achilles (*Purgatorio* 9). Dante's fictional self becomes the third hero in the Western epic genealogy, while the *Commedia* represents the latest epic poem in the wake of Homer, Virgil, and Statius. From this perspective we can better appreciate the importance of Statius' failure with the *Achilleid* for Dante's ambitions: with the *Commedia* he aimed to fulfill the epic genealogy and claim the crown of Christian Homer that—according to Dante's own fiction—Statius had failed to conquer. As Martin Eisner points out with regard to the *Vita nova*, Dante's self-identification as a "new" Homer was an essential device for his "legitimizing" of the emerging literary vernacular.[88]

The *Achilleid*, moreover, provided Dante with a precise lesson on how to supersede the epic standards set by Virgil in the *Aeneid*. In his unfinished epic, Statius closely engages with Virgil's poem but takes Ovid's *Metamorphoses* (13.162–70) as his main model for representing Achilles' sexual initiation in Scyros. As a result,

---

[87] The *accessus* is transmitted in the manuscript Berlin, Staatsbibliothek zu Berlin, Diez B Sant. 4, fol. 169r. Both Latin and translated excerpts are quoted in Woods, *Weeping for Dido*, 55–56.

[88] Martin Eisner has also showed the role of Dante's appropriation of the Homeric subtext as a "touchstone" for the legitimizing of other emerging literary cultures. Eisner, *Dante's New Life of the Book: A Philology of World Literature* (Oxford: Oxford University Press, 2021), 111.

242 DANTE'S EDUCATION

the poem features erotic situations and elegiac interludes.[89] Statius' meddling with subject matters and styles belonging to the genres of elegy and comedy significantly departs from the tragic and heroic themes that defined the epic genre in Virgil's wake.[90] Statius even presents the hero, Achilles, as a psychologically nuanced figure, in contrast with his traditional portrait as the intrepid and pitiless hero.[91] The insertion into an epic poem of erotic subject matter, enriched with elegiac and comic motifs, provides Statius with the means of subverting conventional understandings of the genre. Given the *Achilleid*'s incompleteness, what might have been only an erotic break within a larger epic narrative, much in the style of the fourth book of the *Aeneid*, became a most unconventional generic experiment.

Virgil represents the obvious target of Statius' elegiac remaking of the epic genre. As Federica Bessone eloquently puts it, "once Vergil has been consecrated in the envoi of the *Thebaid*, in his second epic, Statius allows himself to joke with the saints—in Ovidian spirit—and repeatedly cites fragments of Vergil's epic discourse in a context that is at the same time both akin and 'mischievously dishomogeneous' to the *Aeneid*."[92] Whole textual sequences of the *Achilleid* are devoted to the systematic rewriting of passages from and narrative portions of the *Aeneid*. The opening scene, where Thetis' appeal to Neptune to sink Paris' fleet remains unheard, reworks in a minor and parodic key the beginning of the *Aeneid*. Here, with Aeolus' help, Juno sets a storm against Aeneas' fleet, which is then saved by Neptune's intervention. From this comparison, Thetis emerges as a weakened Juno.[93] Achilles' whole sojourn in Scyros, moreover, is a comic restaging of Aeneas' delay in Carthage. The rape and ensuing relationship between the transvestite Achilles and Deidamia can be interpreted as a parody of the affair between Aeneas and Dido.

Peter Heslin also points out that Thetis' attempt to turn her son into a girl mocks the relationship between Venus and Aeneas in the *Aeneid* and provides an important hint about the core strategy of Statius' emulative stance in the *Achilleid*.[94] In the fourth book of the *Aeneid*, Venus pushes Aeneas and Dido into love's trap, but fate compels the hero to continue his journey and the queen of Carthage to commit suicide. The whole fourth book, as Alessandro Barchiesi argues, represents a narrative and metapoetic threat to the poem's epic development: the

---

[89] For excellent discussions of these innovative elements in Statius' experiment with the epic genre, see Federica Bessone, "Allusive (Im-)Pertinence in Statius' Epic," in *Intertextuality in Flavian Epic Poetry: Contemporary Approaches*, ed. Neil Coffee et al. (Berlin: de Gruyter, 2019), 133–68; Heslin, *The Transvestite Achilles*; François Ripoll and Jean Soubiran, "Introduction," in *Stace Achilléide*, 1–99, esp. 51–65. As William Dominik rightly points out, "the *Achilleid* seems to be an attempt at a new type of epic." Dominik, "Statius," 524.

[90] Jenkyns, "Epic and Other Genres," 571.

[91] On this point see Dominick, "Statius," 524.

[92] Bessone, "Allusive (Im-)Pertinence," 138.

[93] For these readings see Bessone, "Allusive (Im)Pertinence," 156, and Heslin, *The Transvestite Achilles*, 103.

[94] Heslin, *The Transvestite Achilles*, 102.

THE END OF THE PURGATORIAL CURRICULUM   243

constraints imposed by fate coincide with those of the epic tradition, and the love between Aeneas and Dido "contradicts the generic canons of epic since it represents, on more levels than one, an intrusion of materials outside and not provided for in the epic code."[95] The superimposition of fate over love, therefore, implies the victory of tradition over poetic deviance. To outdo Virgil, in the *Achilleid* Statius reenacts the fourth book of the *Aeneid* and exploits the metapoetic threat posed to epic by love and elegy.[96] In the end, however, the *Achilleid* reestablishes the status quo: as Ulysses and Diomedes lead Achilles away from Deidamia toward Troy, the dichotomy between epic and love remains irreconcilable, and Statius' comic experiment ends in tragedy.

A keen reader, Dante likely noted this final shortcoming in Statius' experiment and intensified its significance in the *Commedia*. He first turns Statius into a Christian poet, whose new understanding of love should have transcended the thematic constraints imposed by ancient epic and elegy. He then stages the characters of Virgil and Statius leading Dante—the new Achilles—*to* Beatrice. Thus the *Commedia* accomplishes what the *Achilleid* had failed to achieve. As readers have observed, in the scene of Virgil's disappearance and Beatrice's concomitant reappearance, at *Purgatorio* 30, Dante introduces clear allusions to the tragic love between Dido and Aeneas: first, at Virgil's sudden disappearance, Dante quotes Dido and reenacts her abandonment by Aeneas (40–54); then, Beatrice takes up the part of the abandoned women, and Dante turns into the abandoner (55–144). In *Purgatorio* 31, however, forgiveness and redemption provide a resolution to the *Aeneid*'s elegiac impasse, thus also fulfilling the *Achilleid*'s comic experiment.[97] Hence, Statius' "dolce . . . vocale spirto" (sweet . . . poetic recitation) (*Purgatorio* 21.88) turns out to be but an aborted anticipation of the "dolce stil novo" (the sweet new style) (*Purgatorio* 24.57) that Dante claims to have achieved in his fictional dialogue with the poet Bonagiunta. Whatever this allusive expression means, it no doubt describes the new style and subject matter of the *Commedia*, in which epic and love can finally coexist, thanks to the process of moral reeducation undergone by the poem's new Christian hero.[98]

---

[95] Barchiesi, *Speaking Volumes*, 131.

[96] As Heslin shows, Statius' attempt to prove himself a better poet than Virgil is also apparent through other strategies he adopts in the *Achilleid*—for instance, redeploying intertextual similes from the *Aeneid* in a more accurate way and more suitable contexts than Virgil had done in the poem (*The Transvestite Achilles*, 93–103).

[97] On this, see Hagedorn, "A Statian Model," 40. As Robert Hollander puts it, in this scene Dante creates a "Christian romance" that supersedes classical tragedy and elegy. See Hollander, *Allegory in Dante's "Commedia"* (Princeton, NJ: Princeton University Press, 1969), 156.

[98] The meaning of Dante's definition here has been the object of intense critical scrutiny, and a variety of interpretations have been proposed. In recent scholarship, however, the term "style" has been read broadly to mean not only the form but also the content of Dante's innovative poetics. To mention only a few influential discussions on the meaning of "dolce stil novo," see Emilio Bigi, "Genesi di un concetto storiografico: 'Dolce stil novo,'" *Giornale storico della letteratura italiana* 132 (1955): 333–71; Guido Favati, *Inchiesta sul Dolce Stil Nuovo* (Florence: Le Monnier, 1975); Robert Hollander, "Dante's 'dolce stil novo' and the *Comedy*," in *Dante: Mito e poesia; Atti del secondo Seminario dantesco internazionale*, ed. Michelangelo Picone and Tiziana Crivelli (Florence: Cesati, 1999),

244   DANTE'S EDUCATION

Dante perhaps anticipates the exceptional nature of his personal epic already at *Inferno* 2.4–5, where he describes himself in the act of walking after Virgil, while preparing for "la *guerra* / sì del cammino e sì de la *pietate*" (to face the *struggle* [literally, the war]— / of the way and of the pity) (emphasis added). A few lines after that, Dante compares himself to Aeneas, effectively emboding a new type of epic hero (32). Hence, the author's words may also allude to a generic oxymoron, as they define the *Commedia* as a poem in which epic (*guerra*) and elegy (*pietà*) are bound together by the hero's journey of moral and spiritual edification (*cammino*).[99] Hence, Dante indicates here his creative engagement with the subject matter he claimed had not yet been sung in the Italian vernacular—"*Arma vero nullum latium adhuc invenio poetasse*" (as for *arms*, I find that no Italian has yet treated them in poetry) (emphasis added)—which the poem will encompass together with the other two topics that pertain to the lofty style: love and rectitude (*De vulgari eloquentia* 2.2.8). On such a premise, it does not come as a surprise to find that in *Purgatorio* Dante should wish to rewrite the genre of the ancient epic in the way I have described.

In *De raptu Proserpinae*, however, Claudian had already attempted to take the experiment of Statius' *Achilleid* beyond the impasse epitomized by the fourth book of the *Aeneid*. The central themes of *De raptu Proserpinae* are indeed erotic and elegiac. Rather than a tragic parenthesis, a generic and narrative deviance from the epic standards, Claudian makes the violent satisfaction of sexual desire, the victim's lament, and the nuptial resolution the central themes of his poem. The purpose of Claudian's experiment might have been precisely the comic deconstruction of the epic genre.[100] Therefore, the fact that Dante was required to resist Proserpina to complete his training under Virgil's and Statius' guidance may also have a key metapoetic significance that has largely gone unnoted. As already discussed, several elements in Dante's representation of Eden and Matelda's first appearance (*Purgatorio* 28.49–51) echo Claudian's *De raptu Proserpinae*. I propose that, by evoking this school epic at this precise juncture of the poem, Dante intends to acknowledge and silence a direct competitor of his epic experiment. The reason behind this argument becomes more apparent when we observe the terms with which Claudian announces the absolute novelty of his enterprise in the opening lines of the *De raptu Proserpinae*:

263–81, esp. 271–72; Giuseppe Mazzotta, *Dante, Poet of the Desert* (Princeton, NJ: Princeton University Press, 1979), 197–210; and Zygmunt G. Barański, "Canto VIII," in *Lectura Dantis Turicensis: Purgatorio*, ed. Georges Güntert and Michelangelo Picone (Florence: Cesati, 2001), 389–406, esp. 392–94.

[99] Most commentators interpret "pietà" here as meaning "compassion" or "anguish for the infernal torments." For a discussion of this as well as of Dante's many other uses of this term see Antonio Lanci, "Pietà," in the *ED*. It would be helpful to remember that Dante defines elegy as "stilum . . . miserorum" (the style of the unhappy) in the *De vulgari eloquentia* (2.4.5–6).

[100] It is also possible, as Hall ("Introduction," 110) suggests, that in Claudian's eagerness to find a new epic subject matter, he eventually found himself compelled to abandon the project due to its essentially unheroic nature.

THE END OF THE PURGATORIAL CURRICULUM   245

Di, quibus innumerum vacui famulantur Averni
vulgus iners, opibus quorum donatur avaris
quidquid in orbe perit, quos Styx liventibus ambit
interfusa vadis et quos fumantia torquens
aequora gurgitibus Phlegethon perlustrat anhelis;
vos mihi sacrarum penetralia pandite rerum
et vestri secreta poli: qua lampade Ditem
flexit Amor, quo ducta ferox Proserpina raptu
possedit dotale Chaos, quantasque per oras
sollicito genetrix erraverit anxia cursu;
unde datae populis fruges et glande relicta
cesserit inventis Dodonia quercus aristis.

(*De raptu Proserpinae* 1.20–29)

(Ye gods, whom the numberless host of the dead serves in ghostly
Avernus, into whose greedy treasury is paid all that perishes upon
earth, ye whose fields the pale streams of intertwining Styx sur-
round, while Phlegethon, his rapids tossed in spray, flows through
them with steaming eddies—do you unfold for me the mysteries
of your sacred story and the secrets of your world. Say with what
torch the god of love overcame Dis, and tell how Proserpine was
stolen away in her maiden pride to win Chaos as a dower; and how
through many lands Ceres, sore troubled, pursued her anxious
search; whence corn was given to man whereby he laid aside his
acorn food, and the new-found ear made useless Dodona's oaks.)

The central theme of Claudian's epic is not only love's victory, in contrast to the
Aeneid, but precisely love's victory in Hell. All geographical references in this
exordium—Styx, Phlegethon, and Dis—map the same world as the one described
in Dante's *Inferno*. The particular formulation that Claudian uses to introduce the
subject matter of his poem, "qua lampade Ditem flexit Amor" (with what torch
the god of love overcame Dis) anticipates Dante's representation of the "messo
celeste" who alone conquers Dis in *Inferno* 9.[101] More broadly, Claudian's prologue
encapsulates with remarkable precision the core experiment of the *Commedia*:
an epic poem about love both human and divine and its victory over death and
Hell.[102]

---

[101] More to the point, as noted above, some critics suggest that Claudian's *De raptu Proserpinae*
1.32–47 could be a source for Dante's representation of the infernal army and the Furies on top of Dis'
walls, in *Inferno* 9. See Butler, "Claudian's *De raptu Proserpinae* and Dante's Vanquished Giants."

[102] As encapsulated by the poem's last line, where God is identified as "l'amor che move il sole e l'altre
stelle" (*Paradiso* 33.145).

246   DANTE'S EDUCATION

The path, however, that leads to love's victory in Dante's poem is diametrically different from Claudian's, as implied by Matelda's identification with an unviolated Proserpina: the hero of the *Commedia* has to renounce the forceful pursuit of sexual satisfaction and endorse instead the God-oriented love proposed by Beatrice in Eden. In this locus of generic transformation, the *Commedia* supersedes the unfinished experiments of its didactic models, as symbolized by Beatrice's ultimate success in rescuing her "friend" (*Inferno* 2.61), as opposed to Thetis' and Ceres' failure to protect their children in Statius' and Claudian's poems, respectively. Dante's success acquires even greater significance in that both Statius and Claudian were Christian poets—albeit, for Statius, only within the fiction of the *Commedia*. Hence, their failure to supersede the school of the ancient pagan poets prepared the way for Dante's creation of a Christian epic, in which love is integral rather than a hindrance to the heroic journey.

Dante's decision to evoke and silence Claudian at the juncture of *Purgatorio* 28.49–51, and in relation to Matelda, may also have depended on the latter's putative Florentine origin. An erroneous tradition claimed that Claudian was a Florentine poet.[103] This opinion found acceptance among early humanists such as Benvenuto da Imola, Petrarch, Boccaccio, Filippo Villani, and Coluccio Salutati.[104] Claudian's Florentine origin, in conjunction with the subject matter of the *De raptu Proserpinae*, made him an especially relevant precedent for Dante. Claudian's Florentinity may have led Dante to treat him in similar fashion to another local poet who is evoked in the same canto: Guido Cavalcanti. As already pointed out, Dante's description of Matelda's first appearance echoes Guido Cavalcanti's poem, "In un boschetto trova' pasturella." Cavalcanti's specter in these lines coincides with a complex tribute to a poetic model that Dante wishes indirectly to acknowledge here. In the same canto, therefore, and through the

---

[103] The tradition probably derived from Claudian's alleged dependence on a certain prince Florentinus. Geoffrey of Vitry's *accessus* maintains that Claudian worked for the Roman prince Florentinus: "et ipse dictus est Claudius Claudianus, qui in tempore Florentini Romanorum principis valde peritus fuit in rhetorica et in arte poetica. Unde Florentinus ipsum rogavit ut ipsius gesta assumeret describenda." Clarke and Giles, *Commentary of Geoffrey of Vitry*, 23. Florentinus, whom Claudian celebrates in the preface to Book 1, was not an emperor. This mistake was probably the result of the association of Claudian's poem with Statius' *Achilleid*. In *Achilleid* 1.18–19, Statius celebrates the emperor Domitian: "te longo necdum fidente paratu / molimur magnusque tibi praeludit Achilles."

[104] As Giorgio Brugnoli ("Statius Christianus," 14–15) notes, Statius and Claudian were commonly discussed together as Christian poets among proto- and early Italian humanists. Dante certainly had an important role in this tradition with regard to Statius, but Claudian's Christianity was derived from other sources. See the entry "Claudianus, Claudian" in Paget Toynbee, "Index of Authors Quoted by Benvenuto da Imola in His Commentary on the *Divina Commedia*: A Contribution to the Study of the Sources of the Commentary," *Annual Report of the Dante Society of America* 16–25 (1899–1900): 1–54. Filippo Villani argues that Florence's poets inherit the achievements of ancient Rome in a genealogical continuity, and Claudian was the last Florentine poet from antiquity: "After Claudian, who was almost the last poet that ancient times produced, the greed and weak-mindedness of the Emperors, resulted in the decline of poetry." Quoted in Simon Gilson, *Dante and Renaissance Florence* (Cambridge: Cambridge University Press, 2005), 71. On this passage by Villani, see also Michael Caesar, ed., *Dante: The Critical Heritage* (London and New York: Routledge, 1989), 183.

same character—Matelda—Dante conveniently recognizes and eclipses two of his Florentine predecessors: one ancient, Claudian, and one modern, Cavalcanti.

Conclusion

Dante's identification with Achilles in *Purgatorio* 9, the presence of the character Statius in *Purgatorio* and of Claudian's intertext in Eden underlines the mediating role of the *Achilleid* and the *De raptu Proserpinae* in Dante's reworking of the Roman epic genre. At the narrative level, their intertextual presence symbolizes Dante's rite of initiation into the moral order restored by the purgatorial school, as well as the author's epic call to become a poet entrusted with a divine mandate in a corrupt and violent world. But Dante's engagement with these two school poems also fulfills a metapoetic function: while Dante engages with the major epic models, particularly Virgil and Ovid, in both the narrative symbolism of the protagonist's ascent behind Virgil and Statius and in the remaking of a primeval Edenic landscape, he also acknowledges Statius' and Claudian's models of *aemulatio* of the same *auctores maiores*. The integration of these intermediate models foregrounds Dante's original contributions to the genre. Throughout his purgatorial ascent, Dante lays the foundation of a new vision of Christian epic poetry that has superseded the theoretical and narrative dichotomy between love and war. As I will argue in the next chapter, *Paradiso* provides the subject matter to develop this new Christian epic poem in the vernacular. Not surprisingly, the influence of Statius' *Achilleid* and Claudian's *De raptu* does not stop at Lethe's banks but crosses over the border of *Purgatorio* to reappear in the proemial lines of *Paradiso*.

As Chapters 4, 5, and 6 have shown, the moral and spiritual education Dante envisions in his purgatorial "school" also entails a literary reformation of his audience through a close engagement with the key texts of contemporary Latin education. The coincidence of moral and literary reeducation in *Purgatorio* is better understood in light of Dante's encounter with Matelda in Eden. As memories of classical and vernacular texts deceive the pilgrim in preparation for this meeting, school texts' power to harm becomes apparent. While Dante showcases the innovative features of his own poetics, he also provides a corrective to flawed moral, political, and cultural paradigms that were perpetuated by Latin education.

7

"Be Silent, Ovid" (You, Too, Statius and Claudian)

Underground Voices in the Prologue to *Paradiso*

In the eighth *bolgia* of *Inferno*, Dante witnesses the incessant and horrifying serpentine transformations that torment the thieves. These endless transmutations of human and animal bodies give the author an opportunity to reflect on the metamorphoses of ancient literary texts through time and at the hands of readers and emulators. Being an enthusiastic disciple of the ancient poets, Dante tackles the subject with striking agonism:

> Taccia Lucano omai là dov' e' tocca
> del misero Sabello e di Nasidio,
> e attenda a udir quel ch'or si scocca.
> Taccia di Cadmo e d'Aretusa Ovidio,
> ché se quello in serpente e quella in fonte
> converte poetando, io non lo 'nvidio;
> ché due nature mai a fronte a fronte
> non trasmutò sì ch'amendue le forme
> a cambiar lor matera fosser pronte.
>
> (*Inferno* 25.94–102)

> (Let now Lucan fall silent where he tells / of poor Sabellus and Nasidius, / and let him wait to hear what comes forth now! / Let Ovid not speak of Cadmus or Arethusa, / for if his poem turns him into a serpent / and her into a fountain, I grudge it not, / for never did he change two natures, face to face, / in such a way that both their forms / were quite so quick exchanging substance.)

The epic topos of the serpentine metamorphoses and the practice of literary "thievery," implied in the sin of this *bolgia*, fire up Dante's spirit of poetic emulation.[1] In the same spirit, he uses the narrative medium to extend this challenge to his

---

[1] On this particular feature of the Latin epic, see Alessandro Barchiesi, *Speaking Volumes: Narrative and Intertext in Ovid and Other Latin Poets* (London: Duckworth, 2001), 129.

Dante's Education. Filippo Gianferrari, Oxford University Press. © Filippo Gianferrari (2024).
DOI: 10.1093/oso/9780198881766.003.0008

revered master: "per ch'io, acciò che 'l duca stesse attento, / mi puosi 'l dito su dal mento al naso" (and then, to catch my guide's attention, / I held my finger up from chin to nose) (*Inferno* 24.44–45). Pressing a finger against his mouth, the protagonist silences Virgil and invites the reader to appreciate the *Commedia*'s emulative stance toward its classical models. Poetic emulation here coincides with Dante's foray, once more, into the territory of the ancient epic. The vernacular correlative of the *taceat nunc* (be silent) formula is a tribute to the genre, as this implies self-conscious intertextuality, made of allusions to and citations from its own canon. Dante forcefully attempts to insert himself into this ancient poetic lineage, while also thematizing his "anxiety of influence"—both the influence his predecessors exert on him and the one he hopes to have on his readers.[2] Leonard Barkan argues that in the punishment of the thieves, Dante displays "the great pagan vision of metamorphosis" in order for it "to be respected, confronted, saved, and recast in an original form."[3] Arguably, however, Dante's recovery and recasting of this ancient epic topos is fulfilled only much later in the *Commedia*, and only as a result of a renewed understanding of poetic emulation that transcends the anxiety voiced in *Inferno* 25.

Throughout *Purgatorio*, as we have seen, Dante's challenge to the ancient poetic school becomes less overtly agonistic and more syncretistic: the poet systematically explores the merits and limits of pagan poetic wisdom, as encapsulated in the fictional relationship between the protagonist, Virgil, and Statius. Albeit different in character and aims, therefore, the competition with the ancients remains intense at the narrative level. In *Paradiso*, Dante's emulation of the "fair school" of poetry transforms once more in response to the canticle's groundbreaking subject matter: the vision of God. Here the pagan subtext is absorbed and transfigured to become the vessel of the new Christian subject matter. One needs go no further than the two-part prologue to *Paradiso* to appreciate how such renewal is brought about.

In the first canto, Dante promises to recount, by means of his poetry, the mystery of the beatific vision (the *arcana Dei*): "Veramente quant'io del regno santo / ne la mia mente potei far tesoro, / sarà ora materia del mio canto" (Nevertheless, as much of the holy kingdom / as I could store as treasure in my mind / shall now become the subject of my song) (*Paradiso* 1.10–12). This daring ambition heralds the elevation of theme and tone, as well as the atmosphere of heroic enterprise,

---

[2] See Caron Ann Cioffi, "The Anxieties of Ovidian Influence: Theft in *Inferno* XXIV and XXV," *Dante Studies* 112 (1994): 77–100.

[3] Leonard Barkan, *The Gods Made Flesh: Metamorphoses and the Pursuit of Paganism* (New Haven, CT: Yale University Press, 1986), 140.

250   DANTE'S EDUCATION

engendered by the didactic epos of *Paradiso*.[4] The epic prologue then concludes
with an invocation to Apollo:

> O buono Appollo, a l'ultimo lavoro
> fammi del tuo valor sì fatto vaso,
> come dimandi a dar l'amato alloro.
>   Infino a qui l'un giogo di Parnaso
> assai mi fu; ma or con amendue
> m'è uopo intrar ne l'aringo rimaso.
>   Entra nel petto mio, e spira tue
> sì come quando Marsïa traesti
> de la vagina de le membra sue.
>   O divina virtù, se mi ti presti
> tanto che l'ombra del beato regno
> segnata nel mio capo io manifesti,
>   vedra' mi al piè del tuo diletto legno
> venire, e coronarmi de le foglie
> che la materia e tu mi farai degno.
>   Sì rade volte, padre, se ne coglie
> per trïunfare o cesare o poeta,
> colpa e vergogna de l'umane voglie,
>   che parturir letizia in su la lieta
> delfica deïtà dovria la fronda
> peneia, quando alcun di sé asseta.
>   Poca favilla gran fiamma seconda:
> forse di retro a me con miglior voci
> si pregherà perché Cirra risponda.

(Paradiso 1.13–36)

(O good Apollo, for this last labor / make me a vessel worthy /
of the gift of your belovèd laurel. / Up to this point, one peak of
Mount Parnassus / has been enough, but now I need them both
/ in order to confront the struggle that awaits. / Enter my breast
and breathe in me / as when you drew out Marsyas, / out from the
sheathing of his limbs. / O holy Power, if you but lend me of yourself / enough that I may show the merest shadow / of the blessèd
kingdom stamped within my mind, / you shall find me at the foot
of your belovèd tree, / crowning myself with the very leaves / of

---

[4] For a succinct discussion of the two major branches of the Greek epic tradition as derived from
Homer's heroic epic and Hesiod's didactic epos, see Richard Jenkyns, "Epic and Other Genres in the
Roman World," in *A Companion to Ancient Epic*, ed. John Miles Foley (Malden, MA: Blackwell, 2005),
562–73.

which my theme and you will make me worthy. / So rarely, father, are they gathered / to mark the triumph of a Caesar or a poet— / fault and shame of human wishes— / that anyone's even longing for them, / those leaves on the Peneian bough, should make / the joyous Delphic god give birth to joy. / Great fire leaps from the smallest spark. / Perhaps, in my wake, prayer will be shaped / with better words that Cyrrha may respond.)

At the heart of Dante's invocation and, by extension, of his poetic enterprise, lies a striking conflation of classical and biblical motifs—for instance, the merging of the classical topos of the Apollonian inspiration with the authority of St. Paul.[5] The new purpose and balance of Dante's syncretistic emulation of the *auctores maiores*, however, is best exemplified by the striking rewriting of Ovid's *Metamorphoses* that marks both sections of this proem: the author first compares himself to Marsyas and Glaucus (1.19–21, 67–69) and then contrasts his readers with the Argonauts (2.16–18).[6] These two instances of Ovidian appropriations show how emulation has become for Dante an essential means to express the protagonist's journey of transformation beyond the human—"transumanar."[7]

Not only does Dante adapt the Ovidian subtext to the new purpose of his Christian poem: he also thematizes the very process of reinterpretation and rewriting of the ancient source, thus creating what Kevin Brownlee defines as a "dialectic of intertextuality."[8] As this chapter argues, however, such a "dialectic" involves not only Ovid and Virgil; while reenvisioning the classical epic proem and repurposing echoes from the *Metamorphoses*, Dante also draws on the two canonical examples of epic exordia that medieval education derived from Statius' *Achilleid*

[5] The author's self-representation as a "vaso" points readers back to the title of "Vas d'elezïone" (Chosen Vessel) that identifies St. Paul at *Inferno* 2.28. The author had already alluded to the authority of 2 Corinthians 12:3–4 in order to express the ineffability of God's vision: "Nel ciel che più de la sua luce prende / fu' io, e vidi cose che ridire / né sa né può chi di là sù discende (*Paradiso* 1.4–6). On the meaning and intertextual significance of this Pauline reference, see Steven Botterill, "'Quae non licet homini loqui': The Ineffability of Mystical Experience in *Paradiso* I and the *Epistle to Can Grande*," *Modern Language Review* 83 (1988): 332–41, and Giuseppe Ledda, *La guerra della lingua* (Ravenna: Longo, 2002), 243–59. Simone creating what Kevin Brownlee term "labor," which closes the first line of the invocation (1.13), may also refer to St. Paul. See Marchesi, "Epic Ironies: Poetics, Metapoetics, Self-Translation (*Inferno* 18.1, *Purgatorio* 24.52, *Paradiso* 1.13)," *Dante Studies* 131 (2013): 99–117, esp. 112–13.
[6] Two seminal studies on these Ovidian reminiscences remain Kevin Brownlee, "Pauline Vision and Ovidian Speech in *Paradiso* I," in *The Poetry of Allusion: Virgil and Ovid in Dante's Commedia*, ed. Rachel Jacoff and Jeffrey Schnapp (Stanford, CA: Stanford University Press, 1991), 202–13, and Michelangelo Picone, "Dante argonauta: La ricezione dei miti ovidiani nella *Commedia*," in *Ovidius redivivus: von Ovid zu Dante*, ed. Michelangelo Picone and Bernhard Zimmermann (Stuttgart: M&P Verlag, 1994), 191–200. For a recent reconsideration of Dante's reference to the quest of the Argonauts in *Paradiso*, see Vincenzo Vitale, "'Poca favilla gran fiamma seconda': Appunti sugli Argonauti di Dante," in *Giornale storico della letteratura italiana* 194 (2017): 1–37.
[7] On this see Robert Hollander, *Allegory in Dante's "Commedia"* (Princeton, NJ: Princeton University Press, 1969), 202–03.
[8] Brownlee, "Pauline Vision," 204.

252   DANTE'S EDUCATION

and Claudian's *De raptu Proserpinae*. Thus, Dante recreates what we have already termed an "imitative series."[9] Dante's engagement with these two emulative poets appears more prominently in connection with the topoi of the poetic crowning, the divine frenzy, and the seafaring metaphor—all three at the heart of the proem to *Paradiso*. In *Paradiso*'s outdoing of the major Latin epic tradition, these stock epic themes become "tropes of intertextuality" for creative engagement with its literary precursors.[10]

The *Achilleid* in *Paradiso*: Poetic Agon and Laurel Crowning

Dante's invocation to Apollo reworks three stock themes of the epic exordium: *Paradiso* represents the poet's ultimate achievement ("l'ultimo lavoro," 1.13); its completion will be worthy of the beloved laurel crown ("l'amato alloro," 1.15); and it will be the hardest agonistic challenge for him to undertake and win ("l'aringo rimaso," 1.18). These topoi can all be traced back to classical sources. The formulation "ultimo lavoro" (1.13), for instance, reveals the influence of Virgil's "extremum hunc, Arethusa, mihi concede laborem" (This now, the very latest of my toils, / vouchsafe me, Arethusa!) (*Eclogues* 10.1).[11] The theme of the poetic crowning, and particularly Dante's words "che parturir letizia in su la lieta / delfica deïtà dovria la fronda / peneia" (those leaves on the Peneian bough, should make / the joyous Delphic god give birth to joy) (1.31–33), would instead owe to the account of Daphne's myth given by Ovid in *Metamorphoses*:[12]

> ... mihi *Delphica* tellus
> et Claros et Tenedos Patareaque regia servit;
> Iuppiter est genitor; per me, quod eritque fuitque
> estque, patet; per me concordant carmina nervis.
>
> ...
>
> cui deus "at, quoniam coniunx mea non potes esse,
> arbor eris certe" dixit "mea! semper habebunt
> te coma, te citharae, te nostrae, laure, pharetrae;
> tu ducibus Latiis aderis, cum laeta Triumphum
> vox canet et visent longas Capitolia pompas;
> postibus Augustis eadem fidissima custos
> ante fores stabis mediamque tuebere quercum,
> utque meum intonsis caput est iuvenale capillis,

---

[9] See Chapter 6.

[10] Barchiesi, *Speaking Volumes*, 130.

[11] Marchesi, "Epic Ironies," 111–14.

[12] See, for instance, Hollander, *Allegory*, 208–09, and Giorgio Inglese, comm. ad loc., in Dante Alighieri, *Paradiso* (Rome: Carrocci, 2020).

tu quoque perpetuos semper gere frondis honores!"
finierat *Paean*: factis modo laurea ramis
adnuit utque caput visa est agitasse cacumen.

> > (*Metamorphoses* 1.515–18 and 557–67; emphasis added)

(The *Delphic* Land, the Pataraean Realm, / Claros and Tenedos revere my name, / and my immortal sire is Jupiter. / The present, past and future are through me / in sacred oracles revealed to man, / and from my harp the harmonies of sound / are borrowed by their bards to praise the Gods. . . . And thus the God; / "Although thou canst not be my bride, thou shalt / be called my chosen tree, and thy green leaves, / O Laurel! shall forever crown my brows, / be wreathed around my quiver and my lyre; / the Roman heroes shall be crowned with thee, / as long processions climb the Capitol / and chanting throngs proclaim their victories; / and as a faithful warden thou shalt guard / the civic crown of oak leaves fixed between / thy branches, and before Augustan gates. / And as my youthful head is never shorn, / so, also, shalt thou ever bear thy leaves / unchanging to thy glory." / Here the God, / *Phoebus* Apollo, ended his lament, / and unto him the Laurel bent her boughs, / so lately fashioned.)

The metaphor of the creative act as a type of agonistic struggle is indeed an ancient topos, but no specific classical archetype has been identified as the source of inspiration for Dante's "aringo rimaso" (1.18). I contend that the exordium to Statius' *Achilleid* contains all three epic motifs and intertwines with Ovid and Virgil in providing the subtext for Dante's invocation to Apollo.

The *Achilleid* begins by invoking Apollo and petitioning him for the laurel crown:

> tu modo, si veterem digno deplevimus haustu,
> da fontes mihi, Phoebe, novos ac fronde secunda
> necte comas: neque enim Aonium nemus advena pulso
> nec mea nunc primis augescunt tempora vittis.
> Scit Dircaeus ager meque inter prisca parentum
> nomina cumque suo numerant Amphione Thebae.
> At tu, quem longe primum stupet Itala virtus
> Graiaque, cui geminae florent vatumque ducumque
> certatim laurus—olim dolet altera vinci—,
> da veniam ac trepidum patere hoc sudare parumper

254   DANTE'S EDUCATION

> pulvere: te longo necdum fidente paratu
> molimur magnusque tibi praeludit Achilles.
>
> (*Achilleid* 1.8–19)[13]

> (All I require from you, Phoebus Apollo, / is new springs if I have
> drained the old ones dry / with a worthy draught, and to wreathe
> my hair / a second time with auspicious laurel, / for I am not
> knocking at the Aonian grove / as a stranger here, nor are these
> sacred bands / the first to augment my temples. Dirce's land / is
> aware of this, and Thebes has me on her list / of venerable poets
> dating back to Amphion. / And you, Domitian, chief wonder both
> of Italian / and Greek virtuosity, with rival laurels / as poet and
> general (the former long in somber eclipse) / indulge me, permit
> me to sweat for a while / in the dust, trepidatious in preparing /
> my monument to you. Achilles is your prelude.)

While Dante and Statius rewrite the same Ovidian archetype in their exordia, I
argue that some significant parallels between them reveal Dante's close engagement with Statius' intermediary example of emulation.[14] First, both Dante and
Statius introduce the motif of the laurel crown in the context of an invocation
to Apollo, whereas in Ovid's *Metamorphoses* it is the god himself who wishes to
possess Daphne and then to wear the laurel crown. Second, Dante's reference
to the double crowning also points to the intermediary model of the *Achilleid*.
In Ovid's *Metamorphoses*, Apollo wishes his laurel crown to become a trophy to
celebrate both epic triumphs, the military and the poetic: "semper habebunt /
te coma, te citharae, te nostrae, laure, pharetrae; / tu ducibus Latiis aderis, cum
laeta triumphum / vox canet et visent longas Capitolia pompas" (O Laurel! shall
forever crown my brows, / be wreathed around my quiver and my lyre; / the
Roman heroes shall be crowned with thee, / as long processions climb the Capitol
/ and chanting throngs proclaim their victories) (1.560–61). Statius reproduces
this motif in the address to his patron, the Roman emperor Domitian. Statius
praises the emperor for his double achievements as both a poet and a general—
skills, the author complains, that are seldom found together. If we turn to Dante's

---

[13] The lines in Stanley Lombardo's translation (P. Papinius Statius, *Achilleid*, trans. Stanley Lombardo [Indianapolis: Hackett, 2015]) are 11–25.

[14] Pietro Alighieri was the first commentator to note the parallel between Dante's and Statius'
invocations to Apollo; see his comm. (1359–64) *Paradiso* 1.1–36. Awareness of this significant echo
is displayed by Bernardino Daniello, comm. *Paradiso* 1.22–30; Francesco Torraca, comm. *Paradiso*
1.28–33; Tommaso Casini and S. A. Barbi, comm. *Paradiso* 1.29; Bosco and Reggio, comm. *Paradiso*
1.28–30.

UNDERGROUND VOICES IN THE PROLOGUE TO *PARADISO*   255

rewriting of the same motif and compare it to Statius' version, the similarities are arresting:

At tu, quem longe primum stupet Itala
                  virtus
Graiaque, cui geminae florent vatumque
                  ducumque
certatim laurus—olim dolet altera vinci—,
da veniam ac trepidum patere hoc sudare
                  parumper
pulvere: te longo necdum fidente paratu
molimur magnusque tibi praeludit
                  Achilles.
          (*Achilleid* 1.14–19)

Sì rade volte, padre, se ne coglie
    per trïunfare o cesare o poeta,
  colpa e vergogna de l'umane voglie,
          (*Paradiso* 1.28–30)

(So rarely, father, are they gathered /
to mark the triumph of a Caesar or a
poet— / fault and shame of human
               wishes—)

(And you, Domitian, chief wonder both of Italian / and Greek virtuosity, with rival laurels / as poet and general (the former long in somber eclipse), / indulge me, permit me to sweat for a while / in the dust, trepidatious in preparing / my monument to you. Achilles is your prelude.)

Whereas Ovid provides only a generic source for Dante's image of the double crowning, Statius' formulation of the same theme appears almost identical: "vatumque ducumque certatim laurus" (with rival laurels / as poet and general): "per trïunfare o cesare o poeta" (to mark the triumph of a Caesar or a poet). Furthermore, Dante and Statius both lament the long absence of a laurel crowning. In Statius' case, the poet complains that Domitian's shining military career has long detracted from his poetic achievements, whereas Dante denounces the scarcity of suitable candidates for either poetic or military crowning. Albeit for different reasons, both argue for the need of a new poetic crowning—"olim dolet altera vincit" (the former [poetic crown] long in somber eclipse): "Sì rade volte, padre, se ne coglie" (So rarely, father, are they gathered). What we need to appreciate, moreover, is that this particular issue is entirely absent from the Ovidian archetype.

A few other linguistic and thematic parallels buttress the thesis of Dante's engagement with the exordium of the *Achilleid* in *Paradiso* 1:

256 DANTE'S EDUCATION

si veterem <u>digno</u> deplevimus haustu
da *fontes mihi,* Phoebe, novos ac
                    fronde secunda
necte comas.
  (*Achilleid* 1.8–10; emphasis added)

(All I require from you, Phoebus
Apollo, / is new springs if I have
drained the old ones dry / with a
worthy draught, and to wreathe my
hair / a second time with auspicious
laurel.)

vedra' mi al piè del tuo diletto legno
venire, e coronarmi de le foglie
che la materia e tu mi farai <u>degno</u>.
(*Paradiso* 1.22–33; emphasis added)

(you shall find me at the foot of your
belovèd tree, / crowning myself with
the very leaves / of which my theme
and you will make me worthy.)

che parturir letizia in su la lieta
delfica deïtà dovria la *fronda*
peneia, quando alcun di sé <u>*asseta*</u>.
Poca favilla gran fiamma *seconda*
(*Paradiso* 1.31–34; emphasis added)

(that anyone's even longing for them,
/ those leaves on the Peneian bough,
should make / the joyous Delphic
god give birth to joy. / Great fire
leaps from the smallest spark.)

Both poems mention the need to prove oneself worthy of Apollo's crown. Whereas Statius claims to have already done so in his previous works, Dante justifies his demand on the basis of his divine election and the subject matter of *Paradiso* itself: "si veterem digno deplevimus haustu" (if I have drained the old ones dry): "che la materia e tu mi farai degno" (of which my theme and you will make me worthy). Both poets, moreover, represent Apollo's inspiration as a spring they thirst for: "da fontes mihi" (give me new springs): "quando alcun di sé asseta" (when someone is thirsty for it). Finally, Dante uses the term "fronda" to identify the sacred laurel, just as in Statius' reference to the second laurel, "fronde secunda," Once again, both are drawing on the same Ovidian archetype: "frondis honores" (honores of the laurel) (*Metamorphoses* 1.565). Yet, Dante's rhyme of "fronda" with "seconda" is a skillful calque of Statius's "fronde secunda."

The *Achilleid* and its medieval reception also feature two more motifs that give Dante's invocation its distinctive agonistic tone: the poetic agon and the epic challenge. Statius' exordium rehearses the familiar metaphor of the act of writing as an athletic competition. Both texts represent the poet as an athlete—a runner about to enter the racetrack or a fighter approaching the arena:

UNDERGROUND VOICES IN THE PROLOGUE TO *PARADISO* 257

Da veniam ac trepidum patere hoc sudare
parumper
pulvere, te longo necdum fidente paratu
molimur
(*Achilleid* 1.17–19)

(Indulge me, permit me to sweat for a while
/ in the dust, trepidatious in preparing)

ma or con amendue
m'è uopo intrar ne l'aringo rimaso
(*Paradiso* 1.17–18)

(but now I need them both / in
order to confront the struggle that
awaits.)

Dante's mention of the "aringo" as a metonymy for the agonistic endeavor required by the creative act represents a variation on Statius' "pulvere."[15]

The reception of the *Achilleid* and the *De raptu Proserpinae* in medieval schools may also provide some useful context against which to interpret another agonistic element in Dante's invocation to Apollo. We have already seen that Dante introduces *Paradiso* as his ultimate poetic work, "this last labor," which most critics take to mean *Paradiso*'s status as the poem's last canticle. The precedent of Virgil's *Eclogue* 10.1, where the author defines his last eclogue as the "extremum . . . laborem," supports this interpretation. I contend, however, that Dante's definition of *Paradiso* as "ultimo lavoro" may also reflect an understanding of the epic genre that was ingrained in medieval education. In the exordium of the *Achilleid*, Statius gives readers a sense of his career's progression; the poet is new neither to the Muses, "si veterem digno deplevimus haustu," nor to poetic achievements, "fronde secunda," and he presents the *Achilleid* as a particular moment in his relationship with his powerful sponsor, the emperor Domitian (1.15–19), when the poet asks leave to write this poem. Statius also alludes to a planned work on the emperor's achievements, in relation to which the *Achilleid* would be only a preparatory exercise—"give me good leave; / suffer me in my eagerness to sweat awhile in dust. / On you I work in long and not yet confident preparing, / and great Achilles is your prelude" (*Achilleid* 1.17–19). Acknowledging this sense of progression, a medieval *accessus* explains that Statius wished to prove his ingenuity on the subject matter of the *Achilleid* before tackling an epic about the emperor; death, however, prevented

---

[15] In his edition of the *Achilleid*, Dilke points to "sudare" and "pulvere" as metaphors from the arena, which are also used by Cicero and, similarly, by Statius in *Silvae* (4.7.24f.). See Papinius Statius, *Achilleid*, ed. Oswald A. W. Dilke (Cambridge: Cambridge University Press, 1954), comm. ad loc., 82. In addition to the metaphorical language, it should also be noted that medieval *accessus* represented Statius as a poet who participated successfully in several poetic contexts, thus emphasizing his agonistic spirit. See Violetta de Angelis, "Lo Stazio di Dante: Poesia e scuola," *Schede umanistiche* 16, no. 2 (2002): 29–69, esp. 40–45. Statius' agonistic attitude toward his literary forebears is explicit in all his texts. On this topic, see Ernst Robert Curtius, *European Literature and the Latin Middle Ages* (London: Routledge & Kegan Paul, 1953), 162–63, and Laura Micozzi, "Statius' Epic Poetry: A Challenge to the Literary Past," in *Brill's Companion to Statius*, ed. William J. Dominik, C. E. Newlands, and K. Gervais (Leiden: Brill, 2015), 325–42.

258   DANTE'S EDUCATION

the author from fulfilling his plan.[16] In this reading, the *Achilleid* becomes an intermediate work, in preparation for the composition of Statius' ultimate epic poem.

Some glosses transferred this piece of biographical information from Statius' *accessus* to that of Claudian's *De raptu Proserpinae*. As a result, this unfinished poem also came to be regarded as an intermediate and preparatory exercise; Claudian, too, was practicing writing an epic about another Roman prince, Florentinus—who was in fact a Roman nobleman and the poet's patron. Claudian, too, died while carrying out his preparatory exercise. Geoffrey of Vitry's *accessus* to Claudian, for instance, informs readers that

> Claudius Claudianus, qui in tempore Florentini Romanorum principis, valde peritus fuit in rethorica et in arte poetica. Unde Florentinus ipsum rogavit ut ipsius gesta assumeret describenda. Claudianus autem se diffidens tantae materiam describendae posse sufficere praesens opus aggressus est in quo materiam habuit raptum Proserpinae filiae Cereris ad inferos per Plutonem. . . . Intentio actoris est triplex, scilicet ingenii praeacutio et Florentini in aliquo satisfactio et eruditio auditorum. . . . Ideo enim praemittit prologum ut ingenium suum praeacuat ut ad quodlibet opus postea facilius audeat provenire.[17]

> (Claudius Claudian, who lived at the time of the Roman prince Florentinus, was well versed in rhetoric and poetry. For this reason, Florentinus asked Claudian to write about Florentinus' heroic deeds. Claudian, however, doubting his own ability to write of such a subject matter, began this work on Pluto's abduction of Ceres' daughter, Proserpina, to the underworld ... The author's intention is three-fold: to sharpen his intellect; to appease Florentinus with some composition; and to instruct the listeners. . . . Thus, in his premise, he states that the reason for this work is that he may sharpen his intellect and after that dare tackle more easily any given work.)

This alteration of Claudian's professional biography could have been a consequence of the physical proximity between his *De raptu Proserpinae* and Statius' *Achilleid* in scholastic anthologies, as well as their combined use for Latin instruction and their several narrative and structural similarities.

As a result of this confusion, I suggest, medieval education turned a biographical detail of Statius' life into a characteristic of the epic genre. Both poems taught pupils two notions concerning epic poetry: first, that the genre was fitting only for expert poets, who had reached the highest point of their career and

---

[16] "se prius velle acuere ingenium suum in alia materia antequam gesta ipsius describeret; sed morte preventus est." Quoted in Paul M. Clogan, ed., *The Medieval Achilleid of Statius, Edited with Introduction, Variant Readings, and Glosses* (Leiden: Brill, 1968), 21.

[17] Amy Key Clarke and Phyllis M. Giles, eds., *The Commentary of Geoffrey of Vitry on Claudian De raptu Proserpinae* (Leiden: Brill, 1973), 23. The translation is mine.

UNDERGROUND VOICES IN THE PROLOGUE TO *PARADISO*   259

had proved their worthiness in less demanding genres; second, that writing epic poetry on an entirely new subject matter was in itself a competitive challenge that only very few were able to carry out—both Statius and Claudian had failed in their attempts.[18] Not only was the subject matter "epic," therefore, but so too was the very act of writing it: the poet himself would become the contender in a competition he might end up losing.[19] Before embarking on such a difficult enterprise, both Statius and Claudian were first obliged to practice with rather traditional subjects. When we consider again the declaration about the *Achilleid* that Dante puts in Statius' mouth in *Purgatorio*, "ma caddi in via con la seconda soma" (but [I] fell along the way with the second burden) (*Purgatorio* 21.93), we can appreciate how Dante may wish to tap into this motif of the epic failure. In his invocation to Apollo, at *Paradiso* 1, Dante draws on the *Achilleid* to oppose his "ultimo lavoro" to Statius' and Claudian's failed experiments. Thus, Dante claims to have successfully accomplished the ultimate poetic challenge and crowning achievement of any poet's career: an epic poem on an entirely new subject.[20]

Claudian in *Paradiso*: The Poet's Divine Frenzy

The main request in Dante's invocation to Apollo is that the poet be possessed by the god: "Entra nel *petto mio, e spira* tue / sì come quando Marsïa traesti / de la vagina de le membra sue (Enter *my breast and breathe* in me / as when you drew out Marsyas, / out from the sheathing of his limbs) (*Paradiso* 1.19–21; emphasis

---

[18] This progression was in line with medieval views concerning the hierarchy between different literary genres and their respective styles (*genera dicendi*), as exemplified by the famous mnemonic device known as *Rota Vergilii* (Virgilian wheel) and was based on the alleged order in which Virgil wrote his poems. In his commentary on Virgil, Servius had already established the idea that a young poet should exercise his art on the "lower" genres, such as the elegiac or the bucolic, whereas an older and more expert one should write epic and tragic poems. Virgil's oeuvre represented the ideal poetic career. On the *Rota Vergilii*, see Anker Teilgard Laugesen, "La Roue de Virgile: Une page de la théorie littéraire du moyen âge," *Classica er mediaevalia* 23 (1962): 248–73.

[19] In addition, Dante embraces and articulates such a vision of the epic poet in the *Commedia*, where he makes himself the hero of the poem: "Nel mezzo del cammin di nostra vita / *mi* ritrovai in una selva oscura," as well as "Nel ciel che più de la sua luce prende / *fu' io.*" (*Paradiso* 1.4–5; emphasis added).

[20] The topos of singing things never expressed before appears in ancient Greece as the rejection of trite epic material. Choerilus (end of the fifth century), who sought to rejuvenate the epic by introducing historical material, held that the old sagas were worn out and called those happy who served the Muses when the "meadow was still untouched." Quoted by Curtius, *European Literature*, 86. In *Georgica* 3.4, Virgil observes that everyone knows about the twelve labors of Hercules, a subject treated much too often. Horace promises a "song never heard" (*Carmina* 3.1.2). Statius praises Lucan for having forsaken the well-worn tracks: "trita vatibus orbita" (*Silvae* 2.7.51). The *novitas* of the subject matter is a recurrent theme in Dante's oeuvre, as exemplified, for instance, by his *De vulgari eloquentia* (1.1.1) "Cum nemine ante nos" and *Monarchia* (1.1. 3), where he claims that "intemptatas ab aliis ostendere veritates."

260   DANTE'S EDUCATION

added). For this appeal too, critics have generally pointed readers to an Ovidian subtext, possibly alluded to in Dante's wording:

> In nova fert animus mutatas dicere formas
> corpora; di, coeptis (nam vos mutastis et illas)
> *adspirate meis* primaque ab origine mundi
> ad mea perpetuum deducite tempora carmen.
>
> > (*Metamorphoses* 1.1–4; emphasis added)[21]

> (My soul is wrought to sing of forms transformed / to bodies new and strange! Immortal Gods / *inspire my heart*, for ye have changed yourselves / and all things you have changed! Oh lead my song / in smooth and measured strains, from olden days / when earth began to this completed times!)

Dante's rewriting of Ovid, however, appears once again layered and can be shown to engage with the didactic example of Ovidian emulation provided by Claudian's *De raptu Proserpinae*. A learned rhetorical exercise, stuffed with references to the tropes and topoi of the classical epic exordium, Claudian's poem well served the purpose of introducing pupils to the rhetorical nuts and bolts of epic poetry. A commanding metaphor that opens the first book of the *De raptu* is the poet's self-representation as the ancient *vates*, the priest who is possessed by Apollo and serves as mouthpiece of the god.[22] First, Claudian presents the subject of his poem: the vision of Pluto rushing to kidnap Proserpina on his chariot. Next, after Apollo has possessed the poet, the latter describes a ritual scene, which readers have generally interpreted as a reference to the Eleusinian mystery:[23]

> Inferni raptoris equos afflataque curru
> sidera Taenario caligantesque profundae
> Iunonis thalamos audaci promere cantu
> mens congesta iubet. Gressus removete, profani.
> Iam furor humanos nostro de pectore sensus
> expulit et solum spirant praecordia Phoebum.

---

[21] Among the proposers of this intertext, see Brownlee, "Pauline Vision," 206–07.

[22] Claudian shows some evidence of a possible influence from the Orphism that had gained renewed attention in Alexandria in the fourth to fifth centuries. The extent of such influence, however, as well as Claudian's actual stance toward this tradition, is less clear. On the possible traces of Orphism in the *De raptu Proserpinae*, see Marco Onorato, "Introduzione," in Claudio Claudiano, *De raptu Proserpinae*, ed. and trans. Marco Onorato (Naples: Loffredo, 2008), 11–107, esp. 28–40.

[23] Claudian mentions Eleusis at line 11. The Eleusinian mysteries were celebrated yearly in honor of Demeter and Proserpina at the sanctuary of Eleusis.

UNDERGROUND VOICES IN THE PROLOGUE TO *PARADISO* 261

Iam mihi cernuntur trepidis delubra moveri
sedibus et claram dispergere limina lucem
adventum testata Dei. Iam magnus ab imis
auditur fremitus terris templumque remugit
Cecropium sanctasque faces extollit Eleusis.
Angues Triptolemi strident et squamea curvis
colla levant attrita iugis lapsuque sereno
erecti roseas tendunt ad carmina cristas.
Ecce procul ternis Hecate variata figuris
exoritur laetusque simul procedit Iacchus
crinali florens hedera, quem Parthica velat
tigris et auratos in nodum colligit ungues.
Ebria Maeonius firmat vestigia thyrsus.

(De raptu Proserpinae 1.1–19)

(My full heart [mind] bids me boldly sing the horses of the ravisher from the underworld and the stars darkened by the shadow
of his infernal chariot and the gloomy chambers of the queen
of Hell. Come not night, ye uninitiate. Now has divine madness
driven all mortal thoughts from my breast, and my heart is filled
with Phoebus' inspiration; now see I the shrine reel and its foundations totter while the threshold glows with radiant light telling
that the god is at hand. And now I hear a loud din from the depths
of the earth, the temple of Cecrops re-echoes and Eleusis waves its
holy torches. The hissing snakes of Triptolemus raise their scaly
necks chafed by the curving collar, and, uptowering as they glide
smoothly along, stretch forth their rosy crests toward the chant.
See from afar rises Hecate with her three various heads and with
her comes forth Iacchus smooth of skin, his temples crowned
with ivy. There clothes him the pelt of a Parthian tiger, its gilded
claws knotted together, and the Lydian thyrsus guides his drunken
footsteps.)[24]

Several elements in these opening lines point to the relevance of Claudian's
exordium for Dante's invocation to Apollo. The terms the two poets use to request
Apollo's inspiration are nearly identical:

---

[24] The translation is quoted from Maurice Platanauer, ed. and trans., *Rape of Proserpine*, in *Claudian*,
vol. 2 (Cambridge, MA: Harvard University Press, 1922), accessed March 2024, https://www.theoi.
com/Text/ClaudianProserpine.html#1.

262   DANTE'S EDUCATION

Iam furor humanos <u>nostro de pectore</u> sensus expulit et solum *spirant* praecordia *Phoebum.* (*De raptu Proserpinae* 1.5–6; emphasis added)	O buon *Apollo* ... Entra nel <u>petto mio,</u> e *spira* tue sì come quando Marsïa traesti de la vagina de le membra sue. (*Paradiso* 1.13, 19–21; emphasis added)
(Now has divine madness driven all mortal thoughts from <u>my breast,</u> and my heart is filled with *Phoebus' inspiration.*)	(O good *Apollo* ... Enter <u>my breast</u> and breathe in me / as when you drew out Marsyas, / out from the sheathing of his limbs.)

Several elements in Dante's reworking of the Apollonian trope point to Claudian's own remaking of Ovid: Claudian's "spirare" is a closer model for Dante's "spirare" than Ovid's "adspirare"; both Claudian and Dante mention their breasts, "pectore": "petto," whereas Ovid does not; and, finally, both poets summon Apollo precisely, rather than all gods generically. Moreover, Claudian's lines "<u>humanos nostro de pectore sensus / expulit</u>" (driven all mortal / thoughts from <u>my breast</u>) convey another idea that is central to Dante's invocation. In his petition to Apollo, he compares himself to Marsyas when he is flayed alive by the god: "sì come quando Marsïa traesti / de la vagina de le membra sue" (as when you drew out Marsyas, / out from the sheathing of his limbs) (*Paradiso* 1.20–21). This simile, also drawn on Ovid, betokens the poet's purification and liberation from the limits of human nature and art to make room for the divine spirit. Claudian's use of the verb "expulit" means precisely a spiritual emptying that prepares for the poet's possession by Apollo, as Geoffrey of Vitry explains in his commentary:

> *Expulit* i.e. removit. *humana sen.* i.e. humanam scientiam, quia vix sufficit pectus ad divinam, nedum ad utramque. *de nostro pec.* quia pectus meum iam impletur spiritu et sapientia Phoebi.[25]

> (*Driven* i.e. to remove. *Human senses* i.e. human knowledge, because a breast can barely hold the divine knowledge, and cannot contain both. *From my breast.* because my breast is filled with Apollo's spirit and wisdom.)

Dante's reference to Apollo "extracting" Marsyas from his mortal body represents an articulated mythological rendering of the same concept expressed by Claudian in the line "expulit humanos sensus."

---

[25] Clarke and Giles, eds., *Commentary of Geoffrey of Vitry*, 26.

UNDERGROUND VOICES IN THE PROLOGUE TO *PARADISO*   263

More echoes of the exordium of the *De raptu Proserpinae* can be detected in Dante's reworking of the motif of the poet's divine frenzy. Right before experiencing the furor of the Apollonian possession, Claudian has an ecstatic rapture, which he describes as the experience of having his mind transfixed and filled up by the god. The same mystical experience is also described in similar terms by Dante:

Mens congesta (<u>concussa</u>) iubet.[26]

(*De raptu Proserpinae* 1.4; emphasis added)

(My *full* [<u>struck</u>] *heart* [mind or spirit] bids.)

Veramente *quant'*io del regno santo
ne la mia mente potei far tesoro. . .
tanto che l'ombra del beato regno
<u>segnata nel mio capo</u> si manifesti
(*Paradiso* 1.10–11 and 22–23;
emphasis added)

(Nevertheless, *as much* of the holy
kingdom / as I could store as
treasure *in my mind*

. . .

Enough that I may show the merest
shadow / of the blessed kingdom
<u>tamped within my mind</u>.)

In Claudian's version of the ecstatic rapture, the poet's mind appears entirely filled with divine inspiration—"congesta"—and sealed off from the outside world.[27] Geoffrey of Vitry explains: "*mens* i.e. sapientia mea; *congesta* i.e. omni tempore coadunata per favorem Apollinis, Musarum, Palladis, Bachi, Cereris, Proserpinae, et aliorum numinum" (*mind* i.e. my wisdom; *filled* i.e. entirely concentrated by the favor of Apollo, the Muses, Pallas, Bacchus, Ceres, Proserpina, and all the other gods).[28] Dante, too, presents his mind as a chamber in which the image impressed by the divine vision is locked: "quant'io . . . ne la mia mente potei far tesoro" (*as much. . . /* as I could store as treasure *in my mind*). Some manuscripts of Claudian's *De raptu Proserpinae* present the alternative reading "mens concussa" (struck) which conveys instead a sense of the violence with which the divine vision impresses itself on the mind of the poet-seer. Dante also echoes this image when

---

[26] Several manuscripts present "concussa" as an alternative reading for "congesta." The majority of modern editors have elected the variant "mens congesta," whereas J. B. Hall chose the variant "concussa." For a discussion of his critical choice, see J. B. Hall, comm. ad loc., in Claudian, *De raptu Proserpinae*, ed. J. B. Hall (Cambridge: Cambridge University Press, 1969), 190–91. Claire Gruzelier follows Hall's decision in her edition, Claudian, *De Raptu Proserpinae*, ed. and trans. Claire Gruzelier (Oxford: Clarendon Press, 1993), comm. ad loc., 84.

[27] For the interpretation of *congesta* as "full of inspiration," see Marco Onorato's comm. ad loc., 176–77. Onorato points out the defining precedent of Lucan's *Pharsalia* 5.161–97, esp. 177–81, where the prophetess Phemonoe is possessed by Apollo, and her mind is described as filling up with images of the future.

[28] Clarke and Giles, eds., *Commentary of Geoffrey of Vitry*, 26.

264   DANTE'S EDUCATION

he talks about the memory of the vision being engraved in his head: "ombra . . .
segnata nel mio capo" (the merest shadow / . . . tamped within my mind).

Claudian's "mens congesta," moreover, represents a relevant example of the
poet's apostrophe to his own soul, a motif that was developed in late antique poetry
and had one of its archetypes, once again, in Ovid's *Metamorphoses* (1.1).[29] Dante
gestures toward this tradition by calling on his own inspired mind in the opening invocation of each *cantica* of the *Commedia* (*Inferno* 2.7–9 and *Purgatorio*
1.2). In the first one, at *Inferno* 2.7–9, he addresses the Muses and a "lofty genius,"
whose actual meaning and possible sources have proved hard to track: "O muse,
o alto ingegno, or m'aiutate; / o mente che scrivesti ciò ch'io vidi, / qui si parrà
la tua nobilitate" (O Muses, O lofty genius, aid me now! / O memory, that set
down what I saw, / here shall your worth be shown). Critics mostly agree that with
"ingegno," Dante would identify his own mind and talent. Robert Hollander has
argued against this general consensus, noting instead that this would represent the
first case in the history of poetry in which a poet appealed to his own genius. Dante,
moreover, explicitly calls on his own "mente" in the following line, a choice that
would appear redundant. Hollander proposes instead to read the "lofty genius" as
belonging to God.[30] In light of the possible intertextual echo of Claudian's "mens
congesta" (or "concussa") in *Paradiso*, however, the "alto ingegno" of *Inferno* 2
may in fact refer neither to God's mind nor to the poet's, but rather to the divinely
inspired mind of the vatic tradition—the intermediary state between the human
and the divine that the poet-seer reaches when the god possesses him. The proposed interpretation would also explain why Dante addresses his own "mente" in
the following line: "mente" here would identify the capacity of the human mind to
store the memory of the vision—"che scrivesti ciò ch'io vidi" (O memory, that set
down what I saw) (*Inferno* 2.8).[31]

Another token of the vatic tradition shared by both Claudian's and Dante's epic
exordia is the request for Apollo's and Bacchus' joint inspiration. Dante maintains
that he has already received divine assistance from one of Mount Parnassus's two
peaks while completing the previous two *cantiche*. To relate the matter of *Paradiso*, however, he now needs inspiration from both of them: "Infino a qui l'un
giogo di Parnaso / assai mi fu; ma or con amendue / m'è uopo intrar ne l'aringo
rimaso" (up to this point, one peak of Mount Parnassus / has been enough, but
now I need them both / in order to confront the struggle that awaits) (*Paradiso*
1.16–18). Toward the end of his invocation, Dante also names "Cirra," the peak
dearest to Apollo: "forse di retro a me con miglior voci / si pregherà perché Cirra
risponda" (perhaps, in my wake, prayer will be shaped / with better words that

---

[29] Curtius, *European Literature*, 233–34. Besides Ovid's *Metamorphoses* 1.1, see also Lucan's
Pharsalia 1.67, and Statius' *Thebaid* 1.3, 32.

[30] See Hollander, comm. *Inferno* 2.7–9.

[31] As Conrad of Hirsau (*Dialogus*, 43) explains, the bard (*vates*) gets his name from his mental
powers.

UNDERGROUND VOICES IN THE PROLOGUE TO *PARADISO*   265

Cyrrha may respond) (*Paradiso* 1.35–36).[32] Some scholars have pointed out that the two "peaks" of Parnassus were conventional images for Bacchus and Apollo; while the former embodied the gifts of rhetorical and poetic abilities, the latter represented the gifts of divine wisdom.[33] By petitioning the two gods, Dante implies that both gifts are now needed in order to accomplish the superhuman task of retelling the vision of God. Claudian, too, evokes the presence of the two gods. He first claims to be possessed by Apollo and then witnesses a pageant of divinities; among them, Bacchus is described with particular care:

> Cecropium sanctasque faces extollit Eleusis.
> Angues Triptolemi strident et squamea curvis
> colla levant attrita iugis lapsuque sereno
> erecti roseas tendunt ad carmina cristas.
> Ecce procul ternis Hecate variata figuris
> exoritur laetusque simul procedit Iacchus
> crinali florens hedera, quem Parthica velat
> tigris et auratos in nodum colligit ungues :
> ebriaMaeoniusfirmatvestigiathyrsus.
>
> (De raptu Proserpinae 1.11–19)

> (The temple of Cecrops re-echoes and Eleusis waves its holy torches. The hissing snakes of Triptolemus raise their scaly necks chafed by the curving collar, and, uptowering as they glide smoothly along, stretch forth their rosy crests toward the chant. See from afar rises Hecate with her three various heads and with her comes forth Iacchus smooth of skin, his temples crowned with ivy. There clothes him the pelt of a Parthian tiger, its gilded claws knotted together, and the Lydian thyrsus guides his drunken footsteps.)

Claudian implicitly claims that, in addition to the Apollonian *raptus*, he is granted Dionysian inspiration. Geoffrey of Vitry confirms this interpretation in his gloss:

> Foebus dicitur interesse huic operi quia inspiravit ipsi vati . . . Bachus quia deus est potus et vini, et vino modice sumptum acuit ingenium, vel quia deus est sufficientiae sine qua multum studere non valet poeta.[34]

---

[32] For the interpretation of *Cirra* that I propose, see Chiavacci Leonardi, comm. *Paradiso*, 1.36.

[33] For compelling evidence that the two "gioghi" refer to Apollo and Baccus, see Violetta de Angelis, "'. . . e l'ultimo Lucano,'" in *In Dante e la* "bella Scola" della poesia: Autorità e sfida poetica, ed. Amilcare Iannucci (Ravenna: Longo, 1993), 95–149, esp. 136–49. More recently, Alessia Carrai has attempted a comprehensive reconsideration of this image and the different interpretations that have been offered, reasserting the coherence of Dante's appeal to Bacchus at this point in the poem. Carrai, "Bacco e i due gioghi di Parnaso: per l'interpretazione di *Par.* I, 16–18," *L'Alighieri* 54 (2019): 43–61.

[34] Clarke and Giles, eds., *Commentary of Geoffrey of Vitry*, 26.

266 DANTE'S EDUCATION

(Phoebus is said to attend to this work because he inspired the seer himself
... Bacchus because he is the god of drinking and wine, and wine if taken in
small quantity sharpens the creative mind, or because he is god of the sufficiency
without which even much effort is not good for a poet.)

Definitive evidence of Claudian's influence on Dante's self–portrait as poet *vates*
and *sacerdos*, however, is to be found in the opening of *Paradiso* 2, the second part
of the proem to the *Commedia*'s third canticle. Here Dante addresses an unidenti-
fied group of readers, whom he conjures up as sailors on a sea journey; however,
they have been sailing after Dante aboard small boats:

> O voi che siete in piccioletta barca,
> desiderosi d'ascoltar, seguiti
> dietro al mio legno che cantando varca,
>   tornate a riveder li vostri liti:
> non vi mettete in pelago, ché forse,
> perdendo me, rimarreste smarriti.
>
> (Paradiso 2.1–6)

> (O you, eager to hear more, / who have followed in your little bark
> / my ship that singing makes its way, / turn back if you would see
> your shores again. / Do not set forth upon the deep, / for, losing
> sight of me, you would be lost.)

Shockingly, the author forbids them from following him, thus pursuing the open
sea, and invites them to return to shore lest they get lost while trying to follow him. The meaning and purpose of this exhortation have puzzled modern
interpreters and eluded attempts to single out literary precedents of similarly off-
putting rhetorical addresses. Teodolinda Barolini, for instance, claims that Dante
here would be putting "a new spin on the rhetoric of persuasion."[35] As I hope
to demonstrate, however, the novelty of Dante's address should be reconsidered
in light of Claudian's nearly identical invitation in the exordium of his *De raptu
Proserpinae*. Immediately after receiving the divine illumination, Claudian exhorts
the profane readers—those uninitiated to the mystery cult—to step back: "*Gressus
removete*, profani" (*Come not nigh* [literally: step back], ye uninitiate) (*De raptu
Proserpinae* 1.4; emphasis added). Claudian's invitation has been compared to that
of the ancient priest or prophetess who, possessed by a god, turns from the altar to

---

[35] Teodolinda Barolini, *The Undivine Comedy: Detheologizing Dante* (Princeton, NJ: Princeton
University Press, 1992), 55.

UNDERGROUND VOICES IN THE PROLOGUE TO *PARADISO*   267

face the acolytes and invites them to stay away from the priest.[36] A pivotal literary model behind Claudian's rhetorical formula here is in Virgil's *Aeneid*, when the Cumaean Sibyl warns of Apollo's arrival: "procul, o procul este, profane" (away, o souls profane! Stand far away!) (*Aeneid* 6.258). Dante's use of the imperative "tornate" (turn back) in *Paradiso* 2.4, however, resembles Claudian's injunction, "gressus removete" (step back) to a remarkable degree. Once again, while drawing on a traditional epic theme, Dante is engaging with Claudian's intermediate emulation of the same trope. It could be argued, therefore, that Dante's obscure address to the reader in *Paradiso* 2 actually repurposed a long-established rhetorical formula and cliché that had been made popular by medieval Latin instruction. Claudian's remaking of this formula in the fictional context of a religious mystery, moreover, helps shed some light on the meaning of Dante's off-putting address. After dismissing those who are trying to follow him on inadequately "small boats," the poet turns toward a different group of readers, who are instead ready for the journey: "Voialtri pochi che drizzaste il collo / per tempo al pan de li angeli, del quale / vivesi qui ma non sen vien satollo" (You other few who craned your necks in time / to reach for angels' bread, which gives us life on earth, / yet never leaves us satisfied) (*Paradiso* 2.10–12). The specific meaning of this "bread of angels" remains elusive.[37] Clearly, however, this eucharistic image makes a distinction within Dante's audience: the readers who have been feeding on this divine nourishment are elected to contemplate God's mystery; all others should instead withdraw. Dante's use of the "gressus removete" formula, therefore, may evoke the same atmosphere of religious mystery that Claudian had already readapted from Virgil's *Aeneid*. Both Claudian's and Dante's audiences are divided between initiates and uninitiates.

The two proems also share a similar reference to the sacred fires. In the *De raptu Proserpinae*, Claudian has a vision of a long procession "of sacred torches" advancing toward Hera's temple in Eleusis, where every year ritual mysteries were celebrated in memory of Proserpina's kidnapping: "*sanctasque faces extollit*

---

[36] In her commentary, Claire Gruzelier points out that although "the phrase is properly used by a priest celebrating sacred rites," Claudian repurposes it to claim that "he is an imaginative poet with a theme that at least purports to be solemn." Gruzelier, comm. ad loc., 84.

[37] Dante had already used the same image in *Convivio* 1.1.7: "Oh beati quelli pochi che seggiono a quella mensa dove lo pane delli angeli si manuca." Some differences, however, set these two instances apart. For useful comparative readings of Dante's evolving use of this expression from *Convivio* to *Paradiso*, see Paolo Pecoraro, "Il Canto II del *Paradiso*," in *Lectura Dantis Scaligera: Paradiso* (Florence: Le Monnier, 1967). In the Bible, Psalms 77.25, the "panis angelorum" is the manna that fed the Israelites in the desert and figuratively signifies the divine logos and source of all wisdom. See Inglese, comm. ad loc., *Paradiso*, 48. To some readers, the angelic bread would represent the discipline of theological study, thereby making *Paradiso* a reading exclusively for theologians. See, for instance, Vincenzo Placella, "Il pubblico del *Convivio* e quello del *Paradiso*," in *Miscellanea di studi in onore di Raffaele Sirri*, ed. M. Palumbo and V. Placella (Naples: Federico e Ardia, 1995), 365–73, esp. 369. Others, on the contrary, have pointed to the eucharistic allusion and thereby universal scope implied by this biblical imagery. See, for instance, Ambrogio Camozzi Pistoja, "Testo come eucarestia: Linguaggio parabolico nel Convivio di Dante," *Studi danteschi* 84 (2019): 57–100, and Christian Moevs, "*Paradiso* II: Gateway to Paradise," *Le tre corone* 3 (2016): 57–73.

268   DANTE'S EDUCATION

Eleusis" (and Eleusis waves its *holy torches*) (*De raptu Proserpinae* 1.11; emphasis added). Given its particular religious connotation, this imagery provides a new perspective on the rather obscure *terzina* that closes Dante's invocation to Apollo in *Paradiso* 1: "Poca *favilla gran fiamma seconda*: / forse di retro a me con miglior voci / si pregherà perché Cirra risponda" (*Great fire leaps from the smallest spark. /* Perhaps, in my wake, prayer will be shaped / with better words that Cyrrha may respond) (*Paradiso* 1.34–36; emphasis added). Contradictory to some, and obscure to most, the meaning of this tercet has stirred considerable critical debate.[38] It is nonetheless worth noting that, in light of Claudian's readaptation of the vatic tradition, Dante's visualization of a small spark followed by a great fire acquires ritualistic significance. Cesare Goffis already suggested that through this particular imagery, Dante may wish to fashion his readers as participating in a religious procession "in his wake": as if in a nocturnal parade, the poet-priest leads the column holding a torch, and his acolytes, also holding up torches, follow after him; together they create a larger and brighter fire.[39] If the parallel between Dante's and Claudian's texts is more distant in this case, it nonetheless provides a model against which this cryptic imagery can be understood: by drawing on Claudian's intertext in the prologue to *Paradiso*, Dante appropriates the motif of the *poeta vates* to present his new role of divinely inspired poet.

Claudian in *Paradiso*: The Boat of the Argonauts

The exordium of Claudian's *De raptu Proserpinae* provides a striking precedent for the seafaring metaphor that Dante repurposes in the second part of his prologue to *Paradiso*:

O voi che siete in piccioletta barca,	Inventa secuit primus qui nave profundum,
desiderosi d'ascoltar, seguiti	et rudibus remis sollicitavit aquas,
dietro al mio legno che cantando varca,	qui dubiis ausus committere flatibus alnum,
	quas natura negat, praebuit arte vias.
tornate a riveder li vostri liti:	Tranquillis primum trepidus se credidit undis,
non vi mettete in pelago, ché forse,	
perdendo me, rimarreste smarriti.	litora securo tramite summa legens:
L'acqua ch'io prendo già mai non si corse;	mox longos temptare sinus et linquere terras
Minerva spira, e conducemi Appollo,	
e nove Muse mi dimostran l'Orse.	

[38] For an extensive study of this tercet, see Filippo Gianferrari, "'Poca favilla, gran fiamma seconda' (*Par.* I 34): Un proverbio d'autorità," *Le tre corone* (2020): 133–58.

[39] Cesare F. Goffis, "Il canto I del *Paradiso*," in *Lectura Dantis Scaligera* (Florence: Le Monnier, 1968), 29.

Voialtri pochi che drizzaste il collo
per tempo al pan de li angeli, del
                       quale
vivesi qui ma non sen vien satollo,
  metter potete ben per l'alto sale
vostro navigio, servando mio solco
dinanzi a l'acqua che ritorna equale.
  Que' glorïosi che passaro al Colco
non s'ammiraron come voi farete,
quando Iasón vider fatto bifolco.
               (*Paradiso* 2.1–16)

(O you, eager to hear more, / who
have followed in your little bark / my
ship that singing makes its way, /
turn back if you would see your
shores again. / Do not set forth upon
the deep, / for, losing sight of me, you
would be lost. / The seas I sail were
never sailed before. / Minerva fills
my sails, Apollo is my guide, / nine
Muses point me toward the Bears. /
You other few who craned your necks
in time / to reach for angels' bread,
which gives us life on earth, / yet
never leaves us satisfied, / you may
indeed set out, your ship afloat /
upon the salty deep, keeping to the
furrow / I have made, before the sea
goes smooth again. / Those famous
men who made their way to Colchis,
/ when they saw Jason had become a
plowman, / were not as stunned as
you shall be.)

et leni coepit pandere vela Noto.
Ast ubi paulatim praeceps audacia crevit
cordaque languentem dedidicere metum,
iam vagus irrumpit pelagus caelumque
                     secutus
Aegaeas hiemes Ioniumque domat.

Book 1
Inferni raptoris equos afflataque curru
sidera Taenario caligantesque profundae
Iunonis thalamos audaci promere cantu
mens congesta iubet. Gressus removete,
                     profani.
(*De raptu Proserpinae* 1, *preface* 1–12;
                     1.1–4)

(He who first made a ship and clave
therewith the deep, troubling the waters
with roughly hewn oars, who first dared
trust his alder-bark to the uncertain winds
and who by his skill devised a way
forbidden to nature, fearfully at the first
essayed smooth seas, hugging the shore in
an unadventurous course. But soon he
began to attempt the crossing of the broad
bays, to leave the land and spread his
canvas to the gentle south wind; and, as
little by little his growing courage led him
on, and as his heart forgot numbing fear,
sailing now at large, he burst upon the open
sea and, with the signs of heaven to guide
him, passed triumphant through the storms
of the Aegean and the Ionian main.)

Book 1
(My full heart bids me boldly sing the
horses of the ravisher from the underworld
and the stars darkened by the shadow of his
infernal chariot and the gloomy chambers
of the queen of Hell. Come not nigh, ye
uninitiate.)

270 DANTE'S EDUCATION

The two prologues rework the long-established epic motif of comparing poetic endeavor to seafaring and poetic novelty to the journey of the Argonauts. Claudian draws on this theme at the outset of his poem (*De raptu Proserpinae* 1.1), whereas Dante introduces it only in the second half of his proem (*Paradiso* 2.16–18).[40] Claudian deploys this metaphor to represent his own poetic career: after testing his skills in less demanding works, the poet is now daring to tackle a more challenging epic subject matter.[41] In his *Praefatio*, the journey of the Argonauts becomes a metaphor for the power of art to conquer the limits imposed by our human nature: "quas natura negat, praebuit arte vias" (who by his skill devised a way forbidden to nature) (*De raptu Proserpinae, preface* 1.4). Dante makes a similar claim in *Paradiso* 1, where he avers that the subject matter of the third canticle transcends our intellectual powers:

> . . . cose che ridire
> né sa né può chi di là sù discende;
> perché appressando sé al suo disire,
> nostro intelletto si profonda tanto,
> che dietro la memoria non può ire.
>
> *(Paradiso* 1.5–9)

> (. . . he who comes down from there / can neither know nor tell
> what he has seen, / for, drawing near to its desire, / so deeply is
> our intellect immersed / that memory cannot follow after it.)

Notwithstanding his human limitations, Dante will in fact relate the divine vision by means of his poetic song:

Veramente quant'io del regno santo
ne la mia mente potei far tesoro,
sarà ora materia del mio canto.

> *(Paradiso* 1.10–12; emphasis added)

(Nevertheless, as much of the holy kingdom / as I could store as treasure in my mind / *shall now become the subject of my song.*)

audaci promere (prodere) *cantu*
(*De raptu Proserpinae* 1, *preface*
1.3; emphasis added)

(My full heart bids me *boldly sing*)

---

[40] On Claudian's allusion to Jason's journey in these lines, see Gruzelier, comm. ad loc., 81, and Onorato, comm. ad loc., 173.

[41] As Geoffrey's commentary explains, this complex metaphor represents the progress of the poet's career: "Ideo enim praemittit prologum ut ingenium suum praeacuat ut ad quodlibet opus postea facilius audeat provenire, et hoc per exemplum sumptum a Iasone probat apertissime; quemadmodum enim Iason primus nauta, cum maximo timore laborem navigantibus suscepit, viam suam secus littora per aquam minimam primo temptans ut pstea melius et audacius magnum mare auderet ascendere, similiter actor iste suum ingenium cum magna solicitudine in hac materia parva praeacuit ut postea securus ad fortia gesta Florentini describenda conscendat." Clarke and Giles, eds., *Commentary of Geoffrey of Vitry*, 24. The same interpretation is also endorsed by some modern commentators, such as Gruzelier, comm. ad loc., 81.

UNDERGROUND VOICES IN THE PROLOGUE TO *PARADISO*   271

The two texts thus deploy similar terms in order to present the supernatural and superhuman power of poetry. They also exploit the same Argonautic motif of sailing waters never sailed before in order to state both the absolute novelty of their subject matter and the unparalleled poetic challenge they are about to undertake:[42]

L'acqua ch'io prendo *già mai non si corse*;
(*Paradiso* 2.7; emphasis added)

(The *seas* I sail were *never sailed before*.)

Inventa secuit *primus* qui nave
profundum,
et rudibus remis *sollicitavit aquas*
(*De raptu Proserpinae* 1, *preface*
1.1–2; emphasis added)

(He who *first* made a ship and clave
therewith the deep, *troubling the
waters* with roughly hewn oars)

Several verbal and conceptual echoes, moreover, confirm the two poems' similar treatment of the Argonautic motif, as clearly visible:

O voi che siete in *piccioletta barca*,
desiderosi d'ascoltar, <u>seguiti</u>
dietro al mio legno che <u>cantando</u> varca,
(*Paradiso* 1.1–3; emphasis added)

(O you, eager to hear more, / who have
<u>followed</u> in your *little bark* / my ship that
<u>singing</u> makes its way)
metter potete ben per l'<u>*alto*</u> sale
vostro navigio, servando mio <u>*solco*</u>
(*Paradiso* 1.13–14; emphasis added)

(you may indeed set out, your ship afloat /
upon the salty <u>*deep*</u>, keeping to the <u>*furrow*</u>
/ I have made)

et *rudibus remis* sollicitavit aquas
. . .
iam vagus irrumpit pelagus
caelumque <u>secutus</u>
(*De raptu Proserpinae* 1, *preface*
1.2–11; emphasis added)

. . .
audaci promere <u>cantu</u>
(1.3; emphasis added)

(troubling the waters *with roughly
hewn oars*
. . .
now at large, he burst upon the
open sea and, with the signs of
<u>heaven to guide him</u> [literally
<u>"having followed the sky"</u>]

. . .

---

[42] Geoffrey explains that Claudian means to communicate the sense of the newness of his enterprise through the use of the verb "praebuit": "vel *praebuit* i.e. prae aliis habuit, quia nullus ante ipsum habuit artificium navigandi; vel *praebuit* i.e. prior aliis eundo contulit et ostendit." Clarke and Giles, eds., *Commentary of Geoffrey of Vitry*, 25. For a recent and more comprehensive reconsideration of Dante's reuse of the Argonautic motif in *Paradiso*, see Vitale, "Poca favilla gran fiamma seconda."

272 DANTE'S EDUCATION

> My full heart bids me boldly <u>sing</u>)
> Inventa <u>*secuit*</u> primus qui nave
> <u>*profundum*</u>
> (*preface* 1; emphasis added)
>
> (He who first made a ship and <u>*clave*</u>
> therewith <u>*the deep*</u>)

Both poets depict their boats through the use of metonymy ("remis": "legno") as courageously cutting through the high sea, despite their limited human means, and while powered by poetry. The number of verbal similarities between the two versions is noteworthy. One telling difference, however, separates them: whereas Claudian represents the progression of his boat from "litora" to "pelagus"—from shore to the open sea—Dante invites the readers who are not ready to follow him offshore to undertake the opposite journey from "pelago" to "lidi":

> tornate a riveder li *vostri liti*:
> non vi mettete in <u>pelago</u>, ché forse,
> perdendo me, rimarreste smarriti.
>   (*Paradiso* 2.4–6; emphasis added)
>
> (turn back if you would see *your shores*
> again. / Do not set forth upon the <u>deep</u> /
> for, losing sight of me, you would be lost.)

> *litora securo* tramite summa legens
>   . . .
> iam vagus irrumpit <u>pelago</u>
> caelumque secutus
> (*De raptu Proserpinae* 1, *preface* 1.6,
> 11; emphasis added)
>
> (hugging the *shore* in an
> unadventurous course
> sailing now at large, he burst upon
> the <u>open sea</u> and, with the signs of
> heaven to guide him)

The exordia of *Purgatorio* and *Inferno* also present reworkings of this metaphor that can be profitably compared with Claudian's use of the same trope:

> Per correr miglior acque <u>alza le vele</u>
> omai la navicella del mio ingegno,
> che *lascia* dietro a sé *mar* sì crudele;
>   (*Purgatorio* 1.1–3; emphasis added)
>
> (To run its course through smoother
> water / the small bark of my wit now
> <u>hoists its sail</u>, / *leaving* that cruel *sea*
> behind.)

> mox longos temptare sinus et
> *linquere terras*
> et leni coepit <u>pandere vela</u> Noto.
> (*De raptu Proserpinae* 1, *preface* 1.8;
> emphasis added)
>
> (But soon he began to attempt the
> crossing of the broad bays, to *leave*
> *the land* and <u>spread his canvas</u> to
> the gentle south wind.)

Allor fu *la paura un poco queta,*
che nel lago del <u>cor</u> m'era durata
      (*Inferno* 1.19–20; emphasis added)

(Then *the fear* that had endured / in the
lake of my <u>heart</u>, all the night / I spent in
such distress, *was calmed*)
E come quei che con lena affannata,

uscito fuor del *pelago a la riva,*

      (*Inferno* 1.23; emphasis added)

(And as one who, with laboring breath, /
has escaped *from the deep to the shore*)

Ast ubi *paulatim* praeceps *audacia crevi*
<u>cordaque</u> *languentem dedidicere metum*
      (9–10; emphasis added)

(and, as *little by little* his *growing courage* led him on, and as his <u>heart</u> *forgot numbing fear*)
<u>litora securo</u> tramite summa legens
iam vagus <u>*irrumpit pelagus*</u>
caelumque secutus

      (6–11; emphasis added)
(hugging *the shore* in an unadventurous course

      . . .

sailing now at large, he
<u>*burst upon the open sea*</u> and, with
the signs of heaven to guide him)

Inferno 1, however, inverts the seafaring metaphor, as this features in the *De raptu Proserpinae*: instead of growing bolder and pushing the boat out to sea, like Claudian, Dante presents himself as a shipwrecked man attempting to get back to shore. The profound Christian significance of this inversion becomes clearer when compared to Claudian's precedent: Dante cannot begin his navigation into the deep water of the otherworld boastfully by relying exclusively on his own poetic art and intellectual means. As readers of the poem learn soon after, he needs, instead, a divinely ordained guide.[43] It is on this providential premise, one may suggest, that Dante claims to have succeeded in the epic challenge in which both Statius and Claudian had failed.

This seafaring imagery belongs to a long-established tradition that is unique neither to Claudian nor to Dante and represents instead a trope of poetic emulation.[44] As most commentaries on *Paradiso* 1 and 2 observe, moreover, Ovid is the obvious target of Dante's emulation in these cantos. Guglielmo Bellaira, for instance, notes that the lines of *Paradiso* 2.16–17, "a Colco / non s'ammiraron" (in Colchis, were not as stunned), where Dante refers to Jason's men, contain a precise verbal echo

---

[43] The biblical and spiritual undertone of this shipwreck image has been noted by Singleton, who maintains that the *Commedia* begins with a shipwreck. See Charles Singleton, "In Exitu Israel de Aegypto," *78th Annual Report of the Dante Society of America* (1960): 1–24.

[44] On the literary sources of Claudian's adaptation of the Argonautic motif, see Francesca Minissale, "Il *poeta e la nave* (Claud. rapt. Pros. I, 1–14)," *Helikon* 15–16 (1975–76): 496–99.

274   DANTE'S EDUCATION

of Ovid's *Metamorphoses*: "mirantur Colchi" (*Metamorphoses* 7.120).[45] The direct echo of Ovid, however, appears only in the last *terzina* of Dante's second prologue, in *Paradiso* 2. As I have shown, the first fifteen lines instead more closely echo Claudian's adaptation of the theme of the Argonauts' journey. The remarkable number of intertextual echoes of Claudian's preface in combination with similar remakes of the vatic motif suggest that Dante's engagement with the *De raptu Proserpinae* in the prologue to *Paradiso* is thorough and deliberate. Dante may indeed be reflecting on rhetorical formulas and themes that the reception of Claudian in medieval education had successfully linked to the emulation of Roman epic poetry. While engaging with the great Latin epicists such as Ovid and Virgil, therefore, Dante also addresses their imitation and emulation by Claudian and Statius.

Conclusion

The intricate web of textual echoes and imagery from Statius' *Achilleid* and Claudian's *De raptu Proserpinae* that can be detected in Dante's two-part prologue to *Paradiso* shows the stylistic and rhetorical influence that these two school readings exerted on Dante. They distilled the key features of the epic genre and set the standards for the emulation of the *auctores maiores* in medieval schools. Both poems, moreover, establish a distinctively competitive relationship with their ancient models. The emulative stance toward the *auctores*, therefore, must have been a central lesson about the epic genre in medieval education—one that did not fail to impress Dante. What this evidence suggests is that Dante's distinctive emulative stance toward his poetic models was as much a legacy of his Latin education as it was a peculiar feature of his vernacular poetics. He presents the paradisiacal vision as the utterly unprecedented subject matter that will make him worthy of Apollo's laurel and of rivaling the enterprise of the Argonauts, as confirmed in *Paradiso* 33.94–96: "Un punto solo m'è maggior letargo / che venticinque secoli a la 'mpresa / che fé Nettuno ammirar l'ombra d'Argo" (My memory of that moment is more lost / than five and twenty centuries make dim the enterprise / when, in wonder, Neptune at the Argo's shadow stared). In *Paradiso* 1–2, Dante not only repurposes Claudian's version of the Argonaut journey, but also links the topos of the *novitas* to that of the divine *visio*, identifying himself with the *poeta vates*. The *De raptu Proserpinae*, therefore, presented an especially suitable precedent of Dante's epic emulation.

Suggestively, Dante seems already to hint at the importance of Claudian's model at *Inferno* 25, the locus of the poem where he most openly challenges the *auctores*: "Taccia Lucano omai là dov'e' tocca.... Taccia di Cadmo e d'Aretusa Ovidio" (Let Lucan now fall silent where he tells.... Let Ovid not speak of Cadmus or Arethusa)

---

[45] Guglielmo Bellaira, "Un'eco Claudianea in Dante?," *L'Alighieri* 1 (1974): 50–52, at 52.

(94, 97). The exhortation "taccia" addressed to the ancient *auctores* features a precise calque of Claudian's *In Rufinum* (1.283): "Taceat superata vetustas" (Be silent, superseded antiquity), which circulated in florilegia.[46]

In the *Achilleid*, Statius introduces his epic emulation as an attempt to fulfill the Homeric lineage, while also deploying irony and eros to destabilize and deconstruct the standards set by Virgil in the *Aeneid*. In the *De raptu Proserpinae*, Claudian goes a step further and connects his brand of emulation to the absolute novelty of the poem's subject matter: love victorious in the underworld—something as groundbreaking as the voyage of the Argonauts. In *Paradiso*, Dante absorbs both Statius' and Claudian's models of emulation to set a new didactic standard of vernacular epic poetry that embraces all the lofty themes and subjects that no other Italian poem had yet addressed in the vernacular.

---

[46] The parallel has already been noted by Curtius, *European Literature*, 165.

Epilogue

"The School That You Have Followed"

> "Non so se 'ntendi: io dico di Beatrice;
> tu la vedrai di sopra, in su la vetta
> di questo monte, ridere e felice."
>
> *(Purgatorio* 6.46–48)

> ("I don't know if you understand: I speak of Beatrice. / You shall
> see her above, upon the summit / of this mountain, smiling and
> in bliss.")

Among Virgil's several missteps as Dante's guide, this disclosure is perhaps one of the most deceiving and comic. It creates misguided expectations in both his protégé and the reader. If, in fact, Beatrice is all joy and smiles while longing to reunite with her "friend" (*Inferno* 2.61), she is far from showing her happiness on their first encounter in Eden.

When she makes her first appearance and is yet to fully reveal herself, Dante turns toward Virgil in excitement, only to find that his guide has left for good. As the protagonist is still bemoaning the loss of this "gentlest father" and "ancient mother" (*Purgatorio* 30.50 and 52), he turns to face the incarnation of a rather stern and upset "mother" (79). Beatrice's first words to the pilgrim betray angry feelings that seem rather unbecoming for the kind of reunion Virgil had prepared us for:

> "Dante, perché Virgilio se ne vada,
> non pianger anco, non piangere ancora;
> ché pianger ti conven per altra spada."
>
> *(Purgatorio* 30.55–57)

> ("Dante, because Virgil has departed, / do not weep, do not weep
> yet— / there is another sword to make you weep.")

She then proceeds to scold him for having betrayed her memory. After her demise, she claims, he turned away from her and gave himself to "others," thus squandering the divine gifts he had received in his "vita nova":

Dante's Education. Filippo Gianferrari, Oxford University Press. © Filippo Gianferrari (2024).
DOI: 10.1093/oso/9780198881766.003.0009

> "ma per larghezza di grazie divine,
>
> . . .
>
> questi fu tal ne la sua vita nova
> virtüalmente, ch'ogne abito destro
> fatto averebbe in lui mirabil prova.
>
> Ma tanto più maligno e più silvestro
> si fa 'l terren col mal seme e non cólto,
> quant' elli ha più di buon vigor terrestro.
>
> Alcun tempo il sostenni col mio volto:
> mostrando li occhi giovanetti a lui,
> meco il menava in dritta parte vòlto.
>
> Sì tosto come in su la soglia fui
> di mia seconda etade e mutai vita,
> questi si tolse a me, e diessi altrui.
>
> Quando di carne a spirto era salita,
> e bellezza e virtù cresciuta m'era,
> fu' io a lui men cara e men gradita;
>
> e volse i passi suoi per via non vera,
> imagini di ben seguendo false,
> che nulla promession rendono intera.
>
> Né l'impetrare ispirazion mi valse,
> con le quali e in sogno e altrimenti
> lo rivocai: sì poco a lui ne calse!"
>
> (Purgatorio 30.112–35)

("but by grace, abundant and divine . . . / this man in his new life potentially was such / that each good disposition in him / would have come to marvelous conclusion, / but the richer and more vigorous the soil, / when planted ill and left to go to seed, / the wilder and more noxious it becomes. / For a time I let my countenance sustain him. / Guiding him with my youthful eyes, / I drew him with me in the right direction. / Once I had reached the threshold of my second age, / when I changed lives, he took himself from me / and gave himself to others. / When I had risen to spirit from my flesh, / as beauty and virtue in me became more rich, / to him I was less dear and less than pleasing. / He set his steps upon an untrue way, / pursuing those false images of good / that bring no promise to fulfillment— / useless the inspiration I sought and won for him, / as both with dreams and other means / I called him back, so little did he heed them.")

278   DANTE'S EDUCATION

In the following canto, Dante acknowledges the truth in Beatrice's accusations and confesses to have fallen for the false pleasure of earthly things, which pulled him down and away from her (*Purgatorio* 31.34–36). True repentance is followed by forgiveness, and Dante washes away the memory of his past sins in the water of the river Lethe. Before providing the key to interpreting a vision of future political events that will affect the whole of Christendom, however, Beatrice lashes out once more at Dante for having followed a misleading "school":

> "Perché conoschi," disse, "quella *scuola*
> c'hai seguitata, e veggi sua dottrina
> come può seguitar la mia parola;
>   e veggi vostra via da la divina
> distar cotanto, quanto si discorda
> da terra il ciel che più alto festina."
>
> <div align="right">(<i>Purgatorio</i> 33.85–90; emphasis added)</div>

> ("So that you may come to understand," she said, / "the *school* that you have followed / and see if what it teaches follows well my words, / and see that your way is as far from God's / as that highest heaven, which spins the fastest, / is distant from the earth.")

Beatrice's accusations and Dante's confession are both generic at best. Although readers have attempted to pin down the specific biographical and intellectual targets of her criticism, the fact remains that the author elected to be vague on this point. Thus, which false "school" led him near eternal damnation is a question that will continue to haunt readers.[1]

What makes this autobiographical juncture of the poem appear rather generic and universal is its bookishness. Dante here rewrites the topoi of conversion and *retractatio* as they are exemplified by two key texts for the medieval autobiographical genre, Augustine's *Confessiones* and Boethius' *Consolatio*—two authorities Dante had already singled out in *Convivio* (1.2.1) to justify the act of writing about oneself. The same subtexts are at work within the "intertextual grid of the episode"

---

[1] The general interpretation (already found in ancient commentators, such as the Ottimo) is that these cantos are Dante's retraction of his excessive reliance on philosophical inquiry and arguments rather than on theology, a phase of the poet's career that may or may not have coincided with his unfinished *Convivio*. As Paolo Falzone points out, Beatrice's words reject Avicenna's and Albertus Magnus's conception of the divine and prophetic nature inherent in the human soul. Whereas Dante embraced this idea in the *Convivio*, he sets it aside in the *Commedia*. See Falzone, *Desiderio della scienza e desiderio di Dio nel "Convivio"* (Bologna: Società Editrice il Mulino), 53–59. John A. Scott contests this commonly accepted interpretation and argues that Dante's "school" would instead represent the political Guelfism he endorsed in the years corresponding to the fictional time of the *Commedia*. See John A. Scott, "Beatrice's Reproaches in Eden: Which 'School' Had Dante Followed?," *Dante Studies* 109 (1991): 1–23.

recounted in *Purgatorio* 30, as here, for the sole time in the poem, the author names himself "out of necessity" (62–63).[2]

The dramatic buildup to the protagonist's reunion with Beatrice, moreover, obliquely questions the ethical issue of weeping over elegiac poetry. When mourning Virgil's loss, the author ventriloquizes Dido's words in *Aeneid* 4.23 (*Purgatorio* 30.28). This is followed by Beatrice's rebuke of Dante through the threefold repetition of the verb "piangere" (56–57). As Simone Marchesi notes, here Dante may be targeting Augustine's *Confessiones*, in which the saint condemns his younger self for crying in sorrow over Dido's tragic destiny, at the time when he read the *Aeneid* in school:

> quid enim *miserius misero* non *miserante* se ipsum et *flente* Didonis mortem, quae fiebat amando Aenean, non *flente* autem mortem suam, quae fiebat non amando te, deus, lumen cordis mei et panis oris intus animae meae et virtus maritans mentem meam et sinum cogitationis meae? . . . et haec non *flebam*, et *flebam* Didonem extinctam ferroque extrema secutam, sequens ipse extrema condita tua relicto te et terra iens in terram. et si prohiberer ea legere, dolerem, quia non legerem quod dolerem.[3]
>
> (*Confessiones* 1.13.21; emphasis added)

> (*What is more pitiable* than a wretch without pity for himself who *weeps* over the death of Dido dying for love of Aeneas, but not *weeping* over himself dying for his lack of love for you, my God, light of my heart, bread of inner mouth of my soul, the power which begets life in my mind and in the innermost recesses of my thinking. . . . Over this I *wept* not a tear, I *wept* over Dido who "died in pursuing her ultimate end with a sword" [*Aeneid* 6.456]. I abandoned you to pursue the lowest things of your creation. I was dust going to dust. Had I been forbidden to read this story, I would have been sad that I could not read what made me sad.)

Thus, by evoking Augustine's subtext, Dante also invokes the role that elegiac poetry played in education. If on the one hand Beatrice echoes Augustine's stern condemnation, Marchesi argues, on the other hand Dante mitigates it in the same canto by renegotiating the meaning of Virgil's poem in a Christian context.[4]

---

[2] On Dante's engagement with these authorities here, see Simone Marchesi, *Dante and Augustine: Linguistics, Poetics, Hermeneutics* (Toronto: University of Toronto Press, 2011), 178. As commentators have noted, other subtexts are also at play in these cantos. For an extensive discussion of this allusive exchange with a particular emphasis on the key role of the Song of Songs, see Lino Pertile, *La puttana e il gigante: dal "Cantico dei cantici" al Paradiso terrestre di Dante* (Ravenna: Longo, 1998).

[3] The Latin original is quoted from *The Latin Library*, accessed February 2022, https://www.thelatinlibrary.com/; the English translation is from Augustine, *Confessions*, trans. H. Chadwick (Oxford: Oxford University Press, 1991). For a discussion of this passage in relation to *Purgatorio*, see Marchesi, *Dante and Augustine*, 174–85.

[4] Marchesi notes that this option was already contemplated by Augustine in his *De doctrina christiana*, "a text not fully hostile to a recuperation of classical culture" (*Dante and Augustine*, 183).

280 DANTE'S EDUCATION

The critical revision of one's education and the condemnation of elegiac poetry are also central themes of the other key subtext of *Purgatorio* 30, Boethius' *Consolatio*. Beatrice's first appearance clearly reenacts that of Lady Philosophy at the beginning of the *Consolatio*, when she kicks the elegiac muses, who are gathered in tears around the author's bed, out of the room:

> Haud aliter tristitiae nebulis dissolutis hausi caelum et ad cognoscendam medicantis faciem mentem recepi. Itaque ubi in eam deduxi oculos intuitumque defixi, respicio nutricem meam, cuius ab adulescentia laribus obversatus fueram, Philosophiam.[5]
>
> (*Consolatio* 1.pr.3.1–2)

> (Just so the clouds of misery were dispelled, and I drank in the clear light, recovering enough to recognize my healer's face. So, when I looked on her clearly and steadily, I saw the nurse who brought me up, whose house I had from my youth frequented, the lady Philosophy.)

Like Beatrice, Lady Philosophy comes to Boethius in a time of sorrow and tears. She, too, had first met him in his youth and nourished him with wisdom. She had great expectations for her disciple but had to support him along the way and finally, after his betrayal, had to return and show herself again.[6] Under Philosophy's care, Boethius is invited to recover the wisdom he had first received, to put down his lamentations and embrace instead his sorrowful fate. According to both Augustine and Boethius, therefore, a reexamination of one's education is instrumental to the process of conversion. For Augustine, this review coincides with a rejection *tout court* of the literary initiation he had received as part of his grammatical and rhetorical instruction; for Boethius too, it means deposing the elegiac pen in favor of a philosophical brand of poetry that coincides with a recovery of his philosophical training to regain virtue.

While engaging with these authoritative sources to create the final scene of his purgatorial education, Dante establishes his own original formula of *retractatio* and conversion by throwing another school text into the mix. Henry of Settimello had already taken Boethius' *Consolatio* as the model for representing his encounter with Lady Fortune, at the beginning of the second book of his *Elegia*. Henry's words before Fortune sound remarkably similar to Beatrice's first utterances in *Purgatorio* 30:

---

[5] The Latin text is quoted from *The Latin Library*, accessed February 2022, https://www.thelatinlibrary.com/; the English translation is by S. J. Tester, *The Consolation of Philosophy* (Cambridge, MA: Loeb, 1973).

[6] Several other close parallels, both thematic and verbal, link the two texts. For a close comparative analysis of the two, see Luca Lombardo, *Boezio in Dante: La* Consolatio Philosophiae *nello scrittoio del poeta* (Venice: Edizioni Ca' Foscari, 2013), 363–86.

Plange, miser, palmis, <u>Henrice</u>
            miserrime, <u>plange</u>,
et caput et dura pectora *<u>plange</u>, miser*
 	
     (*Elegia* 2.1–2; emphasis added)
 	
(*<u>Strike</u>, unhappy, <u>strike</u>,* with your
hand, oh <u>Henry</u> most *miserable,*
<u>strike</u>, oh *unhappy* one, your
hardened chest and head.)
	"<u>Dante</u>, perché Virgilio se ne vada,
	    non *pianger* anco, non *piangere*
	           ancora;
	ché *pianger* ti conven per altra spada."
	    (*Purgatorio* 30.55–57; emphasis
	           added)
	
	("<u>Dante</u>, because Virgil has departed,
	   / do not *<u>weep</u>,* do not *<u>weep</u>* yet— /
	there is another sword to make you
	          <u>weep</u>.")

Henry seems also to echo Augustine's *Confessiones* by playing on the threefold repetition of "miser." He certainly rewrites Boethius' subtext. Henry's reworking, however, is altogether original, and its influence on Dante is apparent. The three-fold repetition of the verbs "plangere" and "piangere" in both texts is notable. Although Henry's "plangere" in this particular context means "to strike," the verb can also be used to signify "to lament aloud."[7] In a fourteenth-century volgarizza-mento of Henry's *Elegia*, for instance, "plangere" is rendered into the Florentine vernacular as "piagnere."[8] Even more relevant is the fact that Henry, like Dante, repeats this verb three times in conjunction with his self-naming in the poem. This significant feature is unique to the two texts and is found in neither Augustine's nor Boethius' precedents.

In the third book of the *Elegia*, moreover, Lady Wisdom arrives and questions Henry in a way that is also echoed in Beatrice's words in *Purgatorio*. Since Henry's memory has not been erased by the water of the river Lethe, Wisdom compels him to remember what he had learned in school and particularly during his time in Bologna:

> *Que lethea tuus potavit pocula sensus?*
> *Quo tua dormitat mens peregrina loco?*
> *Certe cecus es et tua mens exorbitant: illud*
> *tantillum nescis, quod <u>scola</u> docta dedit.*
>   (*Elegia* 3.15–18; emphasis added)

> (*What drinks of forgetfulness has your reason drunk?* / Where does your wondering mind sleep? / Certainly, you must be blind, and your mind is out of itself: / you don't even know what little the learned <u>school gave you</u>.)

---

[7] See the entry "plango" in Charlton T. Lewis and Charles Short, eds., *A Latin Dictionary* (Oxford: Clarendon Press, 1879), Perseus Digital Library, Tufts University, accessed February 2022, http://www.perseus.tufts.edu/.

[8] Salvatore Battaglia, *Il Boezio e l'Arrighetto* (Turin: UTET, 1929), 225.

282 DANTE'S EDUCATION

> Sensus abit tuus et tuus intellectus oberrat,
> et tua *letheis mens peregrinat aquis.*
> Dic, ubi sunt que te docuit Bononia quondam?
>
> > (*Elegia* 3.69–71; emphasis added)

> (Your reason is lost, your intellect wonders without end / *and your mind loses itself in Lethe's water.* / Tell me, where are the things Bologna once taught you?)

Beatrice, too, asks Dante to remember before the memory of his sins is erased by the water of the river Lethe in Eden: "Che pense? / Rispondi a me; ché *le memorie triste / in te non sono ancor da l'acqua offense*" ("What are you thinking? Speak, for *your memories / of sin have not been washed away by water yet*") (*Purgatorio* 31.10–12; emphasis added). Furthermore, as Boethius' Lady Philosophy before them, both Henry's Wisdom and Dante's Beatrice claim to have been closely guiding their disciples:

"Hec, ego, dic, ubi sunt que tibi sepe dedi? Te multum fovi, docui te, sepe rogavi, et mea secreta sepe videre dedi"	Alcun tempo il sostenni col mio volto: mostrando li occhi giovanetti a lui, meco il menava in dritta parte vòlto.
	. . .
	Né l'impetrare ispirazion mi valse, con le quali e in sogno e altrimenti lo rivocai . . .
(Tell me, where are all the things I have often given you? / I have fed you abundantly, I have taught you, I have often called you / and I have often revealed my secrets to you) (*Elegia* 3. 72–74)	(For a time I let my countenance sustain him. / Guiding him with my youthful eyes, / I drew him with me in the right direction. . . . useless the inspiration I sought and won for him, / as both with dreams and other means / I called him back.) (*Purgatorio* 30.121–35).

Key oppositions, however, separate Dante's rewriting from Henry's subtext: whereas Henry three times exhorts himself to cry and lament his own misery, in good elegiac fashion, Beatrice three times orders Dante *not* to cry; whereas Wisdom wants Henry to recall the memory of the wisdom she had imparted to him, Beatrice wants Dante to remember his past sins and confess them; and, finally but crucially, whereas Wisdom wishes Henry to remember what he had learned in school, Beatrice wants Dante to see the mistakes of the school he had followed and forget them (*Purgatorio* 33.85–87). Considering, moreover, the importance

EPILOGUE   283

of Henry's *Elegia* for Dante's *Vita nova*—as seen in Chapter 2—the reappearance of this school text precisely in conjunction with Beatrice's direct reference to the protagonist's "vita nova" in Eden (30.115) seems deliberate. Its presence coincides with Dante's Christian reconceptualization of the elegiac genre in these cantos, as demonstrated by the concentration of verbs for "weeping," which is higher in *Purgatorio* 30 than in any other canto of the *Commedia*.[9] Arguably, while in his meeting with Beatrice in Eden Dante puts forth an innovative model of Christian (comic) poetry—as observed in Chapter 6—Henry's alternative model of Christian elegy is echoed and set aside.

More important, Henry's faith in the philosophical training he had received in Bologna is replaced in *Purgatorio* by Beatrice's condemnation of the "school" that deceived Dante. Considering the role that Dante grants to a school text such as Henry's *Elegia* at this thickly intertextual moment of *Purgatorio*, it seems reasonable to extend Beatrice's criticism to his contemporary education more broadly. Such rebuke would represent a fitting conclusion to the "curriculum revision" that Dante proposes throughout *Purgatorio*—as detailed in Chapters 4–6. It would dovetail, more generally, with his critical stance toward medieval school texts in his *Vita nova* and *Commedia*. If Beatrice's words are meant to contradict those uttered by Henry's Wisdom, perhaps the "scuola" Dante followed may be a reference to the type of learning offered by contemporary education, particularly the one offered in academic milieus like Bologna. This reading is supported by Beatrice's parallel, albeit more overt, criticism of contemporary schools in *Paradiso* 29.70–75, where she voices the poet's anti-academic stance:

> Ma perché 'n terra per le vostre scole
> si legge che l'angelica natura
> è tal, che 'ntende e si ricorda e vole,
> ancor dirò, perché tu veggi pura
> la verità che là giù si confonde,
> equivocando in sì fatta lettura.
>
> ("But since in schools on earth you still are taught / that the angelic nature is possessed / of understanding, memory, and will, / I will continue, so that you clearly see / how truth is made unclear down there / by such equivocation in its teaching.")

In *Purgatorio* 30–33, Beatrice not only criticizes this type of learning but also points to its positive alternative in Dante's own poetics of vernacular education, here exemplified by her mention of the *Vita nova*: "questi fu tal *ne la sua vita nova* / virtüalmente, ch'ogne abito destro / fatto averebbe in lui mirabil prova" (this man

---

[9] See Hollander, comm. ad loc.

in his new life potentially was such / that each good disposition in him / would have come to marvelous conclusion) (*Purgatorio* 30.115–17; emphasis added). In *Purgatorio* 30–33—as in his last *Egloga* to Giovanni del Virgilio—Dante presents his own vernacular poetry as a form of learning and wisdom deemed as alternative to, and even incompatible with, contemporary schools. Here, Dante presents his own texts as a new and more edifying form of vernacular instruction.

*

The "intrusion" of Henry's subtext in Dante's reworking of Augustine's and Boethius' archetypes of intellectual conversion sums up what this book has argued. In *Purgatorio* 30–33, Dante taps into the cultural literacy he shared with his lay audience to promote his own alternative educational program in the vernacular. His critical rewriting of the culminating scenes of Henry's *Elegia* appealed to highly educated readers as well as to lay ones, whose familiarity with Augustine's *Confessiones* and Boethius' *Consolatio* could not be assumed—a similar audience, in other words, to the one Dante had targeted in the *Vita nova*.

The growing levels of literacy among the laity presented Dante with the opportunity to shape the new vernacular culture. To implement his educational program, he reworked the models provided by the very Latin instruction for which he was designing a vernacular alternative. He found in the Latin school texts an effective means of engaging with a broader lay readership. Since Dante, however, presents his works as the new school for vernacular readers, he deliberately obscures the importance of the didactic precedents that informed them. When he engages with this tradition more openly, he usually does so to criticize it. As well exemplified by Beatrice's rewriting of Henry's Lady Wisdom in Eden, Dante was eager to invoke his own education only to supersede it.

His engagement with Henry's *Elegia* in *Purgatorio* 30 also shows that medieval school texts did not represent an alternative to the classical *auctores* celebrated by Dante in Limbo. Instead, the *auctores minores* read in schools provided influential models for the reception and readaptation of the *auctores maiores* into a new Christian culture and poetics in vernacular. Prosper of Aquitaine's *Liber epigrammatum* proved the prosimetrum's suitability for the type of instruction that Dante carries out in the *Vita nova*. Henry's *Elegia* offered an example of classicizing poetics, autobiographical writing, and a failed attempt to integrate elegiac poetry with the Christian view of sorrow as a necessary path of redemption. The *Ecloga Theoduli* was the key authority for the kind of pastoral syncretism and apologetics undergirding Dante's and Virgil's ascent throughout *Purgatorio*. In the same *cantica*, Statius' *Achilleid* and Claudian's *De raptu Proserpinae* emerge as key paradigms for Dante's stretching of the traditional limits of classical epic poetry and for his reconfiguring of the genre to the Christian education imparted to the "hero" in the *Commedia*. Even in *Paradiso*, where the poet strives to provide a vernacular equivalent to Ovid's and Virgil's poetry, Dante engages with the standards of epic emulation provided by Statius and Claudian. As these examples suggest, Dante's innovative vernacular poetics neither was generated in a vacuum nor resulted from the poet's solitary dialogue with the *auctores maiores* of the Latin tradition. Rather, it entailed a creative reworking of the classical reception showcased by medieval schoolbooks.

As Chapters 3 to 7 show, the three pillars of Dante's distinctive hermeneutic posture toward classical antiquity—emulation, syncretism, and figuralism—are all rooted in his earliest literary education. If medieval Latin education exerted such a pervasive influence on the poet's innovative stance toward classical poetry, then we would be compelled to revise interpretations of the thirteenth century as a century without classical sophistication and of Dante's oeuvre as the product of an isolated genius. Dante instead drew consistently on elementary school texts.

For a medieval intellectual such as Dante, moreover, a moral reeducation "in pro del mondo che mal vive" (to serve the world that lives so ill) (*Purgatorio* 32.103) could not but concern itself with the texts that supplied the basic linguistic and moral education to most literate people. Notwithstanding Dante's continual efforts to link his poem to the canonical major Roman poets—the "bella scola" of *Inferno* 4.94—his project of moral and cultural reform compelled him to confront the texts that made up the educational canon and to adapt them to the needs of his new "sacrato poema" (sacred poem) (*Paradiso* 23.62). The poet's allusions to contemporary scholastic readings bespeak his awareness that language education entailed significant moral implications, as it provided pupils with a system of ethical values and offered them an understanding of pagan and sacred histories. My analysis has suggested Dante's critical stance toward some of the precepts that were ingrained in contemporary education: the strict norms that bound literary genres and styles to different subject matter; the use of ancient Roman history for factional political propaganda; the controversial role of ancient pagan culture and poetry in Christian poetics; and the role of narratives of sexual violence as part of schoolboys' initiation to the epic genre. Through the critical reappraisal of contemporary school texts, Dante began to break free of some of the limitations imposed by contemporary education, devising a new poetics and a program of intellectual, moral, and spiritual education for his readers.[10] In particular, the *Vita nova* and the *Commedia* offered textual models for reading and composing vernacular poetry. Dante's case elucidates how a combination of both imitation and "resistance" to Latin literacy and education gave life to an innovative vernacular culture.[11] Dante's stance toward his own education reflects the deliberate efforts

---

[10] Katharine Breen has similarly argued that medieval vernacular readers' project of imagining a lay English readership depended on Latinate models of the relationship between order and virtue. See Breen, *Imagining an English Reading Public, 1150–1400* (Cambridge: Cambridge University Press, 2010).

[11] For a definition of poetic "resistance" to education, see Jeff Dolven, *Scenes of Instruction in Renaissance Romance* (Chicago: University of Chicago Press, 2007), 27.

286   DANTE'S EDUCATION

of a still marginal vernacular literature to carve a new textual enclave out of the official Latin culture.[12]

As readers close this book, my hope is for them to appreciate what a complex and long-standing influence school readings exert on individuals throughout their lives and on culture more broadly. Even an innovator such as Dante did not entirely wish to ignore what he had read as a pupil. As school readings, moreover, contribute to one's sense of self and of belonging to a community, a poet on a mission, such as Dante, knew that to transform his social and political reality he needed to engage with his readers' education. He recognized that education and literature are powerful means of social and cultural transformation. Arguably, a key feature of his remarkably successful and long-lived poetic enterprise is precisely that it offered itself as a new and more accessible form of instruction, a poetics of vernacular learning. Finally, Dante's reuse of Latin school texts in his vernacular poetics also contains a powerful message of hope and a path for renewal. It shows that even when taught as part of an elitist educational culture, like Latin instruction in the Middle Ages, literary texts have the potential for subverting that very culture. All that is required are creative, critical readers—like the ones Dante envisions for his *Paradiso*:

> Or ti riman, lettor, sovra 'l tuo banco,
> dietro pensando a ciò che si preliba,
> s'esser vuoi lieto assai prima che stanco.
>   Messo t'ho innanzi; omai per te ti ciba;
> ché a sé torce tutta la mia cura
> quella materia ond' io son fatto scriba.
>
> (*Paradiso* 10.22–27)

> (Stay on your bench now, reader, / thinking of the joy you have but tasted, / if, well before you tire, you would be happy. / I have set your table. From here on feed yourself, / for my attention now resides / in that matter of which I have become the scribe.)

---

[12] See Peter Haidu's thesis, in *The Subject of Violence: The Song of Roland and the Birth of the State* (Bloomington: Indiana University Press, 1993), that twelfth- and thirteenth-century Old French texts "constitute a new cultural territorialization" (6). Haidu's thesis has also been endorsed by Sharon Kinoshita, *Medieval Boundaries: Rethinking Difference in Old French Literature* (Philadelphia: University of Pennsylvania Press, 2006), 3–4.

Bibliography

Primary Sources

Ademaro de Chabannes. 1988. *Favole*, ed. Ferruccio Bertini and Paolo Gatti. Genoa: Università di Genova, Facoltà di lettere, Dipartimento di Archeologia, Filologia Classica e loro Tradizioni.

Albertano Da Brescia. 1998. *Liber de doctrina dicendi et tacendi: La parola del cittadino nell'Italia del Duecento*, ed. Paola Navone. Florence: SISMEL.

Arrigo da Settimello. 2011. *Elegia*, ed. and trans. Clara Fossati. Florence: SISMEL.

Augustine. 1991. *Confessions*, trans. H. Chadwick. Oxford: Oxford University Press.

Avianus. 1968. "Fabulae." In *Minor Latin Poets*, ed. J. Wight Duff and Arnold M. Duff, 669–749. Cambridge, MA: Harvard University Press.

Baebius Italicus. 1982. *Baebii Italici Ilias Latina*, ed. Marcus Scaffai. Bologna: Pàtron.

Barney, Stephen A., J. A. Beach, and Oliver Berghof, eds. 2006. *The Etymologies of Isidore of Seville*. Cambridge: Cambridge University Press.

Bastin, Julia, ed. 1930. *Recueil Général des Isopets*. 2 vols. Paris: H. Champion.

Battaglia, Salvatore. 1929. *Il Boezio e l'Arrighetto*. Turin: UTET.

Bernard d'Utrecht. 1977. *Commentum in Theodolum*. 2nd ed. Spoleto: Centro Italiano di Studi sull'Alto Medioevo.

Biblia Latina cum glossa ordinaria. 1992. Turnhout, Belgium: Brepols. [Facsimile reprint of the *Editio Princeps* (Strassburg: Adolph Rusch, 1480–81).]

Boas, Marcus. 1952. *Disticha Catonis*. Amsterdam: North-Holland Publishing.

Boccaccio, Giovanni. 1914. *Il "Buccolicum Carmen,"* ed. Giacomo Lidonnici. Città di Castello: S. Lapi.

Boccaccio, Giovanni. 1992. *Epistole e lettere*, ed. Ginetta Auzzas. In *Tutte le opere*, ed. Vittore Branca, vol. 5.1: 664–68. Milan: Mondadori.

Boccaccio, Giovanni. 2010. *The Latin Eclogues*, trans. David R. Slavitt. Baltimore: Johns Hopkins University Press.

Boldrini, Sandro ed. 1994. *Uomini e bestie: Le favole dell'Aesopus latinus; Testo latino con una traduzione-rifacimento del '300 in volgare toscano*. Lecce: Argo.

Branca, Vittore. 1966. "Poetica del rinnovamento e tradizione agiografica nella *Vita nuova*." In *Studi in onore di Italo Siciliano*, ed. Alfredo Cavaliere, vol. 1: 123–48. Florence: Olschki.

Branca, Vittore. 1989. *Esopo toscano: Dei frati e dei mercanti trecenteschi*. Venice: Marsilio.

Brunetto Latini. 1839. *Il Tesoro di Brunetto Latini volgarizzato da Bono Giamboni*. Venice: Co' tipi del Gondoliere.

Brunetto Latini. 1915. *La Rettorica di Brunetto Latini*, ed. Francesco Maggini. Florence: Galletti e Cocci.

Brunetto Latini. 1981. *Il Tesoretto (The Little Treasure)*, ed. and trans. Julia Bolton Holloway. New York: Garland.

Brunetto Latini. 1993. *The Book of the Treasure (Li Livres dou Tresor)*, trans. Paul Barrette and Spurgeon Baldwin. New York: Garland.

Brunetto Latini. 2007. *Tresor*, ed. Pietro Beltrami. Turin: Einaudi.

Brunetto Latini. 2016. *Poesie*, ed. Stefano Carrai. Turin: Einaudi.

Brunetto Latini. 2016. *La Rettorica*, ed. and trans. Stefania D'Agata D'Ottavi. Kalamazoo, MI: Western Michigan University.

Leonardo Bruni. 1996. "Vita di Dante." In *Opere letterarie e politiche*, ed. Paolo Viti, 539–52. Turin: UTET.

Caesarius Arelatensis. 1953. *Sermones Caesarii uel ex aliis fontibus hausti*, ed. G. Morin. Corpus Christianorum, Series Latina, 103. Turnhout, Belgium: Brepols.

288 BIBLIOGRAPHY

Cecchus Asculanus. 2002. *Acerba [Acerba etas]*, ed. Marco Albertazzi. Trento: La Finestra.

Chambry, Émile, ed. 1925–26. *Aesopi fabulae*. Paris: Les Belles Lettres.

Chellini, Riccardo, ed. 2009. *Chronica de origine civitatis Florentiae*. Rome: Istituto Storico Italiano per il Medioevo.

Claudian. 1922. *Claudian*, trans. Maurice Platnauer, Loeb Classical Library Volumes 135 & 136. Cambridge, MA: Harvard University Press.

Claudian. 1993. *De Raptu Proserpinae*, ed. and trans. Claire Gruzelier. Oxford: Clarendon Press.

Claudianus, Claudius. 1922. *Rape of Proserpine*, ed. and trans. Maurice Platanauer. In *Claudian*, vol. 2. Cambridge, MA: Harvard University Press. https://www.theoi.com/Text/ClaudianProserpine.html#1.

Claudianus, Claudius. 1969. *De Raptu Proserpinae*, ed. John Barrie Hall. London: Cambridge University Press.

Clarke, Amy Key, and Phyllis M. Giles, eds. 1973. *The Commentary of Geoffrey of Vitry on Claudian "De raptu Proserpinae."* Leiden: Brill.

Clogan, Paul M., ed. 1968. *The Medieval Achilleid of Statius, Edited with Introduction, Variant Readings, and Glosses*. Leiden: Brill.

Contini, Gianfranco, ed. 1941. *Le opera volgari di Bonvesin da la Riva*. Rome: Società filologica romana.

Dante, Alighieri. 1857. *Il Convito di Dante Alighieri e le Epistole*, ed. Pietro Fraticelli. Florence: Barbera.

Dante, Alighieri. 1894. *Purgatorio*. In *La Divina Commedia di Dante Alighieri*, ed. Giacomo Poletto, vol. 2. Rome: Desclée, Lefebvre.

Dante, Alighieri. 1927. *La Divina Commedia con le note di Niccolò Tommaseo e introduzione di Umberto Cosmo*. Turin: UTET.

Dante, Alighieri. 1932. *La Vita Nuova*, ed. Michele Barbi. Florence: Bemporad.

Dante, Alighieri. 1969. *La "Vita nuova,"* trans. Barbara Reynolds. Harmondsworth, Middlesex: Penguin.

Dante, Alighieri. 88. *Convivio*. Ed. Cesare Vasoli and Domenico De Robertis. Milan: Ricciardi.

Dante, Alighieri. 1979–88. *De vulgari eloquentia*. In *Opere minori*, ed. Pier Vincenzo Mengaldo, vol. 2, 3–237. Milan: Ricciardi.

Dante, Alighieri. 1981. *Purgatorio*. In *La Divina Commedia di Dante Alighieri*, ed. Manfredi Porena, vol. 2. Bologna: Zanichelli.

Dante, Alighieri. 1994. *La Commedia secondo l'antica vulgata*, ed. Giorgio Petrocchi. 2nd ed. 4 vols. Florence: Le Lettere.

Dante, Alighieri. 1995. *Convivio*, ed. Franca Brambilla Ageno. 2 vols. Florence: Le Lettere.

Dante, Alighieri. 2009. *Inferno*, trans. Stanley Lombardo. Indianapolis: Hackett.

Dante, Alighieri. 2011. *De l'éloquence en vulgaire*, ed. Irène Rosier-Catach, Anne Grondeux, and Ruedi Imbach. Paris: Fayard.

Dante, Alighieri. 2011. "Rime, Vita Nova, De vulgari eloquentia," ed. Claudio Giunta, Guglielmo Gorni, and Mirko Tavoni. In *Opere*, ed. Marco Santagata, vol. 1. Milan: Mondadori.

Dante, Alighieri. 2012. *De Vulgari Eloquentia*, ed. Enrico Fenzi. In *Opere*, ed. Enrico Fenzi and Luciano Formisano, vol. 3, 2–240. Rome: Salerno.

Dante, Alighieri. 2012. *Epistole—Ecloge: Questio de situ et forma aque et terre*, ed. Manlio Pastore Stocchi. Rome: Antenore.

Dante, Alighieri. 2012. *Vita nova*, trans. Andrew Frisardi. Evanston, IL: Northwestern University Press.

Dante, Alighieri. 2014. *Convivio—Monarchia—Epistole—Egloge*, ed. Gianfranco Fioravanti, Claudio Giunta, Diego Quaglioni, Claudia Villa, and Gabriella Albanese. In *Opere*, ed. Marco Santagata, vol. 2. Milan: Mondadori.

Dante, Alighieri. 2016–20. *Commedia*, ed. and comm. Giorgio Inglese. Rome: Carocci.

Della Vedova, Roberto, and Maria Teresa Silvotti, eds. 1978. *Il Commentarium di Pietro Alighieri, nelle redazioni Ashburnhamiana e Ottoboniana*. Florence: Olschki.

De Robertis, Domenico. 1970. *Il libro della Vita nuova*. Florence: Sansoni.

De Robertis, Teresa, et al., eds. 2016. *Codice diplomatico dantesco*. In *Nuova edizione commentata delle opera di Dante*, ed. Enrico Malato et al., vol. 7 t. 3. Rome: Salerno.

BIBLIOGRAPHY 289

Dominici, Giovanni. 1860. *Regola del governo di cura familiare*, ed. D. Salvi. Florence: A. Garinei.

Duff, J. Wight, and Arnold M. Duff, eds. 1968. *Minor Latin Poets*. Cambridge, MA: Harvard University Press.

Durling, Robert M., and Ronald L. Martinez. 1990. *Time and the Crystal: Studies in Dante's Rime petrose*. Berkeley: University of California Press.

Durling, Robert M., and Ronald L. Martinez, eds. and trans. 1996. *Purgatorio*. In *The Divine Comedy of Dante Alighieri*. New York: Oxford University Press.

Fenzi, Enrico. 1991. "*Sollazzo e leggiadria*: Un'interpretazione della canzone dantesca *Poscia ch'amor.*" *Studi danteschi* 63: 191–280.

Fontana, Laura. 1979. "Un inedito volgarizzamento toscano dei *Disticha Catonis.*" In *In ricordo di Cesare Angelini: Studi di letteratura e filologia*, ed. Cesare Angelini, Franco Alessio, Angelo Stella, 46–64. Milan: Il Saggiatore.

Giuliani, Alfredo. *Antologia della poesia italiana: Dalle origini al Trecento*. Milan: Feltrinelli, 1975.

Gualtierus Anglicus. 2005. *L'Esopus*, ed. Paola Busdraghi. Genoa: Università di Genova, Facoltà di lettere, Dipartimento di Archeologia, Filologia Classica e loro Tradizioni.

Hervieux, Léopold, ed. 1884. *Les fabulistes latins: Depuis le siècle d'Auguste jusqu'à la fin du moyen âge*. Paris: Firmin-Didot.

Horace. 1928. *Ars Poetica*, trans. C. Smart and E. H. Blakeney. London: Scholartis Press.

Horsting, Albertus G. A., ed. 2016. *Prosper Aquitanus: Liber epigrammatum*. Corpus Scriptorum Ecclesiasticorum Latinorum, 100. Berlin: De Gruyter.

Huygens, R. B. C., ed. 1970. *Accessus ad auctores, Bernard d'Utrecht, Conrad d' Hirsau: Dialogus super auctores*. Leiden: Brill.

Jacobs, Morton Y., ed. 1963. "Bernard's Commentum in Theodulum, editio princeps." Ph.D. diss., University of North Carolina at Chapel Hill.

Jacques de Vitry. 1885–88. *Sermones vulgares* 16, ed. J. B. Pitra. In *Analecta novissima*. Paris: Typis Tusculanis.

Jahnke, Ricardus, ed. 1898. *Lactantii Placidi qui dicitur commentarios in Statii Thebaida et Commentarium in Achilleida*. Leipzig: Teubner.

Keil, Heinrich, ed. 1855–80. *Grammatici latini*. 8 vols. Leipzig: Teubner.

Langosh, Karl, ed. 1942. *Das "Registrum multorum auctorum" des Hugo von Trimberg: Untersuchungen und Kommentierte Textausgabe*. Berlin: Ebering.

Lentini, Anselmo, ed. 1975. *Ilderico e la sua "Ars grammatica."* Montecassino: In coenobio Casinensi.

Lucanus, M. Annaeus. 1835. *Pharsaliae Libri X*, ed. Carolus Hermannus Weise. Leipzig: G. Bassus. Perseus Digital Library, Tufts University, http://www.perseus.tufts.edu/.

Macrobius, Theodosius. 1963. *Commentarii in Somnium Scipionis*, ed. J. Willis. Leipzig: Teubner.

Macrobius, Theodosius. 1990. *Commentary on the Dream of Scipio*, trans. William H. Stahl. New York: Columbia University Press.

Mancini, Augusto, ed. 1902. "Un commento ignoto di Remy d'Auxerre ai Disticha Catonis." *L'Accademia* 11: 175–98.

Masi, Gino, ed. 1943. *Formularium Florentinum Artis Notariae (1200–1242)*. Milan: Vita e Pensiero.

McCormick, Thomas J., ed. 1995. *A Partial Edition of "Les Fais des Rommains" with a Study of Its Style and Syntax*. Lewiston, NY: Mellen Press.

Munari, F., ed. 1982. *Mathei Vindocinensis: Opera*. 2 vols. Rome: Edizioni di Storia e Letteratura.

Mussato, Albertino. 2020. *Epistole metriche*, ed. Luca Lombardo. Venice: Ca' Foscari.

Neckam, Alexander. 1987. *Novus Aesopus*, ed. and trans. Giovanni Garbugino. Genoa: Università di Genova, Facoltà di lettere, Dipartimento di Archeologia, Filologia Classica e loro Tradizioni.

Orbán, Árpád P. 1973. "Anonymi Teutonici Commentum in Theodoli Eclogam e Codice Utrecht, U.B. 292 editum." *Vivarium* 11, no. 1: 1–42.

Orbán, Árpád P. 1974. "Anonymi Teutonici Commentum in Theodoli Eclogam e Codice Utrecht, U.B. 292 editum (2)." *Vivarium* 12, no. 2: 133–45.

290 BIBLIOGRAPHY

Orbán, Árpád P. 1975. "Anonymi Teutonici Commentum in Theodoli Eclogam e Codice Utrecht, U.B 292. editum (3)." *Vivarium* 13, no. 1: 77–88.

Origenes. 1985. *Homiliae in Exodum (latine Rufino interprete)*. In *Sources Chrétiennes* 321, ed. Maurcel Borret. Paris: Éditions du Cerf.

Osternacher, Johann E., ed. 1902. *Theoduli eclogam recensuit et prolegomenis instruxit*. Urfahr-Linz: Ripariae prope Lentiam.

Paetow, Louis J., ed. and trans. 1914. *The Battle of the Seven Arts*. Berkeley: University of California Press.

Peraldus, Guilielmus. 1668. "Tractatus de peccato linguae." In *Summae virtutum ac vitiorum*. 2 vols. Lyon. https://www.public.asu.edu/~rnewhaus/peraldus_project/Sins%20of%%20tongue%20trial.html

Perrin, Bernadotte, trans. 1914. *Plutarch's Lives*. Cambridge, MA: Harvard University Press.

Perry, Ben E., ed. 1952. *Aesopica*. Urbana: University of Illinois Press.

Petrarca, Francesco. 2004–10. *Seniles*, ed. Ugo Dotti. Turin: Aragno.

Prosper of Aquitaine. 2009. *Ad coniugem suam. In appendice: Liber epigrammatum*, ed. Stefania Santelia, 106–193. (Naples: Loffredo, 2009)

Reijnders, Harry F., ed. 1971. "Americus, *Ars Lectoria*." *Vivarium* 9: 119–37.

Reijnders, Harry F., ed. 1972. "Americus, *Ars Lectoria*." *Vivarium* 10: 41–101, 124–76.

Remigio de' Girolami. 2014. *Dal bene comune al bene del comune: I trattati politici di Remigio dei Girolami († 1319); Nella Firenze dei Bianchi-Neri*, ed. Emilio Panella. Florence: Nerbini.

Rigg, A. George, trans. 2005. *The Eclogue of Theodulus: A Translation*. Toronto: Centre for Medieval Studies, University of Toronto. https://www.medieval.utoronto.ca/research/online-resources/eclogue-theodulus-translation.

Ripoll, François, and Jean Soubiran, eds. 2008. *Stace Achilléide*. Leuven, Belgium: Peeters.

Schmitt, Christian. 1974. "Zum Kanon Eines Bisher Unedierten Theodul-Kommentars." *Germanisch-Romanische Monatsschrift* 24: 1, 1–12.

Segre, Cesare, ed. 1963. *Volgarizzamenti del Due e Trecento*. Turin: UTET.

Segre, Cesare, and Mario Marti, eds. 1959. *Prosa del Duecento*. Milan: Ricciardi.

Selmi, Francesco, ed. 1873. *Dei trattati morali di Albertano da Brescia: Volgarizzamento inedito fatto nel 1268 da Andrea da Grosseto*. Bologna: Romagnoli.

Septimellensis, Henricus. 2011. *Elegia*, ed. Clara Fossati. Florence: SISMEL Edizioni del Galluzzo.

Servius. 1881–1902. *In Vergilii carmina commentarii*, ed. Georg Thilo. 4 vols. Leipzig: Teubner.

Statius, P. Papinius. 2005 [1954]. *Achilleid*, ed. Oswald A. W. Dilke. Cambridge: Cambridge University Press.

Statius, P. Papinius. 2008. *Thebaid: A Song of Thebes*, trans. Jane W. Joyce. Ithaca, NY: Cornell University Press.

Statius, P. Papinius. 2015. *Achilleid*, trans. Stanley Lombardo. Indianapolis: Hackett.

Stussi, Alfredo, ed. 1967. *Zibaldone da Canal*. Venice: Fonti per la Storia di Venezia.

Tassi, F., ed. 1836. *Della miseria dell'uomo: Giardino di consolazione; Introduzione alle virtù, di Bono Giamboni*. Florence: Guglielmo Piatti.

Taylor, Jerome, ed. and trans. 1968. *The Didascalicon of Hugh of Saint Victor: A Medieval Guide to the Arts*. New York: Columbia University Press.

Theodulus. 1997. *Ecloga: Il canto della verità e della menzogna*, ed. Francesco Mosetti Casaretto. Florence: SISMEL Edizioni del Galluzzo.

Thomson, Ian, and Louis Perraud. 1990. *Ten Latin Schooltexts of the Later Middle Ages: Translated Selections*. Lewiston, NY: Mellen Press.

Tuitiensis, Rupertus. 1854. *Liber Exodus*. In *Commentariorum de operibus S. Trinitatis libri XLII. Patrologia Latina*, vol. 167, ed. J. P. Migne, 565–742. Paris.

Villani, Filippo. 1997. *Liber de origine civitatis Florentiae et eiusdem famosis civibus*, ed. G. Tanturli. Padua: Antenore.

Villani, Giovanni. 1991. *Nuova cronica*, ed. Giuseppe Porta. 3 vols. Parma: Guanda.

Vindocinensis, Matthaeus. 1971. *Ars versificatoria*. In *Les Arts poétiques du XIIe et XIIIe siècle*, ed. Edmund Faral, 109–93. Paris: Champion.

BIBLIOGRAPHY   291

Virgilio. 1985. *Eneide*, trans. Luca Canali and comm. Ettore Paratore. Milan: Mondadori.
Willner, Hans, ed. 1903. *Des Adelard von Bath Traktat "De eodem et diverso."* Münster: Aschendorff.

Secondary Sources

Ahern, John. 1976. *"The New Life of the Book: Oral and Written Communication in the Age of Dante."* Ph.D. diss., Indiana University.
Ahern, John. 1990. "The Reader on the Piazza: Verbal Duels in Dante's *Vita Nuova." Texas Studies in Literature and Language* 35: 18–39.
Ahern, John. 1992. "The New Life of the Book: The Implied Reader of the 'Vita Nuova.'" *Dante Studies* 110, no. 2: 1–16.
Ahern, John. 1997. "Singing the Book: Orality in the Reception of Dante's *Comedy."* In *Dante: Contemporary Perspectives*, ed. Amilcare Iannucci, 214–39. Toronto: Toronto Press.
Albanese, Gabriella, and Paolo Pontari. 2017. "Il cenacolo ravennate di Dante e le *Egloghe*: Fiduccio de' Milotti, Dino Perini, Guido Vacchetta, Pietro Giardini, Menghino Mezzani." *Studi danteschi* 82: 311–427.
Albesano, Silvia. 2006. *"Consolatio philosophiae" volgare: Volgarizzamenti e traduzioni discorsive del Trecento italiano.* Heidelberg: Winter.
Albi, Veronica. 2021. *Sotto il manto delle favole: La ricezione di Fulgenzio nelle opere di Dante e negli antichi commenti alla Commedia.* Ravenna: Longo.
Alessio, Gian Carlo. 1986. "Le istituzioni scolastiche e l'insegnamento." In *Aspetti della letteratura latina nel secolo XIII*, ed. Claudio Leonardi and Giovanni Orlandi, 3–28. Perugia: La Nuova Italia.
Alessio, Gian Carlo, and Claudia Villa. 1990. "Il nuovo fascino degli autori antichi tra i secoli XII e XIV." In *La ricezione del testo*, ed. Guglielmo Cavallo, Paolo Fedeli, and Andrea Giardina, vol. 3 of *Lo Spazio Letterario Di Roma Antica*, 473–511. Rome: Salerno.
Alexandre-Bidon, Danièle. 1989. "La lettre volée: Apprendre à lire à l'enfant au Moyen Age." *Annales: Histoire, Sciences Sociales* 4: 953–92.
Allegretti, Paola. 2021. "Dante Alighieri nell'Archivio Apostolico Vaticano: Un documento del 1320." *Dante Studies* 139: 1–23.
Anderson, Harald. 2009. *The Manuscripts of Statius.* 3 vols. Arlington, VA: Self-published.
Antonetti, Pierre. 1983. *La vita quotidiana a Firenze ai tempi di Dante.* Milan: Rizzoli.
Ardissino, Erminia. 2009. *Tempo liturgico e tempo storico nella Commedia di Dante.* Vatican City: Libreria editrice vaticana.
Armour, Peter. 1983. *The Door of Purgatory: A Study of Multiple Symbolism in Dante's Purgatorio.* New York: Clarendon Press.
Artifoni, Enrico. 2021. "Ancora sulla parva letteratura tra latino e volgari," in *Toscana bilingue (1260 ca.–1430 ca.): Per una storia sociale del tradurre medievale*, ed. Sara Bischetti et al., 107–24. Berlin: De Gruyter.
Ascoli, Albert R. 2008. *Dante and the Making of a Modern Author.* Cambridge: Cambridge University Press.
Auerbach, Erich. 1959. *Scenes from the Drama of European Literature.* Minneapolis: University of Minnesota Press.
Auerbach, Erich. 1965. *Literary Language and Its Public in Late Latin Antiquity and in the Middle Ages*, trans. Ralph Manheim. New York: Pantheon Books.
Avesani, Rino. 1965. "Il primo ritmo per la morte del grammatico Ambrogio e il cosiddetto 'Liber Catonianus.'" *Studi Medievali* 6, no. 2: 455–88.
Avesani, Rino. 1967. *Quattro miscellanee medioevali e umanistiche.* Rome: Edizioni di Storia e Letteratura.
Azzetta, Luca. 2018. "'Fece molte canzoni per lo suo amore et come pare a uno suo libreto cui ei pose nome la Vita Nova': Note sui primi lettori della 'Vita nova.'" *Studi Romanzi* 14: 57–91.
Bambeck, Manfred. 1980. "Zur Polemik des Cecco d'Ascoli gegen Dante oder von der Allgengenwart der Allegorese." *Romanistisches Jahrbuch* 3: 73–77.

Banker, James R. 1974. "The *Ars Dictaminis* and Rhetorical Text Books of the Bolognese University in the Fourteenth Century." *Medievalia et Humanistica* 5: 153–68.

Banker, James R. 2003. *The Culture of San Sepolcro during the Youth of Piero Della Francesca.* Ann Arbor: University of Michigan Press.

Barański, Zygmunt G. 1989. "Dante's Three Reflective Dreams." *Quaderni d'Italianistica* 10: 213–36.

Barański, Zygmunt G. 1990. "The 'Marvelous' and the 'Comic': Toward a Reading of *Inferno* XVI." *Lectura Dantis* 7: 72–95.

Barański, Zygmunt G. 1991. "'Comedìa': Notes on Dante, the 'Epistle to Cangrande,' and Medieval Comedy." *Lectura Dantis* 8: 26–55.

Barański, Zygmunt G. 1991. "'Primo tra cotanto senno': Dante and the Latin Comic Tradition." *Italian Studies* 46, no.1: 1–36.

Barański, Zygmunt G. 1994. "Dante commentatore e commentato: Riflessioni sullo studio dell'*iter* ideologico di Dante." *Letture Classensi* 23: 135–58. Ravenna: Longo.

Barański, Zygmunt G., ed. 1995. *"Libri Poetarum in Quattuor Species Dividuntur": Essays on Dante and "Genre."* Reading, UK: University of Reading.

Barański, Zygmunt G. 1995. "The Poetics of Meter: *Terza Rima*, 'Canto,' 'Canzon,' 'Cantica.'" In *Dante Now: Current Trends in Dante Studies*, ed. Theodore J. Cachey, 3–41. Notre Dame, IN: University of Notre Dame Press.

Barański, Zygmunt G. 1996. *"Sole nuovo, luce nuova": Saggi sul rinnovamento culturale in Dante.* Turin: Scriptorium.

Barański, Zygmunt G. 2000. *Dante e i segni: Saggi per una storia intellettuale di Dante Alighieri.* Naples: Liguori.

Barański, Zygmunt G. 2001. *"Chiosar con altro testo."* Florence: Cadmo.

Barański, Zygmunt G. 2004. "Il *Convivio* e la poesia: Problemi di definizione." In *Contesti della "Commedia": Lectura Dantis Fridericiana 2002–2003*, ed. Francesco Tateo and Daniele Maria Pegorari, 9–64. Bari: Palomar.

Barański, Zygmunt G. 2010. "The Roots of Dante's Plurilingualism: 'Hybridity' and Language in the *Vita nova.*" In *Dante's Plurilingualism: Authority, Knowledge, Subjectivity*, ed. Sara Fortuna, Manuele Gragnolati, and Jürgen Trabant, 98–121. Oxford: Legenda.

Barański, Zygmunt. 2013. "'Lascio cotale trattato ad altro chiosatore': Form, Literature, and Exegesis in Dante's *Vita nova.*" In *Dantean Dialogues: Engaging with the Legacy of Amilcare Iannucci*, ed. Maggie Kilgour and Elena Lombardi, 1–40. Toronto: University of Toronto Press.

Barański, Zygmunt G. 2014. "Reading the *Commedia*'s IXs 'Vertically': From Addresses to the Reader to the *Crucesignati* and the *Ecloga Theoduli.*" *L'Alighieri* 44: 5–35.

Barański, Zygmunt G. 2015. "'Oh come è grande la mia impresa' (*Conv.* IV. vii. 4): Notes towards Defining the *Convivio.*" In *Dante's* Convivio: *Or How to Restart a Career in Exile*, ed. Franziska Meier, 9–26. Bern: Peter Lang.

Barański, Zygmunt G. 2015. "Purgatorio 1." In *Lectura Dantis Bononiensis*, vol. 5, *Inferno XXIX–Purgatorio I–II*, ed. Emilio Pasquini and Carlo Galli, 105–33. Bologna: Bologna University Press.

Barański, Zygmunt G. 2015. "Studying the Spaces of Dante's Intellectual Formation: Some Problems of Definition." In *"I Luoghi Nostri": Dante's Natural and Cultural Spaces*, ed. Zygmunt Barański, Andreas Kablitz, and Ülar Ploom, 257–88. Tallinn: Tallinn University Press.

Barański, Zygmunt G. 2017. "On Dante's Trail." *Italian Studies* 72, no. 1: 1–15.

Barański, Zygmunt G. 2020. *Dante, Petrarch, Boccaccio: Literature, Doctrine, Reality.* Oxford: Legenda.

Barański, Zygmunt G. 2021. "The Classics," in *The Oxford Handbook of Dante*, ed. Manuele Gragnolati, Elena Lombardi, and Francesca Southerden, 111–26. Oxford: Oxford University Press.

Barański, Zygmunt G. and Theodore J. Cachey Jr., ed. 2022. *Dante's "Other Works": Assessments and Interpretations*, ed. Zygmunt G. Barański. Notre Dame, IN: University of University Press.

Barbero, Alessandro. 2020. *Dante.* Bari: Laterza.

BIBLIOGRAPHY   293

Barbi, Michele. 1941. *Con Dante e i suoi interpreti*. Florence: Le Monnier.
Barbi, Michele. 1975. "Dante e l'Arte dei medici e speziali." In *Problemi di critica dantesca: Seconda serie*, 379–84. Florence: Sansoni.
Barchiesi, Alessandro. 2001. *Speaking Volumes: Narrative and Intertext in Ovid and Other Latin Poets*. London: Duckworth.
Barkan, Leonard. 1986. *The Gods Made Flesh: Metamorphoses and the Pursuit of Paganism*. New Haven, CT: Yale University Press.
Barnes, Michael H. 2005. "Claudian." In *A Companion to Ancient Epic*, ed. John Miles Foley, 538–49. Malden, MA: Blackwell.
Barolini, Teodolinda. 1984. *Dante's Poets: Textuality and Truth in the Comedy*. Princeton, NJ: Princeton University Press.
Barolini, Teodolinda. 1989. "True and False See-ers in *Inferno* XX." *Lectura Dantis* 4: 42–54.
Barolini, Teodolinda. 1992. *The Undivine Comedy: Detheologizing Dante*. Princeton, NJ: Princeton University Press.
Barolini, Teodolinda. 2019. "Dante's Limbo and the Cultural Other, Or: Injustice on the Banks of the Indus." In *Dante Worlds: Echoes, Places, Questions*, ed. Peter Carravetta, 21–34. Rome: "L'Erma" di Bretschneider.
Barolini, Teodolinda. 2022. *Dante's Multitudes: History, Philosophy, Method*. Notre Dame, IN: Notre Dame University Press.
Bartuschat, Johannes, Elisa Brilli, and Delphine Carron, eds. 2020. *The Dominicans and the Making of Florence (13th–14th Centuries)*. Florence: Firenze University Press.
Barucci, Guglielmo. 2021. "Dante e la favolistica esopica: Mondo classico e tradizione medioevale." In *"Nostra maggior musa": I maestri della letteratura classica nella Commedia di Dante*, ed. John Butcher, 21–36. Città di Castello: Edizioni Nuova Prhomos.
Bates, Richard, and Thomas Rendall. 1989. "Dante's Ulysses and the Epistle of James." *Dante Studies* 107: 33–44.
Battaglia Ricci, Lucia. 2004. "'Come ... le tombe terragne portan segnato': Lettura del dodicesimo canto del Purgatorio." In *Ecfrasi: Modelli ed esempi fra medioevo e Rinascimento*, ed. Giovanni Venturi, 33–63. Rome: Bulzoni.
Battaglia Ricci, Lucia. 2013. "Canto XXIII: 'Imagini di fuor / imagini d'entro': Nel mondo della menzogna." In *Lectura Dantis romana: Cento canti per cento anni; Inferno 2, Canti XVIII–XXXIV*, ed. Enrico Malato and Andrea Mazzucchi, 740–69. Rome: Salerno.
Battistini, Andrea. 2012. "Il 'ver c'ha faccia di menzogna': Lettura di 'Inferno' XVII," *L'Alighieri*, n.s., 40: 67–87.
Bäuml, Franz. 1980. "Varieties and Consequences of Medieval Literacy and Illiteracy." *Speculum* 55, no. 2: 237–65.
Beal, P. 2008. "Pecia System." In *A Dictionary of English Manuscript Terminology 1450–2000*. Oxford: Oxford University Press. https://www.oxfordreference.com/display/10.1093/acref/9780199576128.001.0001/acref-9780199576128-e-0746?rskey=QZJxxH&result=2
Beddie, James S. 1930. "The Ancient Classics in the Medieval Libraries." *Speculum* 5, no. 1: 3–20.
Beer, Janette M. A. 1972. "A Medieval Cato: Virtus or Virtue?" *Speculum* 47, no. 1: 52–59.
Bellaira, Guglielmo. 1974. "Un'eco Claudianea in Dante?" *L'Alighieri* 1: 50–52.
Bellomo, Saverio. 2003. "La *Commedia* attraverso gli occhi dei primi lettori." In *Leggere Dante*, ed. Lucia Battaglia Ricci, 73–84. Longo: Ravenna.
Bellomo, Saverio. 2004. *Dizionario dei commentatori danteschi: L'esegesi della "Commedia" da Iacopo Alighieri a Nidobeato*. Florence: Olschki.
Bertelli, Sandro. 2004. "Nota sul canzoniere provenzale P e sul Martelli 12." *Medioevo e Rinascimento, Annuario del Dipartimento di Studi sul Medioevo e Rinascimento dell'Università di Firenze* 18: 369–75.
Bertini, Ferruccio. 1975. *Il monaco Ademaro e la sua raccolta di favole fedriane*. Genoa: Tilgher.
Bessone, Federica. 2019. "Allusive (Im-)Pertinence in Statius' Epic." In *Intertextuality in Flavian Epic Poetry: Contemporary Approaches*, ed. Neil Coffee, Chris Forstall, Lavinia Galli Milic and Damien Nelis, 133–68. Berlin: De Gruyter.

294 BIBLIOGRAPHY

Bigi, Emilio. 1955. "Genesi di un concetto storiografico: 'Dolce stil novo.'" *Giornale storico della letteratura italiana* 132: 333–71.

Bisanti, Armando. 1993. "La tradizione favolistica mediolatina nella letteratura italiana dei secoli XIV e XV." *Schede Medievali* 24–25: 34–51.

Bisanti, Armando. 2000. "Nota a Gualtiero Anglico, 'Aesopus' 20,10." *Mittellateinisches Jahrbuch* 35: 77–80.

Bisanti, Armando. 2007. "Sull'edizione critica dell' *Esopus* attribuito al cosidetto Gualtiero Anglico." *Schede medievali* 45: 223–49.

Bischetti, Sara, Michele Lodone, Cristiano Lorenzi, and Antonio Montefusco, eds., 2021. *Toscana bilingue: Storia sociale della traduzione medieval*. Berlin: De Gruyter.

Bischetti, Sara, and Antonio Montefusco. 2018. "Prime osservazioni su *Ars dictaminis*, cultura volgare e distribuzione sociale dei saperi nella toscana medievale." *Carte romanze* 6, no. 1: 163–240.

Bischoff, Bernard. 1961. "The Study of Foreign Languages in the Middle Ages." *Speculum* 36: 209–24.

Black, Robert. 1996. "The Vernacular and the Teaching of Latin in Thirteenth- and Fourteenth-Century Italy." *Studi Medievali* 3: 703–51

Black, Robert. 2001. *Humanism and Education in Medieval and Renaissance Italy: Tradition and Innovation in Latin Schools from the Twelfth to the Fifteenth Century*. Cambridge: Cambridge University Press.

Black, Robert. 2004. "The School Miscellany in Medieval and Renaissance Italy." *Segno e Testo* 2: 213–44.

Black, Robert. 2007. *Education and Society in Florentine Tuscany*, 260–76. Leiden: Brill.

Black, Robert. 2011. "Ovid in Medieval Italy." In *Ovid in the Middle Ages*, ed. James G. Clark and Frank T. Coulson, 123–42. Cambridge: Cambridge University Press.

Black, Robert. 2013. "Teaching Techniques: The Evidence of Manuscript Schoolbooks Produced in Tuscany." In *The Classics in the Medieval and Renaissance Classroom*, ed. Junita Feros Ruys, John O. Ward, and Melanie Heyworth, 245–63. Turnhout, Belgium: Brepols.

Black, Robert. 2015. "Education." In *Dante in Context*, ed. Zygmunt G. Barański and Lino Pertile, 260–76. Cambridge: Cambridge University Press.

Black, Robert. 2018. "Between Grammar and Rhetoric: *Poetria nova* and Its Educational Context in Medieval and Renaissance Italy." In *Le poetriae del medioevo latino: Modelli, fortuna, commenti*, ed. Gian Carlo Alessio and Domenico Losappio, 45–68. Venice: Edizioni Ca' Foscari.

Black, Robert, and Gabriella Pomaro. 2000. *La consolazione della filosofia nel Medioevo e nel Rinascimento italiano: Libri di scuola e glosse nei manoscritti fiorentini (Boethius's Consolation of Philosophy in Italian Medieval and Renaissance Education: Schoolbooks and Their Glosses in Florentine Manuscripts)*. Florence: SISMEL Edizioni del Galluzzo.

Boas, Markus. 1914. "De Librorum Catonianorum historia atque compositione." *Mnemosyne*, n.s., 42: 17–46.

Boas, Markus. 1932. "Cato und die Grabschrift der Allia Potestas." *Rheinisches Museum für Philologie* 81: 178–86.

Boccia, Alessandro. 2001. "Appunti sulla presenza di Stazio nella *Divina Commedia*." *Annali dell'Istituto Italiano per gli Studi Storici* 18: 29–45.

Boldrini, Sandro. 1991. "L'Aesopus' di Gualtiero Anglico." In *La favolistica latina in distici elegiaci Atti Convegno Internazionale, Assisi, 26–28 ottobre 1990*, ed. Giuseppe Catanzaro and Francesco Santucci, 79–106. Assisi: Accademia Properziana del Subasio.

Bolgar, Robert. 1954. *The Classical Heritage and Its Beneficiaries*. Cambridge: Cambridge University Press.

Bonaventura, Enzo. 1912–13. *Arrigo da Settimello e l'"Elegia de diversitate fortunae et philosophiae consolation."* *Studi medievali* 4: 110–92.

Borsellino, Nino. 1989. *La tradizione del comico: Letteratura e teatro da Dante a Belli*. Milan: Garzanti.

Bosco, Umberto. 1972. *Dante vicino*. Caltanissetta, Italy: Sciascia.

BIBLIOGRAPHY   295

Botterill, Steven. 1988. "'Quae non licet homini loqui': The Ineffability of Mystical Experience in *Paradiso* I and the *Epistle to Can Grande*." *Modern Language Review* 83: 332–41.

Botterill, Steven. 1994. "'... però che la divisione non si fa se non per aprire la sentenzia de la cosa divisa' (*V.N.* XIV, 13): The *Vita nuova* as Commentary." In *"La gloriosa donna de la mente": A Commentary on the "Vita Nuova,"* ed. Vincent Moleta, 61–76. Florence: Olschki.

Bowden, Betsy. 2000. "Dante's Cato and the Disticha Catonis." *Deutsches Dante-Jahrbuch* 75, no. 1: 125–30.

Breen, Katharine. 2010. *Imagining an English Reading Public, 1150–1400*. Cambridge: Cambridge University Press.

Bremond, Claude, Jaques Le Goff, and Jean-Claude Schmitt, eds. 1982. *L'exemplum*. Turnhout, Belgium: Brepols.

Brilli, Elisa, and Giuliano Milani. 2021. *Dante: Les vies nouvelles*. Paris: Fayard.

Brown, Emerson, Jr. 1971. "Proserpina, Matelda, and the Pilgrim." *Dante Studies* 89: 33–48.

Brownlee, Kevin. 1991. "Pauline Vision and Ovidian Speech in *Paradiso* I." In *The Poetry of Allusion: Virgil and Ovid in Dante's Commedia*, ed. Rachel Jacoff and Jeffrey Schnapp, 202–21. Stanford, CA: Stanford University Press.

Brugnoli, Giorgio. 1969. "Stazio in Dante." *Cultura Neolatina* 29: 117–25.

Brugnoli, Giorgio. 1988. "Statius Christianus." *Italianistica* 17: 9–15.

Brugnoli, Giorgio. 1998. *Studi danteschi*. 3 vols. Pisa: Edizioni ETS.

Brunetti, Giuseppina, and Sonia Gentili. 2000. "Una biblioteca nella Firenze di Dante: i manoscritti di Santa Croce." In *Testimoni del vero: Su alcuni libri in biblioteche d'autore*, ed. Eugenio Russo, 21–47. Rome: Bulzoni.

Burrow, Colin. 2000. "Virgils, from Dante to Milton." In *The Cambridge Companion to Virgil*, ed. Charles Martindale, 79–90. Cambridge: Cambridge University Press.

Burrow Colin, Stephen J. Harrison, Martin McLaughlin and Elisabetta Tarantino. 2020. *Imitative Series and Clusters from Classical to Early Modern Literature*. Berlin: De Gruyter.

Burton, Rosemary. 1983. *Classical Poets in the "Florilegium Gallicum."* Frankfurt am Main: Lang.

Bushnell, Rebecca W. 1996. *A Culture of Teaching: Early Modern Humanism in Theory and Practice*. Ithaca, NY: Cornell University Press.

Busnelli, Giovanni. 1935. "Il Convivio di Dante e un suo nuovo commento." *La Civiltà Cattolica* 86, no. 1: 135–46.

Bynum, Caroline Walker. 1995. *The Resurrection of the Body in Western Christianity, 200–1336*. New York: Columbia University Press.

Cachey, Theodore J. 2001. "Dante's Journey between Fiction and Truth: Geryon Revisited." In *Dante, da Firenze all'aldilà: Atti del Terzo Seminario Dantesco Internazionale, Firenze 9–11 giugno 2000*, ed. Michelangelo Picone, 75–92. Florence: Franco Cesati Editore.

Cachey, Theodore J. 2010. "Cartographic Dante: A Note on Dante and the Greek Mediterranean." *Italica* 87, no. 3: 325–54. [Revised and republished in Jan M. Ziolkowski, ed., *Dante and the Greeks*, 197–226 (Washington, DC: Dumbarton Oaks, 2014)].

Caesar, Michael. 1989. *Dante: The Critical Heritage*. London: Routledge.

Caferro, William. 2015. "Empire, Italy, and Florence." In *Dante in Context*, ed. Zygmunt G. Barański and Lino Pertile, 9–29. Cambridge: Cambridge University Press.

Cagni, Pietro. 2016. "Il messo celeste e la liturgia alle porte di Dite (*Inferno* IX)." *Le Forme e la storia* 9, no. 2 [*Lecturae Dantis: Dante oggi e letture dell'*Inferno]: 229–50.

Cagni, Pietro. 2020. "Osservazioni su un giuramento dantesco (*Inferno* XVI, 124–36)." *L'Alighieri* 55: 5–22.Camozzi Pistoja, Ambrogio. 2009. "Il veglio di Creta alla luce di Matelda: Una lettura comparativa di *Inferno* XIV e *Purgatorio* XXVIII." *Italianist* 29: 27–28.

Camozzi Pistoja, Ambrogio. 2014. "Il quarto trattato del *Convivio*: O della satira." *Le tre corone* 1: 27–53.

Camozzi Pistoja, Ambrogio. 2015. "Profeta e satiro: A proposito di *Inferno* 19." *Dante Studies* 133: 27–45.

Camozzi Pistoja, Ambrogio. 2019. "Testo come eucarestia: Linguaggio parabolico nel *Convivio* di Dante." *Studi danteschi* 84: 57–100.

296 BIBLIOGRAPHY

Campbell, C. Jean. 2008. *The Commonwealth of Nature: Art and Poetic Community in the Age of Dante*. University Park: Pennsylvania State University Press.

Cannon, Christopher. 2008. "Langland's Ars Grammatica." *Yearbook of Langland Studies* 22: 1–25.

Cannon, Christopher. 2009. "The Middle English Writer's Schoolroom: Fourteenth-Century English Schoolbooks and Their Contents." *New Medieval Literatures* 11: 19–38.

Cannon, Christopher. 2014. "From Literacy to Literature: Elementary Learning and the Middle English Poet." *Publications of the Modern Language Association of America* 129, no. 3: 349–64.

Cannon, Christopher. 2016. *From Literacy to Literature: England 1300–1400*. Oxford: Oxford University Press.

Cardini, Franco. 1978. "Alfabetismo e livelli di cultura nell'età comunale." *Quaderni storici* 13, no. 38: 488–522.

Cardini, Franco. 1982. "'Nobiltà' e cavalleria nei centri urbani: Problemi e interpretazioni." In *Nobiltà e ceti dirigenti in Toscana nei secoli XI–XIII: Strutture e concetti*; atto del IV convegno (Firenze, 12 Dicembre 1981), ed. Comitato di studi sulla storia dei ceti dirigenti in Toscana, 13–28. Florence: Papafava.

Carlucci, Alessandro. 2021. "Who Could Understand the *Commedia*? Multilingualism, Comprehension and Oral Communication in Medieval Italy." In *Dante beyond Borders*, ed. Nick Havely, Jonathan Katz, and Richard Cooper, 132–44. Oxford: Legenda.

Carrai, Stefano. 2012. *Dante e l'antico: L'emulazione dei classici nella Commedia*. Florence: SISMEL.

Carrai, Stefano. 2018. "Puntualizzazioni sulla datazione della 'Vita nova.'" *L'Alighieri* 52: 109–15.

Carron, Delphine. 2009. "Présence de la figure de Caton le philosophe dans les proverbes et exemples médiévaux: Ses rapports avec les 'Disticha Catonis.'" In *Tradition des proverbes et des exempla dans l'occident médiéval*, ed. Hugo O. Bizzarri and Martin Rohde, 165–90. Berlin: Walter de Gruyter.

Carron, Delphine. 2010. "*Le héros de la liberté: Les aventures philosophiques de Caton au Moyen Âge latin, de Paul Diacre à Dante*." Ph.D. diss., Université Paris IV et Neuchâtel. https://doc.rero.ch/record/21170/files/00002181.pdf.

Carron, Delphine. 2018. "La figure de Catilina et l'histoire de Florence dans les chroniques (début XIIIe–milieu du XIVe siècle)." *Rassegna Europea di Letteratura Italiana* 51–52: 11–60.

Carron, Delphine, and Christian Tottman. 2010. "Une vie de philosophe philosophique? Le comentum super Dantis Aldigherii Comoediam de Benvenuto Da Imola et l'elaboration de la figure du Catone Dantesco au XIVe siècle Italien." In *Vie philosophique et vies de philosophes*, ed. Bruno Clement, 177–94. Paris: Sens & Tonka.

Carruthers, Mary J. 1990. *The Book of Memory: A Study of Memory in Medieval Culture*. Cambridge: Cambridge University Press.

Casadei, Alberto. 2013. "Il titolo della *Commedia* e l'Epistola a Cangrande." In *Dante oltre la Commedia*. Bologna: il Mulino.

Casaretto, Francesco Mosetti. 1992. "Alle origini del genere pastorale cristiano: L'*Ecloga Theoduli* e la demonizzazione del paganesimo." *Studi Medievali* 33: 469–536.

Casaretto, Francesco Mosetti. 1999. "Discussione sulla lezione di Dronke." In *Ideologie e pratiche del rimpiego nell'Alto Medioevo: Atti della XLVI Settimana di Studio del Centro Italiano di Studi sull'Alto Medioevo; Spoleto, 16–21 Aprile 1998*, 313–19. Spoleto: Centro di Studi sull'Alto Medioevo.

Casaretto, Francesco Mosetti. 2013. "Il caso controverso dell'*Ecloga Theoduli*." *Studi Medievali* 54, no. 1: 329–64.

Ceccherini, Irene. 2010. "Le scritture dei notai e dei mercanti a Firenze tra Duecento e Trecento: Unità, varietà, stile." *Medioevo e Rinascimento* 24: 29–68.

Ceccherini, Irene, and Teresa De Robertis. 2015. "Scriptoria e cancelleria nella Firenze del XIV secolo." In *Scriptorium: Wesen, Funktion, Eigenheiten*, ed. Andreas Nievergelt, Rudolf Gamper, Marina Bernasconi Reusser, Birgit Ebersperger, and Ernst Tremp, 141–65. Munich: Bayerische Akademie der Wissenschaften.

Cestaro, Gary P. 2003. *Dante and the Grammar of the Nursing Body*. Notre Dame, IN: University of Notre Dame Press.

Chabot, Isabella. 2014. "Il Matrimonio di Dante." *Reti Medievali* 15: 271–302.

Cherchi, Paolo. 2018. "The *divisioni* in Dante's *Vita nuova.*" *Le tre corone* 5: 73–88.

Cherubini, Gianfranco. 1995. "Un rigattiere fiorentino del Duecento." In *Studi in onore di Arnaldo d'Addario*, ed. Luigi Borgia, Francesco De Luca, Paolo Viti, and Raffaele Maria Zaccaria, 761–72. Lecce: Conte Editore.

Chiamenti, Massimiliano. 1999. "Corollario oitanico al canto ventottesimo del *Purgatorio.*" *Medioevo e rinascimento* 13: 207–20.

Chiecchi, Giuseppe. 2005. *La parola del dolore: Primi studi sulla letteratura consolatoria tra Medioevo e Umanesimo*. Rome: Antenore.

Chiesa, Paolo, and Andrea Tabarroni. 2013. "Introduzione." In Dante Alighieri, *Monarchia*, ed. Paolo Chiesa and Andrea Tabarroni, xix–lxxxvi. Rome: Salerno.

Chimenz, Siro A. 1955. *Dante*. Milan: Marzorati.

Ciasca, Raffaele. 1927. *L'arte dei Medici e Speziali nella storia e nel commercio fiorentino dal Secolo XII al XV*. Florence: Olschki.

Cioffi, Caron Ann. 1988. "'Il cantor de' bucolici carmi': The Influence of Virgilian Pastoral on Dante's Depiction of the Earthly Paradise." In *Lectura Dantis Newberryana*, ed. Paolo Cherchi and Antonio Critodemo Mastrobuono, vol. 1, 93–122. Evanston, IL: Northwestern University Press.

Cioffi, Caron Ann. 1994. "The Anxieties of Ovidian Influence: Theft in *Inferno* XXIV and XXV." *Dante Studies* 112: 77–100.

Clogan, Paul M. 1963. "An Argument of Book I of Statius' Thebaid." *Manuscripta* 7: 30–31.

Clogan, Paul M. 1964. "Chaucer and the 'Thebaid' Scholia." *Studies in Philology* 61, no. 4: 599–615.

Clogan, Paul M. 1964. "The Manuscripts of the Achilleid." *Manuscripta* 8: 175–79.

Clogan, Paul M. 1965. "Medieval Glossed Manuscripts of the Achilleid." *Manuscripta* 9: 104–09.

Clogan, Paul M. 1968. "The Manuscripts of Lactantius Placidus' Commentary on the Thebaid." *Scriptorium* 22: 87–91.

Clogan, Paul M. 1982. "Literary Genres in a Medieval Textbook." *Medievalia et Humanistica* 11: 199–209.

Coleman, Edward. 2004. "Cities and Communes." In *Italy in the Central Middle Ages*, ed. David Abulafia, 27–57. Oxford: Oxford University Press.

Coli, Edoardo. 1897. *Il Paradiso Terrestre dantesco*. Florence: Carnesecchi.

Colish, Marcia. 1985. *The Stoic Tradition from Antiquity to the Early Middle Ages*. 2 vols. New York: Brill.

Conklin Akbari, Suzanne. 2019. "Where Is Medieval Ethiopia? Mapping Ethiopic Studies within Medieval Studies." *Toward a Global Middle Ages: Encountering the World through Illuminated Manuscripts*, ed. Bryan C. Keene, 82–93. Los Angeles: Getty Publications.

Connolly, Serena. 2012. "Disticha Catonis Uticensis." *Classical Philology* 107: 119–30.

Conte, Filippo. 2013. "Studi sull'*exemplum.*" *Le forme e la storia* 6, no. 1: 277–92.

Copeland, Rita, and Ineke Sluiter. 2009. *Medieval Grammar and Rhetoric: Language Arts and Literary Theory, AD 300–1475*. Oxford: Oxford University Press.

Corbett, George. 2013. *Dante and Epicurus: A Dualistic Vision of Secular and Spiritual Fulfilment*. London: Legenda.

Corbett, George. 2020. *Dante's Christian Ethics: Purgatory and Its Moral Contexts*. Cambridge: Cambridge University Press.

Cornish, Alison. 1989. "The Epistle of James in *Inf.* 26." *Traditio* 45: 367–79.

Cornish, Alison. 2000. *Reading Dante's Stars*. New Haven, CT: Yale University Press.

Cornish, Alison. 2010. *Vernacular Translation in Dante's Italy: Illiterate Literature*. Cambridge: Cambridge University Press.

Corradi, Augusto. 1887. *Notizie sui professori di latinità nello Studio di Bologna sin dalle prime memorie: Parte prima (fino a tutto il secolo XV); Raccolta*. Bologna.

Corti, Maria. 1983. *La felicità mentale: nuove prospettive per Cavalcanti e Dante*. Turin: Einaudi.

298 BIBLIOGRAPHY

Corti, Maria. 2003. *Scritti su Cavalcanti e Dante*. Turin: Einaudi.

Crevenna, Claudia. 2004. "Strategie ricorsive negli *exempla* del *Purgatorio* dantesco." *ACME: Annali della Facoltà di Lettere e Filosofia dell'Università di Milano* 57: 33–54.

Crimi, Giuseppe, and Luca Marcozzi, eds. 2013. *Dante e il mondo animale*. Rome: Carocci.

Cristaldi, Sergio. 1994. *La "Vita nuova" e la restituzione del narrare*. Soveria Mannelli, Italy: Rubbettino.

Curtius, Ernst Robert. 1953. *European Literature and the Latin Middle Ages*. London: Routledge & K. Paul [Originally published as *Europäische Literatur und Lateinisches Mittelalter* (Bern: A. Francke, 1948).]

Dagenais, John. 1994. *The Ethics of Reading in Manuscript Culture: Glossing the Libro de Buen Amor*. Princeton, NJ: Princeton University Press.

D'Alfonso, Rossella. 1982. "Fra retorica e teologia: Il sistema dei generi letterari nel basso medioevo." *Lingua e stile* 17, no. 2: 269–93.

Davidsohn, Robert. 1956–1968. *Storia di Firenze*. 8 vols. Florence: Sansoni.

Davis, Charles T. 1963. "The Early Collection of Books of S. Croce in Florence." *Proceedings of the American Philosophical Society* 107, no. 5: 399–414.

Davis, Charles T. 1965. "Education in Dante's Florence." *Speculum* 40: 415–35.

Davis, Charles T. 1984. *Dante's Italy, and Other Essays*. Philadelphia: University of Pennsylvania Press.

Davis, Charles T. 1988. "The Florentine 'studia' and Dante's 'Library.'" In *The Divine Comedy and the Encyclopedia of Arts and Sciences*, ed. Giuseppe Di Scipio and Aldo Scaglione, 339–66. Amsterdam: Benjamins.

Day, William R., Jr. 2019. "Economy." In *Dante in Context*, ed. Zygmunt G. Barański and Lino Pertile, 30–45. Cambridge: Cambridge University Press.

De Angelis, Violetta. 1984. "Magna questio preposita coram Dante et domino Francisco Petrarca et Virgiliano." *Studi Petrarcheschi* 1: 103–210.

De Angelis, Violetta. 1993. "'... e l'ultimo Lucano.'" In *Dante e la "bella Scola" della poesia: Autorità e sfida poetica*, ed. Amilcare Iannucci, 95–149. Ravenna: Longo.

De Angelis, Violetta. 2002. "Lo Stazio di Dante: Poesia e scuola." *Schede umanistiche* 16, no. 2: 29–69.

De Angelis, Violetta. 2011. *Scritti di filologia medievale e umanistica*. Naples: MD'Auria.

Debenedetti, Santorre. 1907. "Sui più antichi 'doctores puerorum' a Firenze." *Studi Medievali* 2: 327–51.

Deen Schildgen, Brenda. 2002. *Dante and the Orient*. Urbana: University of Illinois Press.

Delcorno, Carlo. 1984. "Nuovi studi sull'exemplum." *Lettere italiane* 36, no. 1: 49–68.

Delcorno, Carlo. 1989. *Exemplum e letteratura: tra Medioevo e Rinascimento*. Bologna: il Mulino.

Delcorno, Carlo. 1994. "Nuovi studi sull'exemplum," *Lettere italiane* 46, no. 3 (1994): 459–97.

Delcorno, Carlo. 1996. "Dante e il linguaggio dei predicatori." *Letture Classensi* 25: 51–74.

Delhaye, Philippe. 1958. *"Grammatica" et "Ethica" au XIIe siècle*. Leuven, Belgium: Éditions Nauwelaerts.

Dell'Oso, Lorenzo. 2016. "Problemi di metodo intorno alla formazione intellettuale di Dante: i cataloghi librari, le tracce testuali, il *Trattatello* di Boccaccio." *Le tre corone* 4: 1–32.

Dell'Oso, Lorenzo. 2019. "Tra Bibbia e 'letteratura di costumanza': Un'ipotesi su 'Ecce Deus fortior me' (*Vita nova*, II 4)." In *Dante e la cultura Fiorentina*, ed. Zygmunt G. Barański, Theodore J. Cachey Jr., and Luca Lombardo, 221–40. Rome: Salerno.

Dell'Oso, Lorenzo. 2020. "*How Dante Became Dante: His Intellectual Formation between 'Clerici' and 'Laici' (1294–1296)*." Ph.D. diss., University of Notre Dame.

De Luca, Giuseppe. 1977. *Scrittori di religione del Trecento: Volgarizzamenti*. Turin: Einaudi.

Devecka, Martin. 2015. "Literacy." In *The Oxford Handbook of the Literatures of the Roman Empire*, ed. Daniel L. Selden and Phiroze Vasunia. Oxford: Oxford University Press. https://doi.org/10.1093/oxfordhb/9780199699445.013.40

Diacciati, Silvia. 2014. "Dante: Relazioni sociali e vita pubblica." *Reti Medievali* 15, no. 2: 243–70.

BIBLIOGRAPHY 299

Diacciati, Silvia, and Enrico Farini. 2017. "Ricerche sulla formazione dei laici a Firenze nel tardo Duecento." *Archivio storico italiano* 651, no. 2: 205–38.

Dolven, Jeff. 2007. *Scenes of Instruction in Renaissance Romance.* Chicago: University of Chicago Press.

Dominik, William J. 2005. "Statius." In *A Companion to Ancient Epic,* ed. John Miles Foley, 514–27. Malden, MA: Blackwell.

Dronke, Peter. 1984. "Dante's Earthly Paradise: Towards an Interpretation of *Purgatorio* 28." In *The Medieval Poet and His World,* 387–405. Rome: Edizioni di Storia e Letteratura.

Dronke, Peter. 1989. *Dante and Medieval Latin Traditions.* Cambridge: Cambridge University Press.

Dronke, Peter. 1994. *Verse with Prose: From Petronius to Dante.* Cambridge, MA: Harvard University Press.

Dronke, Peter. 1997. *Dante's Second Love: The Originality and the Contexts of the "Convivio."* Leeds: Maney.

Dronke, Peter. 1999. "Riuso di forme e immagini antiche nella poesia." In *Ideologie e pratiche del rimpiego nell'Alto Medioevo,* 283–312.

Dronke, Peter. 2001. *"Viaggi al Paradiso terrestre."* In *Dante: Da Firenze all'aldilà: atti del terzo Seminario dantesco internazionale, Firenze, 9–11 giugno 2000,* 93–103. Florence: Cesati.

Drucker, Johanna. 1995. *The Alphabetic Labyrinth: The Letters in History and Imagination.* New York: Thames and Hudson.

Du Cange, Charles du Fresne. 1883–87. *Glossarium mediae et infimae latinitatis.* Niort: Le Favre.

Durling, Robert. 2003. "Guido Cavalcanti in the *Vita nova.*" In *Guido Cavalcanti tra i suoi lettori,* ed. Maria Luisa Ardizzone, 176–86. Florence: Cadmo.

Earl, Donald C. 1961. *The Political Thought of Sallust.* Cambridge: Cambridge University Press.

Eco, Umberto. 1979. *"Lector in fabula": La cooperazione interpretativa nei testi narrativi.* Milan: Bompiani.

Edwards, Audrey T. 1984. "Cultural Literacy: What Are Our Goals?" *English Journal* 73, no. 4: 71–72.

Eisner, Martin. 2021. *Dante's New Life of the Book: A Philology of World Literature.* Oxford: Oxford University Press.

Erculei, Ercole. 2018. "Frogs' Fairy Tales and Dante's Errors: Cecco d'Ascoli on the Florentine Poet and the Issue of the Relationship between Poetry and Truth." In *Miscellanea Mediaevalia* 40: *Irrtum—Error—Erreur,* ed. Andreas Speer and Maxime Mauriège, 669–80. Berlin: De Gruyter.

Fabian, Seth. 2014. "Cecco vs. Dante: Correcting the *Comedy* with Applied Astrology." Ph.D. diss., Columbia University.

Faini, Enrico. 2014. "Ruolo sociale e memoria degli Alighieri prima di Dante." *Reti Medievali* 15: 203–42.

Faini, Enrico. 2017. "Prima di Brunetto. Sulla formazione intellettuale dei laici a Firenze ai primi del Duecento." *Reti Medievali* 18, no. 1: 1–30.

Faini, Enrico. 2021. "Dante *sapiens Tusciae.*" In *Round Table, the International Dante Congress, Alma Dante 2021,* trans. Anna C. Foster. https://www.academia.edu/95721422/Dante_sapiens_Tuscie_english_version_?email_work_card=title.

Faini, Enrico. 2022. "Before the 'Primo Popolo': Politics and the Popular Movement at San Gimignano in the First Half of the Thirteenth Century," in *Disciplined Dissent in Western Europe,* ed. Fabrizio Titone, 49–74. Turnhout, Belgium: Brepols.

Falzone, Paolo. 2010. *Desiderio della scienza e desiderio di Dio nel "Convivio."* Bologna: il Mulino.

Favati, Guido. 1975. *Inchiesta sul Dolce Stil Nuovo.* Florence: Le Monnier.

Fenzi, Enrico. 2005. "Il libro della memoria." In *Dante in lettura,* ed. Giuseppe De Matteis, 15–38. Ravenna: Longo.

Ferrari, Olindo. 1916. "Il mondo degli inferi di Claudiano." *Athenaeum* 4: 333–37.

Ferrucci, Franco. 1990. *Il poema del desiderio: Poetica e passione in Dante,* 91–124. Milan: Leonardo. [Originally published as "Comedìa," Yearbook of Italian Studies 1 (1971): 29–52.]

300 BIBLIOGRAPHY

Filosa, Carlo. 1952. *La favola e la letteratura esopiana in Italia: Dal medio evo ai nostri giorni*. Milan: Casa editrice F. Vallardi.

Fink-Errera, Guy. 1977. "La produzione dei libri di testo nelle università medievali." In *Libri e lettori nel medioevo: guida storica e critica*, ed. Guglielmo Cavallo, 131–64. Bari: Laterza.

Fisher, Bonnie. 1987. "A History of the Use of Aesop's Fables as a School Text from the Classical Era through the Nineteenth-Century." Ph.D. diss., University of Indiana.

Fiorentini, Luca. 2016. "Il Silenzio di Gerione (*Inferno* XVI–XVII)." *Rivista di Storia e Letteratura Religiosa* 2: 213–40.

Fiumi, Enrico. 1953. "Economia e vita privata dei fiorentini nelle rilevazioni statistiche di Giovanni Villani." *Archivio Storico Italiano* 111: 239–41.

Folena, Gianfranco. 1991. *Volgarizzare e tradurre*. Turin: Einaudi.

Fornaciari, Raffaello. 1901. *Studi su Dante*. Florence: Sansoni.

Forti, Fiorenzo. 1965. *Fra le carte dei poeti*. Milan: Ricciardi.

Franceschi, Franco. 1993. *Oltre il "Tumulto": I lavoratoti fiorentini dell'Arte della lana fra Tre e Quattrocento*. Florence: Olschki.

Franceschi, Franco. 2012. ". . . E seremo tutti ricchi": Lavoro, mobilità sociale e conflitti nelle città dell'Italia medieval*. Pisa: Pacini.

Freccero, John. 1986. *Dante: The Poetics of Conversion*, ed. Rachel Jacoff. Cambridge, MA: Harvard University Press.

Freccero, John. 2013. "Allegory and Autobiography." In *The Cambridge Companion to Dante*, ed. Rachel Jakoff, 161–80. Cambridge: Cambridge University Press.

Frosini, Giovanna. 2020. "Il volgare di Dante." In *Dante*, ed. Roberto Rea and Justin Steinberg, 245–65. Rome: Carocci.

Frova, Carla. 1974. *Istruzione e educazione nel Medioevo*. Turin: Loescher.

Fubini, Mario. 1951. *Due Studi Danteschi*. Florence: Sansoni.

Fumagalli, Edoardo. 2012. *Il giusto Enea e il pio Rifeo: Pagine dantesche*. Florence: Leo S. Olschki.

Gaimari, Giulia, and Catherine Keen. 2019. *Ethics, Politics and Justice in Dante*. London: UCL Press.

Gambale, Giacomo. 2009. "Dante, l''Epistula Iacobi' e il 'De Peccato Linguae': Per una lettura filosofica di 'Inferno' XXVI." *Studi Danteschi* 74: 179–98.

Gambale, Giacomo. 2012. *La lingua di fuoco: Dante e la filosofia del linguaggio*. Rome: Città nuova.

Gargan, Luciano. 2014. *Dante, la sua biblioteca e lo studio di Bologna*. Rome: Editrice Antenore.

Garin, Eugenio. 1957. *L'Educazione in Europa, 1400–1600*. Bari: Laterza.

Gehl, Paul. 1989. "Latin Reader in Fourteenth-Century Florence." *Scrittura e civiltà* 13: 387–440.

Gehl, Paul F. 1993. *A Moral Art: Grammar, Society, and Culture in Trecento Florence*. Ithaca, NY: Cornell University Press.

Gehl, Paul F. 1994. "Preachers, Teachers, Translators: The Social Meaning of Language Study in Trecento Tuscany." *Viator* 25: 289–324.

Gehl, Paul. 2008. "Humanism for Sale: Making and Marketing Schoolbooks in Italy, 1450–1650." http://www.humanismforsale.org/text/.

Gentili, Sonia. 2005. *L'uomo aristotelico alle origini della letteratura italiana*. Rome: Carocci.

Gentili, Sonia. 2020. "Poesia e filosofia a Firenze tra Santa Croce e Santa Maria Novella." In *The Dominicans and the Making of Florence (13th–14th Centuries)*, ed. Johannes Bartuschat, Elisa Brilli, and Delphine Carron, 225–41. Florence: Firenze University Press.

Gentili, Sonia, and Sylvain Piron. 2015. "La bibliothèque de Santa Croce." In *Frontières des savoirs en Italie à l'époque des premières universités (XIII–XV siècles)*, ed. Joël Chandelier and Aurélien Robert, 481–507. Rome: École française de Rome.

Gianferrari, Filippo. 2016. "Pride and Tyranny: An Unnoted Parallel between *Purgatorio* 12 and *Policraticus* 8.20–21." *Dante Notes*. https://www.dantesociety.org/publicationsdante-notes/pride-and-tyranny-unnoted-parallel-between-purgatorio-12-and-policraticus.

Gianferrari, Filippo. 2017. "Did Dante Know the *Ilias latina*? Textual Echoes in the Prologue to the *Purgatorio*." *Dante Notes*. https://dantesociety.org/node/120.

BIBLIOGRAPHY 301

Gianferrari, Filippo. 2017. "*Pro patria mori*: From the *Disticha Catonis* to Dante's Cato." *Dante Studies* 135: 1–30.

Gianferrari, Filippo. 2019. "Cato (and His *Distichs*) between Brunetto and Dante: Uses and Misuses of a Patriotic Icon." In *Bono Giamboni, Brunetto Latini e la formazione intellettuale dei laici*, ed. Zygmunt G. Barański, Theodore J. Cachey, and Luca Lombardo, 173–91. Rome: Salerno.

Gianferrari, Filippo. 2020. "'Poca favilla, gran fiamma seconda' (*Par.* I 34): Un proverbio d'autorità." *Le tre corone*, 133–58.

Gianferrari, Filippo. 2021. "Gli *auctores* scolastici nella formazione classica del poeta." In *"Nostra maggior musa": I maestri della letteratura classica nella Commedia di Dante*, ed. John Butcher, 217–33. Città di Castello: Edizioni Nuova Prhomos.

Gianferrari, Filippo. 2023. "*Donne e divisioni*: The Instructional Aim of the *Vita nova*." In *Dante's "Vita nova": A Collaborative Reading*, ed. Zygmunt G. Barański and Heather Webb, 170–82. Notre Dame, IN: University of Notre Dame Press.

Gilson, Simone. 2005. *Dante and Renaissance Florence*. Cambridge: Cambridge University Press.

Glauche, Günter. 1970. *Schullektüre im Mittelalter*. Munich: Bei der Arbeo Gesellschaft.

Glenn, Diana. 1999. "Women in Limbo: Arbitrary Listings or Textual Referents? Mapping the Connections in *Inferno* 4 and *Purgatorio* 22." *Dante Studies* 117: 85–115.

Gmelin, Hermann. 1953. "Dante und die römischen Dichter." *Deutsches Dante-Jahrbuch* 31–32: 42–65.

Goar, Robert J. 1987. *The Legend of Cato Uticenis from the First Century B.C. to the Fifth Century A.D., with an Appendix on Dante and Cato*. Brussels: Latomus.

Goffis, Cesare F. 1968. "Il canto I del *Paradiso*." In *Lectura Dantis Scaligera*, 5–26. Florence: Le Monnier.

Goldthwaite, Richard. 2008. *The Economy of Renaissance Florence*. Baltimore: Johns Hopkins University Press.

Goody, Jack. 1968. *Literacy in Traditional Societies*. Cambridge: Cambridge University Press.

Goody, Jack. 2000. *The Power of the Written Tradition*. Washington, DC: Smithsonian Institution Press.

Gorni, Guglielmo. 2009. "Una *Vita nova* per Cavalcanti, da Beatrice alla Donna Gentile." In *Guido Cavalcanti: Dante e il suo "primo amico,"* 11–29. Rome: Aracne.

Graff, Arturo. 1891. *Miti, leggende e superstizioni del Medio Evo*. 2 vols. Turin: Loescher.

Graff, Harvey J. 1987. *The Legacies of Literacy. Continuities and Contradictions in Western Culture and Society*. Bloomington: Indiana University Press.

Grafton, Anthony, and Lisa Jardine. 1986. *From Humanism to the Humanities: Education and the Liberal Arts in Fifteenth- and Sixteenth-Century Europe*. London: Duckworth.

Gragnolati, Manuele. 2010. "'Rime trasformate e rime assenti': La *performance* della *Vita nova* e le figure di Dante e Cavalcanti." In *Dante the Lyric and Ethical Poet (Dante Poeta Lirico e Etico)*, ed. Zygmunt G. Barański and Martin McLaughlin, 74–91. London: Legenda.

Grandgent, Charles. 1902. "Cato and Elijah: A Study in Dante." *PMLA* 17: 71–90.

Green, R. P. H. 1982. "The Genesis of a Medieval Textbook: The Models and Sources of the *Ecloga Theoduli*." *Viator* 13: 49–106.

Grendler, Paul F. 1989. *Schooling in Renaissance Italy: Literacy and Learning, 1300–1600*. Baltimore: Johns Hopkins University Press.

Grendler, Paul F. 1995. "What Piero Learned in School: Fifteenth-Century Vernacular Education." In *Studies in the History of Art*, vol. 48, 160–74. Washington, DC: National Gallery of Art.

Grimaldi Pizzorno, Patrizia. 1994. "Matelda's Dance and the Smile of the Poets." *Dante Studies* 112: 115–32.

Grubbs, Judith Evans, Tim G. Parkin, and Roslynne Bell. 2013. *The Oxford Handbook of Childhood and Education in the Classical World*. Oxford: Oxford University Press.

Grubmüller, Klaus. 1977. *Meister Esopus: Untersuchungen zu Geschichte und Funktion der Fabel im Mittelalter*. Munich: Artemis.

302   BIBLIOGRAPHY

Guillory, John. 1993. *Cultural Capital: The Problem of Literary Canon Formation*. Chicago: University of Chicago Press.

Guyler, Sam. 1972. "Virgil the Hypocrite—Almost: A Re-Interpretation of *Inferno* XXIII." *Dante Studies* 90: 25–42.

Hagedorn, Suzanne C. 1997. "A Statian Model for Dante's Ulysses." *Dante Studies* 115: 19–43.

Haidu, Peter. 1993. *The Subject of Violence: The Song of Roland and the Birth of the State*. Bloomington: Indiana University Press.

Hamilton, George L. 1909. "Theodulus: A Medieval Textbook." *Modern Philology* 7: 169–185.

Hanna, R., T. R. G. Keightley, A. J. Minnis, and N. F. Palmer. 2005. "Latin Commentary Tradition and Vernacular Literature." In *The Cambridge History of Literary Criticism: The Middle Ages*, ed. A. J. Minnis and I. Johnson, vol. 2, 361–421. Cambridge: Cambridge University Press.

Harrison, Robert P. 1988. *The Body of Beatrice*. Baltimore: Johns Hopkins University Press.

Haskins, Charles H. 1909. "List of Text-Books from the Close of the Twelfth Century." *Harvard Studies in Classical Philology* 20: 76–94.

Haskins, Charles Homer. 1957. *The Renaissance of the Twelfth Century*. Cleveland: World Publishing Co.

Hastings, Rashdall. 1936. *The Universities of Europe in the Middle Ages*. 3 vols. Oxford: Oxford University Press.

Hatcher, Hanna. 1970. "Dante's Ulysses and Guido da Montefeltro." *Dante Studies* 88: 112–17.

Hawkins, Peter. 1985. "Transfiguring the Text: Ovid, Scripture and the Dynamics of Allusion." *Stanford Italian Review* 5: 115–39.

Hawkins, Peter. 1991. "Watching Matelda." In *The Poetry of Allusion: Virgil and Ovid in Dante's Commedia*, ed. Rachel Jacoff and Jeffrey Schnapp, 181–201. Stanford, CA: Stanford University Press.

Hawkins, Peter. 1999. *Dante's Testaments: Essays in Scriptural Imagination*. Stanford, CA: Stanford University Press.

Hazelton, Richard. 1956. "*Two Texts of the Disticha Catonis and Its Commentary, with Special Reference to Chaucer, Langland and Gower.*" Ph.D. diss., Rutgers University.

Hazelton, Richard. 1957. "The Christianization of 'Cato': The *Disticha Catonis* in the Light of Late Mediaeval Commentaries." *Mediaeval Studies* 19, no. 1: 157–73.

Hazelton, Richard. 1960. "Chaucer and Cato." *Speculum* 35, no. 3: 357–80.

Heilbronn, Denise. 1977. "The Prophetic Role of Statius in Dante's *Purgatory*." *Dante Studies* 95: 58–65.

Herlihy, David and Christiane Klapisch-Zuber. 1978. *Les Toscans et leurs familles: Une étude du catasto florentin de 1427*. Paris: Fondation Nationale des Sciences Politiques.

Herren, Michael. 2007. "Reflections on the Meaning of the *Ecloga Theoduli*: Where Is the Authorial Voice?" In *Poetry and Exegesis in Premodern Latin Christianity: The Encounter between Classical and Christian Strategies of Interpretation*, ed. Willemien Otten and Karla Pollmann, 199–230. Leiden: Brill.

Heslin, Peter. 2005. *The Transvestite Achilles: Gender and Genre in Statius' Achilleid*. Cambridge: Cambridge University Press.

Hexter, Ralph J. 1986. *Ovid and Medieval Schooling: Studies in Medieval School Commentaries on Ovid's Ars Amatoria, Epistulae Ex Ponto, and Epistulae Heroidum*. Munich: Bei der Arbeo-Gesellschaft.

Hirsch, Erik D., Jr. 1983. "Cultural Literacy." *American Scholar* 52, no. 2: 159–69.

Hirsch, Erik D., Jr. 1985. "'Cultural Literacy' Doesn't Mean 'Core Curriculum.'" *English Journal* 74, no. 6: 47–49.

Hirsch, Erik D., Jr. 1987. *Cultural Literacy: What Every American Needs to Know*. Boston: Houghton Mifflin.

Hollander, Robert. 1969. *Allegory in Dante's "Commedia."* Princeton, NJ: Princeton University Press.

Hollander, Robert. 1975. "Cato's Rebuke and Dante's Scoglio." *Italica* 52: 348–63.

Hollander, Robert. 1976. "Dante Theologus-poeta." *Dante Studies* 94: 91–136.

Hollander, Robert. 1983. *Il Virgilio dantesco: Tragedia nella Commedia*. Florence: Olschki.

Hollander, Robert. 1984. "Virgil and Dante as Mind-Readers (Inferno XXI and XXIII)." *Medioevo Romanzo* 9: 85–100.

BIBLIOGRAPHY   303

Hollander, Robert. 2001. *Dante: A Life in Works*. New Haven, CT: Yale University Press.

Hollander, Robert. 2010. "Ancora sul Catone Dantesco." *Studi Danteschi* 75: 187–204.

Hollander, Robert. 2013. "Dante's Cato Again." In *Dantean Dialogues: Engaging with the Legacy of Amilcare Iannucci*, ed. Maggie Kilgour and Elena Lombardi, 66–124. Toronto: University of Toronto Press.

Holmes, Olivia. 2000. *Assembling the Lyric Self: Authorship from Troubadour Song to Italian Poetry Book*. Minneapolis: University of Minnesota Press.

Holzberg, Niklas. 2002. *The Ancient Fable: An Introduction*. Bloomington: Indiana University Press.

Honess, Claire E., and Matthew Treherne. 2013. *Reviewing Dante's Theology*. Oxford: Peter Lang.

Hooper, Laurence E. 2012. "Dante's *Convivio*, Book 1: Metaphor, Exile, *Epoche*." Supplement, *MLN* 127: S86–S104.

Hunt, Richard W. 1980. *The History of Grammar in the Middle Ages: Collected Papers*. Amsterdam: J. Benjamins.

Hunt, Tony. 1991. *Teaching and Learning Latin in Thirteenth-Century England: Texts*. 2 vols. Rochester, NY: Boydell & Brewer.

Hyde, J. K. 1979. "Some Uses of Literacy in Venice and Florence in the Thirteenth and Fourteenth Century." *Transactions of the Royal Historical Society* 29: 109–28.

Iannucci, Amilcare. 1973. "Dante's Theory of Genres and the 'Divina Commedia.'" *Dante Studies* 91: 1–25.

Iannucci, Amilcare. 1976. "Ulysses' *folle volo*: The Burden of History." *Medioevo romanzo* 3: 410–45.

Iannucci, Amilcare. 1984. *Forma ed evento nella "Divina Commedia"*. Rome: Bulzoni.

Iannucci, Amilcare A., and Gian Carlo Alessio. 1993. *Dante e la "bella scola" della poesia: Autorità e sfida poetica*. Ravenna: Longo.

Illich, Ivan. 1993. *In the Vineyard of the Text: A Commentary to Hugh's Didascalicon*. Chicago: University of Chicago Press.

Imbach, Ruedi. 1996. *Dante, la philosophie et les laïcs*. Fribourg: Éditions Universitaires; Paris: Éditions du Cerf.

Imbach, Ruedi. 2013. *Le defi laïque*. Paris: Vrin.

Imbach, Ruedi. 2019. "Dante come allievo e maestro." In *"Minima medievalia": saggi di filosofia medievale*, 197–217. Rome: Aracne.

Indizio, Giuseppe. 2012. "Un episodio della vita di Dante: L'incontro con Francesco Petrarca." *Italianistica* 16, no. 3: 71–80.

Indizio, Giuseppe. 2013. *Problemi di biografia dantesca*. Ravenna: Longo.

Inglese, Giorgio. 2015. *Vita di Dante: Una biografia possibile*. Rome: Carocci.

Irvine, Martin. 1994. *The Making of Textual Culture: "Grammatica" and Literary Theory, 350–1100*. Cambridge: Cambridge University Press.

Irvine, Martin, and David Thomson. 2005. "*Grammatica* and Literary Criticism." In *The Cambridge History of Literary Criticism*, ed. A. Minnis and I. Johnson, 13–41. Cambridge: Cambridge University Press.

Iser, Wolfgang. 1978. *The Act of Reading: A Theory of Aesthetic Response*. Baltimore: Johns Hopkins University Press.

Jenkyns, Richard. 2005. "Epic and Other Genres in the Roman World." In *A Companion to Ancient Epic*, ed. John Miles Foley, 562–73. Malden, MA: Blackwell.

Jones, Edith C. 1944. "Avianus in the Middle Ages: Manuscripts and Other Evidence of Nachleben." Ph.D. diss., University of Illinois Urbana-Champaign.

Kallendorf, Craig, and Hilaire Kallendorf. 2002. "'Per te poeta fui, per te cristiano' (*Purg*. 22.73): Statius as Christian, from 'Fact' to Fiction." *Deutsches Dante-Jahrbuch* 77: 61–72.

Kantorowicz, Ernst H. 1951. "*Pro patria mori* in Medieval Political Thought." *American Historical Review* 56, no. 3: 472–92.

Kay, Tristan. 2016. *Dante's Lyric Redemption: Eros, Salvation, Vernacular Tradition*. Oxford: Oxford University Press.

304   BIBLIOGRAPHY

Keen, Catherine. 2018. "'Parlando vommi / con ser Brunetto' (*Inf.* XV 100–101): Dante in dialogo con Brunetto Latini." *Studi danteschi* 83: 73–94.

Keen, Catherine. 2019. "Vernacular Eloquence and Roman Rhetoric between Brunetto and Dante." In *Dante e la cultura fiorentina*, ed. Zygmunt G. Barański, Theodore J. Cachey Jr., and Luca Lombardo, 151–72. Rome: Salerno.

Kinoshita, Sharon. 2006. *Medieval Boundaries: Rethinking Difference in Old French Literature.* Philadelphia: University of Pennsylvania Press.

Koening, John. 1986. *Il "popolo" dell'Italia del nord nel XIII secolo.* Bologna: il Mulino.

Kristeller, Paul Oskar. 1961. *Renaissance Thought: The Classic, Scholastic, and Humanistic Strains.* New York: Harper & Brothers.

Lansing, Richard, ed. 2000. *Dante Encyclopedia.* New York: Garland.

Larkin, Neil M. 1962. "Another Look at Dante's Frog and Mouse." In *Modern Language Notes* 77, no. 1: 94–99.

Laugesen, Anker Teilgard. 1962. "La Roue de Virgile: Une page de la théorie littéraire du moyen âge." *Classica er mediaevalia* 23: 248–73.

Ledda, Giuseppe. 2002. *La guerra della lingua.* Ravenna: Longo.

Ledda, Giuseppe. 2013. "Per un bestiario di Malebolge." In *Dante e il mondo animale*, ed. Giuseppe Crimi and Luca Marcozzi, 92–113. Rome: Carocci.

Ledda, Giuseppe. 2013. "Un bestiario metaletterario nell'Inferno dantesco." *Studi Danteschi* 78: 119–53.

Ledda, Giuseppe. 2014. "Sulla soglia del *Purgatorio*: peccato, penitenza, resurrezione: Per una 'lectura' di *Purgatorio* IX." *Lettere Italiane* 46: 3–36.

Ledda, Giuseppe. 2019. *Il bestiario dell'aldilà.* Ravenna: Longo.

Leo, Ulrich. 1951. "The Unfinished *Convivio* and Dante's Rereading of the Aeneid." *Mediaeval Studies* 13: 41–64

Leonardi, Claudio, and Birger Munk Olsen, eds. 1995. *The Classical Tradition in the Middle Ages and the Renaissance: Proceedings of the First European Science Foundation Workshop on "The Reception of Classical Texts" (Florence, Certosa Del Galluzzo, 26–27 June 1992).* Spoleto: Centro Italiano di Studi sull'Alto Medioevo.

Lewis, Charlton T., and Charles Short. 1879. *A Latin Dictionary.* Oxford: Clarendon Press. Perseus Digital Library, Tufts University, http://www.perseus.tufts.edu/.

Lewis, C. S. 1956. "Dante's Statius." *Medium Aevum* 25: 133–39. [Reprinted in Walter Hooper, ed., *Studies in Medieval and Renaissance Literature* (Cambridge: Cambridge University Press, 1979), 94–102.]

Lewis, C. S. 1958. *The Allegory of Love.* New York: Oxford University Press.

Livi, Giovanni. 1906. *Cultori di Dante in Bologna nei secoli XII e XIV.* Rome: Nuova Antologia.

Livi, Giovanni. 1921. *Dante e Bologna: Nuovi studi e documenti.* Bologna: Zanichelli.

Lombardi, Elena. 2016. "L''invenzione' del lettore in Dante." In *C'è un lettore in questo testo? Rappresentazione della lettura nella letteratura italiana*, ed. Giovanna Rizzarelli and Cristina Savettieri, 23–41. Bologna: il Mulino.

Lombardi, Elena. 2018. *Imagining the Woman Reader in the Age of Dante.* Oxford: Oxford University Press.

Lombardo, Luca. 2010. "Dante, Boezio e la 'bella menzogna.'" In *L'allegoria: Teorie e forme tra medioevo e modernità*, ed. Fulvio Ferrari, 31–55. Trento: Dipartimento di Studi Letterari, Linguistici e Filologici.

Lombardo, Luca. 2012. "'Quasi come sognando': Dante e la presunta rarità del 'libro di Boezio' (*Convivio*, ii. Xii, 2–7)." *Mediaeval Sophia* 12: 141–52.

Lombardo, Luca. 2013. *Boezio in Dante: La* Consolatio Philosophiae *nello scrittoio del poeta.* Venice: Edizioni Ca' Foscari.

Lombardo, Luca. 2018. "'Alcibiades quedam meretrix': Dante lettore di Boezio e i commenti alla *Consolatio philosophiae*." *L'Alighieri* 52: 5–36.

Lombardo, Luca. 2019. "Primi appunti sulla *Vita nova* nel contesto della prosa del Duecento." *L'Alighieri* 60: 21–41.

Lombardo, Luca. 2019. "'Talento m'è preso di ricontare l'insegnamento dei phylosophi': Osservazioni sulla prosa dottrinale a Firenze nell'età di Dante." In *Dante e la cultura fiorentina*, ed. Zygmunt G. Barański, Theodore J. Cachey Jr., and Luca Lombardo, 33–58. Rome: Salerno.

Longo, Nicola. 1996. "L'*exemplum* fra retorica medievale e testo biblico nel *Purgatorio*." In *Memoria biblica nell'opera di Dante*, ed. Enzo Esposito, Roberto Manica, Nicola Longo, and Riccardo Scrivano, 57–98. Rome: Bulzoni.

Lowe, Elias A. 1914. *The Beneventan Script: A History of the South Italian Minuscule*. Oxford: Clarendon Press.

Lummus, David. 2020. *The City of Poetry: Imagining the Civic Role of the Poet in Fourteenth Century Italy*. Cambridge: Cambridge University Press.

Lusini, Gianfrancesco. 2020. "The Ancient and Medieval History of Eritrean and Ethiopian Monasticism: An Outline." In *A Companion to Medieval Ethiopia and Eritrea*, ed. Samantha Kelly, 194–216. Leiden: Brill.

Lutz, Cora E. 1974. "A Medieval Textbook." *Yale University Library Gazette* 49, no. 2: 212–16.

Lynch, Sarah. 2017. *Elementary and Grammar Education in Late Medieval France*. Amsterdam: Amsterdam University Press.

Malato, Enrico. 1995. "Dante." In *Dalle origini a Dante*, vol. 1 of *Storia della letteratura italiana*, ed. Enrico Malato, 773–1052. Rome: Salerno.

Malato, Enrico. 1997. *Dante and Guido Cavalcanti: Il dissidio per la* Vita Nuova *e il "Disdegno" di Guido*. Rome: Salerno.

Mallette, Karla. 2021. *Lives of the Great Languages: Arabic and Latin in the Medieval Mediterranean*. Chicago: University of Chicago Press.

Manacorda, Giuseppe. 1914. *Storia della scuola in Italia: Il medio evo*, vol. 1. Milan: R. Sandron.

Mandruzzato, Enzo. 1955. "L'apologo 'Della rana e del topo' e Dante." *Studi Danteschi* 33: 147–65.

Manescalchi, Romano. 2008. "Una nuova interpretazione del Catone dantesco." *Critica Letteraria* 140: 419–46.

Manescalchi, Romano. 2011. *Studi sulla Commedia: Le tre fiere, Enea, Ciacco, Brunetto, Catone, Piccarda ed altri problemi danteschi*. Naples: Loffredo.

Mangini, Angelo. 2014. "Quel che Catone non sa: Per una nuova lettura di *Purgatorio* I e II." *Studi e problemi di critica testuale* 89: 111–49.

Manitius, Max. 1892. "Beiträge zur Geschichte Römischer Dichter in Mittelalter." *Philologus* 51: 166–71.

Mann, Jill. 1986. "La favolistica latina." In *Aspetti della letteratura latina nel secolo XIII (Atti del primo Convegno Internazionale di studi dell'Associazione per il Medioevo e l'Umanesimo, Perugia 3–5 ottobre 1983)*, ed. Claudio Leonardi and Giovanni Orlandi, 193–219. Florence: La Nuova Italia.

Mann, Jill. 1992. "Medieval Proverb Collections: The West European Tradition." *Journal of the Warburg and Courtauld Institutes* 55: 19–35.

Mann, Jill. 2006. "'He Knew Nat Catoun': Medieval School-Texts and Middle English Literature." In *The Text in the Community: Essays on Medieval Works, Manuscripts, Authors, and Readers*, ed. Jill Mann and Maura Nolan, 41–74. Notre Dame, IN: University of Notre Dame Press.

Mann, Jill. 2009. *From Aesop to Reynard: Beast Literature in Medieval Britain*. Oxford: Oxford University Press.

Mann, Nicholas, and Birger Munk Olsen, eds. 1997. *Medieval and Renaissance Scholarship: Proceedings of the Second European Science Foundation Workshop on the Classical Tradition in the Middle Ages and the Renaissance (London, Warburg Institute, 27–28 November 1992)*. Leiden: Brill.

Marchesi, Simone. 2001. "La rilettura del 'De officiis' e i due tempi della composizione del 'Convivio.'" *Giornale storico della letteratura italiana* 177: 84–107.

Marchesi, Simone. 2007. "Distilling Ovid: Dante's Exile and Some Metamorphic Nomenclature in Hell." In *Writers Reading Writers: Intertextual Studies in Medieval and Early Modern Literature in Honor of Robert Hollander*, ed. Janet Smarr, 21–39. Newark: University of Delaware Press.

306 BIBLIOGRAPHY

Marchesi, Simone. 2011. *Dante and Augustine: Linguistics, Poetics, Hermeneutics*. Toronto: University of Toronto Press.

Marchesi, Simone. 2013. "Epic Ironies: Poetics, Metapoetics, Self-Translation (*Inferno* 18.1, *Purgatorio* 24.52, *Paradiso* 1.13)." *Dante Studies* 131: 99–117.

Marchesi, Simone. 2019. "Classical Culture." In *The Cambridge Companion to Dante's Commedia*, ed. Zygmunt G. Barański and Simon Gilson, 127–39. Cambridge: Cambridge University Press.

Marcozzi, Luca. 2013. "Dante ed Esopo." In *Dante e il mondo animale*, ed. Giuseppe Crimi and Luca Marcozzi, 131–49. Rome: Carocci.

Marrou, Henri Irénée. 1964. *A History of Education in Antiquity*. New York: New American Library. [Originally published as *Histoire de l'éducation dans l'antiquité* (Paris: Le Seuil, 1948).]

Martelli, Mario. 2009. *Ragione e talento: Studio su Dante e Petrarca*. Cosenza, Italy: Falco Editore.

Marti, Mario. 2005. *Da Dante a Croce: Proposte, consensi e dissensi*. Galatina, Italy: Congedo.

Martines, Lauro. 1988. *Power and Imagination: City-States in Renaissance Italy*. Baltimore: Johns Hopkins University Press.

Martinez, Ronald L. 1989. "La 'sacra fame dell'oro' (*Purgatorio* 22, 41) tra Virgilio e Stazio: Dal testo all'interpretazione." *Letture Classensi* 18: 177–93.

Martinez, Ronald L. 1995. Dante and the Two Canons: Statius in Virgil's Footsteps (*Purgatorio* 21–30)." *Comparative Literature Studies* 32: 151–75.

Martinez, Ronald L. 1998. "Mourning Beatrice: The Rhetoric of Threnody in the *Vita nuova*." *MLN* 113: 1–29.

Martinez, Ronald L. 2004. "The Poetics of Advent Liturgies: *Vita Nuova* and *Purgatorio*." In *Le culture di Dante: Studi in onore di Robert Hollander*, ed. Michelangelo Picone, Theodore J. Cachey, and Margherita Mesirca, 271–304. Florence: Cesati.

Martinez, Ronald L. 2015. "Rhetoric, Literary Theory, and Practical Criticism." In *Dante in Context*, ed. Zygmunt G. Barański and Lino Pertile, 277–96. Cambridge: Cambridge University Press.

Mathis, Joseph, ed. 1971. *Divi Thomae Aquinatis De Regimine Principum*. Turin: Marietti.

Mattone, Antonello. 2005. "Biblioteche ed editoria universitaria nell'Italia medievale." *Studi Storici* 4: 877–922.

Mazzotta, Giuseppe. 1979. *Dante, Poet of the Desert: History and Allegory in the Divine Comedy*. Princeton, NJ: Princeton University Press.

Mazzotta, Giuseppe. 1993. *Dante's Vision and the Circle of Knowledge*. Princeton, NJ: Princeton University Press.

Mazzucchi, Andrea. 2004. *Tra Convivio e Commedia: sondaggi di filologia e critica dantesca*. Rome: Salerno.

Mazzucchi, Andrea. 2012. "Per una nuova edizione commentata del *Convivio*." In *Leggere Dante oggi*, ed. Enrico Malato and Andrea Mazzucchi, 81–107. Rome: Salerno.

McDonough, Christopher J. 2008. "Alexander Neckam and the Commentary on the *Ecloga Theoduli*: A Question of Attribution." *Filologia Mediolatina* 15: 249–67.

McKenzie, Kenneth. 1898. "Dante's References to Aesop." *Annual Report of the Dante Society*: 1–14.

Mead, Herman R. 1939. "Fifteenth-Century Schoolbooks." *Huntington Library Quarterly* 3, no. 1: 37–42.

Meier, Franziska. 2015. "Educating the Reader: Dante's *Convivio*." *L'Alighieri* 45: 21–34.

Meneghetti, Maria Luisa. 1984. *Il pubblico dei trovatori: Ricezione e riuso dei testi lirici cortesi fino al XIV secolo*. Modena: Mucchi.

Mengaldo, Pier Vincenzo. 1966. "L'elegia 'umile' (*De vulgari eloquentia*, II, iv)." *Giornale storico della letteratura italiana* 118: 177–98.

Meyers, Lean. 2004. "L'*Églogue de Théodule*: 'Démonisation' ou 'sacralisation' de la mythologie?" In *L'allégorie de l'antiquité à la Renaissance*, ed. Brigitte Pérez-Jean and Patricia Eichel-Lojkine, 335–47. Paris: Champion.

Micozzi, Laura. 2015. "Statius' Epic Poetry: A Challenge to the Literary Past." In *Brill Companion to Statius*, ed. William J. Dominik, C. E. Newlands, and K. Gervais, 325–42. Leiden: Brill.

Minissale, Francesca. 1975–76. "Il *poeta e la nave* (Claud. rapt. Pros. I, 1–14)." *Helikon* 15–16: 496–99.

Minnis, Alistair J., A. B. Scott, and David Wallace, eds. 1988. *Medieval Literary Theory and Criticism, c. 1100–c. 1375: The Commentary-Tradition*. New York: Clarendon Press.

Mocan, Mira. 2020. "Il 'nuovo ludo' dei diavoli e dei dannati: Lettura di *Inferno* XXII." *Dante Studies* 138: 152–75.

Moevs, Christian. 2016. "*Paradiso* II: Gateway to Paradise." *Le tre corone* 3: 57–73.

Molho, Anthony. 1969. *Social and Economic Foundations of the Italian Renaissance*. New York: Wiley.

Montefusco, Antonio, and Giuliano Milani, eds. 2020. *Le lettere di Dante: Ambienti culturali, contesti storici e circolazione dei saperi*. Berlin: De Gruyter.

Moore, Edward. 1968. *Studies in Dante, First Series: Scripture and Classical Authors in Dante*. New York: Greenwood Press.

Mulchahey, Michèle M. 1998. *"First the Bow Is Bent in Study": Dominican Education before 1350*. Toronto: Pontifical Institute of Mediaeval Studies.

Mulchahey, Michèle M. 2005. "Education in Dante's Florence Revisited: Remigio de' Girolami and the Schools of Santa Maria Novella." In *Medieval Education*, ed. Ronald B. Begley and Joseph W. Koterski, 143–81. New York: Fordham University Press.

Munk Olsen, Birger. 1991. *I classici nel canone scolastico altomedievale*. Spoleto: Centro Italiano di Studi sull'Alto Medioevo.

Munk Olsen, Birger. 1995. *La réception de la littérature classique au moyen age (IXe–XIIe siècle): Choix d'articles publié par des collègues à l'occasion de son soixantième anniversaire*. Copenhagen: Museum Tusculanum Press.

Munk Olsen, Birger, Carl Nylander, and Claudio Leonardi, eds. 1994. *L'atteggiamento medievale di fronte alla cultura classica*. Rome: Unione Internazionale degli Istituti di Archeologia Storia e Storia dell'Arte in Roma.

Murari, Rocco. 1905. *Dante e Boezio: Contributo allo studio delle fonti dantesche*. Bologna: Zanichelli.

Murphy, James J. 1981. *Rhetoric in the Middle Ages: A History of Rhetorical Theory from Saint Augustine to the Renaissance*. Berkeley: University of California Press.

Najemy, John. 2004. *Italy in the Age of the Renaissance 1300–1550*. Oxford: Oxford University Press.

Najemy, John. 2006. *A History of Florence, 1200–1575*. Malden, MA: Blackwell.

Nardi, Bruno. 1912. *Sigieri di Brabante nella "Divina Commedia" e le fonti della filosofia di Dante*. Spianate, Italy: Presso l'autore.

Nardi, Bruno. 1930. *Saggi di filosofia dantesca*. Milan: Società Editrice Dante Alighieri.

Nardi, Bruno. 1942. *Dante e la cultura medievale*. Bari: Laterza.

Nasti, Paola. 2007. *Favole d'amore e "saver profondo": La tradizione salomonica in Dante*. Ravenna: Longo.

Nasti, Paola. 2011. "'Vocabuli d'autori e di scienze e di libri' (*Conv*. II xii 5): Percorsi sapienzali di Dante." In *La Bibbia di Dante: Esperienza mistica, profezia e teologia biblica in Dante*, ed. Giuseppe Ledda, 121–78. Ravenna: Centro Dantesco dei Frati Minori Conventuali.

Nasti, Paola. 2016. "Storia materiale di un classico dantesco: La *Consolatio Philosophiae* fra XII e XIV secolo, tradizione manoscritta e rielaborazioni esegetiche." *Dante Studies* 134: 142–68.

Oldfather, William A. 1911. "New Material for the Study of Avianus." *Transactions and Proceedings of the American Philological Association* 42: 105–21.

Oliger, Livarius. 1924. "Servasanto da Faenza O.F.M. e il suo 'Liber de virtutibus et vitiis.'" In *Miscellanea Francesco Ehrle*, vol. 1, 148–89. Vatican City: Biblioteca Apostolica Vaticana.

Ong, Walter J. 1959. "Latin Language Study as a Renaissance Puberty Rite." *Studies in Philology* 56, no. 2: 103–24.

Ong, Walter J. 1971. *Rhetoric, Romance, and Technology*. Ithaca, NY: Cornell University Press.

Ong, Walter. J. 1982. *Orality and Literacy: The Technologizing of the Word*. New York: Methuen.

308   BIBLIOGRAPHY

Onorato, Marco. 2008. "Introduzione." In *Claudio Claudiano, De raptu Proserpinae*, ed. and trans. Marco Onorato, 11–107. Naples: Loffredo.

Orlandi, Stefano, and Tommaso di Matteo Sardi. 1952. *La biblioteca di S. Maria Novella in Firenze dal sec. XIV al sec. XIX.* Florence: Il Rosario.

Orme, Nicholas. 1973. *English Schools in the Middle Ages.* London: Harper & Row.

Orme, Nicholas. 2001. *Medieval Children.* New Haven, CT: Yale University Press.

Osternacher, Johann E. 1915. "Die Überlieferung der Ecloga Theoduli." *Neues Archiv* 40: 329–76.

Padoan, Giorgio. 1960. *Il pio Enea e l'empio Ulisse: Tradizione classica e intendimento medievale in Dante.* Ravenna: Longo.

Padoan, Giorgio. 1964. "Il *Liber Esopi* e due episodi dell'*Inferno*." *Studi danteschi* 41: 75–102.

Padoan, Giorgio. 1965. "Dante di fronte all'umanesimo letterario." *Lettere Italiane* 17: 237–57.

Paetow, Louis J. 1910. "The Arts Course at Medieval Universities with Special Reference to Grammar and Rhetoric." *University of Illinois Studies in Language and Literature* 3: 497–628.

Pagliaro, Antonino. 1967. *Ulisse: Ricerche semantiche sulla Commedia.* Florence: D'Anna.

Pampaloni, Guido. 1995. "Gli Alighieri, Dante e il buon tempo antico (Il canto XVI dell'*Inferno*)." In *Esegesi e filologia*, of *Studi in onore di Arnaldo d'Addario*, ed. Luigi Borgia, Francesco De Luca, Paolo Viti and Raffaele Maria Zaccaria, vol. 2, 437–48. Lecce: Conte Editore.

Panella, Emilio. 2008. "'Ne le scuole de li religiosi e a le disputazioni de li filosofanti' (Dante Alighieri): *Lectio, disputatio, predicatio*." In *Dal convento alla città. Filosofia e teologia in Francesco da Prato O.P. (XIV secolo)*, ed. Fabrizio Amerini, 115–31. Florence: Zella.

Papaleoni, Giuseppe. 1894. "Maestri di grammatica toscani dei secoli XIII e XIV." *Archivio Storico Italiano* 14: 149–52.

Park, Katharine. 1980. "The Readers at the Florentine Studio." *Rinascimento* 20, no. 2: 249–310.

Parkes, Malcolm B. 1975. "The Influence of the Concepts of *Ordinatio* and *Compilatio* on the Development of the Book." In *Medieval Learning and Literature: Essays Presented to R. W. Hunt*, ed. J. J. G. Alexander and M. T. Gibson, 115–41. Oxford: Oxford University Press.

Parkes, Malcolm B. 1991. "The Literacy of the Laity." In *Scribes, Scripts and Readers: Studies in the Communication, Presentation and Dissemination of Medieval Texts*, 275–97. London: Hambledon Press.

Parkes, Ruth. 2011. "The 'Deidamia Achilli': An Eleventh Century Statian-Ovidian Epistle." *International Journal of the Classical Tradition* 18, no. 1: 19–35.

Parodi, Eugenio. 1915. "Gli esempi di superbia punita e il 'bello stile' di Dante." *Atene e Roma* 18: 97–107

Pasquini, Emilio. 1967. "Il canto di Gerione." *Atti e Memorie dell'Arcadia*, serie III, 4: 346–68.

Pastore Stocchi, Manlio. 1962. "Il cristianesimo di Stazio (*Purg.* XXII) e un'ipotesi del Poliziano." In *Miscellanea di studi offerta a Armando Balduino e Bianca Bianchi per le loro nozze. Vicenza, 30 giugno 1962*, ed. Lorenzo Renzi, 41–45. Padua: Seminario di Filologia Moderna dell'Università.

Pecchiura, Piero. 1965. *La figura di Catone Uticense nella letteratura latina.* Turin: Giappichelli.

Pecoraro, Paolo. 1967. "Il Canto II del *Paradiso*." In *Lectura Dantis Scaligera: Paradiso*, 39–64. Florence: Le Monnier.

Pecoraro, Paolo. 1987. *Le stelle di Dante: Saggio d'interpretazione di riferimenti astronomici e cosmografici della Divina commedia.* Rome: Bulzoni.

Pegoretti, Anna. 2006. "Immaginare la veste di un angelo: Il caso di *Purg.* 9, 115–116." *L'Alighieri* 27: 141–51.

Pegoretti, Anna. 2015. "Filosofanti." *Le tre corone* 2: 11–70.

Pegoretti, Anna. 2017. "'Nelle scuole delli religiosi': Materiali per Santa Croce nell'età di Dante." *L'Alighieri* 50: 5–55.

Pellegrin, Elisabeth. 1957. "Les Remedia Amoris d'Ovide texte scholaire médiéval." *Bibliothèque de l'École des Chartes* 115: 172–179.

Pertile, Lino. 1979. "Dante e l'ingegno di Ulisse." *Stanford Italian Review* 1: 35–65.

Pertile, Lino. 1998. *La puttana e il gigante: dal "Cantico dei cantici" al Paradiso terrestre di Dante.* Ravenna: Longo.

Pertile, Lino. 2000. "Ulisse, Guido e le sirene." *Studi Danteschi* 65: 101–18.

BIBLIOGRAPHY   309

Pertile, Lino. 2009. "Canti XXI–XXII–XXIII: Un esperimento eroicomico." In *Esperimenti Danteschi: Inferno 2008*, ed. Simone Invernizzi, 157–72. Genoa: Marietti.

Pertile, Lino. 2010. "Le *Egloghe* di Dante e l'antro di Polifemo." In *Dante the Lyric and Ethical Poet (Dante lirico e etico)*, ed. Zygmunt G. Barański and Martin McLaughlin, 153–67. London: Legenda.

Petoletti, Marco. 2016. "Nota introduttiva," in Dante Alighieri, *Opere di Dante*, vol. 4: Epistole, Egloghe, Questio de aqua et terra, ed. Marco Baglio et al., 491–504. Rome: Salerno.

Petrocchi, Giorgio. 1983. *Vita di Dante*. Bari: Laterza.

Petrucci, Armando. 1972. "Libro, scrittura e scuola." In *La scuola nell'occidente latino dell'alto medioevo*, 313–37. Spoleto: Centro Italiano di Studi sull'Alto Medioevo.

Petrucci, Armando. 1995. *Readers and Writers in Medieval Italy: Studies in the History of Writing*. New Haven, CT: Yale University Press.

Picone, Michelangelo. 1983. "Rito e 'narratio' nella 'Vita nuova." In *Miscellanea di studi in onore di Vittore Branca*, vol. 1, *Dal Medioevo a Petrarca*, ed. Armando Balduino, 154–57. Florence: Olschki.

Picone, Michelangelo. 1987. "La Vita Nuova fra autobiografia e tipologia," in *Dante e le forme dell'allegoresi*, ed. Michelangelo Picone, 59–69. Ravenna: Longo.

Picone, Michelangelo. 1994. "Dante argonauta: la ricezione dei miti ovidiani nella *Commedia*." In *Ovidius redivivus: Von Ovid zu Dante*, ed. Michelangelo Picone and Bernhard Zimmermann, 191–200. Stuttgart: M&P Verlag.

Picone, Michelangelo. 2003. "La *Vita nova* come prosimetro." In *Percorsi della lirica duecentesca*, 238–41. Fiesole, Italy: Cadmo.

Picone, Michelangelo, Theodore J. Cachey, and Margherita Mesirca, eds. 2004. *Le culture di Dante: Studi in onore di Robert Hollander; Atti del quarto Seminario dantesco internazionale, University of Notre Dame (Ind.), USA, 25–27 settembre 2003*. Florence: F. Cesati.

Piron, Sylvain. 2008. "Le poète et le théologien: Une rencontre dans le *studium* de Santa Croce." In *"Ut philosophia poesis": Questions philosophiques dans l'oeuvre de Dante, Pétrarque et Boccacce*, ed. Joël Biard and Fosca Mariani Zini, 73–112. Paris: Vrin.

Pirovano, Donato. 2012. *Poeti del Dolce stil novo*. Rome: Salerno.

Pirovano, Donato. 2020. "Vita nuova." In *Dante*, ed. Roberto Rea and Justin Steinberg, 37–54. Rome: Carocci.

Placella, Vincenzo. 1995. "Il pubblico del *Convivio* e quello del *Paradiso*." In *Miscellanea di studi in onore di Raffaele Sirri*, ed. M. Palumbo and V. Placella, 365–73. Naples: Federico e Ardia.

Poggioli, Renato. 1962. "Dante *poco tempo silvano*: or a 'Pastoral Oasis' in the *Commedia*." *Annual Report of the Dante Society* 80: 1–20.

Pollard, Graham. 1987. *The Pecia System in the Medieval Universities*. London: Scolar Press.

Pomaro, Gabriella. 1980. "Censimento dei manoscritti della biblioteca di S. Maria Novella: Parte I, Origini e Trecento." In *Memorie Domenicane* n.s., 11: 325–470.

Porcelli, Bruno. 1999. "Peccatum linguae, modello mosaico, climax narrativo nel canto di Ulisse." *Critica Letteraria* 72: 9–26.

Porro, Pasquale. 2020. "Dante e la tradizione filosofica." In *Dante*, ed. Roberto Rea and Justin Steinberg, 307–27. Rome: Carocci.

Post, Gaines. 1953. "Two Notes on Nationalism in the Middle Ages." *Traditio* 9: 281–320.

Prosperi, Valentina. 2015. "'Even Children and the Uneducated Know Them': The Medieval Trojan Legends in Dante's *Commedia*." *Medievalia et Humanistica*, n.s., 40: 83–112.

Proto, E. 1912. "Nuove ricerche sul Catone dantesco." *Giornale storico della letteratura italiana* 59: 193–248.

Quinn, Betty N. 1971. "Ps. Theodolus." In *Catalogus Translationum et Commentariorum*, ed. Paul O. Kresteller, Virginia Brown, and Ferdinand E. Cranz, vol. 2: 383–408. Washington, DC: Catholic University of America Press.

Quondam, Amadeo. 1978. "Nascita della grammatica: appunti e materiali per una descrizione analitica." In *Alfabetismo e cultura scritta*, ed. Attilio Bartoli-Langelli and Armando Petrucci, 555–92. Bologna: il Mulino.

310 BIBLIOGRAPHY

Raby, Frederic J. E. 1957. *A History of Secular Latin Poetry in the Middle Ages*. 2 vols. Oxford: Clarendon Press.

Raimondi, Ezio. 1963. "Il Canto I del *Purgatorio*." In *Lectura Dantis Scaligera*. Florence: Le Monnier.

Raimondi, Ezio. 1965. "Notarella dantesca (a proposito di Taide)." *Lettere Italiane* 17: 443–46.

Raimondi, Ezio. 1968. "Analisi strutturale e semantica del canto IX del *Purgatorio*." *Studi Danteschi* 45: 121–46.

Raimondi, Ezio. 1970. *Metafora e storia: studi su Dante e Petrarca*. Turin: Einaudi.

Rajna, Pio. 1902. "Per le 'divisioni' della Vita Nuova," in *Strenna Dantesca*, ed. Giuseppi Passerini and Orazio Bacci, vol. 1: 111–14. Florence, Ariani.

Rand, Edward K. 1930. "A Friend of the Classics in the Times of St. Thomas Aquinas." In *Mélanges Mandonnet: Études d'histoire littéraire et doctrinale du Moyen Age*, vol. 2: 261–81. Paris: J. Vrin.

Rand, Edward Kennard. 1929. "The Classics in the Thirteenth Century." *Speculum* 4, no. 3: 249–69.

Renucci, Paul. 1954. *Dante disciple et juge du monde gréco-latin*. Paris: Les Belles Lettres.

Reynolds, Leighton D., and N. G. Wilson, eds. 1983. *Texts and Transmission: A Survey of the Latin Classics*. Oxford: Clarendon Press.

Reynolds, Suzanne. 1996. *Medieval Reading: Grammar, Rhetoric and the Classical Text*. Cambridge: Cambridge University Press.

Riché, Pierre. 1962. "Recherches sur l'instruction des laics de IXe Siècle." *Cahiers Civil Mediéval* 5: 175–82.

Riché, Pierre. 2006. *Des nains sur des épaules de géants: Maîtres et élèves au moyen âge*. Paris: Tallandier.

Risse, Robert G. 1964. "*An Edition of the Commentary on the Fables of Avianus in Erfurt MS., Amplon. Q.21: The Text and Its Place in Medieval Literary Culture*." Ph.D. diss., Washington University.

Rizzo, Silvia. 2002. *Ricerche sul latino umanistico*. 2 vols. Rome: Edizioni di storia e letteratura.

Roos, Paolo. 1984. *Sentenza e proverbio nell'antichità e i "Distici di Catone": Il testo latino e i volgarizzamenti italiani*. Brescia: Morcelliana.

Rossi, Luca Carlo. 1993. "Prospezioni filologiche per lo Stazio di Dante," in *Dante e la "bella scola" della poesia: Autorità e sfida poetica*, ed. Amilcare Iannucci, 205–24. Ravenna: Longo.

Rouse, Richard H., and Mary A. Rouse. 1982. "*Statim invenire*: Schools, Preachers, and New Attitudes to the Page." In *Renaissance and Renewal in the Twelfth Century*, ed. R. L. Benson and G. Constable, 201–25. Cambridge, MA: Harvard University Press. [Republished in Mary A. Rouse and Richard H. Rouse, *Authentic Witnesses: Approaches to Medieval Texts and Manuscripts* (Notre Dame, IN: University of Notre Dame Press, 1991), 191–255.]

Rubinstein, Nicolai. 1958. "Political Ideals in Sienese Art: The Frescoes by Ambrogio Lorenzetti and Taddeo di Bartolo in the Palazzo Pubblico." *Journal of the Warburg and Courtauld Institute* 21: 179–207.

Russo, Vittorio. 1979. "Strutture innovative delle opere letterarie di Dante nella prospettiva dei generi letterari." *L'Alighieri* 20, no. 2: 46–63.

Russo, Vittorio. 2002. *Il romanzo teologico*. Naples: Liguori.

Ryser, Gabriella. 2017. "A Wedding in the Underworld of Claudian's *De Raptu Proserpinae*." In *Reading the Way to the Netherworld: Education and the Representations of the Beyond in Later Antiquity*, ed. Ilinca Tanaseanu-Döbler, Anna Lefteratou, Gabriela Ryser, and Konstantinos Stamatopoulos, 282–300. Göttingen: Vandenhoeck & Ruprecht.

Sabbadini, Remigio. 1896. *La scuola e gli studi di Guarino Guarini Veronese (con 44 documenti)*. Catania: Galati.

Salvemini, Gaetano. 1960 [1899]. *Magnati e popolani in Firenze dal 1280 al 1295*, ed. Ernesto Sestan. Turin: Einaudi.

Sanford, Eva M. 1924. "The Use of Classical Latin Authors in the Libri Manuales." *Transaction and Proceedings of the American Philological Association* 55: 190–248.

Santagata, Marco. 2012. *Dante: Il romanzo della sua vita*. Milan: Mondadori.

BIBLIOGRAPHY   311

Santagata, Marco. 2016. "Dante e gli speziali." In *Dante und die bildenden Künste: Dialoge—Spiegelungen—Transformationen*, ed. Maria Antonietta Terzoli and Sebastian Schütze, 13–22. Berlin: De Gruyter.

Scaffai, Marco, and Paolo Serra Zanetti. 1980. "Tradizione manoscritta dell''Ilias latina'." In *In uerbis uerum amare: Miscellanea dell'Istituto Di Filologia Latina E Medioevale dell'Università di Bologna*, ed. Serra Zanetti, 205–77. Florence: La Nuova Italia.

Scarano, Nicola. 1905. *Saggi danteschi*. Livorno: Giusti.

Scherillo, Michele. 1896. *Alcuni capitoli della biografia di Dante*. Turin: Loescher.

Schück, Julius. 1865. "Dantes classische Studien und Brunetto Latini." *Neue Jahrbücher für Philologie und Paedagogik* 92: 262–63.

Schulze-Busacker, Elisabeth. 2012. *La didactique profane au Moyen Âge*. Paris: Classiques Garnier.

Scott, John A. 1971. "*Inferno* XXVI: Dante's Ulysses." *Lettere Italiane* 23: 145–86.

Scott, John A. 1972. "Dante's Admiral." *Italian Studies* 27: 28–40.

Scott, John A. 1991. "Beatrice's Reproaches in Eden: Which 'School' Had Dante Followed?" *Dante Studies* 109: 1–23.

Scott, John A. 1996. *Dante's Political Purgatory*. Philadelphia: University of Pennsylvania Press.

Segre, Cesare. 1976. *Lingua, stile e società; Studi sulla storia della prosa italiana*. Milan: Feltrinelli.

Segre, Cesare. 1985. "Oralità e scrittura nell'epica medioevale." In *Oralità. Cultura, letteratura, discorso: Atti del Convegno Internazionale (Urbino 21–25 luglio 1980)*, ed. Bruno Gentili and Giuseppe Paioni, 19–35. Rome: Edizioni dell'Ateneo.

Semola, Mariangela. 1998. "Maria e gli altri *exempla* biblici nei canti X–XXVI del *Purgatorio* Dantesco." In *Memoria biblica e letteratura italiana*, ed. Vincenzo Placella, 9–32. Naples: Istituto Universitario Orientale.

Semola, Mariangela. 2008. "Dante e l'*exemplum* animale: Il caso dell'aquila." *L'Alighieri* 31: 149–59.

Shoaf, Richard. 1978. "'Auri sacra fames' and the Age of Gold (*Purg*. XXII, 40–41 and 148–150)." *Dante Studies* 96: 195–99.

Silverstein, Theodore. 1938. "On the Genesis of *De Monarchia* II, 5." *Speculum* 13, no. 3: 326–49.

Singleton, Charles S. 1949. *An Essay on the "Vita nuova."* Cambridge, MA: Harvard University Press. [Reprinted 1977. Baltimore: Johns Hopkins University Press.]

Singleton, Charles S. 1960. "In Exitu Israel de Aegypto." *78th Annual Report of the Dante Society of America*, 1–24.

Skutsch, Franz. 1905. "Dicta Catonis." In *Realencyclopädie*, ed. August Pauly and Georg Wissowa, col. 358. Stuttgart: Metzler.

Smalley, Beryl. 1971. "Sallust in the Middle Ages." In *Classical Influences on European Culture A.D. 500–1500: Proceedings of an International Conference held at King's College, Cambridge, April 1969*, ed. R. R. Bolgar, 165–75. Cambridge: Cambridge University Press.

Soetermeer, Frank. 1997. *Utrumque ius in peciis: Aspetti della produzione libraria a Bologna fra Due e Trecento*. Milan: Giuffrè.

Soons, A. 1973. "The Didactic Quality of the *Theoduli Ecloga*." *Orpheus* 20: 149–61.

Spitzer, Leo. 1944. "The Farcical Elements in Inferno, Cantos XXI–XXIII." *MLN* 59, no. 2: 83–88.

Starn, Randolph. 1994. *Ambrogio Lorenzetti: The Paazzo Pubblico, Siena*. New York: George Braziller.

Steinberg, Justin. 2007. *Accounting for Dante: Urban Readers and Writers in Late Medieval Italy*. Notre Dame, IN: University of Notre Dame Press.

Steinberg, Justin. 2010. "Dante's First Dream between Reception and Allegory: The Response to Dante Da Maiano in the 'Vita Nova.'" In *Dante the Lyric and Ethical Poet (Dante Poeta Lirico e Etico)*, ed. Zygmunt G. Barański and Martin McLaughlin, 92–118. London: Legenda.

Steinberg, Justin. 2013. *Dante and the Limits of the Law*. Chicago: University of Chicago Press.

Steinberg, Justin. 2016. "Dante's Constitutional Miracles (*Monarchia* 2.4 and *Inferno* 8–9)." *Lettere Italiane* 3: 431–44.

Stillinger, Thomas C. 1992. *The Song of Troilus: Lyric Authority in the Medieval Book*. Philadelphia: University of Pennsylvania Press.

BIBLIOGRAPHY

Stock, Brian. 1983. *The Implications of Literacy: Written Language and Models of Interpretation in the Eleventh and Twelfth Centuries*. Princeton, NJ: Princeton University Press.

Storey, H. Wayne. 1993. *Transcription and Visual Poetics in the Early Italian Lyric*. New York: Garland.

Storey, H. Wayne. 2004. "Di libello in libro: problemi materiali nella poetica di Monte Andrea e Dante." In *Da Guido Guinizzelli a Dante: Nuove prospettive sulla lirica del Duecento; Atti del convegno di studi, Padova-Monselice, 10–12 maggio 2002*, ed. Furio Brugnolo and Gianfelice Peron, 271–90. Padua: Il poligrafo.

Storey, H. Wayne. 2005. "Following Instructions: Remaking Dante's *Vita Nova* in the Fourteenth Century." In *Medieval Constructions in Gender and Identity: Essays in Honor of Joan M. Ferrante*, ed. Teodolinda Barolini, 117–32. Tempe, AZ: MRTS.

Strecker, Karl. 1924. Ist Gottschalk der Dichter der "Ecloga Theoduli." *Neues Archiv* 45: 18–23.

Sznura, Franek. 1998. "Per la storia del notariato fiorentino: I più antichi elenchi superstiti dei giudici e dei notai fiorentini (anni 1291 e 1338)." In *Tra libri e carte: Studi in onore di Luciana Mosiici*, ed. Teresa De Robertis and Giancarlo Savino, 437–515. Florence: Franco Cesari Editore.

Sznura, Franek. 2014. "I debiti di Dante nel loro contesto documentario." *Reti Medievali* 15: 303–21.

Tandoi, Vincenzo. 1969. "Il ricordo di Stazio 'dolce poeta' nella *Satira* VII di Giovenale." *Maia* 21: 103–22.

Tarantino, Elisabetta. 2012. "*Fulvae Harenae*: The Reception of an Intertextual Complex in Dante's *Inferno*." *Classical Receptions Journal* 4, no. 1: 90–126.

Tateo, Francesco. 2008. "Il poema sacro ('Par.' XXV 1–3)." In *Versi controversi*, ed. Domenico Cofano and Sebastiano Valerio, 345–68. Foggia: Edizioni del Rosone.

Tavoni, Mirko. 2011. "Introduzione." In Dante Alighieri, *Opere*, ed. Marco Santagata, vol. 1: 1067–123. Milan: Mondadori.

Tavoni, Mirko. 2015. "Linguistic Italy." In *Dante in Context*, ed. Zygmunt G. Barański and Lino Pertile, 249–59. Cambridge: Cambridge University Press.

Tavoni, Mirko. 2015. *Qualche idea su Dante*. Bologna: il Mulino.

Thiele, Georg. 1985. *Der lateinische Äsop des Romulus und die Prosa-Fassungen des Phädrus. Kritischer Text mit Kommentar und einleitenden Untersuchungen*. New York: Georg Olms.

Thompson, David. 1974. "A Note on Fraudolent Counsel." *Dante Studies* 92: 149–52.

Tilliette, Jean-Yves. 2005. "Grecia Mendax." In *La Grèce antique sous le regard du Moyen Âge Occidental, Actes du 15e Colloque de la Villa Kérylos (Beaulieu-Sur-Mer, 8 et 9 Octobre 2004)*, ed. Jean Leclant and Michel Zink, 11–22. Paris: Diffusion De Boccard.

Todorović, Jelena. 2016. *Dante and the Dynamics of Textual Exchange*. New York: Fordham.

Toja, G. 1965. "Noterelle dantesche." *Studi danteschi* 42: 248–55.

Took, John. 2020. *Dante*. Princeton, NJ: Princeton University Press.

Toynbee, Paget. 1893. "Was Dante Acquainted with Claudian?" *Academy* 44: 488–89.

Toynbee, Paget. 1898. *A Dictionary of Proper Names and Notable Matters in the Works of Dante*. Oxford: Clarendon Press.

Toynbee, Paget. 1899–1900. "Index of Authors Quoted by Benvenuto da Imola in his Commentary on the *Divina Commedia*: A Contribution to the Study of the Sources of the Commentary." *Annual Report of the Dante Society of America*, 16–25. https://archive.org/details/jstor-40165915.

Toynbee, Paget. 1902. *Dante Studies and Researches*. 2 vols. London: Methuen.

Truscott, James. 1973. "Ulysses and Guido (*Inferno* XXVI–XXVII)." *Dante Studies* 91: 47–72.

Tubach, F.C. 1962. "Exempla in the Decline." *Traditio* 18: 407–17.

Uccellini, Renée. 2012. *L'arrivo di Achille a Sciro: Saggio di commento a Stazio; Achilleide 1, 1–396*. Pisa: Edizioni della Normale.

Vaccaluzzo, Nunzio. 1902. "Fonti del Catone dantesco." *Giornale storico della letteratura italiana* 40: 140–50.

Van Egmond, Warren. 1980. *Practical Mathematics in the Italian Renaissance: A Catalog of Italian Abbacus Manuscripts and Printed Books to 1600*. Florence: Istituto e museo di storia della scienza.

BIBLIOGRAPHY 313

Varela-portas de Orduña, Juan. 1995. "Función y rendimiento de la fábula de Esopo en la 'Divina Commedia' ('Inf.' XXIII 1–9)." *Medioevo y Literatura* 4: 439–51.

Vasoli, Cesare. 1965. "Filosofia e teologia in Dante." In *Dante nella critica d'oggi: Risultati e prospettive*, ed. Umberto Bosco, 47–71. Florence: Le Monnier.

Vecchi, Giuseppe. 1961. *Il magistero delle "artes" latine a Bologna nel Medioevo*. Bologna: Pàtron.

Venturi, Giovanni. 2004. "Una lectura Dantis e l'uso dell'ecfrasi: *Purgatorio* X." In *Ecfrasi: Modelli ed esempi fra medioevo e Rinascimento*, 15–31.

Verger, Jacques. 1991. *Educations médiévales: L'enfance, l'école, l'Eglise en Occident, Ve–XVe siècles.* Paris: Service d'Histoire de l'Éducation, Institut National de Recherche Pédagogique.

Verger, Jacques. 1999. *Culture, enseignement et société en Occident aux XIIe et XIIIe siècles.* Rennes: Presses Universitaires de Rennes.

Vescovo, Pier Massimo. 1993. "Ecfrasi con spettatore (Dante, 'Purgatorio' X–XVII)." *Lettere Italiane* 45: 335–60.

Villa, Claudia. 1984. *La "lectura Terentii,"* vol. 2, *Da Ildemaro a Francesco Petrarca*. Rome: Antenore.

Villa, Claudia. 1992. "Per una tipologia del commento mediolatino: L'*Ars poetica* di Orazio." In *Il commento ai testi: Atti del seminario di Asona 2–9 ottobre 1989*, ed. Ottavio Besomi and Carlo Caruso, 19–42. Basel: Birkhäuser.

Villa, Claudia. 2009. *La protervia di Beatrice*. Florence: SISMEL.

Villa, Claudia. 2010. "Il problema dello stile umile (e il riso di Dante)." In *Dante the Lyric and Ethical Poet (Dante Poeta Lirico e Etico)*, ed. Zygmunt G. Barański and Martin McLaughlin, 138–52. London: Legenda.

Vitale, Vincenzo. 2017. "'Poca favilla gran fiamma seconda': Appunti sugli Argonauti di Dante." *Giornale storico della letteratura italiana* 194: 1–37.

Von Moos, Peter. 1988. *Geschichte als Topik: Das rhetorische Exemplum von der Antike zur Neuzeit und die historiae im "Policraticus" Johannes von Salisbury.* New York: G. Olms.

Vredeveld, Harry. 1987. "Pagan and Christian Echoes in the 'Ecloga Theoduli': A Supplement." *Mittellateinisches Jahrbuch* 22: 109–13.

Walther, Hans. 1963. *Proverbia sententiaeque Latinitatis Medii Aevi*. 9 vols. Göttingen: Vanderhoeck & Ruprecht.

Webb, Heather. 2012. "The Inferno from a Purgatorial (and Paradisiacal) Perspective." In *Dante's Inferno*, ed. Patrick Hunt, 49–62. Pasadena, CA: Salem Press.

Weijers, Olga, ed. 1992. *Vocabulaire des écoles et des méthodes d'enseignement au moyen âge: Actes du colloque, Rome 21–22 octobre 1989*. Turnhout, Belgium: Brepols.

Weiss, Roberto. 1948. "Lineamenti per una storia del primo umanesimo fiorentino." *Rivista storica italiana* 60: 349–66.

Wells, David. 1994. "Fatherly Advice: The Precepts of 'Gregorius,' Marke, and Gurnemanz and the School Tradition of the 'Disticha Catonis,' with a Note on Grimmelshausen's 'Simplicissimus.'" *Frühmittelalterliche Studien* 28: 296–332.

Welter, Jean-Thiébaut. 1927. *L'exemplum dans la littérature religieuse et didactique du Moyen Age.* Paris: Guitard.

Weppler, Amanda M. 2016. "Dante's Stazio: Status and the Transformations of Poetry." Ph.D. diss., University of Notre Dame.

Wetherbee, Winthrop. 2008. *The Ancient Flame: Dante and the Poets*. Notre Dame, IN: University of Notre Dame Press.

Wheatley, Edward. 2000. *Mastering Aesop: Medieval Education, Chaucer, and His Followers.* Gainesville: University Press of Florida.

Wieruszowski, Helene. 1943. "*Ars Dictaminis* in the Time of Dante." *Medievalia et Humanistica* 1: 95–108.

Wieruszowski, Helene. 1946. "An Early Anticipation of Dante's 'Cieli e Scienze.'" *Modern Language Notes* 61: 217–28.

Wieruszowski, Helene. 1953. "Arezzo as a Center of Learning and Letters in the Thirteenth Century." *Traditio* 9: 321–91.

314 BIBLIOGRAPHY

Wieruszowski, Helene. 1959. "Brunetto Latini als Lehrer Dantes und der Florentiner." *Archivio Italiano per la Storia della Pietà* 2: 171–98.

Wieruszowski, Helene. 1966. *The Medieval University: Masters, Students, and Learning.* Princeton, NJ: Van Nostrand.

Wieruszowski, Helene. 1967. "Rhetoric and the Classics in Italian Education of the Thirteenth Century." *Studia Gratiana* 2: 169–208.

Wieruszowski, Helene. 1971. *Politics and Culture in Medieval Spain and Italy.* Rome: Edizioni di Storia e Letteratura.

Wilhelm, Julius. 1960. "Die Gestalt des Odysseus in Dantes *Göttlicher Komödie.*" *Deutsches Dante-Jahrbuch* 38: 75–93.

Wilson, Robert. 2013. "Allegory as Avoidance in Dante's Early Commentators: 'Bella menzogna' to 'roza corteccia.'" In *Interpreting Dante: Essays on the Traditions of Dante Commentary*, ed. Paola Nasti and Claudia Rossignoli, 30–52. Notre Dame, IN: University of Notre Dame Press.

Witt, Ronald G. 1995. "What Did Giovannino Read and Write? Literacy in Early Renaissance Florence." *I Tatti Studies in the Italian Renaissance* 6: 83–114.

Witt, Ronald G. 2000. *"In the Footsteps of the Ancients": The Origins of Humanism from Lovato to Bruni.* Leiden: Brill.

Witt, Ronald G. 2012. *The Two Latin Cultures and the Foundation of Renaissance Humanism in Medieval Italy.* New York: Cambridge University Press.

Wolff, Gustav. 1869. "Cato de Jüngere bei Dante." *Jahrbuch der Deutschen Dante-Gesellschaft* 2: 227–29.

Woods, Marjorie Curry. 1996. "Rape and the Pedagogical Rhetoric of Sexual Violence." In *Criticism and Dissent in the Middle Ages*, ed. Rita Copeland, 56–86. Cambridge: Cambridge University Press.

Woods, Marjorie Curry. 2012. "The Teaching of Writing in Medieval Europe." In *A Short History of Writing Instruction: From Ancient Greece to Contemporary America*, ed. James J. Murphy, 3rd ed., 114–47. New York: Routledge.

Woods, Marjorie Curry. 2019. *Weeping for Dido.* Princeton, NJ: Princeton University Press.

Woods, Marjorie Curry, and Rita Copeland. 1999. "Classroom and Confession." In *The Cambridge History of Medieval English Literature*, ed. David Wallace, 376–406. Cambridge: Cambridge University Press.

Woollgar Verrall, Arthur. 1913. *Collected Literary Essays, Classical and Modern*, ed. Matthew Bayfield and James Duff. Cambridge: Cambridge University Press.

Wright, Aaron E. 1997. *The Fables of "Walter of England."* Toronto: Pontifical Institute of Mediaeval Studies.

Yates, Frances. 1966. *The Art of Memory.* Chicago: University of Chicago Press.

Zambon, Francesco. 1994. "Allegoria e linguaggio dell'ineffabilità nell'autoesegesi dantesca dell' 'Epistola a Cangrande.'" In *L'autocommento*, ed. G. Peron, 21–30. Padua: Esdra.

Zambon, Francesco. 2021. *Allegoria: Una breve storia dall'antichità a Dante.* Rome: Carocci.

Zanin, Enrica. 2018. "'Miseri, 'mpediti, affamati': Dante's Implied Reader in the *Convivio.*" In *Dante's* Convivio: *or How to Restart a Career in Exile*, ed. Franziska Meier, 207–21. Oxford: Peter Lang.

Zieman, Katherine. 2008. *Singing the New Song: Literacy and Liturgy in Late Medieval England.* Philadelphia: University of Pennsylvania Press.

Zingarelli, Nicola. 1948. *La vita, i tempi e le opere di Dante.* 2 vols. Milan: Vallardi.

Index

For the benefit of digital users, indexed terms that span two pages (e.g., 52–53) may, on occasion, appear on only one of those pages.

abbaco, 21, 24–25, 24–25 n.26, 26–27, 29–30, 29–30 nn.46–47, 33–34 n.58, 35–36, 37 n.73
ABCs, 94, 152–153, 211–222
Accessus ad auctores, 11–12, 11–12 n. 29, 33–34, 53, 82–83 n.80, 102–104 n.16, 139–142 nn.29–30 and 33, 157–158 n.81, 176 n.22, 209 n.2, 212 n.11
Accursius, 162
  Glossa ordinaria, 162
Achilleid, 8–9, 33–34, 37–38, 66–68, 66–68 n.41, 208–275, 284–285
Achilles, 15, 190, 195–196, 208–275
Adam, 174, 186, 191, 194 n.63, 195–197
Adonis, 192–193, 227
aemulatio, 247
Aesop, 15, 33–34, 38–41, 49–50, 66–68, 74, 82, 97–131, 151–153
  The Cock and the Pearl, 97, 111–112 n.41
  The Frog and the Mouse, 97, 101–110, 109 n.29, 109, 115–117, 122 n.64, 122–124, 126–127, 131
  The Frogs and the Snake, 119–122, 126
Aesopus latinus, 8–9, 37–38, 39f, 102–104, 105–106 n.18, 111 n.36
  Elegiac *Romulus*, 8–9, 39f, 102–104 n.13, n.14, n.15, 104, 105–106 n.17, 121–123
    De mure et rana, 104, 105f, 107, 107 n.26, 122 n.64
    De ranis et ydro, 119
  Romulus vulgaris, 102–104, 102–104 n.12, 105–106 n.17, 110–111 n.32
fabula Aesopica, 113–114
fabula libica, 113–114
Aethiopum terras, 98, 114–115, 170, 179–181, 201
Ahern, John, 22–23 n.14, 57–58 n.8, 59, 59 n.13, 60 n.15, 61–62, 61–62 n.20, 62–63 n.27, 63, 63 n.29, 65–66, 65–66 n.33, 85, 94–95
Aimeric, 33–34, 211–212 n. 7
  Ars lectoria, 33–34
Akbari, Suzanne Conklin, 171, 171 n.12
Alan of Lille, 74, 138 n.20

De planctu Naturae, 74
  Anticlaudianus, 74, 138 n.20
Albi, Veronica, 112–113 n.45, 120–121, 120–121 n.61
Alcuin, 111, 174–175
Alexander Neckam, 102–104 nn.11–12, 106–107 n.20, 111, 175, 178, 178 n.26
  Novus Aesopus, 102–104 n.12, 106–107 n.20, 111
Alexander of Villedieu, 34–35
  Doctrinale, 34–35, 34–35 n.61
alieniloquium, 122, 122 n.64
Alighiero Alighieri, 41–42, 42 n.92, 49 n.113
Alithia, 167–207
Allegory, 2–4, 112–113 n.45, 117, 120 n.60, 120–122, 122 n.64, 127, 129–130, 173f, 202–203, 205, 206
Almeon, 185, 188
Amphesibeus, 205–206
Amphiaraus, 188
Angel, 171, 191, 195–197, 196–197 nn.66–68, 222, 283
Anonymous Teutonicus, 170–171, 178, 178 n.26, 179–181 n.31, 194 n.63
Ante-Purgatory, 190, 208, 222
Apollo, 172–174, 188, 202–203, 248–275
Apollonian, 251, 261, 263, 265
Arachne, 99, 99 n.6, 181–182, 185
arcana Dei, 249–250
Arethusa, 248, 252, 275
Arezzo, 9–10 n.23, 30–31, 35, 37–38, 91–92
Argonauts, 251, 251 n.6, 268, 270, 271, 271 n.43, 272, 274, 274 n.45, 274–275
Aristotle, 3–4, 3–4 n.3, 110–111, 145–146, 151–152
  Politics, 3–4, 3–4 n.3
  Rhetoric, 110–111
arte, arti, 34–35, 45, 47, 49–50
ars dictaminis, 19–20 n.3, 47–50
ars notaria
Athens, 120 n.60, 169, 171, 172–174, 204

316 INDEX

Auctores maiores, 10, 33–35, 37, 47, 49–50, 69
n.42, 71–73, n.50, 238–239 n.83, 247,
251, 274–275, 284–285

Auctores minores, 14, 34–35, 35 n.64, 37–38,
37–38 n.79, 47, 49–50, 69, 70–73, 75,
179–181, 238–239 n.83, 284–285

Auctores Octo, 102–104 n.15, 179–181

auctoritas, auctoritates, 56–57, 71–73, 145–147,
151–154, 159, 160, 162

Auerbach, Ernst, 19–20 n.4, 21, 21 nn.9–10,
22–23 n.14, 94–95 n.91, 133–134,
133–134 nn.7 and 15

Aurora, 190, 195–196

Avesani, Rino, 7–8 n.18, 8–9 n.21, 33, 33 n.56,
102–104 n.15, 135–137 n.14, 183 n.45,
211–212 n.7

Avianus, 33–34, 37–38, 102–104, 102–104 n.11,
nn.15–16, 112 n.43, 114, 122 n.64

St. Augustine (Aurelius Augustinus
Hipponensis), 2, 46–47, 74–75, 82, 82
n.77, 82–83, 114–115, 142–143, 148–149
n.58, 153–154 n.72, 158, 160, 183–184
n.47, 201–202 n.75, 278–279, 279 n.3,
279, 279 n.4, 280–281, 284
Confessiones, 46–47, 278–279, 279 n.3, 281,
284
De civitate Dei, 148–149 n.58, 153–154 n.72,
183–184 n.47

Babel (Tower of), 181–182, 184, 185–187

Bacchus, 172–174 n.16, 263–265, 264–265 n.33,
265

Babrius, 102–104, 102–104 n.11

Badia

Barański, Zygmunt, 5 n.8, 6–7 nn.12–14, 7–8
n.19, 13–14 n.38, 22–23 n.15, 28 n.43,
46–47 n.103, 49 n.113, 53 n.2, 56–57 n.5,
62 n.23, 62–63, 62–63 n.26, 71–73 n.48,
74 n.54, 77–78 n.66, n.69, 97 n.2, 99–100
nn.7–8, 105–106 n.17, 125–126 n.71,
135–137 n.15, 143–144 n.38, 149–150
n.61, 164–165 n.94, 167–168 n.3, 190,
190 n.57, 191 n.58, 202–203 n.76, 204
n.80, 209–211, 209–211 nn.4 and 6, 229
n.64, 238–239 n.83, 243 n.98

Barbero, Alessandro, 20–21 n.8, 41–42 nn.87
and 89, 42, 42 n.91, 42–43 n.94

Barnes, Michael, 209–211, 209–211 n.3,
215–217 n.28, 234 n.71

Barolini, Teodolinda, 57–58 n.9, 98 n.3, 99 n.6,
99–100 n.8, 125–126 n.71, 192–193 n.59,
199 n.72, 200 n.74, 219–222 n.40, 227
n.55, 234–235 n.72, 266–267, 266–267
n.36

Barrators, 100–101, 127–128, 129 n.77
Ciampolo, 106–107, 109, 122–123

Barkan, Leonard, 248–249, 248–249 n.3

Battistini, Andrea, 99 n.4, 99–100, 99–100 n.8,
116 n.56

Bellaira, Guglielmo, 219–222 n.41, 274, 274 n.46

Bellincione Alighieri, 41–42

Bernard of Utrecht, 170 n.8, 178

Bernardus Silvester, 120–121

Benjamin, Walter, 52

Benvenuto da Imola, 106–107, 135, 135 n.13,
135–137 n.15, 138, 138 n.20, 139–142,
238 n.79, 246–247, 246–247 n.104

Bessone, Federica, 241–242 n.89, 242, 242
nn.92–93

Bible, 19–20 n.3, 53, 120–121, 132–133, 170,
189, 266–267 n.38
Old Testament, 174–175, 181–182
Ecclesiastes, 151–152
Exodus, 129–130, 133–134
Genesis, 186, 196–197, 196–197 nn.66–67
Lamentations, 59 n.14, 74, 76–80
Proverbs, 142–143, 151–152
Song of Songs, 151–152 n.68, 171, 278–279
n.2
New Testament, 174–175, 181–182
Acts, 171
Matthew, 97, 132–133 n.1, 171, 200, 200
nn.73–74, 201–202, 205
Revelation, 196–197

Biblioteca Medicea Laurenziana in Florence,
Plutei 24, sin. 12, 66–68, 179 n.29,
214–215, 216f, 218–219, 218–219 n.37,
220f, 225–226 n.53

Bildungsroman, 213, 222, 224

Bischoff, Bernhard, 23, 23 n.18

Black, Robert, 6–7 n.13, 8–9 n.21, 13–14, 13–14
nn.39–40, 14–15, 14–15 n.42, 18–51, 69
n.42, 70–71 n.44, 71–73 nn.48–50, 73–74
n.52, 75, 75 nn.58–59, 111 n.36, 135–137
n.14, 138–139 n.21, 143–144 n.38,
179–181 n.35, 211–212 n.7, 218–219,
218–219 nn.36–37

Boas, Marcus, 7–8 n.18, 33, 33 n.55, 33–34,
102–104 n.15, 135–137 n.14, 179–181,
179–181 n.33, 211–212 nn.7–8

Boccaccio, Giovanni, 29–30 n.47, 38–41 n.83,
n.84, 49 n.113, 69, 69 n.43, 70, 73, 74–75
n.57, 82 n.77, 111 n.36, 115–116 n.55,
181, 246–247

INDEX 317

Boethius (Anicius Manlius Severinus Boethius), 32, 37–38 nn.78–79, 45–47, 46–47 n.104, 47, 49–96, 138, 278–282, 284
  Consolatio philosophiae, 32, 46–47, 50–96, 278–280, 284
bolgia, 97, 100, 101, 108–109, 126, 163–164 n.92, 248–249
Bologna, 4, 29 n.44, 30–31 n.50, 35, 49, 49 n.113, 49–50 n.116, 57–58, 65–66, 130, 162, 181, 202–203, 202–203 n.76, 205, 281, 283
  University of Bologna, 29 n.44, 65–66, 162
Bonagiunta da Lucca, 57–58, 234
  Voi ch'avete mutata la mainera, 57–58
St. Boniface, 32
  Aenigmata, 32
Bono Giamboni, 6–7 n.14, 21
botteghe, 2, 29–30, 29–30 n.46
Bourdieu, Pierre, 12–13
Breen, Katharine, 12–13, 12–13 n.34, 285–286 n.10
Briareus, 181–186, 187 n.51
Brownlee, Kevin, 251 nn.6 and 8, 251–252, 259–260 n.21
Brunetto Latini, 4 n.3, 10–12, 11–12 n.30, 21, 30–31 n.49, 37–38, 48–49, 49 n.113, 54, 54 n.3, 55–56, 55–56 n.4, 62–63 n.27, 64, 69 n.42, 111–112 n.41, 114, 114 n.52, 132–166, 183 n.43, 219–222 n.41
  Rettorica, 11–12, 11–12 n.30, 55–56 n.4, 62–63 n.27, 148, 148 n.54, 154–155
  Tesoretto, 54, 54 n.3, 55–56, 55–56 n.4, 64, 146–147 n.50
  Tresor, 111–112 n.41, 114, 132–166, 183 n.43
  Tesoro volgarizzato, 114 n.52
Bynum, Caroline Walker, 132–133, 132–133 n.2

Cachey, Theodore, 6–7 n.14, 53 n.2, 62–63 n.26, 71–73 n.48, 99–100, 99–100 n.8, 125–126 n.71, 149–150 n.61, 200 n.74, 202–203 n.76
Caesar, Julius, 133–134, 137, 145–146 n.46
Caesarius of Arles, 129–130, 129–130 n.78
Calpurnius (Titus Calpurnius Siculus), 181
Camozzi Pistoja, Ambrogio, 18–19 n.1, 20–21 n.8, 84 n.85, 95–96, 95–96 n.93, 150 n.63, 167–168 n.3, 192–193 n.59, n.62, 209–211 n.6, 266–267 n.38
Campaldino, 42–43
Cancer (Zodiac), 169, 204
Candace (Queen), 171
Cannon, Christopher, 5–6, 5–6 n.10, 7 n.16, 7–8 nn.18 and 20

cantica, 15, 98 n.3, 165–166, 190, 264, 284–285
cantio, 125–126
canzone, 52–96, 125–126, 150–151
Caprona, 42–43
Carolingian, 26–27 n.34, 82, 102–104, 167–168, 174–175 n.17, 181, 202–203, 212
Carrai, Stefano, 52 n.1, 54 n.3, 71–73 n.47, 75–76, 75–76 n.60, 80, 80 n.72, 219–222 n.41, 228 n.59
Carron, Delphine, 6–7 n.14, 28 n.43, 30–31 n.50, 65–66 n.34, 135–137 n.15, 139–142 nn.27–28, 142, 142 nn.34–35, 145–146 n.44, 146–147 n.50, 148 n.53, 148–149 n.57, 165–166 n.97
carta, 35–36
Casaretto, Francesco Mosetti, 169 n.5, 171 n.15, 176–177, 176–177 n.23, 179–181 n.30, 197–198, 197–198 n.69
Castelvetro, Ludovico, 106–107, 106–107 n.25
Catholic Church, 132–133
Catiline (Lucius Sergius), 143–146, 145–146 nn.44–46, 146, 148, 148–149 n.60, 154–155
  conspiracy, 143–144, 148, 154–155
Cato, 15, 33–34, 37–38, 37–38 n.79, 66–69, 82, 114–115, 132–168, 175
Cato Uticensis, 132–166
Cato the Censor (the Elder), 133–134, 137 n.18, 139–142
catus, 137, 139–142
Cavalcanti, Guido, 47–48 n.106, 49 n.113, 53 n.2, 58–59, 77–78, 77–78 n.66, 91–92, 94, 227, 227 n.55, 246–247
  Donna me prega, 77–78, 77–78 n.66
Cecco d'Ascoli (Francesco Stabili), 129–130 n.78, 130
  Acerba, 130
Ceres, 194–195, 215, 215 n.26, 228, 244, 246, 258, 263–264
Certaldo, 69
Cervantes, 132
  Don Quixote, 132
Cestaro, Gary P., 12–13, 12–13 n.34, 223 n.46
caritas
Chartres, 112–113, 112–113 n.45
Chiron, 208, 214
Christ, 142–143, 190, 199–201, 201–202 n.75
Christendom, 7–8, 199, 278
Cirra, 249–250, 264–265, 264–265 n.32, 267–268
Coccia, Michele, 219–222 n.41, 230, 230 n.66
Cicero (Marcus Tullius), 3–4 n.3, 112 n.42, 114, 114 n.51, 132–166, 257 n.15
  De Amicitia, 45

318   INDEX

Cicero (Marcus Tullius) (*Continued*)
   De finibus bonorum et malorum, 137
   De officiis, 137, 151 n.66, 153–154 n.71
   De Inventione, 112, 112 n.42, 114 n.51, 148
   Hortensius, 46–47
   De senectute, 64–65
Claudian (Claudius Claudianus), 37–38 n.78,
      38–41, 208–275, 284–285
   De raptu Proserpinae, 33, 37–38, 187 n.51,
      208–275, 284–285
clericus, clerici, 6–7, 24
Clogan, Paul, 38–41, 38–41 n.80, 138–139 n.24,
      176 n.20, 211–212 n.7, 212–213 n.16,
      n.17, 218 n.35, 234 n.71, 257–258 n.16
Cluny, 212, 218 n.35
comedìa, 63–64, 97–131
comedy, 63–64, 74, 97–131, 225–226, 241–242
Commedia, 8–10, 9–10 n.25, 11–12, 14–15, 21,
      51, 63–64, 64–65 n.30, 66–68, 71–73
      n.51, 95–96, 95–96 n.94, 97–166,
      183–184 n.47, 185 n.49, 191 n.58,
      192–193 n.61, 196–197 n.66, 198, 200
      n.74, 201–202 n.75, 204, 208–249,
      258–259 n.19, 264, 273–274 n.44, 278
      n.1, 282–286
   Inferno, 15, 48–50, 66–68 n.39, 97–166, 183
      n.43, 192–193, 198, 199, 208–276,
      285–286
   Inferno 1, 273–274
   Inferno 2, 241, 244, 246, 251 n.5, 264, 264
      n.30, 276
   Inferno 4, 198–199, 223–224, 233, 233 n.70,
      238–239 n.83, 285–286
   Inferno 8, 116–117, 120, 122, 155–156 n.76,
      164–165 n.94
   Inferno 9, 97–131, 245–246, 245–246 n.101
   Inferno 14, 134, 158–159, 162–164, 192–193
   Inferno 15, 48–50, 143–144, 155–156 n.76
   Inferno 16, 97–98, 98 n.3, 126–127, 129 n.77,
      163–164 n.93
   Inferno 17, 99, 101, 128
   Inferno 20, 125–126, 163–164, 209–211, 233
   Inferno 21, 100–101, 102 n.9, 115–116, 123,
      125–126, 131, 131 n.81, 209–211 n.6
   Inferno 23, 15, 49–50, 66–68 n.39, 97–131
   Inferno 24, 248–249
   Inferno 25, 248–249, 275
   Inferno 26, 223–224, 266–267 n.35
   Purgatorio, 15, 50–51, 71–73 n.51, 85 n.86,
      91–92, 132–247, 249, 251 n.5, 258–259,
      264, 273, 276–286
   Purgatorio 1, 50–51, 133–134 n.5, n.9, 135
      n.13, 135–137, 138 n.20, 155–166,
      223–224, 264, 273

   Purgatorio 2, 155–158
   Purgatorio 6, 276
   Purgatorio 9, 167–208, 222–226, 235 n.73,
      241, 247
   Purgatorio 10, 181–183, 183 n.43, 185,
      188–189
   Purgatorio 12, 167–207
   Purgatorio 21, 187, 192–193 n.59, 205 n.83,
      208–247, 258–259
   Purgatorio 22, 192, 219–222 n.40, 223–224,
      238 n.79, n.80, 238–239 nn.82–83
   Purgatorio 24, 57–58 n.10, 85 n.86, 91–92,
      234, 243, 251
   Purgatorio 27, 192–193, 206–207, 229 n.64,
      232
   Purgatorio 28, 167–168, 191, 194–195,
      194–195 n.64, 208–247
   Purgatorio 30, 71–73 n.51, 192–193, 192–193
      n.59, 197–198, 224–225, 243, 276–286
   Purgatorio 31, 243, 278, 282
   Purgatorio 32, 133, 235 n.73, 285–286
   Purgatorio 33, 133, 278, 282–283
   Paradiso, 7 n.16, 15, 22–23 n.15, 49–50,
      64–65, 110–111, 110–111 n.33, 167–207,
      219–222 n.41, 223, 235 n.73, 245–246
      n.102, 247–275, 283, 284–286
   Paradiso 1, 255, 258–259, 267–268, 270,
      274–275
   Paradiso 2, 219–222 n.41, 266–267, 274
   Paradiso 4, 206
   Paradiso 10, 286
   Paradiso 12, 49–50, 64–65
   Paradiso 18, 198
   Paradiso 19, 15, 199–200, 200 n.74, 201–202,
      201–202 n.75
   Paradiso 23, 285–286
   Paradiso 29, 110–111, 283
   Paradiso 33, 245–246 n.102, 274–275
commentum, 53
compilatio, 63–64, 84
common good, 3–4, 135–137, 143–144,
      148–149, 148–149 n.60, 154, 160
comune, 3, 84, 150–151, 161
Conrad of Hirsau, *Dialogus super*
      auctores, 11–12, 14 n.41, 33–34, 33–34
      n.57, 102–104 n.16, 111–114, 139–142
      n.30, 178, 179–181 n.32, 209 n.2,
      211–212 n.7, 212, 264 n.31
consiglio dei cento, 42–43
Corbett, George, 133, 133 n.3
cultural literacy, 7–8, 21, 284
curriculum, curricula, 5, 7, 7–8 n.18, 13, 13–14
      n.40, 18–51, 73, 82, 114–115, 132–133,
      143–144, 165–166, 176, 179–181 n.32,

209, 211–212 nn.7–8, 218–219 n.39, 225–226, 238–239 n.83, 283

cursus, 47–48

Cyclopes, 205

Cyrus, 181–182, 185

croce, 35–36

Dante Alighieri (other works)
  De vulgari eloquentia, 6–7 n.11, 31–41, 43, 44–46, 52 n.1, 64–65, 75–76, 85 n.86, 125–126, 154, 209–211, 233, 235 n.73, 236–237, 244, 244 n.99, 258–259 n.20
  Convivio, 11–12, 16–97, 105–106 n.18, 111–112 n.41, 112–113, 112–113 n.45, 120–121, 132–166, 214–215 n.22, 219–222 n.41, 235 n.73, 266–267 n.38, 278 n.1, 278–279
  Egloge, 15, 18–19 n.2, 181, 203, 204 n.82, 205–207, 283–284
  Epistula XIII (to Cangrande), 18–19 n.2
  Monarchia, 18–19 n.2, 47–48 n.109, 112–113 n.45, 132–166, 198, 201–202 n.75, 258–259 n.20
  Questio de aqua et terra, 50
  Vita nova, 8–9, 14–15, 42–43, 45, 47–48, 51, 52–96, 114, 241, 276, 282–286

Daphne, 252, 254–255

David (King), 169, 171, 172–174, 181–182, 185

Davis, Charles, 28 n.43, 29–30 nn.45–46, 30–31 nn.48 and 50, 49–50 n.116, 65–66 n.34, 143–144 n.41, 148, 148 n.55, 148–149 n.57, 150 n.62

Deci, 160

Deidamia, 213, 222, 223–226, 242–243

Delcorno, Carlo, 167 n.1, 181–182, 181–182 nn.40–42, 183 nn.43 and 45, 183–184 n.46, n.48, 185 n.49

del Virgilio, Giovanni, 15, 21 n.11, 181, 202–203, 202–203 n.76, 205–206, 283–284

Demeter, 215, 260 n.23

De raptu Proserpinae, 15, 33, 37–38, 187 n.51, 208–275, 284–285

Dialogus super auctores, 11–12, 33–34, 33–34 n.57, 102–104 n.16, 179–181 n.32, 209 n.2, 212

Diana, 167–168 n.2, 187

Diomedes, 213–214, 222, 223 n.45, 224–225, 242–243

Dis, 97–131, 209–211 n.6, 244–246, 245–246 n.101

Disticha Catonis, 8–9, 15, 32–34, 38–41, 71–73 n.50, 73–74, 102–104 n.15, 111, 132–166, 167 n.1, 175, 209

Breves sententiae, 146, 155–156

Epistula Catonis, 146, 150–151, 151 n.65, 155–156

dicta, 167

dictamen, 47–48 n.109, 48–49

dictator, 47–48

Dido, 223–224, 242–243, 279

divisio, divisiones, 53, 56–57, 62, 62 n.23, 65–66 n.34, 70–71, 70–71 nn.44 and 46

divisions, 52 n.1, 62–63, 77–78 n.65, 185

doctrine, 3, 90–91, 94, 114–115, 121–122, 132–133, 132–133 n.1, 143–144, 148, 201–202 n.75, 206

Donati, Gemma, 42

Donatus (Aelius), 35–36, 35–36 n.67, 37, 37 n.74, 37–38 n.79, 43, 44 n.98, 49–50, 111, 175
  Ars minor, 35–36, 35–36 n.67

doctores puerorum, 27–30, 35–36

Dronke, Peter, 56–57 n.7, 70–71, 70–71 n.45, 151–152 n.68, 176–177, 176–177 n.23, 232 n.67

Durling, Robert, 56–57 n.7, 77–78 n.66, 229, 229 n.64

Earthly Paradise, 132–133, 167, 174, 192–193 n.60, 196–198, 232 n.67, 238–239

Eco, Umberto, 189, 189 n.56

Eden, 167–247, 276, 282–284

Eberhard the German, 33–34, 102–104 n.15
  Laborintus, 33–34, 33–34 n.58, 102–104 n.15

Ecloga Theoduli, 8–9, 15, 33–34, 102–104 n.15, 167–207, 209, 228 n.63, 284–285

Egypt, 170

Egyptians, 129–130

Eisner, Martin, 241, 241 n.88

elegiac, 52–53, 73–74, 95–131, 208–247, 258–259 n.18, 279–280, 282–285

elegy, 15, 38–41, 74, 75–76, 75–76 n.63, 76–80, 87–88, 215, 241–243, 243 n.97, 244, 244 n.99, 282–283

Eleusis, 260, 260 n.23, 264–265, 267–268

empire, 139–142, 153–154 n.71, 154, 162–163, 165–166

England, 5–6, 13 n.35, 32, 178 n.26

epic, 15, 32, 38–41, 102 n.9, 122–123, 125–126, 188, 202–203, 208–275, 284–286

epimythium, 107 n.27, 108–109, 111–112 n.41, 127–128, 130–131

epos, 209–211, 249–250, 249–250 n.4

Eriphyle, 181–182, 185, 187–188

Erfurt, Amplon. Q. 21, 114, 114 n.53

eroicomico, 122–123

Esther, 189

320 INDEX

Ethiopia, 167–207
Ethiopians, 170, 200 n.74
Etna (Mount), 205, 231
eulogy, 74
Europe, 7, 10–11 n.27, 12–13, 15, 19–20 n.3,
30–32, 32 n.54, 33–34, 38–41, 38–41
n.81, 59 n.14, 60, 102–104 n.15, 111,
135–139, 167–168, 178 n.26, 179 n.29,
179–181, 179–181 n.30, 211–212, 218
Eurydice, 185, 190
exempla, 171–207, 219–222 n.41

fable, 15, 38–41, 97–131
fabula, fabulae, 81, 97–131, 178, 189 n.56
facta, 76–77, 112–114, 167
favola, 97–131
farce, 122–123, 125
fiction, 11–12, 15, 74–75, 97–100, 131, 178,
238–239, 241, 246
Florence, Archivio di Stato di Firenze, Carte
Strozziane IIIa ser., 72, 68*f*, 70–71, 72*f*
Florence, Biblioteca Medicea Laurenziana, Plut.
91, sup. 4, 179 n.29
Florence, Biblioteca Nazionale Centrale
1,45, 179 n.29
Florence, Biblioteca Nazionale Centrale
Magliabechi VII 931, 40*f*, 105*f*
Florence, Biblioteca Riccardiana, MS 630, MS
630
Florence, Biblioteca Riccardiana, MS 725, MS
630
Fortune (prosopopoeia), 73–74, 280
Francesco da Barberino, 10–11, 37–38, 69 n.42
Francesco da Buti, 66–68, 66–68 n.39, 70,
105–106 n.17, 111, 111 n.36, 111–112,
134 n.9
Freccero, John, 120–121, 120–121 n.62, 232,
232 n.68
Frederick II, Emperor, 151–152
Fronesis (prosopopoeia), 172–174, 176–179

Ganymede, 190, 195–196
Gehl, Paul, 5, 5 n.7, 8–9 n.21, 9–10 n.24, 13–14
n.40, 23 n.18, 18–96, 102–104 n.6, 111
n.36, 135–137 n.14, 179–181, 179–181
nn.34–35, 218–219 n.38
Geoffrey of Visnauf, 34–35
Poetria Nova, 34–35
Gemma Donati, 42
genera dicendi, 78, 258–259 n.18
Geoffrey of Vitry, 218, 218 n.35, 246–247 n.103,
258, 261, 263–265
Gerbert of Aurillac, 212
Geryon, 97–131, 167–168 n.2

Geta, 33–34
Gigantomachy, 167–207
Glaucus, 251
Giovanni Dominici, 38–41 n.83, 82 n.77,
114–115, 114–115 n.54, 179–181,
179–181 n.36
Regola del governo di cura familiar, 38–41
n.83, 82 n.77, 114–115, 114–115 n.54,
179–181, 179–181 n.36
Goffis, Cesare, 267–268, 267–268 n.40
Golden Age, 167–207, 215, 228, 228 n.63
Gorni, Guglielmo, 52–96
Gospel, 132, 151–152, 171, 200–201
Graff, Harvey J., 12–13 n.33, n.37, 19–20, 19–20
nn.4 and 6–7, 22–23 nn.13–14, 25–26
n.30, 66–68 n.37
Gregory the Great, 142–143
Grendler, Paul, 18–51, 61–62, 138–139
Gruzelier, Claire, 215–217 nn.28–29, 217, 217
n.32, 263 n.26, 266–267 n.37, 270
nn.41–42
Guinizzelli, Guido, 57–58, 90–91 n.89, 91–92,
225–226 n.53, 234
Guittone d'Arezzo, 9–10 n.23, 91–92
Guyler, Sam, 106–107 nn.24 and 26, 107

Hades, 226
Hagedorn, Suzanne, 208–209 n.1, 223–224,
223–224 n.47, 224, 224 n.49, 243 n.97
Henna, 208–209, 229, 230–231
Henry of Settimello, 8–9, 15, 37–38, 52–96,
111–112 n.41, 138 n.20, 280
Elegia, 8–9, 15, 37–38, 52–96, 111–112 n.41,
138 n.20, 280
Hera, 267–268
Hero, 192–193, 227
Hesiod, 209–211, 249–250 n.4
Heslin, Peter, 240–241 n.86, 241–242 n.89, n.93,
242–243, 242–243 n.94, n.96
Hilderic of Montecassino, 37, 37 n.75
Adbreviatio artis grammaticae, 37, 37 n.75
historia, historiae, 114, 178
Hollander, Robert, 53 n.2, 77–78 n.65, 99–100
n.8, 102 n.9, 106–107 nn.23–24, 109–110
n.31, 134, 134 nn.8–9, 135–137 n.15,
153–154 n.71, 163–164 n.92, 165–166,
181–182 n.39, 191 n.58, 227 n.56,
236–237 n.76, 243 nn.97–98, 251 n.7, 252
n.12, 264, 264 n.30, 282–283 n.9
Holofernes, 181–182, 185
Homer, 50–51, 69, 208–247, 249–250 n.4
Horace (Quintus Horatius Flaccus), 47–48,
71–73, 71–73 n.50, 99, 99 n.5, 99–100,

99–100 n.7, 202–203, 233, 236–237, 258–259 n.20

Ars poetica, 99, 99 n.5, 99–100 n.7, 236–237

Horsting, Albertus, 82 n.75, 82–83 n.78

Hugh of Trimberg, 33–34, 102–104 n.15

Registrum multorum auctorum, 33–34, 102–104 n.15

Ianua, 35–36, 35–36 n.67

Ilias latina, 33–34, 37–38 n.78, 46, 50–51, 211–213, 240–241

illitterati, 24

imitatio, 50–51

imperium, 153–154, 153–154 n.72

India, 170, 199, 200 n.74

Indus, 199

instructor, 157–158 n.80

integumentum, 112–113, 112–113 n.45

intellectus, 59, 281

invective, 73–74

Irvine, Martin, 12–13, 12–13 n.34, 32 n.54, 33–34 n.60

Isidore of Seville, 111, 113–114, 113–114 n.48, 122 n.64, 123–124

Etymologiae, 113–114, 113–114 n.48, 122 n.64, 123–124

Isopo, 105–106 n.17, 111

Israel, 170

Italy, 2–96, 102–104 n.15, 110–112, 132–207, 211–212 n.7, 218–219, 218–219 nn.37 and 39, 224 n.48, 227–228 n.57

Jacques de Vitry, 33–34, 33–34 n.58

Ad scholares, 33–34

Jenkyns, Richard, 209–211 n.5, 215, 215 n.25, 241–242 n.90, 249–250 n.4

Jeremiah, 76–77, 170 n.7

St. Jerome, 174–175

Jesus, 89 n.88, 121, 171

jeu, 122–123

St. John, 196–197

John of Garland, 75–76

Poetria, 75–76

Judgment Day, 132–133, 171, 199–202

Judith, 185, 189

Jupiter, 186, 193, 199, 201–202 n.75, 205, 239, 252

Justinian (Emperor), 162

Corpus juris civilis, 162

Juvenal (Decimus Junius Juvenalis), 32

Juvencus (Gaius Vettius Aquilinus Juvencus), 32, 82

Keen, Catherine, 143–144 n.42, 149–150, 149–150 n.61, n.62

Lactantius Placidus, 212–213, 212–213 n.16, 240–241, 240 n.85

laicus, laici, 6–7, 24, 24 n.21, 59

latinantes, 35–37

Latona, 118–119, 187, 188

Leander, 192–193, 227

Ledda, Giuseppe, 46–47 n.104, 118–119 nn.58–59, 126–127 n.72, 128 n.75, 129, 129 n.76, 131 n.81, 151–152 n.68, 196–197 n.67, 251 n.5

Lethe, 167–168, 167–168 n.2, 190–193, 197–198, 201–202, 208–209, 230, 247, 278, 281–282

libello, 47–48 n.106, 52–96, 111, 135 n.13, 139–142

Liber Catonianus, 33–34, 38–41, 102–104 n.15, 111, 179–181, 209 n.2, 211–212, 211–212 n.7, 217, 218 n.35

Limbo, 198–199, 199 n.72, 205, 223–224, 238–239 n.83, 284–285

literacy, 2–51, 56–57, 59, 60–61, 61 n.18, 284–286

litterati, 12–13, 18–21, 24, 24 n.22, 59

locus amoenus, 230

Lombardi, Elena, 7–8 n.19, 53 n.2, 56–57 n.8, 59 n.14, 61, 61 n.18, 86 n.87, 94–95 n.91, 95–96 n.94, 134 n.8

Lorenzetti, Ambrogio, 1*f*, 2–3, 2–3 n.1, 3, 3 n.2, 3–4, 3–4 n.3, 4

The Allegory of the Good Government, 1*f*, 3, 17*f*

The Good City, 1*f*, 2, 17*f*

Lot's wife, 191

Love (prosopopoeia), 62–63, 76–77, 80, 85, 87, 88, 234

Lucan (Marcus Annaeus Lucanus), 47–48, 71–73, 132–166, 209–211, 233, 234, 248, 258–259 n.20, 263–264 n.27, n.29, 275

Pharsalia, 133–134 n.5, 134–137, 139, 154, 160, 209–211, 263–264 n.27, n.29

Lucifer, 181–184, 183–184 n.47, 184–185

Lucy, 208

ludo, 97–131

ludus, 122–123, 126–127

Libyan desert, 134, 206

Lynch, Sarah, 5 n.9, 26, 26 n.32, 33–34 n.60, 35–36 n.72

Lyon (Second Council of), 132–133

322 INDEX

Magi, 171

magister, 6–7, 135, 233, 236–237

Malebranche, 97–131, 209–211 n.6
  Alichino, 106–107, 106–107 n.23
  Barbariccia, 106–107, 106–107 n.23, 127–128
  Calcabrina, 106–107, 106–107 n.23

Mann, Jill, 33–34, 33–34 n.60, 97–131, 151–152
  n.67

Marchesi, Simone, 7–8 n.19, 126–127 n.72, 130
  n.79, 151 n.66, 153–154 nn.71–72, 154,
  154 n.74, 219–222 n.40, 238–239 n.82,
  251 n.5, 252 n.11, 278–279 n.2, 279, 279
  n.3, 279, 279 n.4

Marsyas, 172–174, 249–251, 259–262

Martinez, Ronald, 53 n.2, 56–57 n.7, 59 n.14, 78
  n.70, 192–193 n.59, 209–211 n.6,
  219–222 n.40, 229, 229 n.64, 233 n.70,
  234–235 n.72, 238–239 nn.81–83

Matelda, 167–247

Maximianus, 33
  Elegiae, 33

Mazzotta, Giuseppe, 124 n.69, 133–134,
  133–134 n.7, 135–137 n.15, 153–154
  n.72, 160 n.84, 162–163, 162–163 n.90,
  227 n.56, 243 n.98

Medea, 189

Medusa, 120–122

Mengaldo, Pier Vincenzo, 74–75 n.57, 75–76,
  75–76 nn.61 and 63

messo celeste, 118, 245–246

misterium, 178

Milton, John, 167
  Of Education, 167

Mocan, Mira, 122–123, 122–123 n.66, 129 n.77

Montemurlo, 41–42

Moore, Edward, 7–8 n.19, 181–182, 181–182
  n.39, 184 n.48, 189–190, 219–222 n.41

Mussato, Albertino, 181, 187, 187 n.52, 202–203

Muslims, 199

myth, 12–13 n.33, 99 n.6, 112–113, 186,
  187–188, 191, 194–195, 194–195 n.65,
  215, 218, 228, 228 nn.60 and 63, 252

Nemesianus (Marcus Aurelius Olympius), 181

the Nine, 3, 3 n.2, 3–4

Niobe, 181–182, 185, 187–188, 188 n.54, 189

Odofredus, 162
  Summa in usus feudorum Compluti, 162

opuscula, 63–73

Ong, Walter, 12–13, 12–13 nn.33–34, 223, 223
  nn.43–44

Origen (of Alexandria), 129–130

Orpheus, 185, 190, 194–195 n.65

Orphic poems, 215

Ottimo commento, 118–119

Ovid (Publius Ovidius Naso), 15, 32, 47–49,
  71–73, 71–73 n.50, 77–80, 126–127 n.72,

154, 171, 174, 174–175 n.17, 181–182,
  187, 188 n.55, 192–193, 208–275
  Ars amatoria, 225–226, 225–226 n.53
  Ex Ponto, 73–74
  Fasti, 154, 228 n.59
  Heroides, 227
  Metamorphoses, 79–80, 118–119, 172–174,
    187 n.51, 188, 188 n.54, 204 n.81,
    208–275
  Tristia, 73–74

Ovidius puellarum, 33–34

Oxford, Bodleian, Addenda Add. A. 171, 173*f*,
  179–181 n.35

Padoan, Giorgio, 109–110 n.31, 111 n.36, 117,
  117 n.57

Padua, 35, 181

Palazzo Pubblico (Siena), 1*f*, 3, 17*f*

Pamphilus, 33–34, 37–38 n.78, 225–226

Passavanti, Jacopo, 187, 187 n.52

pastorella, 227

patria, 15, 132–166

St. Paul, 251, 251 n.5

pecia, 65–66, 65–66 n.33

Pegoretti, Anna, 6–7 n.14, 28 n.43, 30–31 n.50,
  65–66 n.34, 95–96, 95–96 n.93, 196–197
  nn.66–67

Peraldus, William, 181–182, 181–182 n.42, 183
  De superbia, 181–182

Pergus, Lake, 229–230

periochae, 212–213

Persius (Aulus Persius Flaccus), 32

Pertile, Lino, 5 n.8, 22–23 n.15, 122–123,
  122–123 n.66, 127, 127 n.74, 143–144
  n.38, 204 n.80, 206 n.84, 278–279 n.2

Petrarch, 18–19 n.2, 38–41 n.83, 69, 74–75,
  n.57, 181, 246–247

Petrus Hispanus, 64–65
  Summulae logicales, 64–65

Phaedrus, 102–104, 102–104 nn.11–12,
  106–107 n.20

Phaeton, 112–113

Physiologus, 37–38 n.78, 118–119

Pierre Maurice, 212

Pietro Alighieri, 107, 107 n.26, 108–109 n.28,
  122 n.64, 187 n.51, 188 n.54, 214–215 n.
  22, 219–222 n.41, 254–255 n.14

Pietro da Isolella da Cremona, 44–45
  Summa, 44–45

Pisa, 47–48 n.109, 66–68

Pizzinga, Jacopo, 38–41 n.83, 69, 111 n.36

planctus, 73–74, 76–77, 80

Platonic, 112–113, 206

Plautus (Titus Maccius), 113–114, 123

Plutarch, 137

INDEX 323

Pluto, 192–193, 208–209, 219–222 n.41, 258, 260

podestà, 145

poema sacro, 63–64

poeta, poetae, 33–34, 61, 97, 123, 130, 152–153, 192, 214, 214–215 n.22, 238–239, 249–250, 254–255, 265, 267–268, 274–275

Polyphemus, 206

popolo, 22–23, 22–23 n.15, 25–26, 41–42

Prato, 41–42

Princes, Valley of, 208

priore, 42–43

Priscian (Priscianus Caesariensis), 37, 49–50, 111, 111 n.34

    Institutiones Grammaticae, 37

Priscus, 137

Procne, 167–168 n.2, 189–190

promythium, 108–109, 127–128

Proserpina, 15, 167–247, 258, 260, 260 n.23, 263–264

Prosper of Aquitaine, 8–9, 15, 37–38, 37–38 n.79, 52–96, 114–115, 284–285

    Liber epigrammatum, 8–9, 15, 52–96, 284–285

Prudentius (Aurelius Prudentius Clemens), 37–38, 66–68, 114–115, 174–175, 174–175 n.17, 183 n.43

    Dittochaeon, 37–38, 66–68, 114–115, 174–175, 174–175 n.17, 183 n.43

psalterium, 35–36, 65–66

Pseustis, 167–207

quaderno, quaderni, 64–66

Quintilian (Marcus Fabius Quintilianus), 10 n.26, 111, 111 n.34, 112–113, 122 n.64

ragioni, 70–71, 153–154 n.71, 199

razos, 53, 82–83 n.81

Ravenna, 41 n.85, 202–203, 205

realism, 3–4, 97, 99–101, 114, 127

Rehoboam, 181–182

Remigio de' Girolami, 30–31 n.50, 135, 148–149, 148–149 nn.57 and 59, 154, 160, 161

    De bono comuni, 148–149, 148–149 nn.57 and 59, 154, 160, 161

Remigius of Auxerre, 135, 139–142 n.30, 164–165

Renaissance, 12–13, 13 n.35, 13–14, 61 n.18, 110–111, 135–137 n.14, 179–181, 212, 223, 246–247 n.104

res publica, 162

reverdie, 227

Ricardian poets, 5–6

rime, 52

Roboam, 185

Rome, 59, 132–166, 170, 235

Rome, Biblioteca Vallicelliana, ms. F.1, 139–142, 140*f*, 141*f*, 142–143, 143*f*, 147, 158

Roman republic, 132–166

Rupert of Deutz, 129–130

Saint Martin, 43

Sala de' Nove, 3

Sallust (Gaius Sallustius Crispus), 132–166

    Bellum Catilinae, 137, 143–144, 145–146 nn.44–45

    Oratio Catonis, 143–144, 148

Sanford, Eva M., 33–34, 33–34 n.59, 102–104 n.15, 138–139 n.24

Santa Croce, 30–31 n.50, 56–57 n.7, 218–219

Santa Maria Novella, 30–31 n.50, 70–71

Santo Spirito, 30–31 n.50

Satan, 171, 219–222 n.41

Saul, 181–182, 185

scola, 233, 285–286

Scott, John, 135–137, 135–137 nn.15–16, 155–156 n.75, 165–166, 165–166 n.97, 278 n.1

scuola, scuole, 4, 278, 283

Scylla, 189

Scyros, 208, 213, 222, 239, 241–242

Sedulius (Coelius), 32, 82, 174–175, 174–175 n.17, 218–219, 218–219 n.37

Seneca (Lucius Annaeus Seneca the Younger), 18–19 n.1, 111–112 n.41, 137, 137 n.19, 139–142 n.32, 142–143, 151–152, 154, 165–166 n.97

    De constantia sapientis, 137

Sennacherib, 181–182, 185

sententia, sententiae, 52–96, 132–166, 219–222 n.41

Sheba (Queen of), 171

Sicily, 102–104, 205

Sicilian, 205–206, 228

Siena, 1*f*, 3–4, 4 n.5, 17*f*, 30–31, 37–38

Silver Age, 211–212, 217

Singleton, Charles, 53 n.2, 77–78 n.67, 89 n.88, 118–119 n.59, 133–134, 133–134 n.7, 192–193 n.61, 227 n.55, 273–274 n.44

Smalley, Beryl, 143–144 nn.38–39, 145–146, 145–146 n.47

Solomon, 142–143, 151–152, 151–152 n.68, 152–154, 171

    Proverbs, 142–143, 151–152

sonetto, 49 n.113, 90–91 n.89, 92

sonnet, 58–59, 59 n.14, 77–80, 92

Spitzer, Leo, 78, 78 nn.70–71, 122–123, 122–123 n.66, 124–125, 125 n.70

Stacius, 212, 240–241

Stacius minor, 212

324 INDEX

Statius (Publius Papinius), 8–9, 15, 32–34, 37–38, 37–38 n.78, 38–41, 66–68, 167–275, 284–285
  Achilleid, 8–9, 15, 33–34, 37–38, 66–68, 66–68 n.41, 208–275, 284–285
  Thebaid, 184 n.48, 187 n.51, 188 n.55, 192–193 n.59, 208–247, 264 n.29
  Silvae, 236–237 n.75, 257 n.15, 258–259 n.20
Steinberg, Justin, 49 n.113, 52 n.1, 56–57 n.5, 58–59 n.12, 62, 62 n.22, 62–63 n.27, 98 n.3, 102 n.9, 109 n.29, 135 n.10, 164–165 n.94, 227–228 n.57
Stoicism, 137
  Stoic, 155–156, 159, 159 n.82
Storey, Wayne, 23 n.18, 24 n.20, 57–58 n.9, 58–59 n.11, 62–63, 62–63 n.27, 64, 64–65 n.30, n.32, 94–95 n.92
students, 2, 4, 14, 18–51, 94, 102–104 n.16, 112, 155–156, 167, 174–175 n.18, 175
studium, studia, 4, 4 n.5, 6–7, 28, 29–31, 30–31 n.50, 49, 49 n.113, 79, 206
Styx, 118, 120, 127–128, 244, 245–246
subdivisions, 62, 62 n.23, 91–92
Susanna, 189

tabula, 35–36
Tamiri, 189
teacher, 2, 7–8, 8–9 n.21, 11–12, 15, 18–51, 82, 111–112, 132–166, 178, 187, 214, 225–226, 238–239
tenzone, 85–86, 89
terzina, 183–184, 267–268, 274
Terence (Publius Terentius), 105–106 n.17, 113–114, 123
Tereus, 167–168 n.2, 190
Theocritus, 205
Theodulus, 33–34, 38–41, 114–115, 167–207
Thetis, 208–247
Tithonus, 190, 195–196
Tityrus, 171, 202–204, 204 n.80, 205–206
Tolomeo da Lucca, 160, 162–163
  De regimine principum, 160–163
tragedia, 125–126, 209–211, 233
tragedy, 125, 197–198, 201, 209–211, 215, 233, 242–243, 243 n.97
tragic, 78, 102 n.9, 109, 125–126, 167–168, 190, 192–193, 192–193 n.61, 198, 209–212, 241–244, 258–259 n.18, 279
Trajan (Emperor), 181–183, 183 n.43, 201–202 n.75
transumanar, 251
Trojan War, 213
Troy, 181–182, 185, 187–189, 195–196, 213, 222, 224–225, 239, 240–243

Tuscany, 10–11, 29–30, 35–36 n.66, 37–38, 60 n.17, 71–73 n.48, 105–106 n.19, 138–139

university, 4, 10, 18–51, 58, 59–60, 65–66, 89, 150–151 n.64, 206

Valerius Maximus, 138
vates, 176–177, 260, 264 n.31, 266–268, 274–275
Vatican City, Biblioteca Apostolica Vaticana, Vat. Lat. 1633, 139–142 n.32, 179 n.29
Vatican mythographers, 120–121, 174–175 n.17
Venus, 167–168 n.2, 192–193, 227, 242–243
vidas, 53, 74–75, 82–83 n.81
Villani, Filippo, 66–68, 66–68 n.40, 70, 246–247, 246–247 n.104
  Liber de civitatis Florentiae et eiusdem famosis civibus, 66–68
Villani, Giovanni, 4, 4 n.6, 5, 24–25, 24–25 n.26, 26, 26 n.33, 26–27, 29–30, 29–30 n.45, 37, 47–48, 47–48 n.108, 49 n.113, 55–56 n.4
  Nuova Cronica, 4, 4 n.6, 24–25 n.26, 26 n.33, 47–48 n.108, 55–56 n.4
Vincent of Beauvais, 110–111 n.32, 135, 135 n.13, 139–142
Virgil (Publius Vergilius Maro), 15, 32, 37–38 n.78, 47–48, 49–50 n.116, 69, 71–73, 71–73 n.50, 97–286
  Aeneid, 125–126, 137, 137 n.18, 153–154, 153–154 n.71, 188 n.55, 192–193 n.59, 208–247, 266–267, 275, 279
  Eclogues, 181, 192–193, 192–193 nn.60–61, 252
vitae, 111–112 n.37, 155–156 n.77, 176–177, 212–213
volgarizzamenti, 23, 23 n.19, 24–25, 138–139, 155–156 n.77
  Les Fais des Rommains, 143–144

Walter of England, 102–104, 102–104 n.15, 120 n.60
William of Conches, 75–76 n.63, 120–121
Wisdom (prosopopoeia), 3, 73–74, 80, 90–91, 281, 282–284
Witt, Ronald, 22 n.12, 24–25 n.25, 25–26 n.28, 34–35 n.62, n.64, 35–36 n.68, 44 n.98, 48–49, 48–49 n.112
Woods, Marjorie Curry, 32, 32 n.53, 213 nn.17 and 19, 213 n.20, 214, 214 n.21, 218–219 n.39, 223 n.45, 224, 225–226 nn.51–52, 240–241 n.87

ydioti (*idiotae*), 24, 59

Zanin, Enrica, 20–21 n.8, 95–96, 95–96 n.93
Zephyrus, 230–232